The Man behind the Discourse

The Man behind the Discourse:

A Biography of King Follett

Joann Follett Mortensen

GREG KOFFORD BOOKS
SALT LAKE CITY, 2011

Copyright © 2011 Joann Follett Mortensen.
Cover design Copyright © 2011 Greg Kofford Books, Inc.
Published in the USA.

Cover illustration: Detail from "Main Street Landing and Nauvoo House," May 2, 1907, George Edward Anderson Collection, LDS Church History Library. Used by permission.

All rights reserved. No part of this volume may be reproduced in any form without written permission from the publisher, Greg Kofford Books. The views expressed herein are the responsibility of the author and do not necessarily represent the position of Greg Kofford Books, Inc.

Greg Kofford Books
P.O. Box 1362
Draper, UT 84020
www.koffordbooks.com

2015   14   13   12   11   5   4   3   2   1

Library of Congress Cataloging-in-Publication Data

Mortensen, Joann Follett, author.
 The man behind the discourse : a biography of King Follett / Joann Follett Mortensen.
   p. cm.
 Includes bibliographical references and index.
 ISBN 978-1-58958-036-7
 1. Follett, King, 1788-1844. 2. Follett family. 3. Church of Jesus Christ of Latter-day Saints—History—19th century. 4. Mormon Church—History—19th century. I. Title.
 BX8695.F65M67 2011
 289.3092—dc23
 [B]
                              2011042746

DEDICATION

This work is dedicated to all early converts whose commitment and devotion, efforts, and trials contributed to the establishment, survival, and future success of what is now the Church of Jesus Christ of Latter-day Saints.

Contents

Introduction, ix

Chapter 1	The New Hampshire Beginnings, 1	
Chapter 2	When New Hampshire Meets New York, 15	
Chapter 3	To the Ohio Country: 1819, 33	
Chapter 4	A Family's Religious New Beginning, 1831–32, 45	
Chapter 5	The Mormon Church Comes to Ohio: 1830–31, 59	
Chapter 6	The Center Place of Zion, 1831–33, 65	
Chapter 7	"Bloody Monday": Prelude to a Forced Expulsion, 93	
Chapter 8	The Turmoil Continues: Clay County 1833–35, 109	
Chapter 9	A Spiritual Respite: Kirtland 1835–36, 135	
Chapter 10	From Clay County to Far West, 157	
Chapter 11	At War in Northern Missouri, 185	
Chapter 12	Siege, Surrender, and Extermination, 213	
Chapter 13	The "Old" Man in Prison: April–September 1839, 245	
Chapter 14	Exiles in Quincy, 269	
Chapter 15	The Beginning of Nauvoo, 1839–40, 285	
Chapter 16	Building Up a City, 1840–41, 305	
Chapter 17	1842: "This Most Extraordinary People", 329	
Chapter 18	1843: Hastening the Work, 355	
Chapter 19	Life and Death for the Folletts in Nauvoo, 377	
Chapter 20	The King Follett Discourse: The Prophet's Greatest Sermon, 411	
Chapter 21	The Death of a Prophet: A Church and a Family Move On, 423	
Chapter 22	King's Family after Nauvoo: From 1846 Onward, 451	

Epilogue, 467

APPENDICES
- A   King Follett's Ancestry,   469
- B   The King Follett Discourse,   477
- C   Louisa Tanner Follett, Journal, June 5, 1844–September 8, 1845,   493
- D   The Children of King and Louisa Follett,   517

Bibliography,   541

Index,   579

About the Author,   603

INTRODUCTION

During a session of the general conference held April 6–9, 1844, in the grove near the unfinished temple in Nauvoo, Illinois, Joseph Smith, the Mormon prophet, addressed the large congregation. One of his topics was a tribute to his friend King Follett who had recently died of injuries suffered while digging a well. A history of the early Church describes King as "one who bore the burden, in common with others of his brethren, in the days when men's faith was put to the test."[1] The Prophet prefaced his funeral remarks with these words: "I have been requested to speak by his friends and relatives, but inasmuch as there are a great many in this congregation who live in this city as well as elsewhere, who have lost friends, I feel disposed to speak on the subject in general, and offer you my ideas, so far as I have ability, and so far as I shall be inspired by the Holy Spirit to dwell on this subject."[2]

The address lasted for more than two hours and covered, among other topics, the character of God and the origin, destiny, and exaltation of humankind. It is from his words that day that the concept originated—unique to Mormon doctrine—that God was once like a mortal human being and that human beings can become like God. Many view this sermon, known as the King Follett Discourse, as the Prophet Joseph Smith's greatest address.

Between 1830, the date of the organization of the Church of Christ (later named the Church of Jesus Christ of Latter-day Saints) and Joseph Smith's death in 1844, thousands of individuals made a decision that not only would profoundly affect their present lives, but a decision that they believed would have positive eternal consequences for them, their spouses, and their descendants. That decision was to join a new and oddly nicknamed Mormon Church. The Follett family is part of this larger story.

In reconstructing the story of King Follett, I have come to appreciate that those early converts were ordinary citizens about whom very little would ever be recorded, their stories blending into the larger story of Mormonism. That larger story is dramatic—repeated moves from their original communities through Ohio, Missouri, and Illinois, pulled by the divine mandate to gather with the Saints and pushed by the all-too-frequent hostility of neighbors. They found a permanent homeland, though not initially a peaceful one, in the Valley of the Great Salt Lake in what became Utah. Although much has been written about that larger story, most of them remained "ordinary" individuals—but ordinary individuals whose lives changed dramatically because they chose to obey a man upon whom they saw God's choice resting as his prophet. Stories were handed down in their families and material gleaned from letters and journals—if they were created and if they survived. If King, his wife, Louisa Tanner Follett, or any of their adult children kept journals or wrote autobiographies, I have not been able to find them despite diligent searching. The sole exception is a brief diary of Louisa's covering a short period following King's death. It contains no information about King's early years. As "ordinary" members, their lives only occasionally intercepted leaders or events that gave them brief mentions in the official record.

King Follett became a member shortly after the organization of the Church at age forty-three and spent the remaining thirteen years of his life quietly participating in the people-making and kingdom-building service that set Mormons apart from their neighbors. He died in March 1844, just three months before the Prophet's own death in June. On the day of King's death, the Prophet called him "our worthy brother." One twentieth-century review of his life praises him: "King Follett was indeed a 'worthy brother.' His Christian name aptly reflects his noble nature. Though he never rose to the governing ranks of the Church, he was a quiet inspiration to those with whom he associated, and his life was an excellent example of the virtue of humble, valiant endurance."[3]

Hanging on the wall above my computer where I have spent countless hours over many years researching King's life are two items. One is a print of Norman Rockwell's 1959 painting entitled *Family Tree*. It was a gift from my husband on my birthday in 2005, at a time when I first began to truly believe that a published copy of the biography of King Follett was becoming a reality, that someone else might be interested in what was contained in the numerous files, notes, photos, and correspondence resting on shelves in my home. This painting reminds me that connecting families together and discovering what makes each family member unique and how each fits into community and society in general is what family history research and genealogy is all about. Taped to the bottom of this Rockwell print, is a copy of a pedigree chart of King and Louisa Follett and their children. Very "dog-eared" because of great use over the years, it reminds me that, when I first started research on this project about thirty years ago, the information on that chart, as inaccurate as some of it has now proven to be, along with a very few anecdotal, family-generated items and a little about the King Follett Discourse was all I really knew about the life of the man who was my third great-grandfather and who shared his July 26th birth date with me.

My first encounter with the name "King Follett" came when I was about ten or twelve years. My family lived on the same block with my grandparents, Orren W. Follett and Josephine Merrill Follett, in the small farming community of Pima, Arizona. By that time in my life I had become an avid reader, particularly of fiction. When I visited my grandparents' home, which I often did on the way home from school, there was very little fiction to read, but they did have some volumes of *The History of the Church of Jesus Christ of Latter-day Saints*. It was in these books that I found the name of King Follett. My grandparents knew very little about him other than he was, as they said, "a bodyguard and friend of the Prophet Joseph Smith," and that the Prophet "preached his funeral sermon." At that early age, I was fascinated by the fact that I had an ancestor who had known the Prophet Joseph Smith. About twenty-five years later when I first became interested in genealogy, rather than starting as a family researcher should—"with the known (myself) and working back to the unknown"—I was drawn to King. My first entry in my research log for him is dated 1976. Since that time I have reconstructed King's life from civil and vital records, supplemented by those few early Church records and documents containing his name and the journals of other converts.

Sources

My children learned at a very young age that they would have to spend some holidays and vacation time "cemetery hopping" with me throughout many states, and that I would make one or two extended trips a year to do research in Salt Lake—especially in the days before the internet. With my husband, Irval, the photographer who documented our travels, and often accompanied by my sister Peggy and her husband, Hollis Jones, I have visited each of the places where King and Louisa resided and where their children and their families lived. Each time and in each place events happened that reinforced my belief that King wanted his story told and that we were asking the right questions in the right places.

In his birthplace of Winchester, New Hampshire, we walked into the town hall asking for Follett records, were handed a large book, shown to a room and given permission to copy anything we wanted. The book contained King's original birth record and those of his siblings. Later that day in a local bookstore, we found a book of early maps of Winchester that identified the general area where the Follett property had been. On a visit to the cemetery the next morning, the first person we met and asked about the location of the Follett graves happened to be the caretaker who was also a local amateur historian. He not only showed us Follett graves but pointed out the specific location of the Follett land, so we could visit the site where King was born. That historian also invited us into his office where he provided copies of many generations of general town historical information.

A couple of days later we visited the St. Lawrence County Historical Society in Canton, New York, again asking for information on Folletts and Tanners. Almost before I finished my first question, a gentleman sitting at one of the tables, who "just happened to be there that day" looked up and said, "Oh, you mean King and Louisa Follett," and quickly showed us land records that are the only primary source I have yet discovered that documents when King and Louisa came to that part of New York. Those records are not yet in print and have just within the last year been available on the internet. In Mills County, Iowa, thanks to the efforts of Beverly Boileau, a local historian, we were able to locate the graves of Louisa and two of her children, as well as the land that she purchased and on which she lived until her death. Beverly helped us make a connection with Allen Worthman, a local historian, who shared his wealth of knowledge about the Folletts and the Mormon Church in general in that area. She also provided many printed documents about Louisa and her family from local newspapers and other records.

Over the years, I have had very positive experiences when requesting help and information from numerous historical societies and extended family members. Staff members at the LDS Church History Library in Salt Lake have directly and indirectly assisted in many ways over the years. My letters and emails to LDS Church historians, the Community of Christ archivists, and authors of numerous books and articles have been answered, all with patience and special understanding that I am not a professional researcher. Each of these encounters provided new and additional information, sources to search, and more questions to ask. I sent my daughter Tonya to the LDS Church Archives to ask one question and the individual at the reception desk that day was Christy Best. It turned out that King Follett had baptized one of her ancestors—a fact that I would not have been able to document without that chance encounter. Christy was also of great assistance with research in Nauvoo City records.

There are so many individuals to whom I owe thanks that it is impossible to name them all. A few are due a special mention because they have been responsible for helping me move my research to this finished document:

My husband Irval for willingly being my photographer and my computer mentor, and for his patience as I put my life "on hold" to finish this project;

Dr. David J. Whittaker, Brigham Young University, who assured me early in the project that the topic was one of interest in the Church and worthy of proposing a paper for the Mormon History Association;

The Mormon History Association for allowing me to present my research at its annual conference in 2003 and for publishing my revised article in the *Journal of Mormon History* in 2005.

Dr. Alexander Baugh, professor of Church history and doctrine, Brigham Young University, for his interest in King's story and for his willingness to share his knowledge of the Missouri period of Mormon Church history;

Lavina Fielding Anderson for her tremendous assistance in editing the *Journal* article and for professionalizing this manuscript. She was understanding and encouraging when I asked so many questions and wanted to "do just a little more research";

And finally Greg Kofford, who handed me his business card when I presented an early version of my research at the Sunstone Symposium in Salt Lake in 2003, and said, "When you are ready to publish, contact me." He did not know how long it would take me to be "ready to publish," nor how the fact that he was interested in my research and willing to consider publishing it kept me going over the years since then. Thanks to him for answering my numerous questions about publishing and for having the confidence to support the efforts of an amateur historian to tell King Follett's story—not only as a biography but as a story of a typical early-day Mormon convert.

I must also express gratitude for my father, Afton Follett, first for the heritage he gave me, but also for the confidence he had in my research on the Follett line, even though he kept telling me that it would be hard because they left no record. I only regret that he did not live to see the finished document and the "record" that I was able to find.

Although all of these individuals contributed to this biographical labor of love, the interpretations and any accompanying errors are my responsibility.

I put King's life together by finding often small bits of information in many places and working to make them fit a coherent and reasonable whole. I accept that another author might have reconstructed his life differently. It is not only certain but my greatest hope that missing pieces will yet be discovered. I have taken seriously the admonition of British historian Robert Lacey: "As we set out to explore the past, we should keep in mind the first rule of history: the things that we don't know far outnumber the things that we do. And when we do unravel secrets, the results seldom fit in with our own modern opinions of how life should be."[4]

An Introduction to Mormon Beliefs

To many readers of this biography, the religious message by which King guided his life for thirteen years will be familiar. Other readers, many of whom are King's descendants, will find many new concepts of religious doctrine. An early attempt to explain Mormon beliefs was published in October 1834—in the first issue of the *Messenger and Advocate*, an early Church newspaper.[5] In 1842, Joseph Smith, responding to the request of John Wentworth, editor of the *Chicago Democrat*, wrote a short history of the Church and ended with thirteen "Articles of Faith of the Church of Jesus Christ of Latter-day Saints."[6] Unquestionably, much of the motivation for King and Louisa Follett's decisions, even when they involved life-wrenching consequences, came from their acceptance of Mormon doctrine. Although that doctrine has evolved in significant ways over the past 180 years, the basics that King Follett accepted are:

1. The principles of the true gospel as taught by Jesus Christ were lost from the earth following his death and the death of his apostles.

2. Just as God spoke to biblical prophets, so he could and did speak to modern prophets, of whom the first was Joseph Smith.

3. Joseph began his mission by translating the Book of Mormon, which testified of Jesus Christ's saving mission to the inhabitants of ancient America and which contains the fullness of the gospel. The Book of Mormon was not only a testimony of Christ but a testimony of Joseph as the Lord's prophet. An angel instructed Joseph Smith where to find the ancient plates from which he translated it "by the gift and power of God," as its title page says.

4. The next tasks were the restoration of Jesus's lost church and the priesthood to govern it.

5. Before Jesus's prophesied second coming, all truth must be restored. Mormons could expect continuous revelation as the Lord spoke to their prophet.

6. Those who heard the message of the Mormon elders must gather out of "the world" to prepare a people to receive him. Thus, an important part of conversion was to move to the Church's center place, a location that shifted at least three times during King's lifetime: Ohio, Missouri, and Illinois.

7. All human beings have immortal spirits who lived with God the Father before the creation of the earth. To return to God's presence, they must obey his commandments, including the ordinances of baptism, confirmation, priesthood ordination (for men), and marriage sealings in temples consecrated for that purpose. Individuals could perform these ordinances by proxy for their ancestors, who were free to accept or reject the gospel principles and ordinances.

King Follett's biography is a story of early Mormonism in America, reflected in the life and activities of one convert and his response to these beliefs. Except for his accidental death and the Prophet's comments on that death in his magisterial doctrinal discourse, probably his name would not be known at all except by his descendants. But because of that sermon, few Church members fail to recognize it. Knowing who he was and what he did—understanding the "man behind the discourse"—is more complicated.

Notes

1. *Nauvoo Neighbor*, March 20, 1844, quoted in *History of the Church*, 6:249.
2. Ibid., 6:302.
3. Calvin N. Smith, "King Follett: Quiet Fortitude, Prophet Speaks at Funeral," 10–11.
4. Robert Lacey, *Great Tales from English History*, 2.
5. Oliver Cowdery, "Address," *Messenger and Advocate*, 1, no. 1 (October 1834): 2.
6. *History of the Church*, 4:535–41.

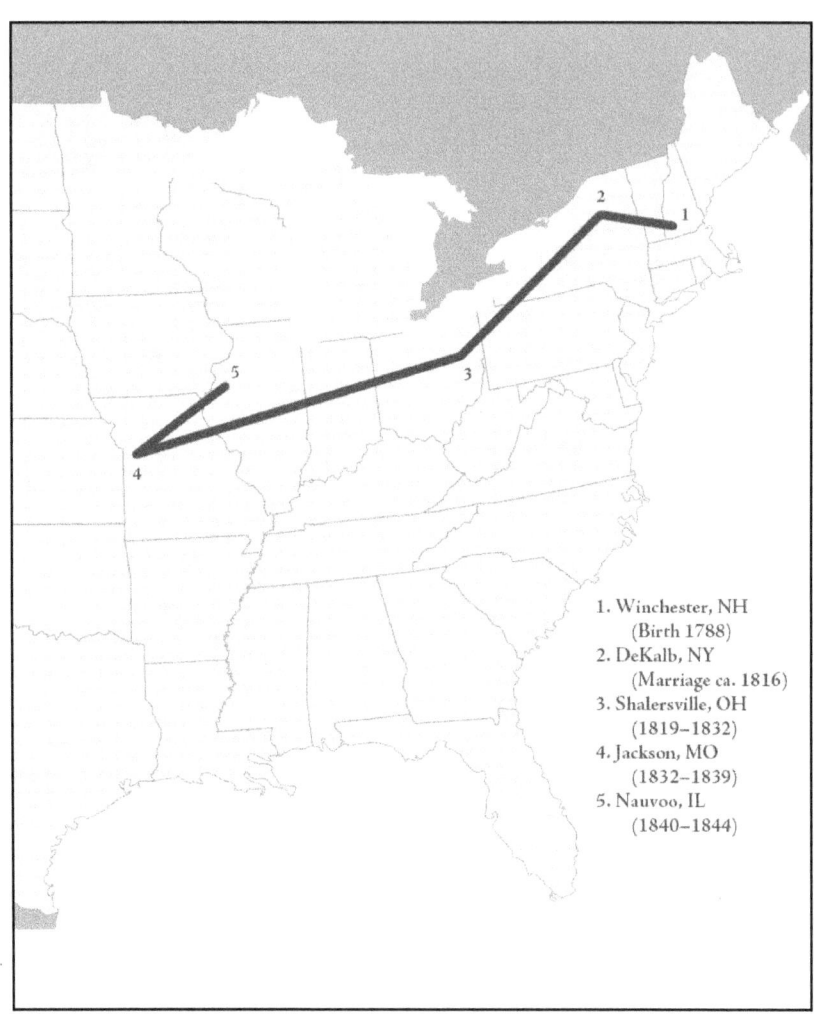

Residences of King Follett, 1788 to 1844.

❊ Chapter One ❊

The New Hampshire Beginnings

King Follett was the descendant of an emigrant ancestor named Robert and four generations of John Folletts, who began their travels in Salem, Massachusetts, and moved with the frontier. (See Appendix A, "King Follett's Ancestry.") His father, the fourth John Follett (1752–1829), arrived with his family in the southeastern corner of New Hampshire (now Cheshire County) sometime after 1768 at about age sixteen. He spent his entire life there—first in Swanzey and later in Winchester, married three wives, fathered at least twelve children, served in the Revolutionary War, purchased and sold land, undoubtedly farmed, and died at a respectable old age. King grew to manhood in that home, learning the traits and attributes that would guide his life.

New Hampshire was originally part of the Massachusetts Colony and drew its European inhabitants primarily from Connecticut and Massachusetts. Because New Hampshire was relatively close to other New England states, many immigrants spent short periods of time en route farther west and north. The Connecticut River, which served as New Hampshire's western boundary, became a convenient method of transportation not only for the westward movement but for those traveling north and south as well. Permanent settlements were few and isolated during the first several decades. The area that became Cheshire County in 1771 was first settled in approximately 1735. Most Native Americans had left the area by that time; however, some fighting between the Indians and the settlers continued over the next twenty-five years. The issue of possession had been settled in the favor of the whites by the time the Follett family arrived in Swanzey ca. 1768. The sparse populace bought and sold land, raised cattle, grew crops, and erected buildings. The entire county numbered 3,557 residents, with 320 in Swanzey and 428 in Winchester.[1] The land was mostly hilly, heavily forested, and well-watered with a network of lakes and ponds. Cattle, sheep, grain, dairy products and other necessities of life could be easily produced and grown. The climate was typical of most of the interior of New England with cold winters, warm summers, and more than adequate rain and snow. It was a perfect place to put down roots, raise a family, and play an active role in growing America.

John Follett Jr. is listed in Swanzey land records in 1772 as receiving a land grant of fifty acres. As his father by that same name may have still been alive in the area until at least 1818 (and was himself the son of another John Follett), it is difficult to always determine which John a record refers to. However, it seems reasonable, since the two Johns were apparently the only individuals by that name in Swanzey, to assume that "Jr." refers to King's father. (After about 1777, King's father moved to Winchester.) In 1773 at age twenty-one, John married the first of his three wives, Christian Belding, daughter of Samuel Belding and Christian King Belding.[2] King's first name—which seems counterintuitive in the generation that fought the Revolutionary War—probably originated as a gesture of respect to Christian, even though she was not King's mother. An 1805 Winchester map shows the Follett and King families living on the same road.[3] John and Christian's three children were born by 1776 on land John owned in Swanzey.[4]

New Hampshire citizens were early supporters of independence from England, so political discussions would have been energetic and frequent. As early as 1760, New Hampshire had organized its town militia into regiments. By the outbreak of the Revolutionary War, the area encompassing Swanzey and Winchester enrolled 1,080 militia as the future state's thirteenth regiment. Swanzey contributed 138 men while Winchester listed 130.[5] To prepare for the coming battles, each town militia had its own "Training Band"—all able-bodied men between ages sixteen and fifty. Indians and Negroes were exempt. Each company in the Training Band, consisting of about seventy privates, officered by a captain, two lieutenants, and an ensign. By law, they furnished their own firearms and equipment and mustered eight times a year.[6] The total number of men in the Continental Army from each colony cannot be determined exactly because many individuals served more than once and were counted each time. The best estimate of New Hampshire's soldiery for the entire war was about 16,000, made up both of regular troops and state militia.[7] When news of Lexington and Concord came, 1,200 troops immediately enlisted in Cheshire County, with New Hampshire's total reaching 10,000 men.[8] Among them was King's father. No battles were fought in New Hampshire; and the state actually benefitted financially, according to a local historian: "Agricultural products were in heavy demand, real estate values increased, and plentiful paper money facilitated the exchange of commodities. Many state inhabitants were significantly richer at the end of the war than at its start."[9]

John Follett's headstone in Evergreen Cemetery, Winchester, New Hampshire, bestows the title of "Captain" upon him; and several sources refer to him as "Revolutionary War Captain" John Follett. However, this rank does not appear in his service records,[10] and a plaque placed at his gravesite in 2005 by the Daughters of the American Revolution refers to him as "Pvt—Continental Line, NH."[11] "Captain" was probably either derived from John's service in one of the local militia units or was a courtesy title.

John Follett (possibly a different man from King's father) was one of more than a hundred men who signed the Association Test document at the request of New Hampshire's Committee of Safety on April 12, 1776. This committee was following up on the Continental Congress's requirement that all men over age twenty-one sign this document indicating their support of the break from England and their willingness to "defend by ARMS" that action; those who refused were required to surrender their arms.[12] John first served in the Swanzey militia, which marched toward Boston on April 21, 1775, only two days after the battle of Lexington, under the command of Lt. Colonel Joseph Hammond. This unit may have joined up with twenty-nine militiamen from Keene, Cheshire County's seat, which left for Boston on April 22, marching through mist, rain, and mud.[13] Some of these soldiers enlisted for eight months, while others, including John, served only a few days. According to the Swanzey town history, he was paid for twelve days of service at Cambridge.[14] Six months later on September 15, he signed a petition requesting that Captain Jeremiah Folsom be appointed lieutenant colonel.[15]

In the fall of 1775 and into 1776, a main focus of the Continental troops was to capture Quebec. By the middle of 1776, major fighting was occurring in Canada and various local groups had been sent north as support. The colonies' fighting forces were now spread throughout New England as well as north into Canada. Once again John participated actively in the fighting, this time as a private in Joseph Whitcomb's Company, Colonel Samuel Ashley's Regiment. His unit marched to Fort Ticonderoga in eastern New York, approximately 128 miles northeast from Swanzey, at the orders of Major General Horatio Gates to reinforce the Army of Ticonderoga. The Town of Swanzey later paid John £1/14/8 for twenty-six days of service and a travel reimbursement of £1/16/8 for 220 miles.[16]

In September 1777 within three days, John and Christian's two- and three-year-old children died of unknown causes.[17] About five months later, Christian died a week after giving birth to a daughter, also named Christian. Mother Christian's headstone reads "Christian (wife of John Follet) d. Feb 10, 1778, ae. 26."[18] The baby survived; and a year later, John married Sybil/Sibel Willard, the daughter of Simon Willard and Catherine Field Willard. She was a descendant of Colonel Josiah Willard, original grantee of the area that became Winchester.[19] Sybil gave birth to two children, then died in 1782.[20] In 1783, John married a widow, Hannah Oak Alexander.[21] This marriage, performed by Rev. Ezra Conant,[22] added six male children to the household during the next ten years. King was the third of these sons.[23] Reverend Conant served as minister for the Winchester Congregational Church until 1806 and was probably part of the family church during King's childhood.

King's mother, Hannah, was the daughter of John Oak and Susanna Allen Oak, born April 20, 1749, in Westborough, Massachusetts.[24] This branch of the Oak family traces its genealogy to a Nathaniel Oak (ca. 1645–1721), who emigrated from Wales. According to a story recorded in a family Bible, the ship wrecked off the coast of Boston. He succeeded in swimming ashore. "In his distress he solemnly promised the Lord if He would preserve him to get to land he would never go onto the water again. This promise he sacredly kept."[25] In 1686, he married Mehitable Rediat in Marlborough, Massachusetts. An Oake family history, states:

"His name is mentioned in the records sometimes as a yeoman and planter and also a gentleman, the latter indicating something of the standing he attained among the townsmen, and the success which was the reward of his industry and thrift." He saw service in the early colonial wars including King Phillip's War in 1675. He died in Marlborough (Northboro), Massachusetts, on February 17, 1721.[26]

Hannah was the fourth child in her family and the first surviving daughter, named for an older sister Hannah who had died at age two. Her father, a "prosperous farmer" in Westboro, was identified in 1749 as "one of the fifteen largest taxpayers in town." He died at age thirty-seven. His only surviving children were Hannah and a brother.[27] Hannah's widowed mother married John Butler and relocated in Shrewsbury, Massachusetts, when Hannah was five, then to Winchester, New Hampshire, twelve years later. In Winchester, Hannah at nineteen married Seth Alexander, a farmer, in 1768. Over the next twelve years, they had eight children, three of whom died young.[28] Seth served as a sergeant and ensign during the Revolutionary War and fought at Ticonderoga in Captain Oliver Capron's Company in the same regiment (Samuel Ashley's) as John Follett.[29] Seth died in December 1780, leaving Hannah with four young children and pregnant with their eighth child, born five months later in May 1781.[30] Seth's will was probated in the Cheshire County probate court in 1781 and settled in 1784. After John and Hannah's marriage, the court appointed John as guardian of Seth's five minor children. The estate was valued at £67/19/9, a third of which constituted Hannah's dower right, while the remaining two-thirds went to John as the children's guardian.[31] Interestingly, Hannah signed these probate papers; but for the rest of her life, she most commonly signed with an "X."

At the time of their marriage in 1783, John had four surviving children from his first two marriages, ranging in age from two to nine, and Hannah had five, ranging in age from two to fourteen—a total of nine children they brought into the marriage. Over the next ten years, they added six sons, all of whom lived beyond infancy and all but one of whom married and raised a family. Thus, King had a total of fourteen surviving siblings, with either Alexander or Follett surnames, most of them boys.

King's father, John, appears to have been a man of some stature, since he appears often mentioned in Cheshire County's land records. He bought and sold at least thirty-five parcels of land over the years.[32] A community history written in 1885 referred to John Follett as "one of the early settlers of Winchester" who had settled on the land then owned by Silas P. Fairbanks and John's grandson Russell Follett. "Here he lived till his death, at a 'good old age.'"[33] Cliff Struthers, the local cemetery caretaker in 1999, referred to a 'Follett Tavern' at one time located on Clark Road, on land now in Mount Pisgah Park.[34] John does not appear as an office-holder in town records although he signed petitions twice. In one, along with about 126 other men, he successfully petitioned the New Hampshire General Court (legislature) for a lottery to build a new road. In the second, John was one of a committee of three men from Winchester, who with a committee of three from nearby Chesterfield, again petitioned the New Hampshire General Court for another lottery to build a road. This petition was denied.[35]

The only other evidence of John's involvement in Winchester affairs centered on religion. After the Revolutionary War, town records reflect much discussion and many decisions about emerging national and continuing local issues, including the need for a larger Congregationalist meetinghouse, the town's . After much confusion over exactly where the center of town was and where the church should be in relationship to that spot, the final committee recommendation on April 14, 1794, was accepted. The town meeting voted to "sell the Pews at Publick Vandue to the highest Bidder" and use the proceeds to buy the land and erect the building. John paid £16/10/- for Pew 42.[36] This building was located "at the base of Meeting House Hill where the Universalist Memorial Church/Center Church in Winchester now stands."[37]

This "town meetinghouse" did dual service as both the town hall and as the Congregationalist house of worship. Winchester, like most New England communities, saw religion as a community duty. The local government hired and dismissed ministers, whose salaries were paid by town funds. Congregational records in Winchester do not give a christening date for King or any of his siblings born prior to 1790. However, they list his three younger siblings born between 1790 and 1794, confirming that the Folletts were Congregationalists.[38] By 1799 when King was eleven, he sang to the accompaniment of the organ in church, an

Winchester Town Hall and Meeting House, built in 1794. Undated postcard in my possession. This building burned in 1909.

unusual evidence of prosperity and commitment. This organ had the distinction of being "one of the very first church organs, if not the first ever constructed, in this country," thanks to the fact that Henry Pratt of Winchester built it in the town.[39]

In this building, the Universalist Society adopted its 'Profession of Faith' in 1803, creating the Universalist Church in the United States.[40] This society took the position that God's mercy would ultimately effect the salvation of all humankind (hence, "universal" salvation), a position considered heretical by the Congregationalists, who adhered to the sterner Calvinist doctrine that some individuals were "elected" to be saved by God's inscrutable will while others were equally "elected" for damnation. The Follett family, however, remained active Congregationalists long after King left Winchester. When John died, his property inventory included "one-half of a pew in central meeting lower floor valued at $8 and a one-fourth pew in gallery central meeting house valued at $3."[41] By 1834, the Congregationalists built their own church, while the Universalists continued to meet in the original building. It was remodeled in 1871 but burned in 1909.[42]

Hannah is not mentioned in any type of public record although her name occasionally appears on a deed. The only documented occasion of her active involvement in public or legal affairs occurred after John's death. Legally, a married woman's identity was subsumed in that of her husband. If she owned land because of an inheritance, it became the property of her husband when she married; if she owned property because of a former marriage, it became her new husband's property when she remarried. According to the county land records, John sold much of his real estate but continued to own a few parcels either individually or jointly with sons Luther and Willard. When he died in March 1829, he and Hannah were living on a farm that "consisted of 125 acres plus 30 acres Garness Mountain plus 50 acres with Eliza and Seth Willard."[43] John did not leave a will. Hannah petitioned that Willard be appointed as administrator of the estate because she "by reason of age and infirmity" was "incapable of tending to any business" (the usual legal formula). For some reason, Luther was appointed instead and received sole title to his father's property. The inventory of estate assets is lengthy—five pages long—and lists land, farm supplies and equipment, animals and household items valued at $1,510.59. As John's widow, Hannah was entitled to her dower right of one-third of the estate's value which she would enjoy during her life but which, upon her death, would revert to the estate's heirs. However, less than a month later, she again appeared before the court, petitioned for her dower right, testified that she had not signed the deed that had transferred the farm's title to Luther, and described her condition as "destitute."[44]

The court, acting on her petition, granted her three parcels of real estate that were equal to one-third of John's total estate, and even divided the farmhouse between her and Luther. She received

> the south front room and the bedroom adjoining with a right to so much of the west end of the cellar as shall be necessary for her use, and occasionally to have the use of the kitchen for the purposes of washing and butchering [?] and also a priviledge in twelve feet in width of the woodshed adjoining nearest to said rooms. Also the west half of bay and the south half of the horse stable in the barn with a priviledge in the barn floor and the use of so much of the barnyard as shall be wanted for the improvement of her share of the barn, also one sixth part of all the manure made on said farm the year last past with the right of laying wood in some convenient place near her said premises to drain water from the well. . . .[45]

It is difficult to tell from the probate records exactly what all of this meant to Hannah financially. After the court specified this division of the property, Luther filed another petition stating that, to pay the debts of his father's estate, it would be necessary to sell all assets, including the

"Capt John Follett Died Feb. 20, 1829 age 77" and "Hannah, wife of Capt. John Follett died April 13, 1838 AE 89." Evergreen Cemetery, Winchester, NH, 2008. Photos courtesy of Christy Menard, Winchester, New Hampshire

buildings in which the court had awarded Hannah spaces. Apparently, though John bought and sold considerable land over the years and had an estate valued at more than $1,500 at the time of his death, his assets were actually smaller than his liabilities. Therefore, exactly how much Hannah ended up with and how she lived the remaining eight years of her life cannot be determined since I found no record of the court's response to Luther's last petition. Likely she lived with and was supported by her children still living in the area. The existing court records do not show that King or any of the other children individually received anything from the estate.

John and Hannah Follett are buried next to each other in a well-cared-for site in Section N of the Evergreen Cemetery (also referred to as Village Cemetery) in Winchester. Their headstones are intact and legible. Between the headstones is a marker commemorating John's service in the Revolutionary War and other family members lie around them. Both lived especially long lives for that era, much longer than King.

The *New Hampshire Sentinel* recorded John's death in a single line: FOLLETT: John Cpt. 76 Wnchstr Feb. 20 [18]29.[47]

Row of Follett headstones, Evergreen Cemetery 2008. Left: (1) "Sibol wife of John died Mar 2, 1782, in her 32 year of her age"; (2) John; (3) Hannah; (4) "John [son of John and Hannah] died July 27, 1816, in his 32 year." "My friends from me a warning take; so that god laws you do not break." [This admonition may indicate some unusual, perhaps criminal, reason for his death.] (5) "Life son of Capt. John & Hannah Follet who was killed by a fall from a frame Oct 21, 1809 in his 20 year." "He fell here lies his moulding frame, ye parents praise gods holy name; who reizns thu natures vast expans and not a sparrow falls by chance."[46] Photo courtesy of Christy Menard, Winchester, New Hampshire.

"Revolutionary War Soldier / JOHN FOLLETT / Pvt - Continental Line, NH / Under Col Isaac Wyman, Samuel Ashby / Born March 5, 1762, Attleborough. Bristol Co. MA/ Died February 20, 1829, Winchester, Cheshire Co. NH / Marker placed by Ashuelet Chapter NSDAR / October 11, 2005." Photo courtesy of Christy Menard, Winchester, New Hampshire.

Notes

1. D. Hamilton Hurd, ed., *History of Cheshire and Sullivan Counties, New Hampshire*, 8.

2. Benjamin Reed, *The History of Swanzey, New Hampshire: From 1734 to 1890*, 340.

3. Edith Adkins, *Early Maps of Winchester New Hampshire, 1733–1892*, 8–9.

4. Reed, *The History of Swanzey*, 340.

5. Ibid., 102–3. For less cumbersome references, I call colonies and territories by their later names as states.

6. James C. and Lila Lee Neagles, *Locating Your Revolutionary War Ancestor: A Guide to the Military Records*, 169–70.

7. Francis B. Heitman, *Historical Register of Officers of the Continental Army during the War of the Revolution, April 1775, to December 1783*, 690.

8. Neagles and Neagles, *Locating Your Revolutionary War Ancestor*, 170.

9. Jere R. Daniell, *Colonial New Hampshire: A History*, 245.

10. Neagles and Neagles, *Locating Your Revolutionary War Ancestor*, 171, lists "Captain Follett's Artillerymen" as a unit from New Hampshire; however, this captain was named Robert, not John. Information courtesy of T. Juliette Arai, Old Military and Civil Records, National Archives and Records Administration. Letter to Joann Mortensen, October 4, 2006.

11. Photograph in my possession, courtesy Christy Menard, Library Director, Conant Public Library, Winchester, New Hampshire.

12. Albert Stillman Batchellor, ed., *Miscellaneous Revolutionary Documents of New Hampshire*, State Papers Series, Vol. 30:81.

13. Yankee Travel Guide, "Captain Wyman's Tavern Named Editor's Choice," 2.

14. Hurd, *History of Cheshire and Sullivan Counties*, 399.

15. "Petition Relative to the Fourth Regiment of Militia, in Isaac W. Hammond, comp. and ed., *Town Papers, Documents Relating to Towns in New Hampshire: New London to Wolfeborough*, 13:20–23.

16. Isaac W. Hammond, comp. and ed., *The State of New Hampshire, Part l, Rolls and Documents Relating to Soldiers in the Revolutionary War, Part 1*, 98. I use "£1/14/8" and similar constructions during the colonial period. The three denominations of currency are pound/shilling/pence.

17. Reed, *The History of Swanzey, New Hampshire*, 340.

18. Walter F. Oakman, comp., "Mount Casear Cemetery" (2d part), *Swanzey Cemetery Records*, Swanzey, N.H., LDS Family History Library, Microfilm #15577, Item 10, 71.

19. Swanzey, New Hampshire, Town Clerk, Records of Marriages, Births, and Deaths, ca. 1741–1915, LDS Family History Library, Microfilm #2200234, item 1, p. 79.

20. Cliff Struthers, Evergreen Cemetery Statistics, unpublished, obtained by personal visit, September 22, 1999. Sybil Willard Follett's headstone is located in Section N 106, 42, Evergreen Cemetery, Winchester, New Hampshire. The inscription reads: "Sibol wife of John died Mar. 2, 1782 in her 32 year of her age."

21. Winchester, New Hampshire, Town Clerk, Records of Marriages, Births, and Deaths, 1733–1930, Microfilm #2208914, Item 3, LDS Family History Library.

22. Frederick Odell Conant, *A History and Genealogy of the Conant Family in England and America: Thirteen Generations*, LDS Family History Library, Microfilm #896781, pp. 251, 267, 277, 576. Ezra Conant was born in Concord September 18, 1763, studied theology at Harvard College, and graduated in 1784.

23. Birth records obtained from Winchester, N.H., Town Hall on personal visit September 22, 1997; copy in my possession. See also New Hampshire, Registrar of Vital Statistics, *Index to Births, Early to 1900*, Microfilm #1000938, ("French-Folsom"), and 1000481 ("Andervil-Allen"). Their oldest son was given the name "John," continuing to the fifth generation the tradition of a male child by that name.

24. Henry Lebbeus Oak, *Oak/Oaks/Oakes—Family Register. Nathaniel Oak of Marlborough, Mass.: And Three Generations of His Descendants . . .*, 17–18. The surname is variously spelled "Oak," "Oake," and "Och"; however, I use "Oak," the spelling used by Hannah's Follett descendants.

25. Ibid., 7.

26. Fred Arthur Oakes, *Oakes and Relatives*, 17–19. Hannah Oak Alexander Follett was in the fourth generation descending from Nathaniel, the immigrant ancestor.

27. Oak, *Oak/Oaks/Oakes*, 11.

28. Ibid., 17–18, 47–48. See also New Hampshire, Registrar of Vital Statistics. *Index to births, early to 1900*. Microfilm #1000481, p. 1321.

29. Isaac W. Hammond, comp. and ed., *The State of New Hampshire, Rolls of the Soldiers in the Revolutionary War, May, 1777, to 1780*, 2:54. Seth Alexander served thirteen days for which he received £2/12 with an additional £3/9/4 for rations and mileage.

30. Oak, *Oak/Oaks/Oakes*, 17–18.

31. New Hampshire, Cheshire County, Probate Estate Files, 1769–1885, Seth Alexander, files 12–13.

32. Cheshire County, New Hampshire, Register of Deeds, 1770–1860, Microfilms #15615, 15617, 15620, 15622, LDS Family History Library.

33. Hamilton Child, *Gazetteer of Cheshire County, N.H., 1736–1885*, 537.

34. Cliff Struthers, caretaker of Evergreen Cemetery and local historian, Winchester, New Hampshire, interviewed September 22, 1999, plus later correspondence in my possession.

35. Isaac W. Hammond, comp. and ed., *Town Papers: Documents Relating to Towns in New Hampshire, "A" to "F" Inclusive*, 11:343–45; and his *Documents Relating to Towns in New Hampshire, Gilmanton to New Ipswich*, 12:223–24.

36. D. Hamilton Hurd, ed. *History of Cheshire and Sullivan Counties, New Hampshire*, 569–70.

37. Tom Haynes, ed., *Sacred and Secular: Historic Meetinghouses and Churches of the Monadnock Region, 1750 to 1850*, 75.

38. "A Book of Records belonging to the Church of Christ in Winchester, — in the State of New Hampshire in New England, 1736–1884." n.p. Photocopy of christenings for the years 1788–1795, courtesy of Alan F. Rumrill, Historical Society of Cheshire County, correspondence dated June 3, 2009, in my possession.

39. Hurd, *History of Cheshire and Sullivan Counties*, 570.

40. Haynes, *Sacred and Secular*, 76.

41. New Hampshire, Cheshire County, Probate Estate Files 1769–1885, "Estate of Captain John Follett," 416.

42. Haynes, *Sacred and Secular*, 76.

43. Child, *Gazetteer of Cheshire County*, 537.

44. New Hampshire, Cheshire County, Administrations, 1823–1869, "Estate of Captain John Follett."

45. New Hampshire, Cheshire County, Probate Estate Files, Dowers Claims, Settlement of Estates of Widows, 1814–1886, 46:52–54.

46. Wording on individual headstones copied during personal visit to Cemetery in 1999. Also courtesy of Cliff Struthers.

47. Photocopy of death listing from the *New Hampshire Sentinel*, p. 34, courtesy Historical Society of Cheshire County, with correspondence dated June 3, 2009, in my possession.

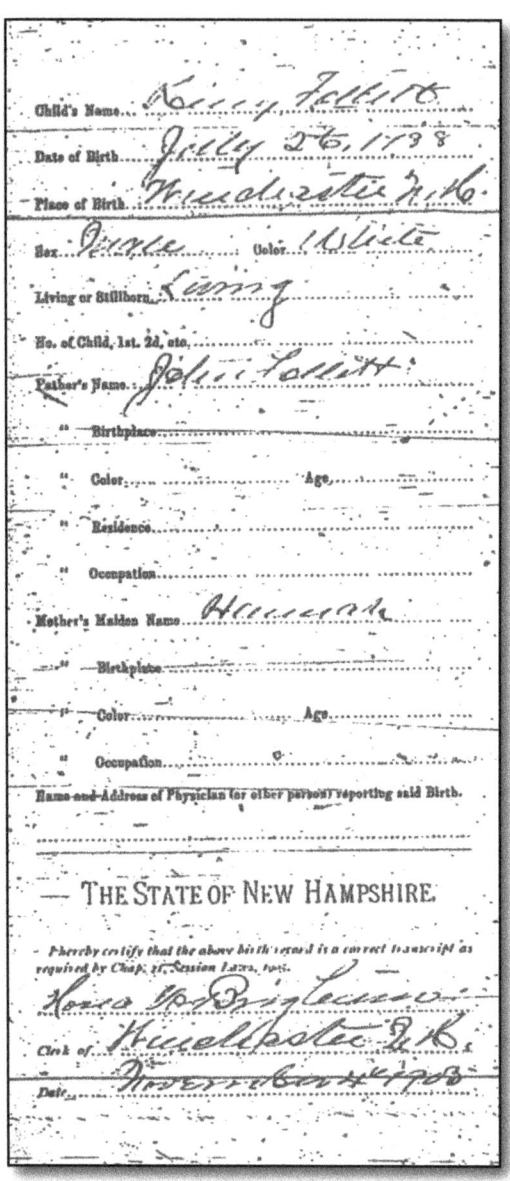

King Follett's birth record, July 26, 1788, Winchester, Cheshire, New Hampshire. Courtesy Winchester Town Hall.

❈ Chapter Two ❈

When New Hampshire Meets New York

It was a hot humid day on July 26, 1788,¹ when King Follett was born, undoubtedly at the Follett home located in the small town of Winchester, New Hampshire.

The earliest known Winchester map is dated 1805, when King was seventeen. It identifies land owned by the Folletts at the north end of a road just east of what was then called Winchester Forest and is now known as Pisgah State Park. A 1983 publication referring to this 1805 map, provides this information about the area: "Next to the forest is the Chesterfield Road, which was well inhabited by 1805. Most of these homesites are now [1983] abandoned. . . . The buildings shown [in 1805] are mostly farmhouses, probably those belonging to the more well-to-do residents."²

Later nineteenth-century maps in the Adkins collection show other land owned by members of the extended Follett family closer to the center of town.

No photograph or written physical description of King survives; but such descriptions exist for two of his sons, and perhaps he shared some of their traits. These sons were Edward, who was six feet one, and Warren, five feet ten. Both had gray eyes, though Follett men of my father's generation were characterized by deep blue eyes.³

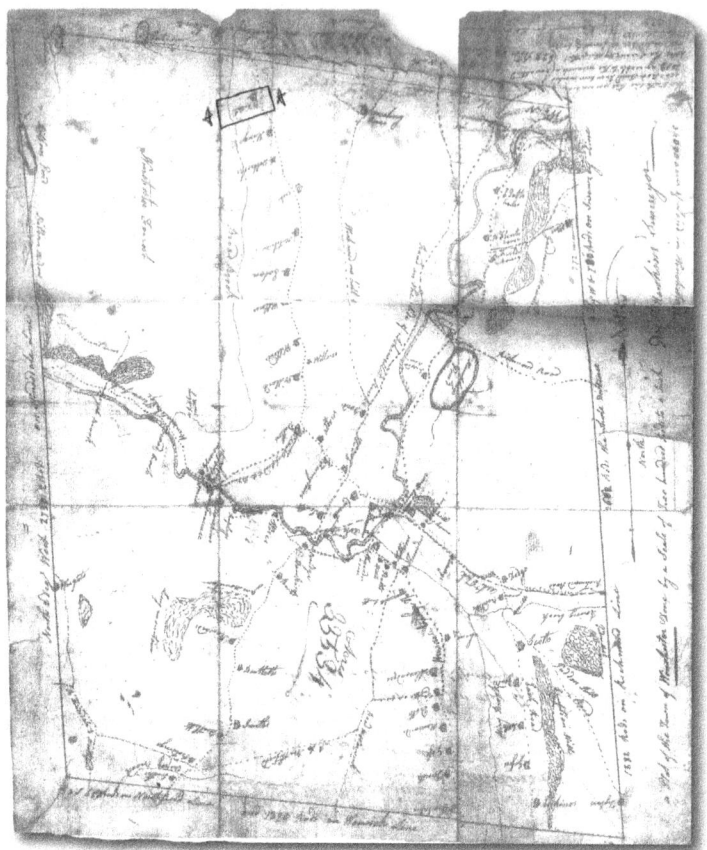

Map of Winchester, 1805. Note in the upper left corner the location of King's birth place on Follett property. Used by permission of Zelda Moore, New Hampshire State Library, Concord, New Hampshire.

When the first national census was taken in 1790, John and Hannah Follett's household included eight males and two females under age sixteen. King was then about two.[4] His birthplace, Cheshire County, was in the southwestern corner of New Hampshire, approximately eighty miles west of Boston. The area was first surveyed in 1733 and settled two years later. In January 1776, New Hampshire was the first colony to declare its independence from England and to form its own state government. After the Follett family moved there in 1777, a town meeting discussed and voted on whether the towns east of the Connecticut River would become part of the new state of Vermont. The citizens of Winchester and thirty-three other nearby communities "voted not to join the union with Vermont,"⁵ but perhaps this early ambiguity about state lines explains why some early Mormon Church records identify his birthplace as Vermont.

The Cheshire County area had grown from 1,300 inhabitants when the Follett family first arrived to a little over 19,000 with 1,209 of them in Winchester in 1788 when King was born.⁶ Also that year, the proposed U.S. Constitution was sent to the states for ratification. After heated debate, the General Court in Concord, New Hampshire, formally ratified the document on June 21, a month before King's birth. This event and the resulting changes in the political, government, and community environment locally and throughout the growing nation would provide the setting in which King lived for the next fifty-six years.

Cheshire County still had frontier characteristics as King grew up. The few frame homes were outnumbered by log houses. No record from the Folletts has survived about life in Winchester during these early years. However, they would probably have had experiences similar to those of the Rixford family who settled in the area in 1782, six years before King's birth:

> The first season he [Simon Rixford] cleared about ten acres of land, built the log cabin.... There were no laid out roads, only paths on which he could ride on horse-back, and the early settlers... built a cabin wherever they might choose a location. Added to the hardships and deprivations attending their pioneer life, was [sic] the depredations on their flocks of sheep by the bears and wolves. Many times he was obliged to leave his bed at night, seize a fire brand, and thus armed drive the wolves from his door. The nearest grist-mill at the time of his settlement was at Northfield, Mass. Hither he and his neighbors wended their way with a bag of corn or rye, the most fortunate carrying it on horseback, the less fortunate, on their shoulders.⁷

King and his siblings grew up in a thick forest of many varieties of trees and dense undergrowth. A modern photograph taken near the site of the Follett home shows vegetation that must be much like that in which King grew up.

King and his brothers learned early to work on the family farm and help provide the necessities of life. Every family grew grains and vegetables for home use and to feed livestock. Berries grew wild and most families kept an apple orchard, using the fruit for food and for liquor, which was consumed or sold. The young men of each family spent long

Peggy Follett Jones, left, and Joann Follett Mortensen standing at the site of John Follett's house, their fourth great-grandfather and King's father, in Winchester. Photo by Irval L. Mortensen, 1999.

hours each day tending crops and animals, for it required everyone's labor to meet daily needs.

Clothes were entirely made at home from flax grown on the property and wool sheared from the family sheep. These items were usually left the natural color or dyed in dark colors like browns, blacks, greens, and blues. Perhaps once a year the average farmer would go to Boston or another large market town where he would trade surplus from the family farm for items that could not be raised, grown, or produced at home. This surplus might consist of butter, cheese, dried and salted pork, beef or poultry, and perhaps excess fabric. Purchased items could include salt, rum, tea, molasses, and small gifts for the children. These items were transported in simple wagons pulled by one or two horses or even oxen. At times goods were carried using panniers, which were two baskets, one suspended on each side of an animal. Horseback riding, often with two people on the same horse, was the usual mode of personal travel prior to 1800.[8] The first post office was not established until 1811, after King was no longer living in the area. Bears, deer, wolves, foxes, and many other animals and birds abounded in the area; typically, King would have spent much time hunting and fishing, both for pleasure and for food for the family.

King, his siblings, and other New Hampshire children would have had the opportunity to receive some formal schooling, since the Province of New Hampshire passed its first law requiring towns to tax its citizens to establish schools in 1693. By 1719 that same body modified that law by requiring every town to hire schoolmasters and, where there were 100 or more families, to establish a school where students would learn reading, writing, and arithmetic.[9] As early as 1770, Winchester had at least three schools; and by 1805, New Hampshire formed school districts and authorized the building and repair of schoolhouses.[10] It is not possible to document King's schooling, nor have I found any records in his handwriting, other than his signature; but he, his numerous siblings, and the neighborhood children would presumably have attended school for at least a part of each year. Furthermore, his father's signature has survived on a number of land purchases and sales. Therefore, he would have understood the value of literacy for his children, particularly his sons. Other suggestions of at least average education are that King, based on his taxes, was about as financially successful as his peers, one document refers to business affairs in New York, and he successfully carried out his duties in the Mormon Church. (See chaps. 5, 8, and 9.)

As King grew to manhood, New Hampshire was, according to a nineteenth-century historian, "distinguished from inhabitants of other sections of our vast country, [only] by their hardihood in danger and patience in suffering, as well as by their sobriety and hospitality." He praised their industry and frugality: "Though few are very wealthy, all are comfortable. . . . No man ever perished here for want of food or raiment" and adds, "Whatever opinion the foreigner may form from the roughness of our exterior . . . he will find hospitality to inhabit every dwelling."[11] These traits, particularly hospitality, were apparent throughout King's life; documentation is not lacking about how willingly he assisted others, especially fellow Church members in Missouri. (See chaps. 8, 11, and 12.)

Because children are not listed by name until the 1850 census, it is difficult to trace exactly how long King lived in New Hampshire during his childhood. The 1800 census, when King would have been twelve, lists John Follett with three males between ages ten and sixteen.[12] The transcription of the 1810 census, taken when King was twenty-two, does not list John, although land records show he was still in the area. Nor does King appear as a separate householder. The holograph census is water stained. At least two entries in the "F's" could be "Follett," but it is impossible to read the first name.[13] Thus, the next document that specifically identifies King is an 1811 land record in St. Lawrence County, New York, when he was twenty-three.[14]

Louisa Tanner, who would become King's wife, was also New England born and bred. Born in 1798 or 1799, when King was about ten, she was the fourth child of Thomas Tanner III and Anna Warren Tanner, then living in Cooperstown, Otsego County, New York.[15] Louisa's Tanner ancestors had settled in Rhode Island in about 1642 and, by 1742, were living in Cornwall, Connecticut, on Indian Lane. Contemporary descriptions mention their large physical stature.[16] Louisa's great-grandfather, Thomas Tanner Sr., enlisted to serve in the French and Indian War (April 21–December 4, 1761). He was a member of the Tenth Company under "Captain Samuel Elmer" in the Second Regiment under Colonel Nathan Whiting.[17]

His namesake son, Louisa's grandfather, born in 1743, served as a second lieutenant of Bradley's Connecticut State Regiment beginning June 10, 1776.[18] A history of his birthplace, Cornwall, Connecticut, provides biographical information about him. He recruited some of the soldiers who served with him and were captured with him at the battle of Fort Washington (near present-day 179th Street, New York City) on November 16, 1776. Following their capture, they were marched by night to Brooklyn and imprisoned on Long Island. Some were held as long as four years, though Tanner was released the following year. During their imprisonment, Tanner took care of other prisoners, including loaning them money for which the legislature reimbursed him £7/8/2. Though "lieutenant" was his official commission, he "was afterward known as 'Capt. Tanner,' and highly esteemed in church and town."[19] Both before and after the war, Thomas Jr. was elected to "Tune the Psalm"[20] at the First Church of Christ in Cornwall and was on the First Church

The Presbyterian Church of Cooperstown, originally built about 1800. This was the home church of the Thomas Tanner family when Louisa Tanner Follett was a small child. Photo by Irval L. Mortensen, 1999.

Committee there for many years. He married Anna Baldwin on October 30, 1765, and they became the parents of six children.[21] Thomas Jr. and wife Anna Baldwin Tanner apparently moved with their son Thomas III and his wife, Anna Warren Tanner, to Cooperstown, New York, as they are buried there in Christ Church Cemetery.[22] (Louisa's mother and her paternal grandmother were both named Anna which, with the proliferation of Thomases, makes sorting out the generations difficult.)

Louisa's parents, Thomas III and Anna, moved from Connecticut to Cooperstown, New York, about 130 miles to the northwest, about 1791. Here they raised their eight children. Thomas was a carpenter and the local sheriff.[23] Louisa was their fourth child and second daughter. Follett family and early Mormon records agree on a birth date of August 3; however, some give the year as 1798 while her obituary states 1799.[24] The 1800 census lists two females under age ten.[25] Civil records are very spotty for that area and period, and their home denomination, the Presbyterian Church, had not yet been built. The first entry in its minutes, dated June 16, 1800, documents that Thomas Tanner and seven others, "having just made a public profession of their faith in Jesus Christ, unanimously and voluntarily entered into a bond of Christian fellowship and communion, and were constituted a regular Presbyterian Church." The same day, those same eight were the first individuals received into membership "having good recommendations from regular churches in New England." Seven months later on January 10, 1801, Anna Baldwin Tanner, Louisa's grandmother, was admitted as a member, confirming that the parents had moved with or shortly after the son, from Connecticut to New York. Six months later on June 4, Louisa's mother, Anna Warren Tanner, also became a member.[26] The church records contain information on the baptisms as infants of three of Louisa's younger siblings (an unnamed child on September 4, 1803; Lucas, on October 6, 1805; and Thomas Warren, February 12, 1809), and the deaths of her grandfather Thomas in 1818 and her grandmother Anna in 1825.[27]

Judge William Cooper of Burlington, New Jersey, headed the first settlement of Cooperstown in 1786.[28] Father of author James Fenimore Cooper and a great land speculator, Judge Cooper chose an elevated piece of land at the foot of Otsego Lake and near the Susquehanna River as his townsite. The lake is often referred to as "the glimmer glass" because of its clarity and shine. In 1803 Judge Cooper led thirty-four Cooperstown residents north approximately 200 miles to settle on another new land purchase he had made on the Oswegatchie River in an area known as DeKalb (a part of which was later named Hermon) in St. Lawrence County, New York. Seth and Elias Alexander, King's older half-brothers, were among those who followed that initial group of settlers during the winter of 1803–4 or the following spring. It is not clear whether they were coming from Cooperstown or direct from New Hampshire.[29] Fifteen-year-old King's location cannot be determined for certain, but he may have accompanied the Alexanders; some undocumented family records state that he lived in Cooperstown prior to moving to St. Lawrence County.[30] About six years later in March 1809 when Louisa was ten, the Tanner family also moved from Cooperstown to St. Lawrence County. Thomas Tanner is listed as one of the very earliest residents of what is now Hermon and served as a town supervisor in 1834–36.[31] A small stream and two roads/streets were named for Thomas Tanner and still carry those names today.[32] Here Louisa grew up on the family farm and, since later records show that she was literate, received some schooling.

St. Lawrence County was named for the great river. Many other rivers and lakes dot the landscape, and the Adirondacks form mountainous highlands. DeKalb was No. 7 of the ten original townships in the county, each ten miles square, all of them created on September 10, 1787. DeKalb consisted of small rocky ridges interspersed by narrow fertile valleys. The local Indians were peaceful and would often visit the small settlements looking for whisky. Early town ordinances imposed a fine of $1.00 on householders who let certain weeds and thistles grow; they also paid a bounty for every wolf and panther scalp—details that suggest living conditions. The first road was officially recorded in 1806, suggesting that the early settlers lived close together.

Seth and Elias Alexander are listed as jurors in 1806[33] and as "electors" who were also identified as "heads of families" in DeKalb in 1807.[34] King may have lived with one of their families. The 1810 census lists in Elias Alexander's household a male between ages sixteen and twenty-six. As Elias was only thirty-three, it is improbable that he had a son of that age; however, King was then twenty-two.[35] Furthermore, the pattern of siblings and members of the extended family following a pioneer relative to new settlements is well established. No other Follett surnames appear in the St. Lawrence County census records until 1840, long after King had left the area. Thus, the next document that specifically identifies King is an 1811 land purchase in St. Lawrence County, New York, made when he was twenty-three.[36]

No records have survived about when and how King and Louisa met. An 1814 document titled "Potter Goff Survey Classification of the Township of DeKalb" states that King owned land that he had purchased in 1811. That neighborhood or ("Division") had fourteen owners and was described as "Choice Lots with handsome improvements, under good cultivation and peopled by able settlers." The description, in short phrases with many abbreviations, is a fascinating glimpse of this acreage: "Bought of Cholan by E Grover nothing then cleared the advance of 50 cents was given, the same as Cholan gave Farr. Follett bought of Grover. 3 years ago, Augt 1811—then cleared 20 acres—$300 was given for the Betterments. *Cleared* now. 20 acres. 4 meadow remains save 6 acres (which is too stony to plough)—ploughland[.] *Stock*—none kept on it. Follett was in Co with Whipple in the distilling business. Having dissolved, F. is undetermined whether to go on his Farm, or else-where to work—(No payments made) on premises. A log house unfinished."[37]

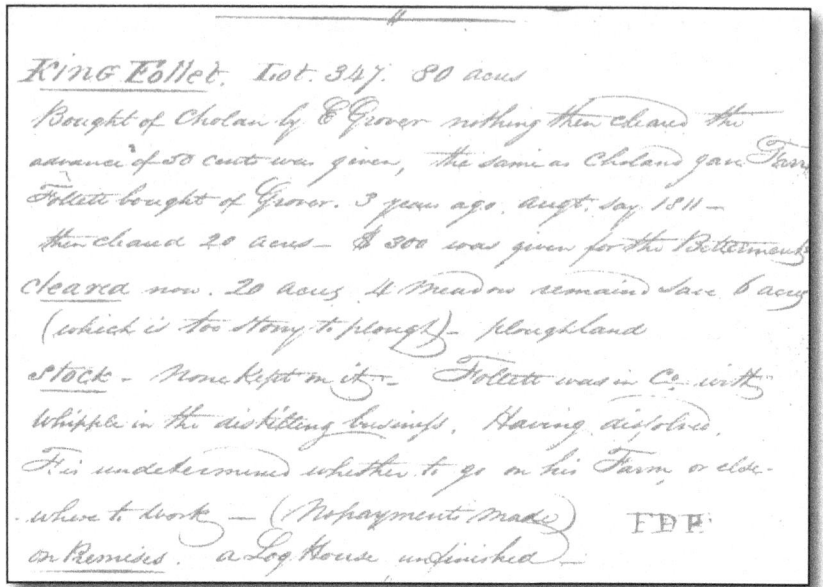

Entry for King Follett's land. "Potter Goff Survey Classification of the Township of DeKalb." 1814.

The current available land records do not state exactly when King bought this land, how much he paid for it, nor when he sold it. Modern records, however, do identify Lot 347 as presently lying on U.S. Route 11, next door to the DeKalb Historical Society Meeting House Museum. A house and a rest area presently occupy the land.[38]

This same "Potter Goff Survey Classification of the Township of DeKalb" shows that Louisa's father owned two tracts of land in the Second Division, described as: "Similar Lots [to the First Division] with smaller improvements occupied by settlers not as capable." Thomas Tanner Jr. owned Lot 336 containing 77 acres, which he used as pasture, and Lot 377 containing 216 acres, which was the family homestead. The Goff survey followed up its "not as capable" statement with a critique of Tanner: "A good matured man, called honest, tho too fond of being at the Hotel, drinking & talking away time, may be called indolent from his paying little attention to farming—not withstanding; all are pleased with him."[39]

DeKalb's Town Meeting Book for 1806–45 mentions King fifteen times, spelling his name both "Follett" and "Follet." The first mention ap-

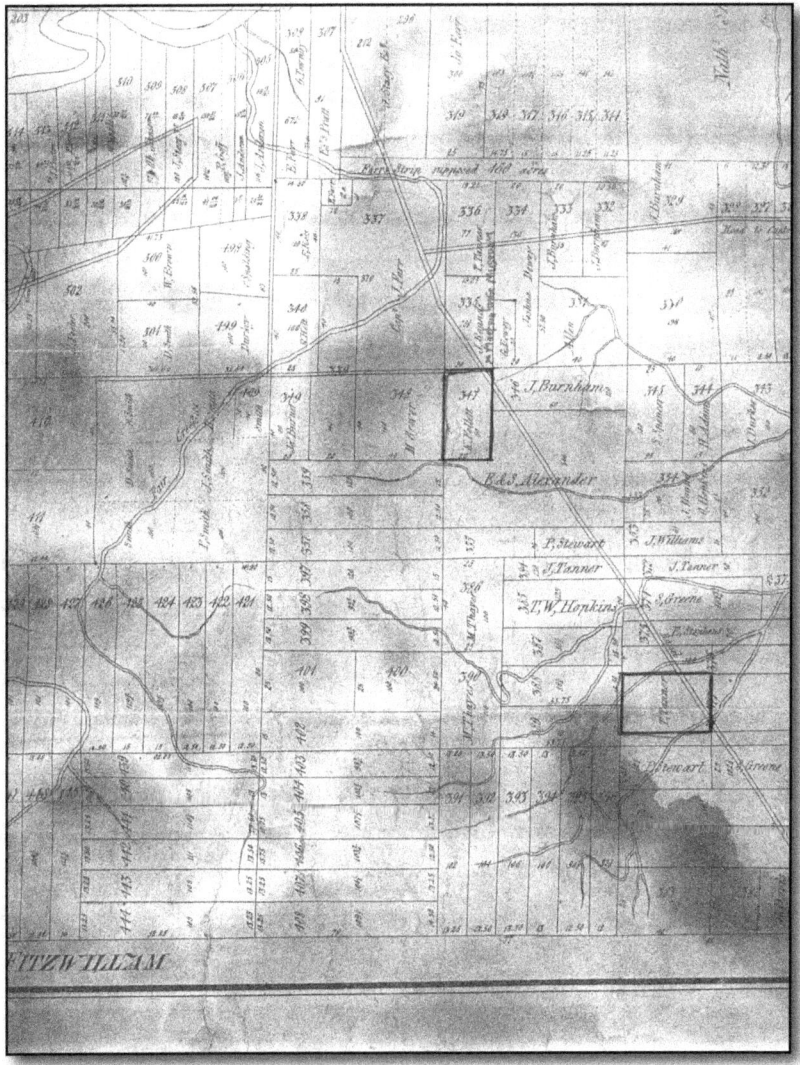

Present site of Lot 347, which King owned in 1811, in DeKalb, New York. Courtesy of DeKalb Historical Association.

pears on March 2, 1813, and contains a "List of town officers chosen and town laws made at the Eighth annual town meeting." King, as one of the "Overseers of Highways, was assigned to District 5 of the fifteen highway districts. While that record does not give a specific job description, town histories and laws of the time throughout New England describe general duties of developing and maintaining roads. The overseer was responsible for recommending when and where a new road might be needed and supervising the residents who were expected to perform road maintenance themselves on the dirt road or series of dirt roads in the area where they lived and owned property. The land owners could also be assessed taxes, at the recommendation of the overseer, to pay for necessary road-repair equipment and could be fined if they failed to show up for assigned roadwork or pay tax assessments. The overseers were required to keep records and submit a report to town officials.[40] King and the overseers took this oath: "We do severally solemnly and sincerely promise and swear that we will in all things to the best of our knowledge and understanding and ability will and faithfully execute and perform the trust reposed in us as Overseers of Highways in the town of Dekalb in the County of St. Lawrence."[41]

The second mention occurs on June 21, 1813, when King's name was added to the jury list. On that same day the Commissioners of Excise granted a license to "Follet & Whipple to retail liquors." This license, which cost five dollars, was good until the first Tuesday of the following May. There is no record of renewal.[42] In February 1814 when the overseers reported the number of days worked (presumably for pay), King reported forty-six[43] and was later (no specific date given) selected as a "Path Master" for District 5. Despite the different title, he was probably being reappointed as a highway overseer, since on March 1, 1814, he again took that oath.[44] His name appears on the 1815 jury list with his future father-in-law, Thomas Tanner, and his two half-brothers, Elias and Seth Alexander.[45] In 1816 he again took the oath for verseer of Highways, this time in District 11, and was paid for twenty-nine days of work.[46] In March 1817 he again took the oath, this time in District 10, and reported working thirty-one days.[47] The 1817 jury list is the final record containing his name.[48]

Northern New York, including St. Lawrence County, was deeply involved in the War of 1812. Neither the military history of the county nor the War of 1812 Pension Index in the National Archives shows King as having served in the war, although he would certainly have been the right age and living close to many important battles. Seth Alexander does appear in the military records.[49]

In about 1815–16, twenty-seven-year-old King and seventeen-year-old Louisa were married in St. Lawrence County. The date comes from her obituary, which states: "When she was ten years of age she removed to St. Lawrence County, New York, where she was married at the age of seventeen to King Follett."[50] I have found no civil or church record of their marriage. Both were members of the Methodist Episcopal Church before converting to Mormonism. In St. Lawrence County, the Methodist Episcopal Society was the first "body of believers . . . to commence their labors in town."[51] About ten members began meeting in DeKalb during the winter of 1811–12. In 1816 Seth and Elias Alexander joined the group,[52] and it seems likely that King and Louisa also became members, but the church "did not form a legal organization until February 25, 1829."[53]

At the time King and Louisa married, the St. Lawrence Methodist circuit was served by three circuit riders: Robert Menshall, Wyat Chamberlin, and John Demster, any of whom could have officiated. Follett family records give a wedding date in both 1815 and 1816, probably mirroring the difference in the same records about whether Louisa was born in 1798 or 1799. The place of the marriage is also listed as both Hermon and DeKalb. Hermon was once part of DeKalb, officially given its own name in 1834, even though the neighborhood of Hermon appears in records of many events before that date. In Louisa's brief diary after King's death in 1844, she visited the Hermon-DeKalb area and mused: "Again I pass the Cottage where I begun first to preform [sic] the duties of a wife and Mother stop and look towards that once loved place . . . [but] he that used to share my joys and sorrow is no more the kind hand that was ever open to admnenster [sic] to my wants is now cold in Death and with my little orphin Boy I am a wandrer alone and unprotected."[54] Louisa's "little orphan Boy" is her youngest son, Warren King, then six years old.

King's and Louisa's first child, Adeline Louisa, was born on December 21, 1816, in DeKalb.[55] As early as 1807, the tensions that led to the War of 1812 in the United States had caused land prices to decline and created general wariness where commerce was involved, especially transactions across the border into Canada. The war began in June 1812 and continued until 1815, heavily impacting northern New York. Unable to make a living, many residents moved away, leaving the region almost deserted. A general depression followed throughout the United States.

Adding to these problems—and causing new ones—was a series of extremely cold years, caused by volcanic ash in the atmosphere. Throughout the northeastern United States and southern Canada, 1815–16 became known as "the year without a summer." Snow in June destroyed crops in the bud. King's name disappears from town records after May 1817, suggesting that they moved away soon after that date—or at least before May 1818 when the new Overseers of Highway were chosen. For the first time since 1813, King was not listed.

By 1819 they were living in Ohio, about 450 miles south and west by modern roads. Their mode of travel is conjectural; but depending on the season, they could have ridden horses, walked, used wagons or sleighs, or a combination. A probable route was traveling overland to Buffalo or Rome, and taking a boat or barge on the numerous rivers, Lake Ontario, or Lake Erie. The Erie Canal, which became such an economic and travel boon for the area, was not yet constructed. Perhaps they traveled with members of the Tanner family or visited them on the way, as Louisa's brother Joseph and his family appear on the 1820 census for Attica Center, New York, which is located east of Buffalo on one possible travel route.[56] Louisa may have been pregnant during the journey as their second child, another John, was born in October 1819 in their new home, in Shalersville, Ohio.

Notes

1. King Follett, Birth Record, Births "F," Winchester Town Records, Winchester Town Hall, Winchester, New Hampshire, personal visit September 22, 1999. Some other sources, primarily early LDS Church records, give his birth date as either July 24 or 25, 1788.

2. Edith Adkins, Early Maps of Winchester, New Hampshire, 1733–1892, 8, 10. I visited Winchester in 1999 and observed that this area was also referred to as Clark Road.

3. Contra Costa County, California, County Clerk, Great Registers, 1867–1898. LDS Family History Library, Microfilm #976458, Edward Follett's registration record, 1892. Photocopies of the original documents of Warren K.

Follett in the Muster Roll of Company B, 29th Iowa Infantry obtained from Beverly Boileau, in my possession.

4. U.S. Census, 1790, New Hampshire, Cheshire County, Winchester, Roll M637_5, image 0065.

5. D. Hamilton Hurd, *History of Cheshire and Sullivan Counties, New Hampshire*, 567.

6. John Hayward, *A Gazetteer of New Hampshire*, 148.

7. Hamilton Child, *Gazetteer of Cheshire County, N. H. 1736–1885*, 542.

8. Benjamin Reed, *The History of Swanzey, New Hampshire: From 1734 to 1890*, 80–84.

9. R. Stuart Wallace and Douglas E. Hall, *A New Hampshire Education Timeline*, n.d.

10. John Farmer, Jacob B. Moore, and Abel Bowen, *A Gazetteer of the State of New Hampshire*, 34–35.

11. Ibid., 36.

12. U.S. Census, 1800, New Hampshire, Cheshire County, Winchester, Roll 20, p. 1066, image 180. This name is transcribed both as John Chollett and John Follett on the current census information recorded on the Ancestry.com website.

13. U.S. Census, 1810, New Hampshire, Cheshire County, Winchester, Roll 23, pp. 122–23, image 70.

14. "Potter Goff Survey Classification of the Township of DeKalb," 1814, pp. A and 5.

15. Elias F. Tanner, *The Genealogy of the Descendants of Thomas Tanner, Sr., of Cornwall, Connecticut*, 42. See the discussion below for the ambiguity on Louisa's birthdate.

16. Ibid., 1, 33–48.

17. *Rolls of Connecticut Men in the French and Indian War: 1755–1762*, 10:277–79. This enlistment record does not include mention of pay.

18. Francis B. Heitman, *Historical Register of Officers of the Continental Army during the War of the Revolution, April 1775 to December 1783*, 532.

19. Edward C. Starr, *A History of Cornwall, Connecticut: A Typical New England Town*, 87, 186–87, 380, 514–15.

20. "Tune the Psalm" referred to giving the pitch for a psalm during a church service. The minister would identify the psalm and read it. Then a deacon (sometimes two, taking turns) would read each line. This step was called "lining the psalm" or "deaconing" it. Someone would then "tune the psalm" by singing it alone; the congregation would then sing it in turn. Joseph Dow, *Joseph Dow's History of the Town of Hampton, from Its First Settlement in 1638, to the Autumn of 1892*, 411.

21. Edward C. Starr, *A History of Cornwall, Connecticut: A Typical New England Town*, 380.

22. Patricia Law Hatcher, *Abstract of Graves of Revolutionary Patriots*, 4:97. See also Royden Woodward Vosburgh, ed., "Records of the Presbyterian Church of Cooperstown in Otsego County, N.Y.," 45–46.

23. Tanner, *The Genealogy of the Descendants of Thomas Tanner*, 33.

24. Louisa Tanner Follett, in AncestralFile; also family records in my possession; "Death of Mrs. Follett," *Malvern (Iowa) Leader*, November 15, 1891, photocopy in my possession.

25. U.S. Census, 1800, New York, Otsego County, Otsego, Roll 25, p. 595, image 43. Three generations of Thomas Tanners make it difficult to determine which man is meant; this census record apparently identifies him as "Jr."

26. Royden Woodward Vosburgh, ed., "Records of the Presbyterian Church of Cooperstown in Otsego County, N.Y.," 111–12.

27. Ibid., 5–7, 45–46.

28. Isaac N. Arnold, *A Centennial Offering: Being a Brief History of Cooperstown with a Biographical Sketch of James Fenimore Cooper*, 19.

29. Samuel W. Durant and Henry B. Peirce, *History of St. Lawrence Co., New York, 1749–1878*, 351–52.

30. Henry Lebbeus Oak, *Oak/Oaks/Oakes: Family Register Nathaniel Oak of Marlborough, Mass.*, 55.

31. Samuel W. Durant and Henry B. Peirce, *History of St. Lawrence Co., New York, 1749–1878*, 351–52.

32. Kelsie B. Harder and Mary H. Smallman, *Claims to Name: Toponyms of St Lawrence County*, 235.

33. Franklin B. Hough, *A History of St. Lawrence and Franklin Counties, New York: From the Earliest Period to the Present Time*, 238, 287–88.

34. Gates Curtis, ed., *Our County and Its People: A Memorial Record of St. Lawrence County, New York*, 507.

35. Ralph V. Wood Jr., *Jefferson and St. Lawrence Counties, New York State, 1810 and 1820 Federal Population Census Schedules: Transcripts and Index*, 61. The 1810 census also lists two males ages twenty-six to forty-five who could have been brothers Elias and Seth, since Seth is not separately listed, even though he had been on a list of electors who were identified as "head of families" three years earlier. Others listed were two females, ages sixteen to twenty-six, who could have been wives of the two Alexander brothers.

36. "Classification of the Township of DeKalb," in "Potter Goff Survey 1814 Town of DeKalb," pp. A, 5. Though the date is given as 1814 in the title, on p. A is written "Drawn 6.8 April 1815."

37. Ibid., p. A. King's property was eighty acres, Lot 347, in the First Division.

38. Virginia Fischer, Town Historian, DeKalb Historical Association, Correspondence and map to Joann Mortensen, December 7, 2006.

39. "Potter Goff Survey Classification of the Township of DeKalb," 1814, pp. A and 63.

40. Andrew W. Young, *The Project Gutenberg E Book of the Government Class Book*, Chapter 16, section 6; Town Highway Records, Benton, Yates County, New York.

41. DeKalb Town Meeting, Book 1, 1806–45, 74, 78.

42. Ibid., 80, 82.

43. Ibid., 83.

44. Ibid., 87, 91.

45. Ibid., 101.

46. Ibid., 106, 111–12.

47. Ibid., 119, 123, 125.

48. Ibid., 127.

49. Hough, *A History of St. Lawrence and Franklin Counties*, 622–24.

50. Louisa Tanner Follett, Obituary, *Malvern (Iowa) Leader*, November 19, 1891.

51. Curtis Gates, ed., *Our County and Its People*, 516.

52. "130 Years of Methodism in DeKalb."

53. Gates, *Our County and Its People*, 516.

54. Louisa Tanner Follett, Diary, September 18, 1844, unpaginated.

55. "Died: West," *Malvern Leader*, August 3, 1884.

56. U.S. Census, 1820, New York, Genesee County, Attica, Roll M33_72, p. 11, image 15.

❋ Chapter Three ❋

To the Ohio Country: 1819

Though King and his brother, Alexander Follett,[1] first appeared on the census and tax records in the small town of Shalersville, Portage County, Ohio, in 1820, they had already lived there for at least part of a year and had moved into an area certainly still considered "the frontier." The town's present location is at the intersection of Ohio State Highways 363 and 44, about half a mile south of Interstate 80. It is not known if the two brothers traveled together or met there by arrangement, nor are the circumstances known that brought them to this somewhat isolated part of northeastern Ohio. Alexander was about eight years King's junior and the only full sibling that King had documented contact with after leaving New Hampshire.

Following the Revolutionary War, the U.S. government as well as most of the New England states began to turn their attention to the land west of the original thirteen colonies. Good farmland in many places in New England was not always readily available. The "Ohio Country" appeared to have the two main ingredients for successful settlement: (1) large areas of fertile, unbroken land, rich in timber for new homes, game animals, and fish; and (2) abundant water, including rivers and proximity to the Great Lakes. Whether it was through bounty lands owned by former military members, a church group seeking greater freedom to worship, or land speculators and developers buying and selling for a profit, the western movement of American civilization gained new impetus during the late 1700s and early 1800s. One author described the movement as having "the dimensions of a mass exodus. . . . Indeed, the majority of New Englanders flooding into the West took the northern route to the Western Reserve, which eventually stretched on to Michigan, Illinois and beyond."[2]

Shalersville lies in the Connecticut Western Reserve, so called because that state had reserved its right to this land. In the years before the American Revolution, New England states claimed rights to land from their eastern borders going westward coast to coast. The land claimed by Connecticut included a "120 mile strip in the Ohio Country" in the northeastern corner of Ohio. In order to settle their Revolutionary War debts, Connecticut sold off all but its Ohio holdings shortly after the war. Part of the remaining area was to be sold and the proceeds used for public education in Connecticut; some land was to be given to Revolutionary War veterans, primarily those from Connecticut, to compensate them for their service. The remaining part of the Western Reserve, 3,000,000 acres, was sold in 1798 to the Connecticut Land Company, a group of thirty-five land speculators. Each parcel was then divided, and most were sold several times over the next years. Townships were surveyed and counties organized.[3] There is no way to determine why King and Alexander Follett chose to move to the Western Reserve or whether they were able to use their father's Revolutionary War service to obtain a right to live on land they cleared in Shalersville.

Portage County was established in 1807 with Ravenna, six miles south of Shalersville, as the county seat. At this time, the entire county had a few hundred inhabitants scattered throughout the county in only four townships, each "a pretty large territory of indefinite size."[4] To encourage settlement, land speculators distributed advertisements throughout the eastern states describing positive attributes of the area and encouraging families to move west. Many did and made a record of their adventures by writing letters home to relatives. The unnamed editor's introduction to information gleaned from the Hoskin Family letters telling of their move to the Western Reserve in 1816 commented: "Many—singly or as family groups—sold their land and homes, packed up everything they owned, and headed for the Paradise in the Western Reserve, promised to them in ads everywhere they looked."[5] Perhaps King and Louisa, like hundreds of others, responded to these promises of a bright future.

As population increased in the Western Reserve during the first part of the nineteenth century, Portage County was one of the slower-growing counties because of its location—not close enough to the major communities and too far south of Lake Erie to benefit from commerce and emigration. However, less than positive reports from early visitors to the area may have been an added reason for Portage County's slow growth. In 1811 a prospective land buyer described Portage County as "a country of dull people, who look pale and sickly.... The Cuyahoga River stank.... [The people] lived much on pumpkin pies."[6] An early doctor who came there to practice was concerned because "most families lived, cooked, ate, slept, dressed and undressed in one room.... People had no manners and preachers were either fanatical or ignorant.... There was plenty of room for improvement."[7]

In 1810, Portage County's population was 2,995; by 1820, shortly after King's arrival, it had increased to 10,095, and by 1830 it had reached 18,820.[8] Shalersville was named for General Nathaniel Shaler of Connecticut who obtained title in the land drawing from the Connecticut Land Company. The first settlers arrived in 1806, the first schoolhouse was built in 1810, the township was organized and the first election held in 1812, and the first store was opened in 1816. Still, as late as 1815, a settler described it as "a wilderness[,] civilization having scarcely left its impress within its borders."[9] Since the first road in the area was not "cut through the unbroken wilderness from Shalersville to Freedom," the nearest township to the east, until 1817, these early settlers lived an isolated existence.[10]

Most of these families were from areas in New England where they had received some formal schooling and considered education important for their children. According to a twentieth-century Ohio historian, "They were greatly distressed when they realized that their children would receive no education unless they, themselves, provided it. Wherever a few families were within walking distance of each other an effort was made to establish a school in one corner of a cabin where children could gather for a few hours of instruction in the three 'R's.'"[11] When the first schoolhouse was built in 1810, it was made of logs with oiled-paper windows and slab seats. Like many schoolhouses, it did double duty for town meetings and activities. Children walked through the woods to and from school and often saw wild animals in the forest.[12]

By the time, the Folletts settled in Shalersville (at least by 1819), the small town had a school, a blacksmith shop, a tannery, a sawmill, a grist

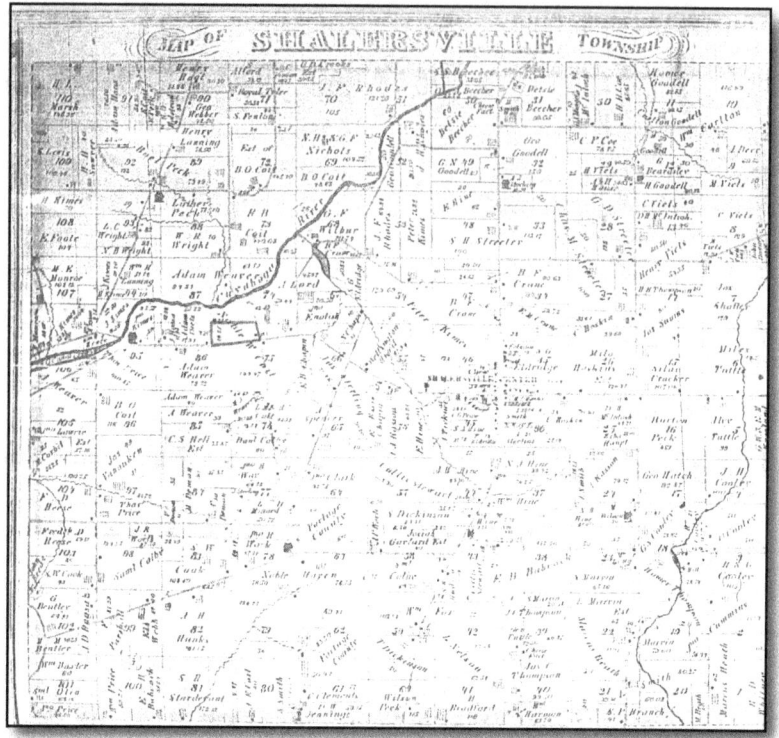

Map of Shalersville township identifying the present location of the land occupied by the Follett family at the intersection of Coits Road and State Route 303, west of the center of town and south of the Cuyahoga River. L. H. Everts, comp. and cartographer, *Combination Atlas Map of Portage County, Ohio*, 143.

mill, a store, and a Congregational church. Frame homes were beginning to replace log cabins. A history of Portage County, while not mentioning the Folletts, gives glimpses of conditions they would have encountered as they traveled from New England and made their new homes.

One family made the journey in four weeks from Massachusetts to Ohio with eight children, including a baby,

> in a large canvas covered wagon by way of Lake Champlain, Rochester, traveling by day and lodging at some unpretentious inn at night, or sleeping in their wagons or beneath the sheltering branches of the trees in some plot of woods by the wayside—the mother with her six-weeks old babe in her arms, sitting in her armchair, which had been removed from the wagon, and through the deep stillness of the night, now and then losing herself in the

broken slumber which tired, worn-out nature enforced. At break of day our travelers were astir and the hasty morning meal prepared, when they again resumed their journey.[13]

Another family arrived from New Hampshire in February with "two horses and a sleigh. They had to cross the river of Mantua on horseback, the water being so high that it was impossible to cross in the sleigh."[14]

Families not only had to create the food, fuel, and fabric for themselves on their individual farms but also find some means of producing commodities that could be sold or traded. One enterprising family who settled two miles north of the center of Shalersville in 1816 combined their large farm with two other endeavors. The wife operated a dry goods store at the farm while the husband also "had a manufactory for pot and pearl ashes [potash], which he sold in Pittsburgh in exchange for dry goods, driving back and forth with a team. The farm was heavily stocked with mules."[15]

Though there is no official documentation of the Folletts in Shalersville prior to 1820, later family, census, and Church records support the birth of King and Louisa's second child, John, on October 26, 1819, in Shalersville.[16] The first time that King appears on a U.S. census as a head of household is along with fifty-seven others in 1820. Apparently the household contained two "Free White Males 16–26," although there is a small mark or smudge on top of that numeral making it difficult to decipher with certitude. The two men must be King and probably Alexander, whose presence is documented in the tax record of 1820 and who had not yet married. Alexander was twenty-four, but some details are contradictory. King was thirty-two, not "16–26," and Louisa was twenty-two, not "26–45," as the census shows. The two children, Adeline and John, appear as one child of each sex under the age of ten. Occupations are listed as agriculture and manufacturing.[17] Perhaps the "manufacturing" was the distillery business, reminiscent of King's occupation in New York. Apples were grown in Shalersville, and apple cider and whiskey were common commodities on the frontier. It also could have referred to the cheese industry, which was important in Portage County from the earliest settlement.[18] Tax records discussed below show that King owned more "cattle" than would have been necessary for one family's dairy needs.

Between 1820 and 1832, King is listed on the county tax records as being taxed on real property only for 1820–26 and only for personal property from 1826–32.[19]

Alexander Follett married Caroline Baker on January 15, 1824, in Shalersville.[20] She was the daughter of Joel Baker, the first settler of Shalersville. Two and a half years later on August 16, 1826, Alexander died with no cause listed. An abstract of newspaper obituaries gives his place of death as Shalersville and his age as about thirty-five. He was a Freemason and "leaves family."[21] "Family" is not defined, so it is not clear whether he and Caroline had children. Alexander was buried in Hillside Cemetery. The wording on the headstone, located on Row 8, is not now legible but a 1995 survey interpreted the wording as "Follett, Ale H. [probably Alex] died Aug 16, 1826 age 33."[22]

The inventory of his estate valued it at $141.06. Among its items were towels, bedding, and tablecloths, household furniture, a spinning wheel, dishes, saddle, barrels, twenty pounds of coarse wool, twelve sheep, a calf, seven yearling steers, a ton of coarse hay, six bushels of rye and wheat "in the mow," a small plow, 39½ bushels of wheat, 25 bushels of rye, and 55½ gallons of whiskey. King and Louisa probably owned similar items. Alexander also held property valued at $67.88 "in common" with William B. Crane: a yoke of oxen, ten hogs, a calf, a three-year old heifer, and a "narrow axe." I could not find any additional information on Crane. However, an entry that might have some relationship to property for which both he Alexander and King were taxed reads: "An unexpired right to the use of thirteen acres of land two years" valued at $20.[23]

These fourteen years in Ohio from 1819 to 1832 turned out to be the longest time that King and Louisa lived in any location during their marriage. During those years, family records support the births of five children. Edward, born about 1821, was dead before 1833 when another son was given the same name. On April 8, 1823, Nancy was born, named for Louisa's older sister, followed by William Alexander, born on December 11, 1826,[24] and named for King's brother who had died four months earlier. Nancy and William Alexander are included on the 1830 census, and their birth dates are documented in Church records of the Missouri and Nauvoo periods. Two daughters, Emily and Mary, were born about 1829 and 1831, but apparently died young.[25] A daughter under age five appears in the 1830 census and could have been

Modern view of land once occupied by the Folletts in Shalersville: 16¾ acres in a quarter of Lot 75, Township 4, Range 8. Photo by Irval L Mortensen, 2006.

either.[26] As King's family grew with the addition of children, a sobering event occurred. King's father, John Follett, died February 20, 1829, in Winchester, New Hampshire, at age seventy-seven. How and when King learned of his father's death cannot be documented.[27]

Although no family information has survived about King and Louisa's stay in Shalersville, here is a list of some typical items and products and their costs taken from a collection of "early" undated Ohio records:

- A good cow sold for $10.00.
- A good horse sold for $25.00. This price suggests that King's $40 horse was an unusually fine animal.
- Supper, bed, and breakfast for a man and his horse at a hotel or tavern were about $.65.
- Meat cost 3.5–5 cents a pound. Eggs sold for 3–4 cents per dozen and potatoes 15–25 cents per bushel. Liquor of any kind was 3 cents a drink. Most everyone accepted a drink before each meal, though few men got drunk.

- Mail had to be picked up at the local post office (if there was one) and postage was 6 cents per item, payable by the receiving party.
- If a young man decided to become an apprentice to learn a trade, he received about $25 per year for three years, with board, washing, and mending included.[28]

Only one other record contains King's name: an 1827 enumeration in Portage County of white males over age twenty-one.[29] The reason for this enumeration is not given, though it may have been for voting, taxing, or military purposes. However, there is a separate record of voters in the county for 1816–56, and King is not listed.[30] It seems likely, however, that Shalersville would have "duplicated" many elements of "New England society" so that "in some ways [it] resembled a Connecticut countryside, thanks to having been settled almost completely by New Englanders with a Puritan background." There were few industries at this period in the Western Reserve "and the region was known for agriculture and dairy products."[31]

Religion, however, was correspondingly important. Some believers strove to replicate the established churches, especially Congregationalism, typical of New England, which insisted that a requirement for full membership was a spiritual experience assuring that the individual had been saved. Others sought a more open approach to membership and a more hospitable approach to participation. Frontier life undoubtedly weakened the rigid structures and hierarchy characteristic of the first New England towns. In isolated areas with limited population and no ordained minister, small groups often met together to worship without any designated leader or dogma. During the early settlement of Portage County, according to an anonymous county history:

> the settlers had to depend upon the stray crumbs that fell from the table of the Lord for their spiritual sustenance. Occasionally some hardy old Methodist circuit rider, or some missionary of the Connecticut Society of Home Missions would come along, but their visits were very infrequent, yet when they did come the occasion was one of great joy and satisfaction. The preacher was well taken care of, and if it was a Sabbath when he preached, the entire township would turn out to hear the word. Denomination, sect and particular belief were all dropped; immersion and sprinkling were not thought of, and the rigid Predestinarian and the absolute Free-Willer clasped

hands around the Altar of the Lord, beneath the overarching branches of some grand old oak, or at the humble cabin of the pioneer.[32]

While the intent of these gatherings may not have been to form new churches, sometimes that happened. About 1816, three settlers who had been raised Episcopalian organized the region's first religious services which were patterned after the Church. By 1824, the Methodist Episcopal Church began holding meetings in Ravenna, the seat of Portage County, ten miles south of Shalersville.[33] If the Follett family attended regular services, it was probably this church, as Louisa's obituary indicated she had been a Methodist Episcopalian before joining the Mormons. During the fall of 1830, four missionaries from the newly organized Mormon Church traveled through the area on their way to Missouri. It was not surprising that people were intensely curious, and some like King and Louisa were also willing to listen.

Notes

1. According to Alexander Follett, birth record, Winchester Town Hall, Birth Records "F," Alexander was born May 7, 1794. Some family records in my possession give the day as May 17. His full name may have been "Seth Alexander Follett." If so he would have been named for King's mother's first husband, Seth Alexander.

2. James W. Brown and Karen Powell, "From New England to Ohio," 154.

3. Judith Sheridan, "The Connecticut Western Reserve."

4. James B. Holmes and Lucille Dudley, *Portage Heritage: A History of Portage County, Ohio; Its Towns and Townships and the Men and Women Who Have Developed Them; Its Life, Institutions and Biographies, Facts and Lore*, 37.

5. "Hoskin Family," *Family History Letters*, 6.

6. Holmes and Dudley, *Portage Heritage*, 40.

7. Ibid.

8. Harold E. Davis, "Sources of Immigration into Portage County," 5.

9. "Shalersville," 4.

10. C. Helen Derby, *Centennial Home Coming in Celebration of the One Hundredth Anniversary of the Settlement of Shalersville Township, Portage County, Ohio, Held at Shalersville Center, August 30, 1906*, 13–23.

11. Margaret Manor Butler, *A Pictorial History of the Western Reserve, 1796–1860*, 61.

12. "Shalersville," 4.

13. Ibid., 2.

14. Ibid., 6.

15. Ibid., 3.

16. Follett family records in my possession. John's birth date and name are also documented in later census and early LDS Church records.

17. U.S. Census, 1820, Ohio, Portage County, Shalersville, Roll: M33_95, p. 60, image 68. This printed transcription as well as the holograph census included with it use the spelling "Fallett."

18. Harry F. Lupold and Gladys Haddas, *Ohio's Western Reserve: A Regional Reader*, 33–36.

19. Ohio, Portage County, Auditor, Duplicate Tax Records: 1816–38, Microfilms #528374, 52375, and 528378. The taxes were divided among four categories: (1) state and canal, (2) county and school, (3) roads, (4) the poor and other township needs. See also Michael Barren Clegg and Eleanor Schindler, comps., *Tax Records of Portage, Summit and Portions of Medina Co[untie]s, Ohio, 1808–1820*. In 1820 and 1821, King was taxed $.167 and $.125 respectively for the "northwest" quarter of Lot 75. For the next four years, Lot 75 is described as belonging to the "southwest" quarter. I could find no reason for this change in description. King paid $.167 for 1822, 1823, and 1825 but $.136 for 1824. He is the "resident proprietor" for 1823, the first year that designation was used, through 1825. Beginning in 1826, he was taxed for personal property: three cattle valued at $24 and taxed $1.56 in 1826; four cattle valued at $32 and taxed $.258 in 1827—the most taxes King paid in any year in Shalersville; a horse valued at $40 (it showed up at the same value through 1832) and nine cattle valued at $72 (mystifyingly collectively taxed only $.84) in 1828; eleven cattle valued at $88 in 1829 which, with the horse, accounted for taxes of $1.184; the horse and five cattle, valued at $40 in 1830 but taxed a mere $70; and the horse and nine cattle valued at $72 in 1831 and taxed $1.008. The last year King and Louisa lived in Shalersville, they reported the horse and only one "cattle" valued at $8 and taxed $.40. The tax records sometimes use the spelling "Fallatt."

20. Betty Widger, extractor, *Portage County, Ohio, Marriages, Vol. 1, 1808–1850*, 36. Alexander paid taxes only on real estate for 1820–25, on a part of Lot 74 and sometimes a part of Lot 75. In 1826, the year after his death, he was listed as owning six cattle valued at $48 with William Crane. Unanswered questions are why both brothers were taxed only for real property for the first six years or why King was taxed only for personal property for the following six years. Did Alexander's death cause the difference? Why was King listed as

a "resident proprietor" for only three of those years and what difference did it make for tax purposes? Were King and Louisa living elsewhere than Lot 75 during the last three years? No owner is listed for Lots 74 and 75 before King and Alexander were taxed in 1820. After they were off the tax rolls, Lots 74 and 75 were listed as belonging to an "unknown owner" after 1825. Deed indexes for the period do not list either King or Alexander as buying or selling land in Portage County.

21. Michael Barren Clegg, comp. and ed., *Portage County, Ohio, Newspaper Obituary Abstracts, 1825–1870*, 2:2.

22. "City of Streetsboro and Shalersville Township 1809–1994," 10:114. The cemetery is south of Route 303 just west of Route 44 in Shalersville.

23. Ohio, Portage County, Probate Court Records, 1808–67, Alexander Follett, Probate Packet #140, September 1826. See also Ohio, Portage County, Probate Dockets, 1819–89, Docket, Vol. 4. The probate was opened in 1826, assets were sold to provide a living for his widow, Caroline, for one year following his death, and the matter was finally closed in 1833.

24. Some sources identify Nancy's middle name as Mariah, Millicent, or the initial "M." Some family records give William's birth date as November 12, 1826, probably because the date was variously given as "12/11/26" and "11/12/26."

25. Follett family records in my possession. Some family records give discrepant birth dates and places and death information. There is no documentation of a birthplace; and since these two children are not listed with the family in any known later records, it is probable that they were born in Shalersville and died in early childhood.

26. U.S. Census, 1830, Shalersville, Portage County, Ohio, Roll 138, p. 252, image 3. That census lists one male, age 40–50 (King was 43); one male age 10–15 (son John was 11); two males under age five (William Alexander was four. The other may have been Edward, with his age misidentified, or possibly a son by Alexander who may have been living with them instead of with his mother); a female age 30–40 (Louisa was thirty-two); another age 10–15 (Adeline was fourteen), a third age 5–10 (Nancy was seven), and one under five (Emily or Mary).

27. Death listing, *New Hampshire Sentinel*, attached to Historical Society of Cheshire County, Letter to Joann Mortensen, June 3, 2009.

28. May Hamlin Harrington, "A Short Historical Sketch of Early Pioneers," 2.

29. Merrible E. Myers, "List of Names of as [sic] Belonging to the Enumeration of the White Males of 21 yrs old and Upward in Portage Co for the year 1827—Located in Probate Court of Portage Co Ravenna Ohio," Western Reserve Historical Society, Cleveland, Ohio, typescript, n.d., unpaginated.

30. Wm. Cumming Johnson Jr., "List of Voters in Portage County, Ohio, 1816–1856," unpaginated.

31. Max H Parkin, "Conflict at Kirtland" A Study of the Nature and Causes of External and Internal Conflict of the Mormons in Ohio between 1830 and 1838," 16.

32. "History of Portage County," 518.

33. Ibid., 532.

❋ Chapter Four ❋

A Family's Religious New Beginning, 1831–32

When the first Mormon missionaries stopped in the Kirtland, Ohio, area on their way west in early November 1830, King and Louisa Follett were beginning their second decade of life in Shalersville with at least four surviving children and probably two little graves in the graveyard. They were far from wealthy, apparently owned no real estate, and certainly lived a simple, hard-working life. In many respects, they were like many other families who joined the Mormon Church, organized not even a year earlier. Although I long to know how they first came in contact with the Church, its missionaries, and its members, neither King nor Louisa left a written record of a family story to be handed down to subsequent generations. Perhaps King was dissatisfied with his current church. Perhaps the general religious excitement prompted by the four young missionaries and their unusual message roused his curiosity and drew him in. Those first missionaries reportedly baptized about a hundred individuals before they continued on their way to Missouri barely three weeks later, but they left behind them a network of the recently baptized who, in turn, preached and baptized. John Murdock, one of these first baptized individuals, was typical of those zealous converts. After his baptism, "I endeavored to bear testimony to my neighbors whom I met by the way. . . . The New York brethren held meeting in Warrensville,[1] four miles west of my house, and I bore testimony to the truth. My wife, Brother Covey and three others were baptized. Brother

Ziba Peterson held meeting in my house the evening before, and I bore testimony to my neighbors."[2]

According to Milton V. Backman, "About twice as many people were baptized in the Kirtland area in one month as had been converted in other parts of the new nation during the first half year of the history of the Restored Church; and the rapid growth continued in Ohio after the missionaries resumed their journey to Missouri."[3] The Book of Mormon, the hallmark scripture of the Restoration, played an important role in conversion, although copies were very rare in Ohio until Joseph Smith arrived on February 4.[4] Parley P. Pratt, who would later become an apostle and also spend time in a Missouri jail with King, had a strong desire to read the book after hearing about it from a Baptist deacon while Pratt was preaching as a representative of the Campbellites in an area near Palmyra, New York. As soon as he laid hands on a copy, "I opened it with eagerness, and read its title page. I then read the testimony of several witnesses in relation to the manner of its being found and translated. After this I commenced its contents by course. I read all day, eating was a burden, I had no desire for food; sleep was a burden when the night came, for I preferred reading to sleep. As I read, the spirit of the Lord was upon me, and I knew and comprehended that the book was true, as plainly and manifestly as a man comprehends and knows that he exists."[5]

Each convert was a candle, newly lit, whose flame might flutter and go out but who could, with equal probability, ignite the faith of relatives, neighbors, or complete strangers. "As clearly enunciated in many revelations recorded by the Prophet Joseph Smith," Backman comments, "the field was white all ready to harvest, and one of the most fruitful fields in the early nineteenth century was northeastern Ohio."[6] King and his family happened to be living in that "fruitful field." While Kirtland was usually the center of the Church in Ohio, "Portage County, some thirty miles south of Kirtland, was easily the second center for Mormonism in Ohio."[7] Here the Folletts had their home.

After spending about nine months in or near Kirtland, Joseph and Sidney Rigdon, accompanied by their families, moved south to the home of early converts John and Elsa Johnson, in Hiram, Ohio, about nine miles from King's home in Shalersville. In this relatively secluded farming area, Joseph and Sidney concentrated on what became known as the Joseph Smith Translation of the Bible, but the young Prophet's presence quickly put northeastern Ohio in the spotlight for those interested in the Church—either to join or to preach against it. Local people were already concerned about this new religion with strange teachings that was attracting many newcomers to the area. The Church quickly became a topic for local newspapers, as it had in New York, through editorials, articles, and letters. It would have been impossible for the Folletts not to have heard about Mormonism, but I cannot identify which elements in the gospel message resonated most deeply with King and Louisa nor what experiences confirmed their faith to the degree that they not only joined the Church but remained faithful to the gospel for the rest of their lives, even though being Mormon in many ways made their lives harder.

Perhaps they had an experience parallel to that of Lydia Clisbee Partridge, wife of Edward Partridge, ordained as the Church's first bishop. Lydia read the Book of Mormon in December of 1830 and accepted baptism from Parley P. Pratt, though Edward was still investigating: "I was induced to believe for the reason," she testified, "that I saw the gospel in its plainness as it was taught in the New Testament and I also knew that none of the sects of the day taught those things."[8] Philo Dibble, another early convert, similarly requested baptism and asserted: "When I came out of the water I knew that I had been born of water and of the spirit, for my mind was illuminated with the Holy Ghost. . . . While in bed that night I felt what appeared to be a hand upon my left shoulder, and a sensation like fibers of fire immediately enveloped my body. . . . I was enveloped in a heavenly influence and could not sleep for joy. The next morning I started home a happy man."[9]

Many of the very early converts were so enthusiastic about their new religion that they immediately went to other family members to tell them the story of Mormonism. There is no evidence that King tried to convert his family; if so, the efforts do not appear to have been successful. The only mention of King and Louisa and their new-found religion in any Follett or Oak ancestral family records that I have found is the notation that King "became a Mormon Elder 1831."[10]

According to BYU religion professor Mark L. McConkie, most Mormon converts were literate and familiar with the Bible and its teachings. Their journals, letters, and other sources depict a people who were "products of their time and reflected the speech patterns and peculiarities of their day, but they wrote well, with feeling and discernment, and communicated artfully what they felt.... They were perhaps more educated in the processes of maintaining a living than in the 'book learning' of the day, but they still wrote with clarity and exactness.... Only occasionally does one wrestle to understand their meaning."[11]

Some were professionals, but most were farmers and artisans. Some grew up on the rough American frontier, yet many others had been raised in refined homes in New England and reproduced that culture as soon as they were able. A vivid summary of these early converts who later became identified as friends of the Prophet Joseph Smith and of the Follett family shows they shared much in common with each other and with neighbors who did not join the church. They were, writes Mark McConkie, "men and women with calloused hands and strong backs ... women who could spin and sew, milk a cow, and bake bread over the open fire; ... men and women who knew how to carve a livelihood out of the land ... [who] lived with mud on their boots and sweat on their brows; the horse, the cow, and the ox were not only their servants, but their friends, on whom they depended for a livelihood ... possessed of the skills to build cities out of wilderness."[12] In addition to these vital abilities, the early converts who followed Joseph Smith were "men and women of extraordinary courage"; they possessed "the faith to follow, the hardiness to survive, and the spiritual sensitivity to know. Many came to Joseph because of inspired dreams and visions; others felt the testimony of missionaries." Most importantly for them and the future of this new religion, they "all came because the Spirit of the Lord directed them to."[13]

Although not even King and Louisa's baptismal date can be determined, all of the available sources agree that it occurred in the spring of 1831. The *Nauvoo Neighbor* published a short biography of King on March 20, 1844, after his death on March 9. This biography, which later was copied into the official *History of the Church*, states: "He was a native of Vermont, and moved many years since into Cuyahoga County, Ohio. There, for the first time, he heard the Gospel preached, [and] united with the Church of Jesus Christ of Latter-day Saints in the spring of 1831."[14] Neither the newspaper nor the *History of the Church* provides a source for this information; and it may have been written by someone who was not well acquainted with him. He was not a native of Vermont, and there is no evidence that he ever lived in Cuyahoga County instead of or in addition to Portage County, where his residence can be firmly documented. The two counties are near each other, and it is certainly possible that he might have been visiting in Cuyahoga County when he first heard about the Church. It is even possible that he was baptized there, but such a conclusion is, of course, conjectural.

Another source, the Kirtland Elders' Quorum Record, places the baptism in St. Lawrence County, New York, in early 1831.[15] Family records submitted to the LDS Ancestral File also give St. Lawrence County as the baptismal site and the birthplace of three children: Emily, Mary, and Edward, born ca. 1829–33.[16] Since other records conclusively place King's family in Ohio during these years, St. Lawrence County cannot be accepted as the children's birth place; and therefore, it seems more likely that the same error was also perpetrated for King's baptismal site. It is remotely possible that King and perhaps other members of the family were visiting either the Alexanders or Tanners in St. Lawrence County when they first heard the gospel and were baptized; but again, such a possibility is conjectural.

Most Follett family records name Ohio as the baptismal site and give a date as the spring of 1831, although without identifying a place or an officiator. Opportunities abounded, however, for King to have been taught the gospel in Shalersville, either by the missionaries en route to or returning from Missouri (they passed through Shalersville). Furthermore, during the year that Joseph Smith and his family lived in the John Johnson home, "Intense missionary activity surrounded Hiram [which was only a few miles from Shalersville], and many converts came from Parkman, Nelson, and Shalersville, which all became Church branches. Others were converted in Ravenna, Streetsboro, Shalersville, and Mantua."[17]

Exact baptismal information exists for two of the Follett children, twelve-year-old John and eight-year-old Nancy. The Journal History of the Church contains a short report of a mission by Peter Whitmer Jr., one of the first four missionaries sent to Missouri: "In the month of August, 1831, I started for the State of Ohio. I arrived home on the 5th day of September, and was taken sick with ague and fever for the space of four weeks; then I labored for some clothing and studied the Scriptures some. On the 11th of October I attended the conference held at Hiram; thence I went to Shalersville, and on December the 4th, I baptized John Follett and Nancy Follett."[18] It seems unlikely that these young children would

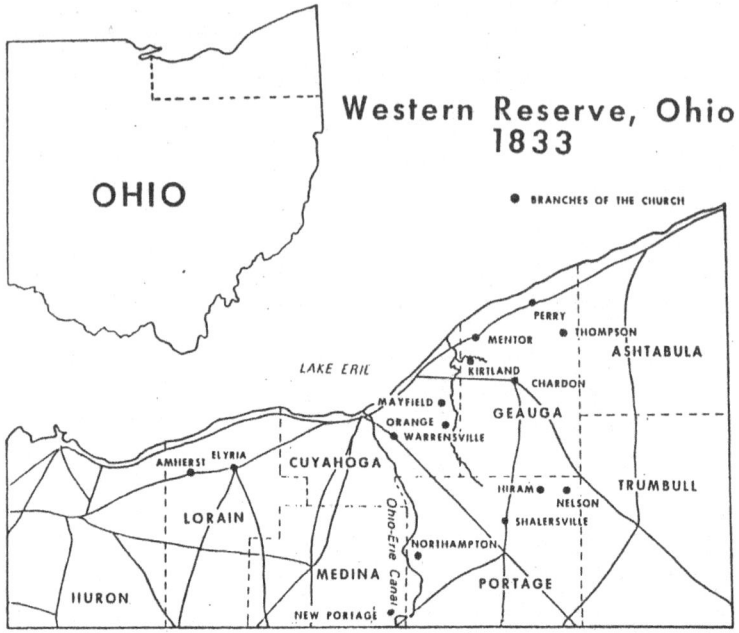

Early LDS branches in the Western Reserve. Cartography by Irval L. Mortensen.

have been baptized unless their parents were already members. And had the parents been baptized at the same time, it seems likely that Whitmer would have included their names. Therefore, an earlier baptism date for King (and probably Louisa) seems probable. King was closely associated with members of the Whitmer family later in Missouri, suggesting that Peter Whitmer may have baptized them, whenever it occurred.

Edward Follett would have been ten, but neither he nor fifteen-year-old Adeline were mentioned in Whitmer's account, suggesting that Edward was already dead at this point and hinting (although once again, this hypothesis is conjectural) that Adeline had been baptized at the same time as her parents. The only baptismal date available on Church or family records for Adeline is a proxy baptism after her death.

An early baptism date for King is supported in Hyrum Smith's 1832 journal documenting his activities as a missionary and also as a member of the Kirtland bishopric. He sold and traded Books of Mormon, and purchased food for the poor. Three times he mentions a "Brother Follett," presumably King, since no other Follett family appears on any civil or church record for Shalersville at that time:

March the 10th took Dinnia Blanchard home with me
March Sold 5 Books to Brother folet of Shulersvill and left 2 more at his hose for to Be Sold.

June th 2D went to Parkmen with Brother Parley Pratt and preached the 3D and Baptised three and Confirmed them from there to the town of Hiram and from thence to the town of Mulersveil[19] and Buayt 19 Sheep Of Brother follet and paid Eght Books which is 10$ and paid 10$ Towoward the Cows that I bought of Him."

June the 27 finished paing for the Sheep and Cow herd of Brother follett."[20]

The fact that King traded sheep for copies of the Book of Mormon and purchased other copies suggests that he was also engaged in missionary activities. Since the total value of his taxable personal property that year was a horse and some cattle valued at $48—but no sheep—taking Books of Mormon valued by Hyrum at $10 in partial payment for nineteen sheep may have represented a substantial donation for King.

Figures on the number of baptisms in 1830–32 are not definite. Max H Parkin, a historian of the Missouri period, cites four sources for membership statistics: (1) The Journal History, December 31, 1830, gives a figure of 100 members in New York and about 150 members in Ohio; (2) John Whitmer said that membership in Ohio during these first two years increased to about 300; (3) an Ohio newspaper in February 1831 estimated members at 400; members; and (4) "By the end of 1831, it is estimated by documents on file at the Church Historian's Office that the Church had a membership of about 2,000, of which 1,500 were in the State of Ohio."[21] By the end of 1831, fifteen branches were functioning in Ohio, one in Shalersville[22] where the Folletts would have attended LDS meetings. These meetings would have been held in someone's home, possibly in a schoolhouse, or perhaps outside when the weather permitted. At least twice, Church leaders came to Shalersville while King and his family lived there. Reynolds Cahoon, an early convert who later served in the Kirtland Stake presidency, and David Whitmer, one of the Three Witnesses to the Book of Mormon, filled a fund-raising mission near Kirtland in November 1831 "to obtain money or property for Brother Joseph and others, in order that they might finish the translation of the Bible." According to Cahoon's diary, he started for Hiram, Ohio, about November 9 and, "On, Tuesday, (Nov.15) I went to Shalersville (Portage County) where we held a meeting with the brethren in the evening, and after laboring with them for some time, Brother David Whitmer sealed them up to eternal life."[23] Although Cahoon does not specify who attended, King and his family probably were invited to donate resources toward the Joseph Smith Translation of the Bible, receive instructions, and be blessed.

Joseph Smith's record shows that, from approximately December 4, 1831, until January 8 or 10, 1832, he and Sidney Rigdon preached "in Shalersville, Ravenna, and other places, setting forth the truth, vindicating the cause of our Redeemer ... by which means we did much towards allaying the excited feelings which were growing out of the scandalous letters then being published in the Ohio Star, at Ravenna" by Ezra Booth, an early convert who had quickly become disenchanted from the Church.[24]

Most of the newly baptized members lived in and around Kirtland. So did Joseph Smith, except for the months he spent in Hiram. Thus, the little town of Kirtland had the status of Church headquarters. The Prophet was twenty-five when he arrived at the Whitney store in Kirtland in February 1831. Since receiving his first vision at age fourteen, he had been ridiculed, persecuted, and misunderstood. His life had been threatened, and he had already had to move from place to place to translate and publish the Book of Mormon. Although he was aware of his human weaknesses, he never tried to deny his mission or refuse to obey what he felt were the Lord's instructions. Kirtland saw Joseph's flowering, not only as his prophetic gifts matured, but also as he assumed the multiplying duties of a growing church. On a very practical level, Joseph not only had new doctrine to learn and teach to others, but the Church was assuming a structure that required administration on various levels. It appears that revelations came primarily when Joseph sensed a need and took it to the Lord in prayer. In fact, he had come to Ohio because John Whitmer, whom he had sent to nurture the new members after the four original missionaries continued to Missouri, wrote asking his immediate assistance to regulate the Church in Kirtland. "As he had done many times before and as he would continue to do in the years to come," summarizes Earl Olson, Church Historical Department librarian, "Joseph inquired of the Lord concerning His will, to which he received in answer a revelation, commanding him to go to Ohio."[25]

In Ohio, Joseph received more revelations than in any other geographical location. The Doctrine and Covenants currently contains 138 sections, 135 of them given to Joseph Smith, and 64 of them received during the Ohio period. These revelations guided the Church's doctrinal and administrative development in its first decade. "The Ohio period was one of great development, expansion, and inquiry in the Church," comments. "As the understanding of the Prophet Joseph Smith expanded, he was ready to receive a deeper insight into the purposes of the Lord. The principle of inquiry . . . brought about many answers which were to set the pattern for Church procedure for the future."[26]

From the time of his baptism in 1831 until sometime after July 1832, King was involved in this learning curve for new Church members. Then the Folletts made the first of several moves because of their religion.

As early as September of 1830, the Prophet had received a series of revelations stating that the "center place" of the Church, the site of the future New Jerusalem, and the location of the temple prophesied in the Bible to which Jesus Christ would return as the resurrected Savior would be in Missouri on land bordering the "Lamanites" (D&C 28:9; 42:35–36; 45:66–67; 52:2, 42; 54:8). The Prophet made his first trip to Jackson County, Missouri, in June and July 1831, and designated the location as "Zion."[27] Members of the Church "established various small settlements in Jackson County in 1831 and 1832," and "the call went out to other members of the Church to 'gather to Zion.'"[28] King and Louisa prepared to obey that call.

In an effort to keep the process orderly, in a revelation on July 20, 1831, instructions were given to Sidney Rigdon and Bishop Edward Partridge to purchase and divide land upon which newly arrived Saints could settle (D&C 57:6–7). Saints already in Jackson County were encouraged to help provide the new arrivals with the necessities of life. Those wishing to go to Missouri had to obtain "a recommend (from the Ohio bishop or three elders) that one was morally trustworthy and financially responsible for acceptance into fellowship and full economic privileges." This recommend would assure Bishop Partridge in Jackson County that these members understood and were willing to live the system of consecrating property to have all things in common that the Saints were attempting to live.[29] Although it was not always their decision, individuals could request to move or they could be asked to move when land became available in Missouri.

On July 5, 1832, Hyrum Smith, as a member of the Kirtland bishopric, went to Shalersville accompanied by Reynolds Cahoon "and gave Brothers Folet and others a recommendation to go to Zion."[30] Apparently none of these recommends have survived, so their exact wording is not known. According to a letter that Joseph Smith wrote to Jared Carter in April 1833, but which was not published until 1844, those who wanted to go to Zion were cautioned to first pay their debts and admonished that the rich "are in no wise to cast out the poor, or leave them behind."[31] The January 1833 issue of the *Evening and the Morning Star*, the Church's newspaper, instructed: "Every soul . . . should settle all his concerns with the world, . . . he should overcome the world, and be ready, when he arrives at the place of gathering to . . . keep the commandments, and do the will of his heavenly Father; otherwise he may not hold communion with the brethren."[32]

It seems likely that the Follett family would have left promptly so that they could reach Missouri before winter set in. The obituary of Adeline, King's oldest daughter, who was born in December 1816, states that she moved to Missouri "in her 16th year,"[33] which could mean that the family traveled in 1832, the year she turned sixteen. King's name did not appear on the tax records in Portage County after 1832; and Edward Moroni Follett was born in Missouri about June 9, 1833.[34] In addition to sixteen-year-old Adeline, the family definitely included fourteen-year-old John, ten-year-old Nancy, and eight-year-old William Alexander, and may have included one or all of the three children whose death dates are not known: the first son named Edward, age about eleven, Emily, about three, and Mary, about one. All three of them were dead by the time the family fled from Jackson County in November 1833.

The journey from Shalersville to Independence was about a thousand miles, traversing most of Ohio, all of Indiana, Illinois, and Missouri, and ending on the border of Kansas. King returned to Kirtland in late 1835, leaving Louisa and the children in Missouri. In the intervening three years, many important events in Church history would occur in both Ohio and Missouri. King and his family would be caught up in those events.

Notes

1. Warrensville was about twenty-five miles from the Follett home in Shalersville.

2. John Murdock, quoted in Richard Lloyd Anderson, "The Impact of the First Preaching in Ohio," 485.

3. Milton V. Backman, Jr. "The Quest for a Restoration: The Birth of Mormonism in Ohio," 347.

4. Dean C. Jessee, ed., *The Papers of Joseph Smith. Vol. 2: Journal, 1832–1842*, xiii. The trip from Fayette, New York, to Kirtland, Ohio, began in January. Joseph's wife, Emma, traveled with him, and they arrived about the first of February. Emma was pregnant with twins, born on April 30, both of whom died three hours after birth. John Murdock's wife, Julia, died giving birth to twins at the same time; and Joseph and Emma adopted these twins, a boy and a girl, like their own Thaddeus and Louisa, naming them Joseph and Julia. Baby Joseph died in infancy. Joseph and Emma eventually had eleven children, four of whom were unnamed and died at birth or were stillborn.

5. Scot Facer Proctor and Maurine Jensen Proctor, eds., *Autobiography of Parley P. Pratt: Revised and Enhanced Edition*, 31–32.

6. Backman, "The Quest for a Restoration," 364.

7. A. J. Simmonds, "John Noah and the Hulets: A Study in Charisma in the Early Church," 7.

8. Lydia Partridge, quoted in Hartt Wixom, *Edward Partridge: The First Bishop of the Church of Jesus Christ of Latter-day Saints*, 3.

9. Philo Dibble, "Philo Dibble's Narrative," quoted in Richard Lloyd Anderson, "Impact of First Preaching in Ohio," 488.

10. Henry Lebbeus Oak, *Oak/Oaks/Oakes: Family Register Nathaniel Oak of Marlborough, Mass.*, 55.

11. Mark L. McConkie, *Remembering Joseph: Personal Recollections of Those Who Knew the Prophet Joseph Smith*, 5.

12. Ibid., 1.

13. Ibid., 19.

14. *History of the Church*, 6:249.

15. Lyndon W. Cook and Milton V. Backman, eds., *Kirtland Elders' Quorum Record 1836–1841*, Appendix, Biographical Index, 82. This appendix contains brief biographies of "elders" during the Kirtland period. The editors do not provide footnotes for the sources of the information.

16. "The LDS Ancestral File is a collection of genealogical information taken from pedigree charts and family group records submitted to the LDS Family History Department since 1978. The information has not been verified

against any official records" Submission numbers: AF92-107062 and 107623; AF93-102145 and 107062; AF97-101604. www.Familysearch.org (accessed October 26, 2004).

17. Karl Ricks Anderson, "Northern Ohio Settlements," 20.

18. Peter Whitmer Jr., Report in Journal History, January 29, 1831, 2. There is no title on p. 1, but an introductory phrase reads: "The following is a brief report written 29 Jan 1831 by Peter Whitmer jun. about his mission to the west." A typed note on p. 2 states: "The original of this report, which is dated Dec. 13, 1831, is on file at the Historian's Office." Although out of the Journal History's usually strict chronological order, it is included with the mission reports of Oliver Cowdery and Parley P. Pratt. This one-page journal entry appears to be the only record of Whitmer's missionary work. One of the eight witnesses of the Book of Mormon, he was born in Fayette, New York, was baptized in June 1830, and left New York for the Lamanite mission in Missouri in October 1830. Bruce N. Westergren, ed., *From Historian to Dissident: The Book of John Whitmer*, 15. Peter Whitmer died of tuberculosis in 1836.

19. Undoubtedly the 'Mulersveil' spelling is an error in translation from Hyrum's original journal to the typescript, as Hyrum identifies King as being from Shalersville in other places in the original journal. Jeffrey S. O'Driscoll, *Hyrum Smith: A Life of Integrity*, 68, transcribed the place name correctly as "Shalersville."

20. Hyrum Smith, Diary, March 10, June 2 and 27, 1832. See also O'Driscoll, *Hyrum Smith*, 68.

21. Max H Parkin, "Conflict at Kirtland: A Study of the Nature and Causes of External and Internal Conflict of the Mormons in Ohio between 1830 and 1838," 45 note 39.

22. Ibid.

23. Journal History, November 1831. David Whitmer was one of the Three Witnesses who testified that he saw the plates containing the Book of Mormon.

24. *History of the Church*, 1:241. Sidney Rigdon was a Baptist minister who first heard of Mormonism from the four original Mormon missionaries to the Lamanites as they passed through Mentor, Ohio, near Kirtland. He was later baptized, became a scribe to Joseph Smith, and served as counselor in Joseph's First Presidency.

25. Earl E. Olson, "The Chronology of the Ohio Revelations," 339.

26. Ibid., 329–30, 349.

27. "Zion" has been variously defined; but during the Kirtland period, it referred to the Church in Jackson County, Missouri, (1831–33). Other meanings include (1) the Church itself, (2) one of the hills in Palestine "upon which Jerusalem is built," (3) "all of North and South America," according to one of Joseph Smith's definitions, (4) "the pure in heart" (D&C 97:21), and (5) its

current meaning as "the people of the covenant throughout the earth" who have gathered "to the stakes of Zion" (D&C 101:17–21). Robert L. Millet, "Zion," 1398; Bruce R. McConkie, *Mormon Doctrine*, 854–55.

28. Van Orden, "From Kirtland to Missouri," 26.

29. Richard Lloyd Anderson, "Jackson County in Early Mormon Descriptions," 291.

30. Reynolds Cahoon, Diary, July 5, 1832; Mary L.S. Putnam and Lila Cahoon, comps. and eds., *Reynolds Cahoon: His Roots and Branches*, 39–40; see also O'Driscoll, *Hyrum Smith*, 68.

31. Joseph Smith, Letter to Jared Carter, Kirtland, April 17, 1833, *Times and Seasons* 5, no. 24 (January 1, 1844): 753. (The *Time and Seasons* was printed in Nauvoo from November 1839 until February 15, 1846.)

32. "Let Every Man Learn His Duty," *Evening and the Morning Star* 1, no. 8 (January 1833): 61. (The *Evening and the Morning Star*, the Church's first newspaper, was published in Independence from June 1832 to September 1834.)

33. "Died: West," *Malvern (Iowa) Leader*, August 1, 1884. Her age is given as sixty-seven years, seven months, and eleven days.

34. Contra Costa County (California) County Recorder, Death Records, 1873–1921, "Register of Deaths, 1:34. Edward's death date is October 27, 1892, age 58 years, 4 months, and 18 days. This would approximate a birth date of about June 9, 1833.

❊ Chapter Five ❊

The Mormon Church Comes to Ohio: 1830–31

At the end of the 1700s, the neighboring states of Vermont and New Hampshire were very much alike geographically and economically. On December 23, 1805, a few months after King's seventeenth birthday when he was probably still living at home, Joseph and Lucy Smith welcomed the fourth of their eleven children, a son they named Joseph for his father. The Smiths were living in Sharon, Vermont, approximately ninety miles northwest of the Follett family home in Winchester, New Hampshire. In 1820 when King had settled in Ohio, Joseph, at age fourteen, began both a spiritual journey that led to the founding of the Church of Jesus Christ of Latter-day Saints and a literal journey that would bring him and King Follett face to face.[1]

This chapter provides a brief overview of Joseph Smith's life and prophetic mission as context for the changes in the Follett family's life. In the absence of personal writings left by the Folletts, tracing events as they developed in the Church provides at least a probable reconstruction of events in the Follett family's experiences and understandings of their new religious identity, even if details within that outline cannot be corroborated. King's activities after baptism centered around what was occurring in the Church. He moved his family to live wherever the Church established its new headquarters. As a result, the Folletts were always at the center of the controversy generated by Mormon conflict with their neighbors in Ohio, Missouri, and Illinois. They shared in the growing experiences of the Church as well.

The Smith family was not wealthy, but they were educated, patriotic, and hard-working. Joseph Sr. and Lucy Mack had married in 1796 and had their eleven children between 1797 and 1821. During Joseph Jr.'s childhood, the family suffered numerous financial setbacks, despite their hard work. By the time Joseph was ten, the family had left Vermont, where three years of protracted cold killed their crops, and moved to Palmyra, Ontario County, New York, near the Erie Canal, finally settling in the adjoining town of Manchester.

As Joseph Jr. entered his teen years, upstate New York was inflamed by religious enthusiasms, which later spread to Ohio and westward. As he recorded in his personal history in the late 1830s, the various denominations competed with each other for converts and debated the correctness of their conflicting doctrines. Revivals became almost annual events, and religious differences in families often caused a loss of harmony in homes. Joseph described it as a time when "the seemingly good feelings of both the priests and the converts were more pretended than real . . . so that all their good feelings one for another, if they ever had any, were entirely lost in a strife of words and a contest about opinions."[2] The Smith family's experience reflected this difference of allegiance. Lucy Mack Smith, two sons, and a daughter aligned themselves with the Presbyterians. Joseph felt "partial" to the Methodists but concluded that the decision was too important to make by himself. As he wrestled mentally and spiritually with this dilemma, he came across this passage in the Bible: "If any of you lack wisdom, let him ask of God, that giveth to all men liberally, and upbraideth not; and it shall be given him" (James 1:5).

Later Joseph described his feelings:

> Never did any passage of Scripture come with more power to the heart of man than this did at this time to mine. It seemed to enter with great force into every feeling of my heart. I reflected on it again and again, knowing that if any person needed wisdom from God, I did; for how to act I did not know and unless I could get more wisdom than I then had, I would never know; for the teachers of religion of the different sects understood the same passage of Scripture so differently as to destroy all confidence in settling the question by an appeal to the Bible. . . . I at length came to the determination to "ask of God."[3]

Joseph sought the privacy of a grove near the family home and prayed to know which of the many churches he should join. He afterward described his answer to that prayer as coming in the form of a vision of the Father and his Son, Jesus Christ. The Savior instructed him to join none of the present churches, as none contained the full truth, but to await further direction. Joseph told members of his family about the vision and went about his usual activities, not knowing what would happen but apparently anticipating the future with confidence. A few days later, he reported his vision to a local minister who sternly told Joseph it was of the devil, the first of many negative explanations and the beginning of a lifetime of persecution. But he staunchly testified of the reality of this experience: "For I had seen a vision; I knew it, and I knew that God knew it, and I could not deny it, neither dared I do it, at least I knew that by so doing I would offend God, and come under condemnation."[4] Indeed, everything that Joseph Smith did or said for the rest of his life confirmed his faith that he had been called of God for an important mission.

As a result of Joseph's emphatic and unwavering belief in this heavenly event, over the next three years, he and his family were frequently treated with scorn by local townspeople. He exerted his efforts with those of his father and brothers to pay for their farm and earn a living. The entire family was greatly saddened by the sudden illness and death of the oldest son, Alvin. In September 1823, after much prayer, Joseph received a visitation from a heavenly being who identified himself as Moroni, who announced three times during that single night that Joseph had been selected to bring forth an ancient scripture created centuries earlier on the American continent by Moroni's people. This record was the Book of Mormon, inscribed on plates that had the appearance of gold and which were buried in a nearby hill. After three years of continued instruction, Joseph obtained the plates.

Although tools called "interpreters" were provided, he translated the book "by the gift and power of God" as predicted in the passage that appears on its title page. The Church's description of this book is as a "volume of holy scripture comparable to the Bible. It is a record of God's dealings with the ancient inhabitants of the Americas and contains, as does the Bible, the fulness of the everlasting gospel."[5] After the translation was complete but before it was published, three other men were selected by revelation to see the plates, an experience about which they testified: "[We] have seen the plates which contain this record, which is a record of the people of Nephi, and also of the Lamanites, . . . And we also know that they have been translated by the gift and power of God, for his voice hath declared it unto us; . . . we have seen the engravings which are upon the plates[;] . . . an angel of God came down from heaven, and he brought and laid before our eyes, that we beheld and saw the plates, and the engravings thereon; and we know that it is by the grace of God the Father, and our Lord Jesus Christ, that we beheld and bear record that these things are true."[6] Shortly thereafter, Joseph received permission to show the plates to eight other men who likewise testified: "[Joseph Smith] has shown unto us the plates of which hath been spoken, which have the appearance of gold; and as many of the leaves as the said Smith has translated we did handle with our hands; and we also saw the engravings thereon, all of which has the appearance of ancient work, and of curious workmanship . . . and know of a surety that the said Smith has got the plates."[7] Though several of these men broke with Joseph Smith as the new church developed, none of them ever renounced his testimony.

After the Book of Mormon was printed in the small community of Palmyra, reactions—both of believers and of unbelievers—intensified, resulting in persecution for Joseph, his family, and other believers. In obedience to revelation, Joseph Smith and five others organized the church, then called the Church of Christ, according to the laws of New York, on April 6, 1830, at the home of Peter Whitmer Sr., whose family had early embraced the new teachings.[8] In addition to the Book of Mormon, which provided evidence of the shattering claim of continued prophecy and of God's love for all of His children everywhere, Joseph Smith was endowed with the priesthood, or the authority to perform ordinances that God recognized, as Jesus had recognized the acts performed by his apostles. This priesthood, bestowed freely upon virtually all male members, made nearly all of the men in the Mormon Church missionaries, who hastened to preach the restoration of the gospel, the need to gather to Zion out of the wicked world, and the immediacy of Christ's second coming.

These claims and the bold challenges to the authority of existing churches intensified both legal and illegal efforts to suppress the new religion. Richard Lyman Bushman, author of a prizewinning biography of Joseph Smith, explains: "Joseph was to become accustomed to ridicule and rough treatment. He lived in a time when citizen vigilantes considered it their duty to discipline disruptive elements in the community."[9]

Among the missionaries called by revelation were four young men who were charged to take the Book of Mormon to the Indian tribes that, displaced by Andrew Jackson's presidential policies, were establishing new homes across the Mississippi River in the Indian Territory. It was these four young men—Oliver Cowdery, Peter Whitmer Jr., Parley P. Pratt, and Ziba Peterson—who packed copies of the Book of Mormon and set out on foot in October 1831 toward Missouri, fifteen hundred miles to the south and west, only six months after the organization of the Church. They were the first missionaries to pass through Ohio, with the results already described. Though sent specifically to Missouri to preach to the Indians—known by their Book of Mormon name as "Lamanites"—these four men's greatest success was among individuals in northeastern Ohio. Mormon historian Richard Lloyd Anderson summarized: "The Ohio labors . . . doubled the membership of the Church and created a solid nucleus for rapid growth and a secure, if temporary, gathering location. . . . More than any other segment of LDS history, early Kirtland reveals why the restored gospel reached independent minds and induced powerful action."[10] It was either these four men or others whom they converted in and around Kirtland at that time who brought the newly restored gospel to the Follett family, then living approximately thirty-seven miles south of Kirtland in the small community of Shalersville.

Notes

1. Numerous histories provide information on the life of Joseph Smith and the Ohio-Missouri-Illinois period. For the general narrative, I drew on George Q. Cannon, *Life of Joseph Smith the Prophet*; *History of the Church*; Richard Lyman Bushman, *Joseph Smtih: Rough Stone Rolling*; and Milton V. Backman Jr., *The Heavens Resound: A History of the Latter-day Saints in Ohio, 1836–1838*. I provide citations for direct quotations.

2. *History of the Church*, 1:3.

3. Ibid., 1:4

4. Ibid., 1:8

5. "Introduction," Book of Mormon, 1981 edition, not paginated.

6. The Testimony of Three Witnesses, Book of Mormon front matter, not paginated. The Three Witnesses were Oliver Cowdery, David Whitmer, and Martin Harris.

7. Ibid. The eight witnesses were Christian Whitmer. Jacob Whitmer, Peter Whitmer Jr., John Whitmer, Hiram Page, Joseph Smith Sen., Hyrum Smith, and Samuel H. Smith.

8. During the Ohio period, the name was changed to the Church of Jesus Christ of Latter-day Saints.

9. Bushman, *Joseph Smith: Rough Stone Rolling*, 116.

10. Richard Lloyd Anderson, "The Impact of the First Preaching in Ohio," 496.

✹ Chapter Six ✹

The Center Place of Zion, 1831–33

Jackson County, Missouri, shared its border with what was then Indian territory. Its seat, Independence, located a little over ten miles from that frontier, was not a likely or logical place for the headquarters of any new religion in the 1830s and would have been rough going for a well-established church. Yet Joseph Smith had received a revelation in 1830 that sent four young missionaries from New York into the county and across the border to preach to the Indians and received a commandment himself on July 20, 1831, to visit the area personally. According to the headnote accompanying Doctrine and Covenants 57, "In contemplating the state of the Lamanites and the lack of civilization, refinement, and religion among the people generally, the Prophet exclaimed in yearning prayer: 'When will the wilderness blossom as a rose? When will Zion be built up in her glory and where will thy Temple stand, unto which all nations shall come in the last days?'"

In response to that earnest plea, the Lord affirmed his intent for Jackson County and particularly Independence, even though the mission to the Indians had not produced any converts. Now instructions came to build a temple, purchase lands, establish a store, and have the Saints gather to Zion. From that moment, Independence has had special status with religious movements that stem from Joseph Smith's teachings. The headquarters of nine such movements currently (2011) exist in this small city,¹ and members of the LDS Church regard it as the site where millennial prophecy will yet be fulfilled.

Independence at the time of Joseph's revelation was located south of the Missouri River and between the Blue River on the east and the Big Blue River to the west. It had "a courthouse built of brick, three stores, and fifteen or twenty houses built mostly of logs hewed on both sides."² The area was growing rapidly because of two economic conditions that reinforced its prime location: (1) the trade between the United States and Mexico on the Santa Fe Trail, and (2) the ongoing fur trade in the Rocky Mountains. Because of its access to important waterways, the town had become a stopping-off point for almost everyone traveling west on either of these two high-profit businesses. Individuals met here to form wagon or pack trains to travel west. Hunters and trappers coming from the West relaxed after a season spent in relative isolation and sold their produce, mostly furs, by shipping them east. It also was the nearest eastern point for the Indians, who lived in the untamed lands that stretched hundreds of miles to the west, to have contact with civilization. All of the characteristics typically found in any frontier community were combined in even greater numbers in Independence to produce an environment in direct opposition to the principles being established by Joseph for his followers.

Because so many of the residents were men living without families, Independence had a well-deserved reputation for roughness. As was usual on the frontier, most men had rifles and probably carried concealed derringers. A number of them were fugitives from the East looking for a place to hide from civilization where their reputations might not follow. Warren Jennings, a Missouri historian, described the male population as "rough and ready," who with an "attitude of fighting" would often meet, fight, and consume alcohol. "Consumption of 'pure unadulterated whiskey' among the early Missourians reached gigantic proportions. . . . Drinking, moreover was not confined to the men alone." Each township had its own military organization, which drilled, trained, perhaps fought each other, and then drank together.³ Another Missouri historian described life as being "uncertain" for the Missourians, "especially for many who had moved several times and who usually had no opportunity for education."⁴ According to a Mormon historian writing in the same time period (mid-1970s), "Few of them [the Missourians] could read or write."⁵ In addition, ownership of slaves was very apparent and considered a sign of wealth and prestige.[6] To Joseph, who had lived in Vermont, New York, and Ohio, all of these places represented civilization by comparison. He described Jackson County and its people as being a "vast wilderness . . . nearly a century behind the times."[7] Most Mormon converts were from New England backgrounds, had Puritan ideals and morals, and at least some formal education. Independence was thus a contested site between cultures.

One cultural clash was the view of appropriate Sabbath day activities. An unnamed Protestant missionary sent to Jackson County by the American Home Missionary Society about 1830 painted this picture of Sunday in Independence: "What I have found here is anything but encouraging. . . . Such a godless place, filled with so many profane swearers, would be difficult to imagine. The majority of the people make a mild profession of Christian religion, but it is mere words, not manifested in Christian living. . . . Christian Sabbath observance here appears to be unknown. It is a day for merchandising, jollity, drinking, gambling, and general anti-Christian conduct."[8] Latter-day Saints, in contrast, had been instructed by revelation on August 7, 1831:

> And that thou mayest more fully keep thyself unspotted from the world, thou shalt go to the house of prayer and offer up thy sacraments upon my holy day. . . .
>
> For verily this is a day appointed unto you to rest from your labors, and to pay thy devotions unto the Most High . . . confessing thy sins unto thy brethren, and before the Lord. (D&C 59:9–10, 12)

The revelation further instructed them to fast and pray with a "glad heart and a cheerful countenance." (D&C 59:15) This is the way King and his family would have expected to observe the Sabbath when they arrived in their new Zion. It is easy to understand why the two cultures would have problems existing side by side.

Independence was only four years old when the four missionaries to the Lamanites "appeared on the ungraded, ungraveled streets of the thriving frontier town" during the winter of 1830–31. In addition to their main mission of "preach[ing] the gospel and bring[ing] the message of the Book of Mormon to Indians beyond the frontier," they were, according to Mormon historian T. Edgar Lyon, "also authorized to locate a favorable place for the members of their rapidly growing church to settle."[9] Joseph made his first visit there in July 1831, dedicated "the land

Site dedicated by Joseph Smith for a temple to be built in Jackson County, Missouri. George Edward Anderson Collection, April 26, 1907. LDS Church History Library. Used by permission.

for the gathering of the Saints," and identified a site upon which temples would be built in Kaw Township.[10]

Before returning to Ohio, Joseph appointed some leaders to remain in Missouri—to purchase land and organize the members who would be moving in from Kirtland and elsewhere. Sidney Gilbert was assigned to establish a store, W. W. Phelps to start a printing shop, and Oliver Cowdery to assist Phelps to "copy, and to correct, and select" the revelations as they were prepared for publication (D&C 57:13). In November 1831, a conference at Hiram, Ohio, had authorized Phelps to begin printing 10,000 copies of the *Book of Commandments*, which would contain the revelations received to that date (D&C 67 heading). However, when printing began in 1833 that number was decreased to 3,000,[11] a still-ambitious print run under the circumstances. During Joseph's brief stay in Missouri, he received six revelations now canonized in the Doctrine and Covenants (Sections 57–62).

Mormons began arriving individually and in groups shortly after Joseph's visit. The most important reason for this migration was the Prophet's revelation a month earlier, designating Missouri as the "place for the city of Zion" and further stating, "Behold, the place which is now called Independence is the center place; and a spot for the temple is lying westward, upon a lot which is not far from the courthouse" (D&C 57:2–3). The urgent message preached by Mormonism's diligent missionaries was to "gather" out of a corrupt and wicked world, to prepare a people and a place for the Lord's second coming before the end times, the millennium, and the final judgment. In Zion, the members would live together in peace and harmony, sharing their material possessions and consecrating their energies and temporal assets toward building up the kingdom of God on earth. Joseph Smith did not attempt to specify the date of the Lord's second coming—a tactic that had invariably ended in disappointment for other religious groups; but he took the relatively unusual step of establishing the physical location of the Second Coming.

Aside from this overriding religious zeal, the timing also offered some practical advantages. Government land was available in Jackson County, usually at $1.25 per acre, which new immigrants and the Church on their behalf could buy. While the new residents certainly had a positive impact on Independence's economy, the personal standards and ethics which they brought with them were in many ways in direct contrast to those already living there.

The surviving descriptions of the area around Independence made by LDS diarists and letter-writers were positive about the fertility and beauty of the country. Surely King and Louisa had heard or read some of these descriptions before leaving Ohio. W. W. Phelps, a convert and journalist from New York, writing from Independence on July 23, 1831, described "rolling prairies, and the rest patches of timber.... The soil is a rich black mould.... [The] prairies are beautiful beyond description.... [It is] a great grazing country."[12]

Washington Irving, a well-traveled American and perhaps the country's best-known writer for his time, visited Independence in 1832 and also praised the countryside: "Many parts of these prairies of the Missouri are extremely beautiful, resembling cultivated countries, embellished with parks and groves.... Some scenery ... only wanted a castle ... to have equalled some of the most celebrated park scenery of

England. The fertility of all this western country is truly astonishing. The soil is like that of a garden."[13]

Joseph Smith's history, compiled later, added a practical note: "The disadvantages here, as in all new countries, are self-evident—lack of mills and schools; together with the natural privations and the inconveniences which the hand of industry, the refinement of society, and the polish of science overcome."[14] Then he reminded his followers of the future of Zion: "All these impediments vanish when it is recollected what the Prophets have said concerning Zion in the last days ... when the splendor of the Lord is brought to our consideration for the good of His people."[15]

The first winter spent in Jackson County (1831–32) was challenging for the Saints. A major concern was food for their animals and themselves. It was too late to plant crops; therefore, they scrimped by and waited for spring: "[They] struggled to cut timber; to build ferries, bridges, mills, dams, homes, outbuildings, and fences; and to prepare some land for cultivation.... As many as ten families lived in each log cabin." Mormon historian Bruce Van Orden noted, "It was not what Zion was, but what it could become, that buoyed them up and lifted sagging spirits."[16] B. H. Roberts, a second-generation Mormon historian, described the difficulties suffered by the Saints during the winter of 1831. They "cheerfully submitted to all kinds of inconveniences, such as several families living in an open, unfinished log room, without windows, and nothing but the frozen ground for a floor [and eating] chiefly beef and a little bread, made of coarse corn meal, manufactured by rubbing the ears of corn on a tin grater. The spirit of peace, union and love, however, was in their midst, and at their prayer meetings, and in their family worship they were blessed with many seasons of refreshing from the presence of the Lord."[17]

By summer 1832, several hundred more Saints arrived, received land from Bishop Partridge, and diligently joined the effort to build up Zion both physically and spiritually. The Folletts were probably among these summer arrivals. Although they left no family record of their travels, John S. Higbee, who joined the church in 1831, and later moved from Hamilton County in Ohio to Jackson County remembered selling his family's possessions for six hundred dollars and traveling a distance of one thousand miles to "Jackson Co Mo to the place where the Lord had pointed out for the gathering of his saints." There they purchased land for $25 per acre and "built a house cleared a few acres of land began to til the earth."[18] Upon arrival in Jackson County at the end of July 1831, Emily Coburn Austin, an 1830 convert in New York, who traveled from Kirtland with the Colesville Branch, commented that "[It was] a strange sight indeed, to see four or five yoke of oxen turning up the rich soil. Fencing and other improvements went on in rapid succession. Cabins were built and prepared for families as fast as time, money and labor could accomplish the work; and our homes in this new country presented a prosperous appearance—almost equal to Paradise itself."[19]

Emily Dow Partridge, the daughter of Bishop Edward Partridge, was eight when her family moved to Missouri in 1832. In an 1874 reminiscence, she commented about small things that had impressed her. Louisa and other women might well have noticed the same things, perhaps overlooked by King and the other men:

> Well, everything was different from the home we had left [in Ohio]—and all seemed so strange in our new home, plenty of Indians and negroes, and the white folks were so different in their customs, and manner of speaking ... and instead of their carrying things in their hands, they would "toat" them on their heads.... Little children were carried or toated a straddle of one hip and some going bare footed in warm weather, and little boys, from two to ten years old running the streets with nothing on but a shirt, everything seemed to be after the stile of the back woodsman.... Their dress was more for comfort than looks.[20]

An anonymously authored history of Jackson County published in 1881 looked back fifty years:

> In those days the ladies made all of the clothing, by spinning and weaving cotton, wool and flax.... [There were] plenty of deer, turkeys and other game, and also plenty of wild honey.... There were a great many Indians passing through the county in those days, camping and hunting. There were also a great many large wolves and snakes.... In the first settling of Jackson county, the first thing any immigrant did was to select a piece of land for a home, put up a log cabin, then go to work making a farm.... The life of the early settler was one of hard toil, with many disadvantages, inconveniences and hardships.[21]

Although no details have survived about the Follett family, they probably lived on land owned by the Church that was made available for their use. There is no record that King bought or sold land in Jackson County.

During the short time—at the longest about two years—that Mormons called Jackson County their Zion, they worked hard and prospered. Although Phelps had every reason to paint an alluring picture for the new immigrants, his enthusiasm was based in fact. In the June 1833 issue of the *Evening and the Morning Star*, he reported: "With little exception the inhabitants of this section of country have had the pleasure of improving one of the most glorious seasons known for a long time.... Wheat is fine and will begin to be harvested by the middle of this month. Much corn has been planted, and it has seldom looked better."[22]

Those who had access to land and were in Jackson County long enough to raise these crops shared what they had with those who came later. Others worked for non-members and for each other. While conditions were typically those of the frontier and the Saints lacked many material possessions, they felt a religious commitment to share what was available. Many principles of the United Order as practiced in Brigham Young's Utah as well as the present-day LDS welfare program had their beginnings in the first years of the Church in Missouri.[23] It was expected that all members would live what was called the law of consecration. They would give title to their personal property to the Church (in this case, Bishop Edward Partridge) and the right to any surplus they were able to raise or obtain, which would then be available for families who needed those particular items. Printed-form documents titled "Certificates of Transfers" or "Deed of Gift" conveyed title back and forth in this scenario.[24] According to a history of Mormon communal efforts, "The six extant deeds of gift [from Jackson County in the 1830s] list household furnishings and clothing as well as livestock, farming equipment and artisan's tools," and reflect values from $34 to $316.[25]

No details have survived of what the Folletts knew about conditions in Missouri before leaving Ohio or details of their journey. Most likely, they would have traveled with other Saints, sharing help and resources along the way. King obtained his recommend in July of 1832. Solomon Hancock, who had joined the Church in New York, "in the summer of 1832 in company with many of our brethren, moved to Missouri and bought land and settled down."[26] The Folletts may have traveled with that group, though it is more probable that King and his family traveled at least part way with a man by the name of Robert Rathbun/ Rathburn/Rathborn. (All three spellings are used in Church records.) Levi Jackman wrote in a journal of his missionary labors as he traveled through eastern Illinois in June 1835: "Passed thru a small town by the name of Grandview, thence thru Parie, the County seat of Edgar. About five miles from this, we found Brother Thomas Guymon.... Br Guyman was baptized by Br Rathborn when he and [illegible word(s)] Follett moved to Zion.... A number of Elders had preached in that place and baptized only two and one of them was then gone."[27] King may have been among these elders. A Robert Rathburn/Rathbun appears in early Church records as having been baptized in the Kirtland area by at least 1831, since he served a mission in Ohio that year and was in Jackson County by 1833. The Kirtland Elders' Quorum Record lists both Robert Rathburn/Rathbun and King Follett as receiving their elder's licenses on March 31, 1836, and being ordained to the office of Seventy in 1836.[28] I hypothesize that the Follett and Rathburn families traveled together and that King and Robert baptized Guymon en route but that, for some reason, Guymon did not "gather" with the Saints at that time.

Those traveling to Zion could have gone partway on the Missouri River, but the majority went by wagon or on foot. Those coming downriver by boat would have disembarked at either the Independence Landing just north of Independence or at Westport Landing about ten miles west and directly north of the Whitmer Settlement where King and his family settled. Some details left by other Saints traveling to Independence may have been true as well for the Folletts' route and the conditions they encountered. When Joseph Smith made his first trip there in 1831, he "went by wagon to the Ohio Canal, by boat and then by stage to Cincinnati, then down the Ohio River, thence to the Mississippi River, and on to St. Louis."[29] From there he and his party walked to Independence by the Booneslick (Boone's Lick) and Santa Fe trails, while others continued by steamer on the Missouri River. On his second trip to Zion in April 1832, he went by wagon, boat, steamer, and stage.[30] Levi Jackman left this reminiscence about the group he traveled with: "In the spring of 1832 a larger company of Saints organized . . . On the 2nd day of May we commenced our journey and on the 6th we arrived at Bever on the Ohio River. Here we chartered the Steamer Messenger and started down the Ohio on the evening of the 7th, arriving at St Louis on the 14th, leaving St Louis on the 20th by land, after shipping our goods for Chariton by water."[31] Bishop Partridge was already in Missouri, but his wife, Lydia, followed with their six children. Daughter Emily Dow Partridge recalled that they were in "a company of Saints under the direction of W.W. Phelps and A. S. Gilbert.... We went down the Ohio River, to Cincinatti in a keel boat. Then we took a steamboat and went up the Missouri River.... When we were within about 100 miles of our destination we met the ice coming down the river so thick that the boat could not proceed.... [A] large Kentucky wagon was procured ... and we started again."[32]

Few areas in Jackson County were politically organized, which may have contributed somewhat to the problems that rapidly developed in response to the influx of Mormons. The "old settlers" were primarily congregated in Independence and two other areas.[33] Under the direction of the Prophet and other Church leaders, the Saints settled in Independence but also in four settlements in Kaw Township,[34] beginning about four miles west of Independence and extending to the county line, which was also the Missouri state line.

Most newly arrived Saints spent at least a few days in Independence, since Bishop Partridge lived there and initially had oversight for the temporal needs of all of the members in Jackson County, including responsibility for purchasing land and assigning acreage to each of the newly arriving families. According to Max H Parkin, "Most Saints lived on Church-owned property, but a few purchased land of their own. They held meetings in a small log building that they constructed on the northeast corner of the Temple Lot close to a house built by Bishop Edward Partridge for his family."[35]

The closest settlement to Independence was the Big Blue or Blue River Settlement on Westport Road, about five miles west of Independence. Here the road and river intersected, making it a natural economic center. Porter Rockwell established a ferry here. By the fall of 1833, the Big Blue Settlement numbered about three hundred Saints, the largest in the county next to Independence.[36] The Rockwell home was also the site of priesthood meetings for the area. On April 6, 1833, the Prophet, eighty priesthood holders, and other members met at the ferry and spent the day "in a very agreeable manner, in giving and receiving knowledge," records the *History of the Church*. "The Saints had great reason to rejoice"

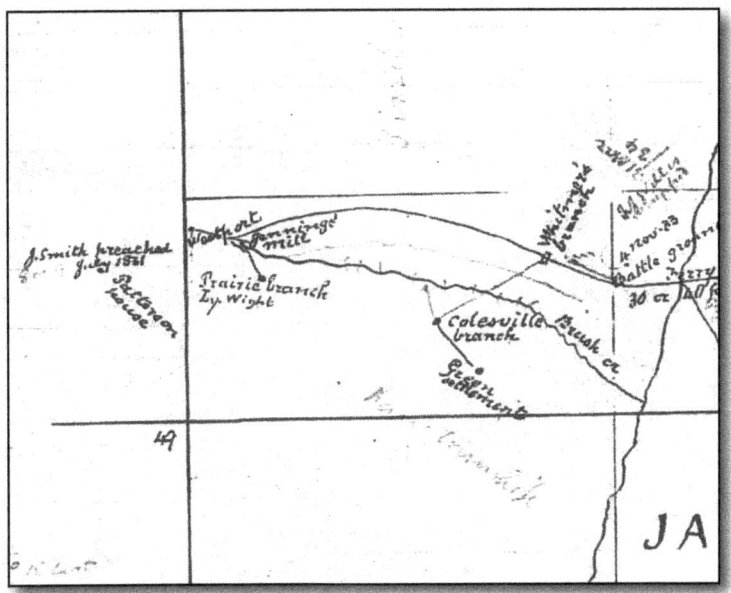

Map of the Mormon settlements in Jackson County. Drawn by Thomas Bullock, 1862. LDS Church History Library. Used by permission.

at this "first attempt" to celebrate the anniversary of the Church's founding, "and those who professed not our faith talked about it as a strange thing."[37] The Folletts presumably were among those in attendance.

Four miles farther west along Westport Road and three miles west of the Blue River was the Whitmer Branch or Settlement, named for the extended David Whitmer family but occasionally referred to as the Timber Settlement/Branch because of its densely wooded location. This site is now north of 31st Street and east of The Paseo Boulevard in Independence.[38] At its center was the Joshua Lewis home where Joseph Smith dedicated a temple site and where the first conference in Zion (Missouri) was held in August 1831. Here King settled his family, among the "144 people" scattered throughout the settlement.[39]

The Colesville Settlement consisted primarily of the Saints who had converted in Colesville, New York, journeyed together to Kirtland, and then became the earliest group, numbering about sixty, to move on to Missouri, arriving in July 1831. They settled about two miles south of

Present site of Timber Settlement (1832–33), Jackson County, Missouri, now at the intersection of 31st Street and The Paseo Boulevard, Independence, Missouri. Photo by Irval L. Mortensen, 2006.

the Whitmers near Brush Creek. Joseph Knight built the county's first gristmill here.

The fifth colony, known as Prairie Settlement, was farthest west from Independence on land that later became Kansas City, Missouri.

These four settlements outside of Independence were linked by a busy roadway system. David Pettegrew "bought 159 acres approximately six miles west of Independence on the Blue River, and on the main road leading to Fort Leavenworth and to the Indian agency." He described the road as "much traveled" and commented that "a great deal of business [was] done" in the area. Furthermore, "stage companies [and] traders passed by bringing news."[40] Beginning in the summer of 1832, LDS branches were organized in each of the four communities west of Independence. The first presiding elder in each of the four were John Corrill (Big Blue), David Whitmer (Whitmer Settlement), Wheeler Baldwin (Colesville Settlement), and Lyman Wight (Prairie Settlement).[41] David Whitmer was thus the Follett family's ecclesiastical leader. By September 1833, there were enough members in the five settlements that they were divided into ten Church units with a presiding high priest over each of them. David Whitmer continued as the Follett family's leader.[42] The November 1833 conference in Jackson County reported "800 members in the several churches."[43]

Upon their arrival in Zion, the Saints diligently began building communities, planning on permanent locations for the future. Solomon Hancock described the members as trying "to live their religion. They preached the gospel, baptized, lay on hand for the reception of the Holy Ghost, attended their meetings and kept the Sabbath day holy unto the Lord, administered the sacrament, prophesized, spoke in tongues and had the interpretations of tongues, and the gifts and powers of healing the sick and casting out devils and we thought that if we erred we wanted to err in judgment as we tried to be honest before God and man."[44] Phelps launched an ambitious publications program from his print shop, in addition to his newspaper. The Colesville School, erected in 1832 in what is now Troost Park, was the first school in the Mormon settlements. It is now marked by a Church-sponsored monument, erected in 1963 at Troost Lake. Bishop Partridge started the second school in Independence, with the log building doing service also for Church meetings. The third school, also a log building, was begun at Cave Spring, near the Whitmer Settlement. Cave Spring was "a place where pioneers going west on the Santa Fe, Oregon and California Trails stopped for water and to camp in the grassy valley."[45] King's three children of school age probably received instruction at this school: John, age fourteen, Nancy, ten, and William Alexander, eight. Seventeen-year-old Adeline was still living at home, and baby Edward was born in June 1833.

King was almost certainly a farmer like most of the other Saints, but by at least December of 1832, he was making business arrangements with Levi Jackman for services and also working on a by-the-task basis for Levi. Jackman's Record Book for 1832–33 reflects numerous transactions between the two men.[46] This record is the earliest documented date of the Folletts' arrival in Jackson County.

Levi provided these services to King:

DATE	TRANSACTION	COST
Dec 12, 1832	6 lights of sash[47]	$0.60
Dec 26, 1832	Making one coffin	$0.37
March 27, 1833	6 lights of sash	$0.60
June 6, 1833	Making one table	$1.50
Oct 14, 1933	Sawing half day	$0.25
Dec 5, 1933	5 baskets of ears of corn	

During the same period, King provided these services to Levi:

DATE	TRANSACTION	COST
Dec 12, 1832	Upper leather for one pr of shoes	
Jan 1833	Drawing one load of husks from cornfield	$0.57
Feb 1, 1833	Per self and oxen 1/4 day drawing timber	$0.25
March 5, 1833	Upper leather for one pair of shoes and garters	$0.50
March 8, 1833	One day killing hogs	$0.50
April 18, 1833	Per self and oxen 1 day clearing garden	$0.70
April 21, 1833	Per self and oxen half day plowing garden	$0.57
April 25, 1833	Per self and boy/bay [?] oxen and horse half day plowing garden	$0.57
June 13, 1833	Horse to go to town one day	$0.20
August 6, 1833	Plowing ground for turnips	$0.50
August 6, 1833	Plowing 2 acres of grownd with oxen and bay	$0.50

The sad mention of a coffin confirms the death of one of King and Louisa's children around Christmas 1832. It could have been Edward, Emily, or Mary—all very young. All three had died by November 1833.

Levi Jackman also had business dealings with several other neighbors. One of them, Nathan West, later married Adeline Follett. On December 4, 1832, Levi paid Nathan $1.20 for "12 lights of sash," and about three weeks later, Nathan bought "25# 9 oz. Pork" from Levi for 75 cents.[48]

By the summer of 1833, however, the Mormon Zion in Jackson County was coming apart. The Saints looked forward confidently to being able to purchase property, build their New Jerusalem, and prepare a temple for the Savior's second coming. But as early as August 1831, seven months before vigilantes in Hiram, Ohio, had attacked Joseph Smith and Sidney Rigdon, a sobering revelation had warned:

> Wherefore, the land of Zion [Jackson County] shall not be obtained but by purchase or by blood, otherwise there is none inheritance for you.
> And if by purchase, behold you are blessed;
> And if by blood, as you are forbidden to shed blood, lo, your enemies are up on you, and ye shall be scourged from city to city. (D&C 63:29–31)

The Saints had every intention of obtaining their land legally, so they hardly needed warnings against being the aggressors. However, as soon as residents of Independence first heard about the visit by Joseph Smith, and his designation and dedication of Jackson County as the center of the Zion for a new religion, local residents began to look at the influx of Mormons as a possible threat to their way of life. Joseph made a second visit to Zion in April of 1832 where he held a conference at which time he was "sustained as the President of the High Priesthood" (D&C 82 heading). During the next year, "alarmed locals watched the growing Mormon numbers. Non-Mormon citizens threw rocks and bricks at Mormon houses or burned haystacks. Mormon children began to wake up with nightmares about 'the mob' coming.[49] A 1902 political history of Jackson County, described conditions by spring of 1833: "By this time Christian settlers had become alarmed and aroused over the incendiary teachings and arrogant acts of the Mormons."[50] Modern-day Mormon historian Alexander L. Baugh summarized the scene with these words: "Their [the Mormons'] growing presence and the cultural, social, political, religious, and economic differences between the local settlers and the Latter-day Saints fostered tension until conflict became the natural outgrowth."[51]

Although probably modern readers will never fully understand the perspective of either the Saints, who so enthusiastically embraced the possibility of their Zion, or that of the old settlers, who eyed the influx of newcomers with increasing misgivings, I have found in my readings that historians have identified at least seven reasons that led to violence against the county's Mormons and their expulsion to Clay and Caldwell counties in the summer and fall of 1833.[52] Reviewing these reasons also illuminates the problems that continued when the Church was forced to move on and which resulted in their eventually having to flee the state of Missouri entirely.

1. Cultural differences played an important role. Most non-Mormons were "transplanted Southerners, most of them from Kentucky and Tennessee, since Missouri had been designated a 'slave state' in the Compromise of 1820.... Most Saints hailed from New England and valued congregational Sabbath worship, education of their children, and refined personal decorum. These values clashed with the 'rough and ready' Missourians, many of whom had come west precisely to avoid any community interference in their lives."[53] Further, "education was felt [by the Missourians] to be either unnecessary or a luxury which would have to await the development of the country."[54] New Englanders had come because they believed God had commanded them to do so. They wanted to build homes, make permanent settlements, and build churches, schools, and their temple. These two groups had very differing reasons for settling in the area and events would suggest that neither group was willing to compromise.

2. Mormonism was a startling religion with teachings that challenged the established religions of the day: a living prophet to whom God communicated, a new book of scripture, the designation of its members as God's "chosen people," lay priesthood that was available virtually universally for its men, an intensive missionary program, the program of "gathering" out of the world into Zion, and—most threatening—the designation of Jackson County as that Zion to which Mormons had a God-given right.[55] Naturally, all of these concepts, but especially the last, were unsettling.

3. By sheer numbers, which were increasing daily, the Mormons were viewed as a political threat. If they voted in a bloc, they would decidedly impact elections and, as the population continued to increase, would soon control the county. Naturally, the old settlers felt threatened by the prospective disfranchisement. "When they [the Mormons] made the difference in the results of an election, it was easy to use them as a scapegoat: 'If it had not been for the Mormons, we [the Missourians] would have won.'" However, the Mormons failing "to take advantage of the highly American institution of the ballot box to improve their situation would have shown a lack of good sense."[56] "It was the prospect of Mormon political supremacy which promised eventual dominance to the Saints and frightened the citizens into believing every rumor about Mormon audacity."[57]

4. Communal elements and the high degree of Mormon cooperation had economic repercussions. The Church bought large parcels of land, then distributed it among members who farmed diligently, traded

products with each other, and made purchases primarily from a Church-owned store. If non-Mormons (called "gentiles" by the Mormons) could be marginalized economically, their livelihood would be threatened. This is exactly what happened as some of the "old settlers were selling their property to the Mormons and moving away. This meant fewer and fewer customers in the stores, and future financial ruin."[58]

5. The religious role assigned to Indians, as expressed in the Book of Mormon, was very different from the general fear and hostility held by Americans generally. Although various individuals and religious groups had long postulated that Indians were part of the lost ten tribes of Israel (not a Mormon belief), Mormonism seemed to offer them a respectful place and fellowship as descendants of a former mighty civilization with a prophetic destiny. Would the Indians join with Mormons to help build their New Jerusalem?[59]

6. Missouri, though not officially allied with either the North or South on issues that would eventually lead to the Civil War, was a state where slavery was legal. Since most of the non-Mormons had emigrated from the South, even if they did not personally own slaves, they supported the right of others to do so. "Property in slaves was often the most valuable possession of the Missouri frontiersman" and "many who did not own slaves aspired to their possession."[60] Would large numbers of "northern" Mormons push for abolition and/or encourage free blacks to settle in Missouri?

7. Mormon historian B. H. Roberts (who did not join the Church until it had relocated in Utah) viewed Missouri as a frontier area that offered refuge for lawbreakers fleeing justice in more eastern states: "Here . . . in a few hours they could cross the line" out of the United States, he wrote. "These outcasts helped to give a more desperate complexion to the already reckless population of western Missouri."[61] The Saints were generally law-abiding except for those cases where they felt that obedience to God's law required them to break human law.

The mutual discomfort of these two cultures was not unexpected. Nor was the determination of Jackson County's old settlers that the Mormons must leave, countered by the equal determination of the Mormons to stay in the land to which God had, they felt, called them. Edwin C. Reynolds, a twentieth-century non-Mormon, summarized:

The combination of church and state practiced by the Mormons in Missouri was out of step with the development of that western commonwealth. Lack of tact, ignorance, and in rare instances, viciousness were to be found among both the Mormons and the "gentiles." Inevitably, a new religious movement that is attractive to the masses obtains the support of some persons who are low in mentality and weak in character. Every frontier in America has attracted and produced some members of society who were inclined toward crime. It would have been remarkable indeed if the Mormons had not encountered serious trouble in western Missouri.[62]

With the Missourians and the Mormons differing in so many areas, it was understandable when tempers and emotions sometimes ruled actions. It rapidly became impossible to tell when a hostile group was technically acting as legal "militia" or as an unauthorized "mob." It was often impossible to determine which role individuals were playing at any given time. However, LDS historian Bruce Van Orden acknowledges that "disobedience and dissension among the Saints contributed to the problems in Jackson County. Latter-day revelations declare that if the Saints had been sufficiently righteous and humble, the Lord would have protected them against their enemies and that they would have remained to build Zion in the county despite their differences with the original settlers."[63] This scenario is, of course, impossible to test.

By early 1833, internal strife and dissension were building among the Saints. Clark V. Johnson, writing in the *Encyclopedia of Mormonism*, summarizes how the year "brought new challenges to the Church in Jackson County. Some members circumvented appointed leaders and ignored their authority to preside. Others tried to obtain property through means other than the revealed laws.... Now there arose a general concern among Missouri Latter-day Saints that their Prophet should move permanently from Ohio to the new Zion."[64] Others did not want to continue the law of consecration, which required living on Church-owned land and contributing their excess to provide for others. With the large number of new immigrants, land values had increased rapidly; and it was profitable to buy and sell plots and farms individually. David Pettegrew, who moved to Jackson County soon after his October 1832 baptism in Indiana, wrote in 1840: "Upon my arrival at Jackson County, we were reproved by the Lord, through revelation, for treating lightly the Book of Mormon and the former revelations, and were to remain under condemnation if we did not repent, and remember the Book of Mormon and the revelations. Soon after this, Bishop Partrage [sic], appointed a solemn assembly in all the branches, which was to be held as a day of confession and repentance, he went from branch to branch exorting, until he had gone through them all."[65] A late twentieth source confirms that these "solemn assemblies in each branch had brought about a new spirit of humility, diligence, and order to the Church."[66] The Church had not been in existence long enough to handle some of these issues quickly, and every request for information was exacerbated by the length of time—three or four weeks, depending on the weather—to get a letter over the nine hundred miles between Missouri and Ohio.[67] The Follett family, having arrived in Missouri by at least December 1832, according to Levi Jackman's account book, must have participated in and learned from one of these solemn assemblies.

In a revelation given to the Prophet on December 16, 1833, the Lord chastised the Saints in Zion: "Behold, I say unto you, there were jarrings, and contentions, and envyings, and strifes, and lustful and covetous desires among them; therefore by these things they polluted their inheritances." Speaking more generally, the revelation continued: Church members "must needs be chastened and tried, . . . For all those who will not endure chastening, but deny me, cannot be sanctified" (D&C 101:4–6). In Jackson County the practicalities of the chastening experience for the Saints had begun and would now follow them indefinitely.

The Mormons had broken no laws and could therefore not be prosecuted in court, but Jackson County residents believed that they could act legally as citizens in the "time-honored American tradition of vigilante action," which had its roots, as Richard Lyman Bushman noted, in the 1700s in New England. The question was: "Can a majority, in defense of the public good as they see it, strip a minority of its rights? The Jackson County citizens believed their procedures were democracy in action . . . [that] they acted purely in self-defense. But for Mormons, Jackson County democracy meant repression and expulsion."[68]

David Pettegrew observed that he saw "non-members who appeared to be honorable men but in the summer of 1833 I watched with horror as these same men persecuted the church. I had never seen men professed [sic] of such spirit."[69] When Phelps published an article in the monthly issue of the *Evening and the Morning Star* in July 1833 about missionary work among slaves and former slaves, some interpreted it to mean that the Church was encouraging blacks to join in great numbers. Although Phelps quickly printed a clarification, this article seemed to be the catalyst for the problems that followed.

As Van Orden relates, "On 20 July 400 or 500 disgruntled citizens met at the Independence courthouse, chose officers, and selected a committee to draft a document outlining their demands of the Mormons. The officers and committee members were some of the leading elected Jackson County citizens."[70] One attendee was Lilburn W. Boggs, then Missouri's lieutenant governor and a resident of Independence, who would play a critical role in the future of the Church in Missouri. Reportedly, he not only attended further meetings of the group but "encouraged the anti-Mormon activity."[71] The committee demanded that Mormons stop moving into the county, that those presently there plan to leave, and that all Church-owned businesses close, including the printing office.[72] Understandably, the Saints refused. Later that day, an estimated three hundred men attacked Phelps's printing office and Sidney Gilbert's store, destroyed most of the unbound sheets of the Book of Commandments, damaged the press, destroyed some furniture, and threatened the Phelps family, who lived above the office. They also pulled Bishop Partridge from his home and tarred and feathered him on the public square.[73] During the next three days, groups of Missourians roamed around the county apparently dealing "with the . . . problem in the forthright manner of the frontier."[74] Van Orden summarizes: "They set fire to haystacks and grain fields and destroyed several homes, barns, and businesses . . . . and community leaders threatened every man, woman, and child with a whipping unless they consented to leave the county."[75] With no other choice, Edward Partridge, Isaac Morley, John Corrill, W. W. Phelps, Algernon S. Gilbert, and John Whitmer signed an agreement dated July 23, 1833, that the Mormons would leave Jackson County beginning in January 1834.[76] A footnote to *History of the Church*, on the same date the agreement was signed, states: "It was at this point, too, that several of the brethren stepped forward and offered themselves as a ransom for the Church, expressing themselves as being willing to be scourged or to die if that would appease the anger of the mob against the Saints. The mob would not accept the sacrifice of the brethren, however, but renewed their threats of violence against the whole Church."[77]

The terms of the agreement required that "Oliver Cowdery, W.W. Phelps, William M'Lellin [sic], Edward Partridge, Lyman Wight, Simeon Carter, Peter and John Whitmer, and Harvey H. Whitlock shall remove with their families out of this county on or before the first day of January next, and that they, as well as the two hereinafter named [John Corrill and Algernon Sidney Gilbert] use all their influence to induce all the brethren now here to remove as soon as possible: one half, say, by the first of January next, and all by the first day of April next."[78] The Saints must have hoped that this agreement would ease tensions and allow them time to finish harvesting summer crops. However, during the next two months, friction between the two groups continued and a petition dated September 28, 1833, was directed "To His Excellency Daniel Dunklin, Governor of the State of Missouri" outlining the events of the past two months and signed "by Edward Partridge and nearly all the members of the Church in Jackson County."[79] The petition "appeal[ed] to the Governor for aid, asking him to raise by express proclamation, or otherwise, a sufficient number of troops, who, with us, may be empowered to defend our rights, that we may sue for damages for the loss of property, for abuse, for defamation, as to ourselves, and if advisable try for treason against the government; that the law of the land may not be defiled, or nullified, but peace be restored to our country."[80]

The petition was presented to Governor Dunklin on October 8, and he wrote back on October 19. The governor affirmed: "No citizen, nor number of citizens, have a right to take the redress of their grievances, whether real or *imaginery*, into their own hands. . . . [and] not being willing to persuade myself that any portion of the citizens of the state of Missouri are so lost to a sense of these truths as to require the exercise of force . . . I would advise you to make a trial of the efficacy of the laws." The governor then directed the church to "obtain a warrant" to see "whether the laws can be peaceably executed or not" and "if they cannot" affirmed that it was his "duty . . . to take such steps as will enforce a faithful execution of them."[81] Following the governor's direction, "the brethren in Zion . . . consulted" with the law firm of Wood, Reese, Doniphan, and Atchison. In a letter dated October 30, the four lawyers proposed to represent the church for a fee of a thousand dollars, for which they would "bring all the suits you may want brought, and attend to them jointly throughout." The correspondence from the law firm further stated that they needed an answer "immediately, for we can be engaged on the opposite side in all probability. We prefer to bring your suits, as we have been threatened by the mob, we wish to show them we disregard their empty bravadoes." The Saints accepted this proposition, and "Brothers Phelps and Partridge gave their note of one thousand dollars, endorsed by Gilbert & Whitney."[82]

Some old settlers, seeing these developments as noncompliance with the agreement to leave, "stepped up their activities to bring about their forceful removal."[83] These escalating developments, according to Reverend Benton Pixley, a local clergyman, "provoked some of the more wild and ungovernable among us [the Missourians] to improper acts of violence, [and] the Mormons began to muster, and exhibit military preparations."[84]

Under these very uncertain circumstances, life had to go on for King and his family, even though they were preparing for another move. The members continued to hold church services wherever possible. Harvey Whitlock baptized eight-year-old William Alexander Follett a member of the Church on August 1, 1833.[85] A brief document recording this event giving only the month and year reads: "William A. Follett a son of King an [sic] Louisa Follett was born at portage County, Ohio December the 11 1825 was baptized in Jackson County Mo august 1833 by harvey whitlock."[86]

In a "Memorial to the Legislature of Missouri," written five years later in December of 1838, Church members alleged that "some time in October the wrath of the mob began again to be kindled, insomuch, that they shot at some of our people, whipped others, and threw down their houses, and committed many other depredations."[87] Some Missouri residents were unwilling to await the decision of the courts and were acting immediately to expel the Saints from the area. During a seven-day period starting on October 31, these vigilante actions centered on the Big Blue settlements and Independence. According to Levi Jackman, Mormon men from the Timber Branch (Whitmer Settlement) "thot it best for their safety to go some two or three miles to a small branch that lived on the edge of the prairie, where the brethren had a grist mill, [probably the Colesville Settlement] and try to save that from the mob.... [They] had been there a few days when word came about problems on the Blue."[88] Since the Folletts lived in the Whitmer Settlement, they had direct knowledge of these events—and probably directly participated in them.

> William A. Follett a son of king
> and Louisa Follett was born at por portay
> County, ohio December the 11 1825
> was baptised in Jackson County Mo
> august 1833 by harvy whitlock

This awkwardly penned document records William Alexander Follett's baptism four months before he turned eight. Courtesy of Wilola Follett.

The first of the attacks occurred on the evening of October 31, 1833. Jackman, who lived in the northwest section of the Whitmer Settlement, described the events:

> A mob party of from 40 to 50, with weapons of death, had come upon our settlement in an hour not looked for, and had commenced throwing down houses, and shamefully beating the men when they could catch them, while the women with their little ones fled to the woods to hide themselves in the brush to save their lives from being taken by the mob The falling of the logs and boards as they fell to the ground, could be heard quite a distance in the stillness of the night and was well calculated to strike horror to the Saints who saw that destruction awaited them.[89]

By the time the raiders rode off, they had torn the roofs off at least ten homes. Many other dwellings were partially destroyed. During the next three days, the mobs struck at the Saints in other Jackson County locations. On November 1, Missourians hammered down doors, broke windows in Independence, and attacked the Gilbert and Whitney store. When Mormons captured one of the mob members and took him before a justice of the peace, that law officer refused to issue a warrant for his arrest. Another group of Missourians attacked the Colesville Branch. The Mormons captured two of their attackers, held them overnight, then released them. On November 2, a mob attacked the Big Blue community, broke into a house, and beat and shot at a man who was sick in bed. Armed members of the Church, coming to the rescue, exchanged shots with the mob, shooting one Missourian in the leg. The next day, several Mormons attempted to obtain a peace warrant from a circuit court judge, citing the governor's letter directing them to use the courts.

The judge delayed in issuing the warrant until November 6, by which time events had moved out of control.⁹⁰

The *History of the Church* acknowledges that not all residents of the county were actively involved in the violence against Church members. But those residents apparently could not or would not mount an active support of the Saints. Some old citizens advised the Mormons to leave as soon as possible because the violence had "enraged the whole county, and the people were determined to come out on Monday and massacre indiscriminately; and, in short, it was commonly declared among the mob, that '*Monday would be a bloody day.*'"⁹¹

Notes

1. "Divergent Paths of the Restoration," description of walking tour led by Steven Shields in the preliminary program of the Mormon History Association annual conference (themed "The Home and the Homeland: Families in Diverse Mormon Traditions,") Kansas City, Missouri, May 27–30, 2010, p. 12.

2. Henry K. Inouye Jr., *Latter Day [sic] Saints in Early Independence Missouri*, front cover.

3. Warren A. Jennings, "'Zion is Fled:' The Expulsion of the Mormons from Jackson County, Missouri," 19–21.

4. Paul C. Nagel, *Missouri: A Bicentennial History*, 121. See *The History of Jackson County, Missouri . . .*,55, 230–31, for a general discussion of early educational law and opportunities.

5. Ivan J. Barrett, *Joseph Smith and the Restoration: A History of the Church to 1846*, 239.

6. Ibid.

7. *History of the Church*, 1:189.

8. Unidentified missionary quoted in Edgar T. Lyon, "Independence, Missouri, and the Mormons, 1827–1833," 16.

9. Ibid., 14.

10. Ibid., 15.

11. Richard Lyman Bushman, *Joseph Smith: Rough Stone Rolling*, 172.

12. W. W. Phelps (Jackson County), Letter, July 23, 1831, quoted in Richard Lloyd Anderson, "Jackson County in Early Mormon Descriptions," 275.

13. Washington Irving, Letter, September 26, 1832, quoted in ibid., 287.

14. *History of the Church*, 1:198.

15. Ibid.

16. Bruce A. Van Orden, "Causes and Consequences: Conflict in Jackson County," 337.

17. Brigham H. Roberts, *The Missouri Persecutions*, 42.

18. John S. Higbee, Reminiscences and Diaries, 1845–1866," n.d., unpaginated.

19. Emily M. Austin, *Mormonism; or, Life among the Mormons, Being an Autobiographical Sketch; Including an Experience of Fourteen Years of Mormon Life*, 67. Emily was the sister-in-law of Newell Knight, one of the leaders of the Colesville Branch, whose members moved as a group from New York to Ohio and on to Missouri. Though she was baptized, her writings reflect discontent with the Church.

20. Emily Dow Partridge Young, "Diary and Reminiscences, February 1874–November 1899," 5.

21. *The History of Jackson County, Missouri* . . ., 298.

22. "The Season," *Evening and the Morning Star*, 2, no. 13 (June 1833): 102.

23. "The United Order" and the "welfare program" refer to organized efforts to care for the needy at various times in the Church's history, with all members contributing assets to make that possible. These types of programs originated from the various revelations, now canonized in the Doctrine and Covenants, regarding the law of consecration.

24. Leonard J. Arrington, Feramorz Y. Fox, and Dean L. May, *Building the City of God: Community and Cooperation among the Mormons*, 22–31.

25. Ibid., 23, 373. See also "Deed Forms Used under the New Order," in William E. Berrett and Alma P. Burton, eds., *Readings in L.D.S. Church History from the Original Manuscripts* . . ., 114–16.

26. Solomon Hancock, quoted in Charles Brent Hancock, "Autobiography (ca. 1882)," 3. Charles was Solomon's son.

27. Levi Jackman, Diary, May 1835–July 1844, June 9, 1835, p. 24 in holograph, and p. 12 in typescript. Some minor wording is different in the two copies. A Thomas Guymon family is listed on the 1830 U.S. Census, Edgar, Illinois, 36.

28. Lyndon W. Cook and Milton V. Backman Jr., eds., *Kirtland Elders' Quorum Record, 1836–1841*, 82, 99.

29. Bruce A. Van Orden, "From Kirtland to Missouri," 26.

30. Bushman, *Joseph Smith: Rough Stone Rolling*, 180–81.

31. Levi Jackman, "Sketch of Life 1851," unpaginated.

32. Emily Dow Partridge Young, "What I Remember, 1884," 5–6. Emily was the daughter of Edward Partridge, the first Presiding Bishop of the Church. Her father was probably not with the family on this journey as he had been sent to Jackson County earlier.

33. Max H Parkin, *Missouri*, 9. The two sites in addition to Independence were Fort Osage, "which by 1831 was a declining, decommissioned federal fort in the northeastern corner of the county" and the "Blue Mills or Hudspeth settlement, a loosely scattered rural neighborhood about nine miles northeast of Independence . . . but it never flourished."

34. Max H Parkin, "Jackson County and Vicinity," 38.

35. Parkin, *Missouri*, 15.

36. William J. Curtis, *Jackson County, Missouri, Mormon Historic Sites*, 48.

37. *History of the Church*, 1:336–37.

38. Curtis, *Jackson County, Missouri, Mormon Historic Sites*, 52.

39. William G. Hartley, *Stand by My Servant Joseph: The Story of the Joseph Knight Family and the Restoration*, 159.

40. David Pettegrew, "A History of David Pettegrew," 12. This surname is frequently spelled "Pettigrew" in later references and by David's living descendants. I use Pettegrew except in quotations.

41. Orson F. Whitney, "The 'Mormons' in Jackson County," in W. Z. Hickman, *History of Jackson County, Missouri*, 196.

42. Donald Q. Cannon and Lyndon W. Cook, eds., *Far West Record: Minutes of the Church of Jesus Christ of Latter-day Saints, 1830–1844*, 65. The Far West Record and the *Kirtland Elders' Quorum Record* are the only two general minute books available for the Joseph Smith period. The *Far West Record* contains minutes of the Far West High Council meetings and conference reports.

43. Whitney, "The 'Mormons,'" 196.

44. Hancock, Autobiography, 3.

45. Curtis, *Jackson County, Missouri, Mormon Historic Sites*, 56.

46. Levi Jackman, Record Book (ca. 1832–1834). This is a holograph unpaginated document and the accounts are not in alphabetical order. By my count, there are a total of 48 individual pages with this entry located on pp. 27–28.

47. Windows set in their frames or windowpanes.

48. Ibid., 25–26.

49. Bushman, *Joseph Smith: Rough Stone Rolling*, 222.

50. *Political History of Jackson County [Missouri]: Biographical Sketches of Men who Have Helped to Make It*, 34.

51. Alexander L. Baugh, "From High Hope to Despair: The Missouri Period, 1831–39," 46.

52. For more detailed discussions of conditions in Missouri at this time, see Van Orden, "Causes and Consequences: Conflict in Jackson County"; Leonard J. Arrington and Davis Bitton, *The Mormon Experience: A History of the Latter-day Saints*; Richard L. Bushman, "Mormon Persecutions in Missouri, 1833"; Robertson, "The Mormon Experience in Missouri, 1830–1839"; Baugh, *A Call to Arms*; Lyon, "Independence, Missouri, and the Mormons, 1827–1833";

Howard Louis Conrad, "Mormonism," 481–87; Warren A. Jennings, "The Expulsion of the Mormons from Jackson County, Missouri," 41–63; *The History of Jackson County, Missouri*, and Clark V. Johnson, "Missouri: LDS Communities in Jackson and Clay Counties," 2:922–25.

53. Van Orden, "Causes and Consequences," 340–41.

54. Jennings, "Zion Is Fled," 21. Van Orden, "Causes and Consequences," 341, states "There were no schools for their children."

55. This was not the first time a religion in America claimed a certain land had been given to a group of people by God. In justifying theft or honest misunderstandings between the Indians and Plymouth inhabitants, Increase Mather, a minister in Boston, "believed that the Puritans lived among 'the heathen people . . . whose land the Lord God of our Fathers hath given us for a rightful possession.'" Quoted in Eric B. Schultz and Michael J. Tougias, *King Philip's War: The History and Legacy of America's Forgotten Conflict*, 20.

56. Arrington and Bitton, *The Mormon Experience*, 50.

57. Bushman, "Mormon Persecutions in Missouri, 1833," 16

58. Lyon, "Independence, Missouri, and the Mormons, 1827–1833," 17–18.

59. Van Orden, "Causes and Consequences," 342; Arrington and Bitton, *The Mormon Experience*, 48.

60. Jennings, "Zion Is Fled," 22–23.

61. Roberts, *The Missouri Persecutions*, 57.

62. Edwin C. McReynolds, *Missouri: A History of the Crossroads State*, 143–44.

63. Van Orden, "Causes and Consequences," 343.

64. Clark V. Johnson, "LDS Communities in Jackson and Clay Counties," 2:924.

65. Pettegrew, "A History of David Pettegrew," 15.

66. Johnson, "LDS Communities in Jackson and Clay Counties," 2:924.

67. William G. Hartley, "Letters and Mail between Kirtland and Independence: A Mormon Postal History, 1831–33," *Journal of Mormon History* 35, no. 3 (Summer 2009): 163–89.

68. Bushman, *Joseph Smith: Rough Stone Rolling*, 223–24.

69. Pettegrew, "A History of David Pettegrew," 16.

70. Van Orden, "Causes and Consequences," 344–45.

71. Ibid., 345.

72. *History of Jackson County, Missouri*, 254–55.

73. Bushman, *Joseph Smith: Rough Stone Rolling*, 123, and Van Orden, "Causes and Consequences," 345. Tarring and feathering was a physical punishment used in the American colonies and on the frontier as a vigilante action. Tar heated until it was liquid was poured or smeared on the victim's naked body; then he was covered or rolled in feathers. In March 1832, Joseph Smith had been tarred and feathered by a mob in Hiram, Ohio; Sidney Rigdon had been dragged outside but the mob members were interrupted before completing the punishment.

74. Jennings, "The Expulsion of the Mormons from Jackson County," 42.

75. Van Orden, "Causes and Consequences," 345.

76. *History of the Church*, 1:394.

77. Ibid., note. The Mormons who offered themselves as a ransom were John Corrill, John Whitmer, William W. Phelps, Algernon S. Gilbert, Edward Partridge, and Isaac Morley.

78. Ibid.

79. *History of the Church*, 1:410–15.

80. Ibid., 1:415.

81. Ibid., 1:424.

82. Ibid., 1:425.

83. Baugh, *A Call to Arms*, 7.

84. Reverend Benton Pixley, quoted in ibid.

85. Newburn Isaac Buff, comp. *Early History of Provo: From March 18, 1849, also Genealogical Information*, 53. A few sources give the year of baptism as 1838 rather than 1833, but 1833 is the year carried forward in most Follett family records and the place as Jackson County, Missouri. Harvey Whitlock, an early convert, was from Massachusetts. In June 1831, he was among the first men to be ordained a high priest. The expectation that worthy fathers would baptize and confirm their children and ordain their sons is a development of the late twentieth century.

86. William A. Follett, Baptismal Certificate, August 1833, photocopy of holograph in my possession, courtesy of Wilola Follett.

87. John P. Greene, *Facts Relative to the Expulsion of the Mormons or Latter Day Saints from the State of Missouri, Under the "Exterminating Order,"* 11. See also Clark V. Johnson, ed., *Mormon Redress Petitions: Documents of the 1833–1838 Missouri Conflict*, 16. Greene is referred to as both a cousin and a brother-in-law of Brigham Young.

88. Levi Jackman, Reminiscences and Journal, 1851–1867, November 4, 1833, unpaginated.

89. Jackman, "Autobiography."

90. Roberts, *The Missouri Persecutions*, 78–79.

91. *History of the Church*, 1:429; emphasis in original.

Chapter Seven

"Bloody Monday": Prelude to a Forced Expulsion

It is difficult for an outside observer to understand the feelings of either the Saints or the Missourians when the sun rose on Monday, November 4, 1833. It goes without saying that such fast-moving and traumatic episodes have at least two versions—and often more. Probably each participant experienced the events in a distinctively personal way, but only some of them left records, and it is from these records that modern readers must try to piece together a whole picture of what happened.

November 4 was well into fall, and all able-bodied men sensed the urgent need to finish harvesting crops that were a necessity for surviving the coming winter. But instead, both groups were diverted into adversarial efforts—the Missourians trying to rid the area of an undesirable group while that same group was preparing to defend itself in what they considered to be their sacred homeland. "Prior to this time," explains historian Alexander Baugh, "it appears none of the Mormons had been or were members of the existing county militia, nor had they organized any type of military unit of their own.... [But now] members living in each of the settlements would have to organize a quasi-military unit of their own" with the understanding that each "would come to the support of the others."[1]

Cordelia Morley Cox, daughter of Isaac Morley, Sr.,[2] was a ten-year-old living in the Whitmer Settlement when these events occurred. Later while living in the Salt Lake Valley, she remembered: "We were threatened day and night. They told us they would burn our houses down over

"Battle of the Blue" site, Jackson County, Missiouri, May 9, 1907, George Edward Anderson Collection, LDS Church History Library. Used by permission.

our heads.... Each night we expected our house would be burned to the ground. We would leave it at night and go away to sleep while the men would stand on guard. The women and children would go to a house away in the woods a mile from where we lived to sleep and come back again before breakfast in the morning.... We could hear the guns all the while but did not know what it meant."[3]

According to the *History of the Church* that was compiled later, the events of Monday morning, November 4, began with the mob commandeering the Church-owned ferry on the Blue River briefly, then moving to Wilson's store.[4] A group of "nineteen Mormons" were chased by "forty or fifty members of the mob" around and to the west of Wilson's store. Realizing they were outnumbered, the nineteen Mormons fled in several directions. The *History* continues: "The mob hunted them, turning their horses meantime into a corn field belonging to the Saints. Corn fields and houses were searched, the mob at the same time threatening women

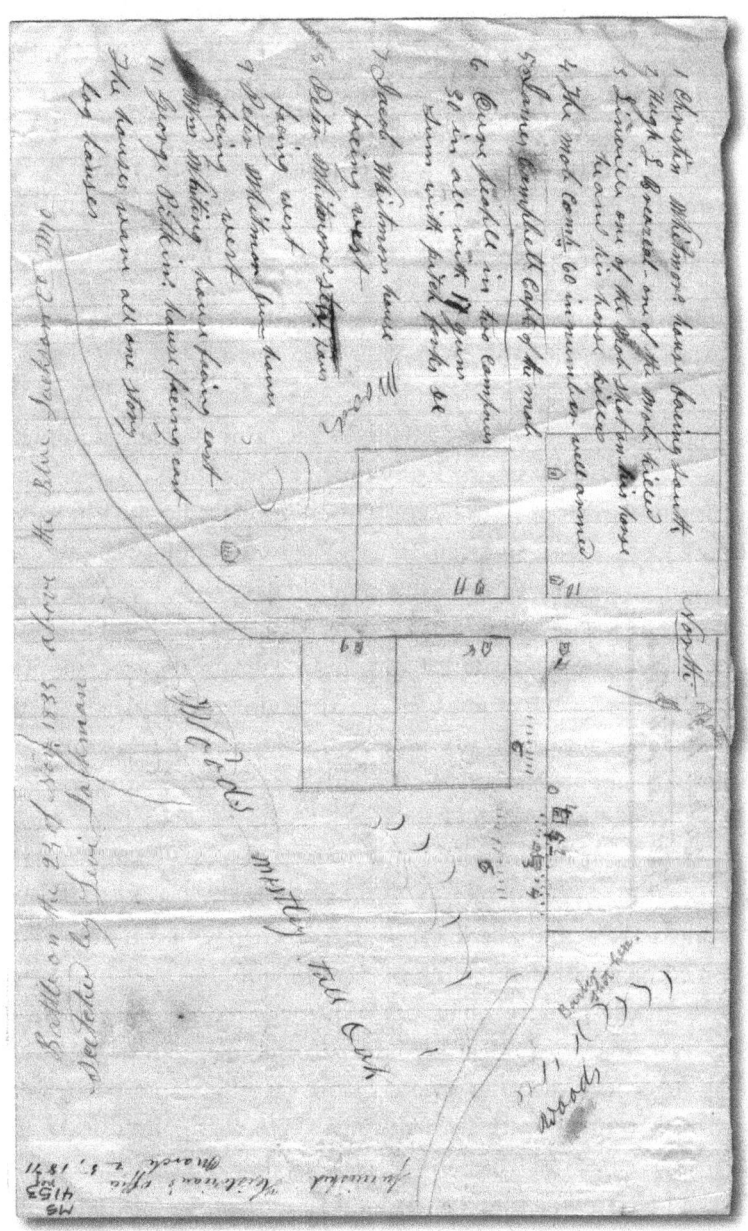

"Drawing of the Big Blue Battle," by Levi Jackman about 1871. Courtesy LDS Church History Library.

and children that they would pull down their houses and kill them if they did not tell where the men had fled. Thus they were employed in hunting the men and threatening the women, when a company of thirty of the brethren from the prairie, armed with seventeen guns, made their appearance."[5] Their leader was David Whitmer and King Follett was probably with this group. The mob "fed their horses in Christian Whitmer's corn field, and took him and pointed their guns at him, threatening his life if he did not tell them where the brethren were."[6] Thus began the battle near the Blue River, variously called the Battle of the Blue, at the Blue, on the Blue, and above the Blue.

Though no official list identifies all thirty who defended the Whitmer Settlement, two sources place King Follett among their number.[7] The circumstantial evidence also leans in that direction. The Folletts were living at the Whitmer Settlement which numbered only 144 members, including women and children, so that the population probably counted only about twenty or thirty adult men. Unless they were bedfast with illness or injury, they would have defended their families and neighbors. Philo Dibble, who was wounded in this battle, recalled King's presence among those who "were engaged" in the fight and further states that Henry A. Cleveland, who was also wounded, was taken to the home of another participant, Nathan West,[8] who later married King and Louisa's daughter, Adeline. West had purchased seventy acres from Mosby S. Owen in Jackson County on September 5, 1832. When Nathan sold twenty acres of that land in 1837 (and another twenty in 1839), Adeline is identified as Nathan's wife on the deed.[9] The Follett family may have lived on some of this land while in Jackson County.

Levi Jackman, a resident at Whitmer Settlement, described its houses as one-story log cabins and the area as wooded with "mostly tall oak." According to his account, thirty male Saints participated in the battle, seventeen with firearms and some with "pitchforks." In contrast, he describes the Missourians as sixty men, all "well armed." About 1871 Jackman drew a map from memory of the area near the Whitmer Settlement where the skirmish occurred.[10]

The Missourians, in addition to threatening Christian Whitmer physically, began to destroy his home located on the east end of town. David Whitmer led his group, including King Follett, from the west toward Christian's home. A group from the Colesville Branch under

Caleb Baldwin's leadership, advanced on the mob from the south armed with pitchforks. Someone in the mob yelled, "Give them hell," and fired. Whitmer's men returned fire. Two of the Missourians were killed and at least one was wounded. One Church member, Andrew Barber died, and at least four men were wounded. The members of the mob fled, pursued for a short distance by the Saints.[11] These events apparently reached their climax in the evening.

Meanwhile, at least four members of the Church—Algernon Sidney Gilbert, Isaac Morley, John Corrill, and William E. McLellin/M'Lellin—had been arrested and jailed in Independence on false charges. A quick trial was in progress late that night when word reached Independence of the skirmish on the Blue River. According to the *History of the Church*, this account described the Mormons as the aggressors, and Missourians rode throughout the county all night telling stories—some true, others false—about the day's events: "Runners were dispatched in every direction under pretense of calling out the militia," reports *History of the Church*, "spreading every rumor calculated to alarm and excite the uninformed as they went; such as that the 'Mormons' had taken Independence, and that the Indians had surrounded it, the 'Mormons' and Indians being colleagued together." Local citizens, some with guns, also gathered around the jail verbally threatening the prisoners. Realizing the potential for violence, the prisoners were "liberated about sunrise, without further prosecution of the trial."[12] The threat of a "bloody Monday" in Jackson County, as later described by Mormon historian B. H. Roberts, had in some ways been realized.[13]

By the morning of Tuesday, November 5, armed Missourians from all over Jackson County arrived in Independence prepared to fight. Simultaneously, led by Lyman Wight, about a hundred Mormon volunteers,[14] presumably including King Follett, began moving east toward Independence from the string of Mormon settlements lying to the west. Lieutenant Governor Boggs called out the state militia under the command of Colonel Pitcher in an apparent attempt to prevent any further bloodshed. However, many members of the armed Missourians from the night before were also militiamen, a predictable circumstance. The situation was tense; and undoubtedly with a little encouragement from the anti-Mormon members of the militia, Colonel Pitcher demanded that the Mormons surrender their weapons to a committee of militiamen and "deliver into his hands certain men to be tried for murder, said to have been committed by them in the battle, as he called it, of the previous evening."[15] Lyman Wight, providing sworn testimony in the Municipal Court of Nauvoo in 1843 regarding conditions in Jackson County at this time, stated that he "here agreed that the Church would give up their arms provided the said Colonel Pitcher would take the arms from the mob. To this the Colonel cheerfully agreed, and pledged his honor with that of Lieutenant Governor Boggs, Owens and others."[16] Even with this agreement, to protect themselves and their families the Saints knew they had to leave Jackson County as quickly as possible. While they tried to prepare for this move and find some place to go, Wight's affidavit continues: "This solemn contract was violated in every sense of the word. The arms of the mob were never taken away, and the majority of the militia, to my certain knowledge, were engaged the next day with the mob . . . going from house to house in gangs of from sixty to seventy in number, threatening the lives of women and children if they did not leave forthwith."[17] This left the Saints with no means to protect themselves and at the mercy of the mob-like militia members. According to the *History of the Church*, "On Tuesday and Wednesday nights, the 5th and 6th of November, women and children fled in every direction before the merciless mob. One party of about one hundred and fifty women and children fled to the prairie, where they wandered for several days with only about six men to protect them. Other parties fled to the Missouri river, and took lodging for the night where they could find it. . . . During this dispersion . . . parties of the mob were hunting the men, firing upon some, tying up and whipping others, and pursuing others with horses for several miles."[18]

King and Louisa were among those forced from their homes with their children. Although they left no record, their experiences were probably similar to the reminiscences of their friend and neighbor, Levi Jackman, of the Whitmer Settlement, who wrote an autobiographical sketch eighteen years later: "I saw one wagon, with one man, and a large company of women with bundles in their hands turning from the road into the woods and then across the prarie to escape a mob who they said had passed towards the Whitmer Settlement, and told them that if they were not gone on their return, they would all be killed."[19] Generally, there was great confusion. Many Saints fled from their homes at night.

Traveling in the dark, family members became separated. They had no time to pack food or clothes and lacked adequate protection from the rain and cold weather. Lyman Wight remembered it as "one of the most stormy nights I ever witnessed, while torrents of rain poured down during the whole night, and streams of the smallest size were magnified into rivers."[20] Everyone headed immediately into a relatively uncertain future. However, what they did know was that Independence to the east was not a safe place for Mormons at this time, and surely an unknown reception awaited them in Indian country to the West. Thus the other side of the Missouri River to the north, as formidable as it might have been, seemed the most logical direction to travel under the present circumstances.

Lyman Wight's son, Orange, who was then ten, recalled, "My father was chased by a mob in a westerly direction and my mother and I and two little sisters were taken by John Higbee in a small boat down the Big Blue River—3 miles—and across the Missouri River to Clay County, MO. We were left on the North bank of the river with a number of others and heard nothing of Father for three weeks.... During our stay on the bank of the river we camped by the side of a big sycamore log about 6 feet in diameter."[21] The Isaac Morley family fared no better: "Father Morley had raised a good garden," recalled his daughter Cordelia, who was ten in 1833. "His vegetables with thirty bushels of potatoes were buried in the ground. His house was not finished and his family was in poor circumstances. We left our home with one team and wagon to take his family, eight in number, and started to find another home. We went into Clay County, Missouri and settled on a piece of low, swampy land."[22]

Several reminiscences written by individuals who participated in these events in Missouri told of the loss of property and crops. John Somers Higbee recorded that, although his wife was ill, they "were driven out with not more than we could carry on our backs not having a team[. L]eft all but a very few things to the enemy and durst not return to get anything that was left."[23] David Pettegrew was able to save only a few personal items: "the Book of Mormon, my bible, a razor and a decantor of composition which my wife had requested me to bring." He had to leave his animals and wagons behind.[24] He tells of stopping by Orrin Porter Rockwell's place where the Missourians had "cut open feather beds, destroyed all of his furniture and all they could lay hands on."[25] Solomon Chamberlin "was driven from Jackson Co Mo with the loss of my inheritance and left my crops on the ground two houses burned and the loss of some cattle."[26] James Bennett lamented, "Our crops at the time were standing in the field, which we could not gather."[27]

The loss of their personal property was serious enough, but even more financially arduous was the permanent loss of their real estate. In Nauvoo, they swore affidavits that recount the loss of "'twenty three acres of land with ten acres of improvement and two houses, wheat and corn" (David Bennett); "loss of improvement of 7 acres and Crop corn and hogs . . . that I never got any Pay for" (David Frampton); and "fourteen acres of corn, twelve acres of corn, fifty acres of land, house and lot" (James Goff).[28] Louisa Follett signed a similar affidavit on behalf of her family. They had heartbreakingly few assets in Jackson County, which meant that these losses in the depth of their poverty were especially cruel. Her claims total $170, consisting of "loss of improvements on land and buildings," $100, $50 worth of "provision and wheat in the ground," and $20 for the "loss of time and expence of mooving from Jackson Co. to Clay Co." These losses mounted as they started over again in Clay and Caldwell counties but again had to leave.[29] Louisa did not claim real estate losses in Jackson County—just improvement on lands and buildings—nor is King listed as owing taxes or laying title to any land. They had been in Missouri for about one year and were probably farming Church-owned property in the Whitmer Settlement or land owned by Nathan West.

As some Missourians were destroying goods and homes, driving families out of their houses, and beating men, other Missourians attempted to persuade their fellow citizens to be more lenient and give the Saints more time and perhaps less threatening circumstances under which to leave. This request only seemed to infuriate those with mob mentality. When a sister of Orrin Porter Rockwell begged the men not to destroy their goods, "one of the Mob replied if she did not go away he would cut her throat from ear to ear pulling out a knife holding it out towards her."[30] By November 8, most of the Saints in Jackson County had been driven from their homes. Near that date, David Pettegrew recalls, between sixty and eighty men "came to my house" in the Whitmer Settlement. "I saw that many of them were painted red and black like Indians and were armed with guns, pistols, swords, bowie knives, club, Etc." After threatening Pettegrew and his family, some of whom were sick in bed, they "destroyed several other houses and property and shot at Sister Sherwood [or Shurwood] and several others as they were running in a cornfield."[31]

Though most of the Mormons went northward to Clay County, a few others went to Lafayette County and other areas to the south and east.[32] Most of those going north made makeshift shelters on the south bank of the Missouri River while they waited in the cold and rain to be ferried across. "Approximately a dozen ferries operated between Jackson and Clay counties, and a principal landing site was Independence Landing, known later as the Wayne City Landing."[33] Many of the Saints had no food, no clothing beyond what they were wearing, or adequate bedding. Most of the twelve hundred [34] individuals who fled from Jackson County at this time huddled together waiting to cross the river. As the Mormon-owned ferry had been confiscated, apparently the remaining ferry owners were all Missourians; and under the circumstances, it might be expected that they charged maximum rates. Unless the Mormons had cash, which is doubtful, at least some could have bartered their few remaining possessions for passage or found ways other than cash to obtain transportation across the river. Mary Elizabeth Rollins Lightner, who was fifteen years old at the time, reported in her biography, written at age eighty-seven, that as some families were camped "on the banks of the Missouri River waiting to be ferried over, they found there was not money enough to take all of them over. One or two families must be left behind, and the fear was that if left, they would be killed." Some of the men decided to try to catch some fish in hopes the ferryman would take them in exchange for passage. They were successful and caught "two or three small fish, and a catfish that weighed 14 pounds. On opening it, what was their astonishment to find three bright silver half dollars, just the amount needed to pay for taking their team over the river. This was considered a miracle."[35] According to LDS historian Max H Parkin, "Operators and their assistants spent at least half a day in making a single round trip across the swiftly moving Missouri." Examples of fares charged were "loaded wagon and team $2; empty wagon and team $1.50; and loaded cart and team $1.00."[36]

The *History of the Church* contains this vivid description:

> The shores of the Missouri river began to be lined on both sides of the ferry, with men, women and children; goods, wagons, boxes, chests, and

provisions; . . . the wilderness had much the appearance of a camp meeting. Hundreds of people were seen in every direction; some in tents, and some in the open air, around their fires, while the rain descended in torrents. Husbands were inquiring for their wives, and women for their husbands; parents for children, and children for parents. Some had the good fortune to escape with their families, household goods, and some provisions; while others knew not the fate of their friends, and had lost all their effects. The scene was indescribable . . . when night came on, they had the appearance of a village of wigwams.[37]

B. H. Roberts, a British convert who joined the Church when it was headquartered in Utah, reports that a baby was born on the river bank during a rainstorm and that a woman died while being ferried across the river.[38]

Those Saints who fled south found themselves in very nearly the same miserable condition. Some lacking bedding took shelter in caves from the rain and bitter winds. David Pettegrew recalled, not only the suffering of his own family, but also "the privations and sufferings of the Saints. They suffered not only from anguish of heart at the loss of home, property, stock and provisions . . . [but also because] no comfort, no relief, could be procured for them constantly exposed to the inclemency of the weather. . . . These were the beginning of days of great trial to us."[39]

It must be stressed that not all non-Mormons living in Jackson County were part of the Missourians that harmed or threatened the Saints and their property or approved of the actions. A modern-day Missouri historian, Thomas M. Spencer, observed that "the newspapers across Missouri spoke out against the actions of the mob in Jackson County" and "there was quite a bit of sympathy in eastern Missouri for the plight of the Mormons."[40] However, those who were not actively involved apparently did not often have the means to help the Mormons or were afraid to overtly interfere on their behalf. According to David Pettegrew, some of the old-time settlers "tried to get people to give up their religion and join a local one and the Mormons would be protected."[41] The non-Mormon vigilantes also offered the Church members an opportunity to stay in Jackson County. Both Pettegrew and Gipson Gates tell of a specific incident which occurred at a Church meeting in the fall of 1833, when a man by the name of Masters came and told them he had been sent by the "mob to tell them if they would forsake their religion and join another religion that they would fight for us."[42]

Undoubtedly a few individuals did so. But King and Louisa followed the majority of the Church members out of the area. A county history written as late as 1923 failed to express sympathy for the struggling Saints, although it accurately noted in its one sentence about the forced exodus from Jackson County: "There was great discomfort and misery among the fugitives as they crossed the river in November, the weather being cold and rainy, and the half-clad women and children suffered severely."[43]

The numbers and names of Church members who fled the county can only be estimated, since, for obvious reasons, no records were created at the time. However, President Brigham Young requested that George A. Smith compile a list of the refugees on March 12, 1864. King, Louisa, their son John, and their son-in-law Nathan West (but not daughter Adeline) are on this list.[44] Obviously because of dissatisfaction with the inadequacy of the first list, a request was made in April conference by George A. Smith for further information. He and Thomas Bullock then prepared the second list on August 27, 1864. The second list is twenty-six pages long with between twenty-five and thirty names on each page, or a total of 650 to 780. If about twelve hundred Saints were living in Jackson County in 1833,[45] this list would account for between half and two-thirds of them; but obviously many names are missing. The list was arranged by name of each individual, the name of the LDS branch in Jackson County he or she had lived in, and whether the individual was alive or dead at the time of the survey. Seven members of the extended Follett family, all of them from Whitmer Branch, appear on this list:

    1. King Follett was "killed in well in Nauvoo."
    2. Louisa is identified simply as "wife" and is not identified as either living or dead.
    3. John Follett "died Council Bluffs."
    4. William Follett, is identified as living in Provo.
    5–6. Adaline Follett and Nathan West were living in "Silver Creek, Iowa," and Nathan is identified as "Apostatized." (See Chapter 22.)
    7. Nancy Follett is identified as living in Illinois.[46]

William Alexander Follett was undoubtedly the source of some of this information, all of which can be corroborated except for Nancy. By 1864, she had been living for more than ten years in Contra Costa County, California, with her second husband, Henry Sanford, and her children. This list is the best evidence for John's approximate death date, sometime after 1846–47 in Council Bluffs. It also provides corroboration that King and Louisa's three youngest children—Edward (born about 1821), Emily (born about 1829), and Mary (born about 1831)—had died before the exodus from Jackson County. Missing from the list is the second son named Edward (possibly born June 9, 1833), who would have been a babe in arms at the time of the flight. By 1864, he was living in California near his sister Nancy.

The painful flight across the Missouri River into Clay County closed a chapter in the Folletts' lives. Like their fellow believers, they had come to Jackson County because of their belief that it was the centerplace of Zion and the destination to which Christ would come to launch his millennial reign. They left Ohio believing that Missouri would be their final home. Within two years, their plans, hopes, and dreams had been torn up by the roots, and they themselves were homeless and persecuted. As Community of Christ historian Ronald E. Romig noted, "For the next few years, hope periodically arose in the hearts of church members that they would once again be allowed to return to their homes [but] . . . Jackson Countians eventually burned most of the abandoned homes to forestall any attempted return."[47] A few did return briefly, sometimes hoping to take possession of their homes again or, more realistically, to sell their property to finance their next move. John Brush of the Big Blue Settlement, returned in January 1834 only to find that those who "had been their nearest neighbors, pillaged their houses of what furniture they had, killed their hogs and cattle, and harvested the corn which they had raised, causing their homes to become deserted wastes."[48] A few were able to sell their property, but it was a buyers' market and they realized small profits. Calvin Beebe, who "built a dwelling house" on the Blue River and "built a Double house anhalf a Mile from indipendance" sold his "lands their at perhaps one tenth of the real value."[49] They also found that the few Mormons who remained in Jackson County had to conceal their affiliation or risk social marginalization and physical abuse. Abigail Leonard, one of the few women who wrote about events, remembered that in February of 1834, three months after the exodus, while she and her family were still living in Jackson County, a group of "men armed with whips and guns about fifty or sixty" threatened her husband and "attacked him with whips & gun sticks."[50]

King and his family had spent at most a year and a half in their new Zion and, like most of their co-believers, had been Mormons for about two years. Would their decision to join the Church have been the same if they could have foreseen the future? They had not been wealthy when they first met the missionaries in Shalersville, Ohio, but they had a warm, comfortable home and did not fear violence. Those two items would be scarce commodities in their lives during the coming years, but they moved on to their next home with the Saints in Clay County.

Notes

1. Alexander L. Baugh, *A Call to Arms: The 1838 Mormon Defense of Northern Missouri*, 7–8.

2. Isaac Morley Sr. was born in 1786 in Massachusetts, was baptized shortly after the Church was organized and served as a counselor to Edward Partridge, the Church's first bishop. The first missionaries to Ohio stayed on the Morley farm in the Kirtland area and Joseph and Emma Smith lived on the Morley property upon their arrival in 1831. Morley was present at and involved with many of the early events of Mormonism and was a leader in Ohio, Missouri and Utah. Cordelia Morley Cox, "Biography of Isaac Morley: A Sketch of the Life of My Father, Isaac Morley, One of the Pioneers to [the] Salt Lake Valley in 1848."

3. Ibid., quoted in Clare B. Christensen, *Before and after Mt. Pisgah: Cox, Hulet, Losee, Morley, Tuttle, Winget, Whiting & Related Families*, 73. See also "Autobiography of Cordelia Morley Cox."

4. This is the same Moses Wilson who met with the group of local Missouri citizens in July 1833 and drew up the agreement outlining the terms under which the church members were to leave Missouri. (See Chapter 6.) Wilson was also identified as being the "main antagonist and anti-Mormon ringleader in that part of the county." Baugh, *A Call to Arms*, 8.

5. *History of the Church*, 1:429–30.

6. Brigham H. Roberts, *The Missouri Persecutions*, 82. Christian Whitmer (1798–1835) was one of the sons of Peter Whitmer Sr., at whose home the Church was organized in 1830. Christian, one of the eight witnesses to the Book of Mormon, was among the Mormons who evacuated Jackson County and settled in Clay County where he died.

7. Christensen, *Before and after Mt. Pisgah*, 75 and Philo Dibble, Journal History, November 4, 1833, 9, and "Statement" April 15, 1851, a one-page holograph document. Christensen's version written after the fact, and Dibble, remembering an event he personally participated in, both identify the Mormon men involved as David Whitmer, Jacob Whitmer, Charles Hulet, Sylvester Hulet, Nathan West, William Whiting, Hiram Page, *King Follett* (emphasis mine), John Forman or Foreman, John Poorman or Porman, Andrew Barber, Philo Dibble, Henry A. Cleveland, and "Father" (no first name) Brace. Dibble alone lists Sheffield Daniels and (no first name) Chaplin or Chapin, while Christensen alone identifies Caleb Baldwin, who led a group of Mormons from the Colesville Branch to give aid; Levi Jackman, who drew a map and wrote a short statement; and George Beebe, "who had been whipped by the mob not long before."

8. Dibble, Journal History, November 4, 1833, 8–9, identifies his list as "partial." Philo Dibble was converted by the Lamanite missionaries who visited the Kirtland, Ohio, area in October of 1830. He lived on twenty acres in the Whitmer Settlement and later moved to Nauvoo, "where he made the cast for the death masks of Joseph and Hyrum Smith after their martyrdom." Max H Parkin, "Missouri," 106.

9. Twylia G. Brand, extractor, *Deeds, Jackson County, Missouri*, "Deeds 1827–1845," 1:8–44, 64, 169, and "Deeds 1845–1851," 2:350. West's property was Section 16, Township 49, Range 33 in Jackson County. In 1844, the sheriff sold ten acres for back taxes. In 1850 Nathan, without Adeline's signature, sold the remaining twenty acres.

10. Levi Jackman, "Drawing of the Battle on the Big Blue River ca. 1871," frame 34. This drawing also appears in Dibble, Journal History, November 4, 1833, 10, and Christensen, *Before and after Mt. Pisgah*, 78.

11. Christensen, *Before and after Mount Pisgah*, 75–76; Dibble, Journal History, November 4, 1833, 1.

12. *History of the Church*, 1:431–32.

13. Ibid., 1:429.

14. Ibid., 1:433.

15. Ibid., 1:433–36.

16. Lyman Wight, "Testimonies Given before the Municipal Court of Nauvoo," in Clark V. Johnson, ed., *Mormon Redress Petitions: Documents of the 1833–1838 Missouri Conflict*, 653. *History of the Church*, 1:435, states that the "brethren surrendered their arms to the number of fifty or upwards."

17. Wight, "Testimonies Given before the Municipal Court of Nauvoo," in Johnson, *Mormon Redress Petitions*, 653–54.

18. *History of the Church*, 1:436.

19. Levi Jackman, "Sketch of Life," 1851, unpaginated.

20. Wight, in Johnson, *Mormon Redress Petitions*, 655. See also discussion of weather conditions in Carrie Polk Johnston and W. H. S. McGlumphy, *History of Clinton and Caldwell Counties, Missouri*, 220; *History of the Church*, 1:437; B. H. Roberts, *The Missouri Persecutions*, 89.

21. Orange Lysander Wight, "Reminiscences, 1903 May–Dec," typescript, 1–2. Orange Wight's mother, Harriett, was pregnant at this time and delivered a baby about two months later in Clay County. When the baby was three days old, her husband, Lyman Wight, left Missouri with Parley P. Pratt to go to Kirtland to confer with the Prophet, leaving Harriett lying "by the side of a log in the woods with a child three days old, and [with] three days' provisions on hand." "History of Lyman Wight," *Millennial Star* 27 (July 22, 1865): 455.

22. Cordelia Morley Cox, "Biography of Isaac Morley: A Sketch of the Life of My Father Isaac Morley, One of the Pioneers to Salt Lake Valley in 1848," 1.

23. John Somers Higbee, "Reminiscences and Diaries, 1845–1866," 2.

24. David Pettegrew, (quoted as Pettigrew) in Ronald E. Romig, *Early Jackson County, Missouri: "Mormon" History Guide. The "Mormon" Settlement on the Big Blue River*, 25.

25. Pettegrew, quoted in ibid., 32.

26. Solomon Chamberlin, "Affidavit" in Johnson, *Mormon Redress Petitions*, 159.

27. James Bennett Bracken, "Statement," November 6, 1881, 9.

28. Johnson, *Mormon Redress Petitions*, 137, 208, 209, 216. During the winter of 1838–39, Joseph Smith instructed Church members to prepare "affidavits of their recent experiences with the design of securing redress from the federal government for the losses they had suffered in Missouri at the hands of mobocrats." The affidavits covered losses in Jackson, Clay, Caldwell, and Daviess counties between 1833 and 1839. The Saints signed and swore to these documents before municipal authorities, then presented their petitions to the federal government more than once during the Nauvoo period.

29. Louisa Follett, Affidavit, in Johnson, *Mormon Redress Petitions*, 201.

30. Oren [sic] Porter Rockwell, "Affidavit," in Clark, *Mormon Redress Petitions*, 527. Harold Schindler, *Orrin Porter Rockwell: Man of God, Son of Thunder*, 16–17, identifies this sister as Electa, age about seventeen.

31. David Pettegrew, "Statements," August 1862.

32. Bracken, Statement, 9.

33. Richard Neitzel Holzapfel and T. Jeffry Cottle, *Old Mormon Kirtland and Missouri: Historic Photographs and Guide*, 163.

34. This is the number given by Joseph Smith Jr., Sidney Rigdon, and Elias Higbee, "The First Memorial," written in Washington City, January 27, 1840, reprinted in Johnson, *Mormon Redress Petitions*, 106. Individual affidavits contained in *Mormon Redress Petitions* confirm this number.

35. Mary E. Lightner, "Mary E. Lightner's Life History," 197.

36. Parkin, "A History of the Latter Day [sic] Saints in Clay County," 41.
37. *History of the Church*, 1:437.
38. Roberts, *The Missouri Persecutions*, 89.
39. Pettegrew, "Statements."
40. Thomas N. Spencer, "Introduction," 9.
41. Pettegrew, "Statements."
42. Pettegrew, "Affidavit," 316l; Gipson Gates, "Affidavit," in Johnson, *Mormon Redress Petitions*, 212.
43. Johnston and McGlumphy, *History of Clinton and Caldwell Counties, Missouri*.
44. "Information Concerning Persons Driven from Jackson County, Missouri, in 1833," fd. 3, unpaginated.
45. The information presented to Congress as a foreword to the "Affidavits" prepared by members of the Church in 1840 and 1842 gives the number of Saints who were "disfranchised and driven from their houses and homes in the County of Jackson" as amounting to "about Twelve hundred souls." Johnson, *Mormon Redress Petitions*, 106, 398.
46. "Information Concerning Persons Driven from Jackson County, Missouri in 1833," fd. 2, unpaginated.
47. Romig, *Early Jackson County, Missouri*, 27.
48. Ibid., 30.
49. Calvin Beebe, "Affidavit," in Johnson, *Mormon Redress Petitions*, 134.
50. Abigail Leonard, "Affidavit," in ibid., 273.

✤ Chapter Eight ✤

The Turmoil Continues: Clay County 1833–35

Situated just north of Jackson County in Missouri, Clay County's history mirrored the same settlement issues as its southern neighbor. Beginning in about 1819 when the first arrivals reached this frontier, they had made their homes along Fishing River and Big Shoal Creek. The area was rich with trees and wildlife. Liberty became the county seat in 1822. When the Mormons began moving into the area, most of them abruptly exiled from Jackson County, Liberty was the only settlement of any size and stood in the center of the area eventually occupied by the Church members. The non-member population then numbered between three and five hundred inhabitants, most of them, like their counterparts in Jackson County, from the South and comfortable with that culture, including its acceptance of slavery. The displaced Indians west of the Mississippi were a source of anxiety. Hunting and trapping were still important; an influx of farmers would change that culture. The local paper described the county as having "rich and fertile soil . . . salubrious climate, a first rate home market . . . [and ranking] among the first counties in the state for wealth, intelligence, [and] population."[1] The same article described Liberty as containing "9 dry goods stores, several groceries, 1 tanyard, a cotton carding and spinning factory, mechanic shops of almost every description and in its vicinity, 1 steam grist and sawmill." In short, located "about three miles from the Missouri River, we are one of the finest tracts of country upon earth."[2]

It is difficult to imagine the conditions the Follett family and the other Saints had to cope with as they clustered on the north bank of the Missouri River in November 1833, huddled against the cold rain. They had managed to cross the river, fleeing Jackson County, most of them in the rain and harsh winter weather. Daniel Berry Rawson, who was about seven years old at the time, from his own personal memories and also perhaps remembering what he had been told by other older family members, later reported stoically: "Grandfather fixed up a team and loaded the family and the few household goods they had kept and moved to the Missouri River, where they loaded on the ferry-boat and were carried across into Clay County. They unloaded upon the sand, stuck willows into the ground and stretched sheets over them for a shelter where they remained for a few days until grandfather could secure another place in the rock piles of Bluffs of the Missouri River."[3]

The anxiety men like King felt, caught between responsibility for their families and the scarcity of options, must have been immense. Levi Jackman, the thirty-six-year-old father of five children whose ages ranged from twenty-one to six years, later recalled that, when it became apparent that they had to leave Jackson County, "attempts were made to go to different counties but the inhabitants refused us admission, and for a time it seemed we must stand still and be murdered all together. But at last we gained admittance into Clay County. . . . As a general thing the people were kind to us."[4]

John Higbee, who was nineteen years of age, later recorded that his family "built shanteys on congress land"—or federally owned land along the banks of the Big Blue—"& stad through the winter our means of sussistence was very limited our living for 5 families for meat depended on my success huntin for wild animals & for our bread we crossed the river in the night time went to my brothers place that was near the river where we got corn out of his field."[5] Emily Coburn, then a twenty-seven-year-old wife and soon to be a first-time mother, in a reminiscence published almost fifty years later, under her then-married name of Emily M. Austin, recalled:

"Log heaps were our parlor stoves, and the cold, wet ground our velvet carpets, and the crying of little children our piano forte; while the shivering, sick people hovered over the burning log piles here and there. . . . The snow covered our sleeping tents, and the scene reminded one of the gathering of the house of Israel." Yet she staunchly affirmed: "Although we did not enjoy the legal rights of civilized citizens, yet we maintained the right of freedom of conscience; neither could we be deprived of the liberty of serving God according to our views."[6]

There, these temporary communities endured the winter, perched precariously on the Missouri's north bank, lacking the means or the energy to move much farther, not knowing where they could go to start over, and above all, lacking on-site leadership. Most of them expected to return soon to their homes. Joseph Smith had taught them that the Lord had designated Jackson County as their Zion, but Joseph was not there. The lag in communications made it impossible for him to get timely information and give relevant instruction, and the Jackson County residents had underscored the message that they would resist with violence any attempt to carry out the religious mandate.

Refugees in Van Buren County to the south fared just as poorly. David Pettegrew, who had made a temporary dwelling for his wife and seven children about thirty miles from his home in Jackson County, reported that three men visited them and "said they came from Jackson County and told us we must leave the place we had stopped at . . . and then said if you don't leave this place your blood will run." His children were barefoot and there was about a foot of snow on the ground. Sister Pettegrew indignantly demanded: "'do you want these children to go out into the snow barefoot that they may freeze[?]'" Their obvious plight apparently abashed the men who backed down but warned gruffly, "Don't let too many warm days go over your heads before you are out of this place."'[7]

The fortunate refugees in Clay County had wagons or tents. The less fortunate improvised tents out of precious bedding strung over low tree branches or made temporary lean-tos by arranging logs against a large tree trunk or bank. They were scattered for about twenty-five miles along the southern border of Clay County from east to west. King and Louisa left no record of how they passed the winter. I hypothesize that they probably stayed by the river for a while but eventually moved north along with others from the Whitmer Settlement. It was certainly critical for them to find land they could farm when spring came, whether as hired hands, on shares, or simply as squatters on unoccupied land.

Reports differ about the reaction of the few (and outnumbered) residents of Clay County. One non-member source reflecting back in

1975 about the history of the Mormons, stated that the "people of Clay welcomed them, feeling they had been badly treated.... The hardships of the Mormons ... had caused the Clay Countians to feel sorry for them."[8] However, W. H. Woodson, who published a county history in 1920, claims: "The people of Clay County did not receive the refugees with open arms, but with suspicion and no little dread. The conduct of the so-called saints in Jackson County was not unheard of or unknown to Clay County."[9] Mormon historian Brigham H. Roberts, who wrote in the late nineteenth and early twentieth centuries, states that the inhabitants of Clay County were "kind to the exiles thrown so unceremoniously upon their hospitality. They were permitted to occupy every vacant cabin, and build others for temporary shelter.... For their acts of kindness the people of Clay County were well repaid in labor performed by the brethren."[10]

As that harsh winter of 1833–34 ground on in Clay County, the Mormons began to spread out, primarily northward towards the county seat of Liberty and then eastward as well, searching for more comfortable places to live, work, and obtain food. The local citizens, according to an anonymously authored modern history, "charitably offered shelter, work, and provisions. The refuges moved into abandoned slave cabins, built crude huts, [and] pitched tents.... Some men found work splitting rails, building houses, and grubbing brush.... Sisters worked in the households of well-to-do farmers, ... [while] others taught school."[11] According to Emily Dow Partridge Young's later reminiscence, a slaughter yard was established on the bank of the river. Here men, women, and children killed "thousands of hogs" and dried and packed the meat. "The brethren were enabled to earn provisions sufficient to keep their families from starving."[12]

Hunger was the most pressing concern. Few of the Saints had been able to pack and move in an orderly way with the result that their supplies had been left behind. Even fewer had money to purchase the necessary items. Some men crossed back over to Jackson County despite the danger, hunted game, and may have hoped to buy corn from sympathetic farmers. They also harvested honey and gleaned in cornfields that had already been harvested. David Pettegrew's experience is probably typical of the results of those excursions. He soon tried to return to his home but reported he was again threatened and told to hurry and get things and that the home of "any man that keep you for the night" would be burned down. He found his home "plundered of everything such as clothing, bed, beding, bed clothes, trunks, pots, kettles, silver spoons, knives and forks, and in fact all my cornfield destroyed, my farming utensils taken away."...We took another trip to our farms a short time afterwards for more provisions and found the people as insolent as ever, in fact our lives were in danger." With the help of Gibson Gates, Pettegrew was able to get a "load of corn."[13]

This return to Jackson County was a precarious adventure for those who undertook it, and many of them suffered as a result. King's son, John, then about fourteen, accompanied Ira Jones Willes,[14] back to Jackson County to locate a stray cow and subsequently prove title to it. They were at the home of a justice of the peace named Manship when they were accosted by Moses Wilson.[15] Though there is no record that John Follett was attacked, Willes was. He recorded: "By advice of the Bishop 1834 March 31st I went to Jackson County to get a cow for one of the brethren and was taken by some of the mob my close [clothes?] was forst [forced?] of and I was compelled to receive from 6 to 8 blows with a hickery whip 4 feet in length to the necked skin."[16] The *History of the Church* described Willes as "a young man, honest, peaceable and unoffending, working righteousness, and molesting no one" and termed the abuse an "unpardonable act."[17]

These attempts by Church members to cross back into Jackson County, even to obtain food, was further documented by a leader of another religion. A letter written in French by a Father Roux from the "Mouth of the River of Kansas, 27 June 1834, to Bishop Rosati, St. Louis County, Missouri," sympathized with the Saints' condition. The writer also worried about the impact this situation would have on his own missionary activities.

> The troublesome situation of the Jackson County people will create for a while some obstacles to our aims. Between them and the Mormons is an implacable hate. They [the Missourians] have chased them from their possessions destroyed their crops, broke their fences, burned their houses and thrown them into distress, that would move even a heart of stone, they keep guard along the Missouri to repel them and take away all hope for them to return to their farms. Everywhere they created generals, chiefs, and armed themselves to the teeth with the most determined resolution to sustain the

bloodiest fight. . . . Combat ideas replace religious ideas and religion does not hold the first place in the Jacksonian hearts."[18]

It had rapidly become apparent that, even if the Church members were to return to Jackson County, it would not be in time to plant crops in the spring of 1834. Therefore, the men began to plant crops on rented land or on "Congress" land, meaning that the federal government held legal title; but "squatting" on the land without permission and improving it usually provided a quasi-legal right that could be validated at the land office later. Although the Folletts left no record, I hypothesize that King, finding himself and his family members in great need, also followed this pattern. Eliza Partridge recalled her family's suffering: "There was already snow on the ground" when the family reached Clay County. "He [her father] found a miserable old house that he could have with one fire place in it. . . . [T]he house [was] open and cold and their cooking and children and husbands and selves all around one fireplace, for stoves were not in use then."[19] The Partridge family lived there through the winter sharing the space with another family. The fact that the Partridges had a roof over their head that they could call a "house" was probably better than many members had. In his role as ecclesiastical leader, her father was also faced with the task of assisting all of the members to find food and shelter and other necessities.

Certainly, all parties concerned, Mormon and non-Mormon alike, expected that the Saints would not become permanent residents. It seems reasonable that Clay County's residents, no matter how they personally felt or believed about the reports flowing over the border from Jackson County, wanted the Mormons to move on in the interests of peace, and certainly the decision about where the Mormons should go was their own business. Nor did the Saints see themselves as more than temporary refugees. They anticipated a quick return to Jackson County and their lands there through legal means. After all, the instructions from Joseph Smith had been to refuse to sell their Jackson County property. But both groups were wrong. The Mormons did not return to Jackson County and consequently, for the two years, they hovered uneasily in Clay County, not rejected by their reluctant hosts but not welcomed either.

In the meantime, the urgent demand for food, shelter, and clothing had to be met without delay, which meant planting spring crops that would provide food for both humans and animals. This problem dominated the second concern, which rested most heavily on the leaders—not only how to regain the Saints' Jackson County lands but providing organization and leadership for the members who were, in search of cropland, scattering throughout southern and eastern Missouri. Alex Baugh, present-day Mormon historian, states that immediately following the arrival of the Church members in Clay County, "efforts were made, particularly through letters and petitions, to make state officials aware of the troubles experienced by the Mormons in Jackson, and requested assistance." The state's attorney general, R.W. Wells, was the first to reply and implied that the Mormons should be allowed to return to their property in Jackson County and to organize themselves into a militia, and also be "supplied with a limited quantity of public arms."[20] Based on this information, on December 6 a petition referencing Wells's reply and signed by W. W. Phelps, John Whitmer, John Corrill, Isaac Morley, Edward Partridge, and A.S. Gilbert, was directed to Governor Daniel Dunklin directly asking that "we may be restored to our lands, houses, and property, and protected in them by the militia of the state, if legal, or by a detachment of the United States Rangers . . .[and] we ask that our men may be organized into companies of Jackson Guards, and be furnished with arms by the state, to assist in maintaining their rights." A further request was made that a "court of inquiry [be] instituted, to investigate the whole matter of the mob against the 'Mormons.'"[21]

While awaiting a reply from the Governor, "the brethren were perplexed most of all as to what course to pursue. . . . They knew not whether it would be best to lease or buy lands in Clay County, whether to prepare for permanent or only temporary residence in that land."[22] At a conference held on January 1, 1834, it was decided that two elders should travel to Kirtland to counsel with Joseph Smith before a final decision was made. Despite the primitive living condition of their families, Lyman Wight and Parley P. Pratt volunteered for this assignment. They started on February 1 and arrived in Kirtland sometime prior to February 24.[23] Meanwhile, correspondence continued between the Missouri Church leaders and Missouri state officials, but it became more and more apparent that, even if the Saints could return to Jackson County, the courts and state would not provide militia or adequate protection against the same kind of vigilante action that had driven them out. Furthermore, the weapons that the Saints had surrendered in Independence were not returned and, in fact, had ended up in the hands of the Jackson vigilantes.[24] Undoubtedly, at least one of these lost weapons was King's.

Within that first year, the Saints in Clay County were joined by other members from Jackson County who had originally scattered to other counties, and who were subsequently forced to leave.[25] Also, there was a "later Mormon push from the East prompted by a vigorous Church policy of gathering to Clay County. This third gathering, authorized by Joseph Smith at Kirtland, Ohio, was intended to collect sufficient numbers in Clay County to mobilize an organized return to Jackson County."[26] All of these members settled in a number of communities throughout southern and eastern Clay County, usually in small groups of a few families. Following their custom in Jackson County, they referred to these little communities by the name of a leading resident. Mormon settlements south and west of Liberty included the Colesville, Hulet, Wight, Phelps, Partridge, Lowrey, Abbott, and Holbrook Settlements. Upper Shoal Creek was unusual in being named for a geographical feature. Mormon settlements east of Liberty were the Gilbert, Turner, Chase, Morley, and Allred Settlements. East Branch Settlement was named for a tributary of the Fishing River.[27] For natural reasons, members tended to cluster with former neighbors they had known in Jackson County, the Kirtland area, or New York, their shared history intensifying the bonds formed by a shared religion.

The Folletts located in the Hulet Settlement.[28] According to Mormon historian A. J. Simmonds, the core of this settlement was "Charles and Sylvester Hulet, Rhoda Hulet Mills and Nathan Ayers and Mary Hulet West" along with "a few other Prairie Branch refugees."[29] These members had been together in the area of the Whitmer Settlement in Jackson County. Church records also identify the Whitmer family as members of the Hulet Settlement. David Whitmer, who had been the Follett family's ecclesiastical leader in Jackson County continued that role in Clay County. This little settlement was the most westerly of the organized LDS communities, lying about ten miles directly southwest of Liberty and about ten miles due north of the Whitmer Settlement in Jackson County about at the intersection of Oak Street Trafficway and I-29, east of U.S. 169.[30]

Distances between these new Mormon settlements were not far even by 1830s standards. Some were near Clay County residents to whom the members could turn for help and from whom they could purchase

Present site of Hulet Branch settlement, ca. 1833–36, Clay County, Missouri, now at the intersection of Oak Street Trafficway and I-29, east of U.S. 169. Photo by Irval L Mortensen, 2006.

or trade for food and shelter. Others had moved to unsettled areas that offered vacant land suitable for farming with a nearby creek, spring, or river. A handful of Latter-day Saints lived in Liberty itself.

Communication within Clay County was largely word of mouth. Undoubtedly there was considerable trading among the separate Mormon communities, combined with visiting and attendance at weekly worship services. As the county seat, Liberty would have drawn the Mormons to do needed shopping and to attend numerous public meetings including the quarterly court proceedings. Modern-day Mormon historian Leland Homer Gentry, states: "Although scattered in various places in western Missouri, they managed to secure a measure of unity by means of postal communication. Moreover, close contact was maintained with the church in Ohio through volunteers who journeyed back and forth between the two states."[31] Another modern-day LDS historian, William G. Hartley, further explains: "Most letters exchanged in the 1831–33 period did so through the U.S. Postal Service which, relying primarily on stage coaches, was agonizingly slow between distant points.

Some decisions had to be made based on inadequate information. As the 1833 crisis in Zion shows, the exchange of letters generated as much or even more frustration than the solutions."[32] He estimated that between Missouri and Ohio "answers [to postal inquiries] took three weeks or more each way."[33]

Though members of a new religion, the Mormons early in Church history established patterns of church attendance that resembled the meeting structure of their former churches. In Ohio and in Jackson County, the Follett family would have usually attended a Sunday morning service followed by a second meeting in the afternoon or evening, part of which was singing hymns, praying, blessing and partaking of the sacrament, and listening to a doctrinal discourse by one of the men. A frequent mid-week meeting was an evening prayer meeting. Characterized by hymns, prayers, and more spontaneous expressions of testimonies, these meetings allowed the participation of women.[34] In addition to these regular church meetings, an important activity whenever missionaries were present was preaching services, well-attended by local members, but also advertised for nonmembers, who were particularly encouraged to attend. However, in Clay County, both because of the disruption and because of the alarm with which Missouri residents regarded Mormon gatherings, "missionaries were told not to preach, and church members were instructed to administer the sacrament only when convenient opportunities arose."[35]

The presence of the Saints just across the county line, accompanied by their pressure for legal redress, caused rumors to grow that the Mormons were arming themselves and preparing to counter-attack in Jackson County. While this may not have been entirely accurate, modern-day historian Richard L. Bushman confirmed that: "From 1834 onwards, Mormons uneasily experimented with various forms of self-protection. Most Mormons were pacific by nature, but a fierce minority longed for battle."[36] The Jackson County citizens, determined to keep the Mormons out, burned approximately 150 of their former homes."[37] David Pettegrew observed that "the old feelings and excitement of Jackson County now began to show itself in Clay. . . . We were now forced to take up arms in self defense."[38] Though he gives no specific date, the chronology of this statement among others in his history would place it during the summer or early fall of 1834.

The steps that Church leaders in Missouri had taken to this point and continued to pursue resulted from Joseph Smith's revelation in December 1833, which instructed:

> Let them [the Saints] importune at the feet of the judge;
> And if he heed them not, let them importune at the feet of the governor;
> And if the governor heed them not, let them importune at the feet of the president. (D&C 101:86–88)

Since efforts with the "judge" and the "governor" had not been successful, the Saints turned to President Andrew Jackson. On April 10, 1834, A. S. Gilbert, Edward Partridge, and W. W. Phelps signed a letter with an enclosed petition for redress, which had an "accompanying handbill, dated December 12, 1833, with assurances that the said handbill exhibits but a faint sketch of the sufferings of your petitioners and their brethren up to the period of its publication." The petition also contained the actual signatures of another 114 Mormons who had suffered persecution at the hands of the Missourians, and were identified at that time as being residents of Clay County. King Follett and Nathan West's signatures appear among them. The petition stated emphatically that Missourians had launched these illegal attacks because of the "beliefs of the Mormons" and emphasized: "We know that such illegal violence has not been inflicted upon any sect or community of people by the citizens of the United States since the Declaration of Independence.... [T]his is a religious persecution."[39] The Saints petitioned for federal troops to ensure their safe return to Jackson County to repossess their property.

However, at least two factors ensured that President Jackson would not take action. One was the "Jacksonian proclivity to see certain types of minority groups as a subversive threat to the existing Jacksonian social structure."[40] The second was the general political philosophy in the United States that saw states' rights as considerably stronger than at present. Because Jackson (or his advisors) could not identify a federal law that had been broken, the government could not send troops into a state unless the governor requested it. For both political and personal reasons, Missouri's Governor Daniel Dunklin, while expressing some sympathy for the Saints' plight and acknowledging "the right of the Mormons to their lands and their constitutional right to arm themselves in self-defense," was unwilling or unable to provide a sufficient number of state troops to offer the support the Saints wanted and needed. He advised them to take "'the eccentricity of the[ir] religious opinions'" elsewhere.[41]

After Parley P. Pratt and Lyman Wight reached Kirtland with a report of the events in Jackson and Clay County, the Prophet Joseph received a revelation on February 24, 1834, assuring the Saints in Missouri, who had previously been told not to give up title or sell the Jackson County lands, that "this is the blessing which I have promised after your tribulations, and the tribulations of your brethren—your redemption, and the redemption of your brethren, even their restoration to the land of Zion, [and] the redemption of Zion must needs come by power" (D&C 103:13, 15). The revelation continued by ordering that Joseph should lead five hundred men, but if that number was not possible "ye shall not go up unto the land of Zion until you have obtained a hundred of the strength of my house, to go up with you unto the land of Zion"(D&C 103:34). This group organized in Ohio to support fellow Church members in Missouri became known as Zion's Camp.

According to Max Parkin's history of events in Clay County, this thousand-mile journey from Ohio to Missouri had three objects: (1) to bring "humanitarian supplies" to the members; (2) "to assist the state in escorting the Saints back to their homes in Jackson County" and (3) "to remain in Jackson County to protect its people after the state troops withdrew."[42] The Prophet's personal leadership emphasized the importance of meeting these objectives and to assure the establishment of Zion in Jackson County.

Recruiting an adequate number of members went slowly; and it was not until almost three months later on May 8 that the Prophet officially organized the camp and the initial group of "about a hundred men, the number eventually doubling as other parties of Mormons trickled in from midwest branches."[43] The final total of 205 reached Clay County on June 18, where they camped on the banks of the Fishing River. By this time, the Missourians had been warned of this Mormon army's approach and were waiting, armed, on the other side of the river. It is likely that at least some members of the Church in Clay County were also armed.

A week after the camp's arrival on June 27, a non-Mormon, John Chauncey of Liberty, wrote to Francis J. Dallam, City Collector of Baltimore, who was considering moving west. After providing a brief and fairly accurate history of the founding of the church, Chauncey made the following general observations: "We are in the midst of war and rumors of war.... The citizens of the county have taken upon themselves to establish a government of their own.... Sometime last fall the sovereign people of Jackson took it upon themselves, for reasons best known to themselves, to drive them from their lands and homes.... They sought refuge in this county, where they have been kindly treated, to the number of 1000."⁴⁴ And specifically regarding Zion's Camp, he wrote:

> Their profet ... put forth a revelation stating that God would restore them again on the land of Zion, and forthwith set about gethering the young men of his church, to the number of 500, all well armed with guns, swords, pistols & knives, and took up his march for this country.... He arrived here a few days since, and is incamp't within a mile of this place with his army. The citizens of Jackson hearing of his movement imbodied themselves for the conflict. Some of the neighboring counties became excited in behalf of Jackson and most of their citizens rushed to the tented field to take part in the conflict.... Negotiations are still going on. How it will terminate time will develop.... My impressions are we shall have more smoke than fire.⁴⁵

Fortunately, tensions did not break into a pitched battle. While the members of Zion's Camp were traveling from Ohio to Clay County, Governor Dunklin "urged the Jackson County leaders to buy out Mormon property" in order to "effect a compromise between the warring parties." Following negotiations between a Jackson County committee and Sidney Gilbert and the church's attorneys, the Jackson County committee "finally proposed to purchase all Mormon lands at double the market value with payment due in thirty days. As an alternative, the Saints could buy all Jackson County lands on the same terms: double the fair price." A few days later the Church made a counter proposal "to buy out the Jackson County citizens at full value—not double value—within a year and not to return until full payment was made. The cost of damages to Mormon property would be deducted from the price."⁴⁶ Neither of these proposals was ever formalized. Church members would have had to go back alone, presumably well-armed, but without support from law officers or the state militia and against what seems to have been a group of very determined Jackson County residents that the Mormons could not again live in the county.

The headnote to Doctrine and Covenants 105, written and/or edited in 1981, describes the situation from the modern Church's perspective: "Mob violence against the saints in Missouri had increased, and organized bodies from several counties had declared their intent to destroy the people." Undoubtedly in response to the Prophet's prayer, he received that revelation (now D&C 105, also called the Fishing River revelation) on June 22. In it, the Lord severely chastised the Saints: "Were it not for the transgressions of my people . . . they might have been redeemed even now" (105:2). Even though that verse said the rebuke applied to "the church and not individuals," the revelation continued with what certainly sounded like individual failures: They were not "obedient to the things which I required at their hands, but are full of all manner of evil" and were not generous "to the poor and afflicted among them" (v. 3) Furthermore, they were "not united according to the union required by the law of the celestial kingdom," which was the only principle upon which Zion could "be built up" (vv. 4–5). The revelation specifically exempted "the first elders of my church" (v. 7) but included LDS branches "abroad" who were withholding financial support because they did not see the Lord delivering his people (v. 8).

The revelation continued by warning that "my people must needs be chastened until they learn obedience" and that "the redemption of Zion" (the return to Jackson County) would have to wait until the people were "prepared, and . . . taught more perfectly . . . concerning their duty" (vv. 9–10). Apparently, in addition to a lack of care for the poor, the Saints had also offended God by not obeying the commandment for "my young men, and middle-aged, to gather together for the redemption of my people, and throw down the towers of mine enemies, and scatter their watchmen" (D&C 105:16).

Unquestionably, this chastisement was difficult for the members of Zions' Camp—and indeed, the entire membership—to fully understand and accept. To make matters worse, two days later, sometime during the late night of June 24 or early morning hours of June 25,[47] an epidemic of cholera broke out among the camp members who had moved from Fishing River to the home of George Burkett located about 2.5 miles from Liberty.[48] Some viewed this catastrophic illness, which did not spare even Joseph and Hyrum Smith, as the Lord's punishment for the disobedience mentioned in the revelation. According to the *History of the Church*, sixty-eight of the camp members contracted the disease; fourteen of them died, including one woman, Betsy Parrish, while Amasa M. Lyman, who had come from Ohio with Zion's camp, recorded a death count of eighteen.⁴⁹ Lyman did not fall ill himself but also obtained shelter overnight at Brother Burkett's home. Here he found that

> some half dozen of the brethren [were] stricken down and all lying on the floor in a small apartment. This was a scene that can be more easily imagined than described, to see men stricken down in a moment, and in a short hour the ruddy glow of health displaced by the palor of death . . . for they are no strangers that are writhing at our feet. . . . I passed the night with the sufferers. . . . Ere I left, I gave a parting look, breathed a hasty prayer, and tore myself away from the scene of death. From this place I went to the residence of Br. King Follett. From this until the organization of the high council, I passed my time with the brethren who had been expelled from Jackson County, by whom I was kindly entertained.⁵⁰

The cholera epidemic site would have been four or five miles directly northeast from King's home in the Hulet Settlement. King therefore was probably among those Clay County Church members who were possibly armed and waiting to assist as needed at the arrival of the rescue group from Kirtland. He and his family also obviously provided aid to at least one member of Zion's Camp—Amasa Lyman—and perhaps to others.

Significantly, the Follett family would certainly have been influenced by the Fishing River revelation's instructions to "carefully gather together" in Clay County, purchase "all the lands in Jackson county that can be purchased, and in the adjoining counties round about," and "find favor in the eyes of the people until the army of Israel becomes very great" (D&C 105:24, 26). The Lord promised to "soften the hearts of the people" so that they would support the Saints' legal claim to their property (v. 27). At that point, this army would then be "guiltless in taking possession of their own lands, which they have previously purchased" (v. 30).

Once Joseph had recovered from his bout of cholera, he visited local members, including "my old Jackson county friends, in the western part of Clay County."⁵¹ He also spent time at the David Whitmer home in the Hulet Settlement.⁵² Surely the Follett family would have eagerly gone to the Whitmer home to visit the Prophet. Also, before his departure, Joseph formally disbanded Zion's Camp and on July 3 organized the second stake (the first was in Kirtland), with David Whitmer, the Follett family's neighbor, as president. This new stake was named the Clay County Stake.⁵³ The Prophet also "spent a week giving instructions."⁵⁴ Obedience to priesthood leaders was constantly an issue during the early days of the Church. Because the Prophet was continually receiving additional doctrine about the Church's organization and doctrine and because means of communication were often erratic and always slow, members often questioned decisions and did not fully understand doctrinal explanations, a problem even with those called to leadership positions as well as missionaries.

Although the Saints' main wish of being restored to Jackson County had not yet been realized, the disbanding of Zion's Camp had diffused the immediate threat of armed conflict, and the Saints knew that they were acting properly in building homes and working industriously to provide for their needs. The Prophet's visit and the organization of the Clay County Stake provided order and structure. The newly appointed stake president along with his "assistants" William W. Phelps and John Whitmer[55] energetically undertook its duties, among them determining the location and condition of the Saints scattered throughout Clay County. The newly formed high council on July 12, 1834, appointed a four-man committee consisting of Edward Partridge, Orson Pratt, Isaac Morley, and Zebedee Coltrin to "set the churches in order" and enumerate the Saints living in Clay County. The specific direction given to these four men was to "visit the scattered brethren and teach them in the ways of truth and holiness, &c."[56] During the rest of July this committee, met with members in eight different parts of the county "privately so as not to arouse suspicion or raise concern."[57] In August "Parley and Orson Pratt, Simeon Carter, and John Corrill were sent to hold public meetings with the Saints 'at twelve different places, to the joy of the scattered brethren.'"[58] It must have been a comfort to the Folletts to feel that the Church was functioning in an organized way, to attend at least one of these meetings, and to listen to the messages brought by these leaders.

One of the few records that provides a direct glimpse of King's activities during this time is Levi Jackman's account book. The two were once again neighbors, as the account book reflects transactions between the two of them in 1834–35. Jackman provided King "horsehide for 2 pair of shoes" (no value assigned) in July 1834, hired out to King in 1835 for "hauling hay [day?]" valued at 50 cents, and sold him "one bushel of corn" for $1.25 in April 1835. King in turn provided "harvesting and planting for Wm 6 days" in July of 1835, for $2.25. This last transaction apparently squared their accounts with each other.[59]

Precisely where the Folletts lived cannot be documented by civil and land records. Land transactions are recorded for other members in and near the Hulet Settlement, but King is not listed among them. Therefore, he did not purchase land, suggesting the family's poverty at this time.

The collection of Hulet siblings and in-laws had joined the Church in Massachusetts, then moved to Nelson Township, near the Folletts in Shalersville, Ohio. The Nelson Branch membership numbered at least sixty members of the Hulet family, and the branch "presented problems as well as strengths, for it seemed to be marked by a strong charismatic trend."[60] The members were "from churches accustomed to revivals" and "the dynamic new religion of Mormonism ... gave them the vision and the courage to act upon that vision ... [and] it changed ... the Hulets from small time provincial farmers into seers in touch with the divine."[61] Both in Ohio and in the Prairie Branch in Jackson County, the Hulet family had been involved with charismatic worship and had apparently accepted that authority to preach the gospel, rather than being derived from ordination, could be bestowed through such spiritual gifts as prophecy and healing. They had claimed direct revelation from God while in Jackson County.[62] Now the Hulets and their extended families and King and his family, who had been neighbors both in Ohio and Jackson County, were members of the same branch settlement in Clay County.

By July of 1834 problems involving doctrine and procedure in the Hulet Branch were brought to the attention of the newly formed high council of the Clay County Stake. Members of that first high council in Clay County were: Simeon Carter, Parley P. Pratt, Wm. E. Mc'Lellin, Calvin Beebe, Levi Jackman, Solomon Hancock, Christian Whitmer, Newell Knight, Orson Pratt, Lyman Wight, Thomas B. Marsh, and John Murdock.[63] King Follett and Nathan West both appear prominently in the only record of these events—the minutes of high council meetings beginning on July 31 and continuing on August 1 and 6. On July 31, the first charge made by Nathan West [was] read by John Whitmer:

> Know ye that, where as, Br. [Samuel] Brown[64] an high priest of this Church of Christ did on the last week come into this Branch [the Colesville Branch] and taught certain of the brethren & sisters things much the reverse of what we had by encouraging them in practising gifts.
>
> And where as said Brown did in an underhanded, (and as we conceive) clandestine manner ordain Sylvester Hulett to the office of high priest; insisting that he had obtained a witness from the Lord for the same, which

witness he said was the promise of performing the ordination on receiving the gift of tongues; which gift he said he had never received before but afterwards said he had been in possession of the same gift for the space of a year.

And whereas, said Brown seemed to undervalue the authority or at least the righteousness of the high Council by charging me not to say any thing that would tend to prejudice their minds that they might not judge righteously.

I therefore, as an Elder of the Church of Christ do earnestly solicit the attention of the council in considering the same.[65]

Testimony was given on July 31 and on August 1 by Leonard Rich, Charles Rich, Br. Brace, Edward Partridge, Hiram Page, Roxa Slade, and Caleb Baldwin. Each testified that they had either had conversation with Brown about the events outlined in the charges or had overheard others speak about them, and that Brown had asked them not to say anything about it.[66] Sylvester Hulet confirmed that the ordination had taken place, although he had told Brown that he [Hulet] "had made application to the Council for an ordination some time since and was rejected." Hulet further testified that Brown "seemed to talk to me in such a manner that understood him to sensure the heads of this Church in some things."[67]

The "charges were sustained by the testimony" and President David Whitmer announced the decision and told Brown "therefore, if you confess all the charges which have been alleged against you to be just, and in a spirit that we can receive it, then you can stand as a private member in this Church, otherwise we have no fellowship for you; and also, that the ordination of Sylvester Hulet, by Samuel Brown, is illegal and not acknowledged by us to be of God, and therefore it is void."[68] Based on the decision "Brother Brown confessed the charges, and gave up his license, but retained his membership."[69] Though King is not mentioned as being present at these proceedings, it is logical he might have been (if the high council meeting was open to anyone other than those who testified) because of his involvement in the continuing issue of the Hulet Settlement regarding the practicing of gifts, a charge that was considered at the next meeting of the high council.

On August 6, the council met again and Nathan West brought another charge, this time against the entire Hulet Branch, (of which he was a member) stating that branch members had "imbibed certain principles concerning the gifts that are thought not to be correct by the greater part of the rest of the Church, which principles seem to have a tendency to cause a split and disunion in the church."⁷⁰ This was technically a charge against his in-laws, the Folletts, as they were members of that branch. Charles English⁷¹ gave testimony and explained that branch members would not "proceed to their temporal business without receiving the word of the Lord" and that "they would not receive the teachings of ordained members even br. Joseph Smith jr. unless it agreed with their gifts." Typically, this "word" came through the gift of tongues with Sylvester Hulet speaking and Sally Crandall (also spelled Crandle) interpreting. English stated that the branch members believed that they "had come up to their privileges more than the rest of the Church. They thought they were right but if they could be convinced that they were wrong, they would retract."⁷² Sally Crandall was the wife of Daniel Crandall. The family had moved to Jackson County in 1832 and resided in the Prairie Branch near the Hulets. Daniel's wife, Sarah (Sally), was thought by some to be "a visionary woman."⁷³

As one example, Sally Crandall claimed that she could "know and see men's hearts." According to Philo Dibble, a member of Hulet Branch, she had seen "the heart of King Follet that it was not right" while Nathan West contributed the mystifying statement that "Sally Crandle saw his heart and that it was full of eyes, also saw eyes in others hearts some had few and some many."⁷⁴ After further discussion and testimony, David Whitmer ruled that "as for the Hulet branch the devil decieved them and that they obtained not the word of the Lord as they supposed they did, but were deceived; and as for the gift of seeing as held by the Hulet branch, it is of the devil saith the Lord God."⁷⁵ The high council endorsed this decision and assigned Amasa Lyman and Simeon Carter to "go and labor with Brother Hulet and Sister Crandall, and others of like faith, and set the truth in order before them."⁷⁶ Although such a situation could lead to disaffection, the majority of those involved apparently accepted this decision and adjusted their behavior. Significantly, despite Sally Crandall's accusation, there is no evidence but that King and Louisa continued a harmonious relationship with branch members, including the Hulet family. Louisa speaks of Sylvester Hulet as being a traveling companion on her trip after King's death and of visiting him while she was in New York.

For the next year, "the Saints, both in Missouri and Ohio, began to enjoy a little peace. The elders began to go forth, two and two, preach-

King's license reads: "To Whom These Presence [sic] May Come: This certifies that King Folliott has ben received into this church of Latterday saints organized on the 6 of April 1830 and has ben ordained an Elder according to the Rules and Regulations of said church and is Duly authorized to Preach the Gospel and act in all the ordainances of the house of the Lord aggreeable to the authority of that office. Given by the Directions of a Conference of Elders held in ["@" or possibly "c"] Monroe County Missouri September 12 – 1835 Jesse Hitchcook Ellis Eames (Clerk)." Location of holograph unknown.

ing the word to all that would hear, and many were added to the Church daily."[77] The burgeoning growth required new procedures for documenting membership and recording ordination and appointment of missionaries. "At each conference of the Church, a clerk was appointed to record certificates and to issue licenses. Consequently, as an elder moved from branch to branch he could be properly identified, and his license enabled non-Mormons to determine the validity of his calling." Men were given a "license" upon ordination to priesthood office and one was given to all missionaries. As these licenses were obviously priesthood based, at that time there was no reference to any type of membership record being given to women. These licenses gave the holder authority to conduct Church business and "enabled the early Church to regulate its internal affairs and control its proselyting system."[78] Doubtless, many men would have agreed with Joseph Smith's younger brother, William, who recalled that receiving his license "made me feel more and more the importance of my mission."[79]

King Follett received his license on September 12, 1835, signed by Jesse Hitchcock and Ellis Eames (Clerk).[80] Although certificates and licenses were usually separate, the wording of King's seems to have covered three purposes: certifying his membership, documenting his ordination as an elder, and licensing him as a missionary.

Monroe County, Missouri, was located in the northeastern part of Missouri, about 170 miles east from King's home in Clay County. It was here near Paris, the county seat, where members of both Zion's Camp and later Kirtland Camp (1838) spent time on their journey between Ohio and Missouri.[81] Also located in Monroe County about fifteen miles from Paris, was the Salt Creek Branch of the Allred Settlement. Parley P. Pratt had served there as an early missionary and at the time of Zion's Camp described the area as "a large branch of the Church."[82] According to King's certificate, an elders' conference (probably missionaries) was held there on September 12 when the clerk issued this license. I know of no reason why King would be in Monroe County, unless he was going to Kirtland, preaching en route, as was customary. He reached Kirtland almost two months later. Levi Jackman recorded: "A Temple was now being built in Kirtland Ohio and many of the first Elders were instructed to go to that place to help on with the work and to preach by the way and I was one of the number. I made my arrangements for going and on the fourth day of May 1835 I took my affectionate farewell of my family."[83] It seems logical that King was one of these elders.

It can be documented that, some time during the fall of 1835, King left his family in Missouri, now consisting of Adeline, age nineteen, John, age sixteen, Nancy, age twelve, ten-year-old William Alexander, and two-year-old Edward. He traveled to Kirtland where he spent seven months during the winter of 1835–36.[84] (See Chapter 9.) An exciting epoch in the growing religion was underway: the House of the Lord was in the final stages of construction in Kirtland and King would participate in its dedication, scheduled for the spring of 1836.

Notes

1. *Upper Missouri Enquirer* (Liberty, Missouri), 1834, quoted in Max H Parkin, "A History of the Latter-day Saints in Clay County, Missouri, from 1833 to 1837," 60.

2. *Upper Missouri Enquirer*, 1834, quoted in *Liberty [Missouri] Tribune*, August 6, 1972, quoted in Max H Parkin, *Missouri*, 213.

3. Daniel Berry Rawson, "A History of Daniel Rawson," 2.

4. Levi Jackman, "A Short Sketch of the Life of Levi Jackman," in "Reminiscences and Journal 1851–1867," 10.

5. John Somers Higbee, "Reminiscences and Diaries, 1845–1866," 2.

6. Emily M. Austin, *Mormonism: Or, Life among the Mormons*, 72–74. Emily refers to her first marriage but does not give the name of that husband.

7. David Pettegrew, "Statements," August 1862, 4.

8. Vera Haworth Eldridge, "Mormons in Clay County," *Discover North*, 4–5.

9. W. H. Woodson, *History of Clay County Missouri*, 245.

10. Brigham H. Roberts, *The Missouri Persecutions*, 92.

11. Church Education System, *Church History in the Fulness of Times*, 137.

12. Emily Dow Partridge Young, "What I Remember, 1884," 18. This specific page is dated November 1834.

13. David Pettegrew, "A History of David Pettegrew," 5.

14. Ira Jones Willes (also spelled Willis in some records) was one of a group of men who left California in July of 1848 after being honorably discharged from the Mormon Battalion. They collected information and made notes about the trail they took from California to Utah. Willes assembled this information in the form of a two-page hand-written document which became a crude self-produced travel guide entitled "Best Guide to the Gold Mines, 816 Miles by Trail." It provided distances and the locations of camping places, hot springs, and rivers. It also contained some information on the goldfields. It was sold to California-bound travelers passing through Salt Lake City, beginning in 1849. A typed reproduction of the guide and an analysis of its historical importance is Irene Dakin Paden, "The Ira J. Willis Guide to the Gold Mines."

15. *History of the Church*, 2:46. Undoubtedly this is the same Moses Wilson who was a leader of the anti-Mormon group during the recent activities in Jackson County.

16. Ira Jones Willes, Diary, March 31, 1834.

17. *History of the Church*, 2:46.

18. Father Roux, Letter written from "the Mouth of the River of Kansas," June 17, 1834, to Bishop Rosati, St. Louis County, Missouri, quoted in Stanley B. Kimball, "Missouri Mormon Manuscripts: Sources in Selected Societies,"

486–87. The original letter is in the St. Mary Pioneer Historical Society of Independence, Missouri.

19. "Life and Journal of Eliza Marie Partridge (Smith) Lyman," 2.

20. Alexander L. Baugh, *A Call to Arms: The 1838 Mormon Defense of Northern Missouri*, 9.

21. *History of the Church*, 1:451–52.

22. Roberts, *The Missouri Persecutions*, 92–93.

23. Scott Facer Proctor and Maurine Jensen Proctor, eds., *Autobiography of Parley P. Pratt: Revised and Enhanced Edition*, 133.

24. *History of the Church*, 1:473–93, quotes the letters.

25. Proctor and Proctor, *Autobiography of Parley P. Pratt*, 122–24.

26. Max H Parkin, *Missouri*, 165.

27. Ibid., 165–212.

28. "Early Branches 1830–1850," *The Nauvoo Journal*, 3, no. 1 (January 1991):15.

29. A. J. Simmonds, "John Noah and the Hulets: A Study in Charisma in the Early Church," 12. Following the death of his first wife, Mary Hulet West, Nathan West married Adeline Follett two years later. "Prairie Branch" is one of the LDS settlements in Jackson County near the Whitmer Settlement where the Folletts had lived. For more information on the Hulet Branch, see A. J. Simmonds, "'Thou and All Thy House': Three Case Studies of Clan and Charisma in the Early Church," 48–50. Sylvester Hulet was born about 1800 in Massachusetts, joined the Church in 1831, moved to Jackson County, and came to the Salt Lake Valley in 1847. Donald Q. Cannon and Lyndon W. Cook, *Far West Record: Minutes of the Church of Jesus Christ of Latter-day Saints, 1830–1844*, 269. Louisa Follett's brief diary, kept while traveling between New York and Nauvoo during 1844–45, mentions traveling part way with Sylvester Hulet; he visited her while she was staying in Parma, Ohio.

30. Parkin, *Missouri*, 169.

31. Leland Homer Gentry, *A History of the Latter-day Saints in Northern Missouri from 1836 to 1839*, 17.

32. William G. Hartley, "Letters and Mail between Kirtland and Independence: A Mormon Postal History 1831–33," 189.

33. Ibid., 164.

34. William G. Hartley, "The McLellin Journals and Early Mormon History," 277–78.

35. Ibid., 162 note 56.

36. Richard L. Bushman, *Joseph Smith: Rough Stone Rolling*, 130.

37. A. S. Gilbert, and W. W. Phelps, Liberty, Clay County, Letter to Governor Daniel Dunklin, May 7, 1834, *Times and Seasons* 6, 20 (January 1846), 1075.

38. Pettegrew, "History of David Pettegrew," 12.

39. "Petition to the President, 10 April 1834, Liberty, Clay County, Missouri," www.farwesthistory.com/petition.asp (accessed June 8, 2005), based on *Times and Seasons* 6 (December 1, 1845): 1041–42 and 6 (December 15, 1845): 1057. The internet site lists the petition's signers. The *Times and Seasons* source does not.

40. R. J. Robertson Jr., "The Mormon Experience in Missouri, 1830–1839, Part 1," 281.

41. Bushman, *Joseph Smith: Rough Stone Rolling*, 242.

42. Max H Parkin, "Latter-day Saint Conflict in Clay County," 250.

43. Bushman, *Joseph Smith:Rough Stone Rolling*, 237.

44. W. D. Hoyt, Jr., "A Clay Countian's Letters of 1834: From John Chauncey of Liberty, Clay County, to Francis J. Dallam, City Collector of Baltimore, Maryland," 352.

45. Ibid., 352–53.

46. Bushman, *Joseph Smith: Rough Stone Rolling*, 242–43.

47. *History of the Church* 2:114, states: "This night [June 24] the cholera broke forth." Amasa Mason Lyman, a member of Zion's Camp wrote: "On the morning of June twenty-fifth the colera suddenly broke out in Zion's Camp." Quoted in Albert R. Lyman, *Amasa Mason Lyman: Trailblazer and Pioneer from the Atlantic to the Pacific*, 49.

48. George Burkett Jr. was born in 1788 in Pennsylvania, joined the Church in Indiana in 1831, fled from Jackson County in November 1833, and settled in Clay County. He is the third great-grandfather of my husband, Irval L. Mortensen. Burkett's short unpublished autobiography in our possession states that the night the camp arrived seventeen people were afflicted. Five died "and the next morning, were buried in an adjoining field." Burkett, Autobiography, 1.

49. *History of the Church*, 2:120. See Albert R. Lyman, *Amasa Mason Lyman*, 51.

50. Amasa M. Lyman, Journal History, June 25, 1834, 1–2; see also Amasa Mason Lyman, "Amasa Lyman's History," *Millennial Star* 27 (12 August 1865): 502–3. Lyman, a diligent missionary, became an apostle and co-founded San Bernardino, California in the early 1850s. He was excommunicated in 1870 for denying that Christ's blood was an essential element of the Atonement. Edward Leo Lyman, *Amasa Mason Lyman, Mormon Apostle and Apostate: A Study in Dedication* (Salt Lake City: University of Utah Press, 2009), chap. 9.

51. *History of the Church*, 2:120.

52. Parkin, *Missouri*, 169–70.

53. Ibid., 177.

54. Bushman, *Joseph Smith: Rough Stone Rolling*, 146.

55. *History of the Church*, 2:124.

56. Cannon and Cook, *Far West Record*, 75.
57. Orson Pratt, quoted in Parkin, *Missouri*, 164.
58. William W. Phelps, quoted in ibid., 164.
59. Levi Jackman, Record Book, ca. 1832–34, 26.
60. Simmonds, "Thou and All Thy House," 49.
61. Simmonds, "John Noah and the Hulets," 6–7.
62. Ibid., 10.

63. *History of the Church*, 2:124. The order of this listing was based on a process whereby lots were cast at the meeting when they were ordained by Joseph Smith "to know who should speak first."

64. Samuel Brown was born in Altstead, New Hampshire, marched in Zion's Camp, served as a doorkeeper in the Kirtland Temple, and later settled in Utah. Cannon and Cook, *Far West Record*, 250.

65. Ibid., 79. Though the charge was read on July 31, the date at the top of the charge is "7th of July, 1834" and the date at the bottom is "July 30, 1834."

66. Cannon and Cook, *Far West Record*, 80–86, quotes the testimony.
67. Ibid., 86.
68. *History of the Church*, 2:137–38.
69. Ibid., 2:138.
70. Cannon and Cook, *Far West Record*, 89.

71. Charles English is not identified in the record, but I believe he may have been related by marriage to Sally Hulet Whiting, an older sister of Sylvester Hulet.

72. Cannon and Cook, *Far West Record*, 89.

73. Larry C. Porter and Ronald E. Romig, "The Prairie Branch, Jackson County, Missouri: Emergence, Flourishing, and Demise, 1831–1834," 18.

74. Cannon and Cook, *Far West Record*, 90. The "heart" filled with "eyes" is unexplained.

75. Ibid., 92.
76. *History of the Church*, 2:141.
77. Ibid., 2:161.
78. Donald Q. Cannon, "Licensing in the Early Church," 105.
79. William Smith, quoted in ibid., 104.

80. A word, possibly "Moderator," is written vertically on the paper, after Hitchcock's name. Jesse Hitchcock was born in 1801 in North Carolina, baptized July 20, 1831, and ordained an elder and high priest. He served on the Clay County High Council, served as Joseph Smith's scribe in 1836, served a mission to Illinois in 1843, and died at Mount Pisgah, Iowa, in 1846. See *Mormon Biographical Registers*, http://byustudies.byu.edu/Indexes/2:38 Ellis Eames (later Ames) was born in 1809 in Geagua County, Ohio, joined the Church there in 1831, served as a president of a conference in Clay County in 1834, and was called on a mission in 1844. A fiddler and a merchant, he moved

to Utah, served as Provo's first mayor, and moved to the Mormon colony of San Bernardino, California, where he died in 1882. www.richardsonfamily.homestead.com/SaraHaskell.html (accessed June 27, 2005).

    81. Parkin, *Missouri*, 539.

    82. Proctor and Proctor, *Autobiography of Parley P. Pratt*, 142.

    83. Jackman, "A Short Sketch of the Life of Levi Jackman," 11.

    84. *History of the Church*, 1:349, 2:301, 2:316, 2:38.

Chapter Nine

A Spiritual Respite: Kirtland 1835–36

In 1835, the population of Kirtland, a small community in northeast Ohio, was growing, and construction was continuing on a stately, white building located in the center of town. Though now referred to as the "Kirtland Temple," King Follett would have heard it described as "the House of the Lord." Mark L. Staker, a modern historian of the Kirtland area, explains: "As soon as the Saints prepared to construct 'a' building, they learned through revelation that it would be 'the' building—a special place where they would be endowed with power. However, the hoped-for-structure in Zion [Jackson County, Missouri] was consistently called 'the temple' while the building in Kirtland was consistently called 'the House of the Lord.'"[1]

Near the end of the year, there were two acknowledged major settlements of early Church converts—Kirtland, Ohio, where the Prophet Joseph continued to reside, and Missouri, primarily Clay County, where the Follett family lived. Congregations and stakes had been established in each place and leadership selected, including stake presidencies and high councils. Adult male members ordained as elders were assigned to serve as missionaries. By this time, the Folletts had been away from the Kirtland area for about three years, and their personal lives and activities in the Church had centered exclusively around events in Missouri. How much contact with members in Ohio they had is not known. How much knowledge they had of specific events there likewise cannot be determined. However, what had happened in Kirtland after the Folletts had moved to Missouri, combined with events of the coming months, would have a great impact on the entire Church membership and on King and his family.

Kirtland was the first gathering place for the Saints. Converts, but also the curious, arrived to investigate further, to settle near other Saints, or to use the town as a stopping-off place to prepare for the journey to Zion in Missouri. When the Folletts left their home in Shalersville in 1832, approximately a hundred Mormons lived in Kirtland. When King returned in 1835, that number had increased to nine hundred with another two hundred living in the surrounding area. The Mormon population continued to grow at a rate of between 200 and 500 annually until 1837, while the non-Mormon population remained relatively stable at between 1,100 and 1,300.[2] Not only do these figures reflect a much larger Mormon population than when King had lived in Shalersville, but the proportion of members to nonmembers had shifted.

Furthermore, King would have noticed a large increase in member-owned businesses. The issues that had plagued and continued to plague Church members in Missouri were also causing conflict in Kirtland. Increased numbers of members meant the potential of greater influence in politics and community affairs. Increased numbers of member-owned businesses also meant less trade with nonmembers and consequently less profit for them. King had been through a similar pattern of events in Missouri and must have felt concerned about the future of Kirtland, especially since issues stemming from the construction and dedication of the temple complicated matters with the community.

The Prophet's arrival in the Kirtland area in February of 1831 had made it the site for an outpouring of revelations—a total of sixty by the end of 1835—and mushrooming organizational issues for the rapidly growing Church. Doctrinal developments spread from this center to other areas where members had gathered or where they were rapidly being baptized. About thirty miles away in Hiram, Ohio, the Prophet and Sidney Rigdon worked on a new "translation" of the Bible. At a Church conference in November 1831, the Prophet was appointed to supervise the first publication of revelations, and he selected sixty-five for inclusion. These were compiled and sent to Missouri to be published as the Book of Commandments. As it was necessary to first establish a Church press, the work was slow, and "the project was still in its initial phase when the Prophet arrived there in April 1832." When violence in Independence in July 1833, interrupted this process, the project shifted back to Kirtland where an expanded edition called the Doctrine and Covenants was published in 1835.[3] The rapid growth in members called for a more formal, expanded structure. Some of those revelations defined the role of the Church president (Joseph Smith), while authority was rapidly bestowed on male members who became counselors, high councilors, and members of priesthood quorums to handle spiritual, judicial, and temporal issues for the members. One of the revelations, received in February 1833 was a law of health, later known as the Word of Wisdom (now D&C 89). Missionaries set out, often on foot, to spread the Restoration message—first to areas where they had family or had previously lived but by 1835 throughout the eastern United States, Canada, and by 1837 to Europe where the British Mission was established.

As the Church in Kirtland grew rapidly, more emphasis was given to the idea of constructing a house of worship to replace the outdoor preaching services or the crowded facilities of a barn, a schoolhouse, or a private home. Such a building, it was envisioned, would contain offices, meeting rooms, and a school. It would indeed be identified as Church headquarters. The Lord had told the Prophet that Ohio was not to be the permanent location of the Church headquarters but that he would "retain a strong hold in the land of Kirtland, for the space of five years" (D&C 64:21). In actuality, the Church was based in Ohio for about seven years, during which time the Prophet continued to receive new understandings about gospel principles and doctrines and during which he trained leaders who could teach the general membership. The very real need to house these functions would produce the first temple built by the new religion.

Obeying the direction of the Lord, Joseph had dedicated a temple site in Jackson County, Missouri, on August 3, 1831, but the Saints had been driven out before construction could begin. As early as December 1832, the first revelation was given to build a "house of God" in Ohio (D&C 88:119). On May 6, 1833, another revelation directed building up the "city of the stake of Zion" in Kirtland. That revelation included details about the building's size and construction. It was to be "a house for the work of the presidency, in obtaining revelations; and for the work of the ministry of the presidency" and "it shall be wholly dedicated unto the Lord for the work of the presidency" (D&C 94:3 & 7). Undoubtedly the members believed they were to construct a meetinghouse like those with which they were familiar from their previous denominations; but the Prophet envisioned a grander building patterned after the biblical temples, one that would not only function as organizational headquarters but also be worthy of heavenly visitors. At this time, Joseph Smith needed further instruction to fully understand the purpose of a temple, but he nevertheless recognized the significance of this building. To erect such a temple was a tremendous task for these Saints, but they faithfully began despite the poverty in which most of them lived.

This project required great sacrifice on the part of members everywhere, all of whom were asked to assist financially no matter where they lived. Though most Mormon men had built or helped build their own homes, very few of them had ever been involved in large public buildings. Benjamin F. Johnson, who labored on the temple, recalled that "there was not a scraper and hardly a plow that could be found among the Saints"[4] in the early stages. Not having detailed architectural plans, the builders relied on information provided to the Prophet and other leaders in a vision.[5] Eliza R. Snow later described how overwhelming the entire project seemed: "At that time . . . the Saints were few in number, and most of them very poor; and, had it not been for the assurance that God had spoken, and had commanded that a house should be built to his name, of which he not only revealed the form, but also designated the dimensions, an attempt towards building that Temple, under the then existing circumstances, would have been, by all concerned, pronounced preposterous."[6]

In spite of these humble circumstances, or perhaps because of them, the Prophet optimistically reported on June 1, 1833: "Great preparations were making to commence a house of the Lord; and notwithstanding the Church was poor, yet our unity, harmony and charity abounded to strengthen us to do the commandments of God."[7] Construction began in May 1833. From then until its dedication almost three years later in March 1836, completing the temple was the primary focus for the members living in Kirtland. Closely related to this project was the intensity with which the Prophet was preparing the members, especially the priesthood leaders, for the spiritual experiences that would surround the dedication and that would occur thereafter in the temple. It was in these circumstances that King Follett made his first documented return to Kirtland after three years' absence.

The *History of the Church* records on Wednesday, November 4, 1835: "King Follet arrived today from Zion."[8] I can only imagine the extent of the sacrifice by Louisa and the children as they stayed in Missouri while he was absent for approximately seven months. Many male members of the Church were often gone for extended periods serving missions and attending to other Church business. Another couple separated during this time were W. W. and Sally Phelps. On November 14, 1835, Phelps, who was in Kirtland, wrote to Sally in Liberty, Missouri: "King Follett arrived from the west since my last letter to you was written. . . . The Elders are coming in every day. . . . The school has commenced."[9] If the Folletts wrote to each other, their letters have not survived; but it may have been from this letter to Sally Phelps that Louisa Follett learned that King had arrived safely.

According to Levi Jackman's diary: "A Temple was now being built in Kirtland Ohio and many of the first Elders were instructed to go to that place to help on with the work and to preach by the way."[10] King was certainly one of the "first Elders." Follett family stories report that King was now a personal friend of the Prophet and may have carried messages back and forth between Missouri and Kirtland over the winter of 1835–36. If so, it may have been a reason for mentioning his arrival in the *History of the Church*; but there is no supporting documentation for this family story. Because he apparently stayed until the temple dedication, it seems more likely that he was drawn to Kirtland because of his obedience to the call for temple labor and the opportunity to participate in the promised temple blessings.

We have no specific information about his activities for his first few weeks in Kirtland. King probably had a difficult time finding a place to stay during these months. Milton Backman's history of Kirtland describes the little town: "Kirtland was crowded. . . . Leaders of the church from Missouri were there, as well as many other members of the priesthood from other parts of the country. The newcomers crowded into the small homes of the Saints, and when the homes and the boarding houses near the temple were filled, the visitors sought accommodations in adjacent communities."[11]

The Newel K. Whitney Store, Kirtland, Ohio, where the School of the Prophets and the School of the Elders were held. Photograph August 7, 1907, George Edward Anderson Collection, LDS Church History Library. Used by permission.

On November 3, the day before King's arrival, the third session of a schooling program for the adult male members, referred to at that time as the "School of the Elders" began, the "school" Phelps referred to in his letter to Sally. Initially a revelation received in December 1832 had instructed the Prophet to establish a "School of the Prophets" (D&C 88:127–41).[12] That school, with fourteen individuals invited to attend,[13] had begun on January 22, 1833, and continued until sometime in April of that year in the apartment where Joseph Smith was living above the Newel K. Whitney store.

The original purpose of the school and its programs of instruction were "doctrine and spiritual instruction," primarily for leaders and future leaders—hence the name: School of the Prophets. Orson Pratt, who was added later, explained that "the men gathered so that they might learn about 'the operations of the Spirit upon the mind of man.'"[14] The school reconvened in November 1834 under the title of "School of the Elders" with an expanded membership, thus preparing them for missions and developing in them a greater understanding of leadership roles. Milton

Backman, Kirtland historian, explained: "Joseph Smith presided over the school and taught various subjects, including theology.... Although the students explored a variety of disciplines, religious topics received the main emphasis."[15] Two sessions of this enlarged group were held, the first beginning in November 1834 and concluding in March 1835, and the second beginning November 3, 1835.[16] Perhaps the school calendar was set to accommodate the need for the men to work in the fields to support their families. When the temple was partially completed, the School of the Elders began meeting there on January 18, 1836.[17] Although no complete list of members has survived for this second session of the School of the Elders, likely it was one reason why King came to Kirtland four months before the temple's dedication.

King may also have worked on the temple. Newel Knight, who had joined the Church in May 1830 in New York, worked on the temple "as my labor was very much needed" and the Prophet told him that "it would be better for me to labor there than to go to school."[18] Perhaps King was able to do both. He probably also visited with friends, participated in social activities, studied, and attended preaching services. W. W. Phelps wrote of the importance of these activities to those who were away from their loved ones: "It is quite natural to see Bishop Partridge, Morley, Carroll, Beebe and many other Zion [illegible] everyday—I sometimes think if it were not for our being together where we can exchange our feelings that time would hang heavy, [illegible] Marsh and I generally see each other every day, and comfort one another by chatting on what is to be!"[19] Perhaps King viewed the Egyptian mummies and rolls of papyrus that the Church had acquired in July 1835 and eagerly awaited Joseph's translation of the papyrus on which, he said, were inscribed writings of Abraham in Egypt (now part of the canonized Pearl of Great Price). According to the *History of the Church*, the mummies were viewed by the Prophet and others at the home of Frederick G. Williams on November 17; on that same day and again on November 23, unnamed individuals visited the Prophet's home to look at the ancient records.[20] Mark Staker adds: "In February of 1836, Joseph Smith also began exhibiting in the building [Johnson Inn] the Egyptian mummies and manuscripts."[21]

King's first documented activity in Kirtland was receiving his patriarchal blessing on December 16 from Joseph Smith Sr., father of the Prophet.[22] His blessing occurred at a "feast for the poor" that was patterned after Jesus's story of a rich man who held a feast for the less fortunate (Luke 14:12–24). Nineteenth-century Protestants also often held such feasts.[23] In February 1835, W. W. Phelps wrote a twelve-verse poem or hymn titled "There's a Feast of Fat Things" (also "The Proclamation") specifically for such feasts that, according to musical historian Michael Hicks, "invited people to the actual feasts in the city and ultimately to the wedding supper of Christ. . . . In the song's twelve verses, Phelps calls on Latter-day Saints to gather everyone into their millennial community."[24] In a "journal" entry, W. W. Phelps described the December 16 feast and names King as one of those who received his blessing:

> I attended a feast at the house of Bro. Zera S. Coles; about sixty guests were present, a number of whom were blessed by Father Joseph Smith, among them being Elijah Fordham, King Follett and Jesse Hitchcock.[25] This was the first and greatest blessing feast I have ever attended. The greatest solemnity and harmony prevailed. The vituals were good and the affair was orderly and enjoyable, though many of those present were young. We sang "There's a feast of fat things," "Adam-Ondi-Ahman," "O Behold the Lord is nigh" etc. The greatest wishes of the guests were that we might soon celebrate a feast in the land of Zion. The weather was very cold.[26]

Mark Staker notes that this type of meeting-feast developed from a revelation given to Bishop Newel K. Whitney in September 1832, which instructed him to "travel round about and among all the churches, searching after the poor to administer to their wants by humbling the rich and the proud (D&C 84:112). Kirtland's growing membership included an influx of poor members who had used all their resources in preaching the gospel and moving their families." Fast meetings were begun where members were asked to "abstain from meals and brought butter, bread, and other food to scheduled meetings." These items were then distributed to the poor. "A pattern developed that combined meetings at which members received patriarchal blessings from Joseph Smith Sr., with a dinner 'for the poor.'"[27] These meetings were held at various homes with other members attending; occasionally the Prophet and his wife, Emma, joined in. The *History of the Church* records that on December 29, 1835, Joseph and Emma attended such a blessing meeting at the home of Oliver Olney where "fifteen persons then received patriarchal blessings under his [Father Smith's] hands. The services were concluded as they commenced. A table was crowned with the bounties of nature; and after invoking the benediction of heaven upon the rich repast, we fared sumptuously; and suffice it to say that we had a glorious meeting throughout, and I was much pleased with the harmony that existed among the brethren and sisters."[28] Ira Ames described a similar meeting held in his home on March 13, 1834: "I received my Patriarchal Blessing under the hands of Joseph Smith Senior at a feast and blessing meeting which I made at my house for the widows and orphans. . . .[I]t was a very pleasant time, a glorious meeting."[29] The pattern for each appeared to be the same: food (apparently both to eat and to contribute to poor Church members), music, blessings by Patriarch Smith, socializing, and most of all being spiritually fed.

No copy of King Follett's blessing has survived within the extended Follett family nor in the collection of patriarchal blessings held by LDS Church History Library. However, H. Michael Marquardt, who transcribed and edited more than 700 blessings bestowed on early Saints by Joseph Jr., Joseph Sr., Hyrum, and William Smith, includes Father Smith's blessing for Jesse Hitchcock on December 16, 1835. Marquardt includes an undated blessing given to Elijah Fordham in a group of blessings which Marquardt states was probably given in 1836.[30] Phelps, who acted as clerk, recorded Hitchcock's blessing given by Joseph Sr. and copied it six days later in Father Smith's Patriarchal Blessing Book. Marquardt describes the usual procedure at that early date: "The persons blessed usually retained the original handwritten blessing. At a subsequent date, they would bring their blessing to a Church recorder to be copied into the official blessing book. That way the blessing would be preserved for future generations. . . . Not all early patriarchal blessings were recorded in Joseph Smith Sr.'s book."[31]

Apparently King's blessing was never officially recorded. Its absence leaves an interesting and perhaps critical piece of his early religious history unrecorded. Lavina Fielding Anderson, a Lucy Mack Smith biographer, explains the importance of these blessings given to members by the Prophet's father:

> In my view, the spiritual hungers of the new members and Joseph Sr.'s personal spirituality intersected in the act of seeking inspiration and articulating blessings, one recipient at a time. I see these blessings as telling new members who they were as Latter-day Saints, what God expected of them, and how He would reward their devotion. These Mormons heard in Father Smith's voice the commendation of God, spelling out the spiritual and heavenly compensation for their earthly sacrifices. I argue that the blessings be-

stowed represent items of greatest desire for the poverty-stricken, socially marginalized, and frequently mocked Mormons and that the blessings articulate compensations—dreams of power, as it were—for perceived lacks. These blessings therefore operate, although inevitably with some slippages, to attach these new Mormons more firmly to the Church.[32]

Phelps's December 18 letter to Sally adds details about living conditions in Kirtland that must have been true for King as well and poignantly expresses what must have been common concerns of the men separated from their families. "My anxiety for your welfare is inexpressible," he wrote, detailing the duties that he knew she was dealing with at home. He encouraged her: "Keep up your faith and pray for the endowment. As soon as that takes place, the Elders will anxiously speed toward their families." Although "health prevails among the brethren generally," the price of food and other supplies was high: "fresh pork, 5-6 cents per lb, and beef from 2 to 2 ½ cents per lb, wheat is $1.12 ½ cents per bushel and rising, corn 75 cents per bushel, cheese 9 cents per lb. by wholesale." Butter was twenty-five cents a pound—so expensive that he had had not had any for weeks. "Without great business or plenty of money a family fares coarse in this part of the country," he summarized, but added more cheerfully, "Work on the Lord's House goes on quite rapidly again."[33]

Recollections of this period indicate that many rich religious experiences accompanied worship in and dedication of the temple during a six-month period beginning in January 1836. Apostle Orson Pratt reminisced about such experiences that occurred during the dedication of the temple: "God was there, his angels were there, the Holy Ghost was in the midst of the people, the visions of the Almighty were opened to the minds of the servants of the living God; the veil was taken from the minds of many; they saw the heavens opened, they beheld the angels of God; they heard the voice of the Lord; and they were filled from the crown of their heads to the soles of their feet with the power and inspiration of the Holy Ghost."[34]

Several members described the dedication-related events as "Pentecostal,"[35] an allusion to a remarkable experience following Jesus's resurrection when the Holy Spirit was poured out on the people, they saw heavenly beings, and spoke in tongues. The Apostle Peter, quoting the Prophet Joel, described such an event:

And it shall come to pass in the last days, saith God, I will pour out of my Spirit upon all flesh; and your sons and your daughters shall prophesy, and your young men shall see visions, and your old men shall dream dreams:

And on my servants and on my handmaidens I will pour out in those days of my Spirit; and they shall prophesy. (Acts 2:17)

Milton Backman summarizes the fifteen-week period between January 21 to May 1, 1836:

> Probably more Latter-day Saints beheld visions and witnessed other unusual spiritual manifestations than during any other era in the history of the Church. There were reports of Saints' beholding heavenly beings at ten different meetings held during that time. At eight of these meetings, many reported seeing angels; and at five of the services, individuals testified that Jesus, the Savior, appeared. While the Saints were thus communing with heavenly hosts, many prophesied, some spoke in tongues, and others received the gift of interpretation of tongues.[36]

The Prophet Joseph, in response to revelations emphasizing the necessity of preparing priesthood leaders like King for a greater level of spirituality, also received instructions to reinstitute the ancient biblical ordinances of washing and anointing in preparation for a special "endowment" of spiritual power. Backman continues: "Joseph Smith taught that the endowment was a gift of knowledge derived from revelation," which consisted of "instructions relating to the laws of God . . . partially designed to help missionaries to serve with greater power." Men ordained to the priesthood "should prepare for this gift by purifying themselves, by cleansing their hearts and their physical bodies."[37] Although the LDS temple ceremony now known as the endowment would not be given until the Nauvoo period, these Kirtland experiences raised the level of spiritual awareness and focused the men on improving their lives, leading their families in righteousness, and teaching the gospel with greater diligence. Matthew S. McBride, in his history of the Nauvoo Temple, states that the Kirtland Temple "served a unique purpose in preparing for future temples. In addition to serving as a site for congregational meetings, prayer meetings, and the administration of the sacrament, the Kirtland Temple was a place of revelation, particularly the revelation of temple-related doctrine and the authority to perform temple ordinances."[38] The prophetic instruction and personal purification, combined with participants' ardent prayers, became the catalyst for the remarkable spiritual experiences associated with the temple.

In an undated letter to Sally, W. W. Phelps described one of these experiences:

> On Sunday January 17 at an early hour all authorities of the church regularly organized meet [sic] in the school room under the printing office, and the Presidents commenced the meeting by confessing their sins and forgiving their brethren and the world.... The Lord poured out his spirit in such a manner as you never [illegible] when I was speaking, which was but few words, the spirit of the Lord came upon me so that I canst not speak and I cried as little children cry and the tears from my eyes ran in streams; the audience, which was the largest ever commenced in this [illegible] room sobbed and wept Aloud; ...There was speaking and singing in tongues, and prophecying as in the day of the Pentacost.[39]

I would like to think that King was present at such an extraordinary meeting or at others attended by "elders"; but even if he was not, the spirit that Phelps describes would have influenced him. The Prophet Joseph began this intense religious period in Kirtland on January 21, 1836, first with the First Presidency, the bishoprics, and the high councilors from Kirtland and Missouri. The next day, the apostles and presidents of the First Quorum of the Seventy joined them. A week later on January 28, the elders, presumably including King, met to "receive their anointing." Joseph moved from group to group, at one point going "to the quorum of Elders in the other end of the room" where he "assisted in anointing the counselors of the president of the Elders and gave them the instruction necessary for the occasion and left the President and his councilors to anoint the Elders, while I should go to the adjoining room."[40] After the quorum presidency was anointed, "President [Alvah] Beman[41] anointed twenty four Elders ... and the Lord poured out his spirit, and some spake with tongues and prophecied. Oh the wonderous blessings of the God of Israel." King Follett was one of the twenty-four elders anointed that day.[42] The *History of the Church* records five additional meetings between then and the temple's dedication on March 27 when the Prophet taught "the elders" about principles of priesthood organization and leadership, the sealing of anointings, and ordinations to priesthood offices. On one of these occasions, the Prophet organized and blessed the first elders' quorum, again in the temple.[43] W. W. Phelps explained the purpose of these meetings to Sally: "We are preparing to make ourselves clean, by first cleansing our hearts, forsaking our sins, forgiving everybody, all we ever had against them; anointing washing the body; putting on clean decent clothes, by anointing our hearts and by keeping all the commandments. As we come nearer to God we see our imperfections and nothingness plainer and plainer."[44]

On February 3, 1836, a list of elders, including King, as candidates for the "Second Quorum of Seventy" was submitted to Joseph Smith. King was one of those ordained on February 28. Joseph Young Sr., Brigham Young's brother, was one of the original Seven Presidents of the First Quorum of Seventies. In his 1878 *History of the Organization of the Seventies*, he lists members of the First and Second Quorums.[45] King's name appears on the list of those in the Second Quorum. Another member of this quorum is James Daley, who later married King's daughter Nancy. Levi Jackman, writing on February 26 to his wife, Angeline, and children in Liberty, Missouri, reported: "I suppose that you have heard that the Second Seventy has been chose and Bro Follett is one of them."[46] King's name also appears on a broadside, printed in Kirtland in April 1836, on a list headed "The Second Seventy Elders."[47]

Recognizing that the early membership and ordination records of the Church had been "imperfectly kept," each of the priesthood quorums in Kirtland on March 3, 1836, adopted "Resolutions on Ordinations and Licenses" at the Prophet's request. This action established a uniform system of documentation, including instructions to send a copy of any licenses "hereafter granted" to Kirtland where the official record would be kept in a book specifically for that purpose. All who had previously received preaching licenses were asked to return their certificate to Kirtland with a letter verifying their worthiness for the office, and they would receive new licenses. In addition, the resolutions called for the Church newspaper to publish a quarterly list identifying those who had received licenses to preach.[48] Though King had received his initial membership/license several months earlier in Missouri, he apparently received a new license that spring, since his name is among those of 263 men published in the *Messenger and Advocate* in July. The list is headed: "Names of Ministers of the Gospel, Belonging to the Church of the Latter Day Saints, whose Licenses Were Recorded, the Preceeding Quarter, in the License Records, in Kirtland, Ohio. Thomas Burdick, Recording Clerk."[49]

Finally, the long-awaited temple dedication took place on Sunday, March 27. Hundreds of Saints crowded into the temple and the nearby

THE TWELVE APOSTLES.

Thomas B. Marsh	Orson Hyde	William Smith
David W. Patten	William E. McLellin	Orson Pratt
Brigham Young	Parley P. Pratt	John F. Boynton
Heber C. Kimball	Luke Johnson	Lyman Johnson

THE SEVEN PRESIDENTS OF THE SEVENTY ELDERS.

Hazen Aldrich	Leonard Rich	Zebedee Coltrin
Joseph Young	Levi Hancock	Lyman Sherman
		Sylvester Smith

THE FIRST SEVENTY ELDERS.

Elias Hutchings	Solomon Angel	Royal Barney
Cyrus Smalling	Henry Harriman	Lebbeus T. Coons
Levi Gifford	Israel Barlow	Willard Snow
Stephen Winchester	Jenkins Salisbury	Jesse B. Harmon
Roger Orton	Nelson Higgins	Heman T. Hyde
Peter Buchanan	Harry Brown	Lorenzo Burns
John D. Parker	Jesaniah B. Smith	Hyrum Stratten
David Elliott	Lorenzo Boothe	Moses Martin
Samuel Brown	Alexander Badlam	Lyman Smith
Salmon Warner	Zerubbabel Snow	Harvey Stanley
Jacob Chapman	Harpin Riggs	Almon Babbit
Charles Kelley	Edson Barney	William F. Cahoon
Edmond Fisher	Joseph B. Noble	Darwin Richardson
Warren Parrish	Henry Benner	Milo Andress
Joseph Hancock	David Evans	True Gliddon
Aldin Burdick	Nathan B Baldwin	Henry Shibly
Hyrum Winters	Burr Riggs	Harrison Burgess
Hyrum Blackman	Lewis Robins	Jedadiah Grant
William A. Pratt	Alexander Whitesides	Daniel Stephens
Zera S. Cole	George W. Brooks	Amasa Lyman
Jesse Huntsman	Michael Griffith	George A. Smith

THE SECOND SEVENTY ELDERS.

John Gould	Joel H. Johnson	William Gould
Stephen Starks	William Terney	Sherman Gilbert
Samuel Phelps	Daniel Wood	William Redfield
Joel McWithy	Edmund Marvin	Truman Angel
Selah J. Griffin	Reuben McBride	John Herritt
Shedrach Roundy	Marvel C. Davis	Jonathan Hampton
Zerah Pulsipher	Almon Sherman	Chauncey G. Webb
King Follett	Isaac H. Bishop	Solon Foster
Joseph Rose	Elijah Reed	William Perry
Robert Culbertson	Rufus Fisher	Milton Holmes
John Young	Dexter Stillman	James Bailey
James Foster	Thomas Gates	Ervin A. Avery
Salmon Gee	Uriah B. Powel	Charles Thompson
Nathaniel Milliken	Amasa Bonney	Joshua Grant
Gad Yale	Jonathan Holmes	Andrew J. Squires
Josiah Butterfield	Ebenezer Page	Erastus Snow
Elias Benner	Loren Babbit	Levi F. Nickerson
Arial Stephens	Lorenzo Young	Edmund Durfee jr
Elijah Fordham	Wilford Woodruff	Nathan Tanner
Robert Rathbun	Levi Woodruff	Henry Willcox
Hiram Dayton	William Carpenter	Edmund M. Webb
Giles Cook	Johnathan Crosby	William Miller
John E. Page	Francis G. Bishop	Stephen Post
		William Bosley

Church Kirtland Broadside showing King Follett as a member of the "Second Seventy Elders," LDS Church History Library. Used by permission.

schoolhouse. I can only wonder where King was and whether he was among those who managed to find a seat in the sacred structure. The program included singing, scripture-reading, prayers, and sermons. The first official sustaining of Church officers and leaders allowed all present to voice their support. Then the Prophet dedicated the completed building to the Lord and his work on the earth, a prayer later canonized as scripture (D&C 109).

Many of those in attendance recorded in their memoirs or in letters to family and friends the spiritual manifestations associated with the dedication, making me wonder what words King would have used to communicate his feelings.

> A glorious sensation passed through the House . . . that elevated their souls. —Truman O. Angell

> This was by far, the best meeting I had ever attended. . . . Gifts of the gospel . . . were enjoyed in a marvelous manner. —William Hyde

> The Spirit of God was poured out profusely, as on the day of Pentecost. We had a most glorious and never to be forgotten time. — Benjamin Brown

> No mortal language [could] describe the heavenly manifestations of that memorable day. The congregation felt the sweet spirit of love and union . . . a sense of divine presence [and] each heart was filled with joy inexpressible and full of glory. —Eliza R. Snow

> This was one of the happiest days in her life. Heavenly influences . . . rested upon the Lord's House and heavenly beings appeared to many. — Nancy Naomi Alexander Tracy[50]

During the following days, additional meetings were held in which unusual spiritual manifestations continued to be seen and shared.

King undoubtedly participated in these powerful experiences until he left Kirtland sometime after the dedication. After such spiritually powerful months, and now holding the priesthood office of a Seventy, King traveled to New York on business. I have found no details about the specific dates or itinerary. He could have returned to his former home in St. Lawrence County, but I hypothesize that his business had to do with the death of his mother-in-law, Anna Warren Tanner, who had died February 17, 1836, in Attica Center, near Buffalo.[51] I have not found a record of her will, but indirect evidence that she may have left

1845 exterior engraving of Kirtland Temple by E. D. Howe. Used by permission of Community of Christ Archives.

money to Louisa and King is suggested by Levi Jackman, who was then preaching in Buffalo. He recorded in his journal on May 3, 1836, "While walking on the sidewalk I found Brother King Follette who had been to that country on business. He had been collecting some money that was due him. Our meeting was joyous. He was my neighbor in Missouri and we were both going home. He let me have some money, and we engaged a passage on the steamer Columbia, to the nearest port to Kirtland."[52] The fact that King had money to share at that time suggests an inheritance.

The two reached Kirtland on May 5; and on May 17 they joined a Brother "McHenery" and family and started for Missouri, driving "a wagon and horses belonging to Brothers David and John Whitmer to go home with, taking the most of the load for them."[53] Jackman stopped off on the way on June 5 to preach and to assist a group of Saints who were planning to leave for Missouri[54] while on June 8 King and the others continued.[55] I have found no documentation of the date King arrived in Clay County, but it must have been a joyous homecoming after his absence of seven months. The next few days must have been filled with vivid descriptions to his eager family and friends of what had happened in Kirtland, but it was already full farming season. Whatever arrangements Louisa had been able to make to raise a crop to feed the family would have immediately absorbed King in hard labor.

There is no way to answer a related question of whether it would have been a surprise to him that he was a father-in-law. On March 13, 1836, his oldest daughter, Adeline Louisa, had married Nathan Ayers West, with the ceremony being performed by Hiram Page.[56] King already had a close relationship with Nathan since they were neighbors in Jackson County. and both had participated in the Battle of the Blue there. They had also been involved in the "charismatic" dispute among the members of the Hulet Branch in Clay County.

Nathan was a widower. His first wife, Mary Hulet West, had died September 6, 1835, leaving five-year-old Tryphena and two-year-old Maria.[57] There is no record that Nathan and Adeline had children of their own, so these daughters are doubtless the females who appear on the 1840 census in Quincy, Adams County, Illinois, one between ages five and ten (Maria) and the other between ages ten and fifteen (Tryphena).[58] A census of Van Buren County, Iowa, conducted on October 23, 1847, shortly after the Follett family left Nauvoo, lists two otherwise unidentifiable female children, one between the ages of five and ten and one between the ages of ten and fifteen in the Nathan West household.[59] Later still, the Wests settled in Mills County, Iowa,[60] and Nathan, an exemplary son-in-law, provided for Louisa and the younger children during King's imprisonment in 1838 and after his death.

However, less joyous news that greeted King was of conflict again escalating between the Mormons in Clay County and the old residents. Another move loomed for the Saints in Missouri.

Notes

1. Mark Lyman Staker, *Hearken, O Ye People: The Historical Setting of Joseph Smith's Ohio Revelations*, 413–14.

2. Milton V. Backman Jr., *The Heavens Resound: A History of the Latter-day Saints in Ohio, 1836–1838*, 139–40.

3. Ibid., 92–93.

4. Benjamin F. Johnson, quoted in Backman, *The Heavens Resound*, 143. Benjamin and his numerous siblings were natives of New York and joined the Church in 1831 when they moved to Kirtland. He became a close friend of the Prophet during the Nauvoo period, and later helped make Mormon settlements in Utah, Arizona, and Mexico.

5. Backman, *The Heavens Resound*, 147–49.

6. Eliza R. Snow, quoted in Karl Ricks Anderson, *Joseph Smith's Kirtland: Eyewitness Accounts*, 155. Eliza was not a member when temple building began. She was baptized in December 1835 and immediately began to support the building financially. She later became a strong woman leader, served as Relief Society general president (1866–87), and was well known for her poetry. Some of her poems became hymn texts, some of which are still in the current (1985) LDS hymnbook.

7. *History of the Church*, 1:349.

8. Ibid., 2:301.

9. W. W. Phelps, quoted in Bruce Van Orden, "Writing to Zion: The William W. Phelps Kirtland Letters (1835–1836)," 568. Phelps, a native of New Jersey, was a journalist, who joined the Church in June 1831 and became a close friend and confidant of the Prophet. Many of his poems are hymns still in use by the Church. A prolific letter writer, his surviving letters "give important details about the lives and teachings of Latter-day Saints as the Church flourished in Kirtland, Ohio," 543. He died in 1872.

10. Levi Jackman, "Diary, May 4, 1835, 8.

11. Backman, *The Heavens Resound*, 284.

12. D&C 95:17 uses the terminology "school of mine apostles."

13. Backman, *The Heavens Resound*, 265: "Orson Pratt was admitted to the school a few weeks later."

14. Orson Pratt quoted in ibid., 266.

15. Ibid., 269.

16. Ibid., 268.

17. Anderson, *Joseph Smith's Kirtland Eyewitness Accounts*, 118.

18. Newel K. Knight, quoted in William G. Hartley, *Stand by My Servant Joseph*, 233.

19. William Wines Phelps, Letter to Sally Phelps, in Phelps, Letters, 1835–41, 69. This particular series of letters are fragments of some of the many letters Phelps wrote. Someone later placed a number at the top of each fragmented page, apparently in an attempt to put them in some type of chronological order.

20. *History of the Church*, 2:316, 319.

21. Staker, *Hearken, O Ye People*, 416. *History of the Church*, 2:396, describes this exhibit as being from "day to day, at certain hours, that some benefit may be derived from them."

22. I have found no primary source verifying exactly when Joseph Smith Sr., was ordained to the office of Patriarch. According to *History of the Church* 4:190, when he died on September 14, 1840, in Nauvoo, the Prophet states that he ordained his father as the Patriarch on December 18, 1833, assisted by Oliver Cowdery, Sidney Rigdon, and Frederick G. Williams. H. Michael Marquardt, comp., *Early Patriarchal Blessings of the Church of Jesus Christ of Latter-day Saints*, viii–ix, gives a different date. He believes that "a compelling argument may be made that Joseph Sr.'s ordination as patriarch occurred ... at or near the time Joseph Sr., was ordained assistant president or president in the First Presidency, which ordination took place on December 6, 1834" by Sidney Rigdon. Further, Marquardt summarizes that: "Joseph Sr.'s ordination as patriarch no doubt occurred before he formally blessed his family on December 9, 1834." Regardless of which date is correct, Joseph Sr. was a Patriarch by the date of King's blessing on December 16, 1835, as many blessings given by Joseph Sr. before that date are recorded.

23. Michael Hicks, "What Hymns Early Mormons Sang and How They Sang Them," 100.

24. Ibid., 100–101

25. It is impossible to determine why Phelps named these three individuals out of all who attended. Elijah Fordham, a native of New York, joined the Church during the Nauvoo period and is best known for his miraculous recovery from an illness after receiving a blessing from the Prophet Joseph in Montrose, Iowa, in July 1839. George Q. Cannon, *Life of Joseph Smith the Prophet*, 313. Jesse Hitchcock issued King's membership/elder's certificate in Missouri in 1835. Zera Smith Cole, who hosted this particular feast, was a native of Vermont and a participant in Zion's Camp and the First Quorum of the Seventy and at this time was running the tannery in Kirtland for the Rigdon family. Staker, *Hearken, O Ye People*, 406.

26. W. W. Phelps, quoted in Journal History, December 16, 1835, 1. Though referred to as "journalizing," this typescript record may be an excerpt from another letter written from Kirtland to Sally Phelps, in Missouri. The entry reads: "Under this date Wm.W. Phelps journalizes as follows:" Then at the bottom of the quotation is hand written "(W.W. Phelps letter)". I have not been

able to locate that specific information in any of his available letters nor have I been able to find a surviving journal in which the entry was made.

27. Staker, *Hearken, O Ye People*, 244.

28. *History of the Church*, 2:346–47.

29. Ira Ames, quoted in Staker, *Hearken, O Ye People*, 244–45.

30. Marquardt, *Early Patriarchal Blessings*, 56, 119–20. He states: "A number of early patriarchal blessings were pronounced without indicating when the blessing was given."

31. Ibid., x.

32. Lavina Fielding Anderson, "Dreams of Power: The Patriarchal Blessings of Joseph Smith Sr.," 1–2.

33. W. W. Phelps, Letter to Sally Phelps, December 18, 1835, Journal History, 4–5.

34. Orson Pratt, October 9, 1875, *Journal of Discourses*, 18:132. Orson Pratt, a native of New York, was baptized in 1831. He was a member of Zion's Camp and the Missouri High Council. He was ordained an apostle in 1835.

35. See Backman, *The Heavens Resound*, Chap. 17, "A Pentecostal Season," esp. p. 292; and Anderson, *Joseph Smith's Kirtland*, Chap. 16, "A Pentecost and a Time of Rejoicing," esp. pp. 170–71, 175–77, where participants use "pentecostal" or "pentecost" as a descriptive word or phrase. See also *History of the Church*, 2:372–428, Chap. 27, subheaded: "Pentecostal Times in Kirtland."

36. Backman, *The Heavens Resound*, 285.

37. Ibid.

38. Matthew S. McBride, *A House for the Most High: The Story of the Original Nauvoo Temple*, xxiv–xxv.

39. William Wines Phelps, Letter to Sally Phelps, [ca. January 1836], in Phelps, Letters, 1835–41, 109.

40. *History of the Church*, 2:386.

41. Also spelled "Alvah" and "Beaman." He was born in Massachusetts and was a friend of the Smith family during the translation of the Book of Mormon. According to Parley P. Pratt, quoted in *History of the Church*, 2:43 footnote, during the translation of the Book of Mormon, Beaman "had assisted him [Joseph Smith] to preserve the plates of the Book of Mormon from the enemy, and had at one time had them concealed under his own hearth." He died in Kirtland in 1836 while serving as "president of the elders."

42. Lyndon W. Cook and Milton V. Backman Jr., eds., *Kirtland Elders' Quorum Record, 1836–1841*, 4, 82–83.

43. *History of the Church*, 2:387–410.

44. W. W. Phelps, Letter to Sally Phelps, January 1836, quoted in Richard Lyman Bushman, *Joseph Smith: Rough Stone Rolling*, 314.

45. Joseph Young Sr., "Names of the Presidents and Members of the First and Second Quorums of Seventies . . .," beginning p. 3. A typographical error gives the year of the ordinations as 1835 instead of 1836.

46. Levi Jackman, Kirtland, Ohio, Letter to Angeline Jackman, Liberty, Missouri, February 26, 1836.

47. Photograph of broadside in Backman, *The Heavens Resound*, Appendix B. A broadside is a large sheet of paper printed on one or both sides announcing a special event. This one lists "The Twelve Apostles," the "Seven Presidents of the Seventy Elders" and the membership of the "First Seventy Elders" and the "Second Seventy Elders." The term "Seventy Elders" indicates men who were elders at the time they were also ordained seventies. I found no further reference to "Seventy Elders," i.e. Third Seventy Elders. Therefore, apparently from this time forward in the Church, elders and seventies were identified in separate quorums as they are today. This broadside reproduction mistakenly lists James Daley as James Bailey. Daley later became one of the presidents of the Second Quorum of Seventies. The broadside list is reproduced in the Journal History, December 31, 1836, 4.

48. *History of the Church*, 2:402–5.

49. "First, [sic] Names of the Elders," Kirtland Ohio, June 3, 1836, *Messenger and Advocate* 2, no. 10 (July 1836): 335–36.

50. Quoted in Backman, *The Heavens Resound*, 299–300.

51. Gertrude A. Barber, comp., "Deaths Taken from the *Otsego Herald* and *Western Advertiser and Freeman's Journal*, Otsego County, N.Y. Newspapers, from 1795–1840," 1:81.

52. Jackman, Diary, May 3, 1836, 19. The fact that King had money to share after spending the previous months in Kirtland when he was probably generating little or no income would support the theory that his trip to the Buffalo area might have had some connection with the death of Anna Tanner, from which he and Louisa benefited.

53. Ibid., May 17, 1836, 19.

54. Ibid.

55. Ibid., June 8, 1836, 19.

56. Rudena Kramer Mallory, comp., *Clay County Missouri Marriages 1821–1881*, 12. Hiram Page was one of the Eight Witnesses to the Book of Mormon. He had been baptized April 11, 1830, and later left the Church.

57. "In Clay County Missouri. . ." *Messenger and Advocate* 2, no. 1 (October 1835): 207–8. "In Clay Co. Mo. on the 6th of September last, Mrs. Mary West, consort [spouse] of Elder Nathan West, after an illness of about eight days, aged [blank in original], Sister West embraced the new and everlasting covenant in 1831, and has been a firm believer in the work of the Lord ever since; she died having obtained a bright hope of a glorious resurrection—her death

was sweet unto her." Some family records date her death as September 5, 1831, in Jackson County, but she is listed as one of the members of the Hulet Family who settled in Clay County in the Hulet Branch. A. J. Simmonds, "John Noah and the Hulets: A Study in Charisma in the Early Church," 12.

58. U.S. Census, 1840, Illinois, Adams County, Roll 54, p. 60.

59. Joe and Madeline Huff, comps., Iowa General Assembly, Census of Clinton, Davis, Louisa, Marion, Scott, Van Buren, and Wapello Counties, Iowa, 1847, 16.

60. *History of Mills County, Iowa*, 631. In the section on "Silver Creek Township," Nathan is listed as one of its early settlers: "He had two children by his first marriage, one of whom, Mrs. Maria Kempton, resides in Glenwood." A Maria Kempton is listed on the 1870 census for Mills County, Iowa, which confirms a birth year of 1835 in Missouri and that she was the younger of Nathan's two children.

❊ Chapter Ten ❊

From Clay County to Far West

As early as the spring of 1836, Church leaders in Missouri began sending exploring missions north, seeking possible settlement sites as alternatives for returning to Jackson County or staying in Clay County. This northern area, consisting either of unorganized territory or newly formed counties, was commonly referred to as the "Far West." A promising location, heavily wooded but close to a reliable water source was Shoal Creek, where Mormon land purchases began in May 1836.[1] Clearly the members did not want to move again so soon; but as a practical matter, Church leaders wanted to be ready if the need arose.

For a while after the Saints arrived in Clay County, they were not perceived as a major problem—and certainly not as a threat—by the residents. Part of this initial reaction was undoubtedly because of the sad condition in which the Saints had arrived and the fact that they tried to take care of themselves as quickly as possible. Also their determination to return to Jackson County initially kept the Clay County residents from worrying about them as permanent residents. But the way the Saints lived, thought, and believed caused the local citizens to take another view. In June 1836, the minutes of a public meeting expressed concern: "The religious tenets of this people are so different from the present churches of the age, that they always have, and always will, excite deep prejudices against them in any populous country where they may locate."[2] By the time of King's return to Clay County, differences in culture, basic religious beliefs and concepts, feelings over slavery, and Book of Mormon teachings that defined the Indians as God's chosen people again became alarming. Like the residents of Jackson County, some of Clay County's residents respected the Saints and could be considered friendly, but others saw more validity in Jackson County's position. As the number of Saints moving into the county from Kirtland and the East increased, spreading throughout the county, these basic differences became more abrasive. A member wrote: "As [Mormon] number[s] increased the older settlers . . . became somewhat alarmed and by mutual agreement were asking that the Mormons move to the North where there was enough unoccupied territory to support a large influx of settlers."[3] One citizen, writing to his brother and sister in North Carolina, expressed the residents' perspective:

> They [Mormons] have been flocking in here faster than ever and making great talk what they would do. . . . They intend to Emigrate here til they outnumber us. . . . They would rule the Contry [sic] at pleasure . . . Borrowing all the money they Can to procure land here & they Buy all on a credit that they Can get and promise the most Anormous [sic] prices ever heard of. They have offered 1000 Dollars for a tract of 80 Acres Sold 12 months ago for 250 Dollars. . . . They have got a revelation from Smith that they Shal have the Missouri By money or Blood and God has Commanded them (they Say) to sell their flocks and Hovels and procede [sic] to the Mo. And Buy land that they may rest & these revelations are witnessed to By the 12 apostles Some of which are amonst [sic] us. They are Still going on in their usual way of lying, raising the dead, Casting out devils, Healing the sick, etc. In this way they have Still been annoying us from day today.[4]

In addition, although the Saints labored diligently to farm and build homes, their poverty was acute. The implications for the local economy, the fear of losing political control, and the perception that the Saints would fight, if necessary, caused both friendly and unfriendly residents to want the Saints to move on.

Beginning in spring 1836 small anti-Mormon planning meetings were held throughout the county in preparation for a general public meeting on June 29 in Liberty (initiated by "friendly" citizens) to begin negotiating with the Mormons regarding their removal from Clay County. The night before that meeting, however, on June 28, an attack on an unnamed Mormon settlement southwest of Fishing River, resulted in the death of one Mormon man due to the severe whipping he received and the harassment of many. Another confrontation occurred about the same time when a group of members seeking to enter the county were turned back by a group of "regulators" led by Jesse Clark. Church members organized 250 men to "confront Clark . . . and protect the roads." This show of force by armed members "inflamed" the Missourians.[5]

Simultaneously, however, the Missourians were gathering and arming in even greater numbers than the Saints. One contemporary estimate is that, during meetings held on July 1 and 2, to organize volunteer companies, Clay County could raise 500 men with another estimated 3,800 coming from the seven nearest counties.[6] Edward Channing, an early twentieth-century historian, commented that these hostile actions focused on the Mormons simply because they "had their own ministers, settled their own disputes among themselves without going to courts of law, and healed their own sick by their own methods, and thereby aroused the jealousies of ministers, lawyers, doctors, and politicians."[7]

The June 29 gathering of citizens adopted a report outlining the reasons why the Saints should leave. The charges as previously enumerated, as well as additional ones, were given; and while not all of those attending vouched for the truthfulness of the statement, "their [the charges] effect has been the same in exciting our community . . . to raise a prejudice against them; and a feeling of hostility, that the first spark may, and we deeply fear will, ignite into all the horrors and desolations of a civil war."[8] Viewing themselves as "mediators" in the situation, the Clay County citizens urged the Saints to stop all new immigration into the county and to move "where the manners, the habits, and customs of the people will be more consonant with their own"—an area "where they may obtain large and separate bodies of land and have a community of their own." Admitting that they had no legal right to force the members to leave, these county representatives argued that war would be prevented if the Mormons left but, if they did not, they would be responsible for whatever happened.[9]

To develop the Church's position in response, a "Public Meeting of the Saints in Clay County, Missouri," was held on July 1. The *History of the Church* described the gathering as a "very large meeting of the Elders of the Church of Latter-day Saints, assembled in Clay county, Missouri." I hypothesize that King, who had returned to Clay County from Kirtland about two months earlier, probably attended. W. W. Phelps was selected to chair the meeting. After much discussion, the Church members acknowledged that they must leave the area or face the prospect of bloodshed, and resolved that they "accept the friendly offer verbally tendered to us by the committee yesterday, to assist us in selecting a location, and removing to it." A written response adopted by those in attendance expressed thanks and appreciation for their treatment in Clay County, reaffirmed that any land they obtained in that county would be through purchase, and confirmed that the Church's position was "just to preach the Gospel to the nations of the earth." The response further stated: "We believe that all men are bound to sustain and uphold the respective governments in which they reside, while protected in their inherent and inalienable rights by the laws of such governments." Under the signatures of W. W. Phelps, Chair, and John Corrill, Secretary, the response was delivered the next day to "the citizens of Clay County,"[10] and a copy was sent to Kirtland. On July 25, Joseph Smith, Sidney Rigdon, Oliver Cowdery, F. G. Williams and Hyrum Smith, penned a response, advising the Saints in Clay County to not be "the first aggressors. Give no occasion, and if the people will let you, dispose of your property, settle your affairs, and go in peace. . . .You know our feelings relative to not giving the first offense, and also of protecting your wives and little ones in case a mob should seek their lives. . . . Be wise; let prudence dictate all your counsels; preserve peace with all, if possible; stand by the Constitution of your country; observe its principles; and above all, show yourselves men of God."[11]

On July 7, prior to receiving this response, Bishop Edward Partridge appealed to Governor Daniel Dunklin on behalf of the Church, seeking at the very least state protection while members were in the process of moving and suggesting that perhaps the President of the United States should be petitioned to intervene. Dunklin rejected the appeal. Max H Parkin summarized Dunklin's response: "His reasoning this time was not that he lacked the authority to act, but that the Saints themselves, he felt, should not contribute to social disorder by being so out of line with popular opinion. He said that in some cases 'public sentiment may become paramount law.' He felt that the Saints had an obligation toward other citizens not to excite their neighbors to hostility."[12] Meanwhile, however, the local citizens had met again on July 2 and agreed to help raise money and find places where the Mormons "will be, in a measure, the only occupants; and where none will be anxious to molest them."¹³ In essence, the governor and citizens of Clay County told the Mormons that, because they were a minority with unique beliefs and ideas, they did not deserve the protection afforded constitutionally to all other citizens and should deal with this situation by living in isolation somewhere else.

By August 1836, about three months after King's return from Kirtland, Mormon families began to leave Clay County and settle in northern Ray County on Shoal Creek where the Church had earlier made some land purchases. The area consisted of a one-square mile plat for a townsite designated Far West. As the number of Saints in that area began to increase, the few local residents quickly became concerned. Both sides negotiated an agreement that went to the state legislature in December, which approved the formation of two new counties, Caldwell and Daviess, from northern Ray County. Caldwell County was located immediately east of Ray County, and later Missourians took the position that the Mormons agreed to settle only in it. Daviess County was directly north of the new Caldwell County with settlement open to anyone. To assure the "isolation" of the Church members and to assure the present residents of Ray County that the Mormons would not move too close, "a proposal was also accepted to establish a six-mile buffer zone, three miles on each side of the dividing line between Ray and Caldwell counties, as a "no-man's land" where neither Mormon nor non-Mormon could settle."¹⁴ An unidentified author, writing in 1886, best describes the roles defined for the three main parties at this time:

> "Let us fix up a county expressly for the Mormons," exclaimed certain politicians and public men. "Let us send all the Mormons in the state to that county and induce all Gentiles therein to sell out and leave." The proposition suited everyone. The Gentiles said, "If the Mormons are willing to go into that prairie county and settle, let them have it and welcome." The Mormons said, "If we may be allowed to remain peaceably and enjoy our religion, we will go into any country that may be set apart for us and no matter how wild, we will make it blossom as the rose. If we obtain political control of a county, we will honestly administer it and be loyal in all things to the state government over us."¹⁵

Approached in that manner, the move to northern Missouri seemed a simple and complete solution for what had been a major problem for Missouri and for the Saints: No one wanted them for neighbors. This time the Saints hoped and planned to settle Caldwell County as "their" county where they could live permanently.

The Folletts' participation in or reaction to these events has not been preserved. The only known civil document containing King's name in 1836 is the Clay County tax list, dated September 5.[16] Names are listed in alphabetical order with no indication of address or location. King had no real estate, and his personal property consisted of one horse valued at $40 and four cattle valued collectively at $50. His tax on this total of $90 was 48 cents. Son-in-law Nathan West owned a horse ($40) and a single "cattle" ($10) for a total of $50, upon which he paid a total of 43 cents. Nathan's tax seems proportionately high compared to King's since he had about half of King's property. Most other members of the Church likewise owned little personal property. The base rate for an adult man was twenty-five cents, with property tax being figured at 12.5 cents every hundred dollars worth of property.[17]

It is not clear when the Folletts moved from Clay County; but they settled near Far West in Caldwell County. In Nauvoo, Louisa added this item to the Mormon petitions for redress sent to Congress: "1835 [sic] To loss of property, time & expence by being Driven from Clay Co. to Caldwell Co. $150.00."[18] The home in Caldwell County was their third in about five years, but they must have felt hopeful that this time they would be unmolested. Most of the few non-Mormons in the area had sold out to the Mormons and moved.

An 1876 atlas of Caldwell County described the area: "Up to the year 1836, there was not a town or a store within the limits of Caldwell County. When an article of merchandise was needed a trip to Richmond was necessary to obtain it. The old settlers, if they desired to cast their votes, had to repair to Richmond for that purpose . . . there being no voting precinct in this county."[19] The county was "about two-thirds prairie and one-third timber. . . . Situated about 140 miles west of the eastern boundary of Missouri and approximately sixty miles south of the State's northern line, . . . [it] encompassed 432 square miles or 276,480 acres of land."[20] Because it was prairie rather than timber, the Missourians felt that it was less valuable and fertile. Those Church members who had initially been sent to purchase land on Shoal Creek had brought back a good report—"that the site was far superior to any they had previously seen; a good grazing country, plenty of timber and good water, and few inhabitants."[21] Alanson Ripley, one of the new Mormon settlers, also described its positive points: "The county of Caldwell is a beautiful elevated prairie country, interspersed with valleys, and beautiful groves of timber; the face of the country is generally high and rolling.... The soil is very productive, insomuch that forty or fifty bushels of corn per acre is but middling yield and equally as good for wheat and all other kinds of grain."[22]

The area around Shoal Creek was soon officially named Far West and became the largest settlement in Caldwell County—the county seat as well as Church headquarters. A year earlier Jacob Hawn, originally from Wisconsin, had established a small Mormon settlement about twelve miles east of Far West also on the Shoal Creek.[23] Before the Saints fled from Missouri in 1839, they had established at least nineteen other towns and settlements and an estimated "2,000 farms," totaling "more than 250,000 acres," most of it purchased in forty-acre parcels for which they had paid $318,000. Caldwell County land records and early Mormon Church records document "344 known Mormons who were original landowners" and "another 238 probable Mormon original landowners during 1836–39."[24]

King Follett was one of the known original landowners. While a few members may have had the good fortune to buy land that was already under or ready for cultivation, he, like many other settlers, bought unimproved land directly from the federal government, but it was not a short or easy process. According to historian Ronald E. Romig,

> When the government advertised land for sale, interested individuals had to travel to the Land Office at Lexington, Missouri, in order to bid on the land. If a bid was successful, and paid in full, the purchaser was issued a receipt for the land. Land could also be purchased by paying four annual installments. When the land payment was complete, land patent paperwork was started. It was often two or more years before the paperwork was actually completed with buyers eventually receiving an official patent certificate for their land.[25]

Records in the land office at Lexington, Ray County, include a receipt for King's payment—$50 cash—for forty acres in Mirabile Township at the rate of $1.25 per acre, plus the Registration Certificate authorizing the commissioner of the General Land Office to issue a patent for this land. Both documents are dated February 13, 1837. A year and a half

Deed to King Follett's land in Far West, Caldwell County, Missouri. Photocopy of original obtained from Bureau of Land Management, General Land Records Office.

later on July 28, 1838, the deed to the property, identifying King as being from Ray County, was finally signed on behalf of President Martin Van Buren. The legal description of the land locates it in "the North East quarter of the North West quarter of Section nine, in Township fifty six, of Range twenty nine, in the District of and subject to sale at Lexington, Missouri, containing forty acres."[26] This description would have placed

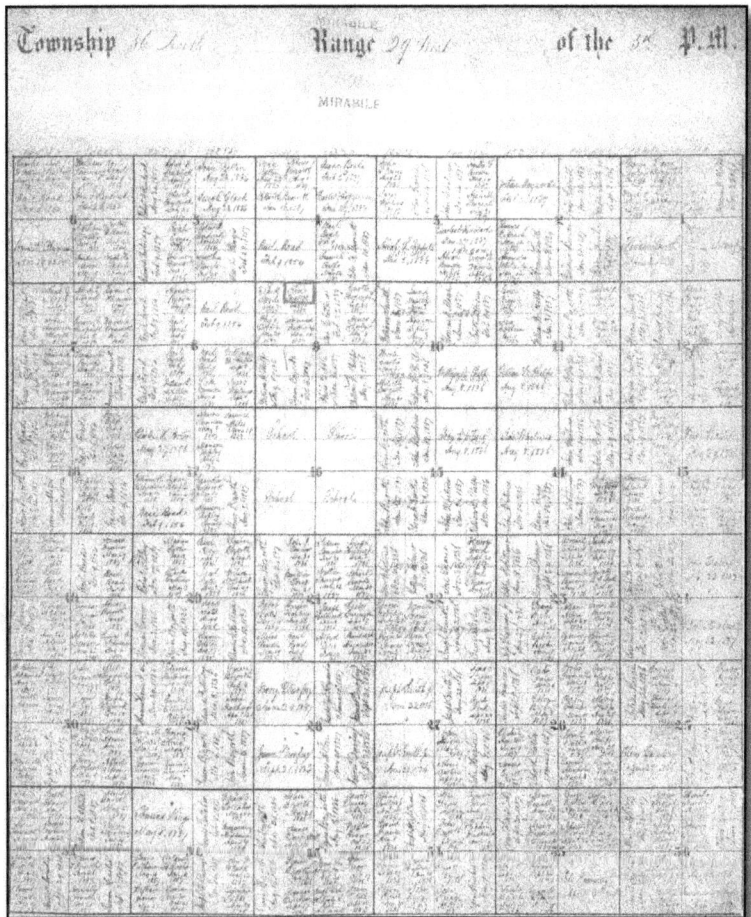

Plat of Mirabile Township, identifying the location of King's land. Caldwell County Recorder's Office, reprinted in Clark V. Johnson and Ronald E. Romig, *An Index to Early Caldwell County, Missouri Land Records*, 11. Used by permission of Ronald E. Romig.

Follett's land 1.5 miles west and ¾ mile north of the center of the original Far West townsite.

This land presently fronts on the south side of NW Rocky Mountain Drive, identified in some places and records as Stinson Drive. During my visits, I took note of the small hill in the center of the acreage, all of which is now farmland with no buildings located on it.

According to a descendant of the Whitmer family, Mirable Township contained meadows "lush enough to promise abundant food for the

Present site of King Follett's land (1837–39), facing south from NW Rocky Mountain Drive. Photo by Irval L. Mortensen, 2006.

horses, cattle and livestock. Decorating this wonderland were also clusters of many different kinds of summer butterflies. . . . Teeming with an abundance of rabbit, prairie chickens, wild turkey, geese and large herds of deer, Far West seemed a haven . . . in many ways. The long stretching banks of Shoal Creek presented a seemingly endless supply of fish. Also nearby were stands of forests to provide much needed building materials."[27] An index to early Caldwell County records document that other land owners who were King's neighbors in the north half of section 9 included Clark Strode and Philo Dibble to the west, Armond Butler to the south, and Amos and Curtis Hodges Sr. and Ira Clothier on the east. In the south half of section 9 were W. W. Phelps, Philo Dibble, and Squire Bozorth.[28] The *History of the Church* reflects some connections that these individuals had with the Folletts and also the diverse activities of Church members who were neighbors in Caldwell County.[29]

Squire Bozorth was one of approximately 176 men who signed a covenant in January 1839 agreeing to help the Saints in "removing from Missouri" to Illinois. King would have then been in jail in Columbia,

Missouri, and Louisa would have needed assistance. Philo Dibble was wounded by a mob during the Battle of the Blue in Jackson County, in which King and his son-in-law Nathan West had participated. Amos Hodge was among those who escorted Joseph and Hyrum Smith's bodies to Nauvoo following the martyrdom at Carthage. He was also called to serve a mission in Vermont.

Curtis Hodges Sr. became the first case tried before the newly organized Kirtland High Council in February 1834. Charged with "loud speaking" in prayer meetings and "error in spirit," he confessed and was forgiven but was later excommunicated for "unchristian like conduct." Two months after King purchased his land, he was a member of this same type of Church governing body, the newly formed high council in Far West, where he would be called on to adjudicate such cases. W. W. Phelps was an early convert who became the Church printer in Missouri, served as a member of the Presidency in Missouri, helped settle Far West, was excommunicated in March 1838 for misuse of Church funds in the purchase of land in Clay County, but was later rebaptized. In letters to his wife from Kirtland during 1835, Phelps had mentioned King as though they were friends.

The *History of the Church* does not mention the other two neighbors, Armond Butler and Clark Strode, by those names. However, William G. Hartley identifies the land just west of King's as belonging to "Clark Slade,"[30] a devout Mormon who had been present at the Church's organization on April 6, 1830.

Phelps's land, located one-half mile east and a quarter mile south of King's forty-acre purchase, was between the Follett land and the townsite. Twenty-four of Phelps's forty acres were used for a burial ground during the time the Saints lived in Far West; but this size represented planning for the future, not present needs. Although the actual numbers and the names of those interred there are not known, tradition estimates that it was the final resting place for perhaps as many as two hundred early Saints.[31]

Soon after King purchased his land in February 1837, the Folletts moved onto their property, built a log home, and planted their first crop. This is the first documented land purchase for the Follett family since they left Shalersville in 1832. By now, King was almost fifty, which made him "old" by the day's standards. Louisa was ten years younger. Yet they certainly had few possessions or material security to show for their past twenty years. Eighteen-year-old John, fourteen-year-old Nancy, twelve-year-old William Alexander, and four-year-old Edward were still living with them. There is no record that Nathan West purchased land in Caldwell County so he, Adeline, and Nathan's two daughters by his first marriage, may have also lived with King and Louisa. Perhaps Nathan and Adeline helped King pay the $50 that was the purchase price; about that time, Nathan and Adeline received $60 from selling their Whitmer Settlement property in Jackson County.[32] Although Nathan and Adeline's residence is not identified, they were definitely living in or near Far West, since Nathan acted as clerk of Far West's high council meetings on April 24 and July 29, 1837.[33]

Far West lay approximately fifty miles north of Independence between Shoal Creek on the north and Goose Creek on the south. Although even town ruins have not survived, it would have been at the crossroads of what is now County Road D (running north and south) and a narrow, presently unnamed county road running east and west. In November 1837, the original town plat of one mile square was enlarged to two,[34] moving King's home closer to the center of town. Roads divided the town into blocks, each containing four acres consisting of four, one-acre house lots. In both Jackson and Clay counties, Church policy encouraged members to either live on Church-owned land or consecrate their property to the Church, thus providing means for sustaining poorer members. However, this policy was suspended in Caldwell County. The Saints were encouraged to form "cooperative farming enterprises" and, according to historian Glen M. Leonard, "set up huge farms managed under a neighborhood organization as a supplement to private—unconsecrated—land."[35] Therefore, a number of the Saints eventually owned both a town lot and a farm. Perhaps King consecrated his land to the Church, then leased it back and farmed it for his family, donating the excess to the Church for distribution to the poor.

Far West's center was a large square where a temple and a school were planned. In March 1840, the Church newspaper *Times and Seasons* described Far West, which had been abandoned in the fall of 1838, in glowing terms: "In one year from the time of the first settlement in Caldwell, there were one hundred to one hundred and fifty dwelling houses erected in that place, six dry goods stores in operation, one grocery, and several mechanic shops. There were in the county, nearly three hundred farms opened and several thousand acres under cultivation; also, four saw and five mills doing good business. Thus we see that in the short space of one year, the solitary place was made glad for them, and the wilderness was converted into a fruitful field."[36]

The speed with which the members established homes and farms did not go unnoticed by nonmembers. Reed Peck, a Missouri Mormon, writes that the non-Mormons expressed the feeling to him that it was as if "by magic that the wild prairies over a large tract were converted into cultivated fields" by the Saints. He claims that visitors to the chief city in Caldwell County were often heard to remark that "no other people of the same number could build a town like Far West and accomplish as much in the agricultural line in five years as the Mormons had in one."[37] In addition, the industry of the Saints was noted by a local judge writing in the 1880s, remembering events he had observed in Clay County:

> The Mormons were, in the main, industrious, good workers, and gave general satisfaction for their employers, and could live on less than any people I ever knew. Their women could fix up a good meal out of what a Gentile's wife would not know how to commence to get half a dinner or breakfast. They had a knack of economizing in the larder, which was a great help to the men, as they mostly had to earn their bread and butter by day's work with wages about half what they are now. The women were generally well educated, and, as a rule, quite intelligent, far more so than the men.[38]

However, this resourcefulness that enabled Church members to quickly become self-sufficient and even prosper aroused local hostilities, too. Jacob Gates later recalled that he and his family were able to quickly get "many of the comforts of life when we first settled in Caldwell County," either by buying from or working for non-members. But as soon as "the church became able to live within themselves then the people . . . arose up against us in order to stop our prosperity and keep us in bondage for they feared least [sic] the revelations which the Lord had given. . ."[39]

For the Folletts and others who had been through so much turmoil since first joining the Church, the chance to settle down, enjoy the benefits of their industry and labor, educate their children, and attend Church services regularly must have been a source of rejoicing. According to William G. Hartley: "The families [in Far West] were busy providing for what they presumed would be a long stay. Their pressing concerns were roofs, firewood and water, fences and barns, and plows and seeds. Being in a solidly Mormon county, the Saints lived together with almost no 'Gentiles' in their midst for the first time in the Church's short history. They enjoyed the right to be governed by their own county and town officers, including judges and law enforcement people, to operate their own businesses, and to control their own land transactions after initial ownership was established."[40]

An early Missouri history describes the Saints' attention to education: "In the fall of 1836 a large and comfortable school-house was built and here courts were held.... The Mormons very early gave attention to educational matters. There were many teachers among them and school-houses were among their first buildings. The school-house in Far West was used as a church, a town hall and as a court-house, as well as for a school-house. It first stood in the southwest quarter of town but upon the establishment of the county seat it was removed to the center of the square."[41] A visitor described "a large frame building, with seats well arranged and a good pulpit,"[42] a floorplan that would work well for either a classroom or a religious service. Thirteen-year-old Nancy Follett and her eleven-year-old brother William Alexander may have attended this school, although no pupils rolls have survived.

The entire Follett family would have attended Sunday worship services and Thursday evening prayer meetings here, the first time they had had access to a Mormon-constructed meetinghouse. Pearl Wilcox, author of a twentieth-century regional history, quotes John Bush, a member of the Plum Creek Settlement south of the Follett land, recounting that members from many of the settlements attended meetings in the schoolhouse in Far West:

> "'We went regularly each Sunday to Far West[;" wrote Bush. "]Few of the Saints had teams, and these worked hard during the week, and the people walked the distance. Sunday after Sunday quite a crowd of men, women, and children could be seen wending their way toward the central city.'... [Wilcox continues:"]Thursday evenings the Saints met in prayer and testimony meetings. In their zeal for the gospel they were truly blessed by love and goodwill toward one another. In Church services, "the burden of instruction given was exhortation to greater faithfulness and more strict compliance with the law, with warnings and prophecies concerning future distress, if they did not."[43]

By April 1837, Far West was chosen as the seat of Caldwell County. John P. Greene, a Mormon, writing about the Church's move to Caldwell County, stated: "Here they were allowed to organize the government for the county." While not identifying all government offices specifically, he reported: "Of the officers then appointed, two of the judges, thirteen magistrates, and all of the military officers, and the county clerk were Mormons. These steps were taken, be it carefully observed, by the advice of the State Legislature; and the officers were appointed in the manner directed by law."[44] Lyman Wight recorded that a county regiment of militia was organized and "an election being called for a colonel of said regiment, I was elected unanimously receiving 236 votes in August, 1837; we then organized with subaltern officers, according to the statutes of the state, and received legal and lawful commissions from Governor Boggs for the same."[45] He stresses this procedure to counter accusations that the Saints acted as unauthorized vigilante units. Alex Baugh, Missouri historian, explains: "Over thirty Latter-day Saint men are known to have received official appointments from either the governor or other state authorities, or they were properly accorded their rank by a sanctioned election in their unit."[46] On March 10, 1838, the high council in Missouri resolved: "That the High Council recommend to all those who hold licences, between the age of 18 and 45, and do not officiate in their respective offices, be subject to military duty."[47] An entry in *History of the Church* explains: "The law of Missouri excused from military duty all licensed ministers of the Gospel, and as nearly all the adult members of the Church who were worthy had received ordination to the Priesthood, it left the community in Far West . . . without militia companies and state arms for its protection; hence the recommendation of the Council that the brethren within the ages specified, and not actively employed in the ministry, place themselves in a position to accept militia service."[48] Baugh continues: "[The] Mormons clearly felt it was not only their public duty to muster, but also recognized that the militia system could be the means whereby they could defend their civil rights. Such was not the case in Jackson or Clay, for the simple reason they were not the majority."[49] King was forty-nine at this point and was thus past the age specified in the high council resolution. His son John, age nineteen, and his son-in-law Nathan West, age thirty-seven, would have fit the age-range for military duty. However, I found no record that included John or Nathan as members of the militia.

As in Independence and Kirtland, plans for a temple were quickly begun. A building committee consisting of Elisha H. Groves, Jacob Whitmer, and George M. Hinkle was appointed on November, 15, 1836, and a site was selected on the northeast corner of the town's central square, about a mile and a half east of the Follett home. Actual groundbreaking and construction began on July 3, 1837. Approximately five hundred men, using "crude tools and wheelbarrows," dug an excavation 80 by 110 feet. I like to think that King, John, and Nathan West joined in this labor, cheerful despite the heat and humidity of high summer in Missouri. Construction continued sporadically until November 1837; then because of financial strictures, Joseph Smith suspended work until the following summer.[50] By the summer of 1838, the tensions leading to the Mormon War in Missouri were in full spate, and the Saints left the barely begun temple behind them when they fled to Illinois in the winter of 1838–39.

The *Far West Record* provides glimpses of King Follett and Nathan West's participation in Church governance. Minutes of three high council meetings record King's presence as a member. The high council had broad responsibilities—some of them verging on what would be assigned to civic and educational authorities today.[51] Though I could not find a record of when he was made a member of the high council, his first appearance, on April 24, 1837, identifies him as "No. 10" on a list of twelve,[52] with Nathan serving as clerk of the council. The only agenda item was hearing an accusation that Lyman Wight[53] was teaching "erronious [sic] doctrine," defined as meaning he had taught that "we the Church were under a telestial law. ... And that the Book of Covinants [sic] and Doctrine was a telestial law and the Book of Commandments ... were a Celestial law." Nathan West's minutes record: "The above is only a sketch of the erroneous doctrine Lyman Wight taught." After hearing the evidence, the presidency, then consisting of John Whitmer and W. W. Phelps, ruled that the accusation was true and that Wight should "make acknowledgment to the Council and also that he go and acknowledge to the Churches where he preached such abominable doctrine." This decision was "unanimously sanctioned" by the high council, including King.[54]

On November 7, 1837, at a general assembly in Far West with the Prophet Joseph Smith in attendance, King participated in the discussion and voting, both as a high councilor and also as a member. Because this gathering was a general assembly, not a priesthood meeting, I like to think that Louisa, Adeline, and Nancy were also present and took part in the voting. The minutes refer to "Elder King Follett." Although offices and titles were quite fluid at that early period, King had been ordained a Seventy in Kirtland, so "Elder" here indicates that he was a male member in good standing. The same title was used for most of the men who spoke unless they were either a "President" or "Bishop."

The development of the formal leadership organization of the Church came over a period of time. At the organization of the Church on April 6, 1830, Joseph Smith was ordained as the "first elder." (D&C 21:10–12) Over the years that leadership role remained the same, though the title evolved. Joseph was ordained as "President of the High Priesthood" at a conference held in Amherst, Ohio, January 25, 1832. Three months later on April 26, 1832, in a general council of the Church held in Jackson County, Missouri, he was sustained in that position (D&C 75 and 82).[55] A revelation on the priesthood recorded on March 28, 1835, gave specific instructions about a "First Presidency": "Of the Melchizedek Priesthood, three Presiding High Priests, chosen by the body, appointed and ordained to that office, and upheld by the confidence, faith and prayer of the Church, form a quorum of the Presidency of the Church" (D&C 107:22). Joseph had been sustained in that position by the Saints in Kirtland with Sidney Rigdon and Frederick G. Williams as his counselors.

The Missouri Saints were now also asked to sustain these three, with Joseph Smith as the "First President of the whole Church, to preside over the same. All were requested (males and females,) to vote—who [sic] was unanimously chosen." Sidney Rigdon was also approved as a counselor; but after much discussion, Hyrum Smith was selected rather than Frederick G. Williams, even though Williams had been nominated by the Prophet.[56] This nomination is puzzling since, by this time, conditions in Kirtland had deteriorated because of the financial situation, and "widespread apostasy resulted." Williams had already become alienated from the Church and had been "removed from office."[57]

Also at this time, David Whitmer was nominated to serve as the "first President of this branch of the Church" in Missouri. Several elders spoke, both for and against Whitmer's nomination; King was one who voiced his approval. Finally, Whitmer was sustained. After a recess of one hour, the congregation took up membership on the high council. Most of those proposed were unanimously approved; however, three objected to George M. Hinkle—one because "he was too noisy," another by "King Follet because of his military office," and a third because he was "a merchant." Despite these objections, Hinkle, an 1832 convert, was unanimously approved.[58] In retrospect, King's objection to Hinkle's combined military and ecclesiastical roles may have been an important point. After the flight to Illinois, Hinkle was excommunicated because of the members' feeling that, as colonel of the Caldwell County militia, he had "betrayed" Joseph Smith and other leaders to the Missouri militia during the siege of Far West, resulting in six months of imprisonment for the Prophet.

On April 14, 1838, the *Far West Record* documents another high council meeting at which the council heard a complaint by Truman Wait that had been made on March 27, 1838, in the elders' quorum against Nathan West but which Nathan had appealed to the high council. Wait complained that Nathan had a 'spirit of dissension" and had opposed the Church's congregational vote on November 7, 1837, "not to support stores and shops selling spirituous liquors, tea, coffee, and tobacco." Furthermore, he was allegedly guilty of "teaching incorrect doctrine in that he said the word of wisdom did not concern our Spiritual Salvation" and "did not consider the word of Wisdom given by Commandment or Constraint." In point of fact, this 1833 revelation, received in Kirtland, specified that the health code was given "not by commandment or constraint, but by revelation and the word of wisdom" (D&C 89:2); but it is also true that the Far West authorities had forbidden the sale or consumption of liquor within the city limits. During the testimony and discussion, Silas Maynard further complained that West had disagreed with the conference action to excommunicate W. W. Phelps (one of the Folletts' neighbors and a family friend) and John Whitmer, both members of the Church presidency in Missouri. The situation that was quickly unraveling through internal dissension and questions about the direction in which Joseph Smith and Sidney Rigdon were taking the

Church. If the ultimate objective was to live in peace with their Missouri neighbors, such questions were actually well placed; but historical events would play out differently.

Speaking in his own defense, Nathan West acknowledged a part of the charge regarding the Word of Wisdom and conceded that he now saw the excommunication differently and "does coincide with" the conference's decision. The high council determined that "Br. West had erred in spirit, therefore feel to admonish him, but do not find anything in him worthy of death or bonds."[59] The minutes do not list King as a member of this council; however, since he was still a member three months later, he may have recused himself because a family member was involved.

The last time King's name appears in the *Far West Record* was July 6, 1838, during a quarterly conference presided over by Joseph Smith Jr. and Sidney Rigdon, when "the Presidents of the different Quorums proceeded to organize their respective Quorums." King led out as "acting President of the Seventies as the Presidents were absent." Sidney Rigdon exhorted each officer to "stand in his place, and perform his duty as it is required at his hand" and counseled: "Because all the Officers in the Church has [sic] more influence ... than he may suspect, therefore, when you speak, let your words be seasoned with grace."[60]

As both an elder and a seventy, King had the authority and responsibility to preach the gospel. I have found no documentation in Church or family records that he was ever officially called as a missionary; but he performed at least four baptisms during 1837–39, apparently away from Far West. Perhaps these baptisms were incidental to other journeys, or he may have served a brief mission for which no record has survived. It is also possible that he preached and baptized at other times and places for which no record exists or for which the records are not now available. The first two recorded baptisms were of Samuel Williams and his son, Newman B. Williams, in 1837 (no specific date), when Newman would have turned eight. One source dates this baptism as September 1837 but without giving a location.[61] Records of Kamas Ward in Utah date this baptism a year later in September 1838; the column labeled "Remarks" includes this notation: "[Newman] remembers sitting on log."[62] Samuel Williams's account book suggests that the Williams family was living somewhere in Ohio but gives a different date: "April the 3 We was Baptised in to the Church of Jesus Christ of latter-day Saints Ad 1837."

Later that same year, they moved to Kirtland.[63] "Samuel Williams" is not an uncommon name; but I hypothesize that the man King baptized is the same one named in *History of the Church* as signing a petition along with many other men to "assist each other to the utmost of our abilities" as the Saints fled from Far West. He was ordained an elder in Commerce (Nauvoo), in October 1839, and "retained" in his office as president of the elders' quorum at a conference on October 6, 1844, also in Nauvoo.[64] He also worked as a stonecutter on the Nauvoo Temple.[65] The Williams family was from Russell, Hampden County, Massachusetts. They are listed in 1852 as members of the Salt Lake Fifteenth Ward.[66]

Another baptism King performed was that of Martin Wood, a twenty-year-old native of Portage County, Ohio, and a son of Henry Wood and Esther Cranmer Wood. Martin's record as a Seventy contains his statement: "Nov 1838 I was baptized in Davis Co Mo by King Follett."[67]

According to Galloway family tradition, Charles Wesley Galloway, born in Pennsylvania in 1826, was "baptized in 1837 when 11 years old by King Follett" and that Charles's father, John Galloway, "died 5 July 1837 in LaSalle County, Illinois." Charles's obituary says that he "joined the Church as a young man in Illinois." I assume, therefore, that the baptism probably occurred in LaSalle County, which is located about 181 miles northeast of Nauvoo. A family group sheet gives the baptismal date as July 1839, which I argue is mistaken since King was in prison in Missouri from March or April to October of 1839. Charles's mother remarried; and by April 1844, the family was living in Nauvoo 11th Ward at Golden's Point Settlement, a farming area south of Nauvoo. Charles was ordained a Seventy in 1848, married in 1849 in Iowa, and moved to the Salt Lake Valley in 1852. After a brief stay in California, he was a farmer and orchard owner in Utah, dying in Meadow, Millard County, on May 29, 1879.[68]

Leavitt family history places Jeremiah Leavitt II and Sarah Sturtevant Leavitt, at Twelve Mile Grove, Will County, Illinois, about a mile and a half east-southeast of the present town of Elwood and just beyond Wilton's northern city limits. The family history is a compilation of memories and journal entries, not all of them specifically dated. Apparently the family moved to Twelve Mile Grove in 1837 and remained there until at least 1840. When they were preparing to move to Nauvoo, Sarah recorded in her memoirs: "Before we left the place there was [sic] a number of elders came and we were made glad indeed. We had not seen a Saint from the time we left Kirtland, and they gave us much instructions and encouraged us so that we felt like urging our passage through all the cares and trials of life until our work was finished on the earth. One of these elders was King Follett." The family history quotes Jeremiah as saying: "I was ordained a teacher under the hand of King Follett (at Twelve-Mile Grove)."[69] Jeremiah repeated that King ordained him at Twelve Mile Grove, still without giving a date, in a brief holograph "Genealogy of Jeremiah Levet" created as part of the "Record of Members of the Sixteenth Quorum of Seventies" in Utah.[70]

I speculate that King could have performed the Galloway baptism and the Leavitt ordination on the same trip or mission, since LaSalle, where the Galloways lived, is 181 miles northeast of Nauvoo while Twelve Mile Grove is an additional 62 miles east.

On January 22, 1838, five years after giving birth to their eighth child, Louisa bore Warren King, their last child and the first of the five sons to be named for his father. "Warren" was the surname of Louisa's mother, Anna Warren, who had died two years earlier. Many family records and LDS Ancestral File information list birth places other than Far West, including Malvern Mills, Iowa, where Warren lived as an adult and where he is buried. However, more detailed biographical information shows his birthplace as Missouri, a few also specifying Caldwell County.

Two months later, King bestowed a "father's blessing" on eleven-year-old William Alexander on March 18, 1838. Joseph Smith Sr. fairly frequently noted in his patriarchal blessings that he was acting because the recipient had no father 'in righteousness" to give such a blessing and, at least once in Kirtland, bestowed a blessing jointly with a worthy father or endorsed the blessing given by such a father.[71] King was a father worthy to bestow such a blessing, and the care taken to make and preserve the record of the blessing suggests its value to William. Although the holograph has apparently not survived, a photocopy of the holograph exists. It shows some underlining, although it is not possible to determine whether these marks were added later. The blessing contains little punctuation, a few misspellings, random capitalization, and some inadvertent repetitions. There is no signature.

> William. Alexander. Follett was born at Portage County, Ohio Dec'r 11 1826
>
> Brother Follett we lay our hands upon thy head in the name of Jesus thy Redeemer and we seal upon thy head a fathers blessing and it shall ever be a great blessing to thee that thou hast a father in the in the new and everlasting Covenant to bless thee and if thou wilt ever listen to the councils of thy father listen to the instructions of thy Mother the blessings of the Heavens and the earth shall be bestowed upon thee and thou shalt grow up into manhood in the Kingdom of thy Saviour and thy name shall ever be registered in the lambs book of life and while thou art in the days of thy Childhood and youth if thou wilt strive to Store thy mind with wisdom and learning thy mind shall expand and thy heart shall be enlarged and the Spirit of the Lord shall be shed abroad in thy heart and while thou art young thou shalt become an Instrument in the hand of the Lord to thrash the nations by the power of his Spirit, and the everlasting priesthood shall be Sealed upon thee. and thou shall push the nations together from the ends of the earth and thy labours shall be crowned with blessings in the Vineyard of the Lord. and thou shalt yet see the gathering of the Saints from the east and from the West. from the North. and from the South and thine Inheritance shall be in Zion
>
> and thou shall become a workman and shall aid in rearing the house of the Lord and the blessing and gift of Architecture shall be given to thee and if thou will live by the words of wisdom the blessing of health Strength and activity shall be bestowed upon thee and thou shall behold and see for thyself the winding up Scene of this Generation and the Stone roll forth from the mountain that shall fill the whole earth and we Seal this fathers blessing upon thee in the name of the Redeemer for ever and ever
>
> Amen & Amen
>
> Given March 18th 1838

A father's blessing, bestowed by King Follett on William Alexander Follett, March 18, 1838, at Far West; photocopy of holograph in my possession.

This father's blessing reads:

> William Alexander Follett was born at Portage County, Ohio Dec 11 1826.[72]
>
> Brother Follett we lay our hands upon thy head in the name of Jesus thy redeemer and we seal upon thy head a <u>fathers blessing</u> and it shall ever be a great blessing to thee that <u>thou hast a father in the in the [sic] new and everlasting Covenant</u> to bless thee and if thou wilt ever listen to the councils of thy father listen to the instructions of thy Mother the blessings of the Heavens and the earth shall be bestowed upon thee and thou shalt grow up into manhood in the Kingdom of thy Saviour and thy name shall ever be registered in the lambs book of life and while thou art in the days of thy <u>Childhood</u> and <u>Youth</u> if thou wilt strive to store thy mind with wisdom and learning thy mind shall expand and thy heart shall be enlarged and the Spirit of the Lord shall be shed abroad in thy heart and while thou art young thou shalt become an Instrument in the hand of the Lord to thrash the nations by the power of his Spirit, and the everlasting priesthood shall be sealed upon thee. And thou shall push the nations together from the ends of the earth and thy labours shall be crowned with blessings in the Vineyard of the Lord.[73] And thou shalt yet see the gathering of the Saints from the east, and from the west, from the north, and from the South and thine Inheritance shall be in Zion and thou Shalt become a workman and shall aid in rearing the house of the Lord and the blessing and gift of archicture [sic] shall be given to thee and if thou wilt live by the words of Wisdom the blessing of health, Strength and Activity Shall be bestowed upon thee and Thou Shalt behold and see for thyself the winding up Scene of this Generation and the Stone roll forth from the mountain that shall fill the whole earth and we Seal this fathers blessing upon thee in the name of the Redeemer for ever and ever
>
> Amen & Amen.
>
> Given March 18th 1838[74]

The promises of future missionary work and being present at the "winding-up scene" were frequent elements in early patriarchal blessings, as were the injunctions to seek knowledge. The promise of a future as an architect is an interesting one, possibly suggesting William's youthful interests and the Saints' renewed focus on building the Far West Temple. I have found no documentary evidence that William ever worked as an architect although he, like most men in Nauvoo, must have contributed his skills and labor to the Nauvoo Temple in Illinois.

Notes

1. Church Education System, *Church History in the Fulness of Times*, 181.

2. Excerpt from "Minutes of a Public Meeting at Liberty, Missouri," June 29, 1836, quoted in *History of the Church*, 2:450–51.

3. Nathan Hale Gardner, "Biographical Sketch of Lucia Streeter Snow," 5.

4. Durward T. Stokes, ed., "The Wilson Letters, 1835–1849: Six Letters from Andersen, Caleb, and Josiah Wilson, Written from Their New Home in Clay County, Missouri, to Their Relatives at Their Old Home in Orange County, North Carolina," 504–5.

5. Max H Parkin, "Latter-day Conflict in Clay County," 255–56.

6. Stokes, "The Wilson Letters, 1835–1849," 508. This source says the total available was 5,300; but adding the specific numbers provided for each county provides a total of 4,300.

7. Edward Channing, *A History of the United States* (1922) 5:488, quoted in "The Wilson Letters," 505 note 31.

8. Public Meeting, Minutes held in Liberty, June 29, 1836, *History of the Church*, 2:450.

9. Ibid., 450–51.

10. *History of the Church*, 2:452–54. These minutes use "citizens of Clay County" from both Mormons and non-Mormons to refer only to non-Mormons, thus implying that neither party considered the Saints true "citizens."

11. Ibid., 2:455.

12. Parkin, "Latter-day Saint Conflict in Clay County," 257.

13. Minutes of the Second Meeting of the Citizens of Clay County, Liberty, July 2, 1836, in *History of the Church*, 2:455.

14. Church Education System, *Church History in the Fulness of Times*, 182.

15. Leland Homer Gentry, *A History of the Latter-day Saints in Northern Missouri from 1836 to 1839*, 23 note 44. Gentry cites *History of Caldwell and Livingston Counties*, 95, but the quotation actually appears on pp. 103–4.

16. Annette W. Curtis, ed., *1836 Clay County, Missouri, State Tax List: All Taxpayers and Land Owners Are Identified Including Mormons and The 1835 Missouri Tax Law*, 2, 18, 47.

17. Ibid., 3.

18. Clark V. Johnson, ed., *Mormon Redress Petitions: Documents of the 1833–1838 Missouri Conflict*, 201. Louisa's dating of 1835 suggests that this was the last year the Folletts spent in Clay County; but I argue that the correct year was 1836. King was in Kirtland during the winter of 1835–36, and Curtis, *1836 Clay County, Missouri, State Tax List*, 14, shows that King was taxed for personal property in Clay County as late as September 1836.

19. Edward Brothers, *An Illustrated Historical Atlas of Caldwell County, Missouri*, 3. Richmond was the county seat of Boone County, lying directly east of Caldwell County.

20. Gentry, *A History of the Latter-day Saints in Northern Missouri*, 29.

21. Emily M. Austin, *Mormonism; or, Life among the Mormons*, 86.

22. Alanson Ripley, "To the Elders Abroad," 39. Ripley was born in New York in 1798 and was a member of Zion's Camp. "He was held for trial at the time of the fall of Far West. The high council directed him to serve as a bishop in Iowa in 1839, but this was reversed in 1841, when the conference failed to sustain him in that position. He was appointed surveyor for Nauvoo in 1841." Donald Q. Cannon and Lyndon W. Cook, eds., *Far West Record: Minutes of the Church of Jesus Christ of Latter-day Saints, 1830–1844*, 285.

23. Alexander L. Baugh, "Jacob Hawn and the Hawn's Mill Massacre: Missouri Willwright and Oregon Pioneer," 1–25.

24. Max H Parkin, *Missouri*, 288 and note 1.

25. Ronald E. Romig, *Early Independence, Missouri: "Mormon" History Tour Guide*, 17.

26. King Follett, Deed, July 28, 1838. See also *United States Land Sales in Missouri, 1827–1903; Index to Land Sales, 1818–1893*, 291.

27. Lorene Elizabeth Burdick Pollard, *Whitmer Memoirs*, 25.

28. John C. Hamer, *Northeast of Eden: A Historical Atlas of Missouri's Mormon County*, 11.

29. *History of the Church*, 3:253; 1:431; 7:135; 2:32–34; 3:284; 4:163–65; 3:7–8, 112, 253.

30. William G. Hartley, "Stand by My Servant Joseph": *The Story of the Joseph Knight Family and the Restoration*, 254–55.

31. "Far West Burial Ground," http://www.farwesthistory.com/mmff-pp.asp (accessed July 4, 2005). For a more detailed discussion of the burial ground's location see Parkin, *Missouri*, 326–27.

32. Twylia G. Brand, *Deeds, Jackson County, Missouri*, 1:44.

33. Cannon and Cook, *Far West Record*, 111, 115–16.

34. Ibid., 121, 125–26. A map in Hartley, *Stand by My Servant Joseph*, 254, places the east boundary of King's land adjoining the west boundary of the enlarged townsite.

35. Glen M. Leonard, *Nauvoo: A Place of Peace, a People of Power*, 11.

36. "A History of the Persecution of the Church of Jesus Christ of Latter Day Saints in Missouri," *Times and Seasons* 1, no. 5 (March 1840): 65–66.

37. Reed Peck, quoted in Gentry, *History of the Latter-day Saints in Northern Missouri*, 30.

38. Judge Joseph Thorp, quoted in *History of the Latter-day Saints in Northern Missouri*, 30.

39. Jacob Gates, Journal, August 1836, Vol. 1, 70–71. Gates was born in Vermont and came directly to Clay County after his conversion. An active Mormon in Missouri and Illinois, he served more than one mission, was a member of the First Quorum of the Seventies, and died in Utah in 1892. Cannon and Cook, *Far West Record*, 262.

40. Hartley, *Stand by My Servant Joseph*, 258.

41. *History of Caldwell and Livingston Counties, Missouri*, 121.

42. Peter H. Burnett, quoted in Pearl Wilcox, *The Latter-day Saints on the Missouri Frontier*, 190–91.

43. John Bush, quoted in ibid., 168–70.

44. John P. Greene, *Facts Relative to. . .*, 18.

45. Lyman Wight, quoted in Johnson, *Mormon Redress Petitions*, 656.

46. Baugh, *A Call to Arms*, 14 and Appendix A. I believe that the James Daily, identified on this list as a sergeant in Samuel Brunson's Co., is probably James Daley, who later married Nancy Follett. See pp. 173, 176.

47. Cannon and Cook, *Far West Record*, 146.

48. *History of the Church*, 3:6.

49. Baugh, *A Call to Arms*, 14.

50. Gentry, *History of the Latter-day Saints in Northern Missouri*, 36.

51. The minutes recorded in the *Far West Record* sometimes use the name "High Council in Zion."

52. It is difficult to tell exactly what the numbering system for the council meetings actually indicated. A footnote in Cannon and Cook, *Far West Record*, 157, regarding the March 24, 1838, meeting notes "that the council changed composition, that is, it had different members, every time it met in this period."

53. Lyman Wight, a native of New York, was baptized in November 1830, was a strong Church member in Missouri and Nauvoo, was called as an apostle by Joseph Smith in 1843, but later broke with Brigham Young, and died in Texas.

54. Cannon and Cook, *Far West Record*, 111.

55. Also see *History of the Church*, 1:242–45 and 267–69.

56. Cannon and Cook, *Far West Record*, 122.

57. Richard Lyman Bushman, *Joseph Smith: Rough Stone Rolling*, 332.

58. Cannon and Cook, *Far West Record*, 122–23.

59. Ibid., 179–81. "Death or bonds" refers apparently to types of punishments for violation.

60. Ibid., 198.

61. Seventies Quorums, Record of Members, 1844–94, Twentieth Quorum Record, Provo, Utah, Family History Library, Microfilm #25554. In September Newman would have just turned eight; his father would have been fifty. This record was created in 1857, after the Williams family had moved to Utah.

62. Kamas Ward, Summit County, Utah, Record of Members: Annual Genealogical Report, 1870–1948, 16:538.

63. Samuel Williams, "Account Book," 158, quoted by Gay Aleen Mitchell, Letter to Joann F. Mortensen, September 29, 2004; photocopy of account book entry in my possession. She is a descendant of Samuel and Newman.

64. *History of the Church*, 3:252, 4:13, 7:297.

65. Keith W. Perkins and Donald Q. Cannon, eds., *Ohio and Illinois*, 124.

66. Samuel Williams, in www.rootsweb.com/~raymondfamily/AlonzoRaymondLineage (accessed July 12, 2005). This database dates Samuel's death as 1855 in Ogden, Utah, and 1915 in Summit, Utah, for Newman. Some of these records give Newman's full name as "Newman Bishop Williams." His mother's name was Ruth Bishop.

67. "Martin Wood," in Seventies Quorums, "Record of Members of the Quorums of the Seventy, 1844–94," 66. Wood next appears on the record in Wellsville, Cache County, as a member of the 17th Quorum of Seventy. He served a mission to England in 1863 and died "on the Weber river, Utah, in October, 1874," leaving a wife and three children. Andrew Jenson, *Latter-day Saint Biographical Encyclopedia*, 3:738.

68. Christy L. Best, Letters to Joann Mortensen, April 16, 2003, and August 30, 2006. She is a descendant of Charles Galloway.

69. Lyman D. Platt, ed., *Jeremiah Leavitt II and Sarah Sturtevant*, 21. Sarah's surname is spelled "Studevant" in Joseph Page Leavitt, *Story of Jeremiah Leavitt (III) and Autobiography of Sarah Studevant*. Joseph is a grandson.

70. "Genealogy of Jeremiah Levet," in "A Record of Genealogies, Biographies etc., appertaining to the 20th Quorum of Seventies," in Seventies Quorum, *Record of Members of the Quorum of Seventy, 1844–94*, Sixteenth Quorum, Item 111. Interestingly, King's grandson, Warren King Follett, married Jeremiah's great-granddaughter Mary Emily Hamblin on August 28, 1871, in Salt Lake City. Follett family records in my possession.

71. See, e.g., H. Michael Marquardt, ed., *Early Patriarchal Blessings of the Church of Jesus Christ of Latter-day Saints*, 181.

72. Many family and Church records give his birth date as November 12, 1825, or 1826.

73. At this point there is a mark that appears to be the top half of an exclamation point, but it is not centered over the period.

74. William Alexander Follett, Father's Blessing, March 18, 1838.

❧ Chapter Eleven ❧

At War in Northern Missouri

> *In 1838 occurred what is commonly known as the Mormon war, although there was but little of real war about it. It was a very respectable war for those days, however, and had some of the elements of genuine martial strife about it.*—an 1881 history[1]

The Follett family and others like them who had moved from Clay County enjoyed a year of relative peace after settling in Far West. They were in a county created especially for them. Had their numbers remained small, perhaps this unique settlement situation would have worked out. But as the Church grew in total membership, converts began moving there in larger numbers, settling not just in Far West but in other settlements throughout the county. In addition, Mormons also began to settle in nearby Daviess County to the east and eventually in other surrounding counties. Many of those moving into the towns and areas east of Far West were new converts who had not been with the Church during the early Missouri persecutions. One of them, Thomas Daniel Stillwell, remembered that, for the first year and a half after arriving with his family in April 1837, they "enjoyed peace," raised ample corn, sweet potatoes, and hogs, kept bees, had everything they needed and were "surrounded with the blessings of heaven and earth. We regretted not the homes we had left behind.... The mobs by this time [fall of 1838] had comenced [sic] their attacks [sic] on Adam mondi amon [sic] in Daviess county and I was called

Major Mormon War sites in Northern Missouri. Milton V. Backman Jr. and Richard O. Cowan, *Joseph Smith and the Doctrine and Covenants*, Map 4. Used by permission of Milton V. Backman.

three times that fall to assist in repelling those attacks. Each of these times we did witnes [sic] many of the houses of the saints in a blase."²

When Caldwell and Daviess counties were created, Missourians assumed that Daviess County would be reserved for nonmembers, though there is not a lot of evidence that the Mormons understood the situation this way. Apparently there were no legal restrictions to prevent Mormons from expanding into that area. When Joseph Smith moved permanently to Far West in March 1838, according to historian Stephen C. LeSueur, "the Mormon population in northwestern Missouri was probably between three and four thousand" but seven months later, "over five thousand Mormons, including several wagon companies with more than two hundred people, migrated to the state. Thousands more were expected.

With Caldwell rapidly filling with immigrants, Mormon leaders made plans to expand throughout the upper counties of Missouri."[3]

During 1838, more than 8,000 Church members moved to Missouri, which not only increased Far West's population but "Mormons soon outnumbered Daviess County Missourians by two to one, and the 40 to 50 Missourians in DeWitt were inundated by 150 to 200 Saints. This dramatic growth led some Missouri extremists to charge that the Mormons were bent on taking over all the western counties of Missouri."[4] One Caldwell County historian emphatically declared that the "more lawless of them [Mormons] strolled about the country taking what they pleased. They largely outnumbered the Gentiles in Caldwell county, and Mormons held all of the important county offices. All efforts, therefore, to punish them for their crimes and misdemeanors were wholly inoperative, and the citizens felt justified in resorting to mob violence and retaliation in kind."[5]

Whether that description is accurate, a modern history of the area describes the conduct of the Church members in this way:

> Unfortunately many Mormons lacked tact, and claimed their Church intended to possess the land—that they were the "chosen people" with the only "true Church." Many of their leaders counseled the Saints to be discreet and live their religion, which the majority did; however, rumors, often unfounded, were enlarged upon, increasing with every telling. Consequently the original landowners felt threatened and were easily stirred up by lawless and angry men, some of them former members of the Mormon Church who roamed the frontier looking for excitement and trouble.[6]

During the nine months between August of 1838 and April of 1839, a chain of events once again culminated in the expulsion of the Mormons, including the Follett family, from an area they had begun to call home. However, this time in addition to religious persecutions and mob violence, activities by Mormons—real or perceived—brought other elements into the picture, elements that modern historian Alexander L. Baugh summarizes as "dissenters, Danites, and the resurgence of militant Mormonism."[7] King's involvement in some of these events can be documented. In other situations, due to proximity, his participation seems reasonable.

When Joseph Smith arrived at Far West in March 1838, he immediately became involved in internal leadership difficulties. For months, dissension had been mounting against the three men serving as the Missouri Stake presidency: David Whitmer, W. W. Phelps, and John Whitmer. The controversy centered on perceived misuse of Church funds in land purchases and general disregard of Church policies and the Prophet's direction. Just before the Prophet's arrival in Far West, the high council had, in an unprecedented move, expelled all three members of the stake presidency from their office. They were later excommunicated, along with Oliver Cowdery, assistant Church president, and other Church leaders for various transgressions. The high council minutes do not identify King specifically as a member of the high council at this time. On April 6–7, 1838, the Church held its first quarterly conference in Far West to celebrate "the [eighth] anniversary of the Church of Jesus Christ of Latter Day Saints and to transact Church business."[8] All members of the Church were invited, and almost certainly the Follett family would have attended. As a part of the business conducted, the sacrament was administered and ninety-five children were blessed.[9] As King's youngest son, Warren King, was just three months old, he could have been one of the children receiving a blessing. One week later on April 13, 1838, Hannah Follett, King's mother died at age eighty-nine in Winchester, New Hampshire.[10] It seems unlikely that King could have received any word of her passing promptly, because of the unrest in his immediate circumstances. In fact, his New Hampshire relatives may not even have known where he was living.

About three weeks later on April 26, the Prophet received a revelation that made "known the will of God concerning the building up of that place and of the Lord's House" (D&C 115). Among the items of business were an official name change to "the Church of Jesus Christ of Latter-day Saints," the designation of Far West as "a holy and consecrated land" upon which "I command you to build a house [temple] unto me, for the gathering together of my saints, that they may worship me," and instructions to lay the temple cornerstones on the "fourth day of July next" (D&C 115:4–10)—in a little more than two months.

The dissenters who had been excommunicated, along with dissenters from Kirtland, quickly began to cause problems for the Church at large and for some individual members. One tactic they used was filing civil lawsuits against the Church in general and against Joseph Smith individually. "He considered these suits 'vexatious,'" comments Baugh, "and partly used by his detractors as a means of tying up his time and draining both personal and Church resources in an attempt to defer [sic] him from his more important spiritual and ecclesiastical responsibilities."[11] In addition, according to John Corrill, Caldwell County's representative to the state legislature, "The dissenters kept up a kind of secret opposition to the Presidency and the Church. They would occasionally speak against them, influence the minds of the members against them, and occasionally correspond with their enemies abroad."[12] Since similar tactics by dissenters in Kirtland had contributed to Joseph Smith's decision to leave Ohio and establish Church headquarters in Far West, Church leaders resolved not to be forced out again by harassment. They, therefore, as a first step, began an active campaign with the aim of expelling the dissenters. Joseph Smith visited settlements throughout the area, preaching against "hasty judgments, or decisions upon any subject given by any people, or in judging before they had heard both sides of a question." He also accused the dissenters of "throwing out insinuations here and there, to level a dart at the best interests of the Church, and if possible destroy the character of its Presidency."[13]

In June, a second step was the organization of Mormon men into a group commonly called the Danites at Far West. A second Danite group was organized at Adam-ondi-Ahman the latter part of July. Modern historians agree that the organization existed, but other areas remain a matter of question: Who were the organizer(s) and leader(s)? What was the group's intended purpose and its actual activities? Who belonged to this organization? What did Joseph Smith and other Church leaders knew about the group, and what was their level of participation?[14] An organization with secret oaths and hand signals, it originally functioned to force the excommunicated dissenters out of the county. This action taken by Church members to solve the problem of "unwanted" citizens seems ironic, considering that the same tactics had been used against the Mormons in Jackson and Clay counties. Eighty-three Mormons signed a letter sent to Oliver Cowdery, David Whitmer, John Whitmer, William W. Phelps, and Lyman E. Johnson, warning: "There are no threats from you—no fear of losing our lives by you, or by any thing you can say or do, will restrain us; for out of the county you shall go, and no power shall save you. And you shall have three days after you receive this communication *to you*, including twenty four hours in each day, for you to depart with your familes [sic] peaceably; which you may do undisturbed by any person; but in that time, if you do not depart, we will use the means in our power to cause you to depart; for go you shall."[15] King's name does not appear on this letter although those of long-time Church friends and neighbors do. Taking the threat seriously, all but Phelps fled to a nearby county; but the plan backfired in that they continued their hostile activities in company with the increasingly concerned Missourians.

The Danites may have taken on other tasks in the coming weeks; but its main purposes seems to have been either protecting the Saints from anti-Mormonism or retaliating against aggressors. A less well known purpose was to provide assistance, food, shelter, and other necessities as the Mormon War escalated during August, September, and October.[16] Luman A. Shurtliff, one of these Danites, later explained: "I was invited to unite with a society called the Danite society. It was got up for our personal defense, also for the protection of our families, property and religion. Signs and pass words were given by which members could know the other wherever they met, night or day. All members must [settle] difficulties if he had any with a member of the society, before he could be received." He and other Church men used the Danite "signs and countersigns to know each other" during the time he was placed on guard in Daviess County to "protect the rights of the Saints there."[17]

In October, the Prophet acting upon advice from General Alexander Doniphan, organized the members of the church into military groups both at Far West and Adam-ondi-Ahman for the purpose of self-protection.[18] Historian Leland Gentry refers to these groups as the "Armies of Israel" whose "commanding officers … held an official commission as Colonel from Governor Lilburn W. Boggs, commander of all the State's troops," and speaks of them as being separate and distinct from the already formed Danites under the direction of Sampson Avard. Gentry explains: "It was natural, however, for enemies of the Church to confuse the activities of the legitimate militia with those of the Danite band."[19] *History of the Church* adds: "And here let it be distinctly understood, that these companies of tens and fifties got up by Avard were altogether separate and distinct from those companies of tens and fifties organized by the brethren for self-defense in case of attack from the mob."[20] Unfortunately, Danite anti-mob activities closely resembled those of anti-Mormon mobs or vigilantes. Joseph Smith took a strong stand in announcing that the Church would no longer suffer persecution passively. The formation of militia units in Mormon towns, though legal, eroded what was at best an uneasy peace in Caldwell County.

Whatever the view of the Danites from within the Church, non-Mormon historians writing of the Danites and their influence, interpreted it as a threatening and actively hostile vigilante group. A 1970s history of Clinton and Caldwell counties, places the date of the formation of the Danites as August 1838. "About this time the 'Danites or Destroying Angels' were organized of the bravest and best of those who were considered true Mormons for the special purpose of burning and destroying. Guns were gathered and put in order and ammunition secured."[21]

The first public appearance of the Danites was July 4, 1838, in Far West. King, Louisa, and their children were probably among the large group of members who attended an Independence Day celebration in the town square. This event was apparently not noted in any civil record as a 1997 publication states that the first Independence Day celebration in Caldwell County was held in Kingston on July 4, 1843—five years later when the Saints had already relocated to Nauvoo.[22] Though all members knew that the Church had been denied certain religious rights guaranteed by the Constitution and although they doubtless felt some uneasiness about the future, their farms were thriving and there was much to celebrate, including the prospect of a temple. The *History of the Church* records that the "order of the day was splendid" and continues: "The procession commenced forming at 10 o'clock a.m., in the following order: First, the infantry (militia); second, the Patriarchs of the Church; the president, vice-president, and orator; the Twelve Apostles, presidents of the stakes, and High Council; Bishop and counselors; architects, ladies and gentlemen. The cavalry brought up the rear of the large procession, which marched to music, and formed a circle, with the ladies in front, round the [temple] excavation."[23] Then the temple's cornerstones were laid in accordance with the revelation received in April. "The southeast cornerstone was laid by the presidents of the stake, assisted by 12 men; then the other three were laid clockwise by other priesthood holders. After each stone was laid, the band played a tune."[24] King had been listed as a member of the high council in April and November of 1837, and two days following this July 4th celebration was identified as being in the leadership of the Seventies. It is therefore likely he was one of the priesthood holders who participated in this ceremony.

The event's main speaker, Sidney Rigdon, then delivered a lengthy oration in which he lauded the freedoms enjoyed in America, including religious freedom, then gave a brief history of persecution suffered by Mormons. Next, he emphasized a new approach for the entire Church, that of resisting abuse and persecution. Obviously becoming more intense as his talk continued, Rigdon issued a powerful warning:

> Our God has promised us a reward of eternal inheritance, and we have believed his promise. . . . The promise is sure and the reward is certain. . . . We have suffered their abuse without cause . . . but from this day and this hour, we will suffer it no more. . . . We warn all men in the name of Jesus Christ, to come on us no more forever, for from this hour, we will bear it no more, our rights shall no more be trampled on with impunity. The man or the act of men, who attempts it, does it at the expense of their lives. . . . We will never be the aggressors, we will infringe on the rights of no people; but shall stand for our own until death. We claim our own rights, and are willing that all others shall enjoy theirs. . . . We this day then proclaim ourselves free, with a purpose and a determination, that never can be broken, "no never! no never!! NO NEVER!!!"[25]

Rigdon, formerly a Baptist-Campbellite minister, was an important early convert, recognized as one of Joseph's advisers and a close friend. A native of Pennsylvania, he acted as scribe to Joseph and at this time was serving as a counselor to Joseph in the First Presidency of the Church. As a gifted and very effective orator, his burning words and impassioned delivery would have had a deep impact. Perhaps more significant, Joseph Smith, who was present, did not modify Rigdon's extreme statements. Furthermore, he gave permission for the oration to be published and distributed. Thus, for whatever reason, it seems logical that Joseph Smith subscribed to these defiant statements.

Emily M. Austin, a young LDS mother with two children, who attended the celebration but who later left the Church, recorded her personal dismay, doubtless shared by nonmembers also attending the celebration. As Rigdon concluded, "Three loud and long cheers and amens rent the air. At this, a very great excitement arose among the old settlers, and Rigdon's life could not have been insured for five coppers. The people were all crazy with excitement, running and rushing to and fro, and tumbling one over another in every direction. I must say I was rejoiced to make exit with my two little children, with the help of my husband."[26]

Even a few days later after the immediate excitement had subsided, the Prophet further endorsed the speech in an editorial in the *Elders' Journal*. He recommended that all Saints obtain a copy of the speech, confirmed its description of unceasing persecution, and affirmed the new policy of defiance: "The persecutors, who are, and have been, continually, not only threatening us with mobs, but actually have been putting their threats into execution; with which we are absolutely determined no longer to bear, come life or come death, for to be mobbed any more without taking vengeance, we will not."[27]

Alexander Baugh summarizes the implications of this event:

> Clearly, by summer of 1838, the Mormon leader's position was that his people were justified in taking up arms against those who perpetrated acts of violence or forced opposition against the Latter-day Saints. This essentially remained the Prophet's position throughout the three months of conflict which followed. . . . The oration generated a newfound militancy in the Church, particularly among Danite leaders and their initiated members. . . . [They] seized the opportunity to strike back, at the same time challenging the local regularly constituted militia as to which organization was in control.[28]

For the Missourians, the new policy became a reason as well as an excuse for even more aggression against the Mormons. For the Mormons, including the Danites, the new policy justified retaliation and even attacking first.

Warren Foote, who had just moved to the Far West area but had not yet been baptized, described his first impressions of the town on September 6: "Far West is situated on a high rolling prairie between Shoal creek on the north, and Goose creek on the south, which empties into Shoal creek a short distance east of Far West. The houses are very scattering, and small, being chiefly built of hewed logs. The basement for the Temple is dug, and the corner stones were laid the 4th of July last. The town contains one printing press, one tavern, and a few small stores, and groceries. It will be a beautiful city, if it is ever built up, as it is intended to be."[29]

However, beneath this lovely surface ran tensions and mistrust. Local Mormon militias sprang up. It seems likely that King would have belonged to his local groups, along with nineteen-year-old John. The involvement of thirteen-year-old William Alexander seems less logical because of his age; however, there is evidence of some involvement of young people. Helen Mar Kimball (later Whitney), the ten-year-old daughter of Heber and Vilate Kimball, recalled that she and her older brother were "fired by the spirit of war . . . [and] prepared for it by making wooden guns, swords and flags, and the latter were hoisted to the topmost part of our fence or cabin . . . and at the martial sound of fife and drum we would start to our feet and march with as much enthusiasm as though we belonged to a regiment of soldiers."[30] As another example, Samuel Kendall, a seventeen-year-old living six miles east of Far West "joined a military company, had a pistol about one foot long and a spear in the end of a long pole with which I trained, stood guard, etc. I was ready to fight in defense of Zion, although I was young and small for my age."[31]

By late summer there were a number of smaller Mormon settlements in four other counties north and east of Far West—Daviess, Clinton, Livingston, and Carroll—and the Mormon population in this area was growing. It was in one of these settlements where the first major incident of the Missouri conflict occurred.

A concern of the old settlers had always been the fear that the increasing number of Mormons meant that, when they achieved a numerical majority, they would control county government. For their part, Church members viewed voting as a privilege guaranteed to them just as to everyone else and some were determined to vote, despite a few threats if they did. August 6, 1838, was election day in Gallatin, a small town consisting of approximately ten cabins in Daviess County. About eleven Saints showed up to vote. One, John Lowe Butler, who lived about thirteen miles away, estimated that "forty to fifty Missourians" were present.[32] Immediately, these men began a barrage of insults against the Mormons, also threatening them not to try voting. Soon a fist fight ensued, and blows were struck by both sides. Butler used a large oak club. "John considered the affair, which lasted but 'two minutes from the first to the last blow,' a minor fracas compared to election fights in [his home state of] Kentucky."[33] A non-Mormon observer, Joseph McGee, "termed the election brawl 'the great knock down between the Mormons and the Missourians.'"[34] Apparently election-day fights were not unusual on the nineteenth-century frontier, especially since alcohol was usually consumed in quantity by the all-male participants.

However, rumors exploded of serious injury and death. Joseph Smith promptly led about 150 men, identified by some as a "Mormon Posse" from Far West to protect members in Daviess County from the threat of retaliation. Because such preparation and immediate action was a Danite goal, it can be safely assumed that at least some of these men were Danites. According to Alexander Baugh, "The men who joined the ranks of the Mormon outfit likely came from parts of both Caldwell and Daviess counties and were a mixed company of Mormon volunteers, regular militia, as well as members of the newly created Danite society. Approximately 120–150 men were recruited."[35]

After speaking with John Butler about threats against him personally, the Prophet instructed him to "go and move them [his family] directly and do not sleep another night there." Butler obediently "started on to far West and my wife folow'd me the next day. We stopt on the west side of far West and went into Folletts farm to live."[36] John left Far West the next day to join a group of men on their way back to Daviess County. Though King had not been at Gallatin for the election, he may have been in the "Mormon posse" or may have gone there with John, leaving both the Butler and Follett families at King's farm. At the least, King and his family willingly gave shelter to the Butler family. They may have shared the same cabin, as the Butlers brought only what they could carry in two wagons. It is not known how long the Butlers stayed with the Folletts before making other living arrangements, but John's wife and children remained in Far West at least for a while.

For the rest of August, through September, and into the middle of October, events escalated rapidly, though the Saints were still acting largely in self-defense. But the line between officially constituted militia and vigilante groups soon became blurred. Albert Rockwood, a thirty-three-year-old member from Massachusetts, noted in his journal on October 22 that the "armies of Isreal [whom he identified as Danites] that were established by revelation from God are seen from my door evry day with their Captains of 10.s50.s&100." The group spent part of each day drilling, then divided into squads to perform such tasks as providing meat, wood, meal, and other provisions, building cabins, caring for the sick, and acting as spies and guards.[37]

The official and legal Caldwell County militia doubtless consisted primarily of Mormons as few nonmembers were living in the county by that time. Church members anticipated that Caldwell County, particularly Far West, would be a main target. Warren Foote reported in his journal on September 6:

> I went up to Far West. The militia of this county, who were all 'Mormons', had been ordered to meet at this place, to take measures to defend themselves against the mob; who were still actively engaged in spreading false reports, to incite the Missourians, to arise and drive the 'Mormons' from the state. The report was, that they had set this day to begin their driving. Their place of operations at this time is in Daviess County, joining Caldwell on the north, and which is very thinly settled. They were not yet bold enough to attack Caldwell County.... The militia at Far West, were ordered not to leave ... under penalty of law, but to hold themselves as minutemen, and be ready at a moments warning, armed and equipped to repel the mob.[38]

I hypothesize that King was probably a member of the county militia at Far West and stayed in the town, unless he was already somewhere else in Caldwell or Daviess County. Louisa and the children probably remained at their home just west of town. Families in the outlying areas would soon be moving into the town itself for protection.

Following the Gallatin incident, harassment of Church members by Missourians in a variety of configurations rapidly increased in counties where members of the Church lived. Some filed affidavits falsely accusing Joseph Smith and Lyman Wight, then a counselor in the stake presidency in Adam-ondi-Ahman, the largest town in Daviess County, of threatening the lives of citizens and of attempting to intimidate Adam Black, a local Justice of the Peace in Daviess County. Reports also circulated that Smith and Wight were going to be arrested.[39] Hoping to avoid violence, the two men agreed to attend a preliminary hearing. Even though evidence was presented that the affidavits were false, the circuit court judge, Austin King, ignored this evidence and "ordered the defendants to stand trial.... Smith and Wight submitted to the verdict without protest, but they believed, as did most Mormons that they were being unjustly persecuted for defending their rights in Daviess County. They regarded King's decision as evidence that they would not receive justice from local government officials."[40]

Judge King's decision seemed designed to satisfy the old settlers rather than insure the rights of the defendants. Unfortunately for Joseph and the Saints, this method of handling conflict at the government and court level was reflected throughout all of the coming events, and the

Saints had considerable evidence for their belief that they would not receive justice from local or state officials. King Follett, one of five who would be arrested in Far West on November 14 or 15, no doubt shared this belief based on his personal experience.

Between August 6 and October 17, Mormons from Caldwell County came at least three times to protect the Saints in Daviess.[41] Both sides wrote to Governor Lilburn W. Boggs appealing for state intervention, even though Boggs, a resident of Independence, had participated in expelling the Mormons from Jackson County in 1833. The state militia was periodically activated to keep the peace, further blurring the line between legal and extra-legal groups.

American frontier history includes numerous episodes during which disagreements erupted into violence, some of it lethal. With tempers on both sides at fever pitch in northern Missouri, relatively minor incidents quickly developed into explosive overreaction, each incident justifying the use of even stronger measures. The same pattern of conflict was repeated in southeast Carroll County at the Mormon settlement of DeWitt on the Missouri River. The Saints had used its steamboat landing as they moved down from Ohio in July 1838. By early October, the Mormon population was estimated at 420, which included a party of approximately 150 members from Canada traveling in thirty wagons. Near the landing, a grove soon became known as Mormon Hill because it was "filled with wagons and tents and was referred to as a 'village of canvas.'"[42] Almost immediately, the old settlers began using physical force and intimidation against the Mormons, ordering them to leave the county in early August. When the Saints refused, the next six weeks saw a pattern of continued harassment with an occasional shot fired by either side. No one was seriously injured; but on September 20, an armed posse demanded that Church members leave within ten days. The Saints responded that they were prepared to fight.

On October 1, a company of Missourians marched on DeWitt, "burning the home of one Mormon family and driving out settlers along the way. Both sides began shooting ... with intermittent firing continuing for several days ... Only one person, a non-Mormon, was wounded."[43] They then settled down to a ten-day siege of the town. Cut off from their farms outside the town, the Saints rapidly ran out of food. "Many of the Saints were also sick due to the adverse conditions, lack of shelter (many were living in wagons), and no medical aid. Silent death was literally staring them in the face."[44] Meetings of participants and mediators failed to resolve the situation, and both sides sought assistance from outside the county. The Missourians received "a steady number of volunteers" as reinforcements, while Joseph Smith and two groups totaling about sixty-two men leaving from Far West on October 5, brought the Mormon defenders to approximately 130.[45] King was apparently in one of these groups since, in 1840, Mormon Elias Higbee, then negotiating with Congress for redress, asked Joseph Smith to "select a number of firm brethren, possessing good understanding, who will tell the truth. . . . I will suggest a few names—Alanson Ripley, King Follett, Amasa Lyman, Francis M. Higbee, as they know concerning the De Witt scrape."[46]

Caldwell old citizens incorrectly estimated the number of armed Mormons in DeWitt as between "five and six hundred" and urged those in adjoining counties to "come by fives and tens, if you cannot come by companies; bring all you can."[47] Several sympathetic nonmembers, perceiving the injustice inflicted on the Saints, sent affidavits to the governor, Lilburn W. Boggs, imploring his intervention. He refused, saying that "the quarrel was between the Mormons and the mob" and they "might fight it out."[48]

The ten-day siege was successful. The Mormons at DeWitt surrendered on October 10 and were given twelve hours to leave. When the victors entered the town, they found that the members were already packing. According to Baugh, "They also noted that the people were in distressful circumstances. . . . [When] two of the most hostile vigilante leaders, saw the deplorable conditions of the women and children they were brought to tears."[49] The beleagured Saints quickly traveled to what they hoped would be safety in Far West. But by the time the DeWitt refugees reached Far West, Saints from all over the surrounding area had already been "pouring into the town of Far West, from day to day, with women, children, goods, provisions, etc: in short, with everything moveable which they had time to bring. Lands and crops were abandoned to the enemy. The citizens were under arms from day to day, and a strict military guard was maintained every night. Men slept in their clothes, with arms by their sides, and ready to muster at a given signal at any hour of the night."[50] King's family in his absence probably stayed in their home just on the western edge of the town limits and may have sheltered other members as they moved to the town itself.

William Huntington noted on an unspecified October 1838 date: "The war become more Severe we [in Daviess County] ware under the necessity Of calling on the brethren at far west For help until they ware under the Necessity of calling on us at diahman For all the forces to be sent to far west."[51]

At a special meeting held at Far West on October 14, four days following the surrender at DeWitt, the Prophet Joseph reaffirmed the Church's position to protect members in Daviess County. Because he made this statement at a Sunday meeting, the Follett family may well have attended. Warren Foote's journal reads:

> October 14, 1838: . . . Joseph Smith preached. He said that those who would not turn out to help to suppress the mob, should have their property taken to support those who would. He was very plain and pointed in his remarks, and expressed a determination to put down the mob or die in the attempt . . . . Joseph said that he wanted all the people (men) of Caldwell County to assemble at Far West tomorrow, [October 15th] in order to find out who will fight, and who will not. He said that the Mormons would have to protect themselves, as they could not put any dependence in the militia of the state; for they were mostly mobocrats. . . .
>
> October 21, 1838: The "Mormons" assembled at Far West last Monday, [October 15th] according to appointment, and about 300 volunteered to go to Daviess County, with Joseph Smith, to assist their brethren, while the rest were to stay, and guard this town.[52]

It seems probable that King was one of these 300 volunteers. The Mormons were taking the offensive. Although officially it was the Caldwell County militia whom the Prophet called out, all of its members were all Mormons and undoubtedly many were Danites. Since this move involved having a county militia sent into Daviess County, to make this mobilization legal, Joseph obtained an "official" call-up from "a Caldwell County judge (probably Elias Higbee)," who was a Mormon, and he "issued the call-out for Mormon volunteers to defend Far West *and* march into Daviess."[53] The Prophet identified the "special object of this march" as protecting Adam-ondi-Ahman and "repel[ling] the attacks of the mob in Daviess county."[54] William Hartley expands that explanation: "Their military purposes were several: to rescue endangered Saints . . . to spy, . . . drive off vigilantes plundering in the county, to destroy buildings housing enemy sympathizers or supplies, to retaliate in kind for Mormon homes that had been burned, to retrieve Saints' possessions ... [and] to forage for food, clothing, bedding, and supplies to support the army and the hard-pressed families at Far West and Diahman. Killing was not a part of the plan, and none occurred."[55]

Warren Foote emphasized that the "Mormons were not the first aggressors, neither did they threaten to murder every thing." When the Missourians found that the "Mormons were too much for them, they set fire to their own houses, and fled into the adjoining counties, and spread the report that the Mormons had burned their houses, and drove them from their homes."[56] When the Prophet arrived at Diahman, he reported seeing homes burned and animals driven off. He expressed strong emotions as he described the suffering of the Saints: "[Members] fled into the town for safety, and for shelter from the inclemency of the weather, as a considerable snowstorm took place.... Women and children, some in the most delicate condition, were thus obliged to leave their homes and travel several miles in order to effect their escape ... almost entirely destitute of clothes, and only escaping with their lives. ... Agnes M. Smith, wife of my brother, ... had traveled nearly three miles, carrying her two helpless babes, and had to wade Grand river."[57]

The Mormons' offensive plan was to attack areas in Daviess County where members had already had troubles or where it was known that the Missouri militia were congregating—primarily, Gallatin, the county seat, and Millport, about three miles to the east. Both were very small towns but were used as Missourian staging areas from which they made forays into the surrounding area. The Mormons believed that Joseph Smith had directed them to find, rescue, and protect Saints still in the area. Some felt that they also had the right to find and take personal property that could be used by Church members; others apparently decided there were no limitations on what they could take or destroy.

On the morning of October 18, a Mormon posse rode to Gallatin, which they looted and set fire to. They then repeated these activities in Millport. By the end of October, most non-Mormons had been forced out of the county. Although no contemporary records exist of these events, later recollections report varied activities and strongly emotional reactions.

George W. Worthington and Joseph H. McGee, nonmember residents of Gallatin, each owned a store. Worthington reported that the

Mormons took his horse, saddle, bridle, and store account books and that both his home and his store were burned. He reported a loss of about $700 worth of property, much of which he later saw in Mormon homes in Diahmon. McGee, who was in Worthington's home when the Mormon attack came, reported that the Mormons took many items from his store, then burned the building. "I saw the Mormons taking the goods out of the store house, and packing many of the articles off on their horses; a number of barrels and boxes were rolled out before the door."[58] McGee added:

> We could stand in our door yard and see houses burning every night for over two weeks. The Mormons completely gutted Daviess county. There was scarcely a Missourian's house left standing in the county. Nearly every one was burned.... The Mormons secured all their property and took it to DeAmmon (DiAhman) and there placed it in what was termed the Lord's Store house, to be issued out to Saints as they might need [it]....
> This was a hard winter on the early settlers of the county. Robbed of all they possessed by the Mormons, and compelled to raise money to enter their homes, or lose them.... Had it not been for the bountiful supply furnished by nature in the way of provisions, many would have suffered.[59]

Benjamin F. Johnson, a Mormon who participated in these events of October 18, in his autobiography acknowledged he served in "foraging companies" that took "whatever we could find, without regard to ownership . . . corn, beef, cattle, hogs, bee stands, chickens, etc." He felt that some Mormons were looters; but "while others were pillaging for something to carry away," he tried to help women and children who were trying to evacuate their homes in a snowstorm.[60]

Supporting the most positive explanation for Mormon activities, Richard Lloyd Anderson cautions: "Non-Mormon families in Daviess County were dispossessed during the last half of October, but careful history should not adopt the propaganda that Mormons indiscriminately burned out Daviess County.... It is risky to make generalizations now or to accept uncritically all those made at the time."[61] He then cited sources that speak of "razing for security" homes where weapons were "held for the use of the mob" or "burning the place used as a base of operations." He concluded: "Survival required taking what was available, a reality only understandable in the light of accounts of Mormons who barely escaped from their homes and were barred from returning to get either possessions or crops."[62] The *St. Louis Republican* editorialized in early December, after the Mormon War's conclusion, that there was no evidence that the Mormons "offered any resistance to the properly constituted authorities of the county, civil and military," but rather that they naturally "desire[d] to protect themselves, their families and their property, from the licentiousness of a mob; and they did, furthermore, retaliate upon some portion of that mob, for burning Mormon houses and Mormon property in one county, by doing a similar act of injustice in another."[63] In fact, the very individuals who had complained to the governor about the Mormons had been the first to carry out the same actions against the Mormons.

James Bennett Bracken, a Mormon, later defended Joseph Smith's directions: "On another occasion when the mob was on us, and some of the brethren would do things they should not have done, such as appropriating to their own use things that did not belong to them, Joseph called us together and said that he felt to because of the acts of men; some, he said, are doing things that will cause the blood of the brethern [sic] to run. He was referring to stealing."[64]

Needless to say, with such heavy destruction being carried out by both sides, any semblance of a normal life became impossible. There is no way to document the extent of the damage inflicted by either side; but instead of the fall harvest's being brought in, crops had been trampled, livestock shot, and homes abandoned, burned, or demolished. Citizens on both sides felt they had to flee for their own safety. Thus, neither side appears to have been the victor, though reports were rampant that the Mormons had driven the Missourians out of Daviess County, even as Mormons were streaming into Far West with reports of being driven out. In the meantime, in spite of letters to the governor from local government officials and citizens groups, Boggs did not respond officially for days. Perhaps he felt that the situation would take care of itself. That is exactly what happened, but not in any positive way.

With the situation in Daviess County at a stalemate, action erupted in Ray, Carroll, Livingston, and Clinton counties with small groups from both sides participating in scattered raids. Some of the non-Mormon citizens, alarmed by reports of Mormon activities and fearing for the safety of their farms, homes, and families, began leaving their homes. By October 22, when Joseph Smith returned to Far West, those reports included the false information that Mormon troops returned to Far

West from terrorizing Daviess County planning to raid Ray County, just south of Caldwell County. The scene was set for the next major "battle" of the war.[65] About fifty or sixty Mormon families were scattered across the northern part of Ray County. On October 24, Captain Samuel Bogart, commander of the Ray County militia, stationed on Crooked River about fourteen miles south of Far West, began patrolling the countryside in Ray County, but also crossed the county line into Caldwell County. A few years later, Hyrum Smith swore an affidavit that Bogart led about 150 men and, in late October, was "sending out his scouting parties, taking men, women and children prisoners, driving off cattle, hogs and horses, entering into every house on Log and Long creeks, rifling their houses of their most precious articles, such as money, bedding and clothing, taking all their old muskets and their rifles, or military implements, threatening the people with instant death, if they did not deliver up all their precious things and enter into a covenant to leave the state or go into the city of Far West by the next morning."[66]

During these raids, Bogart's men took three Mormons prisoners, Nathan Pinkham, William Seely, and Addison Green, and held them at their camp on Crooked River. Fearing that the prisoners might be killed, Judge Elias Higbee mobilized the Caldwell County militia, then all Mormon.[67] Far West was then being guarded twenty-four hours a day with its men ordered "to be ready and on hand at the sounding of a bass drum," as Drusilla Hendricks recalled. "At three taps on the drum my husband would be on his horse in a moment, be it night or day."[68]

Approximately sixty militia members mounted up that night to ride to Crooked River and free the prisoners, the first pitched battle, though a brief one, between the combatants. King's name does not appear among these sixty listed in contemporary records. Reed Peck's testimony, given on oath at the Richmond court of inquiry about three weeks later stated, in reference to participants in the expedition from Far West into Daviess County: "My impression is, that King Follet [sic] was not in that expedition [Daviess County]; but he was captain of 12 men in Far West, under the Danite order, as I understand, as he was neither an officer nor private of militia, and was known and called under the fictitious name of Captain Bull, and his company was called the regulators."[69] This hearing was held immediately after King Follett and four others were added to more than fifty men already arrested.

Crooked River Battleground site, Ray County, Missouri, May 15, 1907, George Edward Anderson Collection, LDS Church History Library. Used by permission.

The context of Peck's testimony would indicate that King's main arena of personal involvement at that time would have been in the Far West area and probably at Crooked River. D. Michael Quinn hypothesizes that King, "acting President of Seventies, age 50," fought at the Battle of Crooked River and that the Mormon participants were Danites.[70] B. H. Roberts, when writing about prisoners still jailed in Missouri in 1839 after the escape of Joseph Smith and others, stated in a footnote: "These were Parley P. Pratt, King Follett, and Morris Phelps. Held on a trumped-up charge of murder because of the part they took in the 'Battle of Crooked River.'"[71] A Follett family tradition has described King as one of the Prophet's bodyguards and characterized him as a "Mormon vigilante" like Orrin Porter Rockwell. Peck's reference to the nickname of "Captain Bull" would support this tradition.[72]

The Battle of Crooked River was described by Albert Perry Rockwood: "A more severe battle perhaps never was fought when we consider the smallness of the number, and the shortness of the time which was about 1

Present site of Crooked River Battle area, Ray County, Missouri. Photo by Irval L. Mortensen, 2006.

½ minutes."[73] However, based on other reports of activities which included the use of guns and ammunition and hand-to-hand contact, it seems that a longer estimate would be more logical. The Mormons forced Bogart and his men to retreat across the Crooked River. At that point, the Mormons, who had rescued the three prisoners, broke off pursuit. One man on each side was killed. Nine Mormons were wounded, two of whom later died. At least six of Bogart's men were wounded.[74] Rumors rapidly circulated that the Mormons had been the aggressors and had killed most (or even all) of Bogart's men. Governor Boggs finally took action but, instead of investigating, sent a letter on October 27 to Major-General John Clark, commander of the Missouri militia: "The Mormons [are] in the attitude of an open and avowed defiance of the laws, and of having made war upon the people of this state.... The Mormons must be treated as enemies, and must be exterminated or driven from the state."[75]

Expecting that the Mormons would now begin a full-scale attack everywhere in northern Missouri, Clark and his subordinates began mobilizing the number of men believed necessary to prevent further bloodshed, a figure estimated at more than five thousand. Whether acting as part of the authorized militia or pushed by their own emotions, the Missourians stepped up their attacks on Mormon settlements and individuals. The Church responded by more urgent instructions to gather to either Far West in Caldwell County or Diahman in Daviess County. According to LeSueur, "Both towns overflowed with refugees.... Over a thousand people gathered at Diahman, where only thirty to forty homes stood. Most families lived in tents or wagons. At Far West, which had a normal population of about two thousand, between three and four thousand Mormons filled the town to overflowing."[76]

In addition to shortages of food and a lack of shelter, the Mormons' sufferings were intensified as the winter weather came on. Anson Call described conditions in Far West beginning October 24:

> The weather continued severely cold.... They killed our cattle, stole our horses, burnt our houses, constantly killing and abusing all that they met with, insulted our women, murdered some of our children. We were not permitted to leave Far West, only to get our firewood. We had not the privilege of hunting our cattle and horses.... We were deprived of holding meetings of any kind. Some few times in the course of the winter, slyly we congregated ourselves in a school-house about 2 miles from Far West to receive instructions from Joseph and others.[77]

About fifteen families who had not yet followed the Prophet's direction to move to Far West and Diahman, along with about fifteen additional families who had just arrived from Kirtland, were at Haun's Mill on Shoal Creek, about sixteen miles east of Far West, close to the border of Caldwell County with Livingston County. This area was one of the earliest Mormon settlements in Caldwell County and, beginning October 25, had previously been the scene of a few minor disagreements between local Mormons and the Livingston County militia. On October 30, more than two hundred Missourians attacked the mill site, killing men and children with guns, knives, and clubs. When the carnage was over, seventeen Saints had been brutally massacred and two more died later.[78] The survivors had saved their lives by fleeing to the nearby woods or feigning death.

Joseph Young, who had just arrived from Kirtland, had been threatened en route "with instant death" and told they could not enter Missouri because they were Mormons. Managing to evade these Missourians, they had just settled into an empty cabin when the attack came about 4:00 P.M. His account paints a horrendous picture of the mob members "charging up to the [blacksmith's] shop," and aiming "directly [through the crevices] at the bodies of those who had there fled for refuge from the fire of their murderers." One Mormon man "was shot with his own gun after he had given it up, and then was cut to pieces with an old corn cutter."[79] Young also told of a nine-year-old who was discovered after the massacre by a Missourian who "presented a rifle near his head and literally blew off the upper part of it ... and boasted of this fiend-like murder and heroic deed all over country."[80] A non-Mormon source, *History of Caldwell County* reports property depredations which followed: "After ... all the able-bodied male Mormons had been killed, wounded or driven away, some of the militiamen began to 'loot' the houses and stables at the mill. A great deal of property was taken.... Those who were in a position to know say that the Mormon hamlet was pretty thoroughly rifled."[81]

News of the attack reached Far West the next day, October 31, where the town was surrounded and under siege by the Missouri state militia under the direction of Major-General Samuel D. Lucas. The Folletts and their neighbors and friends must have expected the worst.

Notes

1. *History of Carroll County, Missouri*, 243.

2. Thomas Daniel Stillwell, Letter to Editor & Readers of the *Lehi Post*, undated, 1–2.

3. Stephen C. LeSueur, *The 1838 Mormon War in Missouri*, 29.

4. Alma R. Blair, "Conflict in Missouri," 46.

5. *History of Carroll County, Missouri*, 247.

6. Beth Shumway Moore, *Bones in the Well: The Haun's Mill Massacre, 1838, A Documentary History*, 22.

7. Alexander L. Baugh, *A Call to Arms: The 1838 Mormon Defense of Northern Missouri*, 33.

8. Donald Q. Cannon and Lyndon W. Cook, eds., *Far West Record: Minutes of the Church of Jesus Christ of Latter-day Saints, 1830–1844*, April 7, 1838, 158. See also *History of the Church*, 3:13–15.

9. Exactly what was meant by "blessing" the children in the early years of the Church isn't clear. If each child was blessed individually, as is the current practice with infants, blessing this number would have taken an excessively long time. The current practice combines blessing and naming, comparable to a "christening," but usually performed by the infant's father in the first sacrament meeting of a month.

10. Death date on Hannah's headstone, Evergreen Cemetery, Winchester, New Hampshire, copied during personal visit in 1999.

11. Baugh, *A Call to Arms*, 35.

12. John Corrill, quoted in ibid., 35.

13. *History of the Church*, 3:27.

14. For analysis of and perspectives on the Danites, see Baugh, *A Call to Arms*; Leland Homer Gentry, *A History of the Latter-day Saints in Northern Missouri from 1836 to 1839*; Leland H. Gentry, "The Danite Band of 1838"; Leland Homer Gentry and Todd M. Compton, *Fire and Sword: A History of the Latter-day Saints in Northern Missouri, 1836–39*, chap. 8; LeSueur, *The 1838 Mormon War in Missouri*; Stephen C. LeSueur, "The Danites Reconsidered: Were They Vigilantes or Just the Mormon Version of the Elks Club?" 35–52; Dean C. Jessee and David J. Whittaker, eds., "The Last Months of Mormonism in Missouri: The Albert Perry Rockwood Journal," 5–41.

15. *Document Containing the Correspondence, Orders, &c.*, 103.

16. Jessee and Whittaker, "The Last Months of Mormonism in Missouri," 23.

17. Myrtle Ballard Shurtliff, *Record of Family and Journal of Luman A. Shurtliff*, 23. Shurtliff was a native of Massachusetts, joined the Church in 1836 in Kirtland, and came to Utah.

18. *History of the Church*, 3:162.

19. Gentry, *A History of the Latter-day Saints*, 117.

20. *History of the Church*, 3:181–82.

21. Carrie Polk Johnston and W.H.S. McGlumphy, *History of Clinton and Caldwell Counties, Missouri*, 234.

22. "July 4th in Caldwell County," 1:49. This short article was originally presented as part of a series of radio programs in 1984.

23. *History of the Church*, 3:41.

24. Max H Parkin, *Missouri*, 311.

25. Peter L. Crawley, "Two Rare Missouri Documents (1834, 1838)," 527. The second document is "Oration Delivered by Mr. S. Rigdon, on the 4th of July, 1838, at Far West, Caldwell County, Missouri (Far West, Missouri: The Journal office, 1838)." Crawley notes that this oration "is exciting inasmuch as it is the only 'book' printed by the Mormon press at Far West." The frontispiece of the original publication contains a quotation from an unidentified source: "Better far sleep with the dead, than be oppressed among the living."

26. Emily M. Austin, *Mormonism: or, Life among the Mormons*, 88.

27. "In this paper, we give . . .," *Elders' Journal of the Church of Jesus Christ of Latter-day Saints*, 4 (August 1, 1838): 54. Two issues of this periodical were published in Kirtland, Ohio, in 1837 while the other two were published in Far West, Missouri, in 1838. Don Carlos Smith, the Prophet's brother, is listed as editor, but this entry lists "Joseph Smith, Jr.," as editor.

28. Baugh, *A Call to Arms*, 39.

29. Garth Homer Killpack, ed., *Autobiography and Journal of Warren Foote*, 28. Warren was born in New York and, after reading the Book of Mormon, went to Kirtland where he joined the Church. He moved with Mormons to Missouri and Illinois, where he was baptized in 1842, and then went to Utah where he died in 1903.

30. Richard Neitzel Holzapfel, ed., "Nauvoo Remembered: Helen Mar Whitney Reminiscences," Part 4, 8.

31. Samuel Kendall Gifford, "Reminiscences, 1864," 4. Gifford was born in 1821 in New York, was baptized in 1833 in Jackson County, and was one of the earlier settlers of Manti, Utah.

32. William G. Hartley, *My Best for the Kingdom: History and Autobiography of John Lowe Butler, a Mormon Frontiersman*, 52.

33. Ibid., 57.

34. Joseph McGee, quoted in ibid.

35. Baugh, *A Call to Arms*, 48.

36. Hartley, *My Best for the Kingdom*, 392.

37. Jessee and Whittaker, "The Last Months of Mormonism in Missouri," 23. Unlike Gentry, Rockwood appears to make no distinction between groups of "10, 50s and 100s" under the direction of Avard as Danites and similar groups formed by the Prophet.

38. Killpack, *Autobiography and Journal of Warren Foote, 1817–1903*, 28.

39. LeSueur, *The 1838 Mormon War in Missouri*, 67–68, 77.

40. Ibid., 83.

41. Parkin, *Missouri*, 362.

42. Ibid., 506–8.

43. LeSueur, *The 1838 Mormon War in Missouri*, 102.

44. Baugh, *A Call to Arms*, 75.

45. Ibid., 73–75.

46. *History of the Church*, 4:87.

47. "Letter to the Citizens of Howard County," October 7, 1838, quoted in Baugh, *A Call to Arms*, 73 note 86.

48. *History of the Church*, 3:157.

49. Baugh, *A Call to Arms*, 74 note 95.

50. Scot Facer Proctor and Maurine Jensen Proctor, eds., *Autobiography of Parley P. Pratt: Revised and Enhanced Edition*, 223.

51. William Huntington, "Reminiscences and Journal, April 1841–August 1846," 4. This statement itself is not dated but the preceding entry with a date is October 1, 1838.

52. Killpack, *Autobiography and Journal of Warren Foote*, 42.

53. Baugh, *A Call to Arms*, 85.

54. *History of the Church*, 3:162.

55. Hartley, *My Best for the Kingdom*, 69.

56. Killpack, *Autobiography and Journal of Warren Foote*, 43.

57. Joseph Smith, quoted in *History of the Church*, 3:162–63.

58. Joseph H. McGee, quoted in *Document Containing the Correspondence, Orders, &c.*, 141.

59. Joseph H. McGee, *Memoirs of Major Joseph H. McGee*, quoted in Rollin J. Britton, *Early Days on Grand River and Mormon War*, 29.

60. Benjamin F. Johnson, *My Life's Review*, 37–39.

61. Richard Lloyd Anderson, "Atchison's Letters and the Causes of Mormon Expulsion from Missouri," 30.

62. Ibid. Anderson's analysis of circumstances in Daviess County are based on his review of letters written by David Rice Atchison, a lawyer hired by the Church after the Mormons were expelled from Jackson County in 1833. During the next five years, Atchison was an important player in Missouri both in civil matters for the Church and as a major general in the Missouri state militia. Thus he, more than most others, might have provided a balanced opinion, having participated in activities of both sides. Atchison was removed from his military post because, during the siege of Far West, he refused to follow Governor Boggs's extermination order.

63. Article in *St. Louis Republican*, reprinting article in *Arkansas Gazette*, December 5, 1838, quoted in Richard Lyman Bushman, *Joseph Smith: Rough Stone Rolling*, 371.

64. James Bennett Bracken, Statement, November 6, 1881, 10–11.

65. Gentry, *A History of the Latter-day Saints in Northern Missouri*, 138–39.

66. Hyrum Smith, "Testimonies Given before the Municipal Court of Nauvoo," in Clark V. Johnson, ed., *Mormon Redress Petitions: Documents of the 1833–1838 Missouri Conflict*, 622.

67. *History of the Church*, 3:169.

68. Drusilla Hendricks, "Drusilla Dorris Hendricks (1810–1881)," in Kenneth W. Godfrey, Audrey M. Godfrey, and Jill Mulvay Derr, eds., *Women's Voices: An Untold History of the Latter-day Saints, 1830–1900*, 89.

69. Reed Peck, Testimony, in *Document Containing the Correspondence, Orders, Etc.*, 119. Reed Peck was an active member of the Church until his

disagreement with Joseph and other leaders during the Missouri conflict prompted him to testify against Church leaders in the November hearing. His testimony, coupled with those of others with similar disagreements, was the reason the Prophet was bound over for trial about events in Daviess County and at Crooked River.

70. D. Michael Quinn, *The Mormon Hierarchy: Origins of Power*, 481. Quinn has constructed his list of those at the Battle of Crooked River from several sources and also cites Peck's testimony (which names King) and that of Sampson Avard (who does not).

71. Brigham H. Roberts, *A Comprehensive History of the Church of Jesus Christ of Latter-day Saints: Century I*, 531 note 27. Accounts vary about King's arrest, the time he spent in jail, and the reason for the arrest. Roberts attributes King's arrest and imprisonment to the same charges (murder) as those against Pratt and Phelps. However, a careful reading of available records does not support that interpretation. See Chapter 12.

72. Peck identifies the aliases of other leaders as Captain Fearnought and Captain Black Hawk.

73. Jessee and Whittaker, "The Last Months of Mormonism in Missouri," 25. Rockwood places the number of Mormon men at 55 and the "Mob No." at about 70.

74. For details of the battle, see Baugh, *A Call to Arms*, 102–8; Gentry, *A History of the Latter-day Saints*, 141–43; LeSueur, *The 1838 Mormon War in Missouri*, 137–42; *History of the Church*, 3:170–72.

75. Governor Lilburn W. Boggs, quoted in Baugh, *A Call to Arms*, 109. Major-General John Clark was then the Missouri militia's commanding officer.

76. LeSueur, *The 1838 Mormon War in Missouri*, 154–55.

77. Ethan L. Call and Christine Shafer Call, *Journal of Anson Call*, 13–14. Anson Call was born in Vermont and owned land in Kirtland (1837–38) where he was ordained an elder. He was in Missouri and Nauvoo and came west to Utah. His reference to "murdered some of our children" must be referring to the events at Haun's Mill as I could find no other source for children being killed in Far West.

78. Moore, *Bones in the Well*, 21.

79. Joseph Young and Jane A. Young, Statement, in Johnson, *Mormon Redress Petitions*, 721–23.

80. Ibid., 723.

81. Quoted in Roberts, *A Comprehensive History of the Church*, 148, note 36.

❊ Chapter Twelve ❊

Siege, Surrender, and Eviction

On October 27, 1838, Governor Lilburn W. Boggs finally took action and issued an order now known as his Extermination Order. Although "extermination" now has only the meaning of "killing," Webster's 1828 dictionary gives a broader first definition: "exterminate: to drive out, to eradicate, annihilate, destroy completely."[1] In retrospect, Boggs's action was reprehensible. Repeatedly requested to provide protection for the Mormons, both from their members and neutral nonmember observers who were upset over the treatment of the Saints, and further asked by his military leaders in the field to come to the area to get a first-hand view of the issues, instead he based his decision to potentially use lethal force against a people and a religion on reports he had received. The validity of those reports was questionable at the best and blatantly untrue at the extreme. Furthermore, Far West was already besieged and a Missouri vigilante unit had already committed the massacre at Haun's Mill before Boggs's order reached them in the field. In essence, he was providing a quasi-legal cover for on-going armed attacks.

There is no way to specifically document the location of King, Louisa, and their children (ages nineteen, fifteen, thirteen, five, and ten months), nor that of daughter Adeline with her husband Nathan West, and his two young daughters, ages eight and five. However, because their home was just west of the town limits of Far West, they were probably still there and, if so, had doubtless welcomed other families who had moved in for protection, either sharing their home or offering places where they could erect makeshift shelters. Far West almost doubled its population during those frightening weeks. Under normal circumstances, the Church members lived in log cabins, one-room frame houses, or even tents if they lacked means to build more substantial homes.[2] Thus, even before the great influx of refugees, most Mormon families would have been living in primitive, crowded dwellings, although many other residents in frontier Missouri may have shared those conditions.

By the time of the attack on Haun's Mill on Tuesday, October 30, but before word of that event reached Far West, a large troop of state militia under General Samuel D. Lucas began approaching Far West from the south. Male Mormons—probably a combination of county militia, Danites, and any man who had a weapon and was willing to use it—moved to meet them from the north, hoping to avoid an invasion of Far West. During a temporary standoff, some negotiations began by representatives of both sides. Obviously doubting that conditions could be resolved, the citizens of Far West took defensive actions. "The militia of Far West guarded the city the past night, and arranged a temporary fortification of wagons, timber, etc., on the south," reported the *History of the Church*. "The sisters, many of them, were engaged in gathering up their most valuable effects, fearing a terrible battle in the morning, and that the houses might be fired and they obliged to flee. The enemy was five to one against us."[3]

Negotiations were continuing the next morning, Wednesday, October 31, when the shocking news of Haun's Mill was delivered to the Prophet Joseph. This was the final blow in many weeks of seeking a peaceful settlement. Outnumbered and threatened with quasi-legal annihilation, thanks to the governor's Extermination Order, Joseph Smith and his advisors had to make a decision quickly. Would they be able to stand off the state militia? If so, for how long? Was there any possibility of a stable settlement? What kind of future would they face in a state that had been so willing to employ violence? If they continued to resist, what would be the ultimate cost in lives and property?

Faced with these facts, Church leaders agreed to more formal negotiations, believing that whatever surrender terms were agreed upon would be handled through the proper government channels. The state's proposal as delivered in writing, by General Lucas, demanded:

1st. To give up their leaders to be tried and punished.

2d. To make an appropriation of their property, all who had taken up arms, to the payment of their debts, and indemnify for the damage done by them.

3d. That the balance should leave the State, and be protected out by the militia, but to be permitted to remain under protection until further orders were received from the Commander-in-Chief.

4th. To give up the arms of every description, to be receipted for.[4]

Lucas also insisted that, while the details were being worked out, five Church leaders including Joseph Smith must be "hostages" to insure compliance. The Prophet, knowing that he did not have the power to protest and that it would be unwise to resist what he believed were the governor's orders, agreed to be considered a "prisoner" overnight (October 31) but expected to be released the next morning. As soon as he and the other four—Sidney Rigdon, Parley P. Pratt, Lyman Wight, and George W. Robinson—arrived in the militia camp, it was apparent that their imprisonment would not be temporary. Rather, filled with unholy glee, the Missourians subjected their prisoners to obscene jeers and threats. They were forced to sleep on the ground in the freezing rain. In the morning, they were still heavily guarded, and two more prisoners joined them, Hyrum Smith and Amasa Lyman. Thus, the state achieved its first demand: the surrender of the Church's leaders.

The *History of the Church* briefly but concisely describes events of Thursday, November 1:

> The officers of the militia held a court martial, and sentenced us to be shot, on Friday morning, on the public square of Far West as a warning to the "Mormons." However, notwithstanding their sentence and determination, they were not permitted to carry their murderous sentence into execution. Having an opportunity of speaking to General Wilson, I [Joseph Smith] inquired of him why I was thus treated. I told him I was not aware of having done anything worthy of such treatment; that I had always been a supporter of the Constitution and of democracy. His answer was, "I know it, and that is the reason why I want to kill you, or have you killed."
>
> The militia went into the town, and without any restraint whatever, plundered the houses, and abused the innocent and unoffending inhabitants and left many desolate. They went to my house, drove my family out of doors, carried away most of my property.[5]

The prisoners were not released as had been anticipated. Rather, the militia began imposing its will on the terrified inhabitants of Far West. The terms of the state's proposal required that the Mormons surrender all their weapons and deed their property to the state to pay for the war's expenses. King was one of the hundreds of men forced to appear in the town square at Far West that morning and submit to the first step of this despoiling. Luman A. Shurtliff described the scene:

> The mob formed a hollow square and we soon, with muffled drums, marched into the place prepared for us. While on our way, each man who had a spear stuck the blade into the ground and broake [sic] it off and then dropped the handle. We formed a square within the square the mob had formed for us. We were faced inward, our backs towards our enemies, they being about sixty feet in our rear. We occupied this position for several hours which gave us time for sober reflection. A short time since, we expected by this time that many of the mob, and perhaps some of us would be in eternity. We had laid our arms down and were sitting or lying on them. In the rear of me I could hear the mob swear to God they would shoot us dead and could hear them talk against us. . . . Many thoughts ran through my mind while sitting on the ground.[6]

William G. Hartley describes Newel Knight's actions: "Newel said that when a bugle sounded, he grabbed his rifle and joined the militia in the town square. Newel and the rest marched in military formation, their band playing Washington's death march, and surrendered their guns. The Saints were now defenseless."[7] John Lowe Butler, with considerable reluctance, surrendered his rifle and sword. "It was councilled by the brethren to lay down our arms for it would be better for Joseph and Hyrum. I laid down mine."[8] However, later his granddaughter "said that John called the surrendering of his arms 'the hardest thing he ever did.'"[9] John also recorded with admiration the defiance of thirty-one-year-old Alexander McRae. He "walked into the middle of the square and looked around him upon the black looking villains. And then swung his sword around his head and threw it, point foremost till it struck the ground and buried it in the ground eight or ten inches, and said 'if you got my arms you have not got my spunk.'"[10]

Even after the Mormons surrendered their arms, the militia held them in the town square, sitting on the ground until about noon. After an initial search of homes to confiscate other weapons, the men were allowed to leave the town square, but the militia posted guards so that no one could enter or leave the city itself. Some families were forced to spend the rest of the day and that night separated by these guards, unable to locate each other or determine the condition of family members. Gunshots and shouts were heard throughout that long and unsettling night. The Saints would have been even more concerned had they known that, only a few miles away, Joseph and the other prisoners were undergoing a mock trial, jokingly referred to as a military court, where their very lives were saved only because Alexander W. Doniphan, also a general in the Missouri state militia, refused to carry out Lucas's order to "take Joseph Smith and the other prisoners into the public square of Far West, and shoot them at 9 o'clock to-morrow morning."[11]

After a long, dreary night, the men of Far West were once again called to the town square early on Friday morning, November 2, where tables had been set up. According to participant John P. Greene: "Whilst the town was guarded, we were called together by the order of Gen. Lucas, and a guard placed close around us, and in that situation were compelled to sign a deed of trust for the purpose of making our individual property all holden, as they said, to pay all the debts of every individual belonging to the church, and also to pay for all damages the old inhabitants of Daviess may have sustained in consequence of the late difficulties in that county."[12] Alexander Baugh adds more details: "On this occasion a table was set up and papers laid out by a committee comprised of three Missouri officials: William Collins (Jackson County), George W. Woodward (Ray County), and Judge Cameron (Clay County), with John Corrill and Morris Phelps representing the Mormons. One by one, each man was escorted up to the table by a guard at the point of [a] bayonet where they signed their names to the documents. Then they held their arm up to the square and acknowledged that they were freely and voluntarily deeding their property over to the state in order to pay for the expenses of the war and the damages done in Daviess County."[13] Like the surrender of weapons the day before, once again the Mormon men recognized they had no choice but to comply. Luman Shurtliff wrote: "If any of us had refused to sign this deed, from all appearances, we would have been shot down or taken to prison or shared a worse fate, if possible."[14] Nathan Tanner's action was typical of the defiance felt by the men. He threw down his pen after signing and said: "It looks like a free volunteered act and deed—at the point of a bayonet."[15]

Under the guise of a search for further weapons, raiding and pillaging by the state troops continued throughout all the northern part of Missouri. No Church member in any location could be free from fear under such circumstances. Thirty-two-year-old Joseph Holbrook in Far West reported the militia's depredations in his autobiography written sometime before 1871: "The mob or militia burnt my house, stole a valuable horse from me, killed my fat hogs, drove off my stock. I had some 300 bushels of the best of corn in the crib taken out of the crib. They fed our oats in the sack, destroyed my hay, and left everything in a state of desolation from one end of the county to the other, abusing the sisters whenever they thought it best to suit their brutal and hellish desires."[16]

Joseph Smith and the six prisoners with him were brought into Far West for display in the town square, then were allowed to briefly bid farewell to their families and gather a few items of clothing before being taken to Independence in Jackson County, a distance of approximately sixty miles. From there, they went on to Richmond in Ray County.[17] Back in Far West, Major-General John B. Clark, whom Governor Boggs had designated commander of the state militia as a part of the Extermination Order,[18] arrived to replace General Lucas "with one thousand six hundred men." An additional "five hundred . . . were within eight miles of the city."[19] He again assembled the Mormon men in the town square on Monday, November 5, and called for the surrender of fifty-six men[20] who were accused of treason, robbery, arson, and murder. They were marched off to Richmond the next day where they joined the Prophet's group for a hearing.[21] (A few days later, King Follett and four others were arrested in a separate action and joined this group in Richmond.) In the square, Clark read out an address, telling the remaining men (including King) that they now had the "privilege of going to your fields and providing corn, wood, etc. for your families" and that "it now devolves upon you to fulfill the treaty that you have entered into."[22] He reminded them that they were required by treaty to leave Missouri but that because of the severe winter weather, they could wait until spring and "for *this* lenity you are indebted to *my* clemency . . . but you must not think of staying here another season, or of putting in crops, for the moment you do this the citizens will be upon you." He added stingingly:

> The character of this state has suffered almost beyond redemption, from the character, conduct and influence that you have exerted, and we

deem it an act of justice to restore her character to its former standing among the states....

You have always been the aggressors—you have brought upon yourselves these difficulties by being disaffected and not being subject to rule—and my advice is, that you become as other citizens, lest by a recurrence of these events you bring upon yourselves irretrievable ruin.[23]

Clark also emphasized that Governor Boggs had stressed in a letter to him: "If the Mormons are disposed voluntarily to leave the state, of course it would be advisable in you to promote that object, in any way deemed proper. *The ringleaders of this rebellion, though, ought by no means to be permitted to escape the punishment they merit.*"[24]

Albert P. Rockwood gave various estimates of the number of Clark's troops. He "arrived with 1600 men as malitia [sic] 600 more within eight miles." When Clark left, Rockwood said that he "came last Sunday with about 3000 men but has now retired." Rockwood also claimed that Boggs called "10,500 men . . . into the field . . . [and] also ordered 19,500 men to stand ready at a moment."[25] These figures seem very high, considering that Missouri's total population at the time, according to U.S. Census records, was 383,702—including women, children, slaves, and men unable to serve in the military.[26] Rockwood also lamented: "These troubles make a sifting in the Church. Many have denied the faith, but they are those that were week [sic] before in most cases. Some however have denied that have long been in good standing."[27] Many of these individuals who denied the faith, especially those in leadership positions, were later excommunicated but not before their testimony at the Richmond hearing in November had a severe impact on Joseph and his companions.

Both groups of prisoners arrived in Richmond on November 9. The large group from Far West had walked approximately thirty miles. Apparently no plans had been made for housing so many prisoners. Three sites are referred to as jails, meaning that Mormon prisoners were incarcerated in all three during this time. The seven, who included Joseph Smith, were lodged in a vacant log house, where they remained until November 28. Apparently considered to be at high risk for escaping, they were all chained with leg-irons about two feet apart. They prepared their own meals from raw materials fetched in. Their guards were reported as both friendly and abusive.[28]

The other group, mostly heads of families, were "penned up in a cold, open, unfinished court house, in which situation they remained for some weeks, while their families were suffering severe privations."[29] When King and his group of four others were arrested on either November 14 or 15, they were initially also kept in this courthouse. The hearing was held in the courthouse's south end on the same floor where the men were being held.

A third site was "a building built for a jail. . . . used after the preliminary hearing for prisoners who were kept longer in Richmond and [who were] not among those sent to Liberty Jail." This site was located at what is now the southeast corner of Shaw and North Main Street.[30] King was imprisoned in this building when he was arrested for a second time in either March or April, 1839, with five other Mormon prisoners. Almost forty years later on June 1, 1878, this jail, then a utility shop, was destroyed when a tornado struck Richmond. This tornado also severely damaged the courthouse, although it is not completely clear whether this was the finally finished 1839 courthouse or a new one, which had been constructed by 1856.[31] All three jails were apparently within two blocks of each other.

The Missouri Mormon Frontier Association and the city of Richmond dedicated a marker on October 15, 2006, at the third site to commemorate all three Richmond jails used during the Mormon War. I attended the ceremony and copied the information on the marker. The names of all of the known Mormon prisoners from all available sources, who were incarcerated at any time in any of these three locations, were inscribed on the marker. King Follett's is one of sixty-names listed.[32] The marker reads:

RAY COUNTY JAIL SITE
Mormon Prisoners Held in Richmond November 1838

The Mormon Prophet Joseph Smith and other church leaders were held prisoners in Richmond, Missouri, while their people were preparing to leave the state of Missouri. The infamous Extermination Order stated that they could be shot on sight if they refused to leave. The Mormon leaders were imprisoned in three locations; in the unfinished courthouse on the square; in a log building in the middle of the block north of the square, which can be seen from Buchanan Street; and here in the Ray County jail. It was in the log building one night that Joseph Smith stood in full majesty of righteous indignation, bound by chains, and ordered the guards in the name of Jesus Christ to cease their vile obscenities. The terrified guards huddled in a corner the rest of the night. Later Joseph Smith and some of the others

Overlooking the town of Richmond, Missouri, May 10, 1907. George Edward Anderson Collection. LDS Church History Library. Used by permission.

were transferred to Liberty Jail. Parley P. Pratt was transferred to this jail. Here he wrote about eighty pages of his memoirs. Parley was later sent to the jail in Columbia. The church leaders were imprisoned until the last of the Mormons had been driven from the state.[33]

Additional research since 2006 suggests possible differences in the specific locations of both the old log house in which Joseph Smith was imprisoned and the location of the unfinished courthouse. In a 2008 issue of the *Missouri Mormon Frontier Foundation Newsletter*, researcher John Craig noted:

> We do know that the prisoners were kept in a vacant old log house. We know that it was north of the Square. Lyman Wight says that it was 20 rods north of the unfinished brick courthouse on the square, that is 330 feet.... Additional information now gleaned from original deeds and records housed in the Richmond County offices, local histories and updated onsite measurements now yield a more accurate conclusion. The best evidence currently available is that the old log court house was not on the block north of the Public Square and no one knows where it was. The old vacant log house was

in the block north of the Public Square and was in the north east quarter of block 46, north of the alley in that block."[34]

During a visit to Richmond in 1907, LDS photographer George Edward Anderson visited what he called the "old jail" site and noted in his diary: "Made negatives of place where old jail stood that Parley P. Pratt and Morris Phelps were confined in. . . . [The] Powell brothers have a blacksmith shop on part of the ground. Showed me the ashes (wood) from the fireplace. Also the bricks etc of foundation. One of the brothers has a key that belonged to the jail, which was demolished by the cyclone which struck Richmond June 1, 1878. . . . The old jail was on the street North of David Whitmer's."[35] A footnote by Anderson's editors states: "The location of the jail is between Shaw and Thornton Streets, one block north of the David Whitmer home."[36]

Regardless of the exact location of these buildings in Richmond, what is important to the Prophet and other prisoners like King Follett were the events that occurred within their walls.

With the Mormons jailed, the next step was to determine whether they should be tried under military or civil laws. "Mormon sources indicate he [General Clark] clearly believed the military statutes should take precedence in the case, and he immediately addressed a letter to the governor's office requesting a ruling. In addition, the major general dispatched an aide to Ft. Leavenworth to secure a copy of the military code. In the meantime, however, much to Clark's disappointment, Circuit Court Judge Austin A. King ruled that the civil courts had jurisdiction"[37] and decided to charge them under civil law with crimes ranging from burglary and robbery to treason and murder. Official proceedings began on November 12 and concluded on November 29. Although many sources refer to it as a "trial" or "court of inquiry," it was actually a preliminary hearing to determine if there was sufficient evidence to hold the defendants for trial. Most of the witnesses were called on behalf of the state (the prosecution), although most of them had been members of the Church at one time but had since defected. A few were still active members who were forced to testify or face prosecution themselves. The prosecution focused on documenting the Mormons' involvement in the Battle of Crooked River as evidence of treason. According to historian Pearl Wilcox, Judge King, who had been involved when Joseph was first arrested in Daviess County and who was a known anti-Mormon, "appeared extremely anxious to fasten the crime of treason upon the prisoners, knowing that if a charge of such character was sustained he could refuse them bail."[38] Mormon attorney Gordon Madsen writing in 2004, however, comments: "Treason can only be committed against the United States, not against an individual state, as clarified by the *Lynch* case in 1814."[39]

The prosecution presented considerable evidence about the Danites, attempting to prove that Joseph Smith not only knew about the group, but actually organized its members and either led them or directed them as they "plundered" the countryside. The entire transcript of the hearing is a 228-page document, of which 131 pages, the "evidence" section, was also published separately. Testimony by thirty-nine prosecution witnesses took up forty-nine of the fifty-two pages of specific testimony in the evidence section. The remaining three pages comprise the testimony for the prisoners by seven witnesses.[40] Interestingly, judging by their names, three of the seven defense witnesses were women, while all prosecution witnesses were male. The remainder of the evidence section consists of printed depositions and affidavits.[41]

Because the printed document lacks careful dates, it is not always clear when a witness actually testified. According to *History of the Church*, witnesses for the prosecution testified from November 13 to November 18.[42] Reed Peck was the tenth witness out of the total of thirty-nine and probably testified on November 14 or 15. His published testimony begins on page 116; and during his testimony, the following statement is inserted in parenthesis on page 119: "At this stage of the examination of Reed Peck, the following named defendants, viz: King Follet [sic], Samuel Bent, Ebberry Brown,[43] William Whitman, and Jonathan Dunham, were brought to the bar of the court, and put upon their trial for the offences alleged against the other defendants; and, time being allowed them to employ counsel, they retired, and again returned to the bar, appearing by their counsel, Messrs. Rees and Doniphan.[44] The examination of Reed Peck was then continued."[45]

Although this record does not provide an exact date, the sequence of events seems clear. King may have been arrested while he was still in Far West and brought to the hearing in Richmond and added as a defendant, perhaps because his name had been submitted as a defense witness. Another possibility is that he came to the hearing on his own, concerned for the welfare of Joseph and his other friends, and was recognized and arrested along with Bent, Brown, Whitman, and Dunham. Either way, King, along with these four, was now charged with the same crimes as most of those initially arrested.

When Peck continued his testimony, which described events in Daviess County when members of the Church were identified as the aggressors, he named several Mormons who participated in those actions. One of his statements was: "King Follet [sic] was *not* [emphasis mine] in that expedition; but he was Captain of 12 men in Far West, under the Danite order, as I understand, as he was neither an officer nor private of militia, and was known and called under the fictitious name of Captain Bull, and his company was called the Regulators."[46] He also provided information about Dunham and described his para-military activities: "Jonathan Dunham was in the last expedition to Daviess and was Captain of a company of 50 . . . called the Fur Company. He went under the fictitious name of Captain Black Hawk. When the men were paraded, they were called out as all belonging to Captain Black Hawks company."[47] No one else provided testimony regarding King during the hearing.

On November 28 at the end of testimony, King was one of six defendants discharged, the "court being satisfied that there is no probable cause for charging a portion of said prisoners, with the offences alleged against them."[48] Many of the histories written shortly after the November hearings and even some modern accounts erroneously include King as among those originally arrested at Far West and found guilty at Richmond. They fail to report that he was released at the end of the testimony but rearrested about four or five months later, either in March or April of 1839.

The sequence of events in the testimony placed King in jail in Richmond for approximately two weeks (November 14 or 15 to November 28), living with the largest group of prisoners in the incomplete courthouse. Edward Partridge painted a bleak picture of conditions for the prisoners at that site: "We were confined in a large open room where the cold northern blast penetrated freely; our fires were small, and our allowance for wood and for food scanty. They gave us not even a blanket to lie upon. . . . The vilest of the vile did guard us and treat us like dogs; yet we bore our oppressions without murmuring."[49] However, another prisoner, Ebenezer Robinson, like Partridge one of the forty-six second group of arrestees, apparently considered the situation more positively.

> Two three-pail iron kettles for boiling our meat, and two or more iron bake kettles, or Dutch ovens, for baking our corn bread in, were furnished us, together with sacks of cornmeal and meat in bulk. We did our own cooking. This arrangement suited us very well, and we enjoyed ourselves as well as men could under similar circumstances. We spread blankets upon the floor at night for our beds, and before retiring, we sang an hymn and had prayers, and practiced the same each morning before breakfast.[50]

It is not clear why the two men reported such different details. The only other account is that of Parley P. Pratt, which was negative and brief. His wife, Mary Ann, and their three children, including an infant, "spent a portion of the winter in the cold, dark dungeon" with the prisoners. According to Pratt, they left on March 17, 1839, "and, with a broken heart returned to Far West." The Pratts exchanged letters after Mary Ann left the jail.[51] There is no evidence that Louisa or other relatives communicated with King during either of his stays in the Richmond jail. Depending on the circumstances of his first arrest in November, she may not have known a great deal about what had happened to him until after his release.

At the end of the hearing, the disposition of the charges against the brethren, originally arrested or added during the hearing, varied. Some had been dismissed before King and the five men in his discharge group were allowed their freedom. Judge King determined that there was sufficient evidence to hold some of the defendants for trial, a few of whom were allowed to post bail. Joseph Smith and Lyman Wight, Hyrum Smith, Alexander McRae and Caleb Baldwin[52] were remanded to "Daviess county to await the action of the grand jury," but accommodations were so inadequate in Daviess County that the prisoners were taken to Clay County and confined in the jail at its county seat, Liberty."[53] There they stayed from November 1838 to April 1839, awaiting trial for treason and murder. Five other men—Parley P. Pratt, Norman Shearer, Darwin Chase, Luman Gibbs, and Morris Phelps—were kept in jail in Richmond to stand trial for the same crimes.[54] Joseph said, "Our treason consisted of having whipped the mob out of Daviess county, and taking their cannon from them; the murder, of killing the man in the Bogart [Crooked River] battle."[55]

Some men, although freed from jail, were far from exonerated, particularly for participation in the Battle of Crooked River. Fearing re-arrest or vigilante action, they immediately fled, crossing Missouri eastward to Illinois, and leaving their families behind. Among them was Edward Partridge, the Presiding Bishop, who left his wife, Lydia, and six children in King Follett's care in Far West and fled to Quincy, Illinois. Daughter Eliza confirmed that when her "father was obliged to leave Far West before his family . . . [he] arranged with Brother King Follett to bring them to Quincy." She does not say when the family made the arduous journey—obviously it was between the end of November 1838 and March/April of 1839—but clearly recollected its rigors: "We had a very uncomfortable time as the weather was cold and we were badly crowded in the wagon, although we did as we had done every time that we moved, left most of our things. We crossed the Mississippi partly in a boat and partly on the ice. Father met us and took us to a house where we were more comfortable than we had been while traveling."[56] Hartt Wixom, biographer of Edward Partridge, states: "In Quincy, the Partridge girls said King Follet [sic] proved a true friend and assisted them in every possible way."[57]

Perhaps King was also escorting some members of his own family out of Missouri, although there is no documentation that they were included. Making the trip east across Missouri to Quincy, just inside the Illinois state line, was a distance of about two hundred miles one way under grueling circumstances. If he made this journey primarily to assist the Partridge family, he certainly showed deep care and compassion at a very stressful time for both the Partridge and Follett families.

The fall and winter of 1838–39 in Far West were difficult for the Follett family and others like them. The "mobs"—whether official members of the state militia or unofficial vigilantes—still roamed the countryside, stealing what they wanted, killing the Saints' livestock, and terrifying the women whose husbands were usually in jail, had fled the state, or were in hiding. Far West continued to swell with refugees as Daviess County's last members crowded into the city. Food was scarce, and going into the fields to harvest any surviving crops was dangerous. The large number of state troops in Caldwell County had to find food and lodging as well. The Prophet's mother, Lucy Mack Smith, described general conditions in November when Joseph was arrested:

The people were all driven in from the country, and there was more than an acre of land in front of our house completely covered with beds, lying in the open sun, where men, women, and children were compelled to sleep in all weather. These were the last who had got into the city, and the houses were so full that there was no room for them. It was enough to make the heart ache to see children in the open sun and wind, sick with colds and very hungry, crying around their mothers for food and their parents destitute of the means of making them comfortable, while their houses, which lay a short distance from the city, were pillaged of everything, their fields thrown open for the horses belonging to the mob to lay waste and destroy, and their fat cattle shot down and turning to carrion before their eyes, while a strong guard, which was set over us for the purpose, prevented us from making use of a particle of the stock that was killed on every side of us.[58]

During King's two-week imprisonment in November, his farm had once again become a haven for those seeking safety. William Huntington Sr., an acknowledged Danite, arrived in Far West on November 26 after an eight-day trip from Diahman with his family. The state had appointed him to a twenty-four-man committee, half Mormons and half Missourians, to sell all business assets as quickly as possible, insure that all members collected their personal items, see that they evacuated the county within three months, and further insure that no other Mormons would enter the county upon penalty of death.

Despite Huntington's official position, he was still at risk. He later recalled: "After my arrival in Far west [sic] with my family I was notified there was Dilligent inquiry and serch For me to take me to richmond I accordingly left my family immediately and went to King Follet's [sic] stayed three days had not left my family but a few minutes When three men arived at the Dore inquired for me under arms Searched the house for me Was not found by them."[59] Huntington's son, Oliver, commented: "Father immediately disappeared, and stayed in King Follet's cornfield."[60] Three days later, after King returned, Huntington finally received a pass to travel back to Daviess County to take care of committee business.

Church members had been told that they could prepare to leave during the winter. In actuality, hoping that something might happen to stabilize the situation, most Saints did not make serious preparations. The Missouri Legislature authorized a one-time payment of $2,000 for their relief, anticipating that it would hasten their departure. However, in December the legislature refused to overturn the governor's

Extermination Order or to repay the Saints for the lands that they had deeded to the state under force. Furthermore, the Prophet was still in jail, and the Saints may have hoped that, if they left immediately, their leaders might be released. The bored and undisciplined state militia could erupt in new violence at any moment. The longer they stayed in Far West, the more impoverished they became. Members with enough funds to leave saw the logic of departing immediately, then sending back their wagons and teams to be used by others.

It was not an easy task to move thousands of people; but by early February, the exodus was officially launched, some going to Iowa but the majority traveling about two hundred miles to Quincy, a journey that took about two weeks. Amanda Smith, a survivor of the Haun's Mill massacre where her husband and one young son had been killed, expressed what must have been the feelings of a great number of women:

> It was cold weather, and they had our teams and clothes, our men all dead or wounded. I told them they might kill me and my children and welcome. They sent word to us, from time to time, saying that if we did not leave the state they would come and kill us. We had little prayer meetings. They said if we did not stop these, they would kill every man, woman and child. We had spelling schools for our little children; they said if we did not stop these they would kill every man, woman and child. We had to do our own milking, cut our own wood; no man to help us. I started on the 1st of February for Illinois without money, mobs on the way; drove our own team; slept out of doors. I had five small children; we suffered hunger, fatigue and cold.[61]

Many families, even pregnant women and little children, traveled primarily on foot, wading through snow and rain. Women gave birth and cared for sick family members under these circumstances. Most of them struggled to find food as they traveled, with some men working for Missourians along the way. Harassment and persecution continued during the journey for most of them. Anson Call and his family, who left in the middle of February, suffered from snow, were forced to camp out in the middle of a prairie, and had a wagon tip over into a creek. Equally icy was their reception: "We found the Missourians universally unwilling to receive us into their houses."[62]

The Church's official position was to help those that needed assistance and to insure that everyone who wanted to leave had the means to do so. A committee coordinated the removal, selling real estate and livestock not needed as draft animals, usually at a great loss, and pooling the proceeds for the greatest advantage. The Removal Committee sent out advance parties to investigate the best route, alert Missourians that the Saints would be passing through, obtain the aid that had been promised during the earlier negotiations, if possible, and even to cache corn for food at specified sites. On January 29 the Removal Committee held a public meeting in Far West and asked male members of the Church to covenant to provide assistance for those who needed it. More than two hundred signed this covenant. Surprisingly, King's name is not on the list—he may have been taking the Partridge family to Illinois—but James Daley, who later married King's daughter, Nancy, did sign.[63] The Prophet sent word from Liberty Jail instructing them to sell even the Jackson County lands, thus abandoning, at least temporarily, the hope of returning to Zion.

Historian William G. Hartley has identified the two most common routes to Illinois. The northern route slanted slightly northeast from Far West, passing near Chillicothe, Shelbyville, and Palmyra. Then it angled directly north to Marion City, from which it ran east across the Mississippi River to Quincy. The second, southern route went east from Far West to Tinney's Grove, Keytesville, Huntsville, and Paris, then angled northwest to join the northern route at Palmyra.[64] Some members may have boarded boats at Richmond, traveled down the Missouri River to St. Louis, and then taken steamships north to Quincy.

Because members were still moving into the Far West area when the Mormon War broke out, an accurate number of evacuees has never been established. At the beginning of the Mormon War, there were probably ten thousand Mormons in the state, most of them leaving before May 1839. Mormon sources usually place estimates at eight to ten thousand. One Missouri source estimated five thousand.[65] Eliza R. Snow, writing to a relative in Ohio in February, reported: "A man just arrived from Ill. who said he counted 220 wagons between this and the Mississippi. It has been judg'd, there were eight thousand of our people in the County."[66]

On the west bank of the Mississippi River, families congregated, waiting their turn to cross. Some had covered wagons or tents. Others were able to improvise shelters. Still others had to sleep on the ground in the snow. When the river was full of huge chunks of floating ice, the refugees had to find someone to take them across in boats or skiffs, dodging the ice as they went, planning to return for their wagons and larger items when the water was again frozen. When the river froze, which it did late in February, the refugees could cross on foot and transport their wagons. Samuel Kendall Gifford, who was eighteen years old in early 1839, recalled: "When we came to the Mississippi River, Father and some other's [sic] cut down two very large cotton wood trees and dug them out in the shape of canoes and lashed them together a sufficient distance apart to admit the wheels of the wagons in which many of the saints crossed the river. They steered their craft between the large cakes of ice that were then floating in the river. While the smaller cakes would pass between the two canoes."67 Thomas Daniel Stillwell, who was then thirty-three, later recalled: "On 14 February 1839 we loaded up our little afects into a wagon and with one small pair of stears we started out with five children in our family and only one pair of shoes amongst them. We went in the direction of Quincy, Illinois and we were ice bound for two weeks after arriving oposit that town. Several of us joined together and built a boat to cross the Mississippi. Before we crossed we unloaded our wagon and sent it back to asist removing the poor and thus to save their lives the mob still threatning them."68

John Greene, who crossed the Mississippi River at Warsaw, echoed the sentiments of all when he said: "This is the first time I have found a place to rest for the last 4 weeks. O Lord thank the Lord."69

Few Mormons remained in Far West by the end of March, but the Folletts were apparently among those who had not evacuated. Where the family lived and how they survived during the winter of 1838–39 is not known, but it seems likely that they stayed on their farm until the weather moderated in the spring. Finally, either in the middle of March or April,70 King was again arrested and jailed in Richmond. Louisa and the nine other members of her immediate family left, probably traveling with others. Perhaps they were one of approximately thirty-six families whom the Removal Committee moved in mid-April to Tinney's Grove where they received rations of "meal and meat" and continued on to Quincy.71 Hartley gives April 20 as the day "the last Mormon settlers left Far West and traveled thirty miles and camped." He adds: "Thus had a whole people, variously estimated at from ten to fifteen thousand souls, been driven from houses and lands and reduced to poverty, and had removed to another State during one short winter and part of a spring.

The sacrifice of property was immense—including houses, lands, cattle, sheep, hogs, agricultural implements, furniture, household utensils, clothing, money and grain. One of the most flourishing counties in the State and part of several others were reduced to desolation, or inhabited only by marauding gangs."[72]

Louisa was in Quincy by May 11, since she signed the affidavit on that day documenting the family's losses in Missouri. The losses for 1838–39, when the family was in Caldwell County, totaled $3,600:

> To loss in land and buildings not gitting the value of them on the account of being obliged by the mob to leave the state: $800.00. To loss of outher property from the same caus such as stock, provisions, furniture &c: 100.00. To loss of time and expences by moving from Missouri to Illenois, and being detained from business previous to removal by the unlawful proceedings of the Mob: 200.00. To loss of the company, and being deprived of the assistance of my husband (King Follett) who is now, and has ben for a long time kept in prison as I think contireary to the Laws of the land: 500.00. To being deprived of rights of citizen ship in the state of Missouri, having ben driven by a mob under the order of govener Boggs from that state to the state of Illenois: 2,000.00.[73]

Louisa's affidavit, like that of many others Mormons, was "Sworn to before C.M. Woods, C.C.C., Adams Co., IL." This part of her affidavit is more detailed than the portions about 1833 and 1835 but is stoical in tone and provides very little insight about how the family lived while in Missouri.

Within two years after the exodus, little was left of what had once been the thriving town of Far West. The total population of northern Missouri had quickly diminished with the exodus of the Mormons. At first, new people moved into the area to occupy the vacant homes. Far West remained the seat of Caldwell County until 1843, then gradually became deserted, the houses torn down or moved to other locations. Farmers began to plow and plant the streets and yards. The hotel became a stable. The cemetery between King's property and the town square was no longer used and eventually disappeared into the landscape.[74] A Missouri historian in 1879, though expressing no sympathy for the Mormons, still wrote somberly: "The old town site is now in the midst of a corn field.... The burying-ground of the Mormons ... is now included within the limits of a farm.... Here are some two or three hundred graves, all more or less obliterated, with scarcely an occasional

The Far West Temple site, May 16, 1907. George Edward Anderson Collection. LDS Church History Library. Used by Permission

rude headstone to mark the presence of a once sacredly-guarded, but long-forsaken and forgotten village of the dead." One of the few remaining houses had been the Prophet Joseph Smith's home: "It is a rude, old-fashioned, one-story frame building, with two rooms.... An unusually large and clumsy stone chimney at the north end of the building is its distinguishing characteristic. Otherwise the structure is an exceedingly ordinary and common-place building, suggestive of anything rather than the residence of the founder of a mighty sect whose wonderful rise and progress constitute an era of history of Missouri."[75] As time passed, all evidence of the town's existence disappeared except for the temple cornerstones, presently identified with a marker.

In 1995, members of the Missouri Mormon Frontier Foundation (MMFF) while on a "Mormon Sites Tour excursion in June to the Caldwell County area" discovered a partially extant pioneer log house that was determined to be on property that had belonged to Charles C. Rich during the Mormon period in Far West. "The center portion was

Marker, dedicated 1968, on the present Far West Temple site. Photo by Irval L. Mortensen, 2006.

log with frame wings on either side, all clapboarded."[76] In 1837 Rich and his family settled in Mirabile Township in Caldwell County on property immediately adjacent to where this pioneer log structure now stands and may have actually been the builders. "The house was later used by James Wallace, a prominent citizen of Caldwell County for whom Wallace State Park was named."[77] For three years MMFF sponsored a highly productive archaeological reconnaissance at the site, unearthing artifactual materials that were consistent with similar items previously uncovered at Far West during its Mormon period. The report concluded that the "log house shows construction characteristics of the Mormons; no nails and a sophisticated 'pentagon notch' system at the corners" and that it had been "moved onto the current foundation and obscured behind thin siding secured with machine forged square nails common in the area after 1840." While the investigation produced no identifying artifacts specific to the Rich family, the "log house and its incorporated construction techniques render it improbable that the original was built by Mr. Wallace, who acquired the property for the last half of the century. By predating him, the log house associates better with the historic claim to the site by Mr. Rich."[78] If so, though the original log house had been added onto and modified, what was found standing is probably typical of homes built by other Church members like King Follett during their stay in Far West. The cabin is located five miles directly south of the Follett farm.[79]

If this surprisingly durable cabin was, in fact, constructed by Rich, then his wife, Sarah DeArmon Pea Rich, recalled it as her honeymoon home with pleasure in her autobiography written in 1885: "Far West was a place everybody lived in log houses so my husband had built a nice little hewed log house and made it ready to live in by the time we were married. It was four miles from Far West near my husband's father's. So I left my father's home in Far West and we moved to our cozy and happy home and we thought we were the happiest couple in all the land.... and our plans were laid for a comfortable and happy home."[80]

An interesting legal point is what happened to the title to Mormon real estate, since the men deeded it to the state under duress, a circumstance that would have voided the transaction. One of the responsibilities of the Removal Committee, established in January 1839, was to convert assets belonging to the church and its members to cash. However, on April 18, according to *History of the Church*, as the members of the committee were leaving Far West in fear for their lives the "mobs staid [sic] until they [the committee] left, then plundered thousands of dollars' worth of property which had been left by the exiled brethren and sister to help the poor to remove.... During the commotion this day, a great portion of the records of the committee, accounts, history, etc., were destroyed or lost, so that but few items can be registered in their place."[81] Further, in April of 1860, the Caldwell County Courthouse in Kingston burned, thus destroying deeds that might have contained land records from the Far West period. A Missouri historian writing in 1876, explains the "Burning of the Records" this way: "The circumstances seem to indicate its destruction was the work of an incendiary, but who the guilty party was has never been ascertained.... Be the motive for the destruction what it may, it was a great misfortune to the people of our County, as it left the origin of many land titles in doubt. Lucky were those who had preserved the old deeds to their lands. The records of both the circuit and county court were wholly destroyed. The Records of deeds and mortgages were also destroyed."[82]

Remains of log cabin, with initial stabilization efforts, in Far West area, Mirabile Township, Caldwell County, believed to have belonged to Charles Rich family. This cabin reflects the type and size of home in which the Follett family would have lived. Photo by Irval L. Mortensen, 2006.

Given this lack of records, it is not possible to document whether King Follett owned land in addition to his Far West farm, purchased in 1837; but an interesting suggestion appears in a letter that son-in-law Nathan West wrote to David Whitmer in 1849. Nathan, Adeline, their children, and fifty-one-year-old Louisa were then living in Atchison County, Missouri. Nathan's letter has not survived, but David Whitmer's answer has, since Oliver Cowdery, acting as David's attorney, answered the letter on November 26, 1849, and retained a copy. Apparently the Follett family believed that King had purchased land from David Whitmer while the Folletts lived in Caldwell County. Cowdery's answer explains that John Whitmer, David's brother, signed a deed for land (not described or located) to King to cover a "certain debt" that David owed King. King "received and accepted the same as he said at the time, in accordance with his previous contract with myself [meaning David]; at the time of receiving said deed, delivered to my brother [meaning John], my note of hand which he had formerly held as evidence of my indebtedness to him, Follett." Apparently the only other thing that David remembered about the transaction was that "someone from Liberty" later asked if King's title to the land was good and David Whitmer had said it was. John Whitmer believed that "Follett must have put this deed into the hands of the Committee that were appointed to settle up business after the church left, and that they, this committee, disposed of this land to some person in Liberty."[83] It would have been King's responsibility to record the deed, but he was either in jail or leaving the state.

There is no way to determine if this deed was King's farm, purchased in 1837. However, since David Whitmer had not owned land in 1837 in Mirabile Township where King's farm was located, it seems more likely that it was a different tract.

At least one of these pieces of land owned by King—either the original piece he purchased or the referenced Whitmer piece—was recorded and remained in his name on official records until the 1860s, as Caldwell County tax records list King Follett as the owner of land subject to sale and "being forfeited to the State" four times in 1862–63 for back taxes accrued in 1860–63. These records were published as "Caldwell County Tax Lists" in the *Caldwell Banner of Liberty/Kingston, Missouri*, a newspaper, on May 20, August 20, and September 2, 1864, and actually covered taxes that had first fallen due in 1855. (King is first listed as owing taxes in 1860.) His name is misspelled on two of the records as "King Tolbett" and "King Tollett." The misspelling may have appeared in the holograph land record or during transcription. An undated transcription note reads: "Not given in this list with the names aere [sic] the acres of each lot, parts of section, section, township, range, state tax, county tax and military tax on land and lots. People with multiple land and lot listings were only transcribed once to save space. The list was placed in alphabetical [order] here to allow for more rapid searches."[84] It is difficult to tell if this transcription note refers to the year, probably 1864, when the newspaper produced the transcription or if it was when the newspaper information was later transcribed to another source or placed on the internet. I did not search the holograph copy of the tax records. In addition to King's name, the list contains the names of other Mormons who lived in the area, several of them close to King's farm in Mirabile Township (Far West). Apparently, most of the land that Far West property-owners deeded to the state under duress in November 1838 was later sold by the state for back taxes.

There is no evidence that Nathan West or David Whitmer knew that King, now five years dead, was still listed as a property owner on the tax records. Their lack of information suggests that the land referenced on the tax sale was King's 1837 purchase from Missouri, not the parcel that the Whitmers deeded to him.

The earliest remaining record I could find for King's initial forty acres in Far West (Mirabile Township) showed J. D. Pope as the owner. By 1897, H. P. Hooper owned those forty acres and an additional fifteen acres to the west.[85] Since Cowdery's letter to West does not describe or locate the land West asked about, tracking its ownership is impossible.

When the Follett family and other Mormons settled in Far West, they looked upon it as a permanent move. They planned to establish homes in northern Missouri, build up their communities, practice their religion, live in peace, and prosper according to their industry. When they left only a few years later, it was as a hated, persecuted, and impoverished group. Many had been imprisoned. King still was. Some had sacrificed their very lives for their religious beliefs.

The closest example of a similar official eviction in the United States was the forced resettlement on reservations of Native Americans and the internment of Japanese American citizens during World War II. Neither group, however, was forced to relocate under a written threat of death like the Mormons in Missouri. William G. Hartley put this action into modern perspective: "Governor Boggs's extermination order called for a nineteenth-century version of what in recent discussions of Serbian treatment of Kosovars is termed 'ethnic cleansing.'"[86] This order remained in force, though obviously not implemented, for 138 years when Missouri's Governor Christopher S. Bond issued Executive Order No. 44 on June 25, 1976. The key sentence reads: "Expressing on behalf of all Missourians our deep regret for the injustice and undue suffering which was caused by this 1838 order I hereby rescind Executive Order Number 44 dated October 27, 1838, issued by Governor Lilburn W. Boggs."[87]

Notes

1. Noah Webster, *American Dictionary of the English Language* (2 volumes; New York: S. Converse, 1828) searched online at www.1828-dictionary.com.

2. Kenneth W. Godfrey, "New Light on Old Difficulties: The Historical Importance of the Missouri Affidavits," 205.

3. *History of the Church*, 3:188.

4. General Samuel D. Lucas, Letter to Governor Boggs, November 2, 1838, quoted in Leland H. Gentry, *A History of the Latter-day Saints in Northern Missouri from 1836 to 1839*, 170–71. The date and content of this document would indicate that the surrender terms were drafted in the field and later conveyed to the governor, rather than coming directly from the governor, as the Extermination Order states.

5. *History of the Church*, 3:190–91.

6. Myrtle Ballard Shurtliff, comp., "Record of Family and Journal of Luman A. Shurtliff," 24.

7. William G. Hartley, *Stand by My Servant Joseph: The Story of the Joseph Knight Family and the Restoration*, 288.

8. John Lowe Butler, quoted in Hartley, *My Best for the Kingdom: History and Autobiography of John Lowe Butler*, 78.

9. Ibid.

10. Ibid.

11. *History of the Church*, 190–91. Parley P. Pratt wrote later that Doniphan said he would "revolt and withdraw his whole brigade . . . if they persisted in so dreadful an undertaking" and further stated 'It is cold blooded murder, and I wash my hands of it.'" Scot Facer Proctor and Maurine Jensen Proctor, eds., *The Autobiography of Parley P. Pratt: Revised and Enhanced Edition*, 236. Doniphan was also an attorney, and apparently at least partially because of this incident, made the decision to defend Joseph Smith and others in the upcoming hearing.

12. John P. Greene, *Facts Relative to the Expulsion of the Mormons or Latter Day Saints, from the State of Missouri under the "Exterminating Order,"* 13–14. Greene, born in New York in 1793, was an early convert who served a mission to the eastern states as early as 1833, moved to Kirtland, then to Missouri, and later to Nauvoo, where he served as city marshal. He prepared this document when a group in Cincinnati requested a concise statement of the Mormon conflict in Missouri.

13. Baugh, *A Call to Arms*, 151.

14. Shurtliff, "Record of Family and Journal of Luman A. Shurtliff," 25.

15. Nathan Tanner, quoted in Alexander L. Baugh, *A Call to Arms: The 1838 Mormon Defense of Northern Missouri*, 151.

16. Joseph Holbrook, *History of Joseph Holbrook, 1806–1885*, 24.

17. *History of the Church*, 3:200–205.

18. Baugh, *A Call to Arms*, 143 note 9.

19. *History of the Church*, 3:201.

20. Ibid., 3:202. The number of men arrested at this time differs according to different sources. Baugh, *A Call to Arms*, 165 note 49, reports that General Clark wrote to Governor Boggs on two different occasions stating the number was forty-six. Steven C. LeSueur, *The Mormon War in Missouri*, 197, confirms the number as forty-six plus the Joseph Smith party of seven: "Fifty-three of the defendants brought to Richmond had been identified during General Clark's two-day investigation in Far West." Albert Perry Rockwood, a resident of Far West, recorded the figure as fifty-one. Dean C. Jessee and David J. Whittaker, eds., "The Last Months of Mormonism in Missouri: The Albert Perry Rockwood Journal," 27.

21. *History of the Church*, 3:202–4.

22. Ibid., 3:202–3.

23. "General Clark's Harrangue [sic] to the Brethren," quoted in ibid., 202–4.

24. Ibid., 204.

25. Jessee and Whittaker, "The Last Months of Mormonism in Missouri," 27.

26. *Encyclopedia of Missouri*, 95.

27. Jessee and Whittaker, "The Last Months of Mormonism in Missouri," 27. Terminal punctuation and initial capitals added.

28. Leland H. Gentry, *A History of the Latter-day Saints in Northern Missouri from 1836–1839*, 190.

29. Proctor and Proctor, *Autobiography of Parley P. Pratt*, 261.

30. Annette W. Curtis, "People and Places: Mormon Prisoners in Richmond," 4. See also Annette W. Curtis, "Historic Sites in Mormon Missouri—Richmond, Missouri."

31. Max H. Parkin, *Missouri*, 237.

32. Annette W. Curtis, emails to Joann Follett Mortensen, July–October 2006, printouts in my possession. The marker lists the prisoners as: Joseph Smith Jr., George W. Robinson, Lyman Wight, Sidney Rigdon, Hyrum Smith, Parley P. Pratt, Isaac Allred, James Allred, Martin C. Allred, William Allred, Caleb Baldwin, Thomas Beck, Lemuel Bent, Ezekiel Billington, Ebenezer Brown, John Buchanan, Darwin Chase, Moses Clawson, Daniel Carn, Benjamin Covey, Sheffield Daniels, Jonathan Dunham, John T. Earl, Elisha Edwards, *King Follett* (emphasis mine), David Frampton, Jacob Gates, Luman Gibbs, George D. Grant, Clark Hallett, George W. Harris, Anthony Head, James M. Henderson, Francis Higbee, John S. Higbee, Chandler Holbrook, Sylvester Hulet, Jesse D. Hunter, Benjamin Jones, George Kimball, Amasa Lyman, Silas Maynard, Alexander McRea[sic], Daniel S. Miles, Isaac Morley,

James Newberry, Elijah Newman, Zedekiah Owens, Ebenezer Page, Edward Partridge, David Pettigrew, Morris Phelps, Thomas Rich, Alanson Ripley, Ebenzer [sic] Robinson, J. Henry Rollins/Rawlins, Daniel Shearer, Norman Shearer, Allen J. Stout, John T. Tanner, Sidney Tanner, Daniel S. Thomas, Alvin G. Tippets, Washington Voorhees, Andrew Whitlock, William Whitman, Joseph W. Younger, [and] Henry Zabriski.

33. Information obtained from attendance at the marker dedication ceremony; photo of marker in my possession.

34. John Craig, "Richmond, Missouri: Update on Location of 'Old Vacant Log House,'" 2.

35. Richard Neitzel Holzapfel, T. Jeffery Cottle, and Ted D. Stoddard, eds., *Church History in Black and White: George Edward Anderson's Photographic Mission to Latter-day Saint Historical Sites—1907 Diary, 1907–8 Photographs*, 75.

36. Ibid., note 166.

37. Baugh, *A Call to Arms*, 160.

38. Pearl Wilcox, *The Latter Day Saints on the Missouri Frontier*, 295.

39. Gordon A. Madsen, "Joseph Smith and the Missouri Court of Inquiry: Austin A. King's Quest for Hostages," 120.

40. Opinions vary about why such a small number of witnesses appeared for the defense. *History of the Church*, 210–11, records that, although more than fifty names were submitted as witnesses, many of them were then arrested or threatened with arrest and that those who did testify were "prevented as much as possible by threats from telling the truth." Baugh, *A Call to Arms*, 169 note 137, records: "There is sufficient evidence given by several Mormons present at the hearing to conclude that Bogart or his emissaries did in fact intimidate some Mormon witnesses as well as incarcerate a number of others so that they could not testify." LeSueur, *The 1838 Mormon War in Missouri*, 212, states: "Although the defense witnesses were intimidated and threatened with prosecution . . . Mormon claims that they were not allowed to testify, to bring witnesses, or to have legal counsel are not true."

41. See *Document Containing the Correspondence, Orders, &c. in Relation to the Disturbances with the Mormons . . .* , 97–228. A second record consisting only of witness testimony was published as *Senate Document 189: Document Showing the Testimony Evidence Given before the Judge of the Fifth Judicial District of the State of Missouri . . .* , February 1841.

42. *History of the Church*, 3:209–12.

43. According to Madsen, "Joseph Smith and the Missouri Court of Inquiry," 126, the correct name is "Ebenezer Brown."

44. All of the Mormon prisoners were represented by Alexander Doniphan and Amos Rees. See *History of the Church*, 3:212, and Baugh, *A Call to Arms*, 160. LeSueur in *The 1838 Mormon War*, 212, refers to the two as "the best-

known defense lawyers in western Missouri." Doniphan, a member of the volunteer Missouri militia as well as an attorney, had only a few days earlier refused to carry out an order to shoot Joseph Smith and others.

45. *Document Containing the Correspondence, Orders, &c.*, 119.

46. Reed Peck, Testimony, quoted in ibid., 119.

47. Ibid.

48. *Document Containing the Correspondence, Orders, &c.*, 149. The other five were "Benj. Jones, Geo. W. Morris, Elijah Newman, Moses Clawson and Daniel Shearer."

49. Edward Partridge, "Family Record," 53.

50. Ebenezer Robinson, "Items of Personal History of the Editor," *The Return* 2 (March 1890): 234.

51. Proctor and Proctor, *Autobiography of Parley P. Pratt*, 267, 287 note 1.

52. *Document Containing the Correspondence, Orders, &c.*, 150. Sidney Rigdon was committed directly to the Clay County jail.

53. *History of Ray County, Missouri*, 276.

54. *Document Containing the Correspondence, Orders, &c.*, 150.

55. *History of the Church*, 3:212.

56. "Life and Journal of Eliza Marie [sic] Partridge (Smith) Lyman," typescript.

57. Hartt Wixom, *Edward Partridge: The First Bishop of the Church of Jesus Christ of Latter-day Saints*, 97.

58. Proctor and Proctor, *The Revised and Enhanced History of Joseph Smith by His Mother*, 408–9.

59. William Huntington, "Autobiography—Journal of William Huntington (1784–1846)," typescript, 6. Huntington was a native of New York where he joined the Church. After two years in Kirtland, he moved to Daviess County, Missouri. His family was one of the first to settle in Commerce (Nauvoo), Illinois.

60. Oliver Boardman Huntington, "Autobiography, 1823–1839," typescript, 38.

61. Amanda Smith, quoted in George Q. Cannon, *Life of Joseph Smith the Prophet*, 303.

62. Ethan L. Call and Christine Shafer Call, eds., *The Journal of Anson Call*, 20.

63. *History of the Church*, 3:250–55.

64. William G. Hartley, "Missouri's 1838 Extermination Order and the Mormons' Forced Removal to Illinois," 17.

65. Gentry, *A History of the Latter-day Saints in Northern Missouri*, 221.

66. Maureen Ursenbach Beecher, ed., *The Personal Writings of Eliza Roxcy Snow*, 262.

67. Samuel Kendall Gifford, "Reminiscences, 1864," 4. Gifford was born in New York and baptized in 1833 in Jackson County, Missouri. In Utah, he

remained active, serving as a Seventy and a patriarch. A chairmaker by profession, he played the fiddle for dances and also taught school. He died in 1907.

68. Thomas Daniel Stillwell, "Letter to Editor & Readers of the Lehi Post," 7. If the birth dates for his children contained in New Family Search (ID number KWGW-MV1) are correct, the children ranged in age from twelve to two years of age, and his wife delivered another child a month later. Stillwell was asked to participate in the "Big Field Company," an experiment in cooperative farming in Far West, which was planned to fence and plant large areas of land to be used by the poor. This was the basis for the system later used in southern Utah to handle large groups of poor immigrants.

69. John Portineus Greene, Diary Entries, November 1–16, 1838, 16. Greene was born in New York, served a mission in 1835, was a member of the Kirtland High Council in 1839, was a member of the Nauvoo City Council in 1841 and served as city marshal in 1843. He died in Nauvoo in 1844.

70. The writings of Parley P. Pratt and Morris Phelps, King's two fellow prisoners in the Columbia jail, disagree on the month. Pratt recalls the date as the middle of April. According to Phelps, the date was March 14. All previous articles and books that I have read about the imprisonment have used Pratt's April date. See Chapter 13.

71. *History of the Church*, 3:319.

72. Hartley, "Missouri's 1838 Extermination Order," 21.

73. Louisa [Tanner] Follett, "Affidavit," 201–2.

74. Wilcox, *The Latter Day Saints on the Missouri Frontier*, 323; and Gentry, *A History of the Latter-day Saints in Northern Missouri*, 228.

75. William F. Switzler, *Switzler's Illustrated History of Missouri, from 1541 to 1877*, 242, 243.

76. Mike Riggs, "Forgotten Sites in Caldwell and Daviess Counties," 3.

77. "An Invitation to Do a Week Long Dig: Log House Archaeological Dig 22–27 June 1998," 1.

78. Paul DeBarthe, David Coit, and Haumana DeBarthe, *Archaeological Reconnaissance of a Caldwell County, Missouri, Log House*.

79. I have visited the site twice. On the first visit in 2002, stabilization work was in progress and a small gift shop was on site. By the second visit in 2006, apparently because of lack of sufficient funding to continue the restoration and also because of some zoning issues, work on the project had halted. However it appeared that someone was living on the property and visitors still had access to it. I do not know its current (2011) status.

80. Sarah Rich, quoted in Richard Neitzel Holzapfel and T. Jeffrey Cottle, *Old Mormon Kirtland and Missouri: Historic Photographs and Guide*, 15.

81. *History of the Church*, 3:323.

82. "Burning of Records," in Edwards Brothers, *An Illustrated Historical Atlas of Caldwell County, Missouri*, 7.

83. Scott H. Faulring, "Letter from David Whitmer to Nathan West Concerning Caldwell County, Missouri, Property Once Owned by King Follett," 127–35.

84. "Caldwell County Tax Lists," 1864.

85. Edwards Brothers, *An Illustrated Historical Atlas*, 37; W. P. Bullock, *Atlas of Caldwell County, Missouri*, unpaginated.

86. Hartley, "Missouri's 1838 Extermination Order," 5.

87. Ibid., 24.

Chapter Thirteen

The "Old" Man in Prison: April–September 1839

Members of the Church were held as prisoners of Missouri in two locations during the winter of 1838–39. At the close of the November hearing in Richmond, the Prophet Joseph Smith, his two counselors in the First Presidency (Hyrum Smith and Sidney Rigdon), Lyman Wight, Alexander McRae, and Caleb Baldwin were taken from Richmond and confined in jail in Liberty, the seat of Clay County. Liberty, located about forty-two miles southwest of Far West, was the first town settled in northern Missouri because of its location on the Missouri River. The other group consisting of Parley P. Pratt, Norman Shearer, Luman Gibbs, Darwin Chase, and Morris Charles Phelps were taken to the Richmond jail. Their families had to fend for themselves or be taken care of by others during these trying months. Both groups were to be held for further court action, but no trial date had been set for any of them. During transport to Liberty, Joseph and his companions were handcuffed and chained in the back of an open wagon. All along the route between the two towns, people came out to view and mock the Mormon prophet. A large crowd was waiting when they reached the jail on December 1. The crude two-story structure that would house them for the next five months was built of limestone blocks and huge oak logs with no sleeping quarters. Inside, it was dark, damp, and filthy. Food was "intolerable." Hyrum later recalled: "Poison was administered to us three or four times. The effect it had upon our system was, that it vomited us almost to death, and then we would lie some two or three days in a torpid, stupid state, not even caring or wishing for life. The poison being administered in too large doses, or it would inevitably have proved fatal, had not the power of Jehovah interposed in our behalf, to save us from their wicked purpose."[1] Hyrum also refused to eat for several days because he overheard a conversation that the guards were trying to feed the prisoners human flesh.

In spite of these conditions, and facing a trial and possible death sentence, the men spent their time discussing Church-related issues and problems, meditating, praying, writing letters, and conversing with visitors. The Prophet's letters to his family and other Church members expressed both hope and frustration, provided counsel and instructions, and assured them that he was aware of their plight. He also wrote letters to the state legislature asking for redress and assistance. Perhaps as a result of one of these letters, Governor Boggs signed an order that the arms surrendered by Church members in Far West, including King, be returned to them. This order, however, was never even partially implemented. An important source of continued support and hope were the revelations that came to the Prophet during this period.

Rumors were rampant that the prisoners were planning to escape, which, in fact, they were. The prisoners made at least one unsuccessful attempt to escape in mid-March, while making several requests for quick legal action both to the Clay County Court and the Missouri Supreme Court, all of which were denied. Meanwhile, an ailing Sidney Rigdon had been released on bail on January 25, 1839, and he quickly left the state with the assistance of his wife, Phoebe, "fearing the Missourians would kill him if he were caught."[2] On April 6 the state moved the remaining four prisoners, first to Daviess County to appear before a grand jury and then to Boone County on a change of venue motion. During this second transfer, the prisoners were "allowed" to escape on April 15, probably because state officials were concerned about negative publicity that the affair had generated and increasing doubts about the state's ability to convict the prisoners. The escapees lost no time, understandably, in leaving the state.[3]

Despite King's brief experience with imprisonment, for unknown reasons he did not follow the body of the Church to Illinois and was still in Far West as late as March or even April 1839. Presumably, the Church members still remaining in Far West were aware of what was happening to the Prophet and others in Liberty Jail. The Prophet wrote letters on at least three occasions, the contents of which could have been shared with King in Far West. Two of them talked of the circumstances and conditions surrounding his imprisonment and provided counsel and advice to the general Church membership. He wrote the first on December, 16, 1838. The second, on March 25, 1839, was also signed by his fellow prisoners. The third was written on March 15 to Presendia Huntington Buell of Clay County in response to a request for an interview. *History of the Church* records frequent visits to the jail by Heber C. Kimball and Alanson Ripley and adds, more generally, that the prisoners "were sometimes visited by our friends." (Was King one of these friends?) On March 17, Parley P. Pratt's wife, Mary Ann, after spending the winter with her husband and three children in the jail, returned to Far West to prepare to leave the state.[4] Emma Smith visited Joseph, accompanied by wives of other prisoners, three times before she left Far West in mid-February 1839.[5] The *History of the Church* records, on Saturday, April 20: "The last of the Saints left Far West."[6]

However, about that time, King was rearrested and jailed in Richmond with the five who had been languishing there since late November 1838. Before the end of 1839, Parley P. Pratt wrote that his wife "tarryed in Far West about a month, and all the Society had gone from the State, but a few of the poor, and widows, and a committee who tarryed behind to assist them in removing. About the middle of April, a gang of robbors [sic] entered Far West armed, and ordered my wife and the committee, and the others, to be gone by such a day, or they would murder them." Pratt gives April 26 as the day the "last of the Society departed from Far West."[7]

Pratt, writing from memory, records that King had "been added [to the prisoners] about the middle of April,"[8] the date commonly used by other historians. However, Morris Phelps states: "On the 13th of March Caldwell Grand Jurors found a bill against Brother King Follet for robbery, who was committed to Richmond jail with us on the 14th."[9] If Phelps is accurate, then King was actually charged in Caldwell County, though I could find no court record in that county, and then was taken to Richmond in Ray County to be jailed.

The charge of "robbery" is also somewhat ambiguous. Sympathetically, Pratt recounted that King "was dragged from his distressed family just as they were leaving the State, being charged with robbery, which meant that he was one of a posse who took a keg of Powder from a gang of ruffians who were out against the Mormons."[10] I have found no further details about where or when this powder keg incident occurred, although an owner is identified in King's trial (discussed below).

Reed Peck's account of the Missouri experience in 1839 did not name the last two Mormon prisoners who were still in Richmond jail in July 1839 (other records show that these two were Luman Gibbs and King Follett), but did provide further information regarding possible charges against them: "Of all that were taken of the Mormons two only remain prisoners in Missouri and I am safe in saying that they are the least guilty. One of them is guilty of standing guard over the Mormon horses while the company marched to attack Bogart on Crooked river. The other is guilty of executing plans laid by S. Rigdon to make the traitors as he termed them service[e]able in defending the cause in Far West."[11] Gibbs was the horse guard, since another record identifies him as present at the Battle of Crooked River and admitting his assignment with the horses.[12] The remaining individual is King. However, Peck does not explain what he meant by "traitors" or "serviceable," so it does not clarify King's role beyond what was already known: that he was willing and able to help defend Far West. Nor does it identify whether this occurred before the city's surrender or afterward, when most Mormons were fleeing from the state.

King left no record of this second imprisonment; but two fellow prisoners did: Morris C. Phelps and Parley P. Pratt. Thus, a rather vivid story of King's life is available for part of the five or six months from his second arrest until September 1839 when he was finally released.

King's second incarceration took place, not in the unfinished courthouse where he had been jailed in November, but in the "new" Richmond Jail that had been either constructed or completed over the winter. He joined Pratt, Phelps, and Gibbs, who had already been there for almost five months. Though the jail was supposedly a newer one, Phelps described it as

> a wriched, filthy prison twostory high, the lower story nine feet square, this was called the dungon all the light being excluded from it in this dungon was

our necsary a large keg which was empied once a week here we had to sleep and stay from 12 to 18 hours in 24 hours the remaining time [spent] in the upper room which was open & cold this upper room we were permited to have a little fire in a stove. our food was mostly boiled corn & bacon rinds.[13]

On March 22, 1839, while still in jail in Liberty, the Prophet had expressed concern for those incarcerated in Richmond Jail. In a letter to Isaac Galland, Joseph reported: "We are informed that the prisoners in Richmond Jail, Ray county, are much more inhumanly treated than we are; if this is the case, we will assure you, that their constitutions cannot last long, for we find ours wearing away very fast; and if we knew of any source whereby aid and assistance could be rendered unto us, we should most cordially petition for it: but where is liberty?"[14]

The Richmond guards were part of the unpleasantness. They made a game of harassing and intimidating the prisoners through the use of foul language and threats to shoot them. The prisoners were allowed occasional visitors, but most of the prisoners' relatives had left Missouri by the time King was rearrested. The wives of both Phelps and Pratt actually stayed in prison with the men for a period of time, hoping that their husbands would be released. Mary Ann Pratt had three children with her, the youngest seven months old.[15] When the release did not come, the women left with the rest of the Saints for Quincy. Phelps would later lament the injustice of "being left, with a few others . . . in prison without money or friends or witnesses to undergo a trial."[16] There is no record that King's family visited him; and indeed, he must have felt great anxiety for them as he knew they needed to quickly seek safety in Illinois. Luman Gibbs's wife also visited him from time to time. Both Phelps and Pratt saw Gibbs as an "apostate" who, to save his life and be granted eventual freedom, turned against the Church and his fellow prisoners but stayed in jail to spy on the other prisoners. As a result of this change of allegiance, Gibbs "went out to dine with the Sheriff or others, or to spend a day with his wife whenever it pleased him to do so."[17]

On May 13, after King Follett had been incarcerated for perhaps two months, Pratt, writing in first person but expressing conditions inflicted upon all of the prisoners, wrote to Judge Austin King, once again objecting to the imprisonment on six somewhat repetitious grounds: (1) no protection of law while residing in Missouri; (2) forceful removal from Clay County; (3) these crimes still go unpunished; (4) wives and family members, together with "about ten thousand of our society, including all my friends and witnesses" have been banished from Caldwell County and now the entire state; (5) "all these inhuman outrages and crimes go unpunished, and are unnoticed by you, sir," and also by all state authorities; (6) "the legislature of the state has approved of and sanctioned this act of banishment." He concluded: "I hereby solemnly protest against being tried in this state, with the full and conscientious conviction that I have no just grounds to expect a fair and impartial trial. I therefore most sincerely pray your honor, and all the authorities of the state, to either banish me without further prosecution; or I freely consent to a trial before a judiciary of the United States."[18]

Judge King visited the jail, took the testimony from all four prisoners, then ordered a change of venue to Boone County, one hundred miles away where they would be jailed at the county seat, Columbia, while awaiting trial. A change of venue is usually granted based on evidence that defendants cannot receive a fair and impartial trial in a given locale, usually the county in which the alleged crimes occurred. It is difficult to see how a trial in Boone County would be considered more "impartial," as conditions for the Mormons had been the same everywhere in Missouri. Pratt had not requested a change of venue, so Judge King's order may have been a public relations gesture to make it appear that "something" was finally being done by the state for the prisoners.

Nine days later on May 22, the sheriff and armed guards chained King and his fellow prisoners in pairs at the wrists and ankles. Phelps described the situation: "We were handcuffed two & two Bro Parley & myself forming the first couple & King Follet & Luman Gibbs the second cuple. These Irons when closed were in the shape of a figure 8 eight & placed around our wrists with the back of our hands together there being no joints in the Irons between our wrists rendered our situation very inconvenient & painfull."[19] This bondage continued for at least the first three days of their journey. Though it was spring, the weather was still somewhat cool. It had been raining for several days and continued most of the five days of the journey. The conveyance in which they rode has been described variously as a "carriage," "coach," or a "wagon." A carriage or coach would have been enclosed and had seats; but a wagon would have had no top, only a railing surrounding the bed high enough to confine the men. If it had seats, it seems doubtful that they would have had springs. Straw in the bed would have provided a little cushioning until the rain soaked it. Curious townspeople came out to watch the prisoners leave. Still, according to Pratt, the men appreciated being out of jail and in the fresh air. "To prisoners who had breathed only a tainted air for half a year the very ground itself seemed to send forth a sweetness which was plainly perceptible to the senses. We enjoyed our ride through that delightful country more than any being could who had never been confined for weary months in a dreary dungeon."[20]

The first day the group traveled forty miles and stopped overnight at an unidentified home. Here, according to Pratt, the prisoners were "stretched upon our backs on the floor, all fastened together with wrist and ankle irons."[21] With this arrangement they could not individually turn or change position. It rained all the next day. Pratt vividly describes that day in King's life:

> In the course of the day we came to a stream which was swollen by the rains. . . . We had to swim over it and stem a swift current. This hindered us for some hours—in crossing over with the horses, wagons, baggage, etc.; and as all of us were engaged in this business, our chains were taken off for the time.
>
> When we had crossed over, put on our clothes, and replaced the baggage, saddles, arms, etc., ready for a start, it was night, and we were very weary and hungry, having had no refreshments during the day. The rain was also pouring in torrents, and the night setting in extremely dark. Four miles of wild country, partly covered with forests and underwoods, still lay between us and the nearest house. Through the hurry of the moment, or for some other reason, they neglected to replace our irons, and our limbs were free. The carriage drove through a thick forest during the extreme darkness, and was several times on the eve of upsetting.
>
> The Sheriff and guards seeing this, rode close on each side, and, cocking their pistols, swore they would shoot us dead if we attempted to leave the carriage, and that if it upset they would shoot us anyhow, for fear we might attempt to escape.[22]

After arriving at a "house of entertainment"—probably an inn or tavern—where they spent the night, they started again the next day. Parley continued:

> When we arrived within four miles of Columbia, the bridge had been destroyed from over a large and rapid river; and here we were some hours in crossing over, in a tottleish [sic] canoe, having to leave our carriage, together with our

bedding, clothing, our trunk of clothing, books, papers, &c., but all came to us in safety after two days. After we had all crossed the river, our guards having swam their horses, mounted them, and we proceeded towards Columbia, the prisoners walking on foot, two being fastened together by the wrists.

After walking two or three miles, Mr. Brown [the sheriff] hired a carriage, and we rode into Columbia. It was about sun-set on Sunday evening, and as the carriage and our armed attendants drove through the streets, we were gazed upon with astonishment by hundreds of spectators, who thronged the streets, and looked out at the windows, doors, &c., anxious to get a glimpse of the strange beings called Mormons.[23]

In Columbia, a new jailer took charge of the four weary prisoners and immediately placed them in another dungeon-like underground room that was much like the previous one—dark, dank, and filthy, having been unused for two years. Exhausted from their days of travel, they collapsed on the bare floor and slept without having eaten all day. The next day they were moved upstairs into better quarters.

This third jail of King's experience was a two-story building, twenty-five to thirty square feet in size, with the prisoners occupying one part and the jailer and his family the other. It was apparently "located near the northwest corner of the public square . . . 'in the same square with the courthouse, being on the north edge of the town.'"[24] No jail records have survived of the prisoners' stay; but the *History of the Church* notes, on May 28, that the prisoners asked for a "special term of court to be holden for their trials."[25] On June 7, Thomas Reynolds, judge of the second judicial circuit court, ordered "a special Term of the Boone Circuit Court be held on the first Monday in July 1839 for the trial of Parley P. Pratt Luman Gibbs and Morris Phelps who are now confined in the jail of the said County upon a charge of Murder and of King Follett who is also confined in said Jail upon the charge of robbery."[26]

Though a trial date of July 1 was set, on June 7, Pratt, Gibbs and Phelps through their attorney requested a continuance, which was granted until the next term of the court in September, as all defense witnesses had obviously left the state. The continuance further ordered that depositions of the (unidentified) witnesses be taken in Illinois and Iowa. Reynolds also issued an order in King's case: "This day came the attorney prosecuting for the State as well as the defendant by his attorney[27] and on the motion of Attorney prosecuting for the state It is ordered by the Court that this cause be Continued until the next term of this Court." A further order issued at the same time commanded the Clerk of the Caldwell Court "to make a full and complete transcript of the records [and] proceedings had in the Caldwell Circuit Court in the State of Missouri In the Cause wherein the State of Missouri is plaintiff and King Follett is defendant."[28]

A week later on June 14, the *History of the Church* reported:

> This evening there was a great excitement about the jail of Columbia, Missouri. Several individuals went and called for the jailer, but he was absent. They next called for the jailer's wife, and offered her money to let the prisoners go, which she declined, and becoming alarmed, raised a cry which brought the whole village together, armed with bowie knives, guns, pistols, etc.; but finding no one there, they soon returned home, except a few to guard the prison. This now brought different individuals to see the prisoners, and by acquaintance those feelings were softened towards the Saints.[29]

The unidentified individuals who offered money for the prisoners' release may have been would-be vigilantes who wanted to bypass the legal system or Church members who had collected money as a ransom.

By July 1, Parley's brother Orson, Phelps's wife, Laura Clark Phelps, and her brother, John Wesley Clark, had arrived from Quincy, bringing letters from family and friends. Perhaps one of them was for King; but if not, the visitors would still probably have known whether Louisa and the children had reached Quincy safely. Before leaving Quincy, Laura had gone to Nauvoo to ask Joseph Smith's advice. According to Morris and Laura's daughter Mary Ann, "He laid his hands on her head and blessed her and told her to go. He said, 'Sister Phelps, perhaps you can accomplish more than we can. We have done our best to get those prisoners liberated, but all our plans have failed.'"[30]

I found no record of exactly when the Caldwell County circuit court's records in King's case reached the Boone County court; meanwhile, events were developing in a different direction. According to Mary Ann Phelps Rich, "The jailer and his wife bragged that they had had several in the prison who had died of old age, because they would just continue their cases and keep them in prison."[31] Whether the prisoners took this rather extravagant claim seriously, they obviously had no reason to believe that Missouri courts would provide legal justice and instead began planning an escape.

Parley P. Pratt wrote that before his brother and Phelps's wife and brother-in-law had arrived at the jail "the Lord had shown me in a vision of the night the manner and means of escape... shown to me on two occasions in the same manner.... Mrs. Phelps had the same thing shown to her in a vision previous to her arrival; my brother, Orson Pratt, also came to us with a firm impression that we were about to be delivered."[32] Parley Pratt says that the prisoners chose July 4 as the day for the escape because it had been a "lucky one for our fathers and our nation" and thus seemed the "proper one to bid farewell to bondage and gain our liberty. In short, we had determined to make that notable day a jubilee to us, or perish in the attempt."[33]

Morris Phelps's version of their plans is somewhat different. He wrote that he had received a personal manifestation on June 27 that he would be free and would reach Nauvoo safely. He told the others of this manifestation, then sought what privacy was available in the dungeon (lower story) to pray: "The whole scenery was before me in open vision as far as to getting [sic] on too [sic] our hourses [sic] & making the start but the time to make the brake [sic] was not given to me."[34] He consulted Parley, because the two of them had earlier made a pact that they would escape together or not at all. After the discussion, they decided to leave on July 3 with Pratt riding the horse that Orson had brought and Phelps on John Clark's horse. Laura Phelps could make her own way back to Quincy on her horse but without the necessity for haste that would obviously propel the prisoners as far as possible at the greatest speed. King was not included in their immediate plans, which Morris Phelps explained this way: "Bro. King Follett a good man had no horse provided for him & his case being a bailable one he was to be kept in the dark as to our making our escape & when we got to Illinois we would raise the money for his bail & send & bring him away."[35] While it is true that robbery was a less serious charge than murder, excluding King from their plans seems unnecessarily practical and even unfeeling.

However, upon arising the next morning, July 2, King shared a prescient dream, which Morris Phelps reported: "As soon as I [Phelps] woke Bro Follett said Brethern I have dreamed a dream or seen a vision.... I dreamed that you [Pratt] & Bro Phelps and myself all broke out of this jail on the evening of the 4 of July when the supper was handed in, Bro Phelps clinched the jailor & down stairs we went you mounted Orson horse Bro Phelps Clarks horse & I mounted Sister Phelps horse & you

& Bro Phelps made good your escape and what become of me after, after I got on to my horse I cannot tell I woke up.[36]

Pratt and Phelps must have been impressed by how closely King's dream resembled the escape they had planned without him. It would have been impossible for them not to have included him at this point. Columbia was holding an enthusiastic July 4th celebration, complete with music, gunfire, and speeches in the town square right in front of the jail. The prisoners decided to participate as much as they could from inside. Requesting a long pole, they "took a white shirt and some read [sic] & black cloth & made a flag in the center place[d] a large red Eagle with the arrows nicely sewed to the white we draped it in mourning by putting a black border around it over the Eagle we placed large letters which read Liberty." They fastened the flag to the pole "and it was thrust out of the uper [sic] window about sixteen foot & lashed with a rope fast to the iron grates of the window."[37] The reaction of the crowd was immediate and exuberant: "[They] would come up and stare at the flag, and reading the motto, would go swearing or laughing away, exclaiming, 'Liberty! Liberty! What have the Mormons to do with celebrating liberty in a damned old prison?'"[38] The silent response of King and his friends was that they would obtain their liberty that very day or become martyrs.

They planned to make it appear that Orson Pratt and John Clark were leaving that evening to go to Illinois and Iowa to obtain necessary depositions to be used in the September trial. Laura Phelps would tell the jailer and his wife that she was going to stay at the jail with Morris and that Orson and John would take her horse with them, bringing it back in a few weeks when she was ready to return home. The group ate lunch consisting of food that Laura Phelps had brought, more provided by the jailer, and still more brought in by the townspeople after they saw the "Liberty" flag. According to Phelps, the townspeople were sharing tasty barbecued ox.[39]

The townsfolk offered toasts outside, and the prisoners responded: "The patriotic & hospitable citizens of Boon County; opposed to tyrena & oppression & firm to original principals of Republican Liberty—may they in common with every part of our wide spreading Country long enjoy the blessing which flow from the fountain of American Independence." This sentiment was "received with loud cheers & called the second best."[40] Then they settled down for the very long afternoon to pass, planning to make their break when the jailer brought in the evening meal.

Each person had a job. Orson Pratt and John Clark had to stay with the horses in a grove about a half mile from the jail, yet be sufficiently visible that the prisoners would know which way to run. Laura's job was to keep the jailer and his wife distracted with conversation so that they would not take the prisoners' supper upstairs while it was still daylight. There were two doors at the top of the stairs leading into the room where the prisoners were kept. The outer door was solid and heavy, and when opened revealed a second door which was usually kept fastened with the food being passed through a window to the prisoners inside. They needed to persuade the jailer to fully open the inside door rather than just passing the coffeepot through, as usually happened. King's job was to yank the door wide open, allowing the prisoners access to the stairway. Morris Phelps would go through the door first and, an experienced wrestler, immobilize the jailer. A lot of variables had to come together perfectly for the escape to succeed!

Under these circumstances, the prisoners must have waited impatiently for footsteps on the stairs, announcing the jailer with food. Perhaps their thoughts centered on the sweet reunion they were anticipating with their family members. Hidden behind this positive outlook, however, there must have been concern about what it could mean to their family members if this attempt were unsuccessful. No one could predict exactly what the townspeople gathered in the square below them would do then. While waiting they "called upon the Lord to prosper us and open our way, and then sang aloud the following lines" that one of them, probably Parley, had composed:

> Lord, cause their foolish plans to fail,
> And let them faint or die:
> Our souls would quit this poor old jail,
> And fly to Illinois—
> To join with the embodied Saints,
> Who are with freedom blest:
> That only bliss for which we pant,
> With them awhile to rest.
> Give joy for grief—give ease for pain,
> Take all our foes away;
> But let us find our friends again
> In this eventful day.[41]

By now Orson Pratt and John Clark had left town, and the prisoners could see "a dry limb of a tree out of the jail window where they would find the horses. The two men were to help them on their journey when they got there." The jailer left the kitchen to take the prisoners' food upstairs to them, leaving Laura in the kitchen.[42]

When the prisoners heard the approaching footsteps, they got in place to receive the food with King in front to jerk open the door so that Morris could stun the jailer and run downstairs with Parley following and King third. As usual, the jailer handed the food through the window but yielded to their persuasion to open the door enough to hand in the coffeepot without spilling it. Parley's version included elaborate allusions to characters from John Bunyon's masterpiece, *Pilgrim's Progress*:

> No sooner was the key turned than the door was seized by Mr. Follett with both hands; and with his foot placed against the wall, he soon opened a passage, which was in the same instant filled by Mr. Phelps, and followed by myself and Mr. Follett. The old jailer strode across the way, and stretched out his arms like Bunyan's Apollion, or like the giant Despair in Doubting Castle, but all to no purpose. One or two leaps brought us to the bottom of the stairs, carrying the old gentleman [the jailer] with us headlong, helter skelter, while old Luman sat and laughed in his corner of the prison, and Mrs. Phelps exclaimed, "O Lord God of Israel, thou canst help." Old Mrs. Gibbs looked on in silent amazement, while the jailer's wife acted the part of the giant despair's wife, Diffidence, and not only assisted in the scuffle, but cried out so loud that the town was soon alarmed.[43]

Laura Phelps, who was watching from the kitchen, heard the jailer call out. His wife, who weighed about two hundred pounds, rushed up the stairs. Mary Ann Phelps related the exciting story she heard from her parents: "The jailer had father clinched, but father jumped down two pairs of stairs, six steps each, with the jailer's wife hanging onto one of his arms. He would get rid of her when he jumped, but she would clinch him again when she again reached him. She could make better progress than he because the jailer held on to him, and in that condition they got down to the kitchen. Here Parley Pratt and Mr. Follet [sic] made their escape, and left father in the hands of the jailer."[44] This setback was only momentary. Phelps immediately broke loose and rushed outside. He, Pratt, and King ran toward the grove where Orson and John were waiting with the horses.

However, once the remaining members of the celebrating crowd still lingering in the town square realized what had happened, they seized weapons and set off in pursuit, soon joined by men from nearby houses. The dash exhausted King, Parley, and Morris after their long confinement. Although Morris reached the grove first, he could not mount his horse without help.[45] Orson Pratt and John Clark helped them all mount, Parley and Morris on the horses belonging to the two men and King on Laura's horse. Pratt later wrote of these tense moments:

> As soon as the prisoners drew near, they were hailed by their friends, and conducted to the horses. They were breathless and nearly ready to faint; but in a moment they were assisted to mount, and a whip and the reins placed in their hands, while the only words interchanged were—"Fly quickly, they are upon you!" "Which way shall we go?" "Where you can; you are already nearly surrounded," "But what will you do? they will kill you if they cannot catch us." "We will take care of ourselves; fly, fly, I say, instantly." These words were exchanged with the quickness of thought, while we were mounting and reining our horses; in another instant we were all separated from each other, and each one was making the best shift he could for his own individual safety.[46]

Parley and Morris galloped out of town, eluding their pursuers. However, King, probably because he was trying to deal with Laura's sidesaddle, was captured almost at once and immediately taken back to the jail. Not realizing that King had not escaped, Parley and Phelps separated, thinking that would be safer than all of them traveling together. For days these two men each traveled by a different route eastward toward Illinois and safety, suffering from lack of food, inclement weather, and often the need to hide by day and travel by night. Word had apparently spread quickly throughout the area between Columbia and the Illinois border to be on the lookout for them, and they were fortunate when they could find a family in an isolated area who was willing to take them in for a night's lodging and meal.[47] Pratt was reunited with his family in Quincy, including his brother Orson who had aided him in the escape. Phelps's children had been left in the care of an elderly woman near Montrose, Iowa,[48] while Laura traveled to Columbia. Now he waited anxiously for word of Laura and what had happened to her at the jail.

Laura Phelps waiting at the jail, heard a "shout of triumph" from the woods, indicating to her that at least one of them had been captured by the quickly forming posse. As Parley later wrote, presumably based on the details she related, she heard the men laughing and cursing, accompanied by the threat: "We've catched one of the damn'd Mormons and we'll roast him alive over a slow fire, damn him." At first she was told it was her husband that had been captured and that they were going to "kill him on the spot." Soon she recognized that the prisoner was King Follett "on whom they were venting their rage, as if he would be torn to pieces."[49] King was riding sidesaddle on her horse, making it impossible for her to pretend that she had not been involved in the jailbreak.

Parley's account continued: "He had been surrounded, overpowered and taken at the time [they] were each separated from the other. He was finally rescued from the mob, and thrust alive into the lower dungeon and chained down to the floor. He remained in this doleful situation for a few days, till the wrath of the multitude had time to cool a little, and then he was unchained by the Sheriff and again brought into the upper apartment and treated with some degree of kindness."[50] In a letter written on July 13, Laura's brother, John W. Clark, states that King was "chained down flat on his back with his hans [sic] chained also among the Flus [sic] for the space of one night."[51]

The jailer vented his feelings in cursing Laura, then ordered her to leave. Some local citizens offered to help, and two men escorted her from the jail. She was later taken in by a Richardson family, whose young son had watched the hullabaloo, concerned about her safety. She stayed with the family for about ten days, hoping to hear some word about the escapees and heartened by the lack of reports that they had been captured. She doubtless learned how King was being treated during this same period.

As Parley continued his narrative, the daring escape, though thwarted, had actually aroused the Missourians' admiration: "They now laughed with him [King] about his adventure, praised him for his bravery, and called him a good fellow. The truth of the matter was, they had no great desire to take the lives of any but those whom they had considered leaders; and since they had discovered that Mr. Follett and Mr. Phelps were not considered religious leaders among our Society, they were in no great danger, except they should happen to be killed in the heat of excitement or passion."[52]

Morris Phelps, who had encountered a member of the posse a few hours after his escape, encouraged their bragging and asked what they had done with the recaptured Mormon. The man answered: "'They tuk him back to prison, I suppose, but it was only the old one. If it had been one o' them tother chaps we would a skinn'ed 'em as quick as [Davey] Crockett would a coon, and then eat 'em alive without leaving a grease spot.'"[53] King was fifty-one,[54] while Pratt was thirty-two and Phelps was thirty-seven. According to Morris's account, the Missourians found King's age a reason to show him some clemency.[55]

Once Laura Phelps was fairly certain that Morris had been able to elude capture, the Richardsons helped recover her saddle and horse and arranged for her to travel toward Illinois with the "mail boy," so that she would not be alone. After traveling for two days on the mail route, she followed the bottoms of the Mississippi River. After riding about fifty miles alone, she was still about six miles from a place where she could count on finding shelter and it was getting dark. For the first time, her courage failed her. At that moment, a young man rode out of the woods and, after a moment of mutual appraisal, he asked, "'I wonder if you are not the woman I am looking for?' She said, 'I believe you are the man I am looking for.' Then he asked what her name was. She told him, after which he told her he was Mr. Follet's son." Morris, fearing that Laura had been jailed for her part in the escape, had sent this young man to find her and give a note saying that "he had arrived safe."[56] The two rode together to a hotel where they stayed, continuing on their way the next day.[57]

This young man was probably King's oldest son, John, then nineteen. (William Alexander, the next son, was thirteen.) This incident provides second-hand evidence that Louisa Follett and her children knew about the jail break and King's recapture. The *Columbia Patriot* on July 6 reported the escape in an article reprinted by the *Quincy Whig*: "The Columbia Patriot of the 6th says, that Parley P. Pratt, Morris Phelps and King Follet, three of them Mormon prisoners, escaped from the jail of this county on the evening of the 4th inst. The Deputy Sheriff, however, retook the last and brought him back to confinement. Pursuit is still made after the other two. Another, Lyman [sic] Gibbs, chose to remain, although he might easily have gotten out."[58]

King remained in the Columbia jail for two and a half months, awaiting trial, probably alone with only the jailer and his family.[59] The court, which convened on September 25, 1839, continued the case of Pratt, Gibbs, and Phelps—more a face-saving gesture than a realistic legal maneuver—and tried King for robbery on the charges originally filed in Caldwell County. According to the original Caldwell County indictment presently in Boone County Circuit Court records, King "was accused of taking from George Walters of Caldwell County, Missouri, his wagon ($100), three horses ($200), a rifle ($20) and other personal goods. He was also charged with taking from Henry and Lucy Ann McHenry, also of Caldwell County, Missouri, two kegs of gun powder and one sword ($40)."[60] The indictment dates the theft from Walters as October 24, 1838.[61] Based on this date, the Walters theft was part of the original charge against King when he was first arrested in November of 1838, while the McHenry matter may have been the "robbery" charge that resulted in his second imprisonment the following spring. A Caldwell County history identifies Henry McHenry as one of the individuals commissioned by the Missouri State Legislature to distribute the $2,000 approved to provide aid to the Mormons in Caldwell and Daviess Counties after the Mormon War.[62] The *History of the Church* confirms that a "Mr. McHenry" was on the commission but states that the actual items distributed consisted only of hogs, which already belonged to the Church members, being rounded up, shot and "cut up and distributed by McHenry to the poor, at a charge of four and five cents per pound; which, together with a few pieces of refuse goods, such as calicoes at double and treble prices soon consumed the two thousand dollars; doing the brethren very little good, or in reality none, as the property destroyed by them, (i.e. the distributing commission) was equal to what they gave the Saints."[63]

This description makes it clear how unhappy the Saints were about the use made of the small appropriation, how uncharitably it was distributed, and how those who needed it the most received little if none. I hypothesize that King may have voiced his opinion of this insult, added to injury, perhaps leading to a clash with McHenry, who retaliated by charging King with robbery.

The Boone County Court record of King's trial reads:

> This day came the attorney prosecuting for the state and the defendant being brought to the bar in the custody of the Sheriff, and it being demanded of him how he will acquit himself and whether he be guilty or not guilty of the charge in said indictment. Saith that he is not guilty and for his trial putteth himself upon the county as likewise does the attorney prose [sic].[64] Acting for the state and thereupon came a jury towit: William C Robinette, Edmund M Forbes, John Dunn, John B Packman, John Murphy,

Lewis Horne, Morris T Ballinger, Isaiah Parks, Frances Connelly, [illegible] Turner, James M West and Thomas U Bryan, who being elected tried and sworn well and truly to try the issue joined herein upon their oaths do say as the Jury find the defendant not guilty. Therefore it is considered and ordered by the Court that the defendant be discharged and go hence without [illegible] his costs.[65]

Some of the names of the jury may be transcribed incorrectly as the microfilm record is difficult to read. Also it appears the order initially was written "Jury find the defendant guilty" with a little extra space between the two words "defendant" and "guilty," and then "not" was entered in a much smaller script and with heavier ink. This could mean that the order was written ahead of time so that "not" could be added if necessary. Or perhaps the original document was written in anticipation of a "guilty" verdict, but the jury members decided otherwise.

The *Missouri Whig and General Advertiser*, published in Palmyra, Marion County, reported: "King Follett, one of the Mormon prisoners, indicted for robbery, was tried at Columbia on the 25ult. The jury, after retiring for a few minutes, brought in a verdict of not guilty."[66] A month later on October 26, 1839, the *History of the Church*, noted: "King Follett, the last of the brethren in bonds in Missouri, had his trial and was set free some time previous to this day."[67]

In 1841, the Missouri Secretary of State requested that the Circuit Court Clerks of Boone, Caldwell, Daviess and Ray Counties provide a "general certificate" regarding the "Mormon difficulties" in their individual counties and provide information as to "Who of the Mormons were indicted? For what crime? What was the final disposition of said indictments?" The "General Certificate" provided by Roger N. Todd, clerk of the Boone Circuit Court, In re. "State of Missouri vs. King Follett: Indictment for robbery," simply states: "This cause was also removed to Boone [c]ounty, by a change of venue, and the defendant removed to the jail in Boone [c]ounty, and having had a trial, was acquitted and discharged from custody."[68]

Undoubtedly King left Missouri as quickly as he could after the verdict. Even though Boone County is a hundred miles closer to the eastern state line than Far West, it would have taken him several days to get home, especially if he had to travel on foot. But I have found no details about that journey. Perhaps his son or son-in-law knew about the date of the trial and made arrangements to meet him with a horse or conveyance. At least he did not need to worry about active pursuit as Parley Pratt and Morris Phelps had done in their flight; but feelings against the Mormons were still high in at least some parts of the state, which may have complicated the need to find nightly shelter and meals.

It must have been with feelings of relief that King crossed the Mississippi into Illinois. When Parley had reached safety the previous July, he immediately found a grove of trees, and "kneeling down kissed the ground as a land of liberty, and then poured out my soul in thanks to God."[69] Perhaps King did, too.

Those thousands of Church members who suffered so much during the Mormon War in Missouri and ended up being forced out of the state would have been heartened by the comments of local historians eighty years later:

> Whatever may be truthfully said about the justice of the handling of the Mormon problem by the state, and however the Mormons may have deserved punishment, the manner, in which they were compelled to leave the state and the suffering which they endured in that journey is one of the most pathetic and deplorable chapters yet written in the history of this people. . . . It can not be denied that there [were] two sides to the controversy, but an impartial observer, in the light of history, is forced to the conclusion that the expulsion of the Mormons from the state was neither justified nor necessary, and was a mistake of the gravest kind on the part of the authorities.[70]

Notes

1. Jeffrey S. O'Driscoll, *Hyrum Smith: A Life of Integrity*, 188.
2. Richard Lyman Bushman, *Joseph Smith: Rough Stone Rolling*, 374.
3. Ibid., 382.
4. *History of the Church*, 3:226–33, 244, 284–86, 289–305.
5. Bushman, *Rough Stone Rolling*, 373.
6. *History of the Church*, 3:326.
7. Parley P. Pratt, "History of the Late Persecution," in Clark V. Johnson, ed., *Mormon Redress Petitions: Documents of the 1833–1838 Missouri Conflict*, 95.
8. Ibid.

9. Morris Phelps, Reminiscences, fd. 2, pp. 24–25. Provenance information in this source reads: "Phelps appears to have written the Missouri part of the account [folders 1 and 2] not long after the events occurred."

10. Scot Facer Proctor and Maurine Jensen Proctor, eds., *Autobiography of Parley P. Pratt: Revised and Enhanced Edition*, 282. This is probably the same gang of robbers referred to by Pratt in footnote 7 above.

11. Reed Peck, *The Reed Peck Manuscript: An Important Document Written in 1839*, 32.

12. During the November hearing in Richmond, Gibbs denied participating in the battle, but admitted his presence there: "I wasn't there at all. I staid back and took care of the horses." Based on his own statement, he was charged with murder. Ebenezer Robinson, "Items of Personal History," 235.

13. Phelps, Reminiscences, fd. 3, p. 1. Provenance information in this source states: "That portion of the manuscript detailing Phelps's escape from Columbia jail (folder 3) was presented to the Historian's Office by Ruth Clark Maughan, a great-great-granddaughter of Morris Phelps, on 1 July 1968."

14. Dean C. Jessee, comp. and ed., *The Personal Writings of Joseph Smith*, 419. Isaac Galland, who owned a large tract of land in southeastern Iowa, initially appeared to be sympathetic to the Mormons and had offered a large tract of land for the refugees' purchase. Galland accepted baptism by Joseph Smith but soon left the Church.

15. The editors of Parley's autobiography identify these three children: "At the time, she was caring for little Parley, two; Mary Ann Stearns, six, and Nathan, seven months." Proctor and Proctor, *Autobiography of Parley P. Pratt*, 286 note 1. "Little Parley" was Parley's son by his first wife, Thankful Halsey Pratt. Mary Ann Stearns was Mary Pratt's daughter by her first husband, Nathan Stearns, and Nathan was Parley's and Mary Ann's first child.

16. Phelps, "Reminiscences," fd. 3, pp. 1–2.

17. Proctor and Proctor, *Autobiography of Parley P. Pratt*, 292.

18. *History of the Church*, 3:353–54.

19. Phelps, "Reminiscences," fd. 3, p. 2.

20. Proctor and Proctor, *Autobiography of Parley P. Pratt*, 297–98.

21. Ibid., 298.

22. Ibid.

23. Pratt, "History of the Late Persecution," in Clark, *Mormon Redress Petitions*, 97–98.

24. Max H Parkin, *Missouri*, 529–30. The building was about in the middle of the south side of today's Ash Street, between 7th and 8th streets.

25. *History of the Church*, 3:368.

26. Boone County, Missouri, Circuit Court Record/Docket Book July 1839 to August 1840, 222.

27. I did not find in the available court records the name of King's attorney for this hearing. However, a recent essay written about the escape from the Columbia jail identifies James S. Rollins "as a lawyer for King Follett, one of the prisoners who was recaptured almost immediately after effecting the jailbreak." Rollins was a Boone County attorney and a state representative and is credited with "shaping the strategy that secured" the location of the University of Missouri in Boone County. Jean A. Pry and Dale A. Whitman, "'But for the Kindness of Strangers': The Columbia, Missouri, Response to the Mormon Prisoners and the Jailbreak of July 4, 1839," 136 note 13.

28. Boone County, Missouri, Circuit Court Record/Docket Book July 1839 to August 1840, 222–23. This record validates Phelps's statement that King was indicted in Caldwell County though originally jailed in Richmond (Ray County), then transferred to Columbia (Boone County). See note 9.

29. *History of the Church*, 3:377.

30. Mary Ann Phelps Rich, "The Life of Mary A. Phelps Rich," 5. I could find no evidence that the State of Missouri ever participated in any discussion to release the prisoners. Perhaps the Prophet is referring to plans that Church members had to "liberate" the prisoners by helping them to escape. Such plans obviously had not succeeded.

31. Ibid., 6.

32. Proctor and Proctor, *Autobiography of Parley P. Pratt*, 301.

33. Ibid.

34. Phelps, "Reminiscences," fd. 3, p. 4.

35. Ibid.

36. Ibid., fd. 3, pp. 4–5.

37. Ibid., fd. 3, p. 5.

38. Proctor and Proctor, *The Autobiography of Parley P. Pratt*, 303.

39. Phelps, "Reminiscences," fd. 3, p. 5.

40. Ibid.

41. Proctor and Proctor, *The Autobiography of Parley P. Pratt*, 309.

42. Rich, "The Life of Mary A. Phelps Rich," 7.

43. Proctor and Proctor, *The Autobiography of Parley P. Pratt*, 310–11.

44. Rich, "The Life of Mary A. Phelps Rich," 7.

45. Phelps, "Reminiscences," fd. 4, p. 7.

46. Proctor and Proctor, *Autobiography of Parley P. Pratt*, 312–13.

47. Neither Pratt nor Phelps give the number of days they traveled nor the dates on which they arrived in Illinois. But based on bits of scattered information in Pratt's autobiography, I believe that his journey took about five or six days, that he arrived about July 9, and that Orson Pratt and Morris Phelps had arrived at least three days earlier. Proctor and Proctor, *Autobiography of Parley P. Pratt*, 313–41.

48. Rich, "The Life of Mary A. Phelps Rich," 4–5. Upon her initial arrival in Illinois, Laura had crossed the Mississippi to the Iowa side to join her father-in-law. She found a place for her and her children—an "old house in the middle of a corn field." Her daughter Mary described it as not fit "for any one to live in as they had stabled horses in it, and it was in a very bad condition. After looking at the place, however, mother decided that any place was better than to be right out of doors, where the sun was getting so very hot." Perhaps Louisa and her family found similar conditions in which to live as they waited for King to join them.

49. Proctor and Proctor, *Autobiography of Parley P. Pratt*, 321.

50. Ibid.

51. John W. Clark, Letter to "Dear Brothers and Sisters" (David H. Clark, Dupage, Mill County, Illinois), July 13, 1839, 1. John states that he had arrived "at home," probably meaning Iowa, a day earlier, after traveling part way on foot and part way on a steamer. At the time of the escape, he and Orson Pratt were left without horses.

52. Proctor and Proctor, *Autobiography of Parley P. Pratt*, 321–22.

53. Ibid., 318.

54. Though I did not find any direct mention of King's age in Pratt's writings, the editors of his autobiography referred to King's age on two occasions. Proctor and Proctor, *Autobiography of Parley P. Pratt*, 287 note 3: "King Follett was fifty-one years old at this time"; and "The 'old one' is King Follett, age fifty-one. In the early nineteenth century the life expectancy of a man was fifty years. Hence, King Follett could have been considered old" (323 note 2). Undoubtedly to Pratt and Phelps, who were nineteen and fourteen years younger respectively, King, who had children their age, would have seemed old.

55. John L. Hart, "Courage a Legend: As She Faced Mobs," *Church News*, June 19, 2004, 12, writing an article in a popular series of historical profiles, calls King "ailing." While it is true that all of the prisoners were debilitated by their lengthy confinement, there is no other reference to King's health. Indeed, his activities in Far West, during the attempted escape, and later in Nauvoo suggest a man in good physical condition, especially for his age.

56. Rich, "The Life of Mary A. Phelps Rich," 10–12.

57. Laura's brother wrote: "Morris Phelps and his wife came home July 18." John Clark, Letter to "Dear Brothers and Sisters," 2. I believe this would mean they returned to the home she had established in Iowa on that date, having previously united in the Quincy area.

58. "The Mormon Prisoners Escaped," *Quincy Whig*, July 20, 1839; reprinted in the *Daily [St. Louis] Missouri Republican*, 15 (Thursday, July 11, 1839).

59. Sometime after the escape, Luman Gibbs "was discharged from custody, and after continuing this cause on the docket for some time, it was dismissed."

Document, 155. Pratt wrote that Luman and his wife Phila later lived in "the little town of Augusta, a few miles from Fort Madison, Iowa Territory." See Proctor and Proctor, *Autobiography of Parley P. Pratt*, 322.

60. Quoted in Alexander L. Baugh, "The Final Episode of Mormonism in Missouri in the 1830s: The Incarceration of the Mormon Prisoners at Richmond and Columbia Jails, 1838–1839," 34 note 100.

61. Alex Baugh, email to Joann Mortensen, November 13, 2008, reporting his notes on the indictment: "See Boone County, Missouri, Circuit Court Records, Miscellaneous, Case No. 1380, fld. 21" in Special Collections, Ellis Library, University of Missouri, Columbia. I believe this reference is to the original indictment out of Caldwell County requested by the Boone County Court. See note 26.

62. *History of Caldwell and Livingston Counties*, 143. The 1840 U.S. Census for Missouri identifies a "Henry McHenry" as living in Blythe, Caldwell County. A "George Walters" is listed as living in Rockport, Caldwell County, in that same census.

63. *History of the Church*, 3:243.

64. King had no money to hire an attorney and the state did not provide one, as would be the case for an indigent defendant today. "Pro Se" (Latin for "For Self" or "in one's own behalf") indicates that King spoke in his own defense in this matter. *Legal Dictionary*, http://definitions.

65. Boone County, Missouri, Circuit Court Record/Docket Book July 1839 to August 1840, 267–68. I suspect the illegible words after "without" means that he did not have to pay court costs, which seems logical as he had been in jail for months with no income.

66. "King Follett . . .," [Palmyra] *Missouri Whig and General Advertiser*, 1, no. 11 (October 12, 1839).

67. *History of the Church*, 4:17.

68. "Certificates," in *Document Containing the Correspondence, Orders, &c.*, 152–55.

69. Proctor and Proctor, *Autobiography of Parley P. Pratt*, 339.

70. Carrie Polk Johnston and W.H.S. McGlumphy, *History of Clinton and Caldwell Counties, Missouri*, 261.

Chapter Fourteen

Exiles in Quincy

While the Extermination Order issued by Governor Lilburn Boggs ordered Mormons out of the state, it did not suggest where they must go. But recognizing their physical and financial burdens, it was obvious that their options were limited. Going west would have placed them in Indian Territory. Going north would take them to unsettled land, and going south would confront them with enemies who had already ejected them. Returning to Ohio was likewise not a possibility, not only because they would have been confronting anti-Mormon feelings that were only a couple of years old, but also because it would have meant a much longer journey in winter for the impoverished Saints. Heading east two hundred miles to Illinois thus seemed to provide the best opportunity. According to a recent Institute manual, "Church leaders who were not in jail had no definite plan for where the Saints should settle. Word reached the leaders that the citizens of Illinois were sympathetic to their plight and would welcome the Saints."[1] However, this source includes no documentation of discussions or negotiations that went into making the decision.

For some time, a few Mormons had been living in Illinois just across the Mississippi River from eastern Missouri. Therefore, at least temporarily, the area around Quincy, Illinois, seemed to be the safest place for the exiled members. The town itself was located on a bluff overlooking the river and was surrounded by good farmland that produced abundant crops for consumption and for sale in other markets. Quincy's estimated population was somewhere between 1,800 and 2,300.[2] Because of

Quincy's location, many Mormon travelers, including Zion's Camp, had traveled through the town going to and from Missouri. Joseph Smith and others had traveled through Quincy when they left Kirtland in 1837. As early as 1832, elders had preached in the area. Quincy, located about forty-five miles directly south of Nauvoo where the Church eventually established its new home, had become the seat of Adams County in 1825. It is presently located where U.S. Highway 24 crosses the Mississippi River, thus connecting Illinois and Iowa.

During the winter of 1838–39, the Saints moved rapidly into the Quincy area, assisted by an eleven-member Refugee Committee of Church priesthood holders, though they were still unsure of how they would be accepted by the residents. During the Church's short history, Mormons had seldom been welcomed in a new area; but the compassion of Quincy's residents earned their unfailing gratitude. Israel Barlow, writing to relatives in Massachusetts, reported in February 1839:

> About 12 families cross the river into Quincy every day and about 30 are constantly at the other side waiting to cross. There is only one ferry boat to cross in. For 3 or 4 weeks past it has been beautiful weather and the roads great for traveling, which has made it very favorable for the brethren but now it is rainy, the roads are mudy [sic] within three days. We look upon our current situation with much sorrow and much anxiety, we must now scatter in every direction [?] hoping [we] can find employment.... We are hungry and they feed us, naked and they clothed us [and] showed much attention and kindness.... Many in this place have great sympathy for us.[3]

Barlow also recorded that the Saints in Quincy were concerned for the fate of the prisoners still in Missouri, afraid that they would never be let out. King Follett, of course, was one of these prisoners.

Samuel Kendall Gifford remembering in 1864 events that happened when he was about eighteen reported: "We landed in Quincy, Illinois where we were received by the citizens of that place. Some of the merchants and leading men of Quincy donated quite freely to help the most destitute of the Saints. Such will be remembered when it is said 'In as much as you have done it unto the least of these, my servants you have done it unto me.'"[4]

Sarah DeArmon Pea Rich, who bore her first child in March 1839 in Burton (near Quincy), described their plight in an autobiographical sketch written sometime after 1885: Her family had "been striped [sic] by the mob of all we possessed except our beds and what little clothing we had. We were very poor having no home and among strangers with the exception of a few of our brethren. . . . The inhabitants of Quincy were very kind to us as a people and done all they could to give our bretheren employment and assisted many that were in need and many were sick they also were cared for an[d] there wants looked after by the people of Quincy."[5]

Lucy Mack Smith and her youngest daughter and namesake, teenage Lucy, were both stricken with cholera shortly after arriving in Quincy. Mother Smith was impressed by the kindness of "the ladies of Quincy" who "sent us every delicacy which could be obtained."[6] Eliza Roxcy Snow simply acknowledged that she "arrived in Quincy, Illinois, where many of the exiled Saints had preceded us, and all were received with generous hospitality."[7] It is to be hoped that Louisa, her children, and later King received the same care when they, too, reached the Quincy area.

An organization called the Democratic Association of Quincy helped focus the community on the needs of the "Mormon exiles." In a series of meetings beginning in early February, the association members appointed a committee to gather information and determine the needs of Church members. These meetings passed resolutions, outlining actions the committee would take. First, they would inform the community that Church members were "entitled to our sympathy and kindest regard" and encourage citizens "to extend to them all the kindness in their power to bestow." Second, the committee members would "use their utmost endeavors to obtain employment for all these people who are able and willing to labour" and to inform the community at large that the Church members wanted only to obtain employment to "save them from starving."[8]

Perhaps the possible political impact of such a large number of prospective voters appealed to both the Democratic and Whig parties, increasing the potential tax base. If so, the same voting issue that had caused problems in Missouri might have benefited the Saints at this time in Quincy. A March editorial in the local paper chastised Missouri's action: "We have no language sufficiently strong for the expression of our indignation and shame at the recent transaction in a sister state."[9] If the town was growing, as it seemed to be, it could provide jobs for workers, though the numbers that arrived in so short a period obviously caused housing and provision problems. However, in addition to these practical reasons, it seems that the people in Quincy simply acted as good citizens. They saw a problem—a people in need—and spontaneously mobilized to help as they could, both as organized groups and as individuals.

No doubt many of the refugees paused only long enough to inquire about job prospects before moving out into the surrounding area and even into nearby counties. Ebenezer Robinson, for instance, recorded that, by his arrival in early February: "Quincy was being overrun with laborers, and hearing there were some parties about forty miles north, in Hancock County, favorable to our people, we concluded to go there."[10] Arriving about March 12, John Lowe Butler stayed "only three to four weeks." Then "wanting to farm as early in the year as possible, [he] moved about ten miles from Quincy—in which direction is not stated. There they rented a farm and planted, knowing that their stay would last only until Church leaders chose a new gathering place."[11] Others "scattered along the Mississippi River from Keokuk, Iowa, to Quincy, Illinois.[12]

It is unknown how many Mormons actually reached Quincy. In 1999, Charles W. Scholz, then Quincy's mayor, described the situation: "For 1,500 Quincyans to provide clothing and shelter during the harsh winter of 1838–1839 to more than 5,000 members of the Mormon Church was an extraordinary act indeed. In modern-day terms the act would be equivalent to our current population taking care of approximately 150,000 men, women, and children in need. This act has been called one of the greatest examples of humanitarian service in the history of our country."[13] Susan Easton Black's description of this event reflects an attitude of a population in Quincy much different than any the Saints had experienced before: "Early Quincy residents compassionately cared for Mormon exiles from Missouri, as one would care for an enduring friend. Residents expressed indignation at the Missouri governor's order. . . . Citizens of Quincy disregarded religious differences and embraced downcast Mormons crossing the Mississippi. The *solicitous reception* by Quincyans during the winter of 1838–1839 is unparalleled in the annals of Mormonism and has never been forgotten. It has become a legacy that epitomizes all that is good in people."[14]

Quincy's humanitarianism extended beyond the Saints. Its citizens aided runaway slaves on the Underground Railway and also Native Americans who were being relocated to the West. The Saints accepted this generosity with gratitude, hoping for a season of peace, an opportunity to purchase land at a reasonable price, and "decent medical care and adequate schooling" for their children.[15]

Though very appreciative of the caring and contributions of necessities given to those in need, Church members quickly focused on finding employment so that they could become self-sufficient. David Pettegrew, in an entry dated January 19, 1839, "took a job chopping wood and boating it."[16] Sarah DeArmon Pea Rich wrote that her husband, Charles, "split rails to get means to pay house rent and get our scanty living for money we had none."[17] Upon his arrival in Quincy, John Somers Higbee "again went to fishing with a net in company with my father's brother."[18] Anson Call, who had obtained a contract to build a railroad, "hired none but the brethren. I kept from 12 to 14 during the Season. I paid my men 20 dollars per month and made but very little more than those I hired."[19] Despite their desperate struggle for bare subsistence, the Saints continued to express gratitude for their blessings. Thomas Daniel Stillwell, writing after his arrival in Utah, summed up: "And all through these times whilst we had been mobbed and driven about imprisoned and in the power of our enemies, called on to sacrifice our home and turned out into the world to start afresh, during all this time we felt happy and cheerful, and felt to thank God for our deliverance, and no spirit of regret for what we had been called upon to sacrifice for the gospel's sake."[20]

I like to think that these descriptions reflected the feelings of Louisa and her children when they reached Quincy—exact date unknown but sometime before May 11, 1839. Fortunately, the grueling winter storms and endless mud had abated with spring, so their physical sufferings were corresponding less. Most likely, she relied heavily on her son-in-law, Nathan, for assistance, and in return she helped daughter Adeline care for Nathan's two young daughters. Twenty-year-old John must have taken a man's share of the work on his shoulders, sharing with Nathan the responsibility for feeding and clothing the family of ten. Sixteen-year-old Nancy may have been available to work as a hired girl in a family that was better off, while fourteen-year-old William Alexander would also have been considered able to shoulder a man's burdens. Louisa, in addition to making a home, would have had primary charge of six-year-old Edward and eighteen-month-old Warren King. It is not known what kind of work they found—or even whether their late arrival worked for or against them. If most of the Saints in or near Quincy had begun to get settled, they may have been in a position to offer employment, especially if early arrivals had been able to find farming opportunities; or it may simply mean that all of the jobs had already been taken.

Whatever plans they made had to be tentative, hanging on the unknown consideration of King's on-going imprisonment. He did not reach Quincy until the first part of October, when the harvest was already well underway. It probably seemed to King and Louisa that he and the other prisoners were all but forgotten by the main body of the Church as it left Missouri and settled in Illinois, but that was not so.

Amasa Lyman who had visited and spent time with King in Far West in June 1834 following the cholera outbreak in Clay County, now went back to Missouri, accompanied by Charles C. Rich, Seymour Brunson, and John Killyon, when King and the other prisoners were being transferred from Richmond to Columbia. To Lyman's dismay, he was thwarted at helping them escape:

> We were frustrated in our intentions to assist Brother Pratt and others, by the misrepresentation of matters between us and them, by Watson Barlow, who came from Quincy to see the prisoners, and was known as a Mormon, while we were traveling incog. On the strength of Barlow's representation I went to Quincy, and returned again to Columbia, but was again defeated as before, and returned leaving our friends to their fate. Brother Pratt told me after, that they were ready to have acted upon our first proposition for their rescue. Our plan was the same as that on which they came out on the fourth of July subsequently.[21]

Watson Barlow is identified in a family source as a "steward of the Prophet," an unusual appellation in Mormonism; evidently, he felt responsible for Joseph Smith's welfare and made more than one trip between Quincy and Far West, attempting to aid all of those in prison, including those both at Liberty and Columbia.[22] Surely these men who had actually seen the prisoners in Columbia reported on their condition to Louisa and the other families waiting in Quincy for their release. Since at least Lyman and Barlow made more than one visit, they also may have carried messages between the prisoners and their loved ones. John W. Clark, after his return to the Quincy area following his participation in the Columbia prison escape, documents that Church members were still attempting to find a way to obtain King's release. On July 19, 1839, he wrote: "Brother Follet [sic] is Bailable and the Brethren has gone to Bale him out.[23]

By the time Louisa and her family arrived in Quincy, even with the help and understanding of local citizens, living conditions were still deplorable. A local historian described conditions in April 1839: "They crowded together in barns, sheds, and many in huts and tents throughout the town. Some of them were almost entirely destitute."[24] Wandle Mace, a recent convert living in Quincy, described living conditions that virtually mirrored those of 1834 when the Saints had been driven across the Missouri River from Jackson County to Clay County: "[I] went down to the riverside and found about 14 or 15 families camped on the river bottom in a most miserable condition. They had crossed the river and could get no farther. Some of them had tried to make a shelter from the wind by placing some poles in the ground and putting a sheet over them. The wind was blowing the snow about them so that the poor children who was hovering over a little fire could get little benefit from it. I returned as soon as possible and made known their situation and in a very short time they were moved into town and made comfortable." Mace brought new arrivals into his own home so that "very many nights the floors, upstairs and down, were covered with beds so closely it was impossible to set a foot anywhere without stepping upon someone's bed."[25]

Mace's home also became a meeting place for worship services. He describes his house as having "two good sized rooms with a good cellar beneath, and one large room above which was reached by stairs on the outside. On the premises was a good stable for my horses and other conveniences that could not be had in the city." The upper room was used for religious meetings and meetings of the Refugee Committee.[26] According to the *History of the Church*, three general conferences were held while the Saints were in Quincy: the first in February 1839 and the second in March—both before Louisa and her family arrived—and the third in May.[27] Joseph Smith presided at this May conference, and Louisa may have attended. She would have fully shared the Prophet Joseph's "peculiar feelings, after having been separated from the brethren so long."[28]

The fact that the Saints continued their worship services, despite their difficult living conditions, impressed the citizens; and one historian recorded: "They kept up their religious services and observances, and were for a time much more numerous than any other religious or ecclesiastical society in the place."[29] The Church did not erect a building in Quincy, but the Saints continued to hold services, even after Nauvoo

Photocopy of Louisa Follett's original handwritten Redress Affidavit. Courtesy of LDS Church History Library.

was founded. A stake was established in Quincy in 1841 but was reduced to a branch in 1842 when most of its members moved to Nauvoo.[30] The only surviving record of the stake and branch membership and meetings in Quincy between 1840 and 1845 does not contain any Follett or West names. This does not mean that the Folletts were not active; many other families known to be in the area also do not appear on the record, so it is obviously incomplete.[31]

Three records confirm the Follett family's presence in Quincy. The first is the Mormon redress petitions that, as noted, Louisa signed on May 11, 1839. This petition was created at the direction of Joseph Smith in a letter written from Liberty Jail between March 20 and 25, 1839. Part of that letter, later canonized as Doctrine and Covenants 123, asks the leaders to gather "up a knowledge of all the facts, and sufferings and abuses put upon them. . . . And also all of the property and amount of damages which they have sustained, both of character and personal injuries, as well as real property" (D&C 123:1–2). The Saints would then present this information to the federal government as a means of obtaining financial reimbursement for the Saints' losses over the years in Missouri, military support against the Missourians, or both.

Louisa's affidavit, which covers all of their losses in Missouri starting in 1833, may have included the losses of Nathan and Adeline West as well as they did not prepare a separate document and the two families undoubtedly lived together at least part of the time. Louisa's affidavit documents losses amounting to $3,920, broken down by years.[32]

In 1833, she listed three claims amounting to $170.00: "To loss of improvemants on land and buldings" ($100); "To loss of provision and wheat in the ground" ($50); "To loss of time and expence of moving from Jackson Co. to Clay Co." 1835 cost them $150 in "loss of property, time & expence by being driven from Clay Co. to Caldwell Co." The most detailed claims are cited for 1838–39, a total of $3,500. The indignation in her voice is almost audible: "To loss of land and buildings not gitting the value of them on the account of being obliged by the Mob to leave the state" ($800); "To loss of time and expences by moving from Missouri to Illenois, and being detained from business previous to removal by the unlawful proceedings of the Mob" ($200); "To loss of the company, and being deprived of the assistance of my husband (King Follett) who is now, and has ben for a long time kept in prison as I think contireary to the Laws of the land" ($500); and "To being deprived of rights of citizen ship in the state of Missouri, having ben driven by a mob under the order of Govener Boggs from that state to the state of Illenois" ($2,000). The sum of all these losses over the six brutal years was $3,920. She swore, "I certify the a bove account to Be Just and true a cording to the Best of m[y] Knowledge" before C.M. Woods, C.C.C.,[33] Adams Co., IL, 11 May 1839, and signed it: "Louisa Follett."

The second document of the extended Follett family's presence in Adams County is its appearance in the 1840 U.S. Census.[34] This census was begun on June 1, was to be completed by November 1, and the original census returns were signed and witnessed on November 2. Both King Follett and Nathan West are listed as heads of separate households. I have filled in the age groups, which is how the census reported the household's occupants until the 1850 census when they started giving specific ages and personal names. On both the holograph census and the printed index, King's name appears as " King Fallat." His household consisted of:

1 Male 50–60 years, King Follett
1 Male 20–30 years, John Follett
1 Male 16–20 years, William Alexander Follett
1 Male 5–10 years, Edward Moroni [his name was misspelled "Maroni"] Follett
1 Male under 5 years, Warren King Follett
1 Female, 40–50 years, Louisa Tanner Follett
1 Female, 15-20 years, Nancy Follett

These ages correspond correctly, as does the same census for the Nathan West family:

1 Male 40–50 years, Nathan West
1 Female 20–30 years, Adeline Follett West
1 Female 10–15 years, Tryphena West
1 Female under 5, Maria West

A handwritten note on the holograph census record states: "Adams County exclusive of the City of Quincy." The modern indexer has interpreted this note to mean: "no township is identified." It seems reasonable, then, that the Folletts and the Wests, like many other Church members, lived outside Quincy, perhaps on land they rented and farmed or as squatters on unclaimed land. However, the fact that the two families are listed on pages 26 and 60, respectively, probably indicates that they were not living next door to each other. And since the census did not begin until June 1, I deduce that neither family moved permanently to Nauvoo until after that date.

The third Follett record in Adams County commemorates a happy occasion for the family: the marriage of King and Louisa's second daughter, Nancy, to James Daley on June 4, 1840.[35] The return of the original license has the signature of Nathan West, Nancy's brother-in-law, as of-

Marriage license of James Daly [sic] and Nancy M. Follett, issued May 30, 1840, with return of the license showing a marriage date of June 4, 1840. Certified copy courtesy of the Adams County Clerk of Court, March 19, 2003.

ficiator, but lists no specific location in Adams County. This authority to marry must have been in his capacity as Church leader, as there is no evidence that he held a civil position in Adams County at that time.

James was born in Marcellus, New York, about 1816, the son of John Daley Jr. and Elizabeth Ennis Daley. The family moved to Florence, Ohio, when James was about seven; here he and other members of his family were converted to the Church in 1832. At age eighteen, James and other family members started on Zion's Camp; but for "some reason

James did not continue, but returned home. Perhaps the leaders felt he was too young."[36] In the spring of 1837, James accompanied his parents, an unmarried brother, and three married siblings to Far West where, in June, he purchased two forty-acre parcels of land near the rest of the Daley family, two miles southwest of the town. This purchase was not far from where Nancy lived with her parents.

James participated in the Battle of Crooked River and fled with his extended family to Quincy in February 1839. There is no record of when or how the young couple met and began courting, but one modern Daley family historian says: "The Daleys probably knew the Folletts quite well inasmuch as King Follett was also . . . in the Battle of Crooked River along with James."[37] This is another family-generated statement providing further evidence that King participated in this battle. (See Chapter 11.)

Members of the Church stayed in the Quincy area for approximately fourteen months—from early 1839 to the spring of 1840. This period was an important respite. Although they knew Quincy was only a temporary stopping place and their living conditions were still restricted, yet they were free from persecution or fears about what would happen to their co-believers. When they began leaving—to Nauvoo and elsewhere—it was the first time that the decision to move was even partially their own. One short paragraph by a local historian writing in 1882, may reflect how this episode of Mormon history was remembered forty years later: "During the winter of 1838–9, the Mormons, in the midst of cold weather, in a suffering condition, in great numbers, being driven from Missouri, took shelter here. They were kindly treated by our citizens, many of the men finding temporary employment in the town."[38]

In 1976, the Church, in cooperation with the Illinois State Historical Society, placed a marker in Washington Square in Quincy that commemorates the Mormons' experiences there.[39] On August 3, 2002, two monuments were erected acknowledging the kindness of the citizens of Quincy to the Saints in 1838–39. One was erected by the City of Quincy in Clat Adams Bicentennial Park at the approximate site where Mormons crossed the Mississippi River. The inscription on the front of the monument reads: "The Latter-day Saints crossed the Mississippi River at this approximate site and were befriended by the citizens of Quincy." The back contains two inscriptions. The first, by Joseph Smith,

Monument dedicated 2002 in Clat Adams Bicentennial Park, commemorating the approximate site where the Saints crossed the Mississippi into Quincy in 1838–39. Photo courtesy of Larry F. Lamb, Quincy, Illinois, 2009.

reads: "The citizens of Quincy (will) be held in everlasting remembrance for their unparalleled liberality and marked kindness to our people, when in their greatest state of suffering and want." Gordon B. Hinckley, Church president when the monument was erected, provides the second statement: "Eternal will be our gratitude for the people of Quincy who provided shelter to the homeless." On that same day another monument was erected by the Williams-Swain family to honor Frederick G. Williams, who served as a second counselor in Joseph Smith's First Presidency. His family had recently discovered his burial location.[40]

Notes

1. Church Education System, *Church History in the Fulness of Times*, 213.

2. Scot Facer Proctor and Maurine Jensen Proctor, eds., *Autobiography of Parley P. Pratt, Revised and Enhanced Edition*, 268 note 6; William H. Collins, Cicero F. Perry, and John Tillson, *Past and Present of the City of Quincy and Adams County, Illinois: Including the Late Colonel John Tillison's History of Quincy, Together with Biographical Sketches of Many of Its Leading and Prominent Citizens and Illustrious Dead*, 77.

3. Israel Barlow, Quincy, Illinois, Letter to Elizabeth H. Bullard, Holliston, Middlesex, Massachusetts, February 27, 1839; capitalization standardized.

4. Samuel Kendall Gifford, "Reminiscences 1864," 5.

5. Sarah DeArmon Pea Rich, "Sarah DeArmon Pea Rich, 1814–1893," 52.

6. Scot Facer Proctor and Maurine Jensen Proctor, eds., *The Revised and Enhanced History of Joseph Smith by His Mother*, 421.

7. Maureen Ursenbach Beecher, ed., *The Personal Writings of Eliza Roxcy Snow*, 15.

8. *History of the Church*, 3:267–71.

9. Editorial, *Quincy [Illinois] Argus*, March 16, 1839, quoted in Anna Scianna, "Missouri's Mormon Past," *Missourian*, October 15, 2006, 1.

10. Ebenezer Robinson, "Items of Personal History of the Editor," *The Return* 2 (April 1890): 241–46. Robinson, a New York native, was baptized in 1835, assisted in printing the Doctrine and Covenants, and edited the *Elders' Journal* and *Times and Seasons*. He was baptized a member of the RLDS Church in 1863 and became the editor of *The Return*.

11. William G. Hartley, *My Best for the Kingdom: History and Autobiography of John Lowe Butler, a Mormon Frontiersman*, 92.

12. Richard Lyman Bushman, *Joseph Smith: Rough Stone Rolling*, 376.

13. "Remarks of Charles W. Scholz, Mayor of Quincy," xv.

14. Susan Easton Black, "Quincy: A City of Refuge," 87; emphasis Black's.

15. Richard E. Bennett, "Quincy, the Home of Our Adoption: A Study of the Mormons in Quincy, Illinois 1838–1840," 86–88.

16. David Pettegrew, "A History of David Pettegrew," 34.

17. Rich, "Sarah DeArmon Pea Rich," 52.

18. John Somers Higbee, Reminiscences and Diaries, 1845–66, typescript, 3.

19. Ethan L. Call and Christine Shafer Call, *Journal of Anson Call*, 20.

20. Thomas Daniel Stillwell, *Reminiscences*, 8.

21. Albert R. Lyman, *Amasa Mason Lyman, Trailblazer and Pioneer from the Atlantic to the Pacific*, 100–102. Lyman was born in 1813, was raised in

New Hampshire, joined the Church in 1832, served several missions, and was a member of Zion's Camp. He was with the Church in Caldwell County, defended Far West, was taken prisoner with the Prophet in Far West, was paraded through Independence, and was released at Richmond.

22. Ora H. Barlow, and Israel Barlow Family Association, *The Israel Barlow Story and Mormon Mores*, 155.

23. John W. Clark, Letter to "Dear Brothers and Sisters" (David H. Clark, Dupage, Mill County, Illinois), July 13, 1839, 2.

24. Gen. John Tillson, quoted in Landry Genosky, ed., *People's History of Quincy and Adams County, Illinois: A Sesquicentennial History*, 483.

25. Wandle Mace, "Biography of Wandle Mace," 9–10.

26. Mace, "Biography of Wandle Mace," 9.

27. *History of the Church*, 3:260, 283, 344.

28. *History of the Church*, 3:345.

29. Gen. John Tillson, quoted in Genosky, *People's History of Quincy and Adams County*, 483.

30. Keith W. Perkins and Donald Q. Cannon, *Ohio and Illinois*, 226.

31. Quincy (Illinois) Branch, Record of Members and Minutes of Meetings, 1840–45.

32. Louisa [Tanner] Follett, "State of Missouri Dr. [Debtor] to Louisa Follett, published as "Affidavit," in Clark V. Johnson, ed., *Mormon Redress Petitions: Documents of the 1833–1838 Missouri Conflict*, 201–2. The holograph has Louisa's signature, but the document itself might be in three different handwritings: (1) the main body, which I believe compares to the signature; (2) a statement: "I certify the above account to be just and true acording [sic]" to the Best of my knowledge" in what appears to be a different hand; (3) a statement "Sworn to before me this 11 day of May. . . ." which appears to be the same handwriting as the signature of C. M. Woods just below who was the "notary" for many of the affidavits. There appears to be a light line drawn below the body of the document, then the "I certify" statement with her signature. followed by another light line before the "Sworn to. . ." statement followed by Woods's signature.

33. C.C.C. confirms that C. M. Woods (Carlo M. Woods) was acting in his capacity as clerk of the circuit court for Adams County, a position he held "from 5 Dec 1838 through 21 Feb 1842." See Clark V. Johnson, *Mormon Redress Petitions*, 755.

34. U.S. Census, 1840, Illinois, Adams County, Roll 54, p. 26.

35. Members of the Great River Genealogical Society, comps., *Marriages of Adams County, Illinois, 1825–60*, 1:28.

36. James D. Martin, *The Story of the John Daley Jr. Family: Westward Pioneers*, 10.

37. Ibid., 24; punctuation standardized.

38. Henry Asbury, *Reminiscences of Quincy, Illinois*, 75–76.

39. Velma Williams Skidmore, "Found at Last: The Final Resting Place of Frederick Granger Williams," 234. I did not find any record that quoted the inscription on this marker.

40. Ibid.

❋ Chapter Fifteen ❋

The Beginning of Nauvoo, 1839–40

During the cold winter of 1838–39, which Joseph Smith, his two counselors, and other Church leaders spent in Liberty Jail, many nonmembers must have envisioned the dissolution of Mormonism. But continue it did at Commerce or Commerce City, Illinois, located on a horseshoe bend of the Mississippi River about fifty miles north of Quincy and now geographically on State Route 96, twenty-five miles south of Burlington, Iowa.[1] Later renamed Nauvoo, no other geographic place name, except Salt Lake City, has so close a connection to the Mormons and their church. According to Glen M. Leonard, LDS historian of the Nauvoo period, the city was located

> on a peninsula-like piece of land jutting out into the Mississippi River. . . . It had been identified by many visitors as one of the most beautiful sites along the river for many miles. A large, level floodplain with wooded bluffs beyond, it measured about two miles north to south and a mile east to west. The flatland rose gently toward the east, nestling against bluffs that rose seventy feet above the river. Small streams of water from the prairie to the east cut through the bluffs toward the river in ravines, nurturing groves of native oak, black walnut, butternut, birch, elm, locust, and sugar maple trees. . . . Nearly forty years before the arrival of the Latter-day Saints, Native Americans abandoned the last of a series of agricultural villages on this Illinois site.[2]

But the decision that made Nauvoo the Saints' gathering place was by no means obvious at first. As soon as Brigham Young and other apostles arrived in Quincy, discussion began about how to meet the immediate physical needs of the members, followed by the related question of whether they should continue to "gather" or whether they would be better served by scattering abroad. The Prophet, though deferring to those leaders who were with the Saints, apparently considered that the law of gathering was still in force. Therefore, Church headquarters needed a permanent location, one where families would have access to good land and be free from hostile neighbors. Although he and others still felt that the Church would eventually return to Jackson County, steps had to be taken in the meantime to care for present members but continue missionary efforts in the United States and abroad. Brigham Young also took the position that gathering was a necessity for the additional reason of mutual protection.

Land was offered to the Church in Lee County, Iowa, whose officials and citizens welcomed the potential population growth. Land was also available for purchase across the Mississippi River from Lee County in and around the new, little town of Commerce, Illinois. As early as February 1839, public meetings were held in Quincy to discuss the issue, but the final decision awaited Joseph Smith's arrival in April, after his escape from Missouri. Within a few days, he and others left to purchase land. The largest acreage was in Iowa, but the headquarters were in Illinois: "660 acres from non-Mormons Hugh and William White, Isaac Galland, and Horace Hotchkiss."[3]

This was the beginning of extensive land purchases in the area, usually bought in the Church's name and on credit. As members moved to the area, they settled on this land and eventually, as their finances permitted, purchased it. King's son John was the first Follett to purchase land in the White Purchase sometime after September 1839. King bought a lot in April 1840 in the Hotchkiss Purchase, and his son-in-law Nathan West, bought land from the Church, also in the Hotchkiss purchase, sometime later. Most people living in frontier America at this time were poor, but many Mormons were genuinely impoverished because of their forced exile. These land purchases and the development of another new city was a tremendous undertaking, both for the Church and for individual families like the Folletts.

Only a few weeks later, Joseph moved his family to Commerce on May 10, 1839. The *History of the Church* records his comments: "I arrived with my family at the White purchase and took up my residence in a small log house on the bank of the river, about one mile south of Commerce City, hoping that I and my friends [by whom he meant Church members] may here find a resting place for a little season at least."[4] This cabin had probably served as the first Indian agency in Illinois. According to Brigham H. Roberts, this collection of houses stood "immediately on the banks of the river" and "scattered between them and what afterwards became the south part of the city of Nauvoo, were one stone and three log houses. It was one of these humble dwellings that Joseph moved into.... Back some distance from the river, however, were other dwellings scattered over the country."[5]

Commerce and Commerce City were initially planned as two separate settlements in Township 6–7, Range 9 of Hancock County.[6] In reality, they existed only on paper, with few actual inhabitants. Joseph described the challenging landscape:

> When I made the purchase of White and Galland, there were one stone house, three frame houses, and two block houses, which constituted the whole city of Commerce. Between Commerce and Mr. Davidson Hibbard's, there was one stone house and three log houses, including the one I live in, and these were all the houses in this vicinity, and the place was literally a wilderness. The land was mostly covered with trees and bushes, and much of it so wet that it was with the utmost difficulty a footman could get through, and totally impossible for teams.[7]

Emma's evaluation of the log house in which she would begin housekeeping has not been preserved. The "flats," or marshy land sloping down to the river were unhealthful. Joseph recognized this problem but foresaw that it could become "a healthful place by the blessing of heaven" for the Saints, who included the Follett family, "and no more eligible place presenting itself, I considered it wisdom to make an attempt to build up a city."[8] As a modern historian, Ronald K. Esplin, commented, "It was the city he built, where he lived and acted, where he died."[9] It was a statement about Joseph, but it also applied to King Follett.

Soon others began to move into the area. That summer of 1839, the Prophet asked all members of the Church, wherever they were living, to move to the newly renamed city. "Nauvoo," he said, was "a Hebrew word meaning 'beautiful.'" The first formal use of the name "Nauvoo" was to place it on the official plat of the city on August 30, 1839. The

United States post office adopted the name change in April of 1840, and in March of that year the city council passed an ordinance incorporating the sites of Commerce and Commerce City into Nauvoo. Once the success of this gathering place seemed assured and the Saints began swarming into the area, other landholders saw advantages in creating subdivisions which were attached to Nauvoo as "additions."[10] In 1845 following the Prophet's death, the town citizens voted unanimously "that henceforth and forever, this city shall be called 'The City of Joseph.'"[11] Although the name is used in Church writings, no action was taken to change it on government and public records.

Church members living in Quincy accepted the call to make this next move. However, they had been accepted so well there, it was difficult for them to think of making another move. Helen Mar Whitney, then about twelve years of age, wrote in 1881 that, although the move was difficult, "nearly everyone realized the Saints had to have a home of their own." She continues: "We were two days on the way, and the journey was quite pleasant" but upon arrival she was quickly "homesick and sick of the country."[12]

> We were surrounded with trees and hazel and other underbrush. The whole country was quite wild, and wolves being plentiful we were treated nightly to their serenades, commencing at sundown and continuing at intervals till morning.... The contrast between that place and Quincy, where we had spent the spring and summer so pleasantly, and everything seemed so delightful to me that it made the dreary looking place anything but interesting; but the scene changed as it were by magic, through the persevering industry of the Saints, and soon instead of a forest the country was dotted over with houses, and gardens and flowers were under cultivation.[13]

The Follett family again left no record of their lives during this period, but the parallel experiences of others provide suggestions of these early Nauvoo years. Not surprisingly, the immediate necessities for survival received primary attention. According to Ebenezer Robinson, who followed the Prophet and his family to Commerce sometime in May, many others moved at that time as well. He like others had to quickly find or make a place to live: "The only chance for a house was the body of a log house situated on high ground in the woods near the river, about one mile north of Commerce. For the want of lumber, were under the necessity of going into the forest and splitting out oak clapboards, or shakes, three feet long, for the roof and doors, which furnished a temporary shelter."[14]

When Sarah DeArmon Pea Rich arrived in Nauvoo from Quincy in the fall of 1839, she wrote:

> And I can assure you my friends, it was a happy time for us to once more feel at home among the saints of God and to be where we could hear words of comfort from the mouth of our Prophet Joseph Smith for we were now where we could attend meeting every Sunday; also where we could visit with our dear brothers and sisters who like ourselves had been driven and robbed and they like us were glad of a resting place out of the reach of those that had sought our lives and the lives of our Prophet and all our leaders who had been delivered from prison by the hand of our heavenly father.[15]

A major challenge was the undrained swamp that lay along the river bank, fostered thousands of mosquitoes, and offered sluggish, impure water. Early arrivals had to immediately drain the land and clear away heavy vegetation before they could plant crops or construct homes. They did not understand the vector of the disease, so many, perhaps most, of them contracted malaria, characterized by cycles of chills and shaking, followed by sweating and high fever, which they called the ague. With little medical care available, they had to help each other; and mortality rates were high. During July, the Prophet himself became ill; but buoyed by the Lord's spirit, he went among the members, laying hands on them and pronouncing priesthood blessings of healing.

Samuel Kendall Gifford, no doubt like many other members, interpreted such illness as a trial. Saints who met the challenge with faith could draw down the Lord's blessings:

> This was a very sickly place and none but Saints could live there and many of them died before they could subdue the destructive elements that filled the air in consequence of the low marshy land that lay right in the midst of the town. But through the perseverance of the Saints coupled with the blessings of God, the swamps were drained, and the land and elements were dedicated, and sickness and death became less frequent. Comfortable dwellings, fruitful fields, orchards gardens, mills and other improvements and comforts sprang into existence to the astonishment of all around.[16]

Eliza R. Snow expressed similar feelings: "The location of the city of Nauvoo was beautiful, but the climate was so unhealthy that several efforts had been made to build it up and as many times abandoned. It seemed to have been held in reserve to meet the occasion, for none but Saints full of faith, and trusting in the power of God, could have established that city. Through the blessings of our Heavenly Father on the indefatigable exertions of the Saints, it was not long before Nauvoo excited the envy and jealousy of many of the adjacent inhabitants."[17]

It is difficult to document the early death rate in Nauvoo, although it was probably higher than other places on the frontier because of the higher percentage of children under age five. Elizabeth Haven Barlow's letters to her family in the East mentions that she had "watched over the *sick, living* and *dead* night and day. . . . [S]sickness and death has been on my right hand and left. Nothing but the power of [G]od has kept me up. I feel sometimes wore out with fatigued (body) and loss of sleep, but that is far from having the ague or my body racked with pain by a raging fever."[18] Surely the Follett family did not escape illnesses of some type; however, they apparently all escaped death. Modern LDS historian Milton V. Backman Jr. points out: "If diseases had not been arrested by innumerable miraculous healings, the number who died in Nauvoo would have been undoubtedly much greater."[19]

Simultaneously with the challenges of beginning a new settlement on the American frontier, the Prophet Joseph launched a massive missionary program, both in the United States and also in England. In August 1839, the Twelve Apostles began their mission to England, leaving Nauvoo and preaching on their way. Some of them were so ill that, according to Elizabeth Haven Barlow, when some of them came to Quincy on their way to New York, they "were not able to set up all day, but they left; saying farewell *friends, farewell ague*, we leave you behind."[20] Others fanned out across the United States to preach the gospel.

After King reached Quincy in October, the extended family wintered in the area and were still there when the 1840 federal census was taken, beginning in June. The *History of the Church* has three related mentions, although it does not identify their residence. The minutes of a Church conference held at Commerce on October 6–8, 1839, note: "Voted that John Daley, James Daley, and Milo Andrus retain their station in the Church." James Daley would become King's son-in-law eight months later. John Daley is James's father, and Milo Andrus is James's uncle. Unfortunately, the minutes include no information about why these three men's membership was being called into question.[21] Possibly

Louisa and the children were in attendance, although King had been released only ten days earlier, and it is not clear that he had reached Quincy by this date. Indeed, a retrospective entry in the *History of the Church* notes on October 26: "King Follett, the last of the brethren in bonds in Missouri, had his trial and was set free some time previous to this day."[22] He had actually been released a month earlier on September 25.

In May 1839, Louisa had signed one of the 491 individual petitions for redress upon which the Saints hoped Congress would take action. On October 29, the Prophet Joseph, Sidney Rigdon, Orrin Porter Rockwell, and Judge Elias Higbee[23] set out for Washington, D.C., to "lay before the Congress of the United States, the grievances of the Saints while in Missouri."[24] A number of events separated the travelers, delaying Smith and Higbee's arrival until November 28. The others joined them on December 23. They carried with them the first appeal which included "a general introductory petition, referred to as a memorial, and many individual petitions,"[25] including Louisa Follett's.[26] In Washington, the men tried unsuccessfully to speak directly to the U.S. Congress but met with several other officials, including an unsatisfactory call (or possibly two) on U.S. President Van Buren. According to Joseph Smith's account, "[He] treated me very insolently, and it was with great reluctance he listened to our message, which, when he had heard, he said: "*Gentlemen, your cause is just, but I can do nothing for you;*" and "*If I take up for you I shall lose the vote of Missouri.*"[27] Discouraged, Joseph Smith left for Nauvoo on February 20, leaving Elias Higbee and others in Washington. Two days later, Judge Higbee wrote of his frustrations after spending a day defending the Church and describing Missouri events to a Senate Committee. He believed that the committee members were going to "rally their forces, viz., by endeavoring to make us [the Church] treasonable characters."[28] Still, hoping he could bring other witnesses to Washington to testify, he asked the Prophet

> to select a number of firm brethren, possessing good understanding, who will tell the truth, and willingly send me their names when they know they are wanted. Send plenty of them. They will get two dollars per day, and ten cents a mile to and from, [as] expense money. Do not send them until their subpoenas get there, for they will not draw expense money only for going home.
>
> I will suggest a few names—Alanson Ripley, King Follett, Amasa Lyman, Francis M. Higbee, as they know concerning the DeWitt scrape;

also send Charles C. Rich, Seymour Brunson, and others. You will know whom to send better than myself.[29]

The Prophet reached Nauvoo on March 4. On March 16, the Nauvoo High Council, responding to Elias Higbee's request, identified thirty-five men—one of them King Follett—and four women. Robert B. Thompson, the Prophet's secretary, was assigned to send the list to Higbee so that he could "order subpoenas for said persons."[30] The next day, March 17, Thompson reported on the action in his letter to Higbee, adding what must have been the welcome commendation "that the greatest satisfaction was manifested . . . with the straightforward and honourable course which you had pursued. . . . [T]here is . . . a fixed determination, to uphold you in your righteous cause and sustain you in your efforts to obtain redress for the injuries which the Saints have borne from their unfeeling oppressors, and in bringing their case before the authorities of the nation."[31]

This wording captures the strong feelings the Saints naturally felt over their time in Missouri. Undoubtedly the thirty-nine selected, including King, were anxious to assist in any way possible; however, the prospective testimony in Washington would not materialize. Senate Judiciary Committee concluded: "It can never be presumed that a state either wants the power or lacks the disposition to redress the wrongs of its own citizens, committed within her own territory, whether they proceed from the lawless acts of her officers or any other persons."[32]

The Saints had too-fresh evidence of how the State of Missouri had responded to petitions for redress. King's thoughts—either about the possibility of traveling to Washington and testifying or relinquishing that idea and turning to more immediate needs—cannot be guessed, given the absence of documentation. At some point after the 1840 census found the Follett family in Quincy, they followed their prophet to Nauvoo. This was his third attempt to build a city that would serve as Church headquarters and as the Church's central city. Although Kirtland was an established town when Joseph reached it in early 1831, it rapidly became a Mormon city, a status it maintained until 1838. The second Mormon city was Far West, Missouri. Nauvoo was the third. The Church's newspaper presented an inviting report of the location city's growth in the fall of 1842: "For three or four miles upon the river and about the same distance back in the country, Nauvoo presents a city of gardens, ornamented with the dwellings of those who have made a covenant by sacrifice, and are guided by revelation.... The City of Nauvoo is regularly laid off into blocks, containing four lots of eleven by twelve rods each—making all corner lots. It will be no more than probably correct, if we allow the city to contain between seven and eight hundred houses, with a population of 14 or 15,000.[33]

Larger plots of land were available outside the town for farming and other projects. Initially no specific neighborhood was set aside for businesses, which were conducted in combination homes-and-shops.[34] Gradually businesses began to cluster around the north-south Main Street in "the flats" near the river, close to the Smith family's home, located "next to the river on the south end of Main Street."[35] Photographic historians Richard Neitzel Holzapfel and T. Jeffrey Cottle describe the first homes: "At first, many homes were simple log cabins or homes made of lumber rafted from Wisconsin. Thomas Gregg, a Warsaw, Illinois, newspaper editor, said that during the heyday the Saints at Nauvoo built about 1,200 hand-hewn log cabins, most of them whitewashed inside, and 300 to 500 frame houses. Using brick and lime made in their own kiln, the Mormons erected 200 to 300 good, substantial brick homes. . . . practical, boxlike structures with gable roofs and single or double brick chimneys built in the end."[36] Holzapfel and Cottle point out that the style of homes varied, depending on the builder's background. Many combined more than one style. "Nauvoo was still a town built primarily of wood when the Saints left the city in 1846.... Several one-story brick residences of only two or three rooms are still in existence [1990] in the main portion of the old city. Their simple, functional form probably represents the residential environment of the average settler in the 1840s. Most of the homes were modest and plain in design."[37]

Land records for Nauvoo and Hancock County show that, in April 1840, even though the Follett family was not yet living in Nauvoo, King had arranged to buy Lot 1, Block 26, in the Hotchkiss Purchase from Joseph Smith, Sidney Rigdon, and Hyrum Smith, who had purchased large parcels of land on behalf of the Church, then made it available in smaller parcels to members moving in. This lot is on the southwest corner of what became the intersection of Partridge and Samuel streets,[38] directly north of the current LDS Visitors' Center. The record of that agreement appears in the "Nauvoo Trustees Land Book, 1836–1842," now housed in the LDS Church History Library. The first page is headed: "Joseph Smith Jun Day Book."[39] King agreed to pay $500 in two installments: $250 on April 1, 1845, and the remaining $250 on April 1, 1850. There is no mention of a down payment. Because King died before 1845, no payments were made and no deed was issued. The entries in this source are listed by block and lot number, not by name of purchaser. Also housed at the LDS Church History Library is a photographic copy of a "Deed" dated April 10, 1840, and made out to King for Lot 1 in Block 26. However, I believe it is misidentified. It is not a deed (none was ever issued, since the Folletts never completed the transaction), but rather a bond that seems to guarantee a purchase price of $1,000, but which repeats that the total amount due from King was $500 with the provisions of two payments of $250 each on the same dates as listed in the Nauvoo Trustee Land Book. This document spells out that, after King made the payments, with an interest payment at an unspecified amount to be "paid annually on the first day of April in each year," Joseph Smith Jr., Sidney Rigdon, and Hyrum Smith agreed to provide a deed.[40] The only signatures on the "Deed" are Joseph's and Hyrum's, along with that of Henry G. Sherwood, their agent.

These terms were very much like those arranged for other Church members. Because they had no cash, they purchased on credit. Some made payments on schedule, but others struggled. A few paid $50 down; for some the payment schedule was annual, over five to ten years. While this type of business arrangement was helpful to members of the Church and Joseph knew it was the only way that most could buy land, it would cause problems for the Church later when the income from these sales fell short of paying the notes due to the original land owners. According to an index created for the files of the Land and Records Office kept by Rowena Miller, the legendary secretary of Nauvoo Restoration, Inc., at one time the "Belnap Collection" at an unidentified depository housed a "xerox of orig." of this "Deed" for this transaction, signed by Joseph and Hyrum.[41] Rowena Miller made a Memorandum on January 6, 1965, apparently to document for some unidentified reason that a "xerox" of this deed did exist and that she had personally seen it:

> Concerning Zerox [sic] copy of a bond for deed covering Lot 1, Block 26 While I was working in the CHO [Church History Office] archives in the basement, Lauritz Petersen brought down a Brother [Ned] Winder,

"Deed" (actually bond) of King Follett's purchase of Lot 1, Block 26, in the Hotchkiss Purchase, Nauvoo, from Joseph Smith, Sidney Rigdon, and Hyrum Smith, who were acting as Church agents. Photograph courtesy of LDS Church History Library.

[owner of] (Winder Dairy) [and secretary of the Church's Missionary Committee] who had a zerox [sic] copy of a bond for deed covering Lot 1, block 26, between Joseph Smith and Hyrum Smith and King Follett, dated April 10, 1840, in the amount of $1,000.00, purchase price of the lot $500.00, $250.00 due on a date, which I did not record, and the balance of $250.00 due in 1845 [sic].

The signatures of Joseph Smith and Hyrum Smith appeared to be written by the same hand, and on examination it appeared that perhaps they, too, were written by H. G. Sherwood, who witnessed the bond for deed, as "agent."

Brother Winder was in the course of neogtiation [sic] with a local antique dealer for the purchase of the document because of the signature of Joseph Smith. The antique dealer is said to have paid $100.00 for it and was asking $150.00 from Brother Winder. Rowena Miller[42]

Since both Rowena Miller and the "Deed" give the figure of $1,000, possibly King made a $500 down payment, and the Trustee Land Book merely noticed the balance due in two installments. None of these records, however, provides a location for the original deed, or bond for deed, or even the location of the photocopy that Rowena Miller saw in 1965. Neither the deed nor the bond appears on land records at the Hancock County Recorder's Office in Carthage, Illinois.[43]

Individuals who initially purchased lots in the same block as King were:

Lot 2: Benjamin Wescott, March 1, 1840, price $450.

Lot 3: Caroline [?], March 27, 1840, price $500, land given back January 14, 1842, no payment made.

Lot 4: Charles Hewlet [probably Hulet], dated March 21, 1840, price $500.[44]

Between 1841 and 1844, King was assessed taxes. The first figure is for personal property and the second for real property:[45]

1841: $83.00, $40.00.

1842: $63.00 + $60.00, $100.00, There is no explanation why he was assessed twice for personal property or why the real property for this year was greater than either the previous or next year.

1843: $33.00, $50.00. The personal property is itemized: a horse valued at $5, cattle at $13, and unidentified, $15.

These consistently low taxes suggest that King and his family were among the poorer Saints. After King's death in 1844, his son John paid $32 in personal property tax and $67 for land taxes.[46] John had pur-

The Beginning of Nauvoo, 1839–40

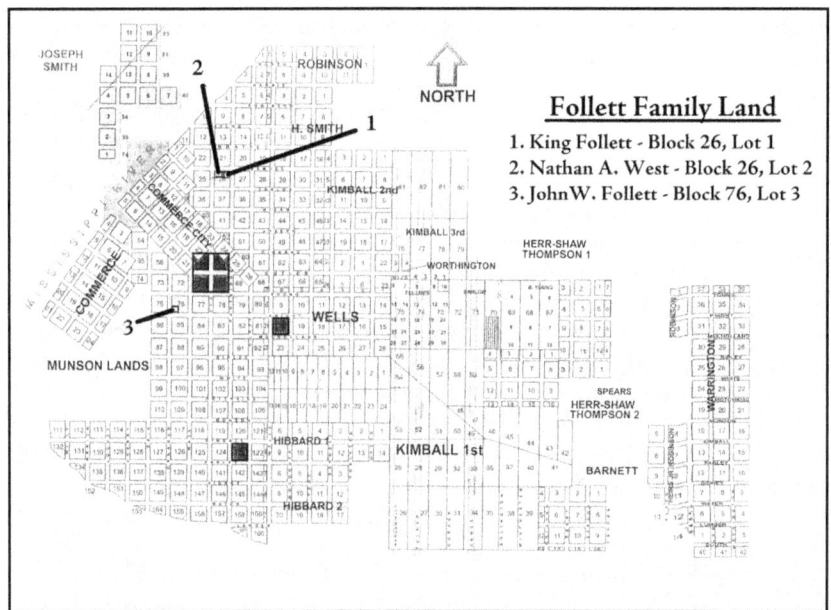

Map of early Nauvoo, courtesy of Nauvoo Restoration, Inc., to which I have added the location of land purchases for the Follett family.

chased land earlier than King in Nauvoo's White Purchase on an unspecified date in 1839, though probably after September 11, as that date is written at the top of the page on which his entry appears. It is described as Lot 3 in Block 69, price $750, with no terms listed. That block was south of the original Commerce City site and is directly southwest of the present LDS Visitors' Center. Lot 1 and 2 in that block were then vacant; Dimick Huntington had purchased Lot 4 that same year for $800.[47] John's lot stands at what is now the southeast corner of the intersection of Granger and Knight streets, six blocks south and two blocks west of his parents' home.[48] Adeline Follett West and Nathan West purchased land, no date specified, apparently previously owned by Benjamin Wescott. It was Lot 2, Block 26, next door to King and Louisa, at the intersection of Carlos and Hyde streets.[49] I found no record of a land purchase by James Daley and Nancy Follett Daley, although a James Daley was taxed for property in 1842.[50]

The city of Nauvoo, as initially planned and laid out by the Church's leaders, consisted of "3733.11 acres," Donald Q. Cannon notes. "In contrast, the Nauvoo of today measures 1842.67 acres, or about 49 percent of the original town. Today only the west-central portion of the original city remains."[51] The contemporary town is clustered "upon the bluffs which rise nearly seventy feet above the Mississippi river. To the west on the 'flats' is the location of the historic city of Nauvoo,"[52] as defined and built during King's lifetime. As originally planned, only one home was to be built on each lot, with a set-back of twenty-five feet from the road. However, as the population increased more than one home was built per lot. Nancy and James Daley may have also lived on the lot that King purchased, at least for a while; King's son, William Alexander, and his wife, Nancy Mariah, may also have lived there later after their marriage in September 1845. Though the "city plat showed the whole area divided into streets and blocks, much of it was just a 'paper' town, which would have to wait for a multitude of settlers to make it a reality. Minutes of the Nauvoo City Council refer, on occasion, to resolutions calling for surveying and opening some of the streets already shown on the original plat."[53]

While Nauvoo was definitely the Church's center, during this period, eventually seventeen additional Mormon communities took shape in Illinois.[54] Because of these additional settlements, Church leaders and missionaries would have places to stay as they traveled outside of Nauvoo, and new converts coming into the area had a choice of places to live that would still be close to other members. In addition, the Church purchased land in eastern Iowa just across the Mississippi River from Nauvoo. These settlements were "considered part of greater Nauvoo [and] were connected to Nauvoo by ferry." Eight branches of the church with members in four communities in Lee County, two townships in Van Buren County, and one town in Des Moines County were organized into the Zarahemla Stake in August 1841. However, this "gathering" period in Iowa did not last long; and because of the "continuing ingathering to Nauvoo," the stake was disbanded in January 1842.[55] This Iowa area, however, would play a more important role in Church history when the Saints began their trek west from Nauvoo in 1846.

The apostolic mission to England and the on-going missionary efforts throughout the eastern United States meant that new converts started arriving in late 1840 and continued to come in swelling numbers throughout the Nauvoo years. The Folletts and other early settlers in Nauvoo soon had neighbors from other states and countries, which changed the culture in which they had been living. What had begun only ten years earlier as a New England religion, now quickly became truly diversified as the Prophet encouraged all Church members to gather to this new "Zion."

As early as May 1839, Joseph wrote to friends, urging them to move to Nauvoo, "reserving lots for them, and speaking of house building and the general development of the city. In July he issued a circular to all members of the Church to urge the principle of the gathering."[56] Some Folletts may have attended the October 1839 general conference in Nauvoo at which Joseph Smith "spoke at some length upon the situation of the Church; the difficulties they have had to contend with; and the manner in which they had been led to this place; and wanted to know the views of the brethren, whether they wished to appoint this a stake of Zion or not; stating that he believed it to be a good place, and suited for the Saints. It was then unanimously agreed upon that it should be appointed a stake and a place of gathering for the Saints."[57]

Almost two years later on January 15, 1841, Joseph issued a "Proclamation of the First Presidency, to the Saints Scattered Abroad," again extolling Nauvoo:

> Let all those who appreciate the blessings of the gospel, and realize the importance of obeying the commandments of heaven . . . prepare for the general gathering . . . make every preparation to come on without delay, and strengthen our hands, and assist in promoting the happiness of the Saints.
> . . .
> From the kind, uniform, and consistent course pursued by the citizens of Illinois, and the great success which has attended us while here, the natural advantages of this place of every purpose we require, and the necessity of the gathering of the Saints of the Most High, we would say, let the brethren who love the prosperity of Zion . . . cast in their lots with us, and cheerfully engage in a work so glorious and sublime.[58]

Thousands of Saints took the gigantic step of gathering to Nauvoo. The question, however, was: How long could the Mormons continue to build Nauvoo without facing the same type of problems they had confronted over the past decade? How soon would their past in Missouri be repeated in Illinois?

Notes

1. Keith W. Perkins and Donald Q. Cannon, *Ohio and Illinois*, 112.
2. Glen M. Leonard, *Nauvoo: A Place of Peace, A People of Promise*, 45–46.
3. James L. Kimball Jr., "Land Ownership in Nauvoo and Vicinity," in S. Kent Brown, Donald Q. Cannon, and Richard H. Jackson, eds., *Historical Atlas of Mormonism*, 64.
4. *History of the Church*, 3:349. The "White purchase" was land that had originally belonged to James White and his relatives who, in 1823, were the first permanent settlers of the "flats" or the area nearest to the river.
5. Brigham H. Roberts, *The Rise and Fall of Nauvoo*, 30.
6. Church of Jesus Christ of Latter-day Saints and Nauvoo Family History and Property Identification Department, "Hancock County: Township and Range," in *Reference Book for Nauvoo Family History and Property Identification Department*, 32.
7. *History of the Church*, 3:375. T. Edgar Lyon, "The Account Books of the Amos Davis Store at Commerce, Illinois," 241–43. Lyon, a modern researcher, reported that this Davis account book indicates that, while residents of the Commerce area were few, those who lived in the area brought their produce to the Davis store to exchange for products and goods. It appears there was also some type of post office where mail was delivered weekly at Commerce via mail coach on the Carthage or Macomb Road. Since the account book contained "ninety-five heads of families (who) had credit accounts on Amos Davis's store ledger before the Mormons arrived there in 1839," there must have been other settlements and farms farther inland. Lyon concludes: "The traditional description of the Commerce area along the river bank has erroneously led us to believe that those few homes were the entire settled part of the Nauvoo peninsula. An analysis of the Amos Davis account books and related records allows us to expand our horizon."
8. *History of the Church*, 3:375.
9. Ronald K. Esplin, "The Significance of Nauvoo for Latter-day Saints," 20.
10. Church Education System, *Church History in the Fulness of Times*, 217.
11. *History of the Church*, 7:394.
12. Richard Neitzel Holzapfel, "Nauvoo Remembered: Helen Mar Whitney Reminiscences, Part 1," 7.
13. Ibid., 7–8.
14. Ebenezer Robinson, "Items of Personal History of the Editor," *The Return* 5 (May 1890): 1.
15. Sarah DeArmon Pea Rich, "Sarah DeArmon Pea Rich, 1814–1893," 57.
16. Samuel Kendall Gifford, "Reminiscences, 1864," 5.

17. Maureen Ursenbach Beecher, ed., *The Personal Writings of Eliza Roxcey Snow*, 16.

18. Elizabeth Haven Barlow, Letter to Dear E, September 28, 1839, in Ora H. Barlow and the Israel Barlow Family Association, *The Israel Barlow Story and Mormon Mores*, 159; emphasis Elizabeth's.

19. Milton V. Backman Jr., *People and Power of Nauvoo: Themes from the Nauvoo Experience*, 15.

20. Barlow, Letter to Dear E, September 28, 1839, 158; emphasis Elizabeth's. See *History of the Church*, 4:9–10 note, for a further discussion of the apostles' illness at this time.

21. *History of the Church*, 4:12. Membership issues with two other men were handled in this same meeting: "Harlow Redfield be suspended until he can have a trial" and "Ephraim Owen's confession for disobeying the Word of Wisdom be accepted."

22. Ibid., 4:17.

23. Elias Higbee, a native of New Jersey, was baptized in 1832, and remained a faithful member, serving in many capacities of leadership, until his death in Nauvoo in 1843. As a Church historian, he helped collect the affidavits about the Saints' losses in Missouri. He had served as a judge in Caldwell County.

24. *History of the Church*, 4:19.

25. Clark V. Johnson, ed., *Mormon Redress Petitions: Documents of the 1833–1838 Missouri Conflict*, 101.

26. Ibid., 201–2.

27. *History of the Church*, 4:80; emphasis in original.

28. Ibid., 4:87.

29. Ibid. This supports the previous discussion regarding King's involvement in the events in Missouri.

30. Fred C. Collier, ed., *The Nauvoo High Council Minute Books of the Church of Jesus Christ of Latter Day Saints*, 3. The minutes span from March 8, 1840, to October 18, 1845, but only this entry names King or any member of his family.

31. Ibid.; see also Elder Robert B. Thompson, "Commerce, Hancock County, Ill.," in Journal History, March 17, 1840, 1.

32. *History of the Church*, 4:92.

33. "Nauvoo," *Times and Seasons* 3, no. 23 (1 October 1842): 936.

34. Leonard, *Nauvoo*, 60.

35. William G. Hartley, *Stand by My Servant Joseph: The Story of the Joseph Knight Family and the Restoration*, 315–16.

36. Richard Neitzel Holzapfel and T. Jeffery Cottle, *Old Mormon Nauvoo and Southeastern Iowa: Historic Photographs and Guide*, 25–26.

37. Ibid., 209.

38. Ida Blum, "History of the Naming," in her *Nauvoo: Gateway to the West*, 193. Blum further states that Samuel Street was named for "Samuel H. Smith, one of the witnesses to [the] Book of Mormon" and that Partridge Street received its name from "Edward Partridge, first bishop in Mormon Church at Nauvoo."195.

39. Nauvoo Trustee Land Book, 1836–42. See also my interview with James L. Kimball Jr., 1999; Susan Easton Black, Harvey Bischoff Black, and Brandon Plewe, comps., *Property Transactions in Nauvoo, Hancock County, Illinois, and Surrounding Communities (1839–1859)*; "King Follett," File 10091, Land and Records Office, Nauvoo, Illinois.

40. "Deed, 1840 Apr 10." MS 21160, LDS Church History Library. I am not able to further explain the $1,000 figure on the "Deed." To complicate matters further, in the LDS Church History Library catalog record, this statement appears: "A document certifying that in return for *$800* [emphasis mine], Joseph and Hyrum Smith and Sydney [sic] Rigdon convey to King Follett lot 1 in block 26 in Nauvoo, Illinois." This deed was donated in 2008 by Brent Ashworth; there is no record of how he obtained this copy.

41. Rowena Miller, indexer, *Index to Historical Collections: Nauvoo Restoration, Incorporated: Rowena Miller Files*; see also Black, Black, and Plewe, *Property Transactions in Nauvoo*, 1335–36. The index was begun in 1962 and the 3 x 5 cards were microfilmed by the Church in November 1973. At that point, they were in Rowena Miller's Salt Lake City office.

42. Rowena Miller, Memorandum, January 6, 1965; see also Christy Best, Church History Archivist, email to Joann Mortensen, June 13, 2008.

43. I searched these records in July 2007. The office staff members who helped me said that many early land records were not recorded before the exodus from Nauvoo.

44. Nauvoo Trustee Land Book, 1836–1842. Charles Hulet was an uncle of Nathan West's first wife, Mary Hulet.

45. The comparatively low value on the real estate probably means that the home was log or frame, not brick. See Hartley, *My Best for the Kingdom*, 107.

46. Kimball, Interviewed by Mortensen, 1999.

47. Nauvoo Trustee Land Book, 1836–1845; see also "John Follett," File #31139, Land and Records Office, Nauvoo, Illinois.

48. Blum, "History of the Naming of the Streets," 193, 195. Knight Street was named after Newell Knight, boyhood friend of the Prophet, and Granger was named after Oliver Granger, who with William Marks and Newel K. Whitney were commanded by revelation to leave Kirtland and go to Missouri.

49. "Nathan West," File #30219, Land and Records Office, Nauvoo, Illinois. According to Blum, "History of the Naming of the Streets," 193, 195, Carlos Street was named for "Don Carlos Smith, brother of Prophet Joseph Smith."

Hyde Street was also known as Carlin Street, "named for Gov. Thomas Carlin." "Hyde" probably referred to Orson Hyde, an apostle.

50. Nauvoo Illinois Assessor, Tax Lists for District No. 3, Nauvoo, Illinois 1840, 1842, 1850, 206.

51. Donald Q. Cannon, "The Founding of Nauvoo," in *Reference Book for Nauvoo Family History and Property Identification Department*, 12.

52. Holzapfel and Cottle, *Old Mormon Nauvoo and Southeastern Iowa*, 3.

53. "Nauvoo Additions," in *Reference Book for Nauvoo Family History and Property Identification Department*, 88.

54. Ibid., 11.

55. Stanley B. Kimball, "Eastern Iowa" in S. Kent Brown, Donald Q. Cannon, and Richard H. Jackson, eds., *Historical Atlas of Mormonism*, 68.

56. Robert Bruce Flanders, *Nauvoo: Kingdom on the Mississippi*, 43.

57. *History of the Church*, 4:12.

58. "A Proclamation of the First Presidency, to the Saints Scattered Abroad," *Times and Seasons* 2, no. 6 (January 15, 1841): 276.

✤ Chapter Sixteen ✤

Building Up a City, 1840–41

In early October 1841, two weeks after the close of the Saints' general conference, Nathan Cheney, a convert living in Nauvoo, wrote to his parents and siblings: "Our people are not so much engaged in cultivating the earth in Nauvoo as they are in building up a City."[1] In it, he captured the focus of the Saints from their arrival at this new gathering place. It is true that they needed to "cultivate the earth" and provide themselves with food, shelter, and clothing. But individually and as a church they quickly began to build up their new city—organizing civil as well as ecclesiastical government, schools, mercantile establishments, law enforcement, and other amenities.

Their location was promising. In May 1841, Edward Hunter, a convert of almost one year, traveled from his home in Philadelphia to Nauvoo. On May 6, he wrote his impressions of Nauvoo to his family:

> Nauvoo is situated in a very pleasant place. The soil is of the first quality and improvements are going on at a rapid rate. I should suppose that there is something like 400 houses here and the chief has been created in the short space of two years.... They have a battalion of men here called the Nauvoo Legion. They are determined that they will no more submit to mobs. They can raise 700 men, efficient for military duty already. There have something like 400 brethren arrived here in about a fortnight.... The corner stones of the temple have been laid.... I'm going up the Mississippi River about 600 miles to help get timber for the Nauvoo House. I get $20 per month and board, and take my pay in land as money here is very scarce. I am very well pleased with the place; it exceeds my expectation.... Baptism for the dead is going on here every week, more or less. There was 450 baptized last fast day

week, and yesterday I saw Brother [William I.]Appleby from New Jersey baptized 34 times for his departed relatives.[2]

Hunter's description focuses concisely on key activities and events that had begun during the previous year: (1) growth in population and Church membership; (2) development of the Nauvoo Legion, authorized by the state's grant of a city charter; and (3) theological issues such as the building of a temple and the introduction of proxy baptisms for deceased relatives. The lives of King and his family would be impacted by each development.

As the leader of the Church, Joseph Smith was the individual ultimately responsible for the temporal and spiritual welfare of its members. He found invigorating the flood of converts moving to the city. On June 1, 1840, the *History of the Church* recorded: "The Saints have already erected about two hundred and fifty-houses at Nauvoo, mostly block houses, a few framed, and many more are in course of construction. The gospel is spreading through the States, Canada, England, Scotland, and other places, with great rapidity.[3]

Five days later the first English converts arrived in Nauvoo. Two weeks later in a "Memorial from Joseph Smith to the Nauvoo High Council" on June 18, 1840, he expressed his gratitude for "the peace and harmony which exist in the Church, and for the good feelings which seem to be manifested by all the Saints, and [he] hopes that inasmuch as we devote ourselves for the good of the Church, and the spread of the kingdom, that the choicest blessings of heaven will be poured upon us, and that the glory of the Lord will overshadow the inheritances of the Saints."[4]

The energetic settling of Nauvoo and the diligence of the members attracted the attention of visitors. A correspondent to the *Joliet Courier* observed in a June 1841 letter:

> The people of the town appear to be honest and industrious, engaged in their usual vocations of building up a town, and making all things around them comfortable. On Sunday I attended one of their meetings, in front of the Temple now building, and one of the largest buildings in the state. There could not have been less than 2,500 people present, and as well appearing as any number that could be found in this or any state. Mr. Smith preached in the morning, and one could have readily learned, then, the magic by which he has built up this society, because, as we say in Illinois, "they believe in him," and in his honesty. It has been a matter of astonishment to me . . . why it is, that so many professing Christianity, and so many professing to rever-

ence the sacred principles of our Constitution (which gives free religious toleration to all), have slandered, and persecuted this sect of Christians.[5]

However, even at this early period, some Nauvoo neighbors envied the success and criticized the accomplishments. Unfortunately these same successes and accomplishments would eventually be the basis for persecution and attack.

From the time the town was first settled until at least 1845, the main occupation and/or business in Nauvoo was construction—homes, businesses, and public buildings. By the time the census was taken in October 1840, there were approximately 2,450 people living in Nauvoo and that number increased by about 30 percent within the next two years.[6] According to historian Donald Q. Cannon, "King Follett was one of those who assisted in transforming swamp-infested Commerce into prosperous Nauvoo. He purchased property on the bluff on the northwest corner of the city (Block 26, Lot 1). His neighbors included Charles Hewlett and Hiram Kimball. He erected a large log house for his family and then went to work as a stonemason."[7] This is the only reference to King as a "stonemason." All other records that mention his occupation call him a "farmer." Perhaps Cannon inferred that King was a stonemason because he died while "wall[ing] up a well."

King's sixteen-year-old son William Alexander would have helped construct the log house for the family. King's other adult son, John, and his son-in-law, Nathan West, may have also helped, but each also owned separate property. Following their move from Quincy, the family undoubtedly camped on their lot in a tent or some other type of temporary dwelling while the house was completed.

As the Follett family built their new home and their new life, they joined with their neighbors in the community life of the Church. An annual conference was held each April in celebration of the Church's founding. Special conferences were also held, sometimes twice yearly in August and October. Regular Sabbath preaching services were held weekly, weather permitting, outdoors as they had been in Missouri. Large crowds gathered initially in an open area near the Prophet's home; later they met in a grove on what became known as Temple Hill.[8] At times of inclement weather, smaller groups met in homes. Here the members listened to the Prophet Joseph and other leaders preach, bear testimony, pray, sometimes speak in tongues, study the scriptures, and sing hymns.[9] "In the style of the

King Follett's lot in Nauvoo. Photo about 1960 by LeRoy Follett.

revivalist camps," describes historian Carol Cornwall Madsen, "they sat on makeshift benches, on the ground, on their horses, and in their wagons, listening to two- and three-hour sermons."[10] This method of worship was one familiar to King and his family since their baptisms.

During Nauvoo's first general conference in October of 1839, the Nauvoo Stake was established with three wards outlined in Nauvoo. Five months later, their boundary lines were changed and a fourth ward was created. By August of 1842, the city's population had grown to the extent that ten wards were needed, each headed by a bishop with responsibility for caring for the poor and providing tithing laborers (one day in ten) for public works.[11] Although no membership records are extant, some deductions can be made from geography. King Follett's land was apparently in the original Nauvoo First Ward. The city's "Record of Members," in essence a census, also places the Folletts in the first ward. It categorized individuals as: "[1] Over 8 and baptized; [2] Under 8; and [3] Over 8 and not baptized." King, Louisa, John W., and William A. are listed as "over 8 and baptized," while Edward M. and Warren K. are "under 8." Though this document is undated, the information had to have been gathered at least by 1841, since Edward M. would have turned eight in that year and would have been baptized. The two older daughters, Adeline and Nancy, were married and not living at home. However, neither they nor their husbands are listed elsewhere in this document.[12]

King was an original member of the Second Seventy Elders, or what was later referred to as the Second Quorum of Seventies, which had been organized in Kirtland in February 1836.[13] He continued that affiliation in Missouri and after arriving in Nauvoo.[14] A notice in the May 1840 *Times and Seasons* instructed the seventies to "meet on the first Sabbath in each month at 9 o'clock, until otherwise ordered. Done by order of the quorum."[15] The notice did not include a meeting location, but it was probably initially in homes or later in Joseph Smith's store. A special building for them, appropriately named the Seventies Hall, would be built and dedicated in December 1844, nine months after King's death.

The specific charge to the Seventies was given to Joseph Smith in Kirtland in 1835: "The Seventy are also called to preach the gospel, and to be especial witnesses unto the Gentiles and in all the world—thus differing from other officers in the church in the duties of their calling." (D&C 107:25) However no records have survived of any specific missionary work or baptisms—if any—that King performed while living in Nauvoo. Likely, however, he would have baptized Edward, who would have turned eight in June 1841.

From the Church's organization in 1830, Joseph Smith had imparted significant doctrinal teachings to the people, many of them very different from the mainstream religions of the period. Nauvoo saw an unprecedented flood of such new doctrines, including baptism for the dead, the full endowment ordinance, and celestial marriage. In their introduction to a collection of essays about Nauvoo, editors Roger D. Launius and John E. Hallwas comment: "Without question the Nauvoo period was the most fertile time for the development of Smith's unique doctrinal conceptions. During that era his ideas concerning the hierarchical nature of eternity, the multiplicity of gods, the possibility of progression to Godhood, celestial and plural marriage, baptism for the dead, and various Mormon temple endowments all came to fruition. Some of these ideas were well outside the mainstream of American religious thought."[16]

As these doctrines and teachings began to unfold, active members embraced them, studying and praying to fully understand their importance and implications. But for others, these new doctrines were a challenge that their faith could not always withstand, and they sometimes decided to leave the Church. Not all of these doctrines were preached publicly, but skeptical nonmembers and hostile former members later used these teachings as one of the reasons for driving the Saints away from Nauvoo.

The Prophet Joseph Smith's first public address about baptism for the dead was on August 15, 1840, when he spoke at the funeral of a member of the Nauvoo High Council, Seymour Brunson, who had died on August 10.[17] However, two years earlier in the July 1838 issue of the *Elders' Journal*, published in Far West, Joseph had written: "All those who have not had an opportunity of hearing the gospel, and being administered to by an inspired man in the flesh, must have it hereafter before they can be finally judged."[18] His use of the word "gospel" referred to the teachings of Jesus Christ in their fullness. This short explanation marked the beginning of a concept that all mortal individuals, regardless of when they lived, must enter Christ's church by baptism and that baptism, an earthly ordinance, could be performed by proxy by the living for the dead.

The main source of the Prophet's funeral sermon that day seems to be a statement by Simon Baker, who was present. He recalled that "during the meeting the Prophet read extensively from 1 Corinthians 15," in which the Apostle Paul referred to baptism for the dead, and stated that Paul was "talking to a people who understood baptism for the dead, for it was practiced among them." He quoted the Prophet as saying that Church members "could now act for their friends who had departed this life, and that the plan of salvation was calculated to save all who were willing to obey the requirements of the law of God."[19] On September 12, 1840, almost a month later, "Jane Neyman requested that Harvey Olmstead baptize her in behalf of her deceased son, Cyrus Livingston Neyman. Vienna Jacques witnessed the proxy baptism by riding into the Mississippi River on horseback to hear and observe the ceremony. A short while later, upon learning the words Olmstead used in performing the baptism, Joseph Smith gave his approval of the ordinance."[20] Jane Neyman's motherly concern thus prompted what was the first documented proxy baptism.

At first, no location was designated for these baptisms. Apparently, any location along the Mississippi River where the water was deep

Main Street Landing and Nauvoo House, Nauvoo, May 2, 1907. George Edward Anderson Collection. LDS Church History Library. Used by permission.

enough close to the shore could be used. According to Alexander L. Baugh, "Traditionally, the Main Street Landing has been the site generally believed to be where baptism, both for the living and the dead, was performed most frequently."[21] This Main Street landing, also called the Nauvoo House Landing, was one of at least four locations where boats bringing new converts and supplies docked.

Soon more instructions followed, notably, that proxies must be of the same sex as the person for whom they were baptized and that an official record of the ordinance must be kept. Individual Church members wrote to knowledgeable relatives, seeking the names of deceased kin and explaining, often with intense emotion, the concept and importance of vicarious baptism. Jonah Ball, apparently a new convert, wrote a series of letters to his nonmember relatives in Massachusetts as he traveled to Kirtland and on to Nauvoo. In a letter from Nauvoo dated May 19, 1843, he wrote: "I want you to send me a list of fathers relations his parents & Uncles & their names, also Mothers. . . . I am determined to do all I can to redeem those I am permitted to."[22] In the middle of a letter from Nauvoo to "Dear Friends" written April 21, 1844, Sally Randall, then a thirty-nine-year-old mother of three boys, reported typical news of health and food. Then, without any specific comment about baptism or the temple, she pled with her own mother in New England:

> I want you should write me the given names of all of our connections that are dead as far back as grandfather's and grandmother's at any rate. I intend to do what I can to save my friends and I should be very glad if some of you would come and help me for it is a great work for one to do alone. It is father's privilege to save his friends if he will come into the church. If not, some other one must do it. I expect you will think this is strange doctrine but you will find it to be true. I want to know whether Lettice was over eight years old when she died. Oh, mother, if we are so happy as to have a part in the first resurrection, we shall have our children just as we laid them down in their graves.[23]

One can only imagine what nonmembers thought when receiving and reading such a document. Perhaps King and Louisa wrote similar pleas to their relatives in New Hampshire and New York. Many proxy baptisms may have occurred before records began during 1840–41. During the next thirteen months, 6,818 documented proxy baptisms were performed in the river, after which Joseph Smith revealed that these ordinances must take place in the as-yet-unbuilt temple.[24] According to these earliest available records, King and his family participated in at least eleven ordinances for their deceased loved ones.[25]

King Follett was proxy for: (1) Alitha Follett, born April 19, 1790, sister;[26] (2) Rachel Stevens Follett, born August 22, 1728, grandmother; (3) John Follett III, born December 11, 1727, grandfather; and (4) John Follett IV, born March 5, 1752, father. Louisa Follett was proxy for (1) Anna Baldwin Tanner, born October 1741, grandmother; (2) Anna Warren Tanner, born about 1769, mother; and (3) Warren Tanner, born 1806, brother. Adeline Follett West was proxy for Alexander Follett, born May 7, 1794, Adeline's uncle and King's brother. Nathan West was proxy for (1) Griffith West, brother; (2) Mary West, mother; and (3) William West, father. Louisa Follett also performed two proxy baptisms on August 13, 1843, when baptisms were then being done in the uncompleted Nauvoo Temple. These were for her sister-in-law, Olive Tanner, the wife of her brother, Harry, and their daughter, Nancy Tanner.[27]

It must have been a humbling yet exhilarating experience for the Follett family. They had sacrificed greatly for their belief in the restored Church and felt strongly about the eternal blessings available to them because of that belief. Now they had the opportunity to ensure that some of their closest relatives could lay hold on the same promise, even across the barrier of death.

It would be interesting to know why King and Louisa selected the candidates they did. King's father was baptized by proxy but not his mother, who was also deceased. Both King and Louisa also had other deceased siblings. Perhaps they did not have enough identifying information. Perhaps they had doubts about the depth of these relatives' religious feelings. It seems more likely to me that they did, in fact, perform these proxy baptisms but that the record did not survive. The fact that King and Louisa did not perform vicarious baptisms for their children Edward, Mary, and Emily provides corroboration that they died before age eight, the revealed age of accountability when a child was believed to be mature enough to make and keep a baptismal covenant (D&C 68:27).

On January 19, 1841, approximately four months after proxy baptisms began, the Prophet received a revelation regarding the proper place for such baptisms: "For this ordinance belongeth to my house, and cannot be acceptable to me [outside a temple], only in the days of your poverty, wherein ye are not able to build a house unto me" (D&C 124:30). This revelation also renewed the instructions to build a temple, which Joseph Smith had first preached about at an October 1840 conference. In this temple, baptisms for the living and the dead would take place, and the fullness of other ordinances, such as the endowment, which had been promised as part of the Kirtland Temple dedication (D&C 124:29–55). A building committee had been appointed in October 1840, but now designing and construction received new attention. The Prophet also began to teach the Saints about the ordinances that would eventually take place in the temple. For the rest of King's life, he would be involved in various ways in helping to make that temple a reality. After his death, his family would participate in some of those important ordinances in the barely completed temple just before leaving Nauvoo.

While the Prophet naturally focused much of his time on doctrinal issues, especially the temple, he also understood the necessity of establishing a more permanent civil government for Nauvoo. During the tumultuous period in Ohio and Missouri, Church members had basically governed themselves through the Church structure with little, if any, distinction between civil and moral laws. The high council in both locations dealt with violators of both types of laws, not unlike the civil/religious structure of early New England communities. The difference was that elected civic leaders in New England also governed religious activity. In the fall of 1840, Joseph Smith and other leaders drafted a petition for a city charter from the Illinois legislature. Other Illinois communities were already functioning under such charters.

On December 16, 1840, the legislature not only granted a city charter but also agreed to two additional requests: one authorizing the establishment of the Nauvoo Legion and the other establishing the University of the City of Nauvoo.[28] A "Proclamation of the First Presidency, to the Saints Scattered Abroad" on January 15, 1841, emphasized the value of each of these three charters to the Folletts and to the Church's entire membership.[29] The Prophet described the city charter as "one of the most liberal charters, with the most plenary powers ever conferred by a legislative assembly on free citizens.... [It] secures to us, in all time to come, irrevocably, all those great blessings of civil liberty which of right appertain to all the free citizens of a great civilized republic: it is all we ever claimed."[30] For the first time, Mormons found themselves in a community that they had built, virtually from the ground up, that was recognized by a state government, and that, at least on paper, guaranteed them all of the political, civic, and religious rights they had been denied in Missouri. The Prophet's rejoicing is obvious: "The City Charter of Nauvoo is of my own plan and device. I concocted it for the salvation of the Church, and on principles so broad, that every honest man might dwell secure under its protective influence without distinction of sect or party."[31]

It was, however, some of these "principles so broad" that would later create hostility against Joseph and the Church.[32] One of the principles, which also appeared in the city charters of Chicago and Alton, Illinois, authorized city governments to pass any law that did not conflict with the U.S. or Illinois constitutions. The distinction between "constitutions" and "laws" would become important later as Nauvoo's leaders made laws for their city. Historian Richard Lyman Bushman commented: "The charter implemented the Jeffersonian principle of distributing power to the level of society closest to the people."[33] Also, the document specified very little actual separation of powers between the government branches and how they functioned. For example, the mayor and city council (representing the legislative branch) could also serve as city justices (representing the judicial branch). Finally, Nauvoo's Municipal Court "with unprecedented powers, especially the granting of writs of habeas corpus"[34] could make ineffective any arrest warrant issued outside the city. In legal terms habeas corpus is a proceeding in which an individual can contest the validity of the foreign warrant. The law passed by Nauvoo under the liberal Nauvoo Charter expanded this usual power under habeas corpus to include the power not only to challenge the legality of the arresting warrant but also the underlying crime upon which the warrant was issued. The effect of this provision was that Nauvoo magistrates, who were either Mormons or friendly, could and did hear and adjudicate complaints from other jurisdictions.[35] In practical terms, when officers from Missouri made attempts to extradite Joseph for trial in Missouri, the Nauvoo Municipal Court, using the broad powers given it in the Nauvoo Charter could legally intervene to protect Joseph. Six such habeas corpus acts were passed by the court between July 1842 and December 1843.[36] These broad principles became particularly troubling to nonmembers living in Hancock County outside of Nauvoo, as well as throughout Illinois, since most of Nauvoo's public officers were Church members. Thus, there was concern that there was not a true separation of church and state within the city and that the civil government was using its powers to protect Church members and especially the Prophet.

In January 1841, public nominating meetings were held, with the first election held on February 1. Regular elections followed over at least the next four years. There are no voting registers for these city elections, so it is impossible to know how active the Follett men were in exercising their franchise. There is no record that any Folletts were elected to a public office in the city. However, the quality of life enjoyed by King, Louisa, and their family was a direct result of the decisions made by the individuals who were elected to office.

Apparently to facilitate members' participation in city elections and activities, on March 1, 1841, the city council divided the city into four political units or "municipal wards," reflecting practice in the eastern United States, where "then and now," William G. Hartley explains, "a ward is a political subdivision of a city. Wards in Nauvoo were civil divisions for police, tax, election, school, and other municipal purposes. When church leaders needed to collect funds or to aid the poor, for convenience they let the city's political ward boundaries serve as assignment districts.

They placed a bishop in charge of each. Those ward units, however, were not Latter-day Saint entities."[37] For these political wards, the town was divided into four quarters at the intersection of Wells and Mulholland Streets.[38] King and Louisa's home was in the first municipal ward.[39]

King's name first appears in Nauvoo City Records with those of eighteen other men on a petition dated August 11, 1841:

> To the hounerable Mayor, Aldermen and City Counsel of the City of Nauvoo.
>
> The petition of the undersigned respectifuly represent that publick convenience requires that part of Partridge street north of Cutler street should be opened and graded that it may be passable; and your petitioners beg leve further to represent, that the contemplated opening will deminish the distance of travel for most of the citisons of the North part of the city in geting to the Temple Lot, lower and south part of the City. Your petitioners, therefore, pray that after due proseedings had, it may be thus opened and graded as in duty bound will ever Pray.[40]

Although Partridge Street had initially been platted, it had not been completed. King's property was six blocks north of Cutler Street. Granting this request would mean that he and others living in north Nauvoo could have a direct route via Partridge Street to the center of town, at least as far as Samuel Street where the Follett property was located.

King also became a member of the Nauvoo Legion. Many cities in Illinois had such local militias, largely holdovers from the earlier century's need to provide protection against Indians and which were still seen as a minuteman army for law enforcement at a county or state level. The periodic muster days were something of civic holidays and were frequently combined with parades and other special events. With Missouri's experience fresh in their minds, however, the Saints took seriously this formalization for self-protection.

In February of 1841, the Nauvoo Legion adopted a resolution "that no [male] person whatever, residing within the limits of the City of Nauvoo, between [sic] the ages of 18 and 45 years, excepting such as are exempted by the laws of the United States, shall be exempt from military duty, unless exempted by a special act of this court;" The resolution set fines for those who failed to show up on the muster days of "the 1st and 6th of April, and the 3rd of July." It also authorized a military "band of music" with a maximum membership of twenty.[41] Although King was fifty-three, well past the age of mandatory membership, he signed up with his son-in-law, Nathan West, age forty-one. Puzzlingly, although his other son-in-law James Daley, and his son, John, were within the mandatory enlistment age, they do not appear in the extant records.[42]

The membership issue became a controversial one as the officers obtained permission for any male regardless of age who lived anywhere in Hancock County to be accepted into membership and further determined that no Nauvoo citizen could enlist anywhere else but Nauvoo. Therefore, though a countywide civil militia unit, the Nauvoo Legion's membership was made up almost totally of Mormons, an item that bothered their neighbors.[43] The actual number of members varies in different sources. In September of 1841, an annual report to the state adjutant general put the number of enlistees at 1,490. In 1843, a total of 1,751 men were listed in the infantry brigade, but there is no surviving record of the cavalry brigade, which had "only one third as many companies as the infantry." A nearby newspaper placed the number at 2,000 while the "editor had heard Joseph Smith claim twice that many fighting men just a few weeks earlier."[44] The authors of the most current history of the legion concluded, based on a report of Joseph W. Coolidge, adjutant, that "the total number of men enrolled in the Nauvoo Legion by June 27, 1844, would have been 3,226." However, they acknowledged that, comparing all enrollment reports, it "is obvious that the total number of soldiers on the June 27 Legion returns varied."[45] Whatever the total number, the Nauvoo Legion quickly became one of the largest and most active militias in the state of Illinois, training often and making regular public appearances as a part of the social and ceremonial life in Nauvoo. John Henry Evans, who wrote a biography of Charles Coulson Rich, a legion member, stated in the early twentieth century: "In size the Legion came to be the largest body of trained soldiery in the United States, excepting only the United States army."[46]

Local militias were not a new concept at that time on the American frontier where, even if a community or county had a sheriff, it lacked back-up law enforcement. Indeed such units date back to colonial days and "provided a steady source of volunteers—or conscripts, if necessary—for the provincial armies which had been created by the colonial governments."[47] They were also instrumental in assisting the formal military units of the original thirteen colonies during the Revolutionary War. The membership of these companies usually consisted of men from the same town. According to a local history of Avon, Massachusetts, "Under the Massachusetts militia system, almost every male between the age of 16 and 60 spent some part of every year in training or in actual combat.... During the times of peace the militia system performed an important social function ... [and] mustered once in May and twice in September.... After a bit of drilling, followed by a practice volley or two, the men would break ranks and join in the fun of a New England picnic. This was a cherished tradition which allowed for a break in the monotonous drudgery of eighteenth century farming."[48]

The strength and popularity of the legion quickly became problematic. The story of the Danites and their paramilitary activities during the Mormon War (1838–39) in Missouri was well known. The Mormons' neighbors were apprehensive to see a group that they perceived to be similar to the Danites, or to actually be Danites, forming in Nauvoo. According to Richard Saunders, writing in 1993, non-Mormon residents of Hancock County perceived it as a "city-controlled militia force." However, Saunders's interpretation of the "General Return for the Second Cohort, 1843," which listed the arms issued by the state to the legion, concludes that "the arms listed are surprisingly sparse and suggest that the Nauvoo Legion was more an organized drill corps than a fighting force.... Thus at no time were the Mormons at Nauvoo really a military threat to the surrounding citizens."[49] Endorsing Saunders's conclusion in their 2010 history of the legion, Bennett, Black, and Cannon state: "The Legion was no better outfitted than any other militia in the state. In fact, there is evidence to suggest that the Legion did not have enough arms."[50] Further, Glen Leonard, a Nauvoo historian, after comparing several sources and reports, determined: "There are good reasons to accept the Legion's 1843 inventory as an accurate accounting of the arms held by the infantry brigade. If the cavalry was equally equipped (an unlikely situation), the Nauvoo Legion would have had around six hundred pieces, plus whatever individuals secured for themselves. In most American militias, the soldiers provided for themselves more often than they had arms furnished to them. That would have increased their defensive capability and, perhaps, explained the discrepancy in numbers."[51]

Whatever the legion's power or numbers, King was one of the early enlistees and remained a member until his death. As early as March 19, 1841, one month after the legion's formation, he was elected a third lieutenant in the First Cohort (mounted).[52] By July 3, he held the rank of

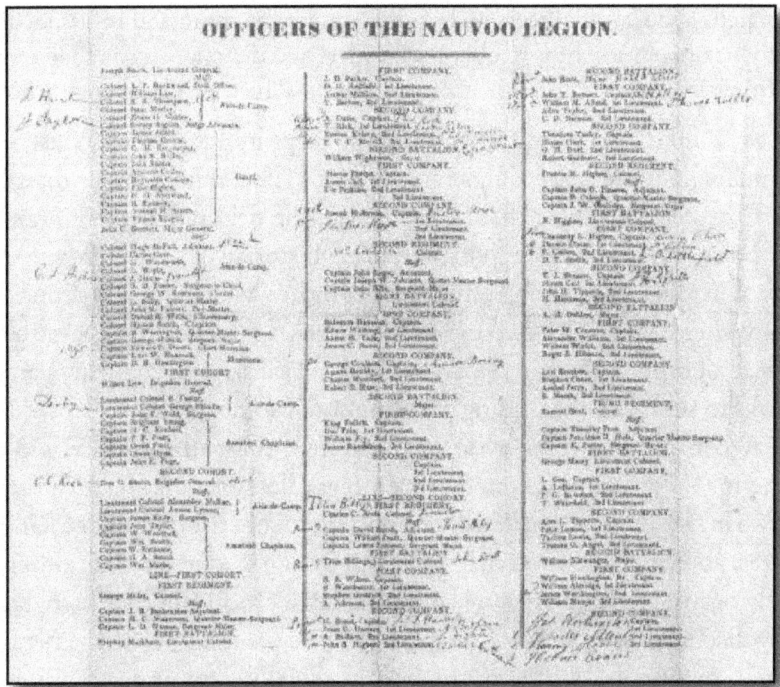

Nauvoo Legion Broadside. Courtesy LDS Church History Library.

captain in the Second Battalion, Second Regiment, First Company, and received that commission as captain from the state on October 16, 1841.[53]

The LDS Church History Library contains a document identified as a "Printed broadside list of Nauvoo Legion officers for the first and second cohorts. Joseph Smith is listed as lieutenant general. Includes handwritten changes.... Provenance for this document has been lost."[54] King's is listed as "Captain" under Second Battalion, First Company.

King's certificate of commission, based on the form of an existing certificate awarded to Joseph Holbrook that same date, would have read:

> To All to Whom these presents shall come—Greeting: KNOW YE, That King Follett having been duly elected to the office of Captain of the 1st Company, 2nd Battalion, 2nd Regiment of the Militia of the State of Illinois, I, THOMAS CARLIN, Governor of said State, for, and on behalf of the People of said State, do commission him Captain of said 1st Company, 2nd Battalion of said Regiment, to take rank from the 3rd day of July, 1841. He is, therefore, carefully and diligently to discharge the duties of said office, by doing and performing all manner of things thereunto belonging; and I do

strictly require all officers and soldiers under his command to be obedient to his orders; and he is to obey such orders and directions as he shall receive from time to time, from the Commander-in-Chief, or his superior officer."[55]

A "Rank Roll of the Nauvoo Legion," kept by Hosea Stout, also a legionnaire, indicates that King's rank was as a "line" officer rather than as a "staff" officer,[56] meaning that he worked in the field rather than in an "office" position. According to John Sweeney, a historian of the legion, a captain "served as the commanding officer of a company which normally consisted of anywhere from thirty-two to sixty-four men. He was to take charge of his men at all times including all parades and roll calls. At all company parades he was to supervise the reading of the duties of companies."[57]

According to the Nauvoo Legion Laws, the oath of office was the same for every commissioned officer, regardless of rank: "I, do solemnly swear (or affirm) that I will support the Constitution of the United States, and this State, and that I will not be engaged in dueling, either directly or indirectly, during my continuance in office; and that I will faithfully discharge the duties of [Captain] in the [unit name] of the Nauvoo Legion of Illinois Militia, to the best of my skill and understanding, so help me God."[58]

On June 3, 1842, the legion minutes state: "The third company of the second regiment, first cohort, commanded by Captain Follet was ordered to be attached to the second battalion of the first regiment, in the first cohort."[59] This note lists King as captain of the "third" company, while all other records place his assignment as the "first" company. The legion was divided into two groups (cohorts), a Roman term but not in use then or now in the American military. The first cohort was designated as "horse troops" while the second was "foot soldiers."

By state militia regulations, the legion, like all local militia units, required training, drills, and reviews. Records have not survived documenting how much time the legion spent in training, specifically what type of training they received, or how prepared they actually would have been if called to active duty. It seems likely that, because their military service was closely associated with the Church and especially because Joseph Smith served as their lieutenant-general and commander, members would have felt a special commitment to their militia responsibilities. Given their location on the frontier and the near-universal experience of hunting, it is also likely that virtually all of the men owned guns and knew how to use them. Charles Rich's biography describes the training site as a "huge parade ground, situated outside the city limits among the farm-lands [where] the legion received its training regularly, after the pattern of the Federal army, from the most skilful experts obtainable; and here the military prophet reviewed his troops."[60] Helen Mar Kimball, Heber C. Kimball's daughter, lived "a little distance from the training ground, where we witnessed many grand displays, as well as on the prairie, where they went to hold a three days' muster."[61] The Rich biography also quotes an artillery officer in the U.S. Army who witnessed one of the drills: "The evolutions of the troops would do honor to any body of armed militia, and closely approximates our regular forces. There are no troops in the State like them in point of enthusiasm and warlike aspect, yea warlike character. Before many years this legion will be twenty, and perhaps fifty thousand strong and still augmenting.[62]

If non-Mormon citizens of Hancock County believed these predictions about the legion's growth, it is understandable why they were concerned. While undoubtedly the prime reason for the Nauvoo Legion's formation was to protect Church members, thus insuring security under all circumstances, a group such as this appears to have also been a vital part of the social, ceremonial, and celebratory experiences of the Saints by drilling and marching on public occasions. King would have participated in these events, leading the men under his command.

The legion's first official appearance was April 6, 1841, the twelfth anniversary of the Church's founding and the day of cornerstone laying for the Nauvoo Temple. According to the *History of the Church*, the day began at 7:30 A.M. with the firing of artillery and cannon. The morning was spent in the first formal review participated in by all members of sixteen companies of the legion: "The appearance, order and movements of the Legion, were chaste, grand and imposing, and reflected great credit upon the taste, skill and tact of the men comprising said Legion. We doubt whether the like can be presented in any other city in the western country."[63]

At noon the legion, led by Joseph Smith, marched to the temple site at the intersection of Wells and Mulholland streets, where they formed a hollow square three men deep around the space marked off for the foundation, the center of which was filled with officers, a band, a choir, and special guests. Louisa and her children must have attended and would have enjoyed seeing the family patriarch in his military role. At the temple site, "short trenches had been excavated at four corners of the intended building to the level of the basement floor, the stone foundation laid, and rough basement walls of unfinished stone raised five feet," described Glen M. Leonard. "... Though the assembled citizens faced an impressive marshaling of soldiers, this was no military proceeding. The Latter-day Saints were about to commence construction of a temple."[64]

With appropriate ceremony, a stone was laid and dedicated at each of the four corners of the exposed foundation. "The occasion doubtless lifted the spirits of many who remembered the Saints' miserable condition two years earlier ... [and] revealed the Saints' pleasure in being a godly civic people," muses Richard Lyman Bushman. "They dedicated the temple surrounded by a city militia under the legal umbrella of a city charter. At last they had become a civic society."[65] On this day of tremendous importance to the legion, Church, and Nauvoo citizens, the legion's members were well enough trained to march and drill like any other military unit of comparable size, carrying appropriate weapons for the time. The state did not issue uniforms to any local militia, leaving each to make decisions about clothing. By about April 1841, its few top officers wore what was described as a full military uniform for the time: coat, pantaloons, epaulets, sash, plumed hat, gloves, spurs, sword, and belt.[66] The cost, more than $200, would have been prohibitive for most legionnaires, especially at first. It is doubtful that King ever owned a uniform, but the legion continued to be an important part of King's life for the three remaining years of his life. As it grew in numbers and importance, it became the pride of Nauvoo.

In addition to the charters issued in early 1841 authorizing the formation of a city government and a local militia, the third charter, as noted above, authorized the establishment of a university. Formal secular education, often combined with religious teachings, had always been important to Church members; and one of the first public buildings they erected in each town they lived in was a school. In "Proclamation of the First Presidency, to the Saints Scattered Abroad" on January 15, 1841, the city council assigned to a board of regents the "general supervision of all matters appertaining to education, from common schools up to the highest branches of a most liberal collegiate course. They will establish a regular system of education and hand over the pupil from teacher to professor, until the regular gradation is consummated and the education finished."[67]

School wardens were appointed in each ward, and teachers were required to prove their competency. Although a stone schoolhouse was apparently built as early as 1839 in Nauvoo, most of the early teaching was actually done in the homes, either by mothers or by teachers hired by the parents. "Such 'subscription' schooling where teachers either moved from house to house and boarded with the family of the pupils or solicited school services in their own homes, was popular in frontier Illinois," notes Brian D. Jackson in his history of education in Nauvoo.[68]

Although not all school records in Nauvoo have survived, none of those extant list King's children even though, by 1842 three Follett children still lived at home: William Alexander, age seventeen; Edward, age nine; and Warren, age four. King's daughter Adeline also had two stepdaughters of school age. However, attendance was not compulsory, and parents had to pay, either in cash or in kind. The charter allowed for school taxation, but there is no record that such taxes were imposed.[69]

As 1841 drew to a close, many ecclesiastical and civil issues had been addressed or at least were in place for later implementation in Nauvoo. Because of the relatively peaceful living conditions, the Saints could focus on building homes and on building up the kingdom of God, both temporally and spiritually. The next years would bring further blessings and challenges for the Follett family in Nauvoo.

Notes

1. Nathan Cheney, Letter to "Dear and Beloved Parents, Brothers, and Sisters, Nauvoo City, October 17, 1841," 3.

2. Edward Hunter, Letter written to his 'Respected Uncle," Nauvoo, May 6, 1841, quoted in Glen M. Leonard, "Letters Home: The Immigrant View from Nauvoo," 91–92.

3. *History of the Church*, 4:133.

4. Quoted in ibid., 4:137.

5. Quoted in ibid., 4:381. The name of the letter writer is not given.

6. Glen M. Leonard and T. Edgar Lyon, "The Nauvoo Years," *Ensign*, September 1979, 12.

7. Donald Q. Cannon, "The King Follett Discourse: Joseph Smith's Greatest Sermon in Historical Perspective," 180.

8. Milton V. Backman Jr., *People and Power of Nauvoo: Themes from the Nauvoo Experience*, 36.

9. Kenneth W. Godfrey, "Some Thoughts Regarding an Unwritten History of Nauvoo," 422.

10. Carol Cornwall Madsen, *In Their Own Words: Women and the Story of Nauvoo*, 12.

11. Ivan J. Barrett, *Joseph Smith and the Restoration: A History of the Church to 1846*, 482.

12. Nauvoo First and Second Wards, Item 4 in List of Members, 1841–45, Records of Members, 1836–48, p. 65.

13. See Chapter 9. See also Lyndon W. Cook, *A Tentative Inquiry into the Office of Seventy 1835–1845*, regarding the terminology used to describe this office, its specific authority, and its place in the priesthood organization of the Church.

14. A book containing an alphabetical list of all members of the Seventies who lived in Nauvoo was located on the second floor of the Seventies Hall in Nauvoo, Illinois, during my visit in 1999. King's name was on that list. Websites about visiting the building state that this list, a typescript in a three-ring binder, is still available.

15. "Notice," *Times and Seasons* 1, no. 7 (May 1840): 112.

16. Roger D. Launius and John E. Hallwas, eds., *Kingdom on the Mississippi Revisited: Nauvoo in Mormon History*, 3.

17. *History of the Church*, 4:179. "Colonel Brunson was among the first settlers of this place. He has always been a lively stone in the building of God and was much respected by his friends and acquaintances. He died in the triumph of faith, and in his dying moments bore testimony to the Gospel that he had embraced."

18. Joseph Smith, "Answers to Questions Asked in No. 2," *Elders' Journal* 1, no. 3 (July 1, 1838): 43. This periodical, edited by the Prophet's brother Don Carlos Smith, was published four times by the Church, twice in Kirtland in October and November of 1837, and twice in Far West in July and August of 1838.

19. Simon Baker, Statement, Journal History, August 15, 1840, 1–2.

20. Alexander L. Baugh, "'For This Ordinance Belongeth to My House': The Practice of Baptism for the Dead outside the Nauvoo Temple," 48.

21. Ibid., 49.

22. Jonah Ball, quoted in M. Guy Bishop, "What Has Become of Our Fathers? Baptism for the Dead at Nauvoo," 93–94. Jonah Randolph Ball (1803–45), the father of a young son at this time, was somewhat estranged from his family because of the Church. Though his letters contain strong feel-

ings about the Church, his request for information on deceased relatives is given without any mention of proxy baptism.

23. Sally Randall, quoted in Kenneth W. Godfrey, Audrey M. Godfrey, and Jill Mulvay Derr, eds., *Women's Voices: An Untold History of the Latter-day Saints, 1830–1900*, 134, 138–39. Sally Carlisle was born in New Hampshire in 1805 and married James Randall. They lived in New York, joined the Church in 1843, and moved to Nauvoo.

24. Bishop, "What Has Become of Our Fathers?" 88.

25. Susan Easton Black and Harvey Bischoff Black, *Annotated Record of Baptisms for the Dead, 1840–1845, Nauvoo, Hancock County, Illinois*, 2:1271–74 and 6:3755–56. See also "Baptisms for the Dead, 1840–1845," A55–56, 162–63, D23; "Nauvoo Baptisms for the Dead in Mississippi River (September 1840–November 1841)."

26. The name and gender as listed on all birth, census, and death records for this sibling of King is "Lifa" or "Life," a male (born 1790, died 1809). The name of "Alitha" and the listing as female on this record must be an error by the recorder at the time as King would certainly have known the name and sex of one of his siblings. Or perhaps King had a sister for whom no other record exists, though this is not likely, especially with the same birth date, unless Lifa and Alitha were twins. My research does not support a female of any age by this name in King's extended Follett family.

27. Black and Black, *Annotated Record of Baptisms for the Dead*, 2:1273.

28. *History of the Church*, 4:248.

29. Quoted in ibid., 4:267–73.

30. Ibid., 4:268.

31. Ibid., 4:249.

32. The implications of these "broad principles," their implementation in Nauvoo, and their impact on Church members are more fully explored in David E. Miller and Della S. Miller, *Nauvoo: The City of Joseph*, 49; Robert Bruce Flanders, *Nauvoo: Kingdom on the Mississippi*, 98–99; Glen M. Leonard, *Nauvoo: A Place of Peace, A People of Promise*, 103.

33. Richard Lyman Bushman, *Joseph Smith: Rough Stone Rolling*, 412.

34. John S. Dinger, "Joseph Smith and the Development of Habeas Corpus in Nauvoo, 1841–44," 140.

35. Ibid., 136.

36. Ibid., 141–66.

37. William G. Hartley, "Nauvoo Stake, Priesthood Quorums, and the Church's First Wards," 58.

38. According to the *History of the Church*, 4:305–6, "all the district of country within the city limits, north of the center of Knight street, and west of the center of Wells street, shall constitute the first ward. North of the center of

Knight street and east of the center of Wells street, the second ward. South of the center of Knight street, and east of the center of Wells street, the third ward. South of the center of Knight street, and west of the center of Wells street, the fourth ward."

39. Lyman De Platt, ed., *Nauvoo: Early Mormon Record Series, Vol. 1*, 13; Susan Ward Easton Black, comp., *Membership of the Church of Jesus Christ of Latter-day Saints, 1830–1848*, 552.

40. Nauvoo (Illinois) City Records, Petitions, 1841, fd. 23.

41. "Legion Resolutions," quoted in *History of the Church*, 4:300.

42. "Index to Mormon Battalion and Nauvoo Legion Soldiers," 30, 36. See also Richard E. Bennett, Susan Easton Black, and Donald Q. Cannon, *The Nauvoo Legion in Illinois: A History of the Mormon Militia, 1841–1846*, 341–401, for a complete list of commissioned and non-commissioned officers and privates in the Nauvoo Legion.

43. Leonard, *Nauvoo: A Place of Peace, A People of Promise*, 116.

44. Ibid., 117–18.

45. Bennett, Black and Cannon, *The Nauvoo Legion in Illinois*, 99–103.

46. John Henry Evans, *Charles Coulson Rich: Pioneer Builder of the West*, 73.

47. William A. Hanna, *A History of Avon, Massachusetts 1720–1988*.

48. Ibid.

49. Richard Saunders, "A Contemporary View of the Nauvoo Legion: The General Return for the Second Cohort, 1843," 51.

50. Bennett, Black, and Cannon, *The Nauvoo Legion in Illinois*, 220.

51. Leonard, *Nauvoo*, 115.

52. "Poll Books and Certificates of Election for Units of the Nauvoo Legion at Nauvoo and Ramus, Illinois."

53. Bennett, Black, and Cannon, *The Nauvoo Legion in Illinois*, Appendix D, 354–55. Though King's name is listed in the Appendix with the rank of captain, his name appears to be the only one with that rank whose name is not also given in a listing of those who "served as captains in the Legion," p. 123 note 52. Because of this omission, King's name is not listed in the index for this source as are others holding that rank.

54. "Officers of the Nauvoo Legion," MS 20447, LDS Church History Library.

55. Joseph Holbrook, Commission document. It contains the date he was elected to the position of captain (April 6, 1841), the date the commission document was issued (October 16, 1841), and the signatures of both the governor and the Illinois Secretary of State.

56. Hosea Stout, *Diary of Hosea Stout: Supplemental Volume Containing Letters, Documents, etc.*, 203.

57. John Sweeney Jr., "A History of the Nauvoo Legion in Illinois," 31.

58. Ibid., 75. The captain's oath is quoted from *Revised Laws of the Nauvoo Legion*, 9.

59. Ibid., 61–62.

60. Evans, *Charles Coulson Rich*, 74.

61. Richard Neitzel Holzapfel, "Nauvoo Remembered: Helen Mar Whitney Reminiscences," Part 4, p. 7.

62. Evans, *Charles Coulson Rich*, 74.

63. *History of the Church*, 4:326–27.

64. Leonard, *Nauvoo*, 234.

65. Richard Lyman Bushman, *Joseph Smith: Rough Stone Rolling*, 424.

66. Leonard, *Nauvoo*, 115–16; see also Glen M. Leonard, "Picturing the Nauvoo Legion," 95–128.

67. Quoted in *History of the Church*, 4:269–70.

68. Brian D. Jackson, "Preparing Kingdom-Bearers: Educating the Children of Nauvoo," 63.

69. Paul Thomas Smith, "A Historical Study of the Nauvoo, Illinois, Public School System, 1841–1845," quoted in ibid., 70 note 14.

❦ Chapter Seventeen ❦

1842: "This Most Extraordinary People"[1]

Because of the large number of individuals and families moving through Nauvoo, its population by 1842 is difficult to determine. Estimates of the maximum during the 1839–46 period when Church members lived in Nauvoo range between 10,000 and 20,000. In July 1841, Heber C. Kimball, who had returned to Nauvoo after a two-year service as a missionary in England, wrote a letter to the editor of the *Millennial Star* in which he commented on the city's progress during his absence:

> You know there were not more than thirty buildings in the city when we left about two years ago; but at this time there are about 1200, and hundreds of others in progress, which will be finished soon. On Friday last seventy Saints came to Nauvoo, led by Lorenzo Barnes, from Chester County, Pennsylvania, in wagons, living by the way. On the next day a company came in wagons, from Canada, all in good spirits, and in two or three days after, they all obtained places to live in. They are coming in from all parts of the vast continent daily and hourly, and the work is spreading in all of this land and calls for preaching in all parts. You will recollect when we built our houses in the woods there was not a house within a half a mile of us, now the place, wild as it was at that time, is converted into a thickly populated village.[2]

A year later in 1842, it was difficult to build homes fast enough to handle all of the new immigrants. A British convert, Ellen Douglas, wrote in June that she was "delighted to find a small house to rent, especially since she had prayed 'that we might have one to ourselves for there is 3 or

4 families in one room, and many have to pitch their tents in the woods or anywhere they can for it is impossible for all to get houses when they come in for they are coming in daily."[3] The Church's *Times and Seasons* in its October 1, 1842, issue commented: "It is one of the few comforts of the saints in this world, to be settled in peace, and witness the rapid growth of their infant city, as a place of safety and gathering for the last days. For three or four miles upon the river and about the same distance back in the country, Nauvoo presents a city of gardens, ornamented. . . . Many of the recent built houses are brick, some one story, and some two stories high, displaying . . . skill, economy and industry."[4]

These flourishing circumstances drew the attention of others. A St. Louis newspaper in 1842 wrote, probably with some exaggeration, that Nauvoo had a population of about 15,000 and was the largest town in Illinois (Chicago was always larger),[5] that, "by their industry in spite of sickness and the many obstacles which they had to contend with, they had accomplished more than any other community had done in the same amount of time." The article further commented on the possible future of this community and Church: "How long the Latter-day Saints will hold together and exhibit their present aspect it is not for us to say. At this moment they present the appearance of an enterprising, industrious, sober and thrifty population, such a population indeed, as in the respects just mentioned, have no rivals east, and we rather guess not even west of the Mississippi."[6]

Even though the Folletts left no reminiscences about their years in Nauvoo, they were presumably a typical Mormon family who would have shared in the life of the town and the Church. Two documents giving glimpses of their life in 1842 are a Church census and a county tax record.

The heading on the first page of the census record reads: "A Record of the names of the Members of the Church of Jesus Christ of Latterday Saints as taken by the lesser Priesthood in the Spring of the year 1842, and continued to be added as the members arrive at the City of Nauvoo, Hancock County, Illinois. Also the Deaths of Members & their Children, and names of Children under 8 years of age."[7]

The "lesser priesthood" refers to men ordained to the Aaronic Priesthood, now teenagers but in Nauvoo, adult males. The Follett family listings begin on the first page, line 23, and read: "King Follett, Louisa Follett, William A. Follett, Edward M. Follett, Warren K. Follett,

Adeline L. Follett, John W. Follett, and Nancy M. Follett." The children are not listed in birth order and the two married daughters, Adeline and Nancy, are listed under their birth names. This census contains no separate listing for their husbands, Nathan West and James Daley.

Lyman De Platt provides additional information about the census:

> Each individual was assigned a group of city blocks to visit. After each list was finished it was signed by the Aaronic Priesthood holder who made it. These lists were then recopied, and became the census.... The census is divided into four main sections according to the civil wards into which the city had been partitioned since March 1, 1841.... These civil wards should not be mistaken for the ecclesiastical wards existing in Nauvoo at this time.[8]

On this record the Folletts were listed as members of the Nauvoo First (City) Ward. This census lists about four thousand people living in more than eight hundred separate dwellings within the city limits. Probably the list was not complete, nor does it include the rest of Hancock County.

The second document, the county tax record, was created about five or six months later in August of 1842. It lists the name of the head of the household, with columns for the individual values of cattle, horses, wagons, clocks, watches, money loaned, stock in trade, other property not enumerated, and personal property. It also provides the coordinates of the real estate on which the personal property is located.[9] The tax rate was ½ percent tax on each of the personal items assessed by the county and ½ percent tax on real estate assessed by the city of Nauvoo. According to Nauvoo historians George and Sylvia Givens, "At the time, such taxes amounted to little more than a dollar per person per year or about an average workman's daily salary. The assessments were apparently quite low."[10] This tax record contains the following information for King and his family:

> Page 206. James Daley [husband of Nancy M. Follett]: Cattle, $20; property not enumerated, $20; Total: $40. Location of real property 7N8W
> Page 223. Nathan West [husband of Adeline M. Follett]: Cattle, $10; property not enumerated, $30; Total: $40. Location of real property 6N8W
> Page 224. King Follett: Cattle, $10; Horses, $10; watches, $10; property not enumerated, $30; Total: $60; Location of real property 6N8W[11]

King's son, John, is not listed on this tax record although he was a land owner at the time. Conversely, this is the only record of which I'm aware that shows James Daley as owning property in Nauvoo. The three pages containing these entries list only a few households in which the evaluations were $30 or under; many were evaluated at more than $100 and some were above $200.[12] The Follett family members were certainly not among the wealthier citizens of Nauvoo.

No Follett men or in-laws are listed as having voted on the official election returns for Nauvoo Precinct, also taken August 1, 1842.[13] King was also not listed in extant records as a voter in any previous place he had lived as an adult, although his possible reasons for not voting are obscure.

As Nauvoo grew in population and purpose, its newly formed city council met often to discuss issues of common concern that had earlier been left to individuals, to the Church, to existing government units, or which had not been addressed at all. Resolutions were passed covering a wide range of topics: regulating weights and measures, auctions, marriages, and "houses and acts of infamy," and establishing a registry of deeds. According to Nauvoo city records, on at least three separate occasions in 1842, King joined with neighbors to petition for specific official action. The first petition was signed on April 4 by thirty-nine men, including King Follett and Nathan West:

> To the honourable, the Council for the city of Nauvoo greeting Whereas an Ordinance has been passed by your honourable Body disanulling wells in the streets—therefore we the undersigned petitioners would humly [sic] represent to your honourable body that the proprietors of the well dug in the street at the junction of Patrige Street with Carlos Street were informed that it was counciled by Lieutenant General Joseph Smith for the Citizens to dig wells as fast as possible as there was much sickness in the City—And where one was not able, for several to Join and dig wells as there were many of that class amongst us who were expelled from Missourie the above being of that number and quite destitute and understanding that such has been practiced in Kirtland as well as other towns and City, they therefore united & sunk a well in the above named streets—This is therefore to petition & pray unto your honourable Body that you will take the above case in to consideration and as may [many] poor & needy are suplyed with water from said well and the proprietors are yet unable to dig wells for them selves, that peradventure your honourable Body may deem it wisdom to grant that the above named well may remain 18 months untill they shall have time to dig others.[14]

On April 8, a notation was made: "Report of the committee is that the well shall stand eight months." It gives no reason rejecting the requested eighteen-month extension. Committee members were "H Smith, H. Kimball and D H Wells."[15]

George and Sylvia Givens note that this power "to provide the city with water, *to dig wells, and erect pumps in the streets* for the extinguishment of fires, and convenience of the inhabitants" comes from Section 8 of the city charter. Thus, providing wells was a duty of the city "for the use of nearby inhabitants, without intruding on anyone's private property."[16] Apparently King, Nathan, and their neighbors wanted the existing well in the intersection to remain open until they could dig their individual wells on their private property.

A similar petition signed by fifty-two citizens requested that a well located on the "First Street West of Wells Street" remain open because it, too, was serving many families who could not afford to dig their own.[17]

King signed a second petition on April 5, the day after the first petition, along with more than eighty other individuals including Nathan West: "To the Honorable City Council of the City of Nauvoo gentlemen we your undersined petitioners pray your honorable body to open Bagbee Street from Parley Street north to Kimble street as it will give us outlet and accommodate us verry much."[18] This petition was granted on April 9. "Bagbee Street" (also "Bagby" and "Bagley" or "Bagly" on other records) was later renamed 24th Street. It ran north and south, while the major roads, Parley and "Kimble" (Kimball), were the major east-west thoroughfares.[19] "Bagbee Street" was located about twelve blocks south and fourteen blocks east of the Follett property; apparently east-bound Nauvoo citizens headed toward the farming land lying east of Nauvoo felt they needed better access to that area.[20]

The third petition, signed by King, Nathan, and ninety-two others, was dated July 18, and reflected concern over the quality of the river water, which was probably related to the marshland near the banks:

> To the Mayor, Alderman and Counselors of the City of Nauvoo—The undersigned citisons of the City of Nauvoo—ask leave to represent to your honourable body, that we believe the health of the City is verry much impuned by consequence of the many rafts of logs, wood, timber etc. that are suffered to lay in the edies, coves and along the river for weeks and months; which caused stagnent water, which when stired by babbling[?] or other ways produces a verry offensive affluvia which [is] injurieous to health— besides it verry much impeads navigation of flat Boats Skifts etc which are almost con[s]tantly passing and repassing—

We therefore request your honourable body to take immediate measures to protect the city against the evle; by passing an audinence to that effect.[21]

From these petitions, it is obvious that King and other citizens were using the authority granted by the city charter to participate in the governance of their city: i.e., affordable culinary water, transportation, and health. This was probably the first time in the ten years since they had moved to Missouri that King and other members of the Church were living where they felt fully confident in exercising their civic rights.

To protect those rights, King continued his involvement in the local militia—the Nauvoo Legion, organized in 1841. The legion's minutes describe the rapid growth, activities, and citizens' response to the organization. King's name is not on the list of those paying assessments or fines. Other than the entries showing that he had joined the Nauvoo Legion and his election as captain, he is mentioned only twice. The first entry, March 26, 1842, reports the results of balloting "to regulate the rank of Captains. . . . King Folliett is 10 of 14."[22] Apparently these new captains, who would be commissioned on July 3, were arranged by rank as the result of a vote. The record contains no explanation about what this "rank" regulation actually meant.

The second entry is the "Pool Book of election of Major General in the Nauvoo Legion, held at Hyrum Smith office on Saturday, August 13, 1842." The candidates were William Law and Lyman Wright. King voted for Lyman Wight. Law was the successful candidate.[23]

It is safe to say that King Follett was involved in other of the legion's activities, leading his troops as their captain. Throughout the United States at this time, having a connection with a military group conferred important social and political status and honor. Those with official positions enjoyed being referred to by that title. "Military trappings were for them a particular symbol of status, prestige, and reassurance in a life so beset with insecurities and deprivations," comments Robert B. Flanders, a historian of Nauvoo.[24] Possibly King was addressed as "Captain Follett" during legion activities, as well as by the normal Church title of "Brother Follett." Parades or marching drills of the legion were held regularly and were special events in Nauvoo, just as with militias in other towns throughout the country. Most of the time, Joseph Smith participated in his role as lieutenant-general with the troops assembling and marching to the Prophet's home for inspection. Legion minutes reflect that each of these events were positive experiences for all citizens.

Early in 1842, Joseph Smith, acting in his role as head of the Nauvoo Legion, issued a general order outlining the need for preparing arms and making assignments for a general parade on May 7, an event at which dignitaries from both Illinois and Iowa would be present. He emphasized his wish that this inspection "pass off in a truly military style, alike honorable to the legion, and creditable to the citizen soldiers."[25] Part of this event would be an evening gala to which officers, wives, and special guests would be invited. Surely King Follett was involved. An unnamed U.S. artillery officer described the successful event on May 8 in a letter to the *New York Herald*: "Yesterday was a great day with the 'Mormons.' Their legion, to the number of two thousand men, was paraded by Gen. Smith, Bennett and others, and certainly made a very noble and imposing appearance. The evolutions of the troops would do honor to any body of armed militia in any States, and approximates very closely to the regular forces."[26]

However, this same letter contained hints of concern over how rapidly the legion would continue to grow in numbers and that, in the future, it might become a "fearful host, filled with religious enthusiasm, and led on by ambitious and talented officers." The writer also speculated that the ultimate goal of the legion and the Church was "perhaps the subversion of the Constitution of the United States; and ... foreign conquests will most certainly follow."[27] Unfortunately, similar reports and speculations played a major role in continuing problems for the Church with their neighbors.

In most ways, King and his family were involved in activities typical of growing communities in frontier America in the 1840s. But in another way, life and activities in Nauvoo were very different. Accommodating the far-flung missionary activities that many of the men engaged in, as well as the influx of new converts, and gathering weekly in good weather for preaching services where they would learn Mormon doctrine were activities geared toward and focused on the commandment to build a temple—a building whose dimensions were approximately "128 feet east to west by 88 feet north to south." When completed it would contain over 11,000 square feet and be one of the largest buildings in the area.[28] The Saints now found themselves in the same condition in Nauvoo as they were when they had started constructing the temple in Kirtland. Very few of them had any experience with this type of construction, and they were busily engaged in building their own homes. However, the fact that the Saints were no longer able to do proxy baptisms in the river was a great impetus for an early completion of at least a part of the building. By November of 1841 the basement rooms "were enclosed by frame walls and were covered by a temporary roof." These rooms included "a temporary wooden font" that was "resting on twelve wooden oxen." The font was dedicated on November 8. On Sunday, November 21, forty proxy baptisms were performed.[29] Hereafter, regular baptisms both for the living and for deceased relatives were performed in this temporary font until a permanent one was installed as part of the completed building. Louisa Follett was baptized by proxy for two of her deceased relatives in this temporary font in 1843. (See Chapter 16.)

Obviously the major concern for Joseph and the Church regarding the temple was how the Church would be able to pay for it. Very few of the members living in Nauvoo during this period had extra cash on hand. Either they were new converts who had just arrived after spending what money they had to move to Zion from Europe or from throughout the United States, or they were long-time members, who had been with the Church during the hectic and tumultuous years in Missouri and were now having to start over, having lost most of their property. It had been determined at the October 1840 conference that a tithing of members' possessions and labor would provide the temple's financial support.

This tithing assessment was applicable to all members of the Church, if possible, wherever they lived. In Nauvoo, this also meant that the Follett men would work every tenth day on the temple without pay. When the city was divided into ten wards, one of the reasons for the division was to organize tithing labor into a steady supply. Families would also pay a tenth of any material items they might have—cash, if possible, livestock, crops, or other items that they grew or made as cottage industries. These items were paid directly to the Nauvoo Temple Building Committee that had been formed at the conference to oversee the construction of the temple. Receipts were issued to members with a value designated on the donation. Later the items donated were given to the Trustee in Trust, set up specifically for that purpose. William Clayton, a temple recorder, explained the bookkeeping system: "All tithings, consecrations, donations, and sacrifices presented for the building of the temple are recorded in a book kept for that purpose in the form of a history, wherein is recorded the names of the donors, the kind of property donated, and the price of the same, or if in money, the amount."[30]

The book in which these donations were initially recorded was referred to as "The Book of the Law of the Lord" and became part of Joseph Smith's papers since he kept, in the same bound book, his "Illinois Journal, 1841–1842." According to Dean C. Jessee:

> The journal is written in a large leather-bound book measuring 11 5/8 x 17 inches, containing 477 pages. Besides the journal, the book contains copies of revelations and a record of donations for the building of the temple at Nauvoo. Illinois. The first three leaves of the book are blank; the fourth contains the title "The Book of The Law of the Lord" in very ornate hand lettering in black ink. Pages 3–25 contain copies of Doctrine and Covenants revelations. The journal begins on page 26 and ends on page 215 but is interspersed with pages that contain lists of donations which then continue unbroken from page 216 to the end of the volume. The front and back covers are unmarked, but the spine of the book is labeled "Law of the Lord."[31]

King Follett's name is not listed in the index to this record.[32]

A temple store, established to handle the donated items, was initially located in the back portion on the main floor of Joseph Smith's Red Brick Store. It was later moved to a location closer to the temple itself. Here those who worked on the temple more than every tenth day and those who held "paid" positions to work on the temple could shop and purchase the items they needed. Except for specialized skills needed in the building, "much of the work on the temple was accomplished by labor tithing. The success of the labor tithe was so marked that it became the means of tithing requested from all able-bodied men who lived in or near Nauvoo."[33] This arrangement would have included King and his sons and sons-in-law. Goods donated to the store were also used to assist the poor in Nauvoo. Eventually, all citizens of the area were allowed to buy from the store, thus assisting the economy of the region.

The importance of the tithing commandment for the temple was stressed to the entire membership of the Church in an epistle issued by the Quorum of the Twelve in December 13, 1841, published two days later in the *Times and Seasons*: "The tythings [sic] required, is one tenth of all any one possessed at the commencement of the building, and one tenth part of all his increase from that time till the completion of the same, whether it be money or whatever he may be blessed with. Many, in this place, are laboring every tenth day for the house, and this is the tithing of their income, for they have nothing else."[34]

Specific direction was given in the epistle about the desirable items to contribute:

> Let the brethren for two hundred miles around drive their fat cattle and hogs to this place, where they may be preserved.... Not the maimed, the lean, the halt, and the blind, and such that you cannot use; it is for the Lord, and he wants no such offering: but if you want his blessing give him the best; give him as good as he has given you. Beds and bedding, socks, mittens, shoes, clothing of every description, and store goods are needed for the comfort of the laborers this winter; journeymen stonecutters, quarrymen, teams and teamsters for drawing stone, and all kinds of provision for men and beast are needed in abundance.[35]

Throughout the winter of 1841–42, work on the temple was slow, perhaps because of the weather. At the quarry, workmen cut and loaded stones, which were then hauled to the temple site, where they were finished as needed for the walls. Nathan Cheney said that there were "probably fifty to seventy people to work every day on the house."[36] When a large number of volunteer workers were needed for a specific project, assignments were made to each of the city wards about what day their male citizens were responsible to work. By this schedule, King, as a member of the First Ward, was responsible for working at the temple on Monday, Tuesday, and Wednesday of each week.[37] Records were kept of the time spent by each worker. Matthew McBride, a modern historian of the Nauvoo Temple, explains these records this way:

> Labor was usually recorded (and corresponding credit given) by the temple committee ... and the crew leaders ... because they were on site and in a position to evaluate the work done. In addition to recording their appraisals of a worker's labor in their "day books," they issued vouchers for a dollar amount that could be redeemed at the "temple store." ... Of course, one tenth of the laborer's wages were deducted as tithing.... Cash and trade donations were appraised every Saturday by the temple recorder.... [T]he donated goods were held in the temple store (and in the case of livestock, in the temple corral). Temple workers then "purchased" goods from the store using the vouchers issued by the temple committee.[38]

Beginning in November of 1841 and continuing through November of 1842, one of those records, now labeled "Building Committee Records,

Daybook A

Date	Page	Item	Value
1841 August	65	To order for meat	$1.00
11/20	118	1.15 1/4 # beef @ 3	3.46
1842 1/19	160	2 oz oil	.50
2/26	188	21 1/2 flower	.53
3/9	196	1 horse	10.00
3/26	217	9# sugar	1.00
4/4	221	7# beans	.19
5/15	265	26# flour	.65
5/18	268	10.9# meat	.81
6/3	282	1/2 bushel meal	.19
6/27	307	11 1/4# meat	.56
6/29	310	1 bushel meal	.38
	314	32 meat or meal	.48
6/30	315	1 rifle gun	14.00
7/1	317	23# beef	1.15
		To order on store	5.00

1841–42" and containing Daybook A and Daybook B, show twenty-five entries for King's purchases at the temple store. He would have used his labor vouchers from his work on the temple, which would have been above and beyond his unpaid tithing labor.[39]

Another item recorded in Daybook A, July 1, 1842, p. 331, lists King and thirteen others as "hauling for Wm Wilke." Each workman was credited with fifteen dollars. Above those names is the notation: "Wm Wilke Sr., 9 loads halling [?] timber Q boards to prairie, 7 loads sand, 1 load lime." Probably Wilke was contributing these items and King and his fellow workmen hauled them to the store. Their labor in doing so was credited to their account at the temple store.

This record also contains two cash payments, both in Daybook B, to King's account. The first is $1.00 on November 13, 1841. It may have been tithing paid. The notation, though not clear, appears to read "By Cwh—8/". The second, $4.00, is dated June 20, 1842, and reads "pd by

Daybook B

Date	Page	Item	Value
1842–7/14	8	1 peck meal	$0.09
8/8	32	13 3/4# flour	.40
		1/2 bushel meal	.19
9/17	91	3 shanks beef	.37
10/14	165	1 pr shoes upper leather	.75
	167	1 pr of upper leather	.75
11/5	197	11 1/2# beef	.34
11/22	217	1 shank	.15
		17 1/2 lbs beef @ 3	.53

Erastus Dodge." Daybook C, which would have preserved the records from 1843, is missing. Daybook D begins in January of 1844 and does not contain any entries for King prior to his death in March of that year. At some point during this period, most of the accounts show a total of purchases and then a total of work credit vouchers or actual cash used to pay off the account. There is no such accounting for King; it may have been in the missing book.

There is one undated entry for a James Dailey (rather than Daley,) which I believe is King's son-in-law, for $3.50 tithing. It is the only other entry in the daybooks or ledgers for any of King's family members.[40]

From this information regarding purchases at the temple store, it looks as if King worked often on the temple in 1842, donating his labor, probably in addition to his usual tithing day. I have found no extant record that establishes King's specific hours worked. His individual labor would be recorded in some small time book from which the store vouchers were issued, most of which have not survived. This donated labor is impressive, considering that he was building a home for his family, planting and raising crops to feed them, and engaged in other civic, religious, and personal activities.

By September of 1842, the walls of the temple were completed to the point that the Prophet requested the installation of a temporary floor so that conference meetings could be held in the temple instead of outside in the grove. Between October 23 and 28, the workmen concentrated on the temporary floor and installing seats. On October 30, the first meeting was held at the temple. The *History of the Church* comments:

> Friday 28: This day the brethren finished laying the temporary floor, and seats in the Temple, and its appearance is truly pleasant and cheering. The exertions of the brethren during the past week to accomplish this thing are truly praiseworthy.
>
> Saturday 29: About ten in the forenoon, I [Joseph] rode up and viewed the Temple. I expressed my satisfaction at the arrangements and was pleased with the progress made in the sacred edifice.
>
> Sunday 30: The Saints met to worship on a temporary floor, in the Temple, the walls of which were about four feet high above the basement; and notwithstanding its size, it was well filled.[41]

Because King redeemed a temple-labor voucher for food six days later, it is very probable that he was one of the men working on the temple during this week in Church history, and also that he and his family attended that first meeting in the temple.

While the men performed most of the skilled work on the temple, the women and older girls provided support in many ways. Some donated money or other items. Many sewed clothing needed for the workers, and most of them cooked and delivered food to the temple site for the men toiling there. In most organized religions, historically the women have focused on caring for the poor and less fortunate. The women of Nauvoo were no different. They had primary responsibility for growing the gardens and cooking the food that nurtured their families and weaving the fabric and sewing the clothes that their families wore. Out of this pattern of supportive service both in their homes and in the larger community came the idea of a formal organization. One of their number, Sarah Melissa Granger Kimball, the wife of nonmember Hiram Kimball, believed that, if the women banded together, they could accomplish even more than they were doing individually. Under her direction, women from her neighborhood[42] met on March 4, 1842, to talk about how this worthy goal could be accomplished. As those who met that day worked to officially organize themselves by developing by-laws and a constitution, the Prophet praised their efforts but said he had "something better for them than a written Constitution." He wanted to organize them "under the priesthood after the pattern of the priesthood."[43] The Prophet met with the women on March 17, 1842, in the Lodge Room above his Red Brick Store and "as-

Reconstruction of Joseph Smith's Red Brick Store in Nauvoo. Photo by Irval L. Mortensen, 2008.

sisted in commencing the organization of 'The Female Relief Society of Nauvoo'... I gave much instruction, read in the New Testament, and Book of Doctrine and Covenants, concerning the Elect Lady, and showed that the elect meant to be elected to a certain work."[44]

The Relief Society minutes frequently record the Prophet's visits and his instruction to the women, thus emphasizing the importance and value of the organization. His organization of these women recognized both their role in the Church and the expansion of that role—a significant step since the Church organization until this time had only male units and leaders. This was the beginning of an organization that has become a "truly distinctive feature of the Church and a unique group among the women's benevolent societies of the day. The women themselves saw their 'society,' as it was commonly and consistently called in the minutes, as more than *simply* a charitable organization. The organization of the society also provided an official 'seal' for the spiritual blessings granted to the sisters in Nauvoo."[45] The Relief Society became the organization through which the Prophet intended to teach the sisters, present doctrine specific to their responsibilities as wives and mothers, and ultimately prepare them for the ordinances and blessings to occur in the temple.

At that first meeting, officers were elected. The Prophet's wife, Emma, was elected president. The minutes list the names of twenty women who were present at that meeting. Those twenty and another six were voted into official membership that day, although in the minutes, a line is drawn through the names of Nancy and Athalia Rigdon, Sidney Rigdon's daughters. When Rigdon broke with Joseph Smith in 1844, his daughters also withdrew from formal participation. At the second meeting, held a week later on March 24, forty-eight additional women became members, including Louisa (spelled "Loisa") Follett in the minutes kept by the secretary Eliza R. Snow.[46] At this second meeting of the organization, the Prophet's mother, Lucy Mack Smith, was touched as she looked at the sisters at the meeting and "hop'd the Lord would bless and aid the Society in feeding the hungry, clothing the naked... [and] said—this Institution is a good one—we must watch over ourselves ... we must cherish one another, watch over one another, comfort one another and gain instruction, that we may all sit down in heaven together."[47]

The organization grew rapidly; and during its first year of existence, seventeen meetings were held. However, there is no record that Louisa's two daughters, Adeline or Nancy, ever became members. By May 1842, the number of women involved had become so large that the Relief Society could not meet in any buildings in Nauvoo. Thereafter, it divided up and met in the home of individual sisters in each of the first Nauvoo wards.[48] Louisa would have met with the women of Nauvoo First Ward who were not only her sisters in the Church, but friends and nearby neighbors. A Necessity Committee was formed in each ward whose purpose was to identify those in need and collect donations for relief.[49] The minutes record donations of cash, food, clothing, and other items at each meeting, which were used to aid those less fortunate. The women also reported on the use of their time and talents for service in the community. Some of the members contributed to others but at times were in need themselves and became recipients of goods and services. "At these meetings, Emma Smith emphasized the society's charge to improve community morals by teaching sexual purity.... The meetings also included reminders of the need to develop personal spirituality by studying the scriptures, praying, and living the commandments."[50] Surely Louisa participated in these activities, and she and other sisters set the pattern of mutual watchcare that still characterizes this thriving organization in every ward in the modern Church.

Maurine Carr Ward, editor of *Mormon Historical Studies*, reported in 2002 that the Nauvoo Relief Society minutes provide the names of 1,341 women who were voted into membership during the two years between March 1842 and March 1844. Because some names were duplicated, she determined that 1,331 was the total membership figure. Using other Nauvoo records, she was able to identify 1,010 of these women, most linked to other family members in Nauvoo. The women ranged in age from under fifteen years to seventy-six. (Louisa was forty-four.) The women were natives of six foreign countries (Canada, England, Ireland, Germany, Scotland, and Wales).[51] The biographical information she provides for Louisa reads: "FOLLETT, Loisa; 24 Mar 1842; Louisa TANNER; b. 3 Aug 1798, Cooperstown, Otsego, New York; parents Thomas TANNER and Anna WARREN; m. 1816 to KING FOLLETT^; D. 15 Nov 1891, Iowa."[52] The mark "^" identified Louisa as one of the members whose husband died in Nauvoo.

The minutes of the Relief Society in Nauvoo are not always detailed enough to determine Louisa's specific activities over the next two years. But it is likely that she participated actively with other women, whether through the formal structure of the Relief Society or informally within her family and neighborhood. The last Relief Society meeting held in Nauvoo was on Saturday, March 16, 1844: "Members convened in the upper room of the Prophet's store where the organization had had its beginning."[53] This was one week after King's death.

As King and his family were busy with activities that were helping to construct and fund the temple, the Prophet Joseph began to expand the concept of the temple, the reason for a temple, and what would occur therein. According to a revelation he had received on January 19, 1841, when the people were told to build a temple, one of the ordinances reserved for the temple was baptism by proxy. But the Lord also stated: "For I design to reveal unto my Church things which have been kept hid from before the foundation of the world, things that pertain to the dispensation of the fulness of times" (D&C 124:41). From this statement and from the temple's physical layout, it was obvious that ordinances other than baptism would occur there. Richard Lyman Bushman, a Joseph Smith biographer, summarizes it this way: "The concept of the temple had steadily expanded since it was first mentioned in a revelation in late 1830. In Independence the temple was understood as a place for the Lord to return—a place to lay His head when He came. In Kirtland, Joseph added administrative offices, a meetinghouse and school, and, more significantly, performed the rituals of washing and anointing in the House of the Lord. In Nauvoo, the ceremonies were further elaborated to include baptism for the dead, endowments, and priesthood marriages."[54]

While the original intent had been to wait until the temple was completed to add the new ceremonies, the work on the temple site seemed slow to the Prophet. He may also have had intimations of his early death or the rise of persecution that would hamper him. In speaking to the Relief Society seven weeks after its organization, he told the sisters that "he did not know as he should have many opportunities of teaching them . . . they would not long have him to instruct them—that the church would not have his instruction long, and the world would not be troubled with him a great while . . . that according to his prayers God had appointed him elsewhere."[55] Perhaps because of these forebodings, he pressed forward with greater haste in teaching his people and initiating them into the temple ceremonies.

The *History of the Church* contains an account of the long-awaited introduction of the endowment ceremony, on May 4, 1842, in the "Lodge Room" on the second story of Joseph's Red Brick Store. At this time, he instructed seven men[56] "in the principles and order of the priesthood, attending to washings, anointings, endowments . . . and all those plans and principles by which any one is enabled to secure the fullness of those blessings . . . . In this council was instituted the ancient order of things for the first time in these last days." The Prophet further said that the things that were made known to these few men this day would soon be available to all the Saints of the last days as soon as "they are prepared to receive, and a proper place is prepared to communicate them, even to the weakest of the Saints."[57] According to a modern historian, it was a year before the Prophet "resumed administering washings, anointings, and endowments to men and women, including his wife, Emma. At the same time, he sealed a number of couples for time and all eternity.... Between May 1842 and his martyrdom on June 27, 1844, the Prophet administered the endowment to most of the Twelve and to about twenty-five other men and thirty-two women.[58] The sealing ordinance would assure couples that their marital bond would transcend death. Following these first endowments, the Prophet reportedly told Brigham Young: "Brother Brigham, this is not arranged perfectly; however we have done the best we could under the circumstances in which we are placed. I wish you to take this matter in hand: organize and systematize all these ceremonies."[59] Brigham Young carried out these instructions, reconstructing and systematizing the temple ordinances in Utah's Endowment House, then in the temples constructed under his direction before his death in 1877.

There is no record that King Follett received these new ordinances before his death in 1844. However, Louisa and the adult surviving children participated in the endowment ceremony in the Nauvoo Temple in 1846 before the Saints left Nauvoo.

Since King did not experience the temple endowment while he was alive, it was necessary for him to receive it by proxy after his death. Church and family records give several dates for his proxy endowment. The first and earliest of these dates in family and Church temple records is November 2, 1877, in the St. George Utah Temple. The relative/proxy for King is his son, William Alexander Follett.[60] This was thirty-three years after King's death and was the first year that endowments for the dead by proxy were performed after the Church members left Nauvoo.

The Prophet Joseph Smith did not refer to any specific revelation or written source when he began the endowment ordinance. It is probable that this, like other teachings of the Church, came to the Prophet by personal revelation which he did not immediately record or at least for which there is no surviving record. Bushman states: "Portions of the temple ritual resembled Masonic rites that Joseph had observed when a Nauvoo lodge was organized in March 1842.... Joseph often requested revelation about things that caught his attention."[61] Matthew McBride, in his history of the Nauvoo Temple, quotes Heber C. Kimball, one of the original Twelve Apostles, who wrote in 1842: "There is a similarity of Priesthood in masonry. Brother Joseph says Masonry was taken from priesthood but has become degenerated, but many things are perfect."[62]

McBride concludes: "These statements hint that Masonry, though 'degenerated' was instrumental in the revelation of the Nauvoo endowment, perhaps in the same way that biblical Christianity, though apostate, was clearly a springboard to the restoration of the fullness of the gospel and the establishment of the Church."[63]

For whatever reason, the Freemasons, which claims to be the oldest fraternal organization in the world, has an interesting presence at this time in Nauvoo and specifically in King's life. As the persecution against the Church began again in Nauvoo, the Prophet used many methods to deflect the hostility characteristic of Missouri. He tried to show nonmembers that Mormons were caring, concerned people who professed and practiced high ideals and beliefs. Several of the Prophet's friends in Nauvoo had been Masons in their communities before joining the Church. In fact, his brother, Hyrum, was a Mason, and revered founding fathers like George Washington, Benjamin Franklin, and Paul Revere were also Masons.

At least one history of Nauvoo recorded that these men reminded the Prophet of the "spirit of brotherhood and brotherly love which supposedly was the very foundation of the Masonic fraternity and characterized Masonic activities. . . . This lofty sentiment corresponded with the high ideals advanced by the Prophet and practiced by his followers. Many prominent and influential men in the state were Masons and the Saints needed them as friends. It was readily conceded that association with the fraternity might help the Saints escape mob persecutions. The Saints wanted peace with all men."[64] Whether this assessment is accurate, it does appear that these Masonic members of the Church petitioned for a lodge to be established in Nauvoo during the summer of 1841.

Although members of the Masonic order in nearby towns did not want the Mormons to join, the request was ultimately granted by Abraham Jonas, the Grand Master of the Grand Lodge of Illinois on October 15, 1841. Perhaps this happened because he saw that Masonic beliefs were similar to the teachings of the Church and therefore had compassion for the Saints. Jonas may also have had a personal reason—the more members who joined, the more friends he could count on when he became a candidate for the Illinois State Legislature.

The men of Nauvoo began to hold meetings on December 29, with the official installation of the Nauvoo Lodge by Grand Master Jonas occurring on March 15–16, 1842.⁶⁵ Jonas later wrote this interesting description of those events:

> While at Nauvoo I had a fine opportunity of seeing the people in a body. There was a Masonic celebration, and the Grand Master of the state was present for the purpose of publicly installing the officers of the new lodge. An immense number of persons assembled on the occasion, variously estimated from five to ten thousand persons, and never in my life did I witness a better-dressed or more orderly and well-behaved assemblage; not a drunken or disorderly person to be seen, and the beauty among the females could not well be surpassed anywhere. During my stay of three days, I became well acquainted with the prophet, the celebrated "old Joe Smith." I found him hospitable, polite, well-informed and liberal. With Joseph Smith, the hospitality of whose house I kindly received, I was well pleased.⁶⁶

The Prophet served as chaplain during the installation, which took place at the grove near the temple. That evening he received "the first degree in Free Masonry in the Nauvoo Lodge" and declared that "the day was exceedingly fine; all things were done in order, and universal satisfaction was manifested."⁶⁷ Heber C. Kimball, who was already a Mason before coming to Nauvoo, reported that the lodge installed a total of forty that day.⁶⁸ Though extant minutes of the lodge and Church history reflect that the Prophet rarely attended meetings, the general membership grew rapidly to 252 by the end of 1842, ten times that of any other lodge in Illinois. The minutes of Thursday, November 2, 1843, announce: "This Lodge [will] proceed to work and confer the degrees of Masonry on all worthy men in this city who desire them."⁶⁹ At that point there were 330 Masons in Nauvoo alone, a total of 506 Mormon Masons in Illinois and Iowa, but only about 227 non-Mormon Masons in all the rest of Illinois. According to James B. Allen, "It is little wonder that, politically, at least, other Illinois Masons began to fear the Mormons in their ranks."⁷⁰

King Follett joined early—in May of 1842—two months after the official installation of the lodge. In the lodge's minutes, beginning in 1841, King Follett is not listed as a founding member, nor was he one of the original petitioners. His signature is, however, found in the by-laws as member #158. The notation "Dead" appears by his signature.⁷¹ On Thursday, May 5, 1842, at a 6:00 P.M. meeting, "Petitions were then presented from the following persons for the honors of masonry, to wit: King Follett, aged 53, a farmer," among others. Two weeks later on Thursday, May 19, again at 6:00 P.M., King Follett is listed among those on whom "the Committee of Investigation ... reported favourably." A week later on May 24, King was "initiated as an Entered Apprentice." Three days later on May 27, "King Follett ... duly passed to the degree of Fellowcraft Mason." On May 28 "King Follet [was] ... duly raised to the sublime degree of a Master Mason and signed the by-laws."[72]

Nathan West is also listed as having signed the by-laws apparently as member #421.[73] He petitioned for membership shortly after King, listing his occupation as a carpenter and joiner. The minutes state that West "applied for membership 6-16-42." On "7-7-42, the Committee report was favorable." However, "the ballot not clear—rejected." "Petitioned again July 6, 1843," this time apparently successfully.[74] Extant lodge records do not list any of the other of the Follett men: John Follett, William Alexander Follett, or James Daley.

King was never a Masonic officer. Minutes of official meetings and events do not always contain names of those attending; those records that do list attendance do not reflect King's name. However, it is likely he was present on Friday, June 24, 1842, when Nauvoo's lodge participated in celebrating St. John's Day, Masonry's traditional festival of St. John the Baptist. The Prophet Joseph "rode in Masonic procession to the grove where a large Assembly of masons & others listened to an address from Prest [President] Rigdon."[75] Wilford Woodruff recorded that "the procession assembled at Joseph Smith's store and marched to the stand near the temple. He estimated 6,000 people were present."[76] Undoubtedly the Follett family members were among this number attending that day. King's name does not appear anywhere in the Nauvoo Lodge Account Book as having paid his dues; however, the first six pages (21-22 and part of 23) are missing.[77] A firm indication that he was an active member is the fact that he was given a Masonic funeral.

The year 1842 had been a busy one, both temporally and spiritually, for King and his family. In addition to all of their other activities, their first grandchild was born to Nancy and James Daley in Nauvoo and was named William King Daley—probably for his uncle, William Alexander Follett, and surely for his grandfather King Follett. William King Daley was born in April of 1842, as calculated from his age at death as "51 years, 5 months."[78] This baby was the first of many born in the Follett family over the next generations to have "King" as a middle name.

Notes

1. "Wonderful Progress of Joe Smith, the Modern Mahomet—Spread of the Mormon Faith, and a New Religious Revolution at Hand," June 17, 1842, *New York Herald*, quoted in Richard Neitzel Holzapfel, "Nauvoo Remembered: Helen Mar Whitney Reminiscences. Part 4," 16.

2. Heber C. Kimball, quoted by Helen Mar Whitney, in ibid., Part 2, 25.

3. Ellen Douglas, Letter to her Father and Mother from Nauvoo, June 2, 1842, quoted in Carol Cornwall Madsen, *In Their Own Words: Women and the Story of Nauvoo*, 7.

4. "Nauvoo," *Times and Seasons* 3, no. 23 (October 1, 1842): 936.

5. Figures by modern Nauvoo historians give better researched estimates of the population of the two cities. "Nauvoo had grown to 2,450 residents when the census of 1840 was taken, making it similar in size to Quincy and Springfield and half the size of Chicago. . . . In 1845, near its peak, the city [Nauvoo] boasted 11,036 inhabitants, while Chicago that same year was not far ahead with 12,088." Glen M. Leonard and T. Edgar Lyon, "The Nauvoo Years," 12. In reality, with a population as fluid as Nauvoo's always was, it would have been very difficult to state a totally accurate figure for its residents at any given period of time.

6. Quoted in Holzapfel, "Nauvoo Remembered, Part 2," 25.

7. Nauvoo First and Second Wards, 1.

8. Lyman De Platt [Lyman D. Platt], comp., "List of Church Members in Nauvoo, I.L. taken from 1842 Census of Nauvoo," 6.

9. Nauvoo Illinois Assessor, Tax Lists for District No. 3 1840, 1842, 1850, Item 5, 163–236. See also "1842 Tax Records, Index of Hancock County, Illinois."

10. George and Sylvia Givens, *Nauvoo Fact Book: Questions and Answers for Nauvoo Enthusiasts*, 100.

11. Nauvoo Illinois Assessor, Tax Lists for District No. 3, 206, 223, 224. It is interesting that the value of King's "cattle" and "horses," necessities on the frontier, were each the same as the value of "watches"—a seemingly luxury item.

12. Ibid.

13. Illinois, Hancock County, Nauvoo Precinct, "Election Returns," August 1, 1842, 1–13.

14. Nauvoo Illinois, City Records, 1841–45, "Petitions 1842—Jan–April," Box 1, fd. 24.

15. Ibid.

16. Givens and Givens, *Nauvoo Fact Book*, 15; emphasis theirs.

17. Nauvoo Illinois, City Records, 1841–45, "Petitions 1842—Jan–April," Box 1, fd. 24. This petition was undated, but the city council adopted it on April 9, 1842.

18. Ibid.

19. Ida Blum, "History of the Naming of the Streets," in Blum, *Nauvoo: Gateway to the West*, 195–96; and Janath R. Cannon, *Nauvoo Panorama: Views of Nauvoo before, during and after Its Rise, Fall and Restoration*, 20–21.

20. Cannon, *Nauvoo Panorama*, 20–21.

21. Nauvoo Illinois, City Records, 1841–45, "Petitions 1842—Jan–April," Box 1, fd. 25.

22. Nauvoo Legion (Ill.) Records, 1841–45, March 26, 1842, fd. 3, p.5.

23. Ibid., fd. 5, p. 1.

24. Robert Bruce Flanders, *Nauvoo: Kingdom on the Missouri*, 112.

25. *History of the Church*, 4:502.

26. [Author not identified], Letter to *New York Herald*, quoted in Holzapfel, "Nauvoo Remembered, Part 2," 16.

27. Ibid.

28. Matthew S. McBride, *A House for the Most High: The Story of the Original Nauvoo Temple*, 43; and Nathan Cheney, Letter to "Dear and Beloved Parents, Brothers and Sisters."

29. Richard O. Cowan, "The Pivotal Nauvoo Temple," in H. Dean Garrett, ed., *Regional Studies in Latter-day Saint Church History: Illinois*, 117; and David R. Crockett, "The Nauvoo Temple: 'A Monument of the Saints,'" 5. For a detailed description of the font see *History of the Church*, 4:446–47.

30. William Clayton, "To the Friends of the Temple," 675.

31. Dean Jessee, *The Papers of Joseph Smith: Journal, 1832–42*, 2:335. The original of this journal is in the First Presidency Archives, LDS Church, Salt Lake City, and is not available for personal research.

32. Christy Best, Archivist, LDS Church History Library, email to Joann Mortensen, August 31, 2007.

33. McBride, *A House for the Most High*, 14–19.

34. "Baptism for the Dead: An Epistle of the Twelve to the Saints of the Last Days," *Times and Seasons* 3, no. 4 (December 15, 1841): 626.

35. Ibid.

36. Cheney, Letter to "Dear and Beloved Parents, Brothers and Sisters."

37. "The Temple of God in Nauvoo," *Times and Seasons* 4, no. 1 (November 15, 1842): 10.

38. Matthew McBride, email to Joann Mortensen, February 17, 2004.

39. Nauvoo Temple Building Committee, Records 1841–52, Daybook A and Daybook B. The original Building Committee (Alpheus Cutler, Reynolds Cahoon, and Elias Higbee) was appointed at the October 1840 general con-

ference. Hyrum Smith replaced Higbee after he died in June 1843. This committee received tithing and donations directly from Church members until the establishment of the Trustee-in-Trust in 1841.

40. Nauvoo Temple Building Committee, Records 1841–52, Ledger A, 1841–42, Reel 3, fd. 1.

41. *History of the Church*, 4:181–82. See also McBride, *A House for the Most High*, 115–16.

42. The Folletts and Kimballs were close neighbors, according to Donald Q. Cannon, "The King Follett Discourse: Joseph Smith's Greatest Sermon in Historical Perspective," 180

43. *History of the Church*, 4:552. Also see Richard Lyman Bushman, *Joseph Smith: Rough Stone Rolling*, 446.

44. *History of the Church*, 4:552.

45. Richard Neitzel Holzapfel and Jeni Broberg Holzapfel, *Women of Nauvoo*, 4; emphasis theirs.

46. Relief Society Minutes, March 24, 1842. Also admitted into membership at the second meeting was Cyrena Merrill, wife of Philemon Christopher Merrill. In the transcribed copy of the holograph minutes, Cyrena's name is entered twice, both as Cirinda Murrill and as Cyrena Murrill. Louisa Follett's great-grandson, Orren W. Follett, and Cyrena Merrill's granddaughter, Josephine Merrill, were married in Pima, Arizona, on January 1, 1902. They are my grandparents.

47. Ibid.

48. Ivan J. Barrett, *Joseph Smith and the Restoration: A History of the LDS Church to 1846*, 507–8.

49. Ida Blum, *Nauvoo: Gateway to the West*, 55–56.

50. James B. Allen and Glen M. Leonard, *The Story of the Latter-day Saints*, 176.

51. Maurine Carr Ward, "'This Institution Is a Good One': The Female Relief Society of Nauvoo, 17 March 1842 to 16 March 1844," 88–90.

52. Ibid., 89, 126. Ward states incorrectly (89): "Louisa Tanner Follett's husband was imprisoned in Liberty Jail." Though several histories make that statement, there is no primary evidence that he was ever in Liberty Jail. He was imprisoned in jails in both Richmond and Columbia, Missouri.

53. Ivan J. Barrett, *Joseph Smith and the Restoration: A History of the LDS Church to 1846*, 507–8.

54. Bushman, *Joseph Smith: Rough Stone Rolling*, 448.

55. Relief Society Minutes, April 28, 1842.

56. *History of the Church*, 5:1–2, lists seven men: General James Adams of Springfield, Patriarch Hyrum Smith, Bishops Newel K. Whitney and George Miller, President Brigham Young, and Elders Heber C. Kimball and Willard Richards. Milton V. Backman Jr., *People and Power of Nauvoo: Themes from*

the Nauvoo Experience, 56, adds the name of William Law to this list without providing a source. Richard Bushman, *Rough Stone Rolling*, 452, gives a figure of nine men, but does not name them.

57. *History of the Church*, 5:1–2.
58. Backman, *People and Power of Nauvoo*, 57.
59. Richard O. Cowan, *Temples to Dot the Earth*, 55 and note 29.
60. Ancestral File, International Genealogical Index, Film Number #170542, p. 328, Ref. #5545, LDS Family History Library, and family records in my possession. Also see Temple Index Bureau, LDS Family History Library, Microfilm #1262904, which lists this same date from St George Temple records.
61. Bushman, *Joseph Smith: Rough Stone Rolling*, 450.
62. Heber C. Kimball, Letter to Parley Pratt, June 17, 1842, quoted in Stanley B. Kimball, "Heber C. Kimball and Family: The Nauvoo Years," 458, and subsequently quoted in McBride, *A House for the Most High*, 98.
63. McBride, *A House for the Most High*, 98–99.
64. Barrett, *Joseph Smith and the Restoration*, 509.
65. James B. Allen, "Nauvoo's Masonic Hall," 43.
66. *Nauvoo Independent-Rustler*, January 25, 1928, quoted in ibid.
67. *History of the Church*, 4:550–51.
68. Kimball, "Heber C. Kimball and Family," 458–59.
69. Mervin Booth Hogan, "The Vital Statistics of Nauvoo Lodge," 5; emphasis his.
70. Allen, "Nauvoo's Masonic Hall," 44. According to Allen's note 15: "There are some slight inconsistencies in the exact figures reported by various people."
71. Freemasons, Nauvoo Lodge Minute Book. The pages containing the bylaws and signatures are not numbered; however, the page with King's signature has what appears to be a (4) in the upper right hand corner. Masonic rules would usually require that everyone sign prior to receiving full membership.
72. Ibid., 6, 45, 54–56, 62, 63.
73. Ibid., no page number given.
74. Hogan, "The Vital Statistics of Nauvoo Lodge," 57.
75. Dean C. Jessee, *The Papers of Joseph Smith: Vol. 2, Journal, 1842–43*, 391.
76. Ibid., 391 note 3.
77. Freemasons, Nauvoo Lodge Account Book. Nathan West's name is also not listed in this account book.
78. "Lafayette (California) Cemetery Records to 1935," in my possession, obtained by personal visit, July 2006. Some censuses give an approximate birth year as 1843. He died on September 7, 1893, in California.

❊ Chapter Eighteen ❊

1843: Hastening the Work

Newspapers near Nauvoo and throughout the eastern United States eagerly reported on Nauvoo and its inhabitants in 1843. Not only were their readers interested in the new city being built by the Saints, but they also found the temple of particular interest. The *Weekly Argus*, published in New York on July 1843, reproduced an article that had earlier been published in the Burlington, Iowa, *Gazette*, headed: "The City of Nauvoo": "Few, we suspect, are aware of the rapid growth and present condition of the city of Nauvoo, the Jerusalem of the Latter Day saints. Notwithstanding but four years have elapsed since the Mormons first made a settlement there, it is estimated that it already numbers from 15,000 to 17,000 inhabitants; and accessions are daily made to the population from the Eastern States and from Europe."[1]

The article went on to describe the town and the temple:

> It is situated at one of the most beautiful points on the river, and is improving with a rapidity truly astonishing. Many of the houses are built in fine style, evincing wealth as well as taste. The Temple, which is destined to be the most magnificent structure in the West, is progressing rapidly, and will probably be completed in the course of the present and succeeding summer. Its style of architecture is entirely original—unlike any thing in the world, or in the history of the world—but is at the same time chaste and elegant. It is said to be the conception of the Prophet, Gen. Smith. It is being built by the voluntary labor of the members of the Church, who devote a certain number of days in the year to the work. If the labor and materials were estimated at cash prices it is supposed that the building would cost something like a million of dollars.[2]

The increase in numbers was not as dynamic as reported. A more accurate figure for the city's population in 1843 was under 12,000; it peaked at 12,000 the next year (1844).[3]

By now the Church in Nauvoo was much different than it had been when it was first organized in New York. Continuing through the early years of its organization, Joseph Smith was basically the leader of the Church but with priesthood and administrative authority widely shared through a network of interlocking quorums, councils, and presidency. Mormons, like all Christians, based their faith in the Bible; but other books of revelation—the Book of Mormon and the Doctrine and Covenants—were also their scripture; and new revelation—like the Book of Abraham and the Book of Moses, first published in the Church's newspaper, promised a continuing stream of divine guidance. Meetings consisted of public preaching services on Sundays, supplemented by midweek prayer services. Church ordinances consisted of baptism, confirmation, the sacrament (or Lord's supper), and priesthood ordination. New couples, firmly believing in the sealing power of the priesthood, sought to have their marriages celebrated by Mormon ecclesiastical leaders.

In Nauvoo, the multi-layered priesthood organization continued to expand, drawing King into membership. The March 1842 organization of the Female Relief Society, to which Louisa belonged, offered expanded opportunities for organized service and sociability. But most important for Nauvoo's 1843 residents were the new ordinances Joseph Smith had introduced: baptism by proxy to assure the salvation of deceased relatives, washing and anointing ceremonies, endowment rituals, and sealing rites (including eternal marriage)—all reasons for building the temple. He urgently encouraged the Saints to continue their work on the temple and, if possible, to accelerate their donations. The Twelve Apostles assumed the missionary burden of also collecting funds for the temple as they traveled throughout the United States and in Great Britain, even though many of those members would never visit the Nauvoo Temple.

The women of the Relief Society continued their work and donations in support of the temple, both as an organization and as individual members. The First Presidency sanctioned and Patriarch Hyrum Smith inaugurated a "penny subscription drive" that his wife, Mary Fielding Smith, and her sister, Mercy Fielding Thompson, implemented. Even poor sisters like Louisa Follett, no matter where they lived, joined in to contribute a penny a week for glass and nails.[4] By December 5, 1844, "there were 50,000 pennies on hand, weighing 343 pounds,"[5] all contributed or collected by the women of the Church. The *Millennial Star* noted the dedication of the sisters and reported: "We believe that the completion of the Temple is as near the hearts of the sisters as to the hearts of the brethren."[6] Individual women "contributed clothing for the workers, and their families, shared their homes with the builders." Others "sold things that they could scarcely spare" while one woman sold "her best china dishes and fine bed quilt." A widow "gave the only possession she had with which, she said, she would grieve to part: her husband's watch. 'I gave it,' she explained, 'to help build the Nauvoo Temple and everything else I could possibly spare and the last few dollars that I had in the world, which altogether amounted to nearly $50.'"[7] One can only imagine what items Louisa might still own that she could also contribute.

Land was also donated to the Church to be sold with the money being used to purchase necessary building supplies. "Among the papers of the office of the trustee is a memorandum of deeds" contributed to the temple—"nearly thirty parcels of land in and near Nauvoo that had been contributed between 1841 and 1844 with a total value of over $5,000," according to historian Matthew McBride.[8] Robert B. Flanders notes: "Between May, 1843, and July, 1844, the county records show [that] 2,558 acres of farm land and an undetermined number of city acres [were] deeded to Joseph Smith as Trustee-in Trust in consideration of 'the love and good will (the grantees) bear the Church of Jesus Christ of Latter Day Saints.' Most of the tracts were no larger than 160 acres."[9]

In September 1843, a reporter for the *Pittsburgh Weekly Gazette*, reported on how he had found the temple during an August visit: "The windows of the upper stories are some fifteen or eighteen feet high, arched over the top in a perfect semi-circle.—The first story above the basement is divided into two apartments, called the outer and inner courts. . . . All the work is of good cut stone, almost white, and it will present a fine appearance when finished."[10] King may have contributed his skills to the temple's stonework.

Another important building material was wood. There were few local sources for lumber because the trees available on the site had quickly been chopped down to make homes and fuel for heating and cooking purposes. Another source had to be found from which to obtain lumber, not only for the temple but for the building of the Nauvoo House, an ambitious structure intended as a hotel for the use of visitors. The numerous homes and businesses being built in the city also created a lively demand for lumber. Church leaders established "the pineries," four sawmills about three or four hundred miles north of Nauvoo in Wisconsin on or near the Black River. Church members were called on missions to cut the wood and process the lumber. Lumber from the pineries built the temple's first baptismal font in the temple out of Wisconsin pine timber (later replaced by cut stone).

According to historian Dennis Rowley, "For four winters, commencing in the fall of 1841 and ending in the spring of 1845, the Latter-day Saints worked the pineries, harvesting an estimated one-and-a-half million board feet of milled lumber, over two hundred thousand shingles, and an undeterminable number of loose logs, hewed timbers, and barn boards. This was enough lumber to build about 215 three-bedroom houses of our day. The harvest from the pineries was floated to Nauvoo on at least a dozen rafts beginning in the spring of 1842."[11]

Though this logging project began in 1841, it was not until 1843 that the project could be considered successful, and records are spotty. The first group, which arrived on the Black River in September of 1841, consisted of about thirty-two: workmen and their family members. The number gradually rose to about a hundred. Possibly as many as two hundred were there during the peak seasons of 1843 and 1844. Some Saints who went to the pineries were termed "semipermanent settlers." They stayed through the harsh winters, working more than one season without going back to Nauvoo. (A season began in the spring as soon as the snow melted and continued until autumn storms forced the closure of the logging operation.) McBride comments that "about one hundred workmen stayed at Black River during the winter of 1842–43 and endured snow that reached depths of twenty-one feet."[12] Such harsh conditions probably account for why most workers were "seasonal," preferring to spend winters in Nauvoo. Some workers participated for a single season, then returned to Nauvoo. Much like Nauvoo, the Black River operations kept an account of the amount of time each man worked. A small store was developed where workers could purchase needed items that were deducted from their work account. When they left, they were given "tithing credit, temple credit, and Nauvoo House stock certificates. On rare occasions, a worker was paid cash."[13]

William Alexander Follett was one of the young men working in the pineries. His name appears on Dennis Rowley's list of 156 men, drawn from Church and civil records about the project, but Rowley does not connect individual names and sources.[14] The only specific source I could find containing William's name is the record kept by Peter Haws covering April-December 1842 for purchases at the store. There are very few readable dates throughout the records, but the first entry appears to be May 20. William's name is found in the following entries:

Sep 22	Repairing gun	$0.12 ½ {difficult to read}
	1 pr pants	5.00
Sep 29	1 pr of pantaloons	5.00
Nov 3	8 oz. web powder	0.13
	1/2 lb. powder	0.25
No date	1 hat at cost	0.31
No date	3 yd stripe	0.94
	6 yr shirting	1.13[15]

While this record establishes William's residence at the pineries during the fall and probably winter of 1842–43 (when the snow reached a depth of twenty-one feet as described above), without other identifying information, it is not possible to determine when he went to the pineries, how long he was gone from the Follett home in Nauvoo, what category of worker he was, or how much he was paid. He would have been almost sixteen when the first group went to the pineries in September of 1841 and nineteen at the end of the last (1845) season. At the time these records were begun in September 1842, he was sixteen, turning seventeen in December. William's work at this period may have taken him away from home at a critical time for Louisa. The previously discussed Nauvoo Temple building records show that King used work vouchers to purchase items from the temple during the entire year of 1842. Thus, for part of this year, Louisa may have been left for many days with no adult male to assist with home duties.

Unfortunately William did not keep a diary or later write a reminiscence; however, other Wisconsin participants did. William Clayton wrote of the first group of workers who left Nauvoo in September 1841: "These brethren spent the Winter in the pine forests, and toiled diligently in their appointed work. They suffered some because of the cold in that northern region, but they made good progress. By the following July, they had succeeded in making up and bringing to Nauvoo a large raft of first-rate pine timber. By this means the prospect of the work was much brightened."[16]

A later logger, Joseph Holbrook, left Nauvoo on May 24, 1843, went by steamboat on the Mississippi River, and then traveled on foot about a hundred miles up the Black River. Because there was no established trail, his party was lost for about two days. His autobiographical sketch recalls his two months' participation:

> Both boats started up the river manned with about ten men to each boat. The river being high and the current strong we were forced to make our way by taking hold of the brush at the bow of each boat and running back to the stern and so continuing through the day. We went twenty five miles per day.
>
> After arriving at the mills all hands were employed in rafting logs to the saw mills and rafting lumber, shingles, square timber, etc. for about six weeks, when we had a raft of 150,000 feet. . . . The country is much broken being somewhat mountainous with long tedious winters. There is some land what might be fertile in the valleys. The streams abound in fish.
>
> Brother Cunningham was drowned this summer above the mills in rafting logs. He got into a whirl in the river and was seen no more.[17]

Mormons in the pineries obviously faced grueling conditions. Common problems were lack of proper food, harsh weather, injuries and the threat of death from the fast-moving river and from climbing and felling trees. The Wisconsin pineries project was a successful venture, providing high-quality and high-quantity pine lumber for the temple at a much lower cost than the Saints would have had to pay for finished lumber in Illinois. When the temple was completed, William and others who worked in Wisconsin, could be as proud of the finished project as King, who worked on the Nauvoo end of the project, and other family members who might also have worked there. If he had been one of those fortunate enough to receive some payment in cash, he would have made a significant contribution toward the Follett family's financial needs.

While physical work continued on the temple, the Prophet concentrated on its spiritual aspects. He had previously introduced washings and anointings in the context of the Kirtland Temple. In Nauvoo, he developed the concept of proxy baptism for dead ancestors, the full endowment ordinance for both the living and the dead, husband-and-wife sealings, and second anointings with the temple as the correct place for these ordinances to occur. Associated with his teachings about eternal marriage came the secret introduction of plural marriage. Although plurality is no longer part of LDS practice, the concept of sealing couples, with the result that their children are also sealed to them, for time and eternity, assumed even greater importance. As early as 1835, when King and other Church leaders were in Ohio for the dedication of the Kirtland Temple, there must have been some teaching that a husband and wife could be together. Although the concept was not fully spelled out, W. W. Phelps described it in a letter to his wife, who was still in Missouri: "A new idea, Sally, if you and I continue faithful to the end, we are certain to be one in the Lord throughout eternity; this is one of the most glorious consolations we can have in the flesh."[18] Four years later in 1839, Parley P. Pratt learned from the Prophet Joseph Smith in Philadelphia: "It was from him that I learned that the wife of my bosom might be secured to me for time and all eternity."[19] Undoubtedly to long-married couples like King and Louisa, the promise of being able to enter the completed temple and be sealed so that they would be together as husband and wife for eternity came as a great blessing.

Since King died before the temple was completed and such sealing ceremonies begun, he and Louisa were not sealed to each other at that time. Just as baptism as taught earlier by the Prophet was necessary for everyone, and was an earthly ordinance, so was sealing and the full endowment, including washing and anointing. However, vicarious or proxy washings and anointings, endowments, and sealings on behalf of the deceased did not begin until 1877, when the St. George Utah Temple was completed. Several of King and Louisa's descendants performed their sealings vicariously, providing several sealing dates. The earliest is February 23, 1928, in the Mesa Arizona Temple.[20]

The revelation that the Prophet dictated on July 12, 1843, regarding eternal marriage also contained commandments relating to plural marriage (now D&C 132). This concept immediately became controversial within the Church and with nonmembers who learned of it. According to the Introduction to Volume 5 of the *History of the Church*, "[There] is indisputable evidence that the revelation making known this marriage law [plural marriage] was given to the Prophet as early as 1831."[21] Joseph never spoke or preached publicly about this controversial concept, but his earliest plural sealing that can be dated was to Louisa Beaman on April 5, 1841. He also taught the commandment privately to his most trusted confidants, including some of the apostles. Neither King Follett nor his sons or sons-in-law were among these men, nor is it known how much they knew about it. Brigham Young and the Twelve embraced the principle along with Joseph Smith's teachings about the centrality of the temple ordinances; and it was an important part of Mormonism in Utah for the remainder of the nineteenth century. Plural marriage was a great test of faith, and many Church members could not accept it, both in the succession crisis immediately after Joseph's death and in succeeding years.

Shortly after Nauvoo became the new gathering area, problems surfaced for the Prophet about the charges still pending against him and others who had escaped from Liberty Jail in 1839. The ultimate goal of the government authorities in Missouri was to extradite Joseph (he also feared an extra-legal kidnapping) so that the cases filed there during 1838–39 could be tried. Unfortunately, despite the initial hospitality of Illinois citizens, an increasing number of them became concerned about the Church's growth and teachings, especially after the disaffected John C. Bennett published an influential series of letters in the summer of 1842 giving a lurid account of polygamy, among other accusations. Bennett had previously been a close friend of the Prophet and a member of the First Presidency but had been excommunicated that spring on several charges, including immorality.[22] Increasing unease was the very real fact that the Church was able to wield significant political power in western Illinois.

In May of 1842, an unknown assailant attempted to assassinate Missouri's former governor, Lilburn Boggs. He survived, and the state of Missouri issued a warrant for Joseph's arrest as an accessory to attempted murder. Bennett's letters included similar accusations. Nauvoo's Municipal Court, acting with the authority given it by the Nauvoo charter, refused to recognize the warrant as valid. The Prophet went into hiding and was out of the public view for most of the summer. A federal court in Springfield, Illinois, quashed the warrant in early January 1843; but the very real fear of other attempts lingered on.

The Nauvoo High Council issued a proclamation proclaiming January 17, 1843, as a day of "fasting, praise, and prayer" for the Prophet's safe return. It assigned the bishops of the ten Nauvoo wards to hold special meetings to which all members were invited and at which time collections could be taken to assist in meeting the legal costs. The Prophet attended "a public meeting in my own house, which was crowded to overflowing. Many other meetings were held in various parts of the city, which were well attended."[23] It is likely that the Follett family along with their friends and neighbors attended the meeting held in the Nauvoo First Ward.

This, however, was only one of several attempts to arrest Joseph and return him to Missouri. By March 1843, the state legislature made an unsuccessful attempt to repeal the Nauvoo charter. The process focused more negative attention on the Church, establishing that the Saints in Nauvoo had a different idea of their rights under the charter than the rest of the state. Later that month word reached Nauvoo that new indictments had been issued against the Prophet and "some hundred others, on the old Missouri troubles, and that John C. Bennett was making desperate threats."[24] It was a troubled summer. In Nauvoo, as in Missouri, individuals who had been excommunicated or who had withdrawn from the Church over disagreements with its leadership were causing problems for the Prophet. This unrest would surely have impacted all members, including the Follett family. In June 1843, the Prophet was "surprised and arrested" by Missouri officers in Lee County, north of Nauvoo, where he and his family were visiting Emma's relatives.[25] Hyrum Smith quickly called for volunteers to protect Joseph and assure his legal rights. More than three hundred men volunteered; 175, including King Follett, were selected to intercept the party and escort the Prophet to Quincy, Illinois, to answer the charges. These men were responding to Joseph's request for "sufficient force to prevent my being kidnapped into Missouri, as I well knew that the whole country was swarming with men anxious to carry me there and kill me, without any shadow of law or justice, Although they well knew that I had not committed any crime worthy of death or bonds."[26]

Albert P. Rockwood, who was the acting adjutant of this escort, called it "the Second Division of the Expedition to Relieve the Prophet."

(A first group had taken a steamship up the river to intercept the arresting party if they tried to come downriver to Missouri.) Rockwood and five others exchanged their riding horses for a horse-drawn wagon. "Having fresh animals, we left most of the detachment in the rear," he recorded, "yet Brother Follet and from five to ten others were up with us, positively charged with fight.... We put our animals at full speed and charged in with drawn swords, our guns and pistols cocked and primed, ready for attack. [Near a village] we concluded that the posse, knowing that we were near by to rescue [Joseph], had taken to the woods to secrete themselves or evade us; therefore Brother Follet [sic] and such others as they came in were ordered to search the timbers."[27]

For generations, my direct line of the Follett family handed down the general information, without details, that King was a "bodyguard of the Prophet." The description given of him verbally by family members which I remember hearing was that he was a "rough and tumble sort of man," much like Orrin Porter Rockwell who fits that description and was actually an official bodyguard. There is no evidence that King was ever specifically called to that position; but his prompt and energetic response to and his activities during this emergency provides a factual basis for the tradition.

While Joseph and the arresting officers from Missouri, accompanied by his citizen escort from Nauvoo, were traveling to Quincy, his attorneys arranged for the hearing to occur in Nauvoo where the municipal court could issue a writ of habeas corpus, a little-known and little-exercised right at that period. (See Chapter 16.) The Saints welcomed their Prophet back with a parade of carriages and band music. John Needham, a recent immigrant from England, wrote: "The city was all alive to see our brother and friend; we shouted him welcome and shed tears of joy to see him again delivered from his enemies. The streets were crowded that he passed through; ... I could not help but weep when I looked at the man and thought of his suffering for the truth."[28]

The Follett family likely joined other Church members in this community-wide event, but the threat of additional attempts shadowed the remainder of the year. On August 19, uneasy non-Mormons in Hancock County held a brazenly titled "Great Meeting of Anti-Mormons" at the courthouse in Carthage, the county seat.[29] The meeting "without distinction of party" appointed a committee to draft a document, presented on

September 6. It concluded that the Mormons "under the sacred garb of Christianity . . . perpetrated the most lawless and diabolical deeds that have ever, in any age of the world, disgraced the human species."[30] A list of resolutions followed and were accepted, helping to explain the events that occurred during the next nine months and climaxing with the murders of Joseph and Hyrum Smith in Carthage in June 1844. The "anti-Mormon" citizens agreed that, among other things:

1. They would resist all wrongs committed by the Mormons, using force, if necessary, and support each other "unto death."

2. Local residents as well as the entire county, other counties, and neighboring states must assert their "rights" against the Church and its prophet.

3. "All good and honest" men must be willing to serve as a "posse" when the arrest of the Prophet was once again sought by Missouri officials.

4. Nearby counties would be asked to form a similar committee and all citizens of Illinois would be asked not to support any political candidate who sought or had support from the Mormons.

5. "If the Mormons carry out the threats they have made in regards to the lives of several of our citizens, we will, if failing to obtain speedy redress from the laws of the land, take summary and signal vengeance upon them as a people. . . . The citizens of course fall back upon their original inherent right of self-defense."[31]

Three months later a group of anti-Mormons in nearby Warsaw, Illinois, also drafted resolutions in regard to the Church, but this time specified threats linked to specific deadlines. Orson Hyde, who had gone to Warsaw, repeated the content of these resolutions to the Prophet: "We will visit the Mormons residing in our vicinity and require them to give up their guns; and such as do it shall dwell in peace; but those who will not do it may have thirteen days to leave in; and if they are not off in that time, we will drive them." Hyde further stated that the anti-Mormon group "also swear that the Mormons shall never raise another crop in that region."[32]

In response to these threats and to protect the Prophet from being kidnapped or rearrested, as well as to ensure that other Church members were not harassed, additional policemen were added to the Nauvoo City police force on more than one occasion. Although the police records seem relatively complete and King Follett's name is not mentioned, such special assignments might also be the source of the family tradition that King was one of the Prophet's bodyguards.

While the Prophet spent a great deal of his time involved in legal issues and sometimes had to go into hiding, he remained involved in Nauvoo's daily activities, in which its citizens—including the Follett family—also participated. The Saints met for Sunday meetings, when the weather was good, in the grove near the uncompleted temple. Often the Prophet spoke at these meetings and hundreds attended. Nonmember Charlotte Haven, observing the Saints walking to meeting on February 19, 1843, described the "Sunday dress of the Saints" this way: "Their dress you would think not very comfortable for a winter's day, many men and boys with straw hats, low shoes, and no overcoats, and women with sunbonnets, calico dresses, thin shawls, or some nondescript garment thrown over the shoulders. Their zeal must surely keep them warm."[33]

She was accurate about the members' zeal, for there were many other formal and informal meetings held in some of the larger public buildings and in homes. It is heartening to think that the Follett home might have been the site for such meetings, although there is no documentation confirming such a supposition. As in Kirtland, there were no buildings built specifically for worship services, except for the temple, while the Saints were in Nauvoo. Evening meetings sometimes were occasions for special blessings given by priesthood leaders. At weekly prayer meetings, those attending read and studied the Book of Mormon and other scriptures. At the regular annual conference, held April 6–8, 1843, the members celebrated the "first day of the fourteenth year of the Church." Joseph Smith was unanimously sustained by those attending as Church president. If King and his family were in the congregation, they would have been part of this reassurance, despite the problems that afflicted all Church members because of rising hostility against Joseph. The Prophet responded by returning "his thanks to the assembly for the manifestation of their confidence, and said he would serve them according to the best ability God should give him."[34]

King, his sons (John W. and William Alexander), and his three sons-in-law (Nathan West, James Daley, and Henry Sanford) all held the priesthood office of Seventy, all in different quorums. (Henry Sanford married King's daughter Nancy on November 17, 1845, following the death of her first husband, James Daley, in late—probably

A reconstruction of the Seventies Hall in Nauvoo. Photo by Irval L. Mortensen, 2008.

December—1844.)³⁵ The Seventies were now organized in quorums, each having seventy members. King had been ordained a member of the "Second Seventy Elders" (later designated as the Second Quorum) in Kirtland while attending the dedication of the temple. He and other seventies participated in the construction of a Seventies Hall in Nauvoo in 1843–44 where the members of the various quorums could be trained for their specific scriptural assignment—missionary work. Bishop Edward Hunter donated the site for the two-story, red brick building. Members of the existing fifteen quorums of seventies were asked to donate time and funds in the construction process. They made their own bricks and obtained lumber by being paid in lumber after unloading rafts and barges at the river.

Simultaneously, three other building projects were ongoing: the temple, the Nauvoo House (hotel), and, for many of them, their own homes. Now they were asked to dig deeper into their pockets and find more hours in the day for another project. A pamphlet containing a brief history of the Seventies Hall, published by Nauvoo Restoration, comments: "They were doing this through the difficult economic times which were the aftermath of the great Panic of 1837, and which in 1843 were still forcing a large part of America to function on a barter and trade economy due to the scarcity of trustworthy money. They had no wealthy men among them. There were no capitalists at Nauvoo, and neither banks nor mortgage lending institutions to assist the seventies in their building project."[36]

When completed over a year later, the Seventies Hall not only served the quorums but also housed Nauvoo's library. It was one of the larger public buildings available, and a variety of groups met there. As a result, it was one of Nauvoo's most important buildings, used for religious, civic and community events.[37]

John W. Follett was a member of the Twenty-ninth Quorum, ordained in Nauvoo on October 26, 1844.[38] The history of that particular quorum gives an official organization date as July 27, 1845, which was actually nine months after John's ordination date. In that same record, however, he is listed as member #15, his birth place as New York which is not correct, and his age is listed as twenty-five, which was probably correct since he was born in 1819. His father is correctly listed as "King Follett."[39]

Apparently there were two men named James Daley (or Dailey), who were Seventies at this time in Nauvoo—one in the Tenth Quorum and one in the Twenty-second Quorum. The James Daley who married Nancy Follett is listed as the sixth president of the Tenth Quorum, but that record does not give a date or place of ordination. Its quorum minutes for December 26, 1844, state: "Elder David McClary ordained one of the junior prest. of 10th Quorum under hand of Prest. Joseph Young and Prest. A.P. Rockwood to fill up the vacancy accompanied by the death of James Daily."[40] This date fits the death date for the James who was King and Louisa's son-in-law.[41]

Nathan A. West was issued his license as a Seventy on April 4, 1841, in Nauvoo and was identified as a Seventy when he was endowed in the Nauvoo Temple on January 8, 1846.[42] There is, however, no indication of his quorum. Henry Sanford is listed as member #35 of the Thirty-fifth Quorum and was ordained on January 26, 1846, at age twenty-eight by his brother-in-law "N A West."[43]

In addition to the religious activities in which King participated in 1843, he was also a member of two civic organizations—the Nauvoo Legion and the Freemasons, as already mentioned. In June 1843, the "ancient York Masons met at the lodge room, being the Anniversary of St.

John's Day." There they walked, in "due Masonic form" to Main Street, "where the corner stone for a Masonic Temple was laid."[44] When completed the next year, it also housed the city police and the Nauvoo Legion. Though there are no official records of how the building was funded, its construction overlapped that of the Seventies Hall and must have added yet another financial burden to its members who, like King, were already helping to fund and construct the Nauvoo Temple and the Nauvoo House. Nor was that all. Another financial burden, also beginning in June 1843, was the construction of an arsenal for the Nauvoo Legion where its members could store their weapons. It was to be built with stone, covered with plaster.[45] However, it was not completed prior to King's death.

Son-in-law Nathan A. West (born in 1801) must have joined the legion at some point, because he was in the age bracket for mandatory membership. He is first listed in legion records on August 19, 1843, as a first lieutenant in the Fifth Regiment, Second Company.[46] Less than three months later on November 7, 1843, Nathan was listed as a drum major.[47] The officers of the legion regularly held their own drills in addition to those of the cohorts (as the division into infantry and cavalry were known). The Prophet often observed and participated in these drills. He was concerned that he might need to call out the militia sometime in the future to protect him and the city.

On a gala occasion on May 6, 1843, Joseph, his staff, his wife, Emma, and other women watched the legion practice and parade on his prairie farm. At that time, he praised the troops: "The officers did honor to the Legion. Many of them were equipped and armed *cap-a-pie* [head to toe]. The men were in good spirits." He spoke of their improvement, "both in uniform and discipline" and called them the "pride of Illinois, one of its strongest defenses, and a great bulwark of the western country."[48] Then reflecting on current events in Nauvoo, with great emotion he told the legion members: "When we have petitioned those in power for assistance, they have always told us they had no power to help us. Damn such traitors! When they give me the power to protect the innocent, I will never say I can do nothing for their good: I will exercise that power, so help me God."[49] These strong words clarify that the Prophet intended to use the legion's armed might, if needed to protect him and the rights of Church members.

In November 1843, King was involved as part of his legion duties in a kidnapping rescue, which could have also supplied part of the basis for the family tradition that he was one of Joseph's bodyguards, although in this case, Joseph was not directly involved and the connection would have been more general law enforcement. On November 19, Philander Avery was captured by vigilantes from Missouri, followed two weeks later by the similar capture of his father, Daniel, on December 2. They were taken across the Mississippi River to Clark County, Missouri, where they were charged with an "alleged crime of horse stealing."[50] *History of the Church* records this episode first on December 4 but includes affidavits dated November 19 and December 2.[51] According to the *Times and Seasons*, the kidnappings occurred on the same day, "about December 4, when the father and son "were decoyed into the neighborhood of Warsaw." The newspaper does not report the source of its information but includes many details, such as, for instance, that nine men, six of them from Illinois and three from Missouri, captured Daniel. The newspaper editorialized: "Being such great sticklers for law and justice, [they] came without process, decoyed and stole—not negroes, but free American citizens, for fear they could not get justice."[52]

In the following days, witnesses prepared affidavits about the event that the Prophet forwarded to Thomas Ford, governor of Illinois, with a letter dated December 6, and asked whether he should call out the Nauvoo Legion to protect its citizens.[53] On December 12, the governor responded, in what the Prophet referred to as a "milk-and-water" letter, that the militia could only be called "to repel an invasion, suppress an insurrection, or on some extreme emergency; and not to suppress, prevent, or punish individual crimes."[54] However, on December 8, four days before Ford's discouragement of mobilizing the militia, Joseph, acting as the city's mayor, ordered Wilson Law, commander of the Nauvoo Legion, "to hold in readiness such portions of the said Nauvoo Legion, which you have the honor to command, as may be necessary to compel obedience to the ordinances of said city and secure the peace of the citizens, and call them out, if occasion require, without further notice."[55]

On December 19, a week after Ford's letter, the Nauvoo Legion, following a parade and inspection, were instructed "to prepare themselves with arms and ammunition and to hold themselves in readiness, for a moment's notice."[56] So while not officially called out, they were placed on alert. These instructions would have included Captain King Follett and First Lieutenant Nathan A. West.

On December 10, J. White, the deputy sheriff of Clark County, Missouri, sent Joseph a letter requesting that witnesses (not named) come to testify as witnesses for the Averys in Marion County. Joseph denounced the request as "a trap to get some more of our people into their power."[57] A Nauvoo justice of the peace issued warrants, based on the testimony of Mormon witnesses, for the arrest of at least eight of the kidnappers, leading to the following entries in *History of the Church*:

> Sunday, December 17: Mr. King Follet [sic], one of the constables of Hancock County, started with ten men this afternoon to arrest John Elliott for kidnapping Daniel Avery, upon a warrant granted by Aaron Johnson, Esq., J.P.
>
> Monday, December 18: After dinner, Constable Follet [sic] returned with John Elliott, a schoolmaster, when an examination was had before Esq. Johnson, in the assembly room. Elliott was found guilty of kidnapping Avery, and bound over in the sum of $3,000 to the Circuit Court of Carthage for trial.
>
> Tuesday, December 19: Brother Chester Loveland told them that he had seen thirty armed men following Constable King Follett some miles on his way, when he had Elliott in custody.[58]

One source from a modern author writing about the Avery kidnapping refers to the arresting official as a "Nauvoo city constable" though he does not identify him by name.[59] The Nauvoo City Council appointed both constables and policemen; however, constables were required to post bonds and King does not appear in city records as having posted such a bond or as being named constable. The fact that he is identified as a constable of the county, not the city, is likewise puzzling, since county records do not include his appointment or election to that position.[60]

Therefore, although there is no official record that King served as one of Joseph's bodyguards or that he officially held a position as a police officer, he did perform enough duties of that type in Nauvoo to give him a secure place in the city's defense. This is, at last, enough evidence to be the foundation of the Follett family tradition.

An ongoing concern for the Prophet was the financial pressure of Nauvoo's cash-strapped economy. He felt that the U.S. government should, in all justice, provide some type of financial relief for the Church members as a result of the Missouri persecutions. He also understood that such relief would amount to an admission by the federal government that the Saints had been wronged by Missouri officials. The first attempt to obtain such relief was in the form of a memorial with attached individual petitions, including Louisa Follett's, which had been sent to Washington in 1839 with no success. In 1840 a similar memorial with other attached petitions (none from the Follett family) was again sent to Washington, basically with the same results. As a third attempt, a memorial dated November 28, 1843, consisted of a single petition signed by 3,419 individuals on one sheet fifty-feet long, rolled like a scroll. Signing this petition were King Follett, Louisa Follett, Nathan A. West, and Adeline Louisa West, all residing in Nauvoo First Ward.[61] Why other adult family members—John Follett, Nancy Follett Daley, James Daley, and William Alexander Follett—did not sign is unknown. After recounting briefly the history of the Church during the Missouri years and previous attempts to obtain relief, the "scroll petition" closes with this declaration, which reflected not only the Prophet's feelings but the sentiments of average Church members like the Folletts and Wests:

> It is true the Constitution of the United States gives to us in Common with all other Native or adopted Citizens, the right to enter and settle in Missouri, but an executive order has been issued to exterminate us if we enter the State, and that part of the Constitution becomes a nullity so far as we are concerned.
>
> Had any foreign State or power committed a similar outrage upon us, we cannot for a moment doubt that the strong arm of the general government would have been stretched out to redress ... our wrongs, and we flatter ourselves that the same power will either redress our grievances or shield us from harm in our efforts to regain our lost property, which we fairly purchased from the general government.
>
> Finally your Memorialists, pray your Honourable body to take their wrongs into consideration, receive testimony in the case, and grant such relief as by the Constitution and Laws you may have power to give.[62]

Though Church leaders had some assistance from the Illinois Congressional delegation when the "scroll petition" was finally presented in the spring of 1844, like the two previous requests, it failed to achieve positive results. And once again, at the close of another year, the Follett family found themselves, along with their fellow Church members, in a precarious position. All they wanted was to live unmolested and peacefully in Nauvoo; anti-Mormon groups from both Missouri and Illinois were now joining forces to keep this from happening.

Notes

1. "The City of Nauvoo," *Weekly Argus*, quoted in Craig J. Ostler, "Nauvoo Saints in the Newspapers of the 1840s," 30.
2. Ibid.
3. Susan Easton Black, "How Large Was the Population of Nauvoo?" 93. Black bases her statement on a "synthesis" of over one thousand sources of "noncensus data" that she studied.
4. "Notice," *Times and Seasons*, 6, no. 5 (March 15, 1845): 847; *History of the Church*, 6:142–43.
5. Ida Blum, *Nauvoo: Gateway to the West*, 52.
6. *Millennial Star*, quoted in *History of the Church*, 6:142.
7. Carol Cornwall Madsen, *In Their Own Words: Women and the Story of Nauvoo*, 20–21.
8. Matthew S. McBride, *A House for the Most High: The Story of the Original Nauvoo Temple*, 162.
9. Robert Bruce Flanders, *Nauvoo: Kingdom on the Mississippi*, 207.
10. David N. White, "The Prairies, Nauvoo, Joe Smith, the Temple, the Mormons, etc.," *Pittsburgh Weekly Gazette*, September 15, 1843, 3, quoted in McBride, *A House for the Most High*, 149–50.
11. Dennis Rowley, "The Mormon Experience in the Wisconsin Pineries, 1841–45," 121.
12. McBride, *A House for the Most High*, 134.
13. Rowley, "The Mormon Experience in the Wisconsin Pineries," 125.
14. Ibid., Appendix 141–42.
15. Nauvoo House Association Records, 1841–1846, "Pinery Accounts, 1842 April–December," unpaginated.
16. George D. Smith, ed., *An Intimate Chronicle: The Journals of William Clayton*, 530.
17. Joseph Holbrook, *History of Joseph Holbrook, 1806–1885: Written by His Own Hand*, 30. He was born in Florence, Oneida County, New York, January 16, 1806, and baptized in Warsaw, Genesee County, New York, on January 7, 1833. He was a member of Zion's Camp, served several missions, and was one of the first members of the Church to settle in Caldwell County. He went to Utah with the Saints and died in Davis County, Utah, in 1885.
18. W. W. Phelps, in Journal History, May 26, 1835, 45.
19. Scot Facer Proctor and Maurine Jensen Proctor, eds., *Autobiography of Parley P. Pratt: Revised and Enhanced Edition*, 361.
20. International Genealogical Index, LDS Family History Library, Microfilm #170707, #641. Wm. H. Follett and Minnie V. P. Follett are listed

as proxies for the sealing of King and Louisa. William Haynes Follett, born in 1874 in Provo, Utah, is the great-grandson of King and Louisa. Minnie Vista Peterson was born in 1873 in Omaha, Nebraska.

21. B. H. Roberts, Introduction, *History of the Church,* 5:xxix.
22. *History of the Church,* 5:2–88.
23. Ibid., 5:252.
24. Ibid., 5:307.
25. Robert Bruce Flanders, *Nauvoo: Kingdom on the Mississippi,* 105.
26. *History of the Church,* 5:448.
27. Ibid., 5:455–56.
28. Maurine Carr Ward, ed., "John Needham's Nauvoo Letter: 1843," 41. Needham wrote this letter on Friday, July 7, 1843, from Nauvoo. Needham was born in Leeds, Yorkshire, England, in 1819, joined the Church in 1837 in Liverpool, and served as a missionary in England from 1838 to 1843. Then he moved to Nauvoo and afterward to Utah where he served as the first manager of the Zion's Co-operative Mercantile Institution (ZCMI), a Church-owned store in Salt Lake City. He died in 1901.
29. *History of the Church,* 5:537.
30. Ibid., 6:4.
31. Ibid., 6:6–7.
32. Orson Hyde, "Affidavit of Orson Hyde—Disclosing Plan to Drive the Saints," December 28, 1843, in *History of the Church,* 6:145.
33. Charlotte Haven, quoted in Richard Neitzel Holzapfel and Jeni Broberg Holzapfel, *Women of Nauvoo,* 87.
34. *History of the Church,* 5:327–28.
35. Dorris Lawton, comp., *Marriage Index, Hancock County, Illinois,* 40.
36. *The Seventies Hall at Nauvoo,* not paginated.
37. David E. Miller and Della S. Miller, *Nauvoo: The City of Joseph,* 126–27.
38. Selections, First Council of 70: Selected Material from Seventies Book B, 1844–48, 51. This record gives his place of ordination as "the City of Joseph." After Joseph's death, the City Council changed Nauvoo's name to honor their fallen prophet.
39. Ibid.
40. Seventies Records, 1844–1975, 10th Quorum, CR 499, Reel 30, 3.
41. Louisa Tanner Follett, Diary, 6.
42. "Nauvoo Illinois Seventies License Records, 21; Nauvoo Temple Endowment Register, December 10, 1845–February 8, 1846, 123.
43. Selections, First Council of 70: Selected Material from Seventies Book B, 260.
44. *History of the Church,* 5:446.
45. Miller and Miller, *Nauvoo,* 101.
46. John Sweeney Jr., "A History of the Nauvoo Legion," 6.

47. Nauvoo Legion (Ill.) Records, 1841–45, 661.

48. *History of the Church*, 5:383–84.

49. Ibid., 384.

50. John Lee Allaman, "Policing in Mormon Nauvoo," 89.

51. *History of the Church*, 6:99, 122–23.

52. "Kidnapping," *Times and Seasons* 4, no. 24 (November 1, 1843): 375–76. Some indication that the newspaper's publication was delayed is that its date precedes the actual kidnappings.

53. *History of the Church*, 6:100–101.

54. Ibid., 6:113.

55. Ibid., 6:104.

56. Ibid., 6:121.

57. Ibid., 6:108. It seems unlikely that a legal process would allow a deputy sheriff of Clark County to request witnesses for a trial in Marion County.

58. Ibid., 6:117–18, 120.

59. Marvin S. Hill, *Quest for Refuge: The Mormon Flight from American Pluralism*, 135.

60. Frank M. Burkett, volunteer at Hancock County Historical Society, email to Joann Follett Mortensen, June 3, 2004.

61. Memorial to Congress, November 28, 1843, MS 2145, fd. 6, 29; see also Clark V. Johnson, ed., *Mormon Redress Petitions: Documents of the 1833–1838 Missouri Conflict*, 563, 589.

62. Johnson, *Mormon Redress Petitions*, 568.

❋ Chapter Nineteen ❋

Life and Death for the Folletts in Nauvoo

By the beginning of 1844, Church members had been in Nauvoo for more than four years. The first had arrived in mid-1839; King and Louisa Follett and their family joined them the next year. Though established and built up as a religious community, Nauvoo was also a river town on the American frontier, located on a major north-south waterway with a rapidly developing river commerce. The Mississippi River was usually frozen during the winter, but a steady flow of steamboats and smaller craft, going both directions, plied its waters during the rest of the year, many stopping daily at Nauvoo. This traffic tied Nauvoo into the regional economy, and steamboats occasionally stopped to let their tourist passengers visit what was considered a colorful local site. Far from being isolated, Nauvoo welcomed merchants, tourists, foreigners, government officials, artists, journalists, ministers, and leaders from local Indian tribes.[1] Richard Neitzel Holzapfel and Jeni Broberg Holzapfel, in their anthology of Nauvoo's women's writings, set the scene: "As many as ten steamers passed by Nauvoo weekly, carrying Indians, soldiers, and various types of goods during the town's early years, and by 1843 some four or five steamboats stopped each day. Not only steamboats but also a wide variety of watercraft plied the currents along Nauvoo's shoreline, including barges, canoes, dugouts, flatboats, keelboats, and log skiffs. These brought a variety of people in contact with the Saints of Nauvoo. As a result, trappers, gamblers, Indians, riverboat men, bartenders, magicians, musicians, roustabouts, slaves, and prostitutes arrived at the wharfs of Nauvoo."[2]

The Church's ferry ran between Nauvoo west across the river to Montrose, Iowa, and its steamboat, the *Maid of Iowa*, transported passengers and freight both across the river and to other settlements along the river. The city maintained two landings, one on the south and the other on the north end of Main Street. Dennis Rowley commented:

> Recent converts to Mormonism immigrating to the United States from Europe and England were brought up the river from New Orleans and St. Louis; supplies were transported to Nauvoo, including food for the laborers on the temple and other public buildings; supplies and personnel for work in the Wisconsin pineries were taken upriver; pleasure excursions were taken by Joseph Smith and many other Mormons; and church services were even held on the decks of the newly acquired steamboat. The *Maid of Iowa* served the Mormons well for two years.[3]

Did some members of King's hard-working family travel on the river for business or perhaps even pleasure? It is impossible to know, given the lack of records; but the sheer number of travelers passing by and converts moving into the city meant that the Folletts had the opportunity to meet and mingle with diverse cultures. Rowley poses the question, but provides no answer, of how the "mentality and outlook of the average Mormon" might have been impacted just by living on the banks of such a great river.[4]

Initially, Nauvoo's residents had few resources beyond their skills, diligence, faith, and willingness to cooperate with each other. However, as early as 1841, a correspondent for the *Joliet Courier*, published in Monmouth, Illinois, reported on a recent visit to Nauvoo that "the people of the town appeared to be honest and industrious, engaged in their usual vocations of building up a town, and making all things around them comfortable."[5] By May 1842 a letter authored by "an observer" in the *Advocate* of Columbus, Ohio, likewise described a recent trip to Nauvoo: "I saw a people apparently happy, prosperous and intelligent. Every man appeared to be employed in some business or occupation. I saw no idleness, no intemperance, no noise, no riot—all appeared to be contented, with no desire to trouble themselves with anything except their own affairs.... I could see no disposition on their part to be otherwise than a peaceable and law-abiding people."[6]

Howard Coray home in Nauvoo built between 1840 and 1846. G. Frank Goulty Collection ca. early 1900s. Courtesy of LDS Church History Library.

Given the lack of ready cash, Nauvoo's economy benefited from public works projects like the temple's construction. In October 1843 the Prophet stated that building the temple "sustained the poor who were driven from Missouri, and kept them from starving; and it has been the best means for this object which could be devised."[7] Writing in *The Ensign* in 1979, James E. Smith confirmed: "Thus the response of the Saints to poverty was increased dedication to common purposes, seeking for 'the greatest temporal and spiritual blessings which always flow from faithfulness and concerted effort,' and not from 'individual exertion or enterprise.'"[8]

Though those first four years found Mormons focused on building their religious community and deflecting anti-Mormonism, in many ways the people, their simple homes and lifestyle were typical of frontier America in the 1840s. According to Donald Q. Cannon, King "erected a large log house for his family," which would certainly be typical for the time and circumstances, but Cannon does not cite any documentation for this fact and I have not been able to find any.[9] Very few photos exist of those early log or frame houses in Nauvoo. Perhaps the Follett family lived in a home similar to one built by Howard Coray, which was still

Reconstructed log house in present-day Nauvoo, now referred to as the Mary Field Garner home. Photo by Irval L. Mortensen, 2008.

standing in the early 1900s.[10] This house was "built near the northwest corner of Young and Barnett streets."[11] That location was approximately five blocks east and five blocks south of the Follett home.

Holzapfel and Holzapfel describe the typical waves of housing construction that likely also applied to the Folletts:

> Like all frontier communities, Nauvoo replaced its first primitive log homes with more substantial structures, maybe somewhat faster in Nauvoo's case, however. On any given block in the city one might find families functioning in two traditional ways. One family would be living in the traditional "first house" or log cabin, where one room encompassed all the family indoor activities, including cooking, eating, socializing and sleeping. The home next door might be a second home, traditionally called the "big house." The big house was usually a two-story brick home, with a kitchen-eating area separated from the sleeping areas, and if circumstances permitted, a parlor apart from all."[12]

Among the reconstructed homes in present-day Nauvoo is one that might reflect the style and perhaps size that King built for his family. This house, undoubtedly intended as a "first house" and originally built by John Workman, was then purchased by William Field for his wife and six children. One of these children was Mary Field (1836–1943). She and her family finally left Nauvoo in 1848, moving to Utah where Mary married William Garner, and they became the parents of ten children. A sign on the restored cabin reads: "The Church Historian['s] office titled her 'The Last Leaf', she was thought to be the last living person to have personally known the Prophet Joseph Smith. Mary Field Garner lived to be 107 ½ years old."[13]

King and Louisa's family economy had, inevitably, slipped down a notch when they sold out in Ohio and took at least some of their portable goods and furniture to Missouri. The period of hostilities and King's imprisonment had again severely reduced the family's economic circumstances. There is no reason to believe that they differed from most of Nauvoo's early residents in owning only basic furniture, homemade wooden utensils, and either a wood-burning fireplace or a cast-iron stove. Such homes could command little privacy. Beds routinely slept at least two adults. Children often slept on pallets or slept three or even four per bed. Some interiors were papered or painted, but most were whitewashed with a lime mixture. Water had to be carried from nearby streams or wells. Baths were often infrequent. Chamber pots and outhouses served basic sanitary needs. Light came from hand-dipped candles and an occasional "lard or grease" lamp. According to Nauvoo historian George W. Givens: "Whatever the form of lighting, it was usually dim, smoky and smelly, but artificial light enabled the women to spin or sew and the men to work or read during the usually brief period between dusk and bedtime."[14]

Louisa Follett, like Nauvoo's other women, sewed the family's clothing by hand—she probably bought the fabric, rather than weaving it on her own loom—and laundered, also by hand, the heavily soiled clothing with home-made lye soap.[15] Some items that would have been difficult to make, such as "shoes, mittens, shirts, socks, stockings, hats, vests, coats, and round-about (wrappers) were available for purchase in Nauvoo."[16]

In her role as wife and mother, Louisa also spent much time on activities related to food and its preparation. She cultivated and dried vegetables and fruit, storing apples and root vegetables like turnips and potatoes in root cellars, made berries into jellies or preserves, and perhaps pickled cucumbers, and converted cabbage into kraut.[17] In addition to fresh milk from the family cow, Louisa would have made cheese and butter. Beef was the most common meat, supplemented by pork, chicken, and fish. "Meat was either salted smoke-cured or pickled. Vinegar and spices were used to improve the flavor. During the Mormon days the smoke house was more important than the summer kitchen, and often they were combined."[18] Corn, which was plentiful, was used in many ways. Though wheat was the basic ingredient in the kitchen for baking, corn was used to assist in the process. Louisa could have used a mixture of "corn meal to which yeast [was] added" and referred to as "'emptin cakes,' the making of which was a regular occurrence in the kitchen at that time. . . . The resulting fermentation was allowed to go on for some time until checked by drying. . . . When used, an emptin cake was broken up in warm water and added to the bread dough. It was then put in a warm place, after which the mass would promptly raise."[19] A typical meal prepared by Louisa for her family could have included some type of meat or fish—fresh or dried—bread, and whatever vegetables and fruit were available. "Families usually ate in the same room where the food was prepared and cooked, indicating that the average home in Nauvoo was rather small."[20] Diaries record both periods of plenty and those of food shortages. One role that the Relief Society assumed was assuring that the hungry had enough food to subsist, although it may not have been a well-balanced diet.

Probably like twenty-two-year-old Bathsheba Wilson Bigler Smith, Louisa found pleasure in modest comforts. George W. Givens describes Bathsheba's homey domesticity, recorded in a June 1844 letter to her husband, George A. Smith, then serving a mission in Illinois, Indiana, and Michigan. She "praised the comfort she had in her home with the flower pots in the windows and new curtains that she made and hung. She had cleaned house, baked a good dinner, and had apples stewing for a pie, preparing for company that evening."[21] Louisa managed the household chores primarily by herself, as her two daughters were married and had homes of their own to care for. Sons Edward and Warren King were ages eleven and six respectively, so they would have helped with some of the chores. William Alexander, age nineteen, was still living at home at least part of the time, and probably assisted her with the heavier chores such as chopping wood and perhaps hoeing the garden.

Bathsheba Smith's letters to her missionary husband, provide insights into a woman's daily chores that may have been typical of Louisa's as well:

> September 2, 1843: I think our gardon will be tolerable good. Our potatoes are poor. Vines are quite good. We begin to have plenty of melons which make many harts rejoice and ours are maid glad. We have a plenty of tomatoes.... Our well is dry.... Our cow does middling well.... With your Fathers [and] others help I shall be enabled to get our house plastered next week.... Josiah let me have fifty feet of lumber and Amos did the carpenter work.... Ickabod got me a gallen of whiskey for pickles. My cowcumbers do well. He said he would get some flower and honey and candells.... I am a bout out of flower now.
>
> June 15, 1844: We have had garden plowed. It looks vary well but wood [do] better if it did not rain so much. The wormes trouble all the neighbor's gardens, but have not mine but little. A great many people have had more or less out of our garden sutch as lettis onions Reddishes and greanes. Indeed I do not know what they would have done if it ware not for us.... Our earley potatoes are getting quite large. The corn is in tossel. Cabbage looks well. Vines rather poore. Tomatoes in blow. Beets quite large. Will soon have peas.... I have soald six pounds of butter since you left.[22]

King was responsible for building and maintaining the house and planting and fencing the acre of land they were buying. Like other Nauvoo residents, he probably also planted grapevines and fruit trees. All of the families in Nauvoo kept small animals, such as chickens, and other poultry, and perhaps pigs, as well as gardens on their acre lot in town, but about a third also purchased farming acreage outside the city limits.[23] There is no record that King ever bought a farm, even though, when King applied for membership in May 1842 in the Freemasons, he gave his occupation as "farmer."[24] King may have hired out to such a farmer or farmed on shares. Likely he participated in a community farm project, formed in February 1843, called the Big Field. George Givens describes it as "a community farm cultivated in common by those unable to buy farms on the outskirts of the city. Its use was regulated by a Board of Trustees. The community farm consisted of six sections of land, or 3,840 acres, east of the city and was one of many projects to aid the poorer Saints who were willing to work the land."[25] Crops raised on this farm included wheat, corn, barley, potatoes, and oats and a variety of vegetables.

Donald Q. Cannon states that King worked "as a stonemason," but does not cite a reference for this information.[26] It is also the only statement I have found that identifies King's occupation specifically as stonemason. Perhaps this is a reference to his work on the temple. (See Chapter 17.) King also had responsibilities with the Nauvoo Legion, the Freemasons, his Seventies Quorum, civic construction projections (e.g., the Seventies Hall and the Masonic Temple), and may also have served one or more short-term missions.

In addition to neighborly bartering or purchase, stores in Nauvoo provided other supplies for those who had money or credit. Amos Davis was operating a store in the spring of 1838 when the first Saints arrived. By January 1842, Joseph Smith opened his Red Brick Store, a two-story structure with the store on the ground floor and an upper level, called the Lodge Room, that served as a meeting place and as the Prophet's office. Perhaps as many as thirty stores existed for various periods during the Nauvoo period, supplying fabric, clothing, shoes, salt, sugar, spices, flour, some patented medicines, and such building materials as nails and glass.[27]

Nauvoo also "had a wide variety of independent artisans or craftsmen skilled in fashioning wood, metal, and textiles into useful products. For example, residents could buy locally produced hats, gloves, shoes, dresses, coats and suits. But virtually all cloth and many other clothing items were imported. So were stoves, tools, pots and pans, tubs, and other manufactured iron items."[28] In 1844, Ellen Douglas in a letter to her parents in England "estimated the number of shops in Nauvoo at one hundred to two hundred compared to a mere two or three shops when she arrived from England two years earlier."[29] This number seems exaggerated unless she was also including workshops and artisans and craftsmen whose homes doubled as shops and stores. A modern Nauvoo source lists at least forty-nine categories of occupations and professions, including such labels as professional schools, horse breeding, musicians, notary public, photography, penmanship/shorthand instructors, professor of phrenology, and lecturers.[30]

Although the cost of living would have varied by season and period, some contemporary sources are helpful. Sally Carlisle Randall, a Nauvoo homemaker, recorded in 1844: "Provisions are very cheap. We can get good pork for four cents a pound, flour for one dollar and fifty cents a hundred, sugar from 8 to 10 cents a pound. Cows are from six to ten dollars."[31] Ann H. Pitchforth, a recent immigrant from the British Isles, wrote to her family in the spring of 1845: "Meat is cheap, two pence [four cents] a pound of choice pieces, one pence a pound the other fowls, one shilling [twenty-five cents] egg two pence [four cents] a dozen. Meat is cheap, but vegetables are high. We hope by next year to grow our own. Cabbages are five cents a piece, turnips are high. Potatoes are high."[32] A modern-day source further explains: "An English pound was valued at approximately $2.50 and since there were 20 shillings to the pound, a shilling would be worth about 12 ½ cents. This was one reason store daybooks of that era listed so many prices in multiples of 6 ¼, which was a six pence or half a shilling. These fractional prices also represented the value of Spanish coins that were so prevalent in the nation. A *real* was worth 12 ½ cents and a *half-real* was 6 ¼ cents"[33] Writing in 1984 historian Kenneth W. Godfrey provided further details on the cost of living: "In 1842 axes were selling in Nauvoo for $16 a dozen, beans were 40 cents a bushel, coal $14 a ton, coffee 13 cents a pound, chocolate 13 cents a pound, feathers 16 cents a pound, cornmeal 25 cents a bushel, dry apples 50 cents a bushel. It was estimated that a rather large family could live on $176 a year."[34]

No Mormons were wealthy. Members' economic status ranged from comfortable to poor; some were very poor. Donald Q. Cannon notes: "According to the 1842 tax list, Follett had $163 in real and personal property, making him some what better-off than most of his fellow citizens."[35] The names are listed on the tax roll that I examined not alphabetically but by the location of real property, though there is no value given for the real property. It is difficult to compare the value of King's real property with other owners in Nauvoo, because of the difference in size and number of lots and farms and because no deeds were recorded for many parcels of real estate. However, a simple comparison of the value for personal property can be made. King's personal property is valued at $60. Examples of larger taxable amounts, particularly those of Church leaders, were: Joseph Smith, $300; Brigham Young, $270; Hyrum Smith, $185; Heber C. Kimball, $205; Wilford Woodruff, $145; Porter Rockwell, $260; and Charles C. Rich, $195. Two owners of lots adjacent to King were listed: Charles Hulett, $100; and Hiram K. Kimball, $120. Others who had been with King through the troubles in Missouri and were now also on the tax rolls in Hancock County were Levi Jackman, $85; John Lowe Butler, $40;

A. P. Rockwood, $65; Reynolds Cahoon, $85; W. W. Phelps, $60; and Philo Dibble, $50. The smallest value I found was $15, many of the Saints having personal property valued between $20 and $100.[36] I see King as close to the bottom of "somewhat comfortable," but probably in the same category as most Mormons at the time.

As already noted in the earlier chapters about the Follett experience in Nauvoo, religious functions met many social needs as well. Sunday preaching services, held morning and afternoon, drew hundreds and sometimes thousands to the grove near the temple where "in the style of the revivalist camps, they sat on makeshift benches, on the ground, on their horses, and in their wagons, listening to two- and three-hour sermons by the Prophet Joseph and other leaders."[37] Adults and children sang, played musical instruments, attended and participated in recitals and drama productions, and enjoyed the performances of the Nauvoo Brass Band and choir. Exhibits and lectures featured visitors to Nauvoo. Returned missionaries shared their experiences. Baseball, bowling, and dancing, especially the "new Cotillion," were popular pastimes. Children played games and attended visiting circuses and other amusements.[38] Some hosted dinner parties. Women frequently paid afternoon calls on each other. Quilting bees combined work with frolics—a substantial potluck supper followed by music, games, and dancing.

Because of the mixed background of the people in Nauvoo, their celebration traditions also varied. Thanksgiving did not become a national holiday until the Civil War; however, New England convert Martha Hall Haven, whose family had previously celebrated the holiday, carried on the tradition in Nauvoo.[39] In 1843, the Prophet's family celebrated Christmas by feasting on special dishes, paying calls on friends and neighbors, exchanging gifts, and being serenaded with carols at 1:00 A.M. by the Rushton family and their neighbors from England. Joseph Smith's history recorded that the singing "caused a thrill of pleasure to run through my soul. All of my family and boarders arose to hear the serenade. . . . My brother Hyrum . . . thought at first that a cohort of angels had come to visit . . . it was such heavenly music."[40]

Illness and death were also facts of life in Nauvoo, and Louisa, like other women in Nauvoo, accepted nursing the sick, delivering babies, and laying out the dead, even though the town had doctors. Among the often-fatal diseases were the ague (malaria), consumption (tuberculosis), chronic diarrhea, and the almost routine childhood illnesses of measles, smallpox, and chicken pox.[41] Children died most frequently of diarrhea, fever, canker, measles, whooping cough, bloody flux, and tuberculosis; adults died most frequently from whooping cough, measles, and mumps. Statistics show that these death causes and their rates in Nauvoo, especially after 1840, were not much different than those in the rest of the country.[42] In addition to these "natural" deaths were fatal accidents from farm and occupation-related incidents involving animals, wagons, other equipment, fires, water, and weapons. It was an occupational accident involving well-digging that claimed King Follett's life in March 1844.

As already noted (Chapter 17), the city regulated and encouraged family and neighborhood wells, to avoid the health issues involved with streams and shallow wells. In addition, George and Sylvia Givens point out, "Shallow wells . . . were so highly impregnated with lime that they left clothes with a grayish hue. Most homes, therefore, had cisterns in which the soft rainwater was stored."[43] Wells in Nauvoo were then approximately twenty to thirty feet deep when they were completed.[44] On Tuesday, February 27, 1844,[45] during winter temperatures when the ground would normally have been at least partially frozen, King, no doubt aided by his sons and sons-in-law and perhaps neighbors and friends, was digging a well on his lot. James Palmer, a neighbor of King's at that time, writing in the mid-1880s, recalled that King "was digging a well for the use of his family."[46] According to a historian's description of well-digging in Texas during the 1840s, "The digger [would be] let down and pulled out by a homemade windlass, and the dirt and rocks were pulled out in big buckets in the same way."[47] The process for digging such a well appears to be simplistic but precise:

> The diggers would first start a hole much bigger than the well would be—perhaps as much as ten to twelve feet in diameter. When the hole became so deep that it was too far to throw the dirt, a second, smaller hole would be started in the center of the first. The dirt would then be thrown onto the first shelf where another worker would throw it to the ground above.
>
> Depending on the depth, usually not over 20 to 30 feet, a second or third shelf might be needed. Once water was reached, rocks would be lowered in buckets to start the walling from the bottom. Walling would then proceed with some of the workers above shoveling dirt behind the wall, filling the outside of the larger hole, and packing it as the wall moved upward.

The walls were so well keystoned together that it is seldom that one sees such wells with collapsed walls today.[48]

This labor-intensive project was frequently hired out by families that could afford it. Though I did not find a record showing the cost of this type of project in 1844, by 1857, Emma Smith paid $65.70 to have a well dug near the Mansion House, which she owned and was running as a hotel and boarding house. More than one-half of this cost was for labor—56 ft. at 62 ½ (cents) for a total labor cost of $35.00.[49] It is very doubtful that King could have afforded to hire someone to help with the digging of his well.

King and his helpers had dug the well to the desired depth, in this case about fifteen feet.[50] This depth was well over his head. He was in the bottom, lining the walls with bricks or stones lowered to him in a bucket. Then the rope or cable holding the bucket broke. It must have been a large container. The *History of the Church* calls it a "tub."[51] It was probably made of oaken staves held in place with metal bands, since all-metal buckets did not replace wooden buckets until later in the century.[52] Colonel Thomas L. Kane commenting on his visit to a deserted Nauvoo shortly after the Saints had left the city, described drawing a drink from "a water sodden well-bucket and its noisy chain."[53] In any case, even empty, the bucket would have been heavy. Filled with stones or bricks, it would have been a lethal missile.

Those above surely shouted to warn King. Perhaps he had only time to look up or perhaps he had time to try and flatten himself against the wall. The bucket did not, apparently, break his skull or his neck; but James Palmer, who recorded his memories of Nauvoo approximately forty years later, said King "was crushed to death by falling rocks and dirt."[54] The injury was not immediately fatal, but he undoubtedly suffered broken bones and internal bleeding, and surely these injuries would have been exacerbated by the difficulties in extracting him from the well. He was carried into his house where he died eleven days later[55] on Saturday, March 9, at the age of fifty-five years, seven months, and twelve days.[56] Death certificates were not issued at that time, and it is not clear whether his death was a direct result of the injury, infection, which could also have been deadly in these days before antibiotics, or related complications, such as pneumonia.

It is impossible to know what type of medical care, if any, he might have had following the accident. The Masonic minutes on the day of his burial record that he "suffered much" during those eleven days."[57] There were a number of doctors in Nauvoo at the time, as well as herbal practitioners. It is possible that bleeding by the use of leeches "to restore a proper balance of the 'humors'" may have still been in use by older physicians. Perhaps some type of patented medicine such as "Dr. Williamson's Pain Soother" or "Dr. Halsted's Magnetic Remedies" sold in a drug store owned by A. T. Terrell on Water Street was used to relieve the pain that King doubtless experienced. "About the only effective treatment, as far as making the patient comfortable, was laudanum" which was made by "dissolving an ounce of opium in a pint of spirits."[58] However, the family may have relied on the advice given by Church leaders. As early as 1841, the Prophet spoke "to a large congregation . . . desiring to persuade the Saints to trust in God . . . and when they were sick, and had called for the Elders to pray for them, and they were not healed, to use herbs and mild food."[59] An editorial in the *Times and Seasons* a year after King's death further emphasized: "Nor are the services of physicians held in so great repute in Nauvoo, that the saints confide in medicine, but rather the commandments of God are looked to as being far more safe than trusting in an arm of flesh."[60] There is no way to determine how the Follett family responded to such advice in caring for King.

At the time of his death, his survivors would have been forty-five-year-old Louisa and their six children: Adeline Louisa Follett West, age twenty-seven; John Follett, age twenty-four; Nancy M. Follett Daley, age twenty; William Alexander, age eighteen; Edward Moroni, age twelve; Warren King, age six, and two-year-old grandson William King Daley.

A number of records exist of King's death. The *History of the Church* on March 9 reads: "Our worthy brother, King Follett, died this morning, occasioned by the accidental breaking of a rope, and the falling of a bucket of rock upon him while engaged in walling up a well, and the men above were in the act of lowering the rock to him."[61]

The *Nauvoo Neighbor* on March 20, 1844, published what might be considered two separate obituaries, or at least a very long obituary in two parts, about King. The first part reads:

> Elder Follett was one of those who bore the burden, in common with others of his brethren, in the days when men's faith was put to the test. He

was a native of Vermont [sic] and moved many years since into Cuyahoga county, Ohio.

There, for the first time, he heard the Gospel preached, united with the Church of Jesus Christ of Latter-day Saints in the spring of 1831, and has been a sharer in the afflictions through which the Saints have passed from that time until the time of his death.

He shared in the violence of Missouri persecution, was cast into prison, and endured many months' imprisonment; and, after long delay, obtained a trial on the charges preferred against him, and was honorably discharged, being acquitted of all the crimes with which a band of wicked persecutors could charge him.

All the persecutions he endured only tended to strengthen his faith and confirm his hope; and he died as he had lived, rejoicing in the hope of future felicity.

Having united with the Church in the forty-first year of his age,[62] he filled up the prime of his life in the service of his God, and went to rest in his fifty-sixth year, being fifty-five years, seven months, and fourteen days old [sic] when he slept the sleep of death.

So the righteous pass, and so they sleep, until the mandate of Him for whom they suffer and in whom they trust shall call them forth to glory, honor, immortality and eternal life.[63]

This part of the obituary is reprinted in the *History of the Church*.[64] The *Nauvoo Neighbor*'s second obituary (or second part), includes a rather flowery sermon on the resurrection by an unidentified author. Samuel M. Brown suggests that the author was possibly Lyman O. Littlefield, who wrote for other papers in the area at that time:

Baptized in 1831, Follett had survived Missouri, including militia and vigilante actions as well as a bout in prison, only to die of a workplace accident among friends, striving to make the city of Nauvoo blossom like a rose. Of any deaths in the city of Nauvoo, this one deserved an explanation.... [This obituary] provides several important glimpses of life and religion in Nauvoo: the importance of martyrdom in explaining premature death, the nature of bereavement in antebellum cultures, the vision of the heavenly society, the emphasis on family bonds ... the use of Masonic rites for burial at this stage in Mormom history, and the description of the funeral procession.[65]

The obituary itself as published and perhaps written by Littlefield[66] follows:

In compliance with the secret promptings of my own bosom, and for the consolation of the bereaved family,—with whom I have often communed within the consecrated penetralia of domestic sociality,—I offer a few reflections upon the death of the deceased—Brother King Follet.

Brother Follet was a member of the Church of Jesus Christ of Latter-Day Saints—firm and uncompromising in the doctrines and principles of eternal truth—and he died triumphing in the liberties of the gospel. He shared in the persecutions of Missouri—was ever at his post in defence of injured innocence and outraged law—ever ready to lay down his life, if necessary, for the cause and the "witness of Jesus." On his death bed, he might very appropriately have exclaimed, in the language of the Apostle Paul, "I have fought a good fight; I have finished my course; I have kept the faith; henceforth is laid up for me a crown of righteousness, which the Lord, the righteous judge, shall give me at that day, and not to me only, but unto all of them also that love this appearing."

Awake!—you mourning bereaved ones: — awake to rejoicing! Let your minds engage a higher theme of contemplation; break forth into gladness, and anticipate the glories of the resurrection; until, swallowed up in excellence and hopes of sublime exaltations, your souls struggle to be released from the thralldom of encumbering clay, and leap into a world of happiness, contentment and joy. Behold him, who has fallen asleep, awake to glory and eternal youth, when the barriers of the tomb shall be burst asunder and the sleep of death be broken by the trump of God. He comes forth to immortality—his body quickened by the spirit of the Lord Jesus—no more to drink from the bitter cup of sickness and pain; but filled with the beatitude and power of Omnipotence, Springs into Liberty and Light and Life.

Why mourn for friends when they fall asleep in Christ? With that illustrious rain of worthies who have been "beheaded for the witness of Jesus, and for the word of God," they will come forth from the solitude of the grave, to live and reign, kings and priests with God, a thousand years, in the Millenium, [sic] when the curse will be removed from the earth—when all creation will be renovated, restored to its primitive state, and clothed in the habiliments of primeval bloom and pristine grandeur—as in the morning of creation when the "morning stars sing together;" when the great *diurnal illuminati* forced from the Creator the divine declaration that the light He had made was good and all created things smiled under the full and benign jurisprudence of the Deity. To die is but complying with the edicts of heaven. Dissolution must ensure; the corporeal system of man must sink into torpidity and decay, in order that the mortal tenement can be regenerated, and all the corruptible particles of the human system be extracted in the grave, that both body and soul may be united in the resurrection in a state of immortality, free from sorrow, pain and distress, and endowed with minds refined and capacious, that they can enjoy the society of angels, comprehend the principles of Jehovah, and mingle in the beatitude of heaven.

Brother Follet's funeral was attended with the highest honors and most marked respect. A procession a mile in length, followed his remains to the "narrow house."[67] The emblems and paraphernalia of the "fraternity," that glittered along the lengthened line, showed that his "fidelity" had entitled him to the benefits of Masonry, under the honors of which, in due Masonic form, he was consigned to the solitude of the grave.[68]

The next week's issue of the *Nauvoo Neighbor*, dated March 27, 1844, carried the regular report of deaths by William D. Huntington, Nauvoo sexton, under the heading: "DEATHS—For the week ending Monday the 11th inst" and one of the six entries is "King Follet, 55y 7m 14d; fall in a well."[69]

James Palmer, a fellow Church member in Nauvoo, writing in the mid-1880s in Utah, recorded his remembrance of King's death entitled: "THE KING FOLLET SERMON. Truthful account of an experience in Nauvoo. When I resided in Nauvoo, Hancock Co., State of Illinois, a brother by the name of King Follet resided nearby.[70] He was digging a well for the use of his family. While he was working below, walling up the well, the cable broke and he was crushed to death by falling rocks and dirt. He was a faithful Latter-day Saint and a true friend to the Prophet Joseph Smith."[71]

Wandle Mace, another of King's contemporaries, described King's death in his autobiography dictated in 1890: "Elder King Follett, who while at work in a well was killed by a tub of stone falling upon him. He was buried with Masonic honors, on the 10th of March, 1844." Then Mace commented, "He [King] was a man faithful to his trust, he suffered persecution and abuse and imprisonment for the sake of the gospel and the testimony of Jesus and never shrank from any duty however unpleasant."[72]

In 1886, Andrew Jenson published this biographical information:

FOLLETT, (King), an honored and worthy Elder of the Church, was born July 24, [sic] 1788, in Vermont [sic], and moved in his youth to Cuyahoga Co., Ohio, where he first heard the Gospel and was baptized in the spring of 1831. From that time he shared with the Saints in their persecutions and afflictions. As he was leaving the State of Missouri in April, 1839, he was dragged away from his distressed family, being falsely accused of robbery, and cast in jail in Richmond, where P. P. Pratt and fellow prison-

> DEATHS—For the week ending Monday the 11th inst.
> Catherine Hopkins, 5y 8d; inflammation on the lungs.
> Mary Ann Holand, 31y; dropsey.
> Seth Cook, 41y; billious colick.
> Selina M. Eldridge, 1y 4m; measles.
> Elizabeth Maryweather, 78y; old age.
> King Follet, 35y 7m 14d; fall in a well.
> Total 6.
> W. D. HUNTINGTON, Sexton.
> DEATHS—For the week ending Monday the 18th inst.
> Ester A. Morrill, 7m 3d; measles.
> Titus Billings, 10y; inflammation on the brain.
> Wm. Jones, 23y; consumption.
> W. D. HUNTINGTON, Sexton.

Photocopy of King's death notice in *Nauvoo Neighbor*, March 27, 1844.

ers had already been confined for months. After suffering in the Richmond and Columbia jails about six months, he finally obtained a trial, and was honorably discharged in October, 1839, being acquitted of all the crimes of which he falsely had been accused. After his release from confinement he was again permitted to join his family and the Saints, in Illinois, and continued faithful and true until his death, which occurred in Nauvoo, Hancock Co., Ill., March 9, 1844. His death was occasioned by the accidental breaking of a rope, and the falling of a bucket of rock upon him, while engaged in walling up a well.[73]

According to historian Donald Q. Cannon, after summarizing one of King's contemporary obituaries:

> King Follett was one of those who assisted in transforming swamp-infested Commerce into prosperous Nauvoo. He purchased property on the bluff on the northwest corner of the city (Block 26, Lot 1). His neighbors included Charles Hewlett and Hiram Kimball. He erected a large log house for his family and then went to work as a stonemason. According to the 1842 tax list, Follett had $163 in real and personal property, making him some what better-off than most of his fellow citizens. He and his wife Louisa had six children and were members of the Nauvoo First Ward. On the morning of 9 March 1844, King Follett was walling up a well when a bucket of rock fell on him, crushing him to death.[74]

The Nauvoo Masonic Lodge minutes for Saturday, March 9, 1844, confirm that twenty-eight members were present that day when the meeting began at 6:00 P.M.[75] The only official item of business on the agenda was to initiate four new members into the organization. When the meeting re-formed as "a Master Masons Lodge," William S. Hathaway announced "the death of brother King, this day and said brother Follet wished to be buried in Masonic Form, whereupon on motion it was resolved that the Lodge adjourn untill tomorrow morning at 10 o'clock."[76]

Given the lack of embalming technology, funerals were typically held the day after death. Coffins would have been available, and Nauvoo's sexton William D. Huntington, "sold 'Ready-made and Made-to-Order Coffins.'"[77] According to George W. Givens, during the Nauvoo period,

> a coffin was usually made of pine and crafted to fit the deceased. It was narrow at the head end, wider at the shoulders, and narrowed back to the smallest width at the feet. Although usually stained or painted black, it was occasionally covered with black cloth, which then required an outer "rough box." For a little extra cost, the coffin could be lined by the coffin-maker or his wife. The lid was either screwed or nailed on after the funeral services, if there were services. Better coffins might have a hinged glass face cover for viewing.[78]

Ida Blum wrote in 1969: "A century ago coffins were made to measure, wide at the shoulders, narrow at the head and very narrow at the foot. Sometimes a carpenter went to the home and took the measurements, sometimes the family sent a piece of string the length of the deceased. Occasionally, a cornstalk was sent cut to the exact length of the corpse."[79]

Families too poor to afford a coffin would wrap the body in fabric and put it directly in the grave.[80] It was the family's responsibility to organize the funeral service and interment. In preparation for King's funeral, relatives, friends, and members of his Masonic Lodge met on March 10, went to the home, and as was the tradition in Nauvoo washed and dressed his body, perhaps wrapped it in a shroud or "winding sheet," and placed it in its coffin.[81]

The *History of the Church* contains three short paragraphs for March 10:

> Frost in the night; beautiful day. South wind.
> Brother King Follett was buried this day with Masonic honors.
> I [Joseph Smith] attended meeting at the stand, and preached on the subject of Elias, Elijah, and Messiah.[82]

At this point, the *History of the Church* includes a "sketch" of the Prophet's address, as reported by Wilford Woodruff.[83] It does not mention King by name nor include even generic references to a death or a funeral. March 10 was a Sunday when the usual preaching service would have been held in the grove. The brief record makes it impossible to tell whether Joseph "attended . . . and preached" at King's funeral, whether the funeral was held in conjunction with a regular Sunday meeting at which the Prophet spoke as usual, or whether there is no connection between the information about King and that about Joseph's address. This information is usually interpreted to mean that the meeting was King's funeral at which the Prophet spoke. If so, it was a very impersonal funeral sermon given while family, friends and fellow Masons were probably preparing the body and attending to the burial, and Joseph Smith did not mention the deceased as he did, for instance, in announcing the doctrine of baptism for the dead during the funeral service for Seymour Brunson. (See Chapter 16.)

As I read the sources, the Masons escorted King's body directly from the home to the cemetery, with no stop for a funeral service:

> The W.M. [Worthy Master] then briefly stated the object of the communication, viz., to carry to the grave a worthy brother, King Follet, who has for some time been a worthy member of our Lodge and continued in good standing while he lived on the earth.
>
> Brother Follet was a man universally respected by a large circle of friends, having the friendship and esteem of all around him, whether he was viewed as a father, a neighbor, a Mason or Christian his character was equally honorable and virtuous. He has borne a large portion of sufferings with the Saints of God, having been amongst the number of those who were so cruelly and inhumanely ejected from the State of Missouri by executive authority at the point of a bayonet, his property destroyed and with his family and friends turned naked and destitute upon the world in a solitary wilderness; but he bore his sufferings with patience, fortitude and courage. He lived long enough to witness the unjust and oppressive conduct of The Grand Lodge of this State towards Nauvoo Lodge in consequence of their religion, and had a disposition with his brethren to contend for his rights as a man and a Mason even though his life must be a forfeit for the attempt. He has been taken away suddenly from the midst of this unfriendly world, and is placed beyond the reach of persecution or oppression from any source. His name will long be remembered with feelings of respect, and be handed down as an ensample for his posterity to copy. He was 55 years of age when he died, he came by his death in consequence of the falling of a well bucket full of stones upon him at the depth of fifteen feet below the surface of the earth, when he was engaged in stoning up a well. He lived eleven days after the accident and suffered much, but he now rests from his labors.

After various remarks from the W.M. the procession was formed in due Masonic form, and proceeded, conducted by the Nauvoo Band to the house of Brother Follet and having arranged the corpse and other necessary preparations proceeded to the place of internment [sic] where the last ceremony was performed as pertaining to this life to the remains of our esteemed friend. The procession was again formed and marched back to the new Masonic Hall. . . . Edwin D. Wooly, Sec Pro Tem — Hyrum Smith, W[orthy]. M[aster].[84]

This document, which makes no mention of a funeral, is the source for the eleven days between the accident and King's death.

Freemasonry had guidelines for transporting the body to the gravesite and the ceremonies preceding internment. Unfortunately, according to Nicholas S. Literski, who has conducted research about Freemasonry in Mormon Nauvoo, "The records of the Grand Lodge of Illinois were almost entirely destroyed by fire in February 1850. Smaller fires of uncertain origin destroyed records in the region surrounding Nauvoo, and many aspects of the relevant history must rely on circumstantial evidence."[85]

Until sometime in the 1860s, individual lodges established their own funeral protocols; later, uniform guidelines were adopted statewide. The oldest printed copy of the ceremony I could find available for Illinois is dated 1877.[86] There is no way of knowing, of course, how closely rites in 1844 followed the 1877 instructions for "Masonic Funeral Services"; but if they were the same, King's body, presumably in a coffin, was placed on some type of vehicle, probably a wagon, possibly decorated with dark plumes.[87] Lodge members formed a procession and marched or rode in "carriages or other conveyances" dressed in "black or dark clothing with significant fraternal adornments." They traveled in two columns five feet apart without speaking. Family, friends, and neighbors followed—some in carriages, others on horseback or on foot. The Nauvoo paper reported that King's procession was a mile in length,[88] a significant community expression of shared grief which must have helped comfort Louisa and her children. Aroet Lucius Hale, a drum major in the Nauvoo Martial Band, the full name of the "Nauvoo Band" that led the procession, recalled in an 1897 letter his remembrance of the band playing for some notable occasions. "Our Band also plyed [sic] at the mock funeral when the Prophet & Hyrum was Buried. I was one of the numbers. Our drums was muffled and trimed with black lace." Perhaps because of the proximity of King's death to that of the Smith brothers, he also added: "Also when King Follet was buried. King Follet was a Free Mason, and was buried under the Masonick Order. King Follet was a grate friend of the Prophet Joseph."[89] (It may be significant that he referred to a "funeral" for the Smiths but being "buried" for King, again suggesting that no funeral was held on the day of the burial.)

At the cemetery, six pallbearers who were fellow Masons, bore King's coffin, on which was resting a white apron, and positioned the coffin over the open grave with the family assembled at the foot, the Masonic officiators at the head, and other lodge members lined up across the top and down the sides. Behind them, all other mourners formed a second line.

Masons offered prayers and an "Exhortation" focusing on "the uncertainty of human life, the immutable certainty of death, and the vanity of earthly ambition"[90] perhaps followed by a brief obituary. The Marshall removed the white apron and handed it to the Master, and the pallbearers slowly lowered the coffin into the open grave. The Master explained that the "white apron was the first gift of masonry to our departed brother; it is an emblem of innocence, and the badge of a Mason. This emblem I now deposit in the grave of our deceased brother." The Master followed by lodge members then each dropped "the evergreen" emblem into the open grave. The instructions spelled out that the evergreen emblem symbolized "an enduring faith in the immortality of the soul. By it we are reminded that we have an immortal part within us that shall survive the grave, and which shall never, never, NEVER die."[91] The "obituary roll" containing King's name, birth and death information, activities as a lodge member, and certification "that the funeral ceremonies were performed by the Lodge, and any matters which may be deemed appropriate or of special interest to the Lodge" was read aloud and later filed in the lodge's archives.[92]

The 1877 instructions also suggested statements of sympathy to the family along these lines:

> Our brother whose remains are to be borne hence and be committed to the earth, was one of our fraternal band, bound by the same ties, and pledged to the same duties. . . .To those of his immediate relatives and friends who are most heart-stricken at the loss we have all sustained, we have but little worldly consolation to offer; we can only sincerely, deeply, and most affectionately sympathize with them in their bereavement; but we can say that he who tempers the wind to the shorn lamb looks down with

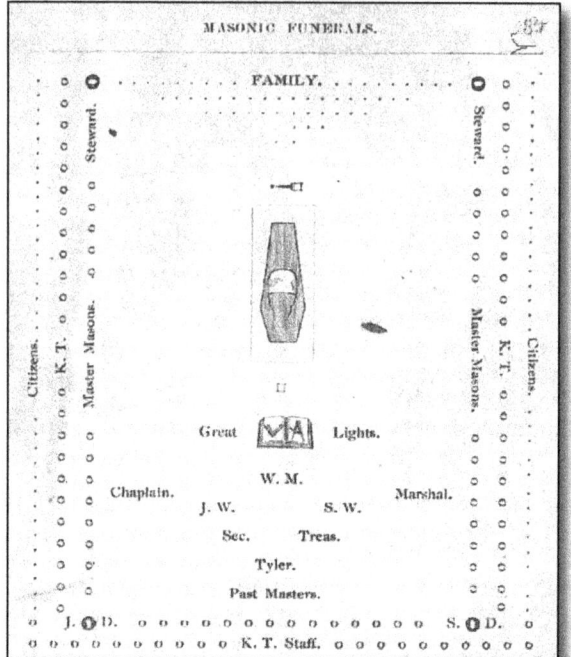

Formation at the gravesite, "Masonic Funeral Services" p. 79.

infinite compassion upon the widow, and the fatherless, in the hour of their desolation; and that their Heavenly Father will fold the arms of His love and protection around those who put their trust in Him.[93]

This statement completed the rites. The procession of Masonic members re-formed in the same order and returned from the gravesite. Louisa and her family returned to their home, accompanied by sympathetic mourners.

No city ordinances regulated burials, so individuals could legally be buried anywhere, even in backyards, although such a selection would have been rare. Numerous small private burial grounds were scattered throughout the city. According to Milton V. Backman, the pre-Mormon residents of the town had already established the "Old Durphy" cemetery. However, by 1844, the main burial site was a cemetery on Parley Street owned by the Church. It is referred to variously as the Parley Street Cemetery, Pioneer Cemetery, Old Pioneer Cemetery, and Old Nauvoo Burial Grounds. Backman explains: "On May 8, 1841, the city

Old unused road into the Old Nauvoo Burial Grounds. This may have been the entrance used by King's funeral possession. Photo by Irval L Mortensen, 2008.

council approved the establishment of this cemetery southeast of the city and lots were being sold at public auction in June 1842. The Old Pioneer Cemetery was divided into 16 blocks each containing 8 lots which included approximately 30 graves or a total of 3,840 grave sites. In the Historic Nauvoo Land and Record's Office is a listing of the burial sites of approximately 100 people."[94] The cemetery's location is about 2.2 miles east of Durphy Street/Highway 96 on Parley Street.

In June 1989, James L. Kimball Jr., an LDS Church History Library employee, estimated during an interview with the *Church News* that this cemetery may have been "about 40 acres. . . . The exact number of graves is unknown. After the Mormons left there, it still would have been used by the people in Nauvoo, although we don't think it was ever filled. We don't know the names of everybody who was buried there."[95]

While the original record of deaths in Nauvoo as "recorded by city sexton William Huntington" contains King's death date, age and cause of death, that record contains no information about the burial.[96] Between 1987 and 1989 Church missionaries in Nauvoo, under the direction of Nauvoo Restoration, Inc. (NRI), compiled a Nauvoo Death List from several sources. The only information given for King contains his death date

Present-day entrance to Old Nauvoo Burial Grounds. Photo by Irval L. Mortensen, 2008.

of March 9, 1844, and identifies only one source, the "Nauvoo Sexton List NRI."[97] A record in the Land and Records Office in Nauvoo, also prepared by NRI, contains an "inventory of markers and graves, etc." from the "Old Nauvoo Burial Ground." King's name, birth and death date, and age at death are correct as given, and Louisa Tanner is identified as his wife. It does not contain a location for his grave, and the area to identify a "Marker Type" contains "0". This confirms King's burial but provides no assistance identifying where he was actually interred in the cemetery.[98]

It is unknown whether King's grave was ever marked; but according to George and Sylvia Givens, "Burials were so common that the graves were often left unmarked with the expectation of later putting up a marker and in the process the location was sometimes lost. . . . Being impoverished, many families could afford nothing more substantial than a wooden marker, which lasted only a few years with no family left in Nauvoo to care for the grave. And finally, for many years the cemetery was abandoned to farm animals that trampled and destroyed many of the more fragile markers."[99]

In 1989, as part of the sesquicentennial commemoration of Nauvoo's founding, members of the Church cleaned up the cemetery, provided a pole fence typical of the period, and stabilized the remaining headstones in their site, thus preserving them from further deterioration. A kiosk at

Outside view of kiosk

Fisk, Lucius
Fisk, Hezekiah
Fisk, Rhoda Walker
Fisk, Sterry (Sterling)
Fisk, William
Fleming, Elizabeth A.
Fleming, Isaac
Fleming, Mariellen (Mary)
Folks (Fox) (Fawkes), Dorothy
Follet, King
Foot, Reuben

On these walls are the names of some of those who died while living in Nauvoo between 1839 and 1846. There are others, we know not who or how many, as time has erased them from our records and our memories. Many of them were children and each of them had a story worth telling. We don't know all of their stories but we do know that they were loved and the Savior knows and loves each one.

Interior of kiosk: King's name on list of deceased and the dedication statement. Photos by Irval L. Mortensen, 2008.

the cemetery entrance contains the names of those known to have died during the Nauvoo period, including King's.

Marilyn Chiat, a member of a different faith, in 2007 was touched by the condition of Nauvoo's "windswept pioneer burial ground." She notes, "This is not a garden cemetery. It's just a plain old cemetery.... You have whole families, mothers, fathers, children. One of the stones says 'Here sleeps a mother and her child in friendship's sweetest ties.' There's

Family statue at the Old Nauvoo Burial Ground. Photo by Irval L. Mortensen, 2008.

a beautiful sculpture that's recently been put there of a mother, father and children gazing out on the graves."¹⁰⁰

Among the few period headstones remaining in the cemetery are scattered newer monuments, erected by descendants. However, unless a grave's exact location can be documented, by policy, new headstones cannot be erected. Thus, King Follett's grave remains unmarked.

Eliza R. Snow, Mormonism's best-known poetess, penned words of appreciation and encouragement that were used at the deaths of several men in Nauvoo. These words must have comforted Louisa and her family. Perhaps this is a most fitting "written marker" for the life and death of King Follett:

> Now he's gone: We'd not recall him
> From a paradise of bliss,
> Where no evil can befall him:
> To a changing world like this.

Old Nauvoo Burial Ground. Photo by Irval L. Mortensen, 2008.

> His lov'd name, will never perish,
> Nor his mem'ry crown the dust;
> For the saints of God will cherish
> The remembrance of the JUST.[101]

Notes

1. William Mulder, "Nauvoo Observed," 96–102.

2. Richard Neitzel Holzapfel and Jeni Broberg Holzapfel, *Women of Nauvoo*, 40–41.

3. Dennis Rowley, "Nauvoo: A River Town," 268.

4. Ibid., 272.

5. *Joliet Courier*, Letter, June 1841, quoted in *History of the Church*, 4:381.

6. Letter to the editor, *Advocate* (Columbus, Ohio), n.d., quoted in *History of the Church*, 4:565.

7. "The Prophet on the Constitution of the United States and the Bible—Temporal Economies," in *History of the Church*, 6:58.

8. James E. Smith, "Frontier Nauvoo: Building a Picture from Statistics," 18. See also *History of the Church*, 4:272.

9. Donald Q. Cannon, "The King Follett Discourse: Joseph Smith's Greatest Sermon in Historical Perspective," 180.

10. G. Frank Goulty, "Nauvoo Photography Collection," ca. early 1900s. LDS Church History Library, PH 1107, fd. 3, item 3. This folder has "Handwritten descriptions at side of photographs, white mounts, early 1900s." G. Frank Goulty was a photographer who lived in Nauvoo in the early 1900s leaving there between 1910–1920. His family came to the United States in 1853; he was born in 1867 and his family lived in Hancock and Adams counties, Illinois, as well as in Missouri.

11. Richard Neitzel Holzapfel and T. Jeffery Cottle, *Old Mormon Nauvoo and Southeastern Iowa: Historic Photographs and Guides*, 49–50. Howard Coray (1817–88) was baptized in March 1840, arrived in Nauvoo in April and married Martha Jane Knowlton (1821–81) in February 1841. He was a schoolteacher, served as a clerk to Joseph Smith and in the tithing office, and also helped compile a history of the Church. Martha aided Lucy Mack Smith, the Prophet's mother, in writing her history; and Howard later assisted with this project. The couple left Nauvoo for Utah in 1846 with the main body of the Saints.

12. Holzapfel and Holzapfel, *Women of Nauvoo*, 38.

13. Information obtained from personal visit to the reconstructed log home in Nauvoo in 2008.

14. George W. Givens, *In Old Nauvoo: Everyday Life in the City of Joseph*, 187.

15. Ibid., 190–91.

16. George Givens and Sylvia Givens, *Nauvoo Fact Book: Questions and Answers for Nauvoo Enthusiasts*, 24.

17. David E. Miller and Della S. Miller, *Nauvoo: The City of Joseph*, 79; Givens, *In Old Nauvoo*, 197.

18. Ida Blum, *Gateway to the West*, 70.

19. Ibid.

20. Kenneth W. Godfrey, "The Nauvoo Neighborhood: A Little Philadelphia or a Unique City Set Upon a Hill?" 93.

21. Bathsheba Wilson Bigler Smith, quoted in Givens, *In Old Nauvoo*, 185. Bathsheba was born in 1822 and baptized in West Virginia in 1837. In 1841 she was married in Nauvoo to George A. Smith, a cousin of the Prophet Joseph Smith. They went with the Saints to Salt Lake City, where George A. served as Church historian, apostle, and counselor in Brigham Young's First Presidency. She served as general president of the Relief Society from 1901 until her death in 1910.

22. Bathsheba Wilson Bigler Smith, Letter to George A. Smith, Nauvoo, September 2, 1843, and June 15, 1844, quoted in Kenneth W. Godfrey, Audrey M. Godfrey, and Jill Mulvay Derr, eds., *Women's Voices: An Untold History of the Latter-day Saints, 1830–1900*, 127–28, 129–30. In a footnote "Josiah" is identified as probably Josiah Walcott Fleming, Bathsheba's brother-in-law. Amos and Ickabod are not identified and I was unable to find more information about them.

23. Givens and Givens, *Nauvoo Fact Book*, 46.

24. Freemasons, Nauvoo Lodge (Ill.) Minute Book, 6.

25. Givens, *In Old Nauvoo*, 66; see also Miller and Miller, *Nauvoo: The City of Joseph*, 79.

26. Cannon, "The King Follett Discourse," 180.

27. Glen M. Leonard, *Nauvoo: A Place of Peace, a People of Promise*, 145–47.

28. Ibid., 159.

29. Ellen Briggs Douglas, Letter to parents, April 14, 1844, quoted in ibid., 158. Ellen Briggs Douglas Parker was baptized in 1838 in Lancashire, England. She and her husband, George Douglas, and children came to Nauvoo in 1842. After George's death, she married John Parker. In 1852, they came to Utah where she died in 1888.

30. Church of Jesus Christ of Latter-day Saints and Nauvoo Family History and Property Identification Department, *Reference Book for Nauvoo Family History and Property Identification Department*, Part 10, 164–87.

31. Sally Carlisle Randall, Letter to her family in New England, addressed to "My Friends," October 6, 1843, quoted in Godfrey, Godfrey, and Derr, *Women's Voices*, 135.

32. Ann H. Pitchforth, Letter to Mother and Father, April 23, 1845, quoted in Holzapfel and Holzepfel, *Women of Nauvoo*, 33.

33. George and Givens, *Nauvoo Fact Book*, 102.

34. Godfrey, "The Nauvoo Neighborhood," 93.

35. Cannon, "The King Follett Discourse," 180.

36. Nauvoo Illinois Assessor, Tax Lists for District No. 3, 1840, 1842, 1850. Microfilm #7706, Item 5. LDS Family History Library.

37. Carol Cornwall Madsen, *In Their Own Words: Women and the Story of Nauvoo*, 12.

38. Godfrey, "The Nauvoo Neighborhood," 88–90.

39. Holzapfel and Holzapfel, *Women of Nauvoo*, 64–65.

40. *History of the Church*, 6:134. See also Holzapfel and Holzapfel, *Women of Nauvoo*, 64, for a short discussion of Christmas traditions in Nauvoo.

41. Holzapfel and Holzapfel, *Women of Nauvoo*, 44–45.

42. Godfrey, "The Nauvoo Neighborhood," 84.

43. Givens and Givens, *Nauvoo Fact Book*, 84.

44. Ibid., 15.

45. King died on Saturday, March 9. I calculate the accident date based on the Masonic record quoted below that King lived 11 days "after the accident." There were twenty-nine days in the leap year of 1844, and I counted the day of death as one of the eleven days.

46. James Palmer, *James Palmer's Travels and Ministry in the Gospel, 1820–1905: Pioneer of 1850*, 63.

47. Gilbert J. Jordan, *Yesterday in the Texas Hill Country*, 27. A windlass consists of a horizontal roller or beam resting on supports, around which a rope or chain is wound, and which raises items it is attached to.

48. Givens and Givens, *Nauvoo Fact Book*, 15. See also Jordan, *Yesterday in the Texas Hill County*, 27.

49. Blum, *Nauvoo: Gateway to the West*, 98. Blum states that this information was taken from a list of expenses found among letters written in 1849 by Major Louis Crum Bidamon, from the goldfields in California to his wife, Emma Hale Smith Bidamon (Joseph Smith's widow).

50. Freemasons, Nauvoo Lodge Minute Book.

51. *History of the Church*, 6:302.

52. "Water from the Well: Buckets, Coopering and Wood."

53. Colonel Thomas L. Kane, "The Mormons: A Discourse Delivered before the Historical Society of Pennsylvania, March 26, 1850," 5. Kane, also a lawyer, first met the Mormons in May of 1846, and became a great friend of the Church though he was never baptized, visiting the Mormon camps in Iowa, assisting at the time of the formation of the Mormon Battalion and the move west.

54. Palmer, *James Palmer's Travels and Ministry*, 63.

55. Freemasons, Nauvoo Lodge Minute Book.

56. Ancestral File and other LDS records give his birthdate as July 24, 25, or 26. According to birth records in Winchester, Cheshire County, New Hampshire, July 26 is the correct date. He thus would have been "55 y 7 m 12d" when he died.

57. Freemasons, Nauvoo Lodge Minute Book 1841.

58. Givens, *In Old Nauvoo*, 117–23.

59. *History of the Church*, 4:414.

60. "The Saints Make Nauvoo," *Times and Seasons* 6, no. 6 (April 1, 1845): 856.

61. *History of the Church*, 6:248.

62. Based on his now known birthdate of 1788, this statement would mean King joined the church in 1829, but I find nothing to support such an early baptism date.

63. "Died," *Nauvoo Neighbor*, March 20, 1844, 2. This obituary spells King's name as "Follet" and mistakenly lists his birthplace as Vermont, rather than

New Hampshire. See Chapter 1. Also see previous discussion regarding his actual age at death based upon his now verified birth date.

64. "King Follett Biography," in *History of the Church*, March 9, 1844, 6:249.

65. Samuel M. Brown (posting as "Sam MB"), "The King Follet(t) Obituary," March 21, 2007, http://bycommonconsent.com/2007/03/21/the-king-follett-obituary/ (accessed November 14, 2011). Brown is the author of *In Heaven As It Is on Earth: Joseph Smith and the Early Mormon Conquest of Death* (New York: Oxford University Press, forthcoming January 2012).

66. Lyman Omer Littlefield (1819–93) was a native of New York who joined the Church in Michigan and at thirteen was the youngest person in Zion's Camp. He worked for the *Times and Seasons* in Nauvoo and wrote *The Mormon Martyrs: A Sketch of the Lives and a Full Account of the Martyrdom of the Joseph and Hyrum Smith*.

67. The use of the phrase in this context would indicate, I believe, a reference to a grave. However, Ida Blum, *Nauvoo: An American Heritage*, 36, defines "narrow house" as "coffin."

68. "Died," *Nauvoo Neighbor*, March 20, 1844, 2.

69. *Nauvoo Neighbor*, March 27, 1844, 3.

70. I was not able to locate land in Nauvoo listed in Palmer's name nor any other reference to where he might have been living at this time.

71. Palmer, *James Palmer's Travels and Ministry*, 63.

72. Wandle Mace, "Autobiography: Journal of Wandle Mace." Mace also accurately remembered King's imprisonment in Missouri, his attempted escape, and his release, and stated "he then made his way to Nauvoo."

73. Andrew Jenson, ed., "Miscellaneous: FOLLETT, (King)," 31. Jenson was born in Denmark in 1850 and immigrated to Utah in 1866, served two missions in Denmark, and began publishing a historical magazine in Danish. At the request of Church authorities, he changed it to an English publication, the *Historical Record*, which he published for five years.

74. Cannon, "The King Follett Discourse," 180. Cannon may be mistaken in giving King's occupation as "stonemason," provides no reference to that information, and incorrectly implies that King was injured and died on the same day.

75. At that time, the Masons were meeting at "Henry Miller's home, as the Masonic Hall would not be completed and dedicated until almost a month later on April 5, 1844, two days before the Prophet Joseph Smith delivered the King Follett Discourse. See James B. Allen, "Nauvoo's Masonic Hall," 46.

76. Freemasons Nauvoo Lodge Minute Book, March 9, 1844.

77. Keith W. Perkins and Donald Q. Cannon, eds., *Ohio and Illinois*, 127.

78. Givens, *In Old Nauvoo*, 126–27.

79. Blum, *Nauvoo: An American Heritage*, 36.

80. Givens and Givens, *Nauvoo Fact Book*, 79.

81. Givens, *In Old Nauvoo*, 127.

82. *History of the Church*, 6:249.

83. Ibid., 6:249–54.

84. Freemasons, Nauvoo Lodge Minute Book, March 10, 1844. Among the 128 attendees was King's son-in-law Nathan A. West.

85. Nicholas S. Literski, "An Introduction to Mormonism and Freemasonry," n.d.

86. John Dorner, Librarian and Curator, Illinois Lodge of Research, email to Joann Mortensen, June 13, 2008. Dorner's email included a scanned copy of a document titled "Masonic Funeral Services," 1877, pp. 75–97. In response to my question about Masonic funeral rites in 1844 in Illinois he stated: "The rituals of Illinois did not fully solidify until well into the 1860's, so depending on the time line, it may be difficult to determine precisely what did happen. However, I can share with you the service as it exists since the 1860's. The ritual is public, and is given to the surviving widow today." The following information about the procession and burial service as it might have applied to King are taken from this document, unless otherwise noted.

87. Blum, *Nauvoo: An American Heritage*, 36, not referring to King's funeral specifically but to funerals in general during the Nauvoo period wrote: "For the funeral the undertaker used a lumber wagon in lieu of a hearse. A post in each corner, topped with a bunch of black plumes, designated it as a burial vehicle."

88. "Died," *Nauvoo Neighbor*, March 20, 1844, 2.

89. Aroet Lucius Hale, Letter to Ebenezer Beesley, ca. 1897, 2. Hale referred to the band as the "Old Timer Nauvoo Martial Band" and said he was giving information about the "old members that used to play in the Nauvoo Legion, Lieutenant General Joseph Smith commanding." This was probably to differentiate between that band in Nauvoo and a similar band in Utah. On a personal note, he stated: "I brought my drum from Nauvoo to the Councill Blouffs helped drum the Mormon Battalion into survise."

90. "Masonic Funeral Services, 90–91.

91. Ibid., 93–94.

92. Ibid., 78–79.

93. Ibid., 86, 95–96.

94. Milton V. Backman Jr., *The People and Power of Nauvoo*, 12, 21 note 3.

95. James L. Kimball Jr., quoted in "Historic Nauvoo Cemetery Being Restored," 11.

96. Nauvoo (Ill.), Sexton, Cemetery Records, 1839–1845.

97. Nauvoo Restoration, Inc. "Old Nauvoo Burial Ground: Church of Jesus Christ of Latter-day Saints," 13.

98. Nauvoo Restoration, Inc., "Old Nauvoo Burial Ground: Inventory of Markers and Graves, etc." Follett, King, Nauvoo RIN 10091. Transcript in my possession, obtained on personal visit to Nauvoo 2008.

99. Givens and Givens, *Nauvoo Fact Book*, 81.

100. Marilyn J. Chiat, online interview in *The Monthly Aspectarian*, on her book, *The Spiritual Traveler, Chicago and Illinois*.

101. Eliza R. Snow, quoted in Backman, *People and Power of Nauvoo*, 20, 22 note 19.

❦ Chapter Twenty ❦

The King Follett Discourse: The Prophet's Greatest Sermon

As described in Chapter 19, it seems somewhat unlikely that a funeral for King immediately preceded his burial on March 10. Thus, the tradition that the Prophet Joseph Smith delivered some type of funeral service for King that day is also probably a mistake. Aroet Lucius Hale, drummer in the Nauvoo Martial Band, called King "a grate friend of the Prophet Joseph,"[1] which suggests that (1) a funeral *was* held but the family found it unsatisfactory and asked Joseph for another address, (2) no funeral was held, but the family made the request for such a commemoration from the Prophet, or (3) prompted by his feelings of friendship, the Prophet independently included some of his most important doctrinal teachings in a sermon known by King's name about three weeks following King's death. The King Follett Discourse was part of the Church's five-day general conference (Friday, April 5–Tuesday, April 9, 1844). Unknown to those attending, this would be the last conference prior to the Prophet's death. The *History of the Church* reported glowingly: "The weather has been beautiful for the conference; and they have been the greatest, best and most glorious five consecutive days ever enjoyed by this generation. Much good was done. Many spectators were present from Quincy, Alton, Warsaw, Fort Madison, and other towns.

When we consider the immense number present, and the good order that was preserved, it speaks much in favor of the morality of the city."[2]

The Prophet had intended to "preach the funeral sermon of King Follett" on Friday but postponed it until Sunday because of "the weakness of my lungs." He explained to the congregation on Friday: "I intend to give you some instruction on the principles of eternal truth, but will defer it until others have spoken."[3] On Friday, Sidney Rigdon preached on the history of the Church, a topic he continued on Saturday until the conference was adjourned because of bad weather. Rigdon was also the only speaker in the Sunday morning session.

At the 2:00 P.M. session, Hyrum Smith spoke for an hour, followed by Joseph Smith, who did not begin speaking until 3:15.[4] However, their attentiveness whetted by Joseph Smith's mention of "principles of eternal truth," the "largest congregation ever seen in Nauvoo . . . assembled."[5] Willard Richards, historian and secretary to the Prophet, reported that the sermon ended at 5:30."[6] Acknowledging that the "actual size of the audience is a matter of dispute," Donald Q. Cannon states that "some of those who attended the conference and kept diaries maintained that 20,000 people" heard the sermon, and also that those "assigned to record the official proceedings of the conference used that figure."[7] He concludes, however, that the figure was inflated. Nauvoo had a population of about 12,000; 20,000 would have exceeded the space available to meet, nor could they have all heard a speaker.[8] The Prophet in his role as mayor "requested the people to keep good order, and observed to the police, who were on the outskirts of the congregation to keep order, 'Policemen, I want you to exercise your authority; and don't say you can't do anything for us, for the constitutional power calls you to keep good order, and God Almighty calls you, and we command you to do it.'"[9] This triple authorization suggests that Joseph was also concerned about the presence of enemies who might disrupt the meeting or even attack him.

All sources refer to the sermon as having been given in "the grove," meaning one of three groves located close to the partially completed temple. Historians are divided, however, whether the grove in question was the East Grove (also called the "Temple Stand," "the grove east of the temple," or simply "the grove"). The East Grove was on a one-acre lot on the southeast corner of Knight and Robinson Streets (lot 2, block 16).[10] According to George and Sylvia Givens, however, "the grove" usu-

Reconstructed speaker's stand and log benches in one of the groves in modern Nauvoo. Photo by Irval L. Mortensen, 2008.

ally referred to the West Grove, unless one of the other two groves was identified:

> For example, on June 16, nine days after the King Follett Discourse, Joseph gave a sermon on the Christian godhead, and it was specifically mentioned that the sermon was in the Grove east of the Temple. It is also of interest to note that the day preceding the discourse on April 6, the meeting was in the East Grove but that was specifically mentioned and as Joseph's journal mentions, a "brisk" breeze was blowing that day and that would have encouraged the authorities to move that day's meeting to the east grove. The next day when the discourse was given, no breeze is mentioned and neither is the "east grove." Furthermore, an attendee, Edward Stevenson, recalled in his journal, "the weather was lovely and the surrounding river and the Iowa side with its sloping hills looks lovely." Such a view would be possible only from the West Grove.[11]

Regardless of the exact location, there would have been a speakers' stand and some benches, but most of the congregation sat on the ground, in buggies, or on horses.

Though there is no record of how many people could be seated in such an arrangement, the minutes of the General Conference of October

2, 1841, stated: "met in the grove" and "the several quorums were arranged and seated in order."¹² Ann Pitchforth described the scene of members assembled in a general conference. "It was a fine sight. In the center the Twelve Apostles, then the women with hundreds of parasols, then the men. On the outside were the carriages and the horses."¹³

The spring weather was fine as Joseph Smith began his sermon but then became blustery. Mary C. Westover recalled:

> I was at the funeral service of King Follet [Follett], which was held in the Nauvoo Grove. There was a heavy thunderstorm arose and as it increased the people became frightened and started to go home; but before anyone left the Prophet arose and told the multitude if they would remain still and pray in their hearts the storm would not molest them in their services. They did as they were bidden, the storm divided over the grove. I well remember how it was storming on all sides of the grove, yet it was as calm around us as if there was no sign of a storm so nearby.¹⁴

Amasa Potter likewise recalled the dramatic weather when Joseph Smith was speaking at

> the funeral of Elder King Follett, who was crushed to death in a well. The subject of baptism for the dead was dwelt upon, and when he had spoken about thirty minutes there came up a heavy wind and storm. The dust was so dense that we could not see each other any distance, and some of the people were leaving when Joseph called out to them to stop and let their prayers ascend to Almighty God that the winds may cease blowing and the rain stop falling, and it should be so. In a very few minutes the winds and rain ceased and the elements became calm as summer's morning. The storm divided and went on the north and south of the city, and we could see in the distance the trees and shrubs waving in the wind, while where we were it was quiet for one hour, and during that time one of the greatest sermons that ever fell from the Prophet's lips was preached on the great subject of the dead.¹⁵

Three men on Joseph Smith's staff—Willard Richards, private secretary and historian, William Clayton, another private secretary, and Thomas Bullock, clerk—were the usual recorders for Church conferences. On this particular day a fourth man, Apostle Wilford Woodruff, took notes "on the crown of his hat, while standing in the congregation" and transferred the information to his journal, according to historian Donald Q. Cannon. "Other people attending the conference kept brief notes on the sermon, but the current published version of the King Follett Discourse was constructed from the notes" of these four.¹⁶ Bullock's and

Reenactment of the King Follett Discourse, grove near the temple, July 2008. Jeffrey Hale Dickamore portrays the Prophet Joseph Smith. Photo by Irval L. Mortensen. Used by permission of Jeffrey Hale Dickamore.

Clayton's notes were the primary sources for the sermon's first publication, which was in the Church's *Times and Seasons* on August 15, 1844.[17] According to historian Stan Larson, the "version in general use today is an 'amalgamation' made in 1855 by Jonathan Grimshaw," then a clerk in the Church Historian's office. It uses all four sources.[18] Larson produced another version in 1978, using Bullock as the basic text, then clarifying, adding, or deleting using the other three. Larson appraises the accuracy of the foundational accounts:

> It may, in all fairness, be wondered just how accurate the reports of the King Follett Discourse are. In an absolute sense, it is impossible to determine since there is no way to recover the words actually spoken that day in April of 1844 and thereby judge the accuracy of the reports. However, it should be noted that the reports have no irreconcilable parts—no contradictory statements—and it is sometimes quite amazing how easily the various accounts combine.
>
> A high degree of agreement and harmony exists among them. There is no evidence that any account was made by copying and/or expanding

any other account. Every indication points to the Bullock, Clayton, and Richards versions' being written as Joseph spoke; this fact deserves emphasis. Of all the speeches given by Joseph Smith, this one has the greatest contemporary manuscript support, which certainly strengthens claims of its reliability and authenticity.[19]

The Prophet began his sermon with a request for the "prayers and faith" of those in attendance for his own strength to speak and calm weather. He also implored the faith of his listeners so that "I may have the instruction of Almighty God and the gift of the Holy Ghost, so that I may set forth things that are true and which can be easily comprehended by you, and that the testimony may carry conviction to your hearts and minds of the truth of what I shall say." He also expressed his own faith that "there is strength here, and I verily believe that your prayers will be heard."[20]

In addition to the new doctrine that the Prophet Joseph intended, he obviously meant at least part of his address to pay tribute to his friend, King Follett, as several passages refer to King, the Follett family, and King's status after death. The initial paragraph reads:

> Beloved Saints, I will call [for] the attention of this congregation while I address you on the subject of the dead. The decease of our beloved Brother, Elder King Follett, who was crushed in a well by the falling of a tub of rock, has more immediately led me to this subject. I have been requested to speak by his friends and relatives, but inasmuch as there are a great many in this congregation who live in this city as well as elsewhere, who have lost friends, I feel disposed to speak on the subject in general, and offer you my ideas, so far as I have ability, and so far as I shall be inspired by the Holy Spirit to dwell on this subject.[21]

He then spoke powerfully to those who grieved for dead loved ones:

> How consoling to the mourners when they are called to part with a husband, wife, father, mother, child, or dear relative, to know that, although the earthly tabernacle is laid down and dissolved, they shall rise again to dwell in everlasting burnings in immortal glory, not to sorrow, suffer, or die any more, but they shall be heirs of God and joint heirs with Jesus Christ....
>
> The mind or the intelligence which man possesses is co-equal [co-eternal] with God himself. I know that my testimony is true; hence, when I talk to these mourners, what have they lost? Their relatives and friends are only separated from their bodies for a short season; their spirits which existed with God have left the tabernacle of clay only for a little moment, as it were;

and they now exist in a place where they converse together the same as we do on the earth.

...I want to reason more on the spirit of man; for I am dwelling on the body and spirit of man—on the subject of the dead. I take my ring from my finger and liken it unto the mind of man—the immortal part, because it had no beginning. Suppose you cut it in two; then it has a beginning and an end; but join it again, and it continues one eternal round. So with the spirit of man.[22]

Speaking directly to Louisa and her family, the Prophet added a historic promise:

You mourners have occasion to rejoice, speaking of the death of Elder King Follett; for your husband and father is gone to wait until the resurrection of the dead—until the perfection of the remainder; for at the resurrection your friend will rise in perfect felicity and go to celestial glory, while many must wait myriads of years before they can receive the like blessings; and your expectations and hopes are far above what man can conceive for why has God revealed it to us?

I am authorized to say, by the authority of the Holy Ghost, that you have no occasion to fear, for he is gone to the home of the just. Don't mourn, don't weep. I know it by the testimony of the Holy Ghost that is within me; and you may wait for your friends to come forth to meet you in the morn of the celestial world.[23]

It seems unlikely that anyone but Joseph Smith understood the developing doctrine in this sermon. Contemporary readers understand this assurance to mean that the deceased would be resurrected as a celestial being, destined for the highest degree of exaltation. This is a promise that all members of the Church seek but which few are given in mortality.

Because of the growing anti-Mormon sentiment in western Illinois and rising resistance from disaffected members, it might have been expected that the Prophet would respond to accusations made against the Church. Instead, his discourse reaffirmed some doctrines that were then a part of the growing Church but, more importantly, explained ideas based on new revelation. Some of these complex topics were the character of God, the multiplicity of Gods, the relationship of God to human beings, and the origins and destiny of humankind. From this sermon originated the concept, unique in Mormon teachings, that Lorenzo Snow, a later Church president, recapitulated in an easy-to-remember and oft-quoted epigram: "As man is now, God once was; as God is now, man may be."²⁴ The concept that human beings could become gods has been treated by many traditional Christians as nonscriptural and even blasphemous; but it was the basis for the full endowment and sealing ordinances administered in the completed Nauvoo Temple and remains so for Church members today.²⁵ George Q. Cannon, who wrote an early biography of Joseph Smith and served as counselor to three Church presidents, described the sermon's influence:

> [The Prophet] uplifted the souls of the congregation to a higher comprehension of the glory which comes after death to the faithful. His address ceased to be a mere eulogy of an individual, and became a revelation of eternal truths concerning the glories of immortality.... The multitude were held spellbound by its power. The Prophet seemed to rise above the world.... [He] wanted his brethren to grasp some of the sublimities comprehended by his own inspired soul. Those who heard that sermon never forgot its power. Those who read it today think of it as an exhibition of superhuman power and eloquence.²⁶

The experience of delivering the sermon was a taxing one for the Prophet, certainly physically, because of having to talk loud enough for the large crowd to hear, and perhaps spiritually as well, because of the depth of the new revelatory doctrine he was presenting. He had postponed beginning his sermon on Friday because of weakness in his lungs and instead delivered it on Sunday. On the Monday following, he had intended to continue the topic but was unable to. The *History of the Church* records that the session that day began at 9:45 A.M.

> He [Joseph] requested Elder Brigham Young to read 1ˢᵗ Corinthians, 15ᵗʰ chapter, as his own lungs were injured. Elder Brigham Young said—to continue the subject of President Smith's discourse yesterday, I shall commence by reading the 15ᵗʰ chapter of 1ˢᵗ Corinthians, from an old Bible; and requested W.W. Phelps to read it. Prayer by Elder Brigham Young, after which the choir sang a hymn.
>
> President Joseph Smith said:—It is just as impossible, for me to continue the subject of yesterday as to raise the dead. My lungs are worn out. There is a time to all things, and I must wait. I will give it up, and leave the time to those who can make you hear, and I will continue the subject of my discourse some other time.²⁷

Because of his death the following June, he was not able to continue as he had planned.

No documentation survives about the response of King's family and friends to the sermon (titled a "discourse" by the Prophet himself) that would forever be associated with King's death as "the King Follett Discourse." Certainly they would have been comforted to be told by their prophet that they would once again see King Follett and recognize him as they had on earth. Joseph Fielding, a British convert, recorded in his journal: "Joseph's Discourse on the origin of Man, the Nature of God and the Resurrection was the most interesting Matter of this time."[28] More than fifty years later, Aroet L. Hale recalled it as "the gratest sermon that was ever preached in our Church."[29] Mary C. Westover, a young girl in 1844, wrote in 1906: "I thought as I sat there that the Lord was speaking through Joseph."[30] Donald Q. Cannon reported in 1978: "My research assistants and I read some three hundred journals at the LDS Church Archives and at Brigham Young University. Most did not comment on the discourse, however those who did comment made meaningful observations."[31] According to Cannon, examples of these observations were:

> Wandle Mace: "a remarkable discourse" and "this most interesting and instructive conference."
> Edward Stevenson: "Grand funeral sermon of King Follett."
> Erastus Snow: "All were highly edified and highly delighted."
> Joseph Lee Robinson: The Prophet's statements amazed him and caused him to wonder.
> Alfred Cordon: "I was much delighted with the teachings and doings of the conference."[32]

Some members, especially recent converts, who did not know a great deal about the doctrines, having been converted through their belief in Joseph as a modern-day prophet or through reading the Book of Mormon, were already struggling with such concepts as temple ordinances and the plurality of wives, if they were aware of the latter doctrine. Sarah Hall Scott, a recent convert from New England, in a letter to her mother in April 1843, had spoken glowingly of the Church in general and specifically the previous April conference which had just concluded the previous week: "We go to meeting near the temple every Sunday. I do love to hear the *Prophet* preach; there was over thirty baptized last Sunday in the river. Joseph baptized quite a number of them; there was about fifteen [hundred] people at the meeting; we have the meetings in a grove near the temple. A great many thousand people attended the conference.

It closed Tuesday last."[33] However, her view changed dramatically over the next year, perhaps at least in part because of the doctrine taught in the King Follett Discourse. She wrote again to her mother in June 1844: "I believe there are hundreds of honest hearted souls in Nauvoo ... [but] Any one needs a throat like an open sepulcher to *swallow down* all that is taught here."[34] In June 1844, dissidents published the only issue of the *Nauvoo Expositor* and singled out the sermon's plurality of Gods as being "one of the most direful in its effects that has characterized the world for many centuries. We know not what to call it other than blasphemy."[35]

Over the more than a century and half since that day in the grove, the principles presented and taught during the funeral sermon for King have become a major and important doctrine of the Church of Jesus Christ of Latter-day Saints. Those doctrines also continue to this day to be controversial throughout the worldwide religious and literary community, whenever Mormon doctrine is discussed. In 1993 Harold Bloom, a twentieth-century literary critic, called the discourse "one of the truly remarkable sermons ever preached in America."[36] In a recent publication centered on revelations of the Restoration, Joseph Fielding McConkie, professor of ancient scripture, and Craig J. Ostler, professor of religion, both at Brigham Young University, when identifying the "vehicles of the restoration," referred to the King Follett Sermon as one of those "inspired utterances ... the greatest discourse ever delivered by the Prophet Joseph Smith." They further explain that "the greatness of the discourse lies in the spirit and power of the doctrines taught."[37] While the doctrines were meant for every Church member then and now, King Follett's name will always be the only one intricately tied to those doctrines. Calvin N. Smith, in a *Church News* article, summarized the connection between the man and the sermon:

> [The sermon] focused on the breathtaking possibilities of man should he prove faithful in mortality. As such, it was a fitting tribute to King Follett who had indeed proved faithful and true to his covenants. In a sense, it was a tribute not only to King Follett as a person, but also to the thousands of saints like him who, then and now, discharge their church responsibilities quietly, bravely and consistently.
>
> The King Follett sermon is not only a timeless tribute to man's kinship with Deity, though that in itself would make it a truly outstanding doctrinal sermon. But studying that great speech in the light of the life of the man who inspired it gives hope to all who, with quiet fortitude and patient

endurance, resolve, as King Follett did, to defend and advance the gospel by good works and excellence of example.[38]

Notes

1. Aroet Lucius Hale, Letter to Ebenezer Beesley, ca. 1897, 2.
2. *History of the Church*, 6:326.
3. Ibid., 6:287-88.
4. *History of the Church*, 6:298–302.
5. Ibid., 6:297.
6. Donald Q. Cannon, "The King Follett Discourse: Joseph Smith's Greatest Sermon in Historical Perspective," 182 and note 16.
7. Ibid., 182.
8. Ibid., note 15.
9. *History of the Church*, 6:297.
10. Keith W. Perkins and Donald Q. Cannon, eds., *Ohio and Illinois*, 169–70, 175.
11. Edward Stevenson, quoted in George Givens and Sylvia Givens, *Nauvoo Fact Book: Questions and Answers for Nauvoo Enthusiasts*, 51.
12. *History of the Church*, 4:423.
13. Ann Pitchforth, undated letter to family in England, quoted in Givens and Givens, *Nauvoo Fact Book*, 51.
14. Mary Westover, quoted in Mark L. McConkie, *Remembering Joseph: Personal Recollections of Those Who Knew the Prophet Joseph Smith*, 117, 452. Mary Westover was born in 1836, moved to Illinois in 1838 and later to Nauvoo, and arrived in Salt Lake in 1847. She was married to Charles Westover.
15. Amasa Potter, quoted in ibid., 130, 444. Potter, a native of Ohio, was baptized in 1847, came to Utah in 1848, served a mission to Australia, worked in the Manti Temple, and was buried in Payson, Utah, in 1911.
16. Cannon, "The King Follett Discourse," 182–84.
17. Stan Larson, "The King Follett Discourse: A Newly Amalgamated Text," 195 note 4. "Conference Minutes," *Times and Seasons* 5, no. 15 (August 15, 1844): 612–17.
18. Larson, "The King Follett Discourse," 195 note 4. See also Jerald F. Simon, "Thomas Bullock as an Early Mormon Historian," 80–81. For the Grimshaw text, see Appendix B; see also *History of the Church*, 6:302–17.
19. Larson, "The King Follett Discourse," 194.
20. *History of the Church*, 6:302–3.

21. Ibid., 6:302.

22. Ibid., 6:306, 310–11.

23. Ibid., 6:315.

24. Clyde J. Williams, comp., *The Teachings of Lorenzo Snow: Fifth President of the Church of Jesus Christ of Latter-day Saints*, 1.

25. For a modern interpretation of the sermon, see Richard Lyman Bushman, *Joseph Smith: Rough Stone Rolling*, 533–37.

26. George Q. Cannon, *Life of Joseph Smith the Prophet*, 479.

27. *History of the Church*, 6:318.

28. Andrew F. Ehat, "'They Might Have Known That He Was Not a Fallen Prophet': The Nauvoo Journal of Joseph Fielding," 148.

29. Hale, Letter to Ebenezer Beesley, 2.

30. Mary C. Westover, quoted in McConkie, *Remembering Joseph*, 117.

31. Cannon, "The King Follett Discourse," 186 note 32.

32. Ibid., 186–87.

33. Sarah Hall Scott, Letter to Abigail Hall, April 13, 1843, quoted in Richard Neitzel Holzapfel and Jeni Broberg Holzapfel, eds., *Women of Nauvoo*, 102–3. Sarah and her sister, Martha Hall Haven, and their husbands arrived in Nauvoo from New England in 1843. Sarah and her husband left Nauvoo and the Church before the end of 1844.

34. Sarah Hall Scott, Letter to Abigail Hall, June 16, 1844, 103.

35. "Preamble," *Nauvoo Expositor* 1 (June 7, 1844): 2.

36. Harold Bloom, *American Religion: The Emergence of the Post-Christian Nation*, 95.

37. Joseph Fielding McConkie and Craig J. Ostler, *Revelations of the Restoration: A Commentary on the Doctrine and Covenants and Other Modern Revelations*, 317, 1078–79. They also list as other "vehicles of the restoration" the Book of Mormon, the Doctrine and Covenants, the Book of Abraham, the Book of Moses and the Joseph Smith Translation of the Bible. For other superlatives applied to this sermon, see Cannon, "The King Follett Discourse," 179; Preston Nibley, *Joseph Smith the Prophet*, 503; George Q. Cannon, *Life of Joseph Smith, the Prophet*, 479; and Joseph Fielding McConkie, "A Historical Examination of the Views of the Church of Jesus Christ of Latter-day Saints and the Reorganized Church of Jesus Christ of Latter Day Saints on Four Distinctive Aspects of the Doctrine of Deity Taught by the Prophet Joseph Smith," 135.

38. Calvin N. Smith, "King Follett: Quiet Fortitude, Prophet Speaks at Funeral," 11.

❊ Chapter Twenty-One ❊

The Death of a Prophet: A Church and a Family Move On

On June 27, 1844, Joseph Smith and his brother Hyrum were murdered in Carthage, the seat of Hancock County, by a mob while the Mormon leaders were under a guarantee of safety given personally by Governor Thomas Ford. It was the beginning of the end for Nauvoo.[1]

Three months before King's death, the *History of the Church* records that New Year's day of 1844 was marked by "a cold, blustering rainstorm."[2] Those descriptive adjectives about the weather might also describe other conditions in Nauvoo, since relationships between members and nonmembers in most of Illinois had not only cooled, but were deteriorating rapidly. Joseph Smith knew that the time had come to seriously consider moving the Church farther west, away from its persecutors. When Nauvoo was first settled, Mormons had anticipated that it would be a safe place until the "Missouri troubles" were settled and they could return to that state. But each year had made it clearer that returning to Missouri en masse was not a possibility. Yet living in Nauvoo as a gathered society was becoming increasingly difficult. Brigham Young later recalled in a public sermon in Utah: "Joseph contemplated the move for years before it took place.... In the days of Joseph we sat many hours at a time conversing about this very country. Joseph said, 'If I were only in the Rocky Mountains with a hundred faithful men, I would then be happy.'"³ In August 1842, the Prophet prophesied:

> that the Saints would continue to suffer much affliction and would be driven to the Rocky Mountains, many would apostatize, others would be put to death by our persecutors or lose their lives in consequence of exposure or disease, and some of you will live to go and assist in making settlements and build cities and see the Saints become a mighty people in the midst of the Rocky Mountains.⁴

Politicians and newspapers throughout the nation were free with suggestions about where the Church should go. Nauvoo's newspaper, the *Times and Seasons*, quoted the *Quincy Whig*'s advice:

> If [Smith] will listen to a word from us, we would advise him to locate his new Jerusalem, away to the far West, in the Oregon country and there to build his temple and govern the Saints in his own way. In that case the advantages would be two-fold: for himself and folness, [sic] for there would be no danger of their molestation in the enjoyment of their peculiar notions in that distant country;—to the Government, the location of himself and followers would be an advantage, because it greatly needs settlers in that region; and doubtless, [the] Government would do something, right handsome for Joseph, in the grant of a gift of lands, &c. if he would guarantee the emigration of any number of settlers.⁵

By January of 1844, however, those discussions and plans became even more important, as issues were reaching a critical point. It was difficult to separate religious from civil issues. Many of the same reasons why the Church members were not accepted in Missouri had also been problems in Nauvoo; some were temporal and some were spiritual. As businessmen in the area surrounding Nauvoo watched the city's economic growth, they appeared to be jealous of Mormon merchants' prosperity, the number of homes being built, and the industry of Church members. Civic leaders and politicians were concerned about the impact that the rising number of Mormons had on voting. Enemies of the Church spread rumors and stories that exaggerated the crime rate until individuals who had never been to the city believed that it was close to being a den of iniquity. Local newspaper editors supplied negative impressions of the Church to a national press eager for sensational stories.⁶ The Church's teachings had always seemed unusual compared to traditional beliefs; but reports of polygamy, credibly circulated by former insiders like John C. Bennett, outraged the national moral sense. Church leaders, including Joseph Smith, repeatedly denied these allegations publicly; but the fact that they *were* engaged in polygamy—facts well known to true insiders—created inner turmoil and confusion even among the faithful. Doctrinal innovations, like those in the King Follett Discourse, only created more questions for nonmembers and proved challenging for members, the number of whom is impossible to determine.

Concerned about the members' safety and by the state and federal government's inability or lack of desire to protect the Saints, the Prophet and other leaders had met on January 29, 1844, about six weeks before King's death, to discuss the upcoming U.S. presidential campaign. The two announced candidates were Martin Van Buren and Henry Clay, neither of whom showed much interest in protecting the Saints' civil liberties. The enthusiastic group of Mormons resolved to "have an independent electoral ticket, and that Joseph Smith be a candidate for the next Presidency; and that we use all honorable means in our power to secure his election." A month later on February 7, Joseph issued his platform: "Views of the Powers and Policy of the Government of the United States."[7] On March 1, the *Times and Seasons* publicly announced the Prophet's candidacy. Many outsiders saw this move as another red flag about the Mormon political threat and "saw only one way to reverse the trend: challenge Joseph Smith's dominant political influence as a threat to American individualism and democracy."[8]

Also in early spring, two groups formed whose activities would have lasting impact on the Church, the Prophet, and the Follett family. The first was a group of nonmembers who brazenly called themselves "the Anti-Mormons." In a "convention" at Carthage on February 17, 1844, they made plans to force the Mormons out of Nauvoo. One of their resolutions was designating March 9 as a day of "fasting and prayer, wherein the pious of all orders are requested to pray to Almighty God that He would speedily bring the false Prophet Joseph Smith to deep repentance, or that He will make a public example of him and his leading accomplices."[9] Probably few Mormons paid any attention. Certainly, the Folletts did not, since it was the day when death ended King's sufferings.

The second group was former Mormons who had been expelled or who had disaffiliated and who, on April 28 formed the Reformed Mormon Church, headed by William Law, a former counselor in Joseph

Smith's First Presidency. As Glen M. Leonard, a specialist in Nauvoo history, explains:

> They repudiated the mingling of Church influence in civic life and pledged support for the repeal of the Nauvoo charter.... The little group of dissenters denounced Smith as a fallen prophet and pledged themselves to accept what they termed the religion of the Latter-day Saints as originally taught by Joseph Smith from the Bible, the Book of Mormon, and the Book of Commandments. This was their way of rejecting the newly revealed temple theology with its ordinances and practices as well as the controversial practice of plural marriage. In response, Joseph Smith labeled his opponents false prophets.[10]

One of their goals was to "publish their views and to 'expose' the secret and abominable teachings of the Mormon hierarchy in an opposition newspaper, to be named *The Nauvoo Expositor*."[11] By May, these dissidents and others began to file criminal complaints and lawsuits against the Prophet in court in Carthage, the county seat, for polygamy, false swearing, and receipt of stolen property. On June 7, a thousand copies of the first (and only) issue of the *Nauvoo Expositor* were published. Offended by the paper, its editor, and its contents, Joseph Smith as mayor met with the Nauvoo City Council; and in a day of lengthy meetings, the council decided to shut the newspaper down. According to Glen Leonard, the council declared the paper a public nuisance, citing "the respected English legal authority Blackstone who held 'that a libelous print or paper, affecting a private individual, may be destroyed.'"[12] Joseph Smith ordered the city marshal to destroy the paper and its press, which, "with a force from the Nauvoo Legion standing by as a backup," he did the same day.[13] Whatever the legal merits of the city's position, the action was widely regarded as an attack on the Constitutional guarantee of a free press.

This action did not dampen the intense feelings on both sides. On June 11, Francis M. Higbee, who had written against the Prophet in the *Nauvoo Expositor*, swore out a "writ before Thomas Morrison, a justice of the peace at Carthage" against Joseph Smith and others "for riot, in destroying the *Nauvoo Expositor* press, the property of William and Wilson Law and others," on the previous day. On June 24, the Prophet and seventeen others, acting on promises of protection by Governor Thomas Ford, went voluntarily to Carthage, the county seat, where Joseph and a varying number of friends were incarcerated in the Carthage Jail to await trial or some other settlement of the issue.[14]

Late in the afternoon of June 27, a large "group of vigilantes from the disbanded Warsaw militia had assembled with others privy to their plans. About two hundred in number, they acted not as militiamen but as independent citizens seeking to settle the Mormon question outside the law."[15] They stormed the jail in disguise, killed Joseph and Hyrum Smith, and severely wounded John Taylor. Willard Richards, the fourth Mormon in the prison at that time, escaped unharmed.

Church members were devastated. The *Times and Seasons* carried a black headline: "Awful assassination of JOSEPH AND HYRUM SMITH! The pledged faith of the State of Illinois stained with innocent blood by a Mob!"[16] Newspapers throughout the United States responded to the news with regret and "editorial dismay," denounced the vigilante action "as a threat to American principles," and rebuked the state of Illinois for lawlessness. Glen M. Leonard, Nauvoo historian, wrote: "Editors bemoaned this trend of spreading lawlessness even more than the singular event in Hancock County. They expressed no liking for Joseph Smith or the Latter-day Saints and some even judged the Prophet worthy of the punishment even while they deplored the way he died.... Within Illinois, some papers justified the mob's actions as the last resort when the law failed to bring Joseph Smith to justice through the courts."[17] Governor Ford acknowledged: "'Most well informed persons condemn in the most unqualified manner the mode in which the Smiths were put to death, ... but nine out of every ten ... [express] their pleasure that they are dead.'"[18] Louisa Follett, who had left Nauvoo on June 5 and was in Parma, Ohio, when she heard about the assassinations, had emotions typical of most of the horrified and bereaved Saints: "A great man has fallen to stain with blood the free born rits of this great republic."[19]

During these first months of 1844 and up to the deaths of the Smith brothers in June, I have found no records giving insight into Follett family activities. Life continued in Nauvoo much as it had for months. New members of the Church continued to arrive in Nauvoo, most of them from Europe. The activities that King would have been involved in just prior to his death were still important to the city and other Church members. Work continued on the temple at an ever-increasing pace. The Seventies Hall was still under construction. The Masonic Hall was dedi-

Nauvoo Masonic Hall, May 1907, George Edward Anderson Collection, LDS Church History Library. Used by permission.

cated on Friday, April 5, just before the Church conference at which the Prophet delivered the King Follett Discourse.

I have also found no information confirming whether Louisa's extended family in New York knew of King's death. However, on June 5, three months after King's death and three weeks before the Smith brothers' murders, she left Nauvoo to visit her family in New York, with a stop in Ohio, accompanied by her youngest son, six-year-old Warren. Her oldest daughter, Adeline, and husband, Nathan West, and perhaps Nathan's two daughters, Maria and Tryphena, also traveled partway with her. Eleven-year-old Edward stayed in Nauvoo, either with one of his older brothers, John or William Alexander, or perhaps with his sister Nancy Daley, who was expecting her second child.

Louisa took a steamboat south to St. Louis. Levi Jackman, King's friend from Missouri, was also on board as one of the scores of Mormon men called on short-term missions to "electioneer" for Joseph Smith's presidential candidacy. He noted: "This season Brother Joseph wanted a large number of Elders to go out on missions, and I concluded to go for one. Accordingly on the fifth of June, I started in company with Bro

Nauvoo Masonic Hall, restored and presently referred to as the Cultural Hall. Photo by Irval L. Mortensen, 2008.

Enoch Burnam. We went aboard a steamer and landed at Fulton. It was the steamboat Riley. The Captain did not charge us anything for our passage. Brother Nathaniel West and his wife, and her mother Sister Follett were on the same boat. They had started for the state of Ohio for a visit."[20]

Louisa Follett kept a diary/journal on this trip—the only personal record known from her, King, or any of their children. It reflects Louisa's personality and gives views about the family and her faith in and support of Mormonism. The fact that she began the diary on the first day of her journey suggested the symbolic importance she attached to this journey, her first as a widow. It obviously marked a significant new stage of her life. Regrettably, she did not continue to keep it throughout her remaining years. It ends one year and three months later on September 7, 1845, when she returned to Nauvoo; even more regrettably, there is a six-month gap between September 17, 1844, and March 9, 1845, and

Photocopy of first pages of Louisa's diary. Courtesy Iowa State Historical Society.

another three-month gap between May 7 and August 19, 1845. In addition to a history of her travels, the journal also contains poetry—some of it obviously her own. (See Appendix C.)

Three days after leaving Nauvoo, the group arrived at St. Louis where they turned east, following the Ohio River through Kentucky and Indiana and on to Cincinnati. The weather was so hot that Adaline fainted and a "gentleman kindely offerd us his state room with two births for our better accomadations" (2). The next few days, they passed landmarks and cities in West Virginia and Pennsylvania. On Sunday, June 16, six-year-old "Warren fell into the river which has greatly anoid my peace through the day" (4). The fact that she was annoyed, rather than frightened, suggests that Warren was skylarking about but, even in the river, was not in serious danger. In an introspective entry, Louisa mused: "I am now fifteen hundred miles from Nauvoo, a stranger in a strange land, without money, and no kind friend that is acquainted with my circumstances, to take an interest in my welfare. The earth to me is a tiresome place and when it will assume a different aspect I cannot tell.

The Death of a Prophet: The Church and a Family Move On

... I longe to rest at my Sisters, where I can clame the kindred ties of natural affection" (5). This sister was fifty-five-year-old Nancy Tanner Burnham. She and her husband, Isaac, appear on the 1840 U.S. Census in Parma, Ohio. Their daughter Louisa, named for her aunt (as Louisa had named her own daughter Nancy for this sister), would have been about twenty-nine at the time of this visit.

The next day, June 17, at Beaver, Pennsylvania, Louisa, Warren, Adeline, and Nathan transferred from the steamboat to a canal boat to travel to Cleveland. On June 21, she wrote: "We are now in sight of the County Seat of Portage, where I have often wandered in gone by days. It reminds of endearing associations then formed but long since broken off. To a sensative mind that is formed to aprecite joys and sorrows, there is much to ocupi the mind" (6–7).

The Portage County seat, Ravenna, is just six miles south of Shalersville, where the Follett family lived from 1819 to 1832. After more than two weeks of travel, they reached the home of Louisa's sister, Nancy, in Parma, Ohio, on June 22 for a protracted stay. "To my great joy and satisfaction found them all well and glad to see me"(8). Despite the pleasure of being with her older sister, Louisa obviously felt lonely being away from other Church members, for on July 9, she "was agreeable surprisd by the arrival of Bro Sylvester Hulit, as he was on a visit in the neighborhood to visit some relitives. While we conversd we [w]itness'd strong proofs of setarian blindness—When O when will the veil be rent and the hearts of this gentile generation become subject to the power of inspiration" (9). The Folletts and Hulets had been close friends in Missouri where they were both in the Hulet LDS Branch in Clay County.

On July 14, she was alarmed to read in a Cleveland newspaper a report of the Smith brothers' murders. Her first reaction was disbelief. "As yet, I cannot give much credit to the report but wait for better authenticated reports" (9). However, a week later on a Sunday afternoon, with obvious distress, she received a report that she had to accept:

> I have just recievd and read a Nauvoo Nieghbor containing the mournful but authenticated entelegence of the Death of the Prophet and his brother. The helish design has atlength ben purpretrated and a great man has fallen to stain with blood the free born rits of this great republic.— Alass my heart bleeds at the remberances of those sceanes that have spred devastation, desolation and death over our once happy land. Where will

those scenes of mabicatic violenc end? My hart trembles at the coming events—although I am not presant as on every ocasion preceding this, yet I feel a deepe sympathy in all the afflicttions of my friends at Nauvoo.

Her overwrought feelings groped for expression, and she burst out with imprecations that took the form of poetry:[21] "Oh wretched murders! For human blood you've slain the Prophets of the living God

> who've borne oppression from there erly youth.
> To plant, on earth, the principles of truth
> Oh Illinos thy soul has drank the blood
> Of Prophets marterd for the Cause of God
> Now Zion mourns—she mourns an earthly head
> The Prophet and the Patriarch are dead. (9–10)

Louisa stayed at her sister's for thirty-one days, but I cannot document where Adeline and Nathan and her son Warren were during this time. She left there the morning of August 21, "accompaned by my Bro. in-law and sister" to travel to Cleveland on the *Constitution*, a canal boat, to Buffalo, New York. The next day, she traveled by train to Attica Village, where she hired a buggy to take her to the home of her brother Joseph in Attica Center. Because she uses the word "I" all through this entry, I believe that she boarded the canal boat and traveled alone to Buffalo. Together she, Joseph, and his wife, Florilla, visited their brother William also in Attica Center, where she met her "aged Father once more and realized all that pleasure that I had anticipated after a long and painful abscene" (10). If this was the first time she had visited her family since moving to Shalersville by 1819, the "painful" absence she mentions would have been about twenty-five years. In that time, she had borne eight children, buried three of them, and lost her husband. Her mother and brother Thomas Warren had also died, and she visited their graves in Attica Center. Though she was "tenderly treated" by her father, brother, and family, she still felt the sting of bereavement, writing that she was "sorounded with much to outward appearance calculated to produce happiness; but Oh! Thear is a vacuum within that remains unsatisfied which outward apperances cannot satisfy" (11). Louisa's three brothers had moved to Attica Center about the same time that King and Louisa had moved to Ohio. Louisa's parents had joined her brothers later.

On September 17, she and her seventy-nine-year-old father set out for St. Lawrence County, New York, to visit more relatives. (I still cannot determine where Adeline, Nathan, and Warren were at this point.) She and her father probably first traveled by train to Rochester, then by steamer to Ogdensburgh, and finally by stage to Hermon, where she and King had been married in 1816. Poignantly, she wrote:

> I am now where my eyes meet the wandering gaze of meny that I have known in gone by days.... From the place where I now write, I can look and behold the Parental dwelling where I once had a home, where I was once greeted by the fond and affecttionate imbrace of a Kind Father and Mother Brothers and Sisters, but now how strangly altered.... It was the place of my youthful days, the morning of my life.... Again I pass the Cottage where I begun first to preform the duties of a wife and Mother Stop and look towards that once loved place, but no kind Husband meets my fond imbrace he that used to share my joys and sorrow is no more. The kind hand that was even open to admnenster to my wants is now cold in Death and with my little orphin Boy I am a wandrer alone and unprotected.(12)

She also used her diary as a sort of account book, recording these transactions under the heading:

> Credit to Zenah Tanner:
> To two Pounds of butter
> To two of Shugar
> To two of Honey
> To one quarter of Tea
> To making two Pair of Shoes
>
> Credit to Gorge Ellis:
> One bushel of buck wheat
> To one Dollar twenty five Cents (14)

I believe that Zenah Tanner is a relative, though I have not been able to identify the relationship. She also used this part of her diary to record several pages of melancholy prose and poetry.

At this time, she had been gone from Nauvoo nine months. It was her last entry for six months; and during that time, her activities and even her location cannot be traced with great accuracy though I believe she stayed in the St. Lawrence County area, either in DeKalb or Hermon.

In the next entry dated DeKalb, March 9, 1845, the one-year anniversary of King's death, Louisa records her reflections about that event and her feelings:

> How solom is the reflections of my mind to day, as I sit pensive and alone, while memory calls up those scenes that transpired one year ago. It is the aniversary of that painful season when I commited to the colde and silent grave, the companion of my youthful days. The painful and trying event comes fliting back on my memory, with a redoubled sensation. Oh! How my heart mourns afresh, when I feel that I am left alone and unprotected to endure the winds of adversity in a colde and unfeeling world—Great God, thou who hast hitherto ben my helper in times of trouble and deepe distress, do not I intreate the[e] abandon me in this hour of tribulation Oh! Strengthen my heart and flesh that I murmer and faint not; but help me to acknowledge thy hand and kiss the rod and him who hath appointed it—Strengthen me for every event or thy providanc that doth yet awaite me and hasten the time when I shall praise the[e] in more exalted strains. (19)

On March 31 she records news from Nauvoo that two of "my much loved and valued friends" had died. "James Daily, very muched loved and worthy Sone-in-law is gone the way of all the Earth he rests from all the turmoils and suffering of this world of pain and anxiety, and while my tears flow on account of his suden removal, his freed spirit has gone to greet the numerous company that had gaind the port before him—He has left a weepeing Companion and two little Boys to mourn, how I wish to be where I can see Nancy, and afford her a Mothers sympathies" (20). She does not give James's death date but it was before December 1844. (See Chapter 17.) There is no record of James Daley's death in the extant sexton records of Nauvoo. The second death Louisa mentions was: "I Barkdoll [sic] a youth of eightteen" who was "lovely in life and happy in Death therefore I will not sorrow as those that have no hope, thank God he rests from opression—" (20). The sexton records have this entry: "Isah Barkdoll," death date as January 9, 1845, "19 years, 11 months 3 days old," cause of death "fever."[22]

The next month on April 21, as Louisa was planning her return to Nauvoo, she stayed with Seth Alexander, King's half-brother, in DeKalb. She left there by stage, went to Ogdensburgh where she took passage on the *Lady of the Lake* for Rochester, and spent ten days in Attica with her father and friends. Her father accompanied her to Buffalo where she boarded the *General Harrison* for Cleveland, then went by carriage to Nancy's in Parma, where she spent the late spring and summer. Here she penned these words of meditation on May 13, 1845:

I feel a greatful sense of gratitude swell my bosom while I remember that I have ben mercifully preserved while alone and unprotected I have traveled the distance of five hundred miles by land and water, and now contrary to my expecttations when I reached here, I shall be under the nesessety of spending the summer in Parma, notwithstanding the disappointment I feel to acknowledge the hand of the Lord in it and feel vary happy in the family of my Sister that treat me with every feeling of tenderness and respect, as allso my Son in-law with whome I reside a part of the time. (21)

The son-in-law would have been Nathan West and her daughter Adeline (and probably Nathan's two daughters), although Louisa does not record where exactly the family was living or what Nathan was doing to earn a living in or near Parma. This entry would indicate that the West family arrived in Parma when Louisa did but stayed there while she visited her family in New York. I still am not able to determine if Warren was with his mother or with his aunt and uncle.

The entries between May 13 and the middle of August when she left Parma for Nauvoo, again contain poetry, some of it copied from other sources, and miscellaneous entries.

On Louisa's return journey to Nauvoo, she retraced her route from Parma to St. Louis. She was obviously lonely and downhearted and does not mention Nathan and Adeline. It seems that she was traveling alone with little Warren and was concerned about money. When she arrived in Cincinnati on August 24th, she spent two dollars a piece to purchase passage for her and her son, then "went on board with a heavy heart prayin the Lord to send me some simpathising friend that would take an interest in our wellfair, I did not wait long for the desired blessing, I soon found a family of Mormons bound for Nauvoo with whome I became acquainted who kindly renderd us the assistance we kneeded" (27–28). In her last entry, dated Sunday, September 7, she talks about her longing to see the "City of the Saints and meet the warm embrace of my Children and friends" and to once more meet "in the assembly of the Saints." At 10 o'clock that morning, "we safely landed at the Stone House where we meet with a most cordial welcom from our friends and relitive[s] in Nauvoo" (30–31).

She quickly went to her "former place of residence," presumably the home King had built, then her son John took her to the temple where she "vewd with wonder and amazement the magnificenc of that butiful Structture." She did not stay in King's house—which may have been rented or perhaps had even been sold—but went to the home of her daughter Nancy, on Young Street, who had been widowed the year before and had married Henry Sanford. In a few days "we" (presumably Louisa, Warren, and possibly Edward) moved to the "Lower Stone House" (31)—the building owned by James White on the site of the "Montrose Crossing, or steamboat landing" that was probably serving as a hotel or boarding house.[23]

Her diary ends on an emotional note: "Allthough my health is much impaired yet when I take a retrospective vew of the past, I fee[l] that I have abundant reson to bless God, that amidst the danger to which I have ben exposd that I have ben mercifully preserved and brought to join my afflictted family and Bretheren in Nauvoo" (31). Louisa's fifteen-month absence had been a time of turmoil and change, not only for her personally but for the city and its people. She must have hoped for repose but instead found preparations underway for the Church members to move once again.

In her absence, various claimants to replace Joseph Smith as Church President, like Sidney Rigdon, James J. Strang, and others, had appealed to the Saints for their allegiance; but it was Brigham Young, president of the Quorum of the Twelve, who had articulated the vision of Joseph and carried it out with unwavering purpose. Even as he accepted the necessity of moving the Saints out of Illinois, he held before them the two greatest achievements of Joseph's last years: publicly the completion of the temple, and privately the continuation and even great expansion of plural marriage. Most of the Twelve shared this vision, in part because Joseph's extension of the endowment and ordinance of second anointing, even before the completion of the temple, made his vision real. The Quorum of the Twelve with Brigham at its head led the Church from August 9, 1844, to December 5, 1847, when the First Presidency was reorganized at Kanesville, Iowa. By October 8, 1848, the new organization "had been . . . unanimously sustained by all the major divisions of the church."[24]

If Louisa had continued her diary during these tumultuous months, a clearer picture would have formed of how the Follett family made the decisions that it did. It is easy, in retrospect, to see that accepting Brigham Young's leadership involved a full commitment to travel to the new Zion in Utah, and perhaps a secondary commitment to the possibility of plural marriage, but such an assumption was much less automatic for the Saints between 1844 and 1847, as Louisa's own history shows. What is clear, however, is that they remained committed to Joseph Smith and Mormonism, although they understood it in different ways.

The unity of the Saints and their continued presence in Nauvoo kept concerns high about the Mormons' political power. In December 1844, the state legislature amended the Nauvoo charter and cancelled it altogether the next month. The Twelve responded by organizing a government that used the existing ecclesiastical structure to also serve as a town government. They renamed Nauvoo the "City of Joseph" in tribute to their fallen prophet. The name was later changed to the "Town of Nauvoo" and, with Governor Thomas Ford's assistance, again became a civil unit under Illinois law. However, the ecclesiastical government was the reality, and the civil government was the shadow. As Glen Leonard describes it, "Nauvoo's need for basic civil government—maintenance of a peaceful society through simple regulations, police protection, and a judicial system under a town government . . . had been resolved, and the system worked because of a consensus within the community."[25] The repeal of the charter meant that the organization to which King had devoted so much of his time—the Nauvoo Legion—no longer had the same legal power as an organization, though it was not officially disbanded. Brigham Young took the place of the Prophet as the military unit's leader and it "continued important both as an instrument of internal social control and as a potential means of defense."[26]

Instead of people leaving Nauvoo, "the state census of 1845 showed Hancock to be the most populous county in the state with 22,559 inhabitants, and Nauvoo the largest city with a population of 11,036.[27] The religious life of the community continued with Sunday meetings, general conferences, and quorum meetings. New branches, wards, and stakes were organized, and the leaders provided instruction on Church doctrine. The Seventies Building, which had been started prior to King's death, was dedicated on December 26–30, 1844, and was immediately pressed into service for a variety of Church and civic meetings in addition to those of the Seventies' quorums.

The major focus of construction, however, was the temple—the centerpiece of Joseph's city and also of the new ordinances he was establishing at the time of his death. For two months after his death, work had halted; but by August 24 the Twelve and the Temple Committee again stressed the urgency of finishing the building as soon as possible; and this emphasis provided a telling reminder to all that they were carrying on Joseph's work. It almost certainly provided reassurance to many confused members that the Prophet's death did not also mean the end of Mormonism.

Work continued during the winter of 1844–45, with a call being made in December for fifteen carpenters to work on the interior.[28] King's son, John, was not one of the fifteen named; but according to Temple Building Committee Records, he worked 8.5 days between December 12 and 28, 1844, including Christmas day, and 6.25 days between January 1 and 31, 1845.[29] On January 14, 1845, the Twelve announced in the *Times and Seasons*:

> Great numbers of carpenters, masons, and other workmen are daily engaged in this arduous undertaking, so that not only is stone being prepared, but the sash, flooring, seats, and other things are progressing rapidly; and it is our design, if possible, so to rush the work forward that the building will been closed, and certain portions of it in that state of forwardness, so next fall; that the elders of Israel may be prepared by the power and spirit of the great Jehovah, to fulfill with dignity and honor, the great work [the endowment] devolving upon them to perform.[30]

Two months later on March 15, a decision was made "to put all our help on the Temple," and Brigham Young announced the next day "the temporary halt of many activities, including missionary work."[31] The capstone was laid May 24, 1845. By the time Louisa returned to Nauvoo in September 1845, the temple was almost complete.

During her absence, her daughter Nancy and her husband, James Daley, had a second son, named James Marion, closely followed by the father's death. Though James Marion's birth year is given in later census records and in his obituary as December 18, 1845,[32] he must have been born in 1844, since Louisa, upon learning in March 1845 of her son-in-law's death, lamented in her diary that "He [James] has left a weepeing Companion and two little Boys to mourn."[33] Further, the Seventies' records show that James Daley died in or prior to December of 1844. (See Chapter 18.) And finally, Nancy Follett Daley married Henry Sanford, on November 17, 1845.[34] This marriage date would further help support a birth date for Nancy's second son by James Daley prior to this second marriage. A third family event, which occurred shortly after Louisa's return to Nauvoo, was the marriage of her son, William Alexander Follett, on September 29, 1845, to Nancy Mariah Fausett.[35]

Although extant records do not identify any other Follett family activities, they undoubtedly were involved in the many Church and community events that made up the city's life. The need for industry was as intense as it had ever been. To promote stability, Church leaders encouraged members to act as though their presence in Nauvoo was permanent. Crops were planted and harvested, new homes were constructed, and businesses were developed. The Church also focused on home industries and trade associations to provide for the poor and accumulate a surplus of goods against being forced to leave Nauvoo. Despite their natural mistrust of nonmembers, President Young encouraged them in April 1845 to "learn to suffer wrong rather than do wrong, and by so doing we will outstrip all our enemies and conquer the evil one. . . . Peace reigns among this people which is Zion. Union and true charity dwells with this people."[36]

During the months following the murders of the Smith brothers, an uneasy peace existed between Church members and nonmembers around Nauvoo. But early in 1845, state officials warned Church leaders to leave Nauvoo or face continual harassment and perhaps open attacks. Governor Ford advised: "It would be good policy for your people to move to some far distant country. Your religion is new and it surprises the people as any great novelty in religion generally does. They cannot rise above the prejudices excited by such novelty. . . . If you can get off by yourselves you may enjoy peace; but surrounded by such neighbors I confess that I do not foresee the time when you will be permitted to enjoy quiet."[37]

Mob activity began again in outlying settlements during the summer of 1845, and citizens of Nauvoo were constantly alert to the presence of strangers who might also be enemies. Mosiah Lyman Hancock, who was eleven years old in the summer of 1845, recalled that these strangers, whom he called "fop[s]" or "dude[s]" "would come into town, sit on a shingle pile and whittle and whistle."[38] As a method of encouraging these strangers to leave town quickly, Howard Coray and others "organized the men and boys, who had no occupation, into a group known as the Whittling Deacons."[39] Its members would surround the strangers and begin whistling and whittling themselves. Hancock said he joined the "whistling and whittling band" made up of Nauvoo citizens. "We kept a 'good watch' made these (strangers) 'cross the great River' by whistling and whittling them."[40] He also recalled: "We boys formed a company called the 'Sons of Heleman [sic].' . . . I was second Lieutenant, and we drilled quite a lot."[41] William Byram Pace, who was thirteen years old in the summer of 1845, remembered: "All the boys from eight years and up, not capable of bearing arms, were organized into what was called Boy Companies to learn drill and discipline. Then they were attached to the Nauvoo Legion as reserves. This was no paper hat play, but sober reality. The companies were invariably uniformed with white pants, a kind of blouse or sailor shirt, a sailor hat and wooden guns."[42] Perhaps Edward, who would have been eleven or twelve in 1845, and perhaps even Warren, age six or seven, would have participated in these groups. If so, they were following their father's example in helping protect their family and other Church members.

Louisa must have been concerned that fall with the resurgence of vigilante actions against Church settlements surrounding Nauvoo. Hostile groups of armed men burned homes and haystacks, destroyed possessions, and ran off the livestock. Church leaders encouraged these Saints to move into Nauvoo for protection, where they were taken in by other families. Although it is not clear where Louisa and little Warren took up their residence, their extended family may have been among those providing hospitality to refugee Saints. Charles Brent Hancock, whose family lived in the Morley Settlement, was one of those who quickly came to Nauvoo: "The brethren sent their teams to help us, and the mob kept on a burning houses, barns, fences, and everything that would burn as they marched in double file as soldiers. . . . They number[ed] from about fifty to sixty and wore the worst clothes and hats that I have ever seen men wear, and they were blacked and lived like Indians as they took from the houses that they were burning for living and subsistence, and burned what they could not 'carry away' and destroy."[43]

Church leaders initially believed that withdrawing the Mormons from the area outside Nauvoo would reduce some of the anti-Mormon feelings throughout the area. This plan, however, did not work, probably because the non-Mormons interpreted the emphasis on completing the temple as a signal that the Church intended to stay. Although Governor Ford made some effort to reduce violence against the Saints by the use of the state militia, the general hostility meant that the militia was less diligent than it needed to be. Finally in early October, Brigham Young and other leaders agreed that its members would not plant winter crops and would leave the following spring.[44] During the first general conference held in the nearly completed temple (October 4–6, 1845), Church leaders presented the plan to leave to more than "4,000 persons present within the walls of the [Nauvoo] temple and a large concourse of people without."[45]

The Twelve and Council of Fifty had discussed such plans and made initial preparations, but this conference was the first introduction of this move to the entire membership. Undoubtedly Louisa and her children attended this historic conference or quickly learned the details of the announcement. They were no strangers to such moves; but unlike Missouri, it appeared that they had some time to acquire draft animals and wagons, prepare foodstuffs, and sell what they must leave behind—although, in a buyer's market, they must have realized that they might be called on simply to abandon their possessions. Again, it was a time of stress and testing. Some Church members were too traumatized to face yet another departure. Others were disoriented by the fact that Church leaders announced no clear final destination except "west." Furthermore, the Saints had proved their faith by their unremitting efforts to finish the temple; was God really requiring them to leave it?

By December 1845, the rooms in the top floor of the temple were ready to be used for the endowment ceremony. On December 10 the first ordinances were held and continued until February 1846. According to historian Robert B. Flanders, "Only those who could produce vouchers that their tithe had been paid in full were to be admitted."[46] Apparently the endowments were given by appointment and "these appointments usually came from the Twelve."[47] The records show that Louisa, her adult sons, daughters, and their spouses were some of the more than five thousand Church members who received their endowments. Temple sessions were held every day except Sunday, beginning early in the morning and ending late at night.

The Nauvoo Temple Endowment Register recorded the following Follett family members and their endowment data:

> Follet, John W.—no record of Washing and Anointing; Endowment 7 Feb 1846 Third Company[48]

Follet, Louisa—Washing and Anointing and Endowment 12 Jan 1846 Second Company[49]

Follet, William A. and his wife Nancy Maria Fossett Follet—Washing and Anointing and Endowment 28 Jan 1846, First Company[50]

Sanford, Nancy M. Follett and her husband Henry Sanford—For Nancy Washing and Anointing and Endowment 7 Feb 1846; for Henry no record for Washing and Anointing, Endowment 7 Feb 1846, both Fifth Company[51]

West, Adaline L. Follett and her husband Nathan A. West—Washing and Anointing and Endowment 8 Jan 1846, Third Company[52]

In addition to endowments, "2,420 living couples were sealed to each other in the Nauvoo Temple, and 369 deceased spouses were sealed to living companions."[53] On January 15, 1846, Heber C. Kimball sealed Nathan Ayers West for time and eternity to three women: Mary Smith Hulet, Adaline Louisa Follett, and Louisa "Turner." A footnote in the published record gives this woman's birthdate, thus identifying her as Louisa Tanner.[54] The original sealing record confirms that Nathan Ayers West was sealed to all three women on January 15, 1846, at 1 P.M., with the witness for Mary Smith Hulet being Amasa M. Lyman and for the other two women being John D. Lee.[55]

Why Louisa would have been sealed to her son-in-law rather than her husband is difficult to understand. Some living individuals were being sealed at that same time to deceased spouses, so Louisa could have been sealed to King; but if she was, no record of it has survived. Perhaps the source is incomplete and she was sealed to King but his name was accidentally omitted. In another, possibly analogous case, one Mormon widow, Elizabeth Kirby, "worried that she 'could not obtain her blessings as she was,' since she had not been married 'for time and eternity' to her first husband, so she decided that 'the best thing she could do' was to marry her husband's hired hand, John Heward, who had come to Nauvoo from their native Canada to assist her after her husband died."[56]

This type of a marriage sealing was done to provide eternal blessings and also spiritual support for the trek westward. It did not mean that those who were so sealed would necessarily live together as husband and wife. Indeed, there is no indication in any known record that Nathan West ever recognized Louisa as a plural wife or that she was ever listed as such. In fact, this record of temple sealings is the only place such a sealing is ever recorded. No earlier family researcher has apparently no-

Nauvoo Temple ca. 1845, no photographer identified. Used by permission of LDS Church History Library.

ticed it, nor has that information ever been carried forward in Follett family records. In fact, this marriage is presently a disputed relationship in the LDS Church's new FamilySearch records.

These sealings in Nauvoo fulfilled Joseph Smith's promises of celestial marriage, taught to the Saints before his death. The faithful Saints also firmly believed that their participation in the temple ordinances would provide them with the strength they needed to face a very uncertain future. As Joseph Holbrook wrote after receiving his endowments: "I felt greatly blessed for the opportunity of receiving the little I did for it gave me keys of knowledge for me to improve upon until I could get more."[57] Newel Knight recorded in his diary on January 31, 1846, "My soul has been filled with the love of God. I feel his spirit burning within me day by day. The blessings I have received this winter, have doubly repaid me for all I have done towards building this house."[58]

Though King did not live to participate in the ceremonies in the Nauvoo Temple, there remains to this day an interesting connection between him and that temple. A well was dug in the basement of the original Nauvoo Temple to provide water for the baptismal font. Forty years later in 1886, when Apostle Franklin D. Richards visited Nauvoo from Salt Lake, he saw that the well was still functioning and that animals were being watered from it. He "drank from it and found the water clear and delicious to the taste."[59] In 1909, John Zimmerman Brown, a

Reconstructed Nauvoo Temple. Photo by Irval L. Mortensen, 2008.

professor at the University of Utah, reported after visiting Nauvoo: "All that is now left of the sacred edifice is the old well that supplied water for the baptismal font. Not a single stone of the building is left in place. This well, which was in the east end of the basement, is now equipped with a pump and is used for culinary purposes."[60]

Almost sixty years later in 1968, the Church planned to rebuild part of the temple on the original site. This structure would have been a visitors' center and would have contained a restored or rebuilt temple well. This plan was never realized.[61] In 1999, Church President Gordon B. Hinckley announced that the Church planned to build a fully functional temple in Nauvoo for sacred ordinances using the original temple's "footprint." That temple was dedicated in 2002. During the construction, the bricks from the original temple's well were excavated and used to build a well on Lot 26—the land King had owned.[62]

Though no signage identifies it as such, this small monument is a fitting modern tribute to King Follett—a stalwart early Church member

View of well constructed with brick from the original temple well on King's land in Nauvoo. Photo by Irval L. Mortensen, 2008.

Close-up of well with a wooden bucket presently on King's land in Nauvoo. Photo by Irval L. Mortensen, 2008.

who remained steadfast in his testimony from his conversion in 1831 until his unexpected death in 1844. His efforts and determination assisted Church leaders and members in setting the foundation of the Restoration from which the Church of Jesus Christ of Latter-day Saints has developed into the worldwide organization it has now become.

Notes

1. Robert Bruce Flanders, *Nauvoo: Kingdom on the Mississippi*, 306.
2. *History of the Church*, 6:155.
3. Brigham Young quoted in Milton V. Backman, Jr., *The People and Power of Nauvoo*, 134.
4. *History of the Church*, 5:85. See Backman, *The People and Power of Nauvoo*, 134–36.
5. *Quincy Whig*, September 24, 1842, quoted as "To the Editor of the Times and Seasons. Cold Comfort," *Times and Seasons* 24, no. 3 (October 15, 1842): 953.
6. George W. Givens, *In Old Nauvoo: Everyday Life in the City of Joseph*, 104–5.
7. *History of the Church*, 6:188, 197–209.
8. Glen M. Leonard, *Nauvoo: A Place of Peace, a People of Promise*, 304.
9. *History of the Church*, 6:221.
10. Leonard, *Nauvoo*, 360.
11. Flanders, *Nauvoo*, 308.
12. Leonard, *Nauvoo*, 364.
13. Ibid., 365.
14. *History of the Church*, 553–54.
15. Leonard, *Nauvoo*, 393.
16. "Awful Assassination of JOSEPH AND HYRUM SMITH! The pledged faith of the state of Illinois stained with innocent blood by a Mob!" *Times and Seasons* 5, no. 12 (July 1, 1844): 1.
17. Leonard, *Nauvoo*, 404–5.
18. Ford, Letter to W. W. Phelps, July 22, 1844, quoted in ibid.
19. Louisa Tanner Follett, Diary, July 21, 1844, 9. In November 1997 I obtained a photocopy of the holograph and a typescript dated July 1979 from the files of the Iowa State Historical Society (ISHS), along with two letters from Gertrude Follett Colby, Beaumont, Texas, a great-granddaughter of King and Louisa. In her first letter dated September 1, 1977, Gertrude requested

that the original of the diary be returned to her after she had loaned it for filming. She wrote that the original "was in a lock box around my home many years—though somewhere it was certainly nearly destroyed." In her second letter, dated September 21, she acknowledged the return of the diary and stated: "It is a shame the original has been so abused in the many years. But guess we are lucky to have the part of her [Louisa's] journey. I had not thought of what I might do with the diary. Never dreamed anyone would be interested in publishing it or even be interested at all, except family. . . . For the present, the little diary will go back in the lock box where it has been since 1910." I have not been able to locate anyone who knows about the "lock box" or what may have happened to the diary. The original diary was not paginated; some of the entries as dated by Louisa appear to be out of chronological order. I cite herein the page numbers assigned by the ISHS copying process, have retained original spelling and have added terminal punctuation and initial capitals to quotations from the diary where needed. Though Gertrude Colby, ISHS, and the card catalog of the LDS Church History, which has a copy of the ISHS typescript, use the title "diary," Louisa describes it as a "journal." It is divided into four Sections: Section 1 ("Louisa Follett Journal from Nauvoo to Ohio," June 5–21, 1844), Section 2 (ca. June 22–September 17, 1844), Section 3 ("Louisa Follett, Linden, Missouri," March 9–May 7, 1845); and Section 4 ("Journal from Parma Ohio to Nauvoo," August 9–September 8, 1845). Louisa and some of her family may have settled for a time in Linden after leaving Nauvoo in 1846–47. See Appendix C for a typescript of the holograph which I prepared in March 2011.

20. Levi Jackman, "Diary, 1835 May–1844 July," June 5, 1844, 21. Although catalogued as a diary, this section is more accurately a memoir.

21. For a discussion of the poetic impulse to communicate grief and distress at the murders, with many additional examples both published and unpublished, see Davis Bitton, *Millions Shall Know Brother Joseph Again: Perceptions and Perspectives*, Chapter 9, "The Saints Mourn: Martyrdom Poetry."

22. Nauvoo (Ill.), Sexton Cemetery records, unpaginated. It is possible Isah was a good friend of Louisa's son, William Alexander, who was the same age.

23. Keith W. Perkins and Donald Q. Cannon, eds., *Ohio and Illinois*, 117; Carol Cornwall Madsen, *In Their Own Words: Women and the Story of Nauvoo*, 15.

24. *History of the Church*, 7:246.

25. Leonard, *Nauvoo*, 472–73.

26. Flanders, *Nauvoo*, 325.

27. Ibid., 321–22.

28. Matthew S. McBride, *A House for the Most High: The Story of the Original Nauvoo Temple*, 189.

29. Nauvoo Temple Building Committee, Carpenter Time Book C, 14.

30. "An Epistle of the Twelve to the Church of Jesus Christ of Latter-day Saints in All the World," *Times and Seasons* 6, no. 1 (January 15, 1845): 779.

31. McBride, *A House for the Most High*, 195.

32. "James M. Daley Pioneer Dies," *Contra Costa [California] Gazetteer*, July 28, 1923.

33. Follett, Diary, March 31, 1845, 20.

34. Dorris Lawton, comp., *Marriage Index, Hancock County, Illinois*, 40. The license is numbered #1025 but gives no officiator. Henry Sanford was born July 4, 1818, in New York, the son of Fran Sanford. He was baptized on August 27, 1844, and was ordained a Seventy in Nauvoo. See Sanford, Henry, on "Early Latter-day Saints Database."

35. Nancy Mariah Fausett was born in Maury, Tennessee, in 1827, the daughter of William McKee Fausett and Matilda Carolina Butcher Fausett. The family was in Macoupin County, Illinois, by 1835 and joined the Mormon Church there about 1837. This information is taken from family records in my possession, LDS Ancestral File, and International Genealogy Index records. The family name is also spelled as Fossett and Fawcett.

36. Brigham Young, quoted in Leonard, *Nauvoo*, 474.

37. "Letter of Governor Ford on the Organization of Town Government within Nauvoo," to General Brigham Young, Springfield, April 8, 1845, in *History of the Church*, 7:397–98.

38. Mosiah Lyman Hancock, "Autobiography," n.d., 26.

39. Ida Blum, *Nauvoo: Gateway to the West*, 35.

40. Mosiah Lyman Hancock, "Autobiography," 26.

41. Ibid., 25. "Sons of Heleman" (sic) is an allusion to a group in the Book of Mormon (Alma 53–57).

42. William Byram Pace, Autobiography, 2.

43. Charles Brent Hancock, Autobiography, 28.

44. *History of the Church*, 7:449.

45. Hosea Stout, Diary, October 6, 1845, 2:70.

46. Flanders, *Nauvoo*, 335.

47. McBride, *A House for the Most High*, 271.

48. Nauvoo Temple Endowment Register, December 10, 1845–February 8, 1846, 329.

49. Ibid., 141.

50. Ibid., 211.

51. Ibid., 338.

52. Ibid., 123.

53. Richard O. Cowan, quoted in McBride, *A Temple of the Most High*, 293.

54. Lisle G Brown, comp., *Nauvoo Sealings, Adoptions, and Anointings: A Comprehensive Register of Persons Receiving LDS Temple Ordinances, 1841–*

1846, 102, 328. See also Lyndon W. Cook, *Nauvoo Marriages, Proxy Sealings, 1843–1846*, 68. Neither source provides sealing information for Nancy M. Follett and her husband, Henry Sanford, or William Alexander Follett, and his wife, Nancy Mariah Fausett.

55. "Sealings in the Temple at Nauvoo, Hancock County, Illinois," 1841–1846, 545.

56. Elizabeth Kirby, quoted in Madsen, *In Their Own Words*, 34 note 66.

57. Joseph Holbrook, *History of Joseph Holbrook, 1806–1885: Written by His Own Hand*, 35.

58. Newel Knight, quoted in William G. Hartley, *Stand by My Servant Joseph: The Story of the Joseph Knight Family and the Restoration*, 369–70.

59. Franklin D. Richards, quoted in McBride, *A House for the Most High*, 367–68.

60. John Zimmerman Brown, quoted in ibid., 368.

61. Jay M. Todd, "Nauvoo Temple Restoration," 11.

62. Tour guide's comments during my personal visit to Nauvoo for the temple dedication in June 2002; notes in my possession. The well as it now stands is not necessarily a replica of King's intended well nor is it necessarily located where he was digging the well when he died. In fact because of possible road changes, it may actually be near but not on King's land.

❊ Chapter Twenty-Two ❊

King's Family after Nauvoo: From 1846 Onward

"For Nauvoo, it was not the 'enduring stone' but rather the 'keeping of the spiritual' which lasted."[1] Just a few months after Louisa Follett returned to Nauvoo in September 1845, she and her family moved rather hurriedly once again—this time west across the Mississippi River into Iowa. The arrangement that Church leaders had negotiated with their hostile neighbors and state government officials would have allowed the Mormons to winter in Nauvoo, finish the temple, conduct the all-important ordinances there, and prepare for their trip west. However, conditions in the town deteriorated so sharply that it was no longer comfortable or safe for the Saints to remain. Church leaders made the decision that the members should begin moving across the river before the appointed time, perhaps thus surprising their enemies who might have been planning to cause more problems. The Church faced the rumored threat that martial law might be declared with state militia being sent into the city.

By the end of January 1846, Brigham Young and other leaders knew that they had to leave as soon as possible. On February 4, 1846, the crossing of the Mississippi began. The group's first stop was at Sugar Creek just west of the river, in Lee County, Iowa, where a number of Mormons already lived, some of whom joined the Nauvoo group on their westward journey. Sugar Creek became the staging ground for members leaving the Nauvoo area as they began the long and mud-choked journey across Iowa.

Church leaders worked with those left in Nauvoo to insure that they could move all who needed to leave at that time. Many members lacked the money to buy necessary supplies and equipment. Contributions were gathered from those better off to help the poverty stricken. According to Nauvoo historian Glen M. Leonard, "Widows with limited means qualified for help."[2] Louisa Follett may have been one of these widows, or she, eight-year-old Warren, and thirteen-year-old Edward, may have traveled with her adult children. During February, those left behind in Nauvoo continued work on the temple building itself, while others worked to provide the opportunity for more members to complete endowments and sealings in the edifice. "From early January until the final company left the temple on February 7, endowment groups received the ordinances six days a week, with sessions underway some days from early morning until late at night," reported Glen Leonard.[3] As Joseph Holbrook prepared his family to leave Nauvoo, he recorded that, on February 6, he "went in the temple at Nauvoo and received my washings and anointing in the house of the Lord, it being at the closing of giving indowments; there was a great crowd so that near five hundred passed through their ordinances in the last twenty-four hours, but I felt greatly blessed for the opportunity of receiving the little I did for it gave me keys of knowledge for me to improve upon until I could get more."[4] The next day on February 7, John and Nancy, and Nancy's second husband, Henry Sanford,[5] were among the "upwards of six hundred"[6] who attended. Ordinances were discontinued that very day. Two days later on Sunday, February 9, Brigham Young

> met with the Council of the Twelve in the southeast corner room of the attic of the Temple. We knelt around the altar, and dedicated the building to the Most High. We asked his blessing upon our intended move to the west; also asked him to enable us some day to finish the Temple, and dedicate it to him, and we would leave it in his hands to do as he pleased; and to preserve the building as a monument to Joseph Smith. We asked the Lord to accept the labors of his servants in this land. We then left the Temple.[7]

Over the next months, the Church members who chose to leave Nauvoo as part of the exodus led by the General Authorities began their journey west. Most of them "crossed into Iowa from March through June,

Parley Street leads down to the Mississippi River today. Photo by Irval L. Mortensen, 2008.

leaving primarily those too old, too sick, or without the means of travel . . . in Nauvoo." That group finally left the middle of September and "camping out on the Iowa shore, became known as the Poor Camp."[8] The total number of residents in the city itself was about ten thousand, with several thousand living in the outlying areas.[9] As with the exodus from Missouri, the bitter winter weather caused great suffering. This time, however, some of them were initially better prepared and outfitted with covered wagons. A few had tents and livestock. However, many simply were not ready. As they prepared to endure in Nauvoo until spring ameliorated the weather, they also worked to prepare to leave. Nevertheless as Church members gathered, most often in the snow, at the foot of Parley Street, and looked across the frozen Mississippi River, they knew they had to leave.

Comparatively few of the Saints were able to sell their homes and farms for fair prices. Since it was a buyer's market, many of their neighbors who wished to appropriate their belongings simply waited until the Mormons left. Joseph Holbrook reported that he sold an eighteen-acre farm previously valued at $300 for twenty-five bushels of corn, which he was later able to sell for only 10 cents per bushel, thus making a grand total of $2.50 profit.[10] Myron Abbott, then nine years old, later wrote that "a man came to our house and told my mother that he would give her ten dollars for our property if she would leave the furniture and give the Deeds to him. Mother told him that was a very small sum for so much property. His reply was you have got to leave any how and you can tak that or nothing."[11] John Steele told of leaving his furniture and everything in his house, including a clock on the wall, as though they were just gone out for a visit. After leaving, he needed to return to get a hammer and "found three of our enemies quarreling who should have the clock. I opened my toolchest, took out my hammer, closed the lid and sat down upon it, and heard them awhile, then started on my journey."[12] Poignantly, Lewis Barney recorded crossing the river and looking back at Nauvoo and the temple, "the spire of which was then glittering in the bright shining sun. This last view of the Temple was witnessed in the midst of sighs and lamentations all faces in gloom and sorrow bathed in tears at being forced from our homes and Temple that had cost so much toil and suffering to complete its erection."[13] James Jones, a convert who arrived in the Nauvoo area in 1844, wrote sad news in May 1846 to his son Henry who had remained in England. James's wife (Henry's mother) had died on the sea voyage, and two adult sons had died of malaria in Nauvoo. In spite of these circumstances and while preparing to leave Nauvoo with his daughter, James emphatically expressed positive feelings: "In the midst of mobs and persecution that house [temple] is built. The Lord has accepted the same at our hands. It is consecrated and in that house I myself with thousands more have received our washings, anointings, and endowments. . . . Now this one thing is worth all and more than all the sorrows and afflictions I have had to pass through."[14]

On February 28, Brigham Young writing from the Saints' encampment at Sugar Creek, Iowa, summarized the experience of the Saints:

> The fact is worthy of remembrance that several thousand persons left their homes in midwinter and exposed themselves without shelter, except that afforded by a scanty supply of tents and wagon covers, to a cold which effectually made an ice bridge over the Mississippi river which at Nauvoo is more than a mile broad. We could have remained sheltered in our homes

had it not been for the threats and hostile demonstrations of our enemies, who, not withstanding their solemn agreements had thrown every obstacle in our way, not respecting either life, liberty or property, so much so, that our only means of avoiding a rupture was by starting in midwinter.

Our homes, gardens, orchards, farms, streets, bridges, mills, public halls, magnificent Temple, and other public improvements we leave as a monument of our patriotism, industry, economy, uprightness of purpose and integrity of heart; and as a living testimony of the falsehood and wickedness of those who charge us with disloyalty to the constitution of our country, idleness and dishonesty.[15]

Colonel Thomas L. Kane, a non-member friend of the Church who would be of great help to the members as they spent time at Council Bluffs, Iowa, on their trek west, visited Nauvoo, arriving in "late September" when most of the Saints had left. Glen Leonard, Nauvoo historian, described Kane's visit. "Those evacuated after the Battle of Nauvoo had just departed, along with a number of new citizens, creating the impression that the city's entire population had vanished in a day. . . . Four years later, Kane's interest in pleading the Mormon cause in Washington led him to remember his 1846 visit again [and] Kane described the scene in prose crafted to win the sympathy of his listeners for the unfairness of the forced evacuation."[16]

The town lay as in a dream, under some deadening spell of loneliness, from which I almost feared to wake it. For plainly it had not slept long. There was no grass growing up in the paved ways. Rains had not entirely washed away the prints of dusty footsteps. Yet I went about unchecked. The spinner's wheel was idle; the carpenter had gone from his work-bench and shavings, his unfinished sash and casing. Fresh bark was in the tanner's vat, and the fresh-chopped lightwood stood piled against the baker's oven. The blacksmith's shop was cold; but his coal heap and ladling pool and crooked water horn were all there, as if he had just gone off for a holiday. No work people anywhere looked to know my errand. If I went into the gardens, clinking the wicket-latch loudly after me . . . and draw [sic] a drink with the water sodden well-bucket and its noisy chain . . . no one called out to me from any open window, or dog sprang forward to bark an alarm. I could have supposed the people hidden in the houses, but the doors were unfastened; and when at last I timidly entered them, I found dead ashes white upon the hearths, and had to tread a tiptoe, as if walking down the aisle of a country church, to avoid rousing irreverent echoes from the naked floors.[17]

There is no record, of course, of what Louisa and her children left behind in Nauvoo nor what their thoughts were as they started west.

The initial plan when the Saints began leaving Nauvoo was that a small, vanguard group would immediately continue on west and begin a settlement in the Rocky Mountains. The rest of the group would travel as fast as possible, hoping to reach the Missouri River on Iowa's western border by April, then continue to their destination during the summer. But in Sugar Creek, a severe winter snowstorm hit, and it became apparent that so large a group could not traverse Iowa in those conditions. They had neither adequate shelter nor clothing and certainly not enough food to make the long trip. It became quickly apparent that to survive they needed to supply their own needs. The southern part of Iowa was primarily public land, and with adequate rainfall and fertile soil, the Saints used implements intended for use in Salt Lake. "So the Mormon migration turned into a plowing and planting operation."[18] Thousands of Saints spread out over Iowa in early 1846, clustering in way stations where, as soon as the weather permitted, they planted crops. They traded with or worked for Iowa and Missouri residents, earning money to prepare them for the rest of the journey. The best-known of these stopping points were named Garden Grove and Mount Pisgah. By late June, Winter Quarters, now Florence, Nebraska, was established on the land owned by the Pottawatomie Indians on the west bank of the Missouri River,[19] across from Kanesville, now Council Bluffs, Iowa. By the fall of 1846, most of the Saints were away from the turmoil in Nauvoo, three hundred miles to the east. As Carol Cornwall Madsen notes, "More than ten thousand Latter-day Saints had reached the Missouri River, setting up camps on both sides, nearly four thousand of them settling Winter Quarters on the west side of the Missouri. Hundreds more were scattered in the camps and settlements throughout Iowa. Until forced to move back to the Iowa side of the Missouri in 1848, Winter Quarters was the headquarters of the Church at the Missouri. From 1848 to 1852, Kanesville, formerly Miller's Hollow, on the east bank of the Missouri, served as the center of the Church activity in Missouri."[20]

From these settlements, more than four hundred Mormon men joined the U.S. Army in the Mormon Battalion in July 1846 as part of the U.S. military's participation in the Mexican War. Between the early spring of 1846 and that of 1847 when Brigham Young led the vanguard company west, departing in April, it was a time of faith and determination, but also confusion and suffering. Some members struggled to decide whether to continue west as soon as possible, to find ways to earn enough for supplies, even if it took several years, or listened to the messages of those who questioned Brigham Young's leadership and formed small colonies either in the area or elsewhere in the Midwest and East. Many, no doubt, drifted away from any organized religion.

Sometimes families were united in their choice, but the Folletts are an example of a family whose members made several choices. It is not known exactly when Louisa's family left Nauvoo or even if they traveled together. Their whereabouts over the next few years document their personal choices, and the records of other Mormons in the same areas can provide insight into the challenges the Folletts must have encountered after leaving Nauvoo. There is adequate evidence to trace Louisa and her surviving children until their deaths. Although they had spent their first fifteen years as Latter-day Saints within Mormonism's gathering places, they moved to a variety of locations as time passed.

Louisa Tanner Follett, 1798–1891

The earliest known record of Louisa's whereabouts after leaving Nauvoo is the 1847 Iowa State Census for Van Buren County. It lists Nathan A. West as a head of a family group of seven individuals, unidentified by name, sex, or age. Nathan and Adeline, Louisa's daughter, appear to have had a close relationship with Louisa, and a family tradition (mistaken as it turns out) indicates that Louisa lived and died in Van Buren County.[21] It seems logical that Louisa was one of the other six individuals, along with Adeline, his two daughters, Maria and Tryphena, by his first marriage, and Louisa's sons, fourteen-year-old Edward and eight-year-old Warren. The census was commissioned in January 1847 and closed that August, with the return dated October 25, 1847. It enumerates 10,203 residents but does not provide any specific locations in the county.[22]

It also seems logical that Louisa's family and many other Church members passed through Van Buren County as they moved west from the Sugar Creek area in Lee County. One route taken by the Mormons through Van Buren County during the winter of 1846–47 passed through the area between Farmington and Bonaparte.[23] At Bonaparte, they would have ferried across the Des Moines River. Ropes and cables connected to grooved wheels positioned the ferries against the current as ferrymen poled the loaded flatbed boats to the other side. According to a local historian, "The Journals express many different reactions to the scenes along the way. For some it meant merely a jolting ride, pleasant or painful, depending on the weather. For others it involved hard work, as some of the men split rails, built fences and homes for the local settlers, or worked on the farms in exchange for means to continue their journey."[24]

Nathan West and his family, probably accompanied by Louisa Follett and her sons, lived in Farmington, Iowa, at least briefly. Samuel Kendall Gifford, who was twenty years old when he left Nauvoo in February of 1846, reached Lee County at an unspecified date, where he "went to Farmington, Iowa. I boarded with Nathan West and made chairs, settees, etc."[25] Nathan West was probably also making furniture, since later censuses listed him as a "joiner," meaning a carpenter specializing in furniture and complicated woodworking. Gifford was in Farmington until at least September 1846 when the "battle of Nauvoo" erupted between the incoming citizens who were bent on sweeping the few remaining Saints out of the city. "I could hear all the cannons fired in the Nauvoo Battle," commented Gifford.[26] This event marked the end of this chapter of Mormon history in Nauvoo.

Sometime between 1847 and September 25, 1850, Louisa moved approximately 265 miles farther west to live with her daughter Nancy and son-in-law Henry Sanford. The 1850 census of Atchison County, Missouri, lists "Louisa Follett age 49" among its 1,648 inhabitants.[27] Seventeen-year-old Edward and twelve-year-old Warren were not living in the Sanford household. Atchison County is in northwest Missouri adjacent to the southwest corner of the Iowa border. North across the state line from Atchison County was Mills County, Iowa, established in 1852, where Louisa eventually settled. Mormons traveling across Iowa in 1846-47 passed through this area to reach Kanesville/Council Bluffs. According to a tourism pamphlet, "A number of families came back to the Mills County area to establish farms and grow food for their continued march westward. They established communities at Rushville, Coonville, Cutler's Camp and Farm Creek." These settlements "were not towns, but only a few log cabins."[28]

When the Iowa State Census was enumerated in July of 1856, Louisa was again with Nathan and Adeline West living in Silver Creek

Warren Follett's red brick home in Mills County where Louisa was living at the time of her death. Undated photo courtesy of Janet Fuller, 2002.

Township, Mills County. She was identified as a widow, age fifty-eight. Eighteen-year-old Warren, a farmer, was in the same household. The census notation states they had lived in Iowa for ten years,[29] confirming a departure from Nauvoo in 1846. By June of 1858, she and Warren jointly purchased forty acres and then, the next year, May 5, 1859, bought another nine acres, both in Silver Creek Township.[30] Subsequent censuses document her legal residence in this same area of Iowa. She spent the rest of her life in Mills County.

In the 1860 federal census on July 16, she was living with Adeline and Nathan West at Mount Olive Post Office, in Silver Creek, Mills County.[31] The 1870 census, taken on September 2, shows her living with Warren, and his wife, Virginia Ann ("Jenny") Dunlap Follett, at Malvern Post Office, still in Silver Creek Township.[32] In 1880, she was at in the same location.[33] Warren became a prosperous farmer, later building the fine brick home in which Louisa lived until her death in 1891.

Descendants of Warren King Follett have two cane-bottomed chairs—one a rocker— which they say belonged to King and Louisa

Photos of two chairs said to have belonged to King and Louisa Follett. Courtesy of Caron Whitesides, 2002.

Follett. The chairs then became successively the property of Warren, his son Charles, and Charles's daughter Gertrude Follett Colby. If that history is correct, they are the only known tangible possessions I am aware of that had belonged to either King or Louisa.[34]

No information has survived about why Louisa stayed in the Midwest instead of traveling to Utah. No doubt the fact that Warren and Adeline settled in this area was a strong attractor, although the same questions remain about why they also chose not to travel farther west. Their brother, William Alexander Follett, settled in Utah, but only after serving with the Mormon Battalion and spending additional time in the Council Bluffs area. Frances Marian Huff Minthorn, a great-neice of Warren's wife, Virginia "Jenny" Dunlap Follett, recorded in a document referred to by Minthorn as a "journal" (year not given): "When Louisa Follett and her children came across Iowa from Nauvoo, and bought land in Mills County, she was going blind. The Follett land was north of the Cattle Trail, now U.S. Highway 34, north of James Dunlap's land."[35] According to Gertrude Follett Colby, Louisa's great-granddaughter, the issue was one that troubled many of the Saints as they left Nauvoo. "My father mentioned that his grandmother (Louisa) and his father had come west with the Mormons—learning that they might practice polygamy in Utah, 'had dropped off in Iowa.'"[36]

It is also possible that, like others, Louisa became disheartened with the leadership of the Twelve in the turmoil following the deaths of Joseph and Hyrum Smith. In 1996 Danny L. Jorgensen, Cutlerite historian, wrote: "Sometime in the fall of 1847, a temporary Mormon camp was established along a creek and against a hillside grove at a now-obscure location in what was then Pottawattamie County, Iowa. This place in southwestern Iowa eventually came to be known as Alpheus 'Cutler's Camp at the Big Grove on Silver Creek.'"[37] By March 1848 Cutler, whom Joseph Smith had called as one of the Council of Fifty in Nauvoo and assigned a special mission to the Indians, settled with his family and others in the Silver Creek area and was the "president of a branch of the Church."[38] Jorgensen identifies the Follets [sic] as one of the "other Latter-day Saint families living at Silver Creek or nearby."[39] By the fall of 1848, disagreement developed between Cutler and the high council in Council Bluffs, who "viewed the teachings and claims of Cutler's more-zealous followers as heretical." The council tried to "coerce" the "Cutlerites" to follow Brigham Young to Utah. When this failed, some were disfellowshipped, Cutler's mission was "suspended" and "they excommunicated him in April 1851."[40] Mildred H. McBeth in a compilation of information on the Cutler family reported that "Alpheus Cutler began to call the people's attention to the 3 books—the Bible, Book of Mormon and Book of Covenants, and told them that they did not need to go to Utah or submit to rule or teaching of Brigham Young and his associates." She noted that in 1853, he baptized eighteen, and by 1856 had "baptized 102 members into the Cutlerite church."[41] Cutler and his followers lived in the Silver Creek community until 1852–53 when they either moved on elsewhere (some to Utah) or scattered throughout southwestern Iowa to find better living conditions.[42]

Five other individuals, including Nathan West, were also cut off for "aiding and abetting Father Cutler and promulgating his insidious views."[43] I have found no record showing that Louisa Follett joined the Cutlerites, though she lived near or among them for a few years. However, after her son-in-law was excommunicated, her feelings about moving west to Utah must have changed. On Monday, July 6, 1863, Louisa became a member of the Reorganized Church of Jesus Christ

Louisa Tanner Follett, n.d. Photo courtesy of Wilola Follett, 1998.

of Latter Day Saints (now Community of Christ). She was baptized by W. W. Blair, an early RLDS missionary, probably in or near Manti, Iowa, where Blair had "stopped" three days earlier during his missionary travels. Seven other individuals were baptized that day, one of them Tryphena Redfield,[44] the sister of Nathan West.[45] Louisa's decision to join the RLDS Church would have affirmed her testimony of Joseph Smith as prophet and the truthfulness of the Book of Mormon but would have expressed her belief that true priesthood authority rested with Joseph Smith III, not with Brigham Young.

The next mention of Louisa Follett that I have found is a quotation in Frances Minthorn's Journal: "'Granny' was the name that my mother (Viola Dunlap) [and] the Follett children called Warren's mother, Louisa. By 1885, she was 90 years old and blind. My mother loved Aunt Jenny's ma-in-law. She loved her dearly, so dearly."[46]

On April 22, 1886, the *Malvern Leader* published a birthday tribute to Louisa: "EIGHTY-SEVEN—Mrs. Louisa Follett, mother of W. K. Follett, of Silver Creek township, is perhaps as old as any other, if not the oldest person in the county. Mrs. Follett has passed the eighty-seventh milestone in life's journey and not until within a few months has her remarkable age appeared to rest heavily upon her. Now however she seems to be failing and a good portion of the time is unable to leave her bed."[47]

Five years later, this same newspaper published Louisa's obituary:

Louisa Tanner Follett's headstone, Malvern Cemetery. Photo courtesy of Beverly Boileau, 2008.

Mrs. Louisa Follett, mother of W. K. Follett, died at the home of her son in Silver Creek Township Sunday morning, Nov.15, [1891,] and was buried in Malvern Cemetery Monday afternoon, Rev. W. J. Watson officiating, the funeral services occurring at the home. Mrs. Follett's maiden name was Louisa Tanner and she was born in Otsego County, New York, Aug. 3, 1799. When she was ten years of age she removed to St. Lawrence County, New York, where she was married at the age of seventeen to King Follett. About 1820 she with her husband moved to the Western Reserve in Ohio, residing there until 1830. They again took up their march for the West, this time settling in Caldwell County, Mo. Ten years later they removed to Hancock County, Ill., where her husband died in 1844. In 1846, with her children she came to Iowa returning to Missouri for a short time and then coming to Silver Creek Township in 1848. The last 26 years of her life were passed in the home of her son, W. K. Follett. Deceased and her husband, early in their married life, united with the M E Church. At the organization of the Mormon Church at Kirtland, Ohio, they joined that church and followed it in all its wanderings until 1848. She was the mother of nine children, two of whom E. M. and W.K., the youngest sons, survive her, the former living in California."[48]

Louisa Follett was buried on November 16, in the Malvern Cemetery, Fairview, in Section N Row 2. The cemetery record reads: "Follett, Louisa, d 15 Nov 1891, 92y 3m 12d."[49]

No type of probate record was filed upon Louisa's death, which indicates she had no will or assets in her name that required distribution through the court system. That would mean she no longer had title to the real estate she purchased with Warren when they first arrived. She had shared the home of one or another of her children all of the time that the family was in Iowa. Louisa Follett had outlived her husband by fifty-four years. One of the unique beliefs of the religion King joined in 1831 is that he, his wife, and children will continue to live together as a family for eternity. King Follett—a quiet and humble man described by the Prophet Joseph Smith as a "beloved" and "worthy" brother—also left an earthly legacy for all of his descendants, both in and outside of the Mormon Church—a legacy of determination, dedication, and fortitude. For additional information on King and Louisa's children and descendants, see Appendix D.

Notes

1. Glen M. Leonard and T. Edgar Lyon, "The Nauvoo Years," 15.
2. Glen M. Leonard, *Nauvoo: A Place of Peace, a People of Promise*, 553.
3. Ibid.
4. Joseph Holbrook, *History of Joseph Holbrook, 1806–1885: Written by His Own Hand*, 35. Holbrook, a native of New York, was an early Mormon convert. He went to Utah where he served as the first mayor of Bountiful, Utah.
5. Nauvoo Temple Endowment Register, December 1845 to February 8, 1846, 338.
6. *History of the Church*, 7:580.
7. Ibid.
8. Givens, *Nauvoo Fact Book*, 170.
9. Leonard, *Nauvoo*, 551.
10. Holbrook, *History of Joseph Holbrook*, 35.
11. Myron Abbott, "History of Abigail Smith Abbott," 69.
12. John Steele, quoted in Loren N. Horton, "The Worst That I Had Yet Witnessed: Mormon Diarists Cross Iowa in 1846," 70.
13. Lewis Barney, "Autobiography and Diary 1878–1883," 26.
14. James Jones, Letter to Henry Jones, May 19, 1846, in Henry Jones, Correspondence, 1844–1895. MS 7188, LDS Church History Library.

15. *History of the Church*, 7:603.

16. Leonard, *Nauvoo*, 618–19.

17. Thomas L. Kane, "The Mormons: A Discourse Delivered before the Historical Society of Pennsylvania, March 26, 1850," 4–5.

18. David E. Miller and Della S. Miller, *Nauvoo: The City of Joseph*, 208–9.

19. Leonard, *Nauvoo*, 579–82.

20. Carol Cornwall Madsen, ed., *Journey to Zion: Voices from the Mormon Trail*, 36.

21. About thirty-five years ago, my family and I met LeRoy Follett who lived in Van Buren County, Iowa, and who, though not King's descendant, had done some family research on King. LeRoy assured me that his family "knew" that Louisa was buried in Van Buren County. With my family, I spent all of one rainy and discouraging day locating and searching through all of the cemeteries in the county. Many of them were very overgrown with weeds and mature shrubs. It was not until a few years later that I located Louisa's death and burial records across the state in Mills County.

22. Joe and Madeline Huff, comps., *Census of Clinton, Davis, Louisa, Marion, Scott, Van Buren, and Wapello Counties, Iowa, 1847*, items 10–16.

23. Ralph Arnold, "Van Buren County," in Susan Easton Black and William G. Hartley, eds., *The Iowa Mormon Trail: Legacy of Faith and Courage*, 199.

24. Marion Flakes, "Bonaparte on the Mormon Trail through Van Buren County," 1.

25. Samuel Kendall Gifford, "Reminiscences 1864," 7.

26. Ibid.

27. U.S. Census, 1850, Missouri, Atchison County, Roll M432_391, Image 303.

28. Mills County, "Explore Mills County: Find the Mormon Traces," brochure.

29. *Iowa State Census Collection, 1836–1925*, Iowa, Silver Creek Township, Mills County, Roll IA_62, Line 10, Family Number 13.

30. Beverly Boileau, Mills County researcher, email to Joann Mortensen, February 24, 2001.

31. U.S. Census, 1860, Iowa, Mills County, Silver Creek Township, Roll M653_336, p. 96, Image 113.

32. U.S. Census, 1870, Iowa, Silver Creek, Mills County, Roll M593_411, p. 98, Image 197.

33. U.S. Census, 1880, Iowa, Mills County, Silver Creek, Roll: T9_356; p. 354, image10; Enumeration District: 131, Image :0224.

34. Caron Colby Whitesides, Letter to Janet Fuller, Mesa, Arizona, March 30, 1994, copy in my possession. Caron, the third great-granddaughter of King Follett, stated that the chairs "were re-caned in about 1984."

35. Frances Marian Huff Minthorn, Journal, quoted in Alice May Minthorn Hall, email to Joann Mortensen, December 4, 2002.

36. Gertrude Follett Colby (Beaumont, Texas) Letters to Mrs. Joyce Giaguinta (Iowa City, Iowa), September 1 and September 21, 1977.

37. Danny L. Jorgensen, "Cutler's Camp at the Big Grove on Silver Creek: A Mormon Settlement in Iowa, 1847–1853," 39.

38. Ibid., 42.

39. Ibid., 46 note 2.

40. Ibid., 42–43.

41. Mildred H. McBeth, *Alpheus Cutler: A Different Approach*, 45–46.

42. Journal History, April 20, 1851, 2. See Jorgensen, "Cutler's Camp at the Big Grove on Silver Creek," for further details on the Cutlerite sojourn at Silver Creek.

43. Journal History, April 20, 1851, 2.

44. Nathan named one of his daughters Tryphena after this sister.

45. W. W. Blair, quoted in Barbara J. Bernauer, Assistant Archivist, RLDS Church Archives, email to me February 23, 2001; photocopy in my possession.

46. Minthorn, Diary, undated, in Alice Minthorn Hall, email to Mortensen, December 4, 2002. Frances's mother's name was Viola Amelda Dunlap Huff, niece of Virginia "Jenny" Dunlap Follett.

47. "Eighty-Seven," *Malvern [Iowa] Leader*, Thursday, April 22, 1886. Photocopy of newspaper clipping courtesy of Beverly Boileau.

48. "Death of Mrs. Follett," *Malvern [Iowa] Leader*, Iowa, November 15, 1891. Photocopy of newspaper clipping courtesy of Beverly Boileau. Some of the dates in this obituary are different from those of other records, reflecting the fact that obituaries reflect the information of surviving relatives.

49. *Mills County, Iowa Cemeteries*, Microfilm #1421802, Item 4, page 89, LDS Family History Center. Information verified by personal visit to the cemetery in 2001.

Epilogue

Presuming to be an expert on someone else's life, or indeed even writing a biography, is an awesome responsibility. Writing this story as fiction would have been easier. No one else can tell the story of an individual's life in the exact way it was lived or in the way that individual would tell the story. "The history of the world is the biography of great men," was one of the inscriptions once located on a wall in the Library of Congress. Others might not place my third great-grandfather, King Follett, in that category of "great men" but I would. Over the thirty years of my personal research, which has ultimately resulted in this biography, I have become acquainted with this man. His presence and spirit have guided my hand and my mind as I have studied and written. He has wanted his story told—that I know. Not, I believe, that he saw himself as any different from others who lived during his time and were early Mormon converts. In fact, I believe he would readily admit he was just one of many who early developed a testimony of the Church, its teachings, and its Prophet.

The research on King's life has benefited me in two important ways—other than just providing information for his biography. The first and most important has been the knowledge I have gained about Church history and the life of the Prophet Joseph Smith. I thought I knew a lot about both of these topics, but I had to learn more in order to put King's life into perspective, because he left no written record. The second benefit is being able to trace his children and their families down to the present time and to successfully obtain a personal contact with at least one descendant of all but one of his children who left descendants.

While visiting the Saints Cemetery in Nauvoo, Illinois in the summer of 1998, I shared the story of King Follett's life and death with my son,

Hal, his wife, Jeanna, and their two small children. As we walked around the old cemetery, we talked about how exciting it would be to find some information that would lead us to the exact spot where King Follett was buried so that we could, as a family project, erect a headstone to this individual who was our Mormon convert ancestor. Granddaughter Halie, who was then six, listened as we talked, and then asked if we could pray before we left so that "Father in Heaven would help us to find the right spot." A few weeks later, she telephoned to tell me that "she had been thinking" and she "knew where King was buried." Then she described in clear detail a spot close to a headstone we had viewed during our visit. This particular site was the grave of a child. Whether she was impressed because there was a child buried there or because her prayer was truly answered, we may never know.

Until King's gravesite is located so that it can be marked with an appropriate monument, my hope is that King would see this effort to tell his story by his third great-granddaughter as an accurate representative of the life he lived and as a written monument worthy of his remembrance by others.

Joann Follett Mortensen
Safford, Arizona
May 2011

❊ Appendix A ❊

King Follett's Ancestry

The United States of America can be a name-conscious society, resulting in a booming business in family surnames, colorful family crests, and equally colorful emigration stories. While some of those stories may not be fully accurate, descendants look backward for meaning as they carrying forward their surname into a new generation. Early Folletts were no exception.

From my research, I have found a general consensus that "Follett" is French (or Norman), appeared between the eleventh and twelfth centuries, and was relatively common in Scotland, Wales, Ireland, and England. Its spellings include Folliott, Folliotte, Foliot, Folluit, Folyet, LaFollete, and leFolet, to name a few. Defined as "merry, frolicsome, foolish or gay," it apparently described someone with those characteristics.[1] The most common modern pronunciation is "FALL–ut," and the most common modern American spelling is "Follett," or occasionally "Folet." Both spellings appear for King's surname, even on records produced while he was living and even when he signed his own name. I use Follett consistently except in quotations.

The first mention that I have been able to find in an American record of the Follett surname is a John Follett who signed the Dover (Massachusetts) Combination of 1640, establishing an agreement "to combine ourselves into a body politique . . . [to] more comfortably enjoy the benefit of . . . all such Orders as shal bee concluded by a major part of the Freemen of our Society."[2] A Robert Follett, relationship to John Follett unknown but possibly a brother, appears in Salem, Massachusetts,

Since there are no known photos of King Follett, nor any items, journals, or letters that can be documented as belonging to him, these signatures are the only personal record generated by him. (1) top: Nauvoo (Illinois) Records, 1841–45, "Petitions, January-April 1842," Box 1, fd. 24; (2) Freemasons, Nauvoo Lodge (Ill.) Minutebook, October 1841–February 1846; the signature pages are not numbered although King's appears to be on page 4; (3) Memorial to Congress, November 28, 1843, MS 2145, fd. 6, 29; all in LDS Church History Library.

when he married Persis Black in 1655. Robert was King Follett's great-great-great-grandfather.[3] "Robert" and especially "John" appear frequently in early Follett family records, although both names were so common that they tend to confuse rather then illuminate research efforts.

The Historical Collections of the Essex Institute published in Salem, Massachusetts, beginning in 1859, describe Robert (or Rob)'s professions variously as a fisherman, shoreman, husbandman (farmer), and owner of a vessel and waterfront property. Deeds document his ownership of more than 130 acres and probably two dwellings. In addition to appearing in land transactions, he also served on juries and grand juries. In 1686 he was one of two men "Chosen Cullors of fish for this yeare." In 1689 he was one of five designated "Cutters of ffish" and he was paid two shillings for "work done on the high wayes."[4] Robert and Persis, who was the daughter of John Black and Susanna Shockley Black, were admitted as members of the First Church of Salem; and their children, including their son John, King's great-great-grandfather, were baptized there.[5] Robert's name was one of at least forty-two citizens identified as "chief inhabitants" who petitioned unsuccessfully against granting a license for a "house of entertainment that would sell beer, ale and cider." Robert's name also appears as "Inspector to Families," meaning that he was in some way responsible for a number of families living in a certain area of the town, defined in one source as Robert Follett's Ward. Among his responsibilities and other tasks, he had to obtain the signatures of every man over age sixteen in his ward on an oath of allegiance to England in 1678. There is no indication about whether he signed the oath himself. He also signed a petition from residents for a larger meetinghouse because of an increase in the population. He was taxed at the "country rate" of 3 shillings in April 1683.[6]

Most Follett family records, not all of which are equally reliable, indicate he moved to Attleborough, Massachusetts, probably by 1694. Neither his nor Persis's death appears in Salem's records, nor is his will in Salem probates. However, his death occurred after August 4, 1704, when a deed dated August 3 was recorded giving "all of his homestead, being a farm of about 130 acres of arable pasture and meadow ground, and all his other real-estate whatsoever, and all his cattle, horses, sheep, and other creatures whatsoever" to his two youngest sons Isaac and Benjamin.[7]

Then follow four generations of John Folletts: Robert's son, grandson, great-grandson, and great-great-grandson. Then comes King Follett.

Generation 1: John Follett (1669–ca. 1718)

King's great-great-grandfather was born in Salem to Robert and Persis Follett. In 1694, he married Martha Kellum/Cullum. At least their first two children were born in Salem though I have found no baptism records for these children in their parents' church. The third child was apparently born in Salem but not baptized until after the young family had moved to Bristol County, Massachusetts, settling in Rehoboth (later Seekonk) east of Providence, Rhode Island. Their remaining three children were baptized in the Newman Congregational Church in Rehoboth.[8] There is no record of John being involved in community affairs while the family lived in Rehoboth, but it is interesting that the available town records during that period stress procuring and retaining the services of a schoolmaster to teach reading, writing, grammar, and arithmetic.[9] Thus, John and Martha's children could have received some formal schooling though they lived on the frontier.

The family made a short move to Attleborough, also in Bristol County. Martha died there in 1706 at age thirty-six, twelve days after giving birth to Samuel, her sixth child. She was "the first that was buried in ye old Buring Ground," later known as the "Old North Burying Ground" or "Hatch's Burying Ground."[10] Graves were not marked so that the Indians would not know how many residents had died. At one time there was a small Follett family burial yard in Attleborough, but those buried there were not apparently King's direct line. There are no current identifiable locations of any of King's ancestors' graves in Attleborough.

Though I found no record of John's remarriage, he and his second wife, Sarah Fuller, had other children, beginning in 1708.[11] John acted as selectman or town clerk, for 1705, probably 1706, again in 1707 and 1709–15.[12] It is difficult to determine whether these two positions were elective or appointive, but the town clerk, at least, was elected from those serving as selectmen. Between 1715 and 1717, the family moved approximately fifty miles west where John was "excepted an inhabitant in Ashford, Connecticut." On August 17, 1717, "the Town Do grant to John Follet Jr one Hundred Acres of Land and he Doth Engage to the Towns use five Pounds of Money When the Town Shall give him a full confirmation."[13] Ashford land records at that time show other transactions of a John Follett and a John Follett Jr., both as buyer and seller. Were they father and son or the same individual under two names? A history of Ashford shows that an individual identified as "John Follet 2d." was one of forty-five men who, on March 5, 1718, "gave bonds, drew lots and were admitted proprietors of Ashford. A few of these new proprietors were residents of "Windham and Pomfret the remainder were then residents of Ashford."[14]

The available vital records do not show any Follett births or deaths while the family was in Ashford. However, John must have died within a year after the family's move to Ashford, because the family moved back to Attleborough before August of 1718 when his will was filed there.

The gross value of his property was £360 18 shillings. This inventory included the 100 acres in Ashford, Connecticut.[15] The estate reimbursed the expenses of Sarah Fuller Follett and son John who made more than one trip from Massachusetts to Connecticut to inventory, pay taxes, and sell the 100 acres. This land transaction in Ashford is recorded along with several others at the same time to individuals surnamed Fuller, suggesting that they were Sarah's relatives. If so, that may be why he had a claim and title to land in that area. No record of his burial place or exact death date has been located either in Attleborough or Ashford, other than the 1718 probate record in Attleborough.

Generation 2: John Follett (1695–1747)

King's great-grandfather and the next John Follett who descended from Robert is often called John Follett Jr. on early family records. Born in Salem, Massachusetts, he moved with his parents to Attleborough, then traveled to or lived in Ashford, Connecticut, with his father prior to John Sr.'s death. He was involved in the probate of his father's estate in 1718 along with his stepmother, Sarah Fuller Follett. John married Mary Bishop in Attleborough in 1720; and they had five daughters and one son—the next John.[16] The Bishop family into which John married was one of Salem's first settlers, but one source states they were better known for the fact that Bridget Bishop was tried, condemned, sentenced to death, and hanged on Witch Hill in June 1892.[17]

Little is known about the life or activities of this third John who died in Attleborough in 1747. When his will was probated, his property consisted mostly of real estate evaluated at approximately £1700.[18]

Generation 3: John Follett (1727–ca. 1818)

King's grandfather was born in Attleborough, Bristol County, Massachusetts, grew up there and married Rachel Stevens in 1748. Her family had settled early in the area. After the births of eight children in Attleborough,[19] John and Rachel moved about forty miles northwest and settled in Dudley, Worcester County, Massachusetts, where at least two more children were born.[20] No Folletts appear in the town records of Dudley during the four years of the family's residence.[21] They then traveled north about eighty-five miles across Massachusetts to what was probably a less populated area and settled in Swanzey, Cheshire County, in the southwest corner of New Hampshire before 1768, where another son was born. Two of their sons, identified as John Jr. (King's father) and Benjamin, were among the young men spoken of by a local historian: "There was a large increase of inhabitants in the town between 1762 and 1777. This was largely made up of young men who came and established permanent homes, and many of whom eventually became prominent and influential citizens."[22] Few other details are available on either John or Rachel, and I could not find a will or probate record for either. However, John may still have been alive at ninety-one years, as a Follett genealogy, published in 1975, states that John posted a bond in 1818 in a guardianship for his grandson, Walter Follett Jr.[23]

As the threat of Indian raids lessened and the frontier moved further west, the Follett men kept moving, perhaps motivated by the need for more fertile land and/or the appeal of adventure. No record of their motivations or of whether their wives and children also moved willingly has been preserved. In addition to the challenges of frontier living were political disagreements with England that culminated in the Revolutionary War. The last of the four John Folletts, King's father (1752–1829) played a role in that historic event as a young man.

Notes

1. Frank R. Holmes, *Directory of the Ancestral Heads of New England Families, 1620–1700*, lxxxv.

2. Everett S. Stackpole and Lucien Thompson, *History of the Town of Durham, New Hampshire (Oyster River Plantation)*, 1:5–6, 23–24.

3. Birth records confirming four generations of John Folletts connecting Robert Follett to King Follett are: (1) John Follett, son of Robert and Persis Follett, born July 10, 1669; (2) John Follett, son of John (1669) and Martha Follett, born July 29, 1695 *Vital Records of Salem, Massachusetts, to the End of the Year 1849, Vol. 1 Births*, p. 311; (3) John Follett, son of John (1695) and Mary Follett, born December 11, 1727 and (4) John Follett (King Follett's father) son of John (1727) and Rachel Follett, born March 5, 1752. *Vital Records of Attleborough, Massachusetts to the End of the Year 1849*, p. 117.

Appendix A: King Follett's Ancestry

4. Essex Institute, *Town Records of Salem, Massachusetts, 1680–1691*, Vol. 3, pp. 2, 16, 158, 164, 206, 209, 247, 252. I believe that this title is "culler," meaning that he inspected fish and perhaps graded them as they were sold. Early Massachusetts law created a position "culler of fish" in each Province with the responsibility to "cull all merchantable fish" for which the culler received one penny per quintal (hundredweight) of fish, with the cost shared between the seller and the buyer. Isaiah Thomas and Ebenezer T. Andrews, eds., *The Perpetual Laws of the Commonwealth of Massachusetts*, 3:150.

5. Essex Institute, *Records of Baptisms of First Church of Salem, Massachusetts*, 7:126.

6. Sidney Perley, *The History of Salem, Massachusetts*, 3:66, 78, 116, 153–54, 419.

7. Essex County (Massachusetts). Register of Deeds, *Deeds, 1839–1866; Index to Deeds, 1640–1879*, 16:129.

8. Elisha L. Turner, transcriber, "Baptisms, from Rehoboth Church Records," 15:67–72.

9. Leonard Bliss Jr., *The History of Rehoboth, Bristol County, Massachusetts*, 132–34.

10. Essex Institute, *Vital Records of Attleborough, Massachusetts to the End of the Year 1849*, 118, 670. This burying ground may have later been referred to as the "present-day Woodcock Historic Burial Ground." Eric B. Schultz and Michael J. Tougias, *King Philip's War: The History and Legacy of America's Forgotten Conflict*, 110.

11. Essex Institute, *Vital Records of Attleborough, Massachusetts to the End of the Year 1849*, 117.

12. John Daggett (author) and Amelia Daggett Sheffield (editor and completer), *A Sketch of the History of Attleborough: From Its Settlement to the Division*, 633–34.

13. Ashford, Connecticut, Town Clerk, *Proprietor Records 1705–1770*.

14. Ellen D. Larned, *History of Windham County, Connecticut*, 223.

15. "John Follett, Attleboro, 1718."

16. Essex Institute, *Vital Records of Attleborough, Massachusetts*, 116–17.

17. Helen and Warren Burns, *Branches of My Family Tree: The Follett Branch*, 19. Mary Bishop Follett was the granddaughter of an Edward Bishop and his first wife, Hannah. After Hannah died, Edward married Bridget Oliver in 1680.

18. "John Follett, Attleboro, 1747."

19. Essex Institute, *Vital Records of Attleborough, Massachusetts*, 117–18.

20. *Vital Records of Dudley, Massachusetts, to the End of the Year 1849*, 1:57. Burns and Burns, *Branches of My Family Tree*, 21, quote *Vital Records of Dudley, Massachusetts*, 2:154, as identifying three children born during this period, but I did not find a birth record of a third child.

21. *Town Records of Dudley, Massachusetts*.

22. Benjamin Reed, "The History of Swanzey, New Hampshire: From 1734 to 1890," 63–64.

23. Mrs. William Follett, "The Follett Family," *Connecticut Nutmegger* (West Hartford, Conn.: Connecticut Society of Genealogists, 1975) 8:158–59. John is identified by "1727," apparently his birthdate. There is no citation for this guardianship and I have not been able to locate it.

❀ Appendix B ❀

The King Follett Discourse

Joseph Smith Jr. et al., *History of the Church of Jesus Christ of Latter-day Saints*, edited by B. H. Roberts, 2d ed. rev. (6 vols., 1902–12, Vol. 7, 1932; rpt., Salt Lake City: Deseret Book, 1978 printing): 6:302-17. The bracketed insertions are in *History of the Church*.

    Beloved Saints: I will call [for] the attention of this congregation while I address you on the subject of the dead. The decease of our beloved brother, Elder King Follett, who was crushed in a well by the falling of a tub of rock, has more immediately led me to this subject. I have been requested to speak by his friends and relatives, but inasmuch as there are a great many in this congregation who live in this city as well as elsewhere, who have lost friends, I feel disposed to speak on the subject in general, and offer you my ideas, so far as I have ability, and so far as I shall be inspired by the Holy Spirit to dwell on this subject.

    I want your prayers and faith that I may have the instruction of Almighty God and the gift of the Holy Ghost, so that I may set forth things that are true and which can be easily comprehended by you, and that the testimony may carry conviction to your hearts and minds of the truth of what I shall say. Pray that the Lord may strengthen my lungs, stay the winds, and let the prayers of the saints to heaven appear, that they may enter into the ears of the Lord of Sabaoth, for the effectual prayers of the righteous avail much. There is strength here, and I verily believe that your prayers will be heard.

Before I enter fully into the investigation of the subject which is lying before me, I wish to pave the way and bring up the subject from the beginning, that you may understand it. I will make a few preliminaries, in order that you may understand the subject when I come to it. I do not calculate or intend to please your ears with superfluity of words or oratory, or with much learning; but I calculate to edify you with the simple truths from heaven.

The Character of God

In the first place, I wish to go back to the beginning—to the morn of creation. There is the starting point for us to look to, in order to understand and be fully acquainted with the mind, purposes and decrees of the Great Eloheim, who sits in yonder heavens as he did at the creation of the world. It is necessary for us to have an understanding of God himself in the beginning. If we start right, it is easy to go right all the time; but if we start wrong we may go wrong, and it will be a hard matter to get right.

There are but a very few beings in the world who understand rightly the character of God. The great majority of mankind do not comprehend anything, either that which is past, or that which is to come, as it respects their relationship to God. They do not know, neither do they understand the nature of that relationship; and consequently they know but little above the brute beast, or more than to eat, drink and sleep. This is all man knows about God or His existence, unless it is given by the inspiration of the Almighty.

If a man learns nothing more than to eat, drink and sleep, and does not comprehend any of the designs of God, the beast comprehends the same things. It eats, drinks, sleeps, and knows nothing more about God; yet it knows as much as we, unless we are able to comprehend by the inspiration of Almighty God. If men do not comprehend the character of God, they do not comprehend themselves. I want to go back to the beginning, and so lift your minds into more lofty spheres and a more exalted understanding than what the human mind generally aspires to.

I want to ask this congregation, every man, woman and child, to answer the question in their own hearts, what kind of a being God is? Ask yourselves; turn your thoughts into your hearts, and say if any of you have seen, heard, or communed with Him? This is a question that may occupy your attention for a long time. I again repeat the question—What kind of a being is God? Does any man or woman know? Have any of you seen Him, heard Him, or communed with Him? Here is the question that will, peradventure, from this time henceforth occupy your attention. The scriptures inform us that "This is life eternal that they might know thee, the only true God, and Jesus Christ whom thou hast sent."

If any man does not know God, and inquires what kind of a being He is,—if he will search diligently his own heart—if the declaration of Jesus and the apostles be true, he will realize that he has not eternal life; for there can be eternal life on no other principle.

My first object is to find out the character of the only wise and true, God, and what kind of a being He is; and if I am so fortunate as to be the man to comprehend God, and explain or convey the principles to your hearts, so that the Spirit seals them upon you, then let every man and woman henceforth sit in silence, put their hands on their mouths, and never lift their hands or voices, or say anything against the man of God or the servants of God again. But if I fail to do it, it becomes my duty to renounce all further pretensions to revelations and inspirations, or to be a prophet; and I should be like the rest of the world—a false teacher, be hailed as a friend, and no man would seek my life. But if all religious teachers were honest enough to renounce their pretensions to godliness when their ignorance of the knowledge of God is made manifest, they will all be as badly off as I am, at any rate; and you might just as well take the lives of other false teachers as that of mine. If any man is authorized to take away my life because he thinks and says I am a false teacher, then, upon the same principle, we should be justified in taking away the life of every false teacher, and where would be the end of blood? And who would not be the sufferer?

The Privilege of Religious Freedom

But meddle not with any man for his religion; all governments ought to permit every man to enjoy his religion unmolested. No man is authorized to take away life in consequence of difference of religion which all laws and governments ought to tolerate and protect, right or wrong. Every man has a natural, and, in our country, a constitutional right to be a false prophet, as well as a true prophet. If I show, verily, that I have the truth of God, and show that ninety-nine out of every hundred professing religious ministers are false teachers, having no authority while they pretend to hold the keys of God's kingdom on earth, and was to kill them because they are false teachers, it would deluge the whole world with blood.

I will prove that the world is wrong, by showing what God is. I am going to inquire after God; for I want you all to know Him, and to be familiar with Him; and if I am bringing you to a knowledge of Him, all persecutions against me ought to cease. You will then know that I am His servant; for I speak as one having authority.

God an Exalted Man

I will go back to the beginning before the world was, to show what kind of a being God is. What sort of a being was God in the beginning? Open your ears and hear, all ye ends of the earth, for I am going to prove it to you by the Bible, and to tell you the designs of God in relation to the human race, and why He interferes with the affairs of man.

God himself was once as we are now, and is an exalted man, and sits enthroned in yonder heavens! That is the great secret. If the veil were rent today, and the great God who holds this world in its orbit, and who upholds all worlds and all things by His power, was to make himself visible,—I say, if you were to see him today, you would see him like a man in form—like yourselves in all the person, image, and very form as a man; for Adam was created in the very fashion, image and likeness of God, and received instruction from, and walked, talked and conversed with Him, as one man talks and communes with another.

In order to understand the subject of the dead, for consolation of those who mourn for the loss of their friends, it is necessary we should understand the character and being of God and how He came to be so; for I am going to tell you how God came to be God. We have imagined and supposed that God was God from all eternity. I will refute that idea, and take away the veil, so that you may see.

These are incomprehensible ideas to some, but they are simple. It is the first principle of the gospel to know for a certainty the character of God, and to know that we may converse with Him as one man converses with another, and that He was once a man like us; yea, that God himself, the Father of us all, dwelt on an earth, the same as Jesus Christ Himself did; and I will show it from the Bible.

Eternal Life to Know God and Jesus Christ

I wish I was in a suitable place to tell it, and that I had the trump of an archangel, so that I could tell the story in such a manner that persecution would cease forever. What did Jesus say? (Mark it, Elder Rigdon!) The scriptures inform us that Jesus said, as the Father hath power in himself, even so hath the Son power—to do what? Why, what the Father did. The answer is obvious—in a manner to lay down his body and take it up again. Jesus, what are you going to do? To lay down my life as my Father did, and take it up again. Do you believe it? If you do not believe it you do not believe the Bible. The scriptures say it, and I defy all the learning and wisdom and all the combined powers of earth and hell together to refute it. Here, then, is eternal life—to know the only wise and true God; and you have got to learn how to be gods yourselves, and to be kings and priests to God, the same as all gods have done before you, namely, by going from one small degree to another, and from a small capacity to a great one; from grace to grace, from exaltation to exaltation, until you attain to the resurrection of the dead, and are able to dwell in everlasting burnings, and to sit in glory, as do those who sit enthroned in everlasting power. And I want you to know that God, in the last days, while certain individuals are proclaiming His name, is not trifling with you or me.

The Righteous to Dwell in Everlasting Burnings

These are the first principles of consolation. How consoling to the mourners when they are called to part with a husband, wife, father, mother, child, or dear relative, to know that, although the earthly tabernacle is laid down and dissolved, they shall rise again to dwell in everlasting burnings in immortal glory, not to sorrow, suffer, or die any more, but they shall be heirs of God and joint heirs with Jesus Christ. What is it? To inherit the same power, the same glory and the same exaltation, until you arrive at the station of a god, and ascend the throne of eternal power, the same as those who have gone before. What did Jesus do? Why, I do the things I saw my Father do when worlds came rolling into existence. My Father worked out His kingdom with fear and trembling, and I must do the same; and when I get my kingdom, I shall present it to My Father, so that He may obtain kingdom upon kingdom, and it will exalt Him in glory. He will then take a higher exaltation, and I will take His place, and thereby become exalted myself. So that Jesus treads in the tracks of

His Father, and inherits what God did before; and God is thus glorified and exalted in the salvation and exaltation of all His children. It is plain beyond disputation, and you thus learn some of the first principles of the gospel, about which so much hath been said.

When you climb up a ladder, you must begin at the bottom, and ascend step by step, until you arrive at the top; and so it is with the principles of the gospel—you must begin with the first, and go on until you learn all the principles of exaltation. But it will be a great while after you have passed through the veil before you will have learned them. It is not all to be comprehended in this world; it will be a great work to learn our salvation and exaltation even beyond the grave. I suppose I am not allowed to go into an investigation of anything that is not contained in the Bible. If I do, I think there are so many over-wise men here that they would cry "treason" and put me to death. So I will go to the old Bible and turn commentator today.

I shall comment on the very first Hebrew word in the Bible; I will make a comment on the very first sentence of the history of creation in the bible—*Berosheit*. I want to analyze the word. *Baith*—in, by, through, and everything else. *Roch*—the head. *Sheit*—grammatical termination. When the inspired man wrote it, he did not put the baith there. An old Jew without any authority added the word; he thought it too bad to begin to talk about the head! It read first. "The head one of the Gods brought forth the Gods." That is the true meaning of the words. *Baurau* signifies to bring forth. If you do not believe it, you do not believe the learned man of God. Learned men can teach you no more than what I have told you. Thus the head God brought forth the Gods in the grand council.

I will transpose and simplify it in the English language. Oh, ye lawyers, ye doctors, and ye priests, who have persecuted me, I want to let you know that the Holy Ghost knows something as well as you do. The head God called together the Gods and sat in grand council to bring forth the world. The grand councilors sat at the head in yonder heavens and contemplated the creation of the worlds which were created at the time. When I say doctors and lawyers, I mean the doctors and lawyers of the scriptures. I have done so hitherto without explanation to let the lawyers flutter and everybody laugh at them. Some learned doctors might take a notion to say the scriptures say thus and so; and we must believe the scriptures; they are not to be altered. But I am going to show you an error in them.

I have an old edition of the New Testament in the Latin, Hebrew, German and Greek languages. I have been reading the German, and find it to be the most [nearly] correct translation, and to correspond nearest to the revelations which God has given to me for the last fourteen years. It tells about Jacobus, the son of Zebedee. It means Jacob. In the English New Testament it is translated James. Now, if Jacob had the keys, you might talk about James through all eternity and never get the keys. In the 21st. of the fourth chapter of Matthew, my old German edition gives the word Jacob instead of James.

The doctors (I mean doctors of law, not physic) say, "If you preach anything not according to the Bible, we will cry treason." How can we escape the damnation of hell, except God be with us and reveal to us? Men bind us with chains. The Latin says Jacobus, which means Jacob; the Hebrew says Jacob, the Greek says Jacob and the German says Jacob, here we have the testimony of four against one. I thank God that I have got this old book; but I thank him more for the gift of the Holy Ghost. I have got the oldest book of the world; but I have got the oldest book in my heart, even the gift of the Holy Ghost. I have all the four Testaments. Come here, ye learned men, and read, if you can. I should not have introduced this testimony, were it not to back up the word *rosh*—the head, the Father of the Gods. I should not have brought it up, only to show that I am right.

A Council of the Gods

In the beginning, the head of the Gods called a council of the Gods; and they came together and concocted [prepared] a plan to create the world and people it. When we begin to learn this way, we begin to learn the only true God, and what kind of a being we have got to worship. Having a knowledge of God, we begin to know how to approach Him, and how to ask so as to receive an answer.

When we understand the character of God, and know how to come to Him, he begins to unfold the heavens to us, and to tell us all about it. When we are ready to come to him, he is ready to come to us.

Now, I ask all who hear me, why the learned men who are preaching salvation, say that God created the heavens and the earth out of nothing?

The reason is, that they are unlearned in the things of God, and have not the gift of the Holy Ghost; they account it blasphemy in any one to contradict their idea. If you tell them that God made the world out of something, they will call you a fool. But I am learned, and know more than all the world put together. The Holy Ghost does, anyhow, and he is within me, and comprehends more than all the world; and I will associate myself with him.

Meaning of the Word Create

You ask the learned doctors why they say the world was made out of nothing, and they will answer, "Doesn't the Bible say He *created* the world?" And they infer, from the word create, that it must have been made out of nothing. Now, the word create came from the word *baurau*, which does not mean to create out of nothing; it means to organize; the same as a man would organize materials and build a ship. Hence we infer that God had materials to organize the world out of chaos—chaotic matter, which is element, and in which dwells all the glory. Element had an existence from the time He had. The pure principles of element are principles which can never be destroyed; they may be organized and re-organized, but not destroyed. They had no beginning and can have no end.

The Immortal Intelligence

I have another subject to dwell upon, which is calculated to exalt man; but it is impossible for me to say much on this subject. I shall therefore just touch upon it, for time will not permit me to say all. It is associated with the subject of the resurrection of the dead,—namely, the soul—the mind of man—the immortal spirit. Where did it come from? All learned men and doctors of divinity say that God created it in the beginning; but it is not so; the very idea lessens man in my estimation. I do not believe the doctrine; I know better. Hear it, all ye ends of the world; for God has told me so; and if you don't believe me, it will not make the truth without effect. I will make a man appear a fool before I get through; if he does not believe it. I am going to tell of things more noble.

We say that God Himself is a self-existing being. Who told you so? It is correct enough; but how did it get into your heads? Who told you that man did not exist in like manner upon the same principles? Man does exist upon the same principles. God made a tabernacle and put a spirit into it, and it became a living soul. (Refers to the Bible.) How does it read in the Hebrew? It does not say in the Hebrew that God created the spirit of man. It says, "God made man out of the earth and put into him Adam's spirit, and so became a living body."

The mind or the intelligence which man possesses is co-equal [co-eternal] with God himself. I know that my testimony is true; hence, when I talk to these mourners, what have they lost? Their relatives and friends are only separated from their bodies for a short season: their spirits which existed with God have left the tabernacle of clay only for a little moment, as it were; and they now exist in a place where they converse together the same as we do on the earth.

I am dwelling on the immortality of the spirit of man. Is it logical to say that the intelligence of spirits is immortal, and yet that it has a beginning? The intelligence of spirits had no beginning, neither will it have an end. That is good logic. That which has a beginning may have an end. There never was a time when there were not spirits; for they are co-equal [co-eternal] with our Father in heaven.

I want to reason more on the spirit of man; for I am dwelling on the body and spirit of man—on the subject of the dead. I take my ring from my finger and liken it unto the mind of man—the immortal part, because it had no beginning. Suppose you cut it in two; then it has a beginning and an end; but join it again, and it continues one eternal round. So with the spirit of man. As the Lord liveth, if it had a beginning, it will have an end. All the fools and learned and wise men from the beginning of creation, who say that the spirit of man had a beginning, prove that it must have an end; and if that doctrine is true, then the doctrine of annihilation would be true. But if I am right, I might with boldness proclaim from the house-tops that God never had the power to create the spirit of man at all. God himself could not create himself.

Intelligence is eternal and exists upon a self-existent principle. It is a spirit from age to age and there is no creation about it. All the minds and spirits that God ever sent into the world are susceptible of enlargement.

The first principles of man are self-existent with God. God himself, finding he was in the midst of spirits and glory, because he was more intelligent, saw proper to institute laws whereby the rest could have a privilege to advance like himself. The relationship we have with God places us in a situation to advance in knowledge. He has power to institute laws to instruct the weaker intelligences, that they may be exalted with Himself, so that they might have one glory upon another, and all that knowledge, power, glory, and intelligence, which is requisite in order to save them in the world of spirits.

This is good doctrine. It tastes good. I can taste the principles of eternal life, and so can you. They are given to me by the revelations of Jesus Christ; and I know that when I tell you these words of eternal life as they are given to me, you taste them, and I know that you believe them. You say honey is sweet and so do I. I can also taste the spirit of eternal life. I know that it is good; and when I tell you of these things which were given me by inspiration of the Holy Spirit, you are bound to receive them as sweet, and rejoice more and more.

The Relation of Man to God

I want to talk more of the relation of man to God. I will open your eyes in relation to the dead. All things whatsoever God in his infinite wisdom has seen fit and proper to reveal to us, while we are dwelling in mortality, in regard to our mortal bodies, are revealed to us in the abstract, and independent of affinity of this mortal tabernacle, but are revealed to our spirits precisely as though we had no bodies at all; and those revelations which will save our spirits will save our bodies. God reveals them to us in view of no eternal dissolution of the body, or tabernacle. Hence the responsibility, the awful responsibility, that rests upon us in relation to our dead; for all the spirits who have not obeyed the Gospel in the flesh must either obey it in the spirit or be damned. Solemn thought!—dreadful thought! Is there nothing to be done?—no preparation—no salvation for our fathers and friends who have died without having had the opportunity to obey the decrees of the Son of Man? Would to God that I had forty days and nights in which to tell you all! I would let you know that I am not a "fallen prophet."

Our Greatest Responsibility

What promises are made in relation to the subject of the salvation of the dead? and what kind of characters are those who can be saved, although their bodies are mouldering and decaying in the grave? When His commandments teach us, it is in view of eternity; for we are looked upon by God as though we were in eternity; God dwells in eternity, and does not view things as we do.

The greatest responsibility in this world that God has laid upon us is to seek after our dead. The apostle says, "They without us cannot be made perfect"; for it is necessary that the sealing power should be in our hands to seal our children and our dead for the fulness of the dispensation of times—a dispensation to meet the promises made by Jesus Christ before the foundation of the world for the salvation of man.

Now, I will speak of them. I will meet Paul half way. I say to you, Paul, you cannot be perfect without us. It is necessary that those who are going before and those who come after us should have salvation in common with us; and thus hath God made it obligatory upon man. Hence, God said, "I will send you Elijah the prophet before the coming of the great and dreadful day of the Lord; he shall turn the heart of the fathers to the children, and the heart of the children to their fathers, lest I come and smite the earth with a curse."

The Unpardonable Sin

I have a declaration to make as to the provisions which God hath made to suit the conditions of man—made from before the foundation of the word. What has Jesus said? All sins, and all blasphemies, and every transgression, except one, that man can be guilty of, may be forgiven; and there is a salvation for all men, either in this world or the world to come, who have not committed the unpardonable sin, there being a provision either in this world or the world of spirits. Hence God hath made a provision that every spirit in the eternal world can be ferreted out and saved unless he has committed that unpardonable sin which cannot be remitted to him either in this world or the world of spirits. God has wrought out a salvation for all men, unless they have committed a certain sin; and every man who has a friend in the eternal world can save him, unless he has committed the unpardonable sin. And so you can see how far you can be a savior.

A man cannot commit the unpardonable sin after the dissolution of the body, and there is a way possible for escape. Knowledge saves a man; and in the world of spirits no man can be exalted but by knowledge. So long as a man will not give heed to the commandments, he must abide without salvation. If a man has knowledge, he can be saved; although, if he has been guilty of great sins, he will be punished for them. But when he consents to obey the gospel, whether here or in the world of spirits, he is saved.

A man is his own tormentor and his own condemner. Hence the saying, They shall go into the lake that burns with fire and brimstone. The torment of disappointment in the mind of man is as exquisite as a lake burning with fire and brimstone. I say, so is the torment of man.

I know the scriptures and understand them. I said, no man can commit the unpardonable sin after the dissolution of the body, nor in this life, until he receives the Holy Ghost; but they must do it in this world. Hence the salvation of Jesus Christ was wrought out for all men, in order to triumph over the devil; for if it did not catch him in one place, it would in another; for he stood up as a Savior. All will suffer until they obey Christ himself.

The contention in heaven was—Jesus said there would be certain souls that would not be saved; and the devil said he would save them all, and laid his plans before the grand council, who gave their vote in favor of Jesus Christ. So the devil rose up in rebellion against God, and was cast down, with all who put up their heads for him. (Book of Moses—Pearl of Great Price, ch. 4:1–4; Book of Abraham, ch. 3:23–28.)

The Forgiveness of Sins

All sins shall be forgiven, except the sin against the Holy Ghost; for Jesus will save all except the sons of perdition. What must a man do to commit the unpardonable sin? He must receive the Holy Ghost, have the heavens opened unto him, and know God, and then sin against him. After a man has sinned against the Holy Ghost, there is no repentance for him. He has got to say that the sun does not shine while he sees it; he has got to deny Jesus Christ when the heavens have been opened unto him, and to deny the plan of salvation with his eyes open to the truth of it; and from that time he begins to be an enemy. This is the case with many apostates of the Church of Jesus Christ of Latter-day Saints.

When a man begins to be an enemy to this work, he hunts me, he seeks to kill me, and never ceases to thirst for my blood. He gets the spirit of the devil—the same spirit that they had who crucified the Lord of Life—the same spirit that sins against the Holy Ghost. You cannot save such persons; you cannot bring them to repentance; they make open war, like the devil, and awful is the consequence.

I advise all of you to be careful what you do, or you may by-and-by find out that you have been deceived. Stay yourselves; do not give way; don't make any hasty moves, you may be saved. If a spirit of bitterness is in you, don't be in haste. You may say, that man is a sinner. Well, if he repents, he shall be forgiven. Be cautious; await. When you find a spirit that wants bloodshed,—murder, the same is not of God, but is of the devil. Out of the abundance of the heart of man the mouth speaketh.

The best men bring forth the best works. The man who tells you words of life is the man who can save you. I warn you against all evil characters who sin against the Holy Ghost; for there is no redemption for them in this world nor in the world to come.

I could go back and trace every object of interest concerning the relationship of man to God, if I had time. I can enter into the mysteries; I can enter largely into the eternal worlds; for Jesus said, "In my Father's house are many mansions; if it were not so, I would have told you. I go to prepare a place for you." (John 14:2). Paul says, "There is one glory of the sun, and another glory of the moon, and another glory of the stars; for one star differeth from another star in glory. So also is the resurrection of the dead." (1 Cor. 15:41). What have we to console us in relation to the dead? We have reason to have the greatest hope and consolation for our dead of any people on the earth; for we have seen them walk worthily in our midst, and seen them sink asleep in the arms of Jesus; and those who have died in the faith are now in the celestial kingdom of God. And hence is the glory of the sun.

You mourners have occasion to rejoice, speaking of the death of Elder King Follett; for your husband and father is gone to wait until the resurrection of the dead—until the perfection of the remainder; for at the resurrection your friend will rise in perfect felicity and go to celestial glory, while many must wait myriads of years before they can receive the like blessings; and your expectations and hopes are far above what man can conceive; for why has God revealed it to us?

I am authorized to say, by the authority of the Holy Ghost, that you have no occasion to fear; for he is gone to the home of the just. Don't mourn, don't weep. I know it by the testimony of the Holy Ghost that is within me; and you may wait for your friends to come forth to meet you in the morn of the celestial world.

Rejoice, O Israel! Your friends who have been murdered for the truth's sake in the persecutions shall triumph gloriously in the celestial world, while their murderers shall welter for ages in torment, even until they shall have paid the uttermost farthing. I say this for the benefit of strangers.

I have a father, brothers, children, and friends who have gone to a world of spirits. They are only absent for a moment. They are in the spirit, and we shall soon meet again. The time will soon arrive when the trumpet shall sound. When we depart, we shall hail our mothers, fathers, friends, and all whom we love, who have fallen asleep in Jesus. There will be no fear of mobs, persecutions, or malicious lawsuits and arrests; but it will be an eternity of felicity.

A question may be asked—"Will mothers have their children in eternity?" Yes! Yes! Mothers, you shall have your children; for they shall have eternal life, for their debt is paid. There is no damnation awaiting them for they are in the spirit. But as the child dies, so shall it rise from the dead, and be for ever living in the learning of God. It will never grow [in the grave]; it will still be the child, in the same precise form [when it rises] as it appeared before it died out of its mother's arms, but possessing all the intelligence of a God. Children dwell in the mansions of glory and exercise power, but appear in the same form as when on earth. Eternity is full of thrones, upon which dwell thousands of children, reigning on thrones of glory, with not one cubit added to their stature.

I will leave this subject here, and make a few remarks on the subject of baptism. The baptism of water, without the baptism of fire and the Holy Ghost attending it, is of no use; they are necessarily and inseparably connected. An individual must be born of water and the spirit in order to get into the kingdom of God. In the German, the text bears me out the same as the revelations which I have given and taught for the past fourteen years on that subject. I have the testimony to put in their teeth. My testimony has been true all the time. You will find it in the declaration of John the Baptist. (Reads from the German.) John says, "I baptize you with water, but when Jesus comes, who has the power (or keys) He shall administer the baptism of fire and the Holy Ghost." Great God! Where is now all the sectarian world? And if this testimony is true, they are all damned as clearly as anathema can do it. I know the text is true.

I call upon all you Germans who know that it is true to say, Eye. (Loud shouts of "Aye.")

Alexander Campbell, how are you going to save people with water alone? For John said his baptism was good for nothing without the baptism of Jesus Christ. "Therefore, *not* leaving the principles of the doctrine of Christ, let us go on unto perfection; not laying again the foundation of repentance from dead works, and of faith towards God, of the doctrine of baptism, and of laying on of hands, and of resurrection of the dead, and of eternal judgment. And this will we do, if God permit." (Heb. 6:1–3).

There is one God, one Father, one Jesus, one hope of our calling, one baptism. All these three baptisms only make one. Many talk of baptism not being essential to salvation; but this kind of teaching would lay the foundation of their damnation. I have the truth, and am at the defiance of the world to contradict me, if they can.

I have now preached a little Latin, a little Hebrew, Greek, and German; and I have fulfilled all. I am not so big a fool as many have taken me to be. The Germans know that I read the German correctly.

The Second Death

Hear it, all ye ends of the earth—all ye priests, all ye sinners, and all men. Repent! Repent! Obey the gospel. Turn to God; for your religion won't save you, and you will be damned. I do not say how long. There have been remarks made concerning all men being redeemed from hell; but I say that those who sin against the Holy Ghost cannot be forgiven in this world or in the world to come; they shall die the second death. Those who commit the unpardonable sin are doomed to *Gnolom*—to dwell in hell, worlds without end. As they concocted scenes of bloodshed in this world, so they shall rise to that resurrection which is as the lake of fire and brimstone. Some shall rise to the everlasting burnings of God; for God dwells in ever-lasting burnings and some shall rise to the damnation of their own filthiness, which is as exquisite a torment as the lake of fire and brimstone.

I have intended my remarks for all, both rich and poor, bond and free, great and small. I have no enmity against any man. I love you all; but I hate some of your deeds. I am your best friend, and if persons miss their mark it is their own fault. If I reprove a man, and he hates me, he is a fool; for I love all men, especially these my brethren and sisters.

I rejoice in hearing the testimony of my aged friends. You don't know me; you never knew my heart. No man knows my history. I cannot tell it: I shall never undertake it. I don't blame any one for not believing my history. If I had not experienced what I have, I would not have believed it myself. I never did harm any man since I was born in the world. My voice is always for peace.

I cannot lie down until all my work is finished. I never think any evil, nor do anything to the harm of my fellow-man. When I am called by the trump of the archangel and weighed in the balance, you will all know me then. I add no more. God bless you all. Amen.

❦ Appendix C ❦

Louisa Tanner Follett, Journal, June 5, 1844– September 8, 1845

I received from the State Historical Society of Iowa a photocopy of what I assume is a microfilm of the holograph (location of holograph now unknown). In making this typescript copy for publication, I have retained the original spelling, grammar, and punctuation. The original is unpaginated, but the section numbers and page numbers were apparently added by the historical society at the time it made its photocopy or microfilm. In most cases, two of the small (4x6") pages were filmed on one 8.5 x 11 page. Typescript March 2011 by Joann Follett Mortensen.

Section 1—June 5–21, 1844

Louisa Follett's Journal from Nauvoo to Ohio

Page 1

[chronologically out of order]

DeKalb March the 9th—Written by the Exile of Missouri

        The Last Farewell

            Farewell Father—Oh how tende,
            Are the chords that bind is here,

Jesus help me to surrender,
All I love without a tear.

Farewell Sister—do not press me,
To thy tender, throbbing heart,
Oh; no longer now distress me,
Sister—<u>Siter we must part</u>.

<u>Saccred to the memory of a Friend</u>
Farewell pale and silant Brother,
How I grieve to pain you so,
Father—Father Sister Brother,
Jesus calls Oh; let me go.

If distance e're should us devide
And we no more each other see
If friends more dear with you abide
I pray the still remember me.

Should e're thy futer hours of joy
By sorrows stormes o'er cloudied be
If brightened hope thy peace destroy
I pray the still remember me

The world may promis bliss secure
But trust it not—twill soon decay
Then seek for pleasures which endure
And never, never fade away

Wednesday
June the fifth 1844
I bade farewell to Nauvoo procedede down the river as far as Nashvill tied up for the knight, Started again at seven stuck on the rappids with difficulty gt of and made for shore—

Started again passed Warsaw at eleven O'Clock, Quincy at two we are now going at a rappid rate. Passed Hanibel sunset Louisan at nine O'Clock, on the morning of the 7th within a few miles of Alton all well in good spirits and company vary agreeable.

Friday eleven O'Clock
I am now in St Louis the great matropilis of Missouri, as soon as we stoped Cards weare presented from the Steamer "Belle Air" when we

soon made arangements for our passage as far as Bever, we shall be ready to start by four—This is a wonderful place for buisness, everything is all bustle, and confusion and if I may judge it is the great emporilim of the west

Page 2

Saturday June the 8th
This morning we are in St. Louis detaind by unfare promises by the Captain how long we shall be here is quite uncertain one thing I know it is quite an uncomfortable place, Twelve O Clock we are now just leaveing St Loui are under good head way down the river—June ninth we are this morning in the Ohio, we enterd the mouth last knight about twelve O Clock, nine this morning we passed the mouth of Cumberland river at a place called Smith Vill

Sunday the 10th
Have had a vary agreeable time with those on board meny of the Cabbin passengers have ben down to here us talk, I felt no embarrisment in portraying to them our percecution and suffering while thay gave a listing eare one with whome I became more conversant with then the rest was a gentleman from Indiana of preposessing abilities he stops to knight at Evens Vill we are under great head way and proceding with good speede up the Ohio; we came to Evens Vill a little past midnight—Shawney Town yesterday at four in the affternoon

The wether is becoming vary warm the Boat so crowded that it is quite uncomfortable, however I think I feel better then when I cam on board Traviling would be my choice if I had plenty of mony, changings of sceanes has had a tendency to greatly enliven my spirits and turn my from those melencholy scenes that have long prayed upon my thoughts This after noon Adaline was taken fainting a gentlemen kindely offerd us his state room with two births for our better accomadations, which we vary thankfuly accepted

Tuesday 11th we are now lying at a place called Madison—I feel vary unwell this morning having caught cold last knight while passing through the locks at the falls of the Ohio at Luivill

Page 3

This morning I felt vary much cast down through the want of menes to make my journey comfortable, none can realize the vicisitudes of traveling with out menes more than myself unless the Lord provids and gives me friends my tears will afften flow apace I have met with some warm hearted frinds but as yet have not had courage to disclose to them my nesessity—

Passed Warsaw about seventy five miles below Cincinati Shall reach there to knight

Six O Clock this morning, we are passing a town Called St Patrick built by the Roman Catholics

June the 13th
Arived at Cinanati at two O Cl at knight, staid till morning Changed Boats from the "Bell Aire" to the Cutter for Bever, such annother jam pile I never saw, we had to make our beads on the floor and then there was not room for all to lay down we left the City at half ten and are now under good head way

The steam is so high that it makes the Boat tremble

We passed Mays Vill at five O Clock and Portsmouth at twelve, last knight a man was drowned at a place called Ripley.

This morning we stoped at Sandy Creek which divids knentucky from Virginia on the east side of the Ohio river, and the State of Ohio on the west, passed Guyhon river stoped and got ice—at two O Clock passed german Town a small vilage on the east side of the river Galapolies at four, at five Keneway river Point Plesant on the Virginia side, a butiful situation the farmes flourishing and butiful This morning the fourteenth Parkers Burgh, came to Marietta a butiful city on the Ohio side we shall reach Beever to knight some time, the Muskingum river enters into the Ohio at Marietta 5 O Clock Sunrising at Sisters Vill

Page 4

June the 21st [This date is out of order and appears smudged]
This evening passed Wheling about dark, parted with two gentleman that had been vary friendly to me.

This Morning the 14th passed Stubenville & Wheling ten miles below Bever—we have had with the excepttion of being crowded had a plesant voyge, we hope in a few days to meet our friends that we have not seen for a long time, I am now many miles from Nauvoo, and when I shall again see them I know not—I left the Cutter at twelve to day and landed at Beaver, where we expect to stay till we go on board a Canall Boate for Cleveland—to-day is the eleventh day since I left home, I am now on bord a wharfe Boat and shall have to tarry till monday, when I hope a gain to renew my journing and soon meet my sister, and rest from the fatiages of traviling for a little season

My head feeles vary much affected with the motion of the Boate and the loss of our company on board, make me feil vary lonesom, we had much talk and bond with the passengers and some of them became vary friendly, thay expressed there regard for us at parting and wished us much success

Sunday the 16th on the Wharfe Boat at Bever
To day is the sabbath, but to me it has afforded me no rest to the soul or bodye, the continual stopping and the unlading of fraight from the Steam Boats, the gazeing at passengers, with strange faces has made me quite weary of the place, could I greatt the face of one solatary friend how would it relieve the feelings of my uttmost diconsolate heart

This morning Warren fell into river which has greatly anoid my peace through the day

Page 5

I am now fifteen hundred miles from Nauvoo a stranger in a strange land, without money, and no kind friend that is acquainted with my circumstances, to take an interest in my wellfare,—the earth to me is a tiresome place and when it will assume a different aspect I cannot tell— Beever is not as flourishing a place as I had expected, Philips Burgh on the opisit side of the river is a place of conciderable concinquence, settled by jermans, it lies twenty miles below Pitsburgh, we are now one hundred miles from Cleveland, I longe to rest at my Sisters, where I can clame the kindred ties of natural affecttion—

Monday the 17th

We are still lying at the Wharfe Boat where we have ben treated vary kindly particular by the agent, who is a good natured entelegent young man, posessing qualities that are vary preposessing may God make him a polished shaft in his quiver, that his talents may be improved to that advantage that will reflect honor to his Maker—

O could I stay with friends so kind, How would it clean my drooping mind

Monday three O Clock

We have just com on bord the Canall Boat, called Indiania, the Cabbin is vary warm and crowded with passingers, I have just taken the parting hand with one that has treated us with every mark of tenderness and kindness—we have ben with him two days and he has chargd us nothing Mr Veasey the jentleman that had the agency of the buisness of the Boat has gretly interested me in his favor, he is a man of worth and entelegence and deserves the friendship of every virtious and sensible person

Page 6

As for me I allways find some that is entitled to more of my friendship then others, and the reson why is, where I find entelegence then I find that, which clames my highest attention—

Morning of the 18th

I slept tolerable well except the idea that haunts me a sleepe or a wake that I am a stranger in a strange land without money—O how little the rich think or feel for those that poverty and opression has deprived of the nesessary comforts of life, since I commenced this journey I have often see the the business of life presented before me, but could not obtain them for the want of menes—O Lord let some kind hand be touchd to adminerster to my wants that an evidance may remain that thou art still mindful of one that is made desolate by the hand of corroding time

Tusday noon—crossed the line out of Peansylvania in to Ohio, passed through youngs, town, at one O Clock not so much crowded with passengers, the weather vary warm the Boat mooves forward slowly This after noon I have had a warm and spirited confab with a Methodist Priest, he appeared to have a form of godliness but destitute of that knowledg that gives the power—I felt a degre of regard for him as a person of preposessing apperance, but sincerely pittied him, for the darkness with which his mind was enveloped,—

June 21th
Wednesday AM
We are now in sight the County Seat of Portage, where I have often wandered in gone by days, it reminds of endearing asociations then formed but long since broken off

Page 7

To a sensative mind that is formed to apreciate joys and sorrows, there is much to ocupi the mind—

Eleven O Clock we are now at the County Seate of Portage Ravenna the first person that met my wandering gaze was Alonzo Henry and Sister Whiting, with whome we conversed for the spase of an hour we then parted, she has gone to Nauvoo and we persue our way onward, this affternoon the conversation was again renewed with the Methodist Priest his darkness with regard to the authority of the Priest hood was so great that it was not heard for a woman to wind him up in his narrow covering

Section 2

Ca. June 22, 1844–September 17, 1844
[Not all entries in this section are in chronological order.]

Page 8

June 22d, we arivd in Cleveland at five in the after noon, staid on borde the boat rose erley in the morning, walked up to the Stage Office to engage a passage to Parma waited till eight O'Clock, found that I had ben left, got my trunk put in the store house went on shore found a young man that agreed to carry me for one dollar,—left Cleaveland at ten, took dinner at Marriss tavern, got to my sisters at three in the after noon, to my great joy and satisfacton found them all well and glad to see me

I would not forgit to mention a circumstance that occurred with the Methodist Priest, after all all our confabs on the subject of Mormonism he came to me just as the Boat was ready to start said he regarded me with a peculiar friendship, that I manifested a firmness not easey to be shaken, wished me a prosperous journey affecttionately took my hand

and bid me farewell thus ended my short acquaintance of four days with one to whome I bore a strong testimony of what I knew and most assurdly believed, may the Lord give him a heart to believe unto righteouness that with the mouth confession may be made unto salvation

Page 9

Tusday July the 9th Parma
This after noon I was agreeable surprisd by the arival of Bro Sylvester Hulit, as he was on a visit in the neighborhood to visit some relitives, while we conversed we sitnessed [sic] strong proofs of setarian blindness—when O when will the veil be rent and the hearts of this gentile generation become subject to the power of insperation

July the 14th
Sunday Evening this day I have attended meeting in company with my Sister and family, since I returned a Cleaveland paper was handed to me containing several accounts of the late desturbances in Nauvoo—it reports that the Prophet is no more and that Hyrum his Brother is dead allso as yet I cannot give much credet to the report but wait for better authenticated reports

July the 21st Parma Sunday After noon
I have just recieved and read a Nauvoo Nieghbor containing the mournful but authenticated entelegence of the Death of the Prophet and his brother—The helish desire has atlength ben purpretrated and a great man has fallen to stain with blood the freeborn rits of this great republic—Alass my heart bleeds at the remberances of those sceanes that have spred devastation desolation and death over our once happy land Where will those scenes of mobicatic violenc end my hart trembles at the coming events—although I am not presant as on every every ocasion preceding this yet I feel a deepe sympathy in all the afflicttions of my friends at Nauvoo

> Oh wretched murders! ??? for human blood
> you've slain the Prophets of the living God
> Who've borne oppression from there erly youth
> To plant, on earth, the principles of truth

Page 10

> Oh Illinos thy soul has drank the blood
> Of Prophets marterd for the Cause of God

> Now Zion mourns—she mourns an earthly head
> The Prophet and the Patriarch are dead

August 21st Attica Center

This morning accompaned by my Bro. in-law and sister, I bid farewell to Parma, came to Cleveland, went on bord the Constitution bound for Buffalo left the Pier at twelve O'Clock, got under good head way, we had not ben out long before the passengers began to fall like men in battle, the dead swells rolled heavely which caused much sickness, on the morning of 22d we arived at Buffalow, but too late to take the morning Carrs, staid at Huffs <u>Hotell</u>, till four was convayed to the Depo where I was comfortable seated in the train for attica, I had a most delightful passage the distance of thirty one miles in two hours, stayed at the Depo in Attica Village, took some refreshment hired a buggy to convey me to my Brother's where I found them all well

23d this morning Brother Joseph and Wife accompanied me to Brother Williams, where I met my aged Father once more and realized all that pleasure that I had anticipated after a long and painful abscene, Attica is a delightful place, its luxurant hills present a butiful prospect, it is a place that is calculated to please the Eye and gladden the heart

August the 25th

This day after the servises of the Church was over, in company with my Father, Brother & Wife I visited the graves of my dear departed Mather and Brother, While treading beside their lonely and narrow resting place I truly felt thankful that God had spared me to gaze on the green turfs that entombed thear precious remains, more to be desired was this privilege then silver and gold, faith had hitherto enabled me to look forward to this time, and I now felt perfectly satisfied that thear, I beheld all that remained of those that I once

Page 11

loved and revered on earth, and felt the time not far distant when I should again meet them in the glorious morning of the resurrection in a glorified state, to be no more subject to Sickness Death and sorrow—
"Time was thay life like me posessed and time will be when I shall rest"

Septtember the 7th

This morning I had an introduction to a Mrs Kinkum the widdow of the late Mr Kinkum, author of the english grammer now so extensively in use, she is from the City of N.Y. a lady of preposessing apperance and accomplishments—I could not refrain from tears when I contrasted my situation with hers, all though we had both ben alike unfortunate in the loss of our husbands, yet prosperity was still sheding its rays of consolation to the one and withholding from the other.

Oh that I could over-come this spirit of native pride and ambition, and bring my mind to a humble acquiesance and submition to the vecisitudes of this life—

I am now at my Bro Williams where I am vary tenderly treated by my Father and family, and am sorounded with much to outward appearance calculated to produce happiness but Oh! Thear is a vacuum within that remains unsatisfied which outward apperances cannot satisfy—

Septtember the 17
This morning I left my Bro Williams in company with my Father for St Lawrance County, we left the Depo at halfe past ten O Clock, for Rochester where we arived at two in the after noon staid till four and then was conveyed to the landing where we had to wait till twelve O Clo at knight, when we repaired to the river, went on bord the Rochester bound for Ogdensburgh, stoped at Oswego, took breckfast with Courtland Copper tutchd at Kingston, arived

Page 12

arived at Ogdensburgh at nine at Knight, set of in the Staige at three for Hermon when we arived at four in the after noon, found our friends all well and meet with a warm reception—I am now where my eyes meet the wondering gaze of meny that I have known in gone by days, O how the corroding hand of time has invaded their once youthful formes, and silverd one their locks furrowed their cheeks and tell that the days of meny are allmost numbered—

From the place where I now write, I can look and behold the Parental dwelling where I once had a home, where I was once greeted by the fond an affecttionate imbrace of a kind Father and Mother Brothers and Sisters, but now how strangly altered, I see no more those smiling and happy faces, I no longer here the voice of tenderness at my coming, allass;

the voice of a kind mother and Bro is still in Death, and the once peacful mansion is now dserted, O how mournful and desolate is the place, how changed, it was the place of my youthful days the morning of my life—I look and weepe in silant medittation while none but him, that seeth in secret is a witness the mournful reflecttions of my heart Again I pass the Cottage where I begun first to preform the duties of a wife and Mother Stop and look towards that once loved place, but no kind Husband meets my fond imbrace he that used to share my joys and sorrow is no more the kind hand that was ever open to admnenster to my wants is now cold in Death and with my little orphin Boy I am a wandrer alone and unprotected, O God thou Eternal Father give me fortitude and resignation that I may encounter these tryals as one that is seekeing a nother and a better Country even a heavenly one that when meeting and parting is at an end, I may injoy rest eternal at thy right hand

Page 13

whene all tears shall be wiped away and whene parting shall never more come—

At present my life is a composition of joy and sorrow. I am it is true a mong friends but thay do not fiel the sorrow that often swell my anxious bosom—but with the Poet I can say

> When a few more years I've wasted
> When a few more spring are one
> When a few more griefs I've tasted
> I shall fall to rise no more

Benington September the 1st, 1844.

What a variety of painful and pleasing thoughts dos the recollection of past years excite in the mind, I have seen days of prosperity and gladness, and days of adversity and sorrow, I have enjoyed the love of relitives and friends and conversed with the wise and the good

But meny of those who were nearest and dearest to me, are gone down to the grave; and I stand like a tree sorounded with a new jeneration—The spring is past; the summer is ended; the autumn is allmost closeing and winter is at hand. Shall I indulge in sadness and grief? no; I will most thankfully aknowledge the devine goodness. I have enjoyd numberless blessings and I now put my severiest trials among them What blessings in providance have I to recount: God has preserved me and done "all things well" I have had friends and benefacttors. The evile that I feared did not befall me: and good things that I never expected have been granted Truly it becomes me to be thankful

Page 14

[The following is inserted here, with no date or explanation.]

Credit to Zenah Tanner
To two Pounds of Butter
To two of Shugar
To two of Honey
To one quarter of Tea
To making two Pair of Shoes

Credit to Gorge Ellis
One Bushel of buck wheat
To one Dollar twenty five Cents

Sunday August the 11th Parma Ohio [This entry is out of chronological and geographical sequence.]

The time has come, when I must bid farewell to Parma, and go to other place acrost Lake Eries rooling waters; Farewell to these my lonely walks and solitary places, where oft I've loved to wander; in twilights pensive shade; and think on those that heaven has formed for happiness and friendship—

Farewell while thus I go perhaps to never more retrace these much loved walks of silant prayr and medittation—Oh that kind heaven would now in mercy prosper me to meet and clame a Fathers blessing Twas this that caused me thus to wander forth in lonelyness a Widdow to see and here my Father bless me e're he dies And then to tread beside the ashes of my Mother, and there to lift my prayer to heaven that I may meet her, when God shall say my work on earth is done, it is enough, rest from the toils and troubles of this weary life

Page 15

> The last Interview
>
> Here in this lovely place where first I saw thee
> I come my friend beneath the moon's pale ray
> To gaze once more, through struggling tears upon thee
> And then to tear my broken heart away;

I dare not linger near thee as a Brother
I feel my burning heart would still be thine
How could I hope my passionate thoughts to smother
While yealding all the sweetness to another
      That should be mine
But fate hath willed it—the decree is spoken
Now life may lengthen out its weary Chain
For reft of thee, its loveliest links are broken
May we but clasp them all in heaven again
Thear are sweet meetings of the pure and fond
Oh joys unspeakable to such are given
When the sweeat ties of love that here are riven
      Unite beyond
A glorious charm from heaven thou dost inheret
The gift of angels unto the belongs
Then breathe thy love in music that thy spirit
May whisper to me thro' thine own sweet songs
And though my coming life may soon resemble
The desert spots thro' which my life may flee
Though round thee then wilde worshipers assemble
My heart will triumph if thine own but tremble
      Still true to me
Yes thou will then be mine in your blue heaven
And now farewell! Farewell! I dare not lengthen
These sweete sad moments out—To gaze on thee
Is bliss indeede, yet it but serves to strengthen
The love that now amounts to agony
This is our last farewell—our last fond meting
The world is wide and we must dwell apart
My spirit gives the now the last fond greeting
With lip to lip while pulse to pulse is beating
      And heart to heart
Farewell! Farewell! Our dreames of bliss is over
All, save the memory of our plighted love
I now must yeald the to a happier lover
Yet Oh, remember, thou art mine above
Tis a sweet thought, and while by distance parted
I will twine upon our hearts a holy spell
But the sad tears beneath thy lids have started
And I alass, we both are broken hearted
      Dearest Farewelle

Page 16

[Louisa apparently copied this poem in two parts, neither complete, and in two places. For reading convenience, a single version is presented here, from versions on pp. 16–17 and p. 24 of the holograph]

Lady Byrons Farewell

Fare the well inconstant lover
If thy fickle flame was love
Though our transient joys are over
I can near inconstant prove

Man may bost of deathless passion
Swear his love shall near decline
But unfixt his changeful passion
Womans fate may change like mine

Once I thought I might believe the
Might on Byrons othe rely
But my armes did scarse receive thee
Ere thy othes unheded died

From parentel armes you took me
Stole me from my Mothers care
Then in wantonness forsook me
For some more admired fair

Prayrs and tears were unvialing
Naught thy purpos could beguile
Not a wife her wooes bewailing
Not a lovely infants smile

Heaven has formed the for unkindness
Seald thy heart to all thats mild
Dimed thy sight to moral blindness
Left the maturs waywards child.

Nay I must not cannot chide the
What thou hast not who can blame
Virtue is what heaven's denied the
And the world has done the same

Think not I can near forget the
No thy griefs will all be mine
I shall weepe when foes beset the
Smile when fortune's sun shall shine

Must I can I shall a Mother
Hate the Father of her child
Mercy heaven my anguish smother
At that name my infant smiled

Page 17

Around his grave let there be seene
Young hyacinth's forever green
The sweetest rooses of the year
In quick sucsession shall appear

To deck his grave in morning flowers
The clowds shall weepe in falling showers
The lily there shall hang its head
In <u>mourning for the lovely Dead</u>

To deck his grave in morning flowers
The clowds shall weepe in falling shower
The lily then shall hang its head in
In mourning for the lovely Dead

Smiled to think she had a Father
To protect her growing years
Unsuspectting orphan other
Drown they eyes in flood's of tears

Father no sweet babe thou hast not.
All his care you must forego—
Others peace thy griefs may blast not
But thou hast the keenest woo

Orphan babe my care shall even
Guard the from the ills of life
Death alone hath power to sever
Byrons babe and Byrons wife

July the 15ᵗʰ [This entry is out of chronological sequence.]

It requires not time nor proof to make virtuous hearts coalaeasce! There is a language without sounds, a recognition independent of the visual Organ, which acknowledges the kindness of congenial souls allmost the moment they meet The virtuous mind knoweth its brother in the dark

Page 18

The love of friendship that heavenborn principle, that pure affecttion which units congenial spirits here, and with which the Creator will hereafter connect in one blest fraternity, has but one cause, the universal fareness of its object That bright perfecttion which speaks of unchangeableness and immortality is a something so excelant that I ever wish to partake its essance, to share its attainments of true and lasting happiness These are ames aims and joys of real love and friendship, it has nothing selfish; in every desire it soars above this earth; and anticipats the ultimatum of its joys the moment when it shall meet its partner before the throne of God

Section 3

March 9–May 7, 1845

Louisa Follett
    Linden
        Missouri

Comfort ye Comfort ye may People

Page 19

De Kalb March the 9ᵗʰ 1845

How solom is the reflections of my mind to day, as I sit pensive and alone, while memory calls up those scenes that transpird one year ago. It is the aniversary of that painful season, when I commited to the colde and silent grave, the companion of my youthful days

The painful and trying event comes fliting back on my memory, with a redoubled sensation. Oh! How my heart mourns afresh, when I feel that I am left alone and un<u>protect</u>ed to endure the winds of adversity in a colde and unfeeling world–

Great God, thou who hast hitherto ben my helper in times of trouble and deepe distress, do not I intreate the abandon me in this hour of tribulation Oh! Strengthen my heart and flesh that I murmer and faint not; but help me to acknowledge thy hand and kiss the rod and him who hath appointed it—Strengthen me for every event of thy providanc that doth yet awaite me and hasten the time when I shall praise the in more exalted strains

Page 20

The Lord has spared me to survie a long and dreary winter—I hail the returning Spring with increasing delight hopeing that it will prove favorable in restoreing me to my friends and family in the <u>Far West</u>
Nine long months have I ben seperated from kind and sympathiseing friends and Children—and my heart yearn with increasing desire to fold them to my warm and affecttionate imbrace—
Should kind heven prove propitious to my wishes I hope soon to prove the enduring love and friendship of those who on ocasions the most trying have ever ben ready to extende the hand of tenderness and affecttion Should my life be protracted, a few weaks longer, I must again endure the painful feelings of biding friends fare well, with the expecttation of never again beholding them in time, how much I shall stand in kneed of timely consideration, to prepare me with fortitude for the event

DeKalb March the 31st
In a letter recently received from Nauvoo, I have been informed of the Death of two of my much loved and valued friends

James Daily very muched loved and worthy Sone-in-law is gone the way of all the Earth he rests from all the turmoils and suffering of this world of pain and anxiety, and while my tears flow on account of his suden removal his freed spirit has gone to greet the numerous company that had gaind the port before him—He has left a weepeing Companion and two little Boys to mourn, how I wish to be where I can see Nancy, and afford her a Mothers sympathies—

I Bankdoll a youth of eightteen has been cut down by the ruthless hand of death, and left an afflicted Mother Brothers, and Sister to mourn his erly departure—he was lovely in life and happy in Death therefore I will not sorrow as those that have no hope, thank God he rests from opression—

Page 21

[The contents of this page obviously fit in the middle of Page 23 so I have moved it there.]

Page 22

April 21st
I took an affecttionat farewell of my friends in Hermon, came to DeKalb, aranged my affairs for my entended journey, staid at Bro Seth Alexanders, next day came to my Sisters and meet my Brothers for the last time, it was a painful ocason I could scarsely say farewell, as I felt thear last affecttionat imbrace and vewed their retireing forms, as thay wended their way from me, alass thought I, must we never behold each other again while veiled in mortality; and I never again share in thair protection and council, my heart was deepely pained with the reflecttion, and I felt for a few moments all the bitterness of a painful sepperation— Friday the 25, I left DeKalb in the Stage for Ogdensburgh, whene I arived on the morning of the 26th took passage on board the Lady of the Lake for Rochester

    Benington May 7th 1845
    Thou art gone—thou couldst not go—
    True friends can never part;
    Our prayer is one, our hope is one,
    And we are one in heart!
    Nor place nor time, can e'er divide
    The souls which frienship seals
    But still the changing scene of life
    Their mutual love reveals

    Thy form and look in memory's glass
    I still distinctly see
    Ty voice and words, in fancy's ear
    Are whispering still to me
    The stars that meet thy pensive eye
    Are presant still to mine
    The moonlight which sorounds thy path
    Around my footstepts shine

    Oh tis one scene of parting here
    Love watchword is—Farewell

And allmost starts the flowing tear
Ere dried the last that fell
Tis but to feel that one most dear
Is needful to the heart
And straight a voice is muttering near
Impervious, ye must part!

Page 23

Came to Oswego and spent the Sabbath, embark'd again on monday, morning landed at Rochester in time to take the Evening Carrs, reached attica a little after eight in the evening staid till the next day, then visited my friends in that place, found them all well and glad to see me. I staid tenn days and then in company with my Father, again took the Carrs and came to Buffalo where I paid my fare on board the General Harrison, for Cleveland my Father staid on board, till the Bell gave the signal for our departure, I then took an affecttionate leave of my aged Father for the last time, and he returned to Attica, while I was borne with swift rapidity on the rolling waters of Lake Erie to Cleveland where I arived the next day at tenn O Clock, I was convayd in a Carriag to the American House where after resting my selfe a little, I walked out in scerch of some one to

[Contents of Page 21]

take me to Parma, but finding no oppertunity to that purpos, I accidental met with a gentleman, who kindely took me to his boarding house which proved to be a place kept by a friend and acquaintance of mine, where I spent four days vary plesantly, and then hired a man to carry me to Parma where I arived on the 13th of May and found my friends in that place all well and glad to see me, and here let me say that I feel a greatful sense of gratitude swell my bosom while I remember that I have ben mercifully preserved while alone and unprotected I have traveled the distance of five hundred miles by land and water, and now contrary to my expecttations when I reached here, I shall be under the nesessety of spending the summer in Parma, notwithstanding the disapointment I feel to acknowledge the hand of the Lord in it and feel vary happy in the family of my Sister that treat me with every feeling of tenderness and respect, as allso my Son in law with whome I reside a part of the time

Page 23 [continued]

Can I forgit my native land that lovely spot of Earth
And call another Clime my own, that never gave me birth
Can I forgit that native land that gave me friends so dear
Who sympathizd in all my fears and gave me tear for tear

Can I forgit my native land, while Sisters kind are there
And Brothers too, who always sought to know my wish and care
Can I forgit my native land that dear enchanting place
When first I felt a Fathers love a Mothers kind embrace

And last of all can I forgit that holy place of God
When first I felt my sins forgiven clensed by a Saviour's blood

DeKalb St Lawrance March the 23d [date out of sequence]

Page 24

[repeats part of "Lady Byrons Farewell,"]

Page 25

The White Pilgrim

I came to the spot where the white Pilgrim lay
And pensively stood by the tomb
And in a low whisper I herd something say
How sweeatly I sleepe here alone—

The Tempest may howle and the loud thunder rool
And gathering stormes may arise
Yit Calm are my feelings at rest is my Soul
And the tears are all wip'd from my Eyes—

The cause of my master propeled me from home
I bid my companion farewell
I left my sweeat children which for me do mourn
In far distant regions to dwell—

I wandered a stranger an Exile below
To publish salvation abroad
The trump of the gospell endeavored to blow
Inviting poor siners to God—

And when among strangers and far from my home
No kindred or relitive nigh

I met the contagion and sank in the tomb
My spirit to mansions on high—

Go tell my Companion and Children most dear
To weepe not for Joseph though gone
The same hand that led me through scenes dark and drear
Has kindly assisted me home—

Louisa Follett St Lawrance N.Y.

Smile to think she had a Father
To protect her growing years
Unsuspecting Orphin other
Drown thy Eyes in flood's of tears

Father no sweeat Babe thou hast not
All his care you must forego
Others peace thy griefs may blast not
But thou hast the keenest woe

Orphin Babe my care shall ever
Guide the from the ills of life
Death alone hath power to sever
Byron's Babe and Byron's wife—

Hermon Village, March the 23d [date out of sequence]

Section 4

Aug. 19–Sept. 8, 1845

Journal from Parma Ohio to Nauvoo

Page 26

August 19th
Tis morning I bid my Sister and family farewell, and was conveyed to Cleveland in a Carriage where we went on Board a Canall Boat bound for Beever. Left Cleveland on the 20th just as the Bell rung for tien O Clock

Saturday the 23d

Came to Beever about seven O'Clock Passage two Dollars a piece, the wether is vary warm and oppressive and I am quite unwell; my journey looks long and dreary—

Sunday 24th we are now waiting for a Boat from Pitsburgh to carry us to Cincinati, this after noon we went on board the

Page 27

"Alagana Bell" our prospects are rather discouragn, the Boate is heavy loded and accomodations poor, we are now tied up for the knight, slept vary well dureing the knight, started this morning the 25th, passed Stubenville at six, came on well till we came to a place called The Three Sisters where we now stick fast on the bottom The water is so low in the River that we meete with meny hindeans may the Lord grant me faith and patienc to carry me through this trying journey–

August 26 we left Wheling this morning at Seven O Clock, and are now under good head way down the river. Our accomadations are vary poor together with the warm wether renders our journey vary unpleasant We are now among strangers with but little mony, and how we shall prosicute our journey is yet in futurity

This Evening 6 O Clock we passed Marietta a butiful City on the Muskingum, came on well met with no obstructtion tied up for the knight at a small town called Hocking on the Virginia side—

This morning we are moveing with swift rapidity on the waters of the Ohio, shall reach Cincinati to morrow This morning the 27th we arived at Cincinati, hear I meet

Page 28

with a severe tryal, however Summoning all the fortitude I could I put on my Bonnet and walked out on the wharfe and engaged our passage to St Louis for two Dollars a piece on board the Columba, I went on board with a heavy heart prayin the Lord to send me some simpathising friend that would take an interest in our wellfair, I did not wait long for the desired blessing, I soon found a family of Mormons bound for Nauvoo with whome I became acquainted who kindly renderd us the assistance we kneeded—the Boate is crowded with German and Swiss Emigrants I am now passing the North Bend on the Ohio, and allso the Mansion of the late General Harrison, the place where his remains lay are in full vew

Sunday the 30th
We got to Louisvill, and stoped for the knight—we are now passing the falls of the Ohio through the locks, two days more and I hope to be in St Louis—To day Septtember the lst we passed Evens Vill at four O Clock, the Wabash at teen in the Evening

Tusday the 2d we stoped at a fine town on the Kentucky side at the mouth of Tenesee River we are now fifty miles from the mouth of the Ohio and expect to be in St Louis to morrow

Page 29

I long to ship for the last time and reach the place of my distination, I feel nearly worn down with my long protracted journey, Monday twelve O Clock we passed the mouth of the Ohio at a small town called Cairo two hundred miles from St Louis we are crowded with negros on one side and the Dutch on the other a more degraded set I never saw. Tusday the 3d we are now in sight of the Barracks six miles below St Louis, the day and knight has ben vary warm and all on board feel the efects.

Wednsday six O Clock
We landed in St Louis the great emporium of the west Staid dureing the knight on board the Negros and Musketoes being vary troublesom—

Thursday Morning
We engaged a passage on borde the Ohio, after being at the trouble of conveying our things on board we had to engage annother Boate the Pilot and hands having left we accordingly went on bord the Petosi bound for Galena we staid in St. Louis two days left friday six O Clock, slept well dureing the knight but awoke sick in the morning having caught a heard Cold Saturday the 6 has been a day of but a little comfort the Boate is heavy laden and moovs vary slow—

Page 30

The time is protracted in which I anticipated meeting my friends and Children in Nauvoo, Sunday the 7th we are now in sight of the City of Quincy, my heart takes courage thinking I am near the place of my destination my health is rather better this morning, O how I long to gaze one more on the beloved City of the Saints and meet the warm embrace of my Children and friends; this is the third Sunday that I have been confined to a Steam Boate I long once more to meete in the assembly of the Saints and again be privileged with hearing the words of eternal life. I have left Babalon for the last time, and thanks be to God for his preserveing care dureing my long and protracted journey,

Last evening was a troublesom knight, we came to the foot of the rappids a little after dark, when the Boate had to be unladed which caused much confusion; at day light we started and came over stuck for halfe an hour, we at length got safe over which brought in sight of the beloved City we are now lying at Nashvill waiting for the lighten [lighter]—

Page 31

At ten O Clock we safely landed at the Stone House where we meet with a most cordial welcom from our friends and relitive in Nauvoo, I repaired to my former place of residence where I took dinner, and then in company with my eldest sone I visited the Temple, where I vewed with wonder and amazement the mgnificenc of that butiful Structture—from thence I visited my Daughter on Young Streete and spent the knight and returned home, after a few days we moved to the Lower Stone House where we are vary comfortable situated for the presant—

Allthough my health is much impaird yet when I take a retrospecttive vew of the past, I fee that I have abundant reson to bless God, that amidst the danger to which I have ben exposd that I have ben mercifully preserved and brought to join my afflictted family and Bretheren in Nauvoo—

❦ Appendix D ❦

The Children of King and Louisa Follett

Adeline or Adaline Louisa Follett West, 1816–84

Like most women of her generation, Adeline's name appears in few public written records. However, her whereabouts as an adult can be traced with fair accuracy through census records, that show where she lived every ten years until her death. Family records in my possession and some other written records spell her name "Adeline," the spelling I have used; however, some sources spell it "Adaline," including her obituary below. In September 1847, the Iowa State Census shows Adeline and her husband, Nathan Ayres West, living in Van Buren County, Iowa. At an unspecified later date, the family moved farther west to District 21, Pottawattamie County, Iowa. Here they would have had the company of thousands of other Mormons, most of them waiting to move to Utah. The 1850 census, enumerated on November 29, lists Adeline and Nathan (a "joiner," or fine carpenter), along with Adeline's brothers, sixteen-year-old Edward and thirteen-year-old Warren.[1] (Louisa Follett was living with her other daughter Nancy and husband Henry Sanford in Atchison County, Missouri.) By July of 1856, Adeline, Nathan, and Louisa—but not Edward or Warren—appear on the Iowa State Census in Silver Creek Township, Iowa, where Nathan's occupation is given as "Farmer."[2] On the 1860 federal census, taken July 16, Adeline and

Nathan are listed as living at Mount Olive Post Office, Silver Creek Township, Mills County, Iowa. Nathan's occupation is given as farming with real estate valued at $4,000 and personal property at $1,000.[3]

By September 2, 1870, the family's location is unchanged, but the real estate is valued at $3,000, and their next-door-neighbors are Warren Follett (Adeline's brother) and his family, including Louisa Follett.[4] By July 1, 1880, the same information is given, but with no dollar value put on Nathan's property.[5] On each of these records, Adeline is identified as either "housekeeping" or "at home."

A local history states that among early residents who arrived between 1851 and 1855 were "N. A. West and W. K. Follett."[6] An 1881 history of Mills County contains a short biography of Nathan A. West, his first marriage, and his second marriage to Adeline L. Follett on March 17, 1836. After eight years in Illinois (without mentioning Nauvoo),

> he was allured by the attractions of Iowa to its borders and in 1848 he permanently located in Mills county, being one of its first settlers; in fact lived in the territory when it was a part of Pottawattamie county. He has thus seen this section of the state reclaimed from its native wilderness, and its towns grow up to their present dimensions and prosperity.... His principle [sic] pursuit through life has been that of farming. His farm of eighty acres lies in section twenty. At the first election in Silver Creek township he was elected justice of the peace, and has continued to hold that office almost continually since. He has held various other township trusts.[7]

Interestingly, the article does not mention any branch of Mormonism—LDS, RLDS, or Cutlerite—, the family's participation in Mormonism, or the impact of Mormon settlement in that area of Iowa. However, Nathan (and perhaps Adeline, although her name is not mentioned) joined the Cutlerite movement in the Silver Creek area and was excommunicated with Cutler on April 20, 1851, during a Mormon conference held under Orson Hyde's direction at Kanesville, Iowa. The grounds given for the total of six excommunications were "aiding and abetting Father Cutler, and promulgating his insidious views."[8]

Nathan signed the notice of Adeline's death in 1884:

Died

> WEST—On the 1st day of August, 1884, Adaline Louisa, wife of N. A. West, aged 67 years, 7 months and 11 days.
>
> Mrs. West was the first child of King and Louisa Follett, and was born in St. Lawrence county, N.Y., on the 21st day of December, 1816.

In early childhood she removed with her parents to Ohio, and when in her 16th year to Missouri, where in March, 1836, she became the wife of Mr. West, who in 1848 settled in Mills county. She was a kind and affectionate wife, and endeared herself to all who became acquainted with her, who all join speaking to her praise.

And now for myself and all those connected with her, I here tender my sincere thanks to my friends and neighbors for their kind sympathy and assistance in our affliction. N. A. West.[9]

Adeline did not have any biological children but helped raise Nathan's two daughters by his first marriage and also one grandchild. Three months later, Nathan married Julia A. Johnson Fleming, in Glenwood, Mills County, Iowa, on November 11, 1884.[10] Three and a half years later, Nathan died on May 8, 1888. He and Adeline are both buried in the same plot with Louisa in the Malvern Cemetery.[11]

John Follett, 1819–ca. 1849

King Follett continued the family tradition of naming the oldest son "John." On some records, he is also identified as John W. or John Wesley. When he was about twenty-six or twenty-seven, he left Nauvoo with the rest of the family sometime after February 1846. A few months later, he married Elizabeth M. Daley on November 12, 1846.[12] She was the sister of James Daley, who, before his death in 1844, had been married to John's sister, Nancy. *The Early Latter-day Saints Database* notes that Emer Harris performed the ceremony.[13] Emer was a brother to Martin Harris, one of the Three Witnesses to the Book of Mormon. A biographical sketch of Emer states that he and his family had moved to Pottawattamie County, Iowa, by the fall of 1846,[14] which is very probably the site of the marriage. A membership record of the LDS Mill Branch, Iowa, organized April 28, 1847, lists among its members John W. Follett, age twenty-seven, a Seventy, and Elizabeth M. Follett, age twenty-one.[15]

The only other information I have found about John during this period is contained in a biographical sketch of Lyman Stephen Wood, the son of Elizabeth's sister Hannah Daley and Gideon Durfy Wood. In his list of aunts and uncles, he identifies his aunt Elizabeth Millicent as the wife of "John Follett, (son of King Follett) who died some two or three years later," adding that Elizabeth "never to my knowledge joined the Church."[16] This information, based on a marriage date by at least

1846 and a death date of "two to three years later" would place John's death around 1848 and 1849. One family record in my possession with no identifying source gives his death date as 1849.[17]

In a search of the 1850 federal census for Iowa, I did not find a listing for John or Elizabeth Follett. However, in the listing for Isaac Nelson, who is the husband of Elizabeth's sister Hilea Daley Nelson, is a female named Elizabeth, age twenty-three, born in Ohio, and a female named Alwilda, age four, born in Ohio.[18] Though the surname of these two individuals is given as Nelson, I believe they are Elizabeth Follett and a daughter born to her and John. This record would support a death date for John prior to November 15, 1850, the date this census was taken. Elizabeth Follett and Alvilda Follett are each listed as individuals living in Pottawattamie County on an 1851 census of sixteen Iowa counties.[19] The 1852 Iowa State Census for Kanesville Division, Pottawattamie County, again lists Elizabeth Follet as "head of family" with one other female (no name or age listed) in the same household.[20] An 1856 Iowa census listing with Isaac Nelson as the head has a record for Elizabeth Follett, age thirty-one, and Alwelda Follett, age eight.[21]

Although I have found no official birth record for this daughter of John and Elizabeth, family records in my possession, corroborated by my own research, identify a daughter named "Alvilda, Awilda, or Alvadilla" (sometimes with the first name of Mary), born August 28, 1848, who married H. Martin Wright in Wyoming in 1873. She died in Salt Lake City in 1917 at age seventy, which also supports a birth date of 1848. Her death certificate gives her father's last name as "Follette" and her mother's as "Daly." Those same family records show Elizabeth marrying W. A. Ellis in Harrison County, Iowa, on July 1, 1857. They appear together in the 1860 federal census of Magnolia, Harrison County, Iowa. Ellis's occupation is given as physician, with two daughters: twelve-year-old "Alvadilla" Follett and two-year-old Ann Ellis. Elizabeth and Ann both died in 1863 and are buried in Calhoun Cemetery, Calhoun, Harrison County, Iowa, when Alvilda would have been about fifteen. I have found no further record of her until her marriage ten years later in Wyoming.[22]

Nancy M. Follett Daley Sanford, 1823–74

After leaving Nauvoo, Nancy M. (her middle name is given variously as both Millicent and Mariah) and her second husband, Henry Sanford, along with Nancy's two sons from her first marriage to James Daley (then deceased), first settled in the northwest corner of Missouri (now Atchison County) adjacent to what is now Fremont County, Iowa. Atchison County was established in 1845 but the northern border between the two states was not permanently established until 1849. Westbound travelers frequently moved through the area, including Mormons leaving the Midwest. Therefore, it had a very mobile population with 1,648 individuals listed on the 1850 census, dated September 25.

The household of Henry and Nancy Sanford in that enumeration included Nancy's two sons, nine-year-old William Daley and five-year-old James Daley, Nancy's mother, Louisa Follett, and two children born to Nancy and Henry: four-year-old Mary (making her birth year 1846 though later census and family records and Mary's obituary give her birth year as 1848 and 1849[23]) and three-month-old "Newill W.," born about January 1850. Both of these children are listed as being born in Missouri,[24] suggesting that they moved to that state immediately after leaving Nauvoo. Newill does not appear on the 1860 census, suggesting his death. He also does not appear on any early Follett family records. Nancy and Henry had another child while still living in Missouri: Farmer Sanford, born February 2, 1851. (See his biographical sketch below.)

The 1850 census lists Henry's occupation as "Stage Contract" (presumably stage driver or freighter), a rough and dangerous but viable occupation in a frontier town of that era. By September 1852, three years after the California gold rush began in 1849, the Sanfords had arrived in Contra Costa County, California. It is not known whether they started to move to the Salt Lake Valley with the other Latter-day Saints, then continued on to California for unknown reasons, or whether their move had something to do with Henry's occupation. According to the biographical sketch of their son, Farmer Sanford, "born in Atchison county, Missouri, February 2, 1851," the family "first located about one mile from the present site of the town of Walnut Creek. Here his parents resided for one year, and then moved to Martinez, where they remained for two years. His father next moved to, and purchased the hotel at Lafayette, where he [his father] followed hotel-keeping until 1859. His parents then embarked in farming."[25]

On August 9, 1866, forty-eight-year-old Henry Sanford registered to vote in Township 21 of Contra Costa County; he appeared first on the 1867 voting list.²⁶ In the 1860 federal census, enumerated July 9, the family was living at Post Office Lafayette/Alamo. Henry's occupation is given as a farmer, with real estate valued at $3,000 and personal property at $1,170. The two Daley sons' surname is spelled "Dayle." Mary and Farmer are listed along with four-year-old Kate, who was born after the family arrived in California. Nancy's brother, "Edward Folette" is listed as a laborer, and Hiram Smith, age forty-one and a "Dr. of Medicine," is residing with them.²⁷

By August 6, 1870, the Sanfords were living at Township Two, Martinez, Contra Costa County, and a third daughter, Minnie, was nine. The only other children still living at home were Farmer, a farm laborer, and Kate, attending school. Nancy was "keeping house" and Henry is listed as a farmer with real estate valued at $3,000 and personal property at $1,000.²⁸

Four years later, Nancy died. Her obituary appeared in the local newspaper:

DIED

SANFORD—At Cottonwood Grove, Merced County, July 9, [1874]
    Mrs. Nancy M. Sanford, aged 51 years 3 months and 1 day.
    The deceased, whose maiden name was Follette, was born in Ohio, April 8, 1823, and married to James Daily, June 2, 1841.
    She was left by his decease in 1845 with two boys, William and James, and was married in 1846 to her late husband, Henry Sanford, with whom she crossed the plains in 1852, settling on arriving here, in this county, where they resided until their removal to Cottonwood Grove, Merced County, two years ago. By her second husband she had four sons, who, together with their father and the two sons by former marriage, are left to mourn the loss of the most devoted and loving friend and counselor they have known on earth.

> And still the evening sunshine shed
> Its beauty o'er that tomb;
> Like heaven's own hope, to mitigate
> Earth's too unkindly doom.²⁹

This obituary contains significant errors. Nancy married James Daley in 1840, he died by December 1844, and she and Henry were married in November 1845. I believe Henry died in 1881, but he could not have simultaneously predeceased and survived her. She and Henry

Appendix D: The Children of King and Louisa Follett 523

Headstone for Nancy and Edward on common grave in Lafayette Cemetery. Photo by Irval L. Mortensen, 2006.

had only two sons (only Farmer lived to maturity) and three daughters (all of whom did survive her).[30]

Nancy was first buried in Fales Cemetery, a small, private cemetery in the southwestern part of present-day Walnut Creek. In 1947, the remains of thirty-one interments, including Nancy and her brother, Edward Follett, were removed to the Lafayette Cemetery, to make way for a freeway. All of them were buried together in "Mass Grave Plot 4," with a headstone that reads "Pioneers of San Ramon Valley," followed by a list of names. Nancy's entry reads "Jancy [sic] M. Sanford."[31] "[The monument] erroneously calls them 'San Ramon Valley Pioneers' rather than Walnut Creek Pioneers."[32]

A letter of inquiry from "Walt," no surname, regarding the disposition of the headstones from the original Fales Cemetery, to the Walnut Creek Historical Society in 1978 and its answer specifies: "One bone from each grave was to be transferred to the Lafayette cemetery by agreement with the freeway construction contractor at the time the freeway was built to Alamo. I questioned the disposition of the HEADSTONES. Answer: 'I guess they went with all the dirt that was dumped.'"[33]

Many descendants of Nancy with the surname Daley still live in Contra Costa County. Her son Farmer was the last of her Sanford descendants, as he had only one daughter who I do not believe lived to adulthood.[34]

Edward Follett, 1821–ca. 1827

The only record I have been able to find on this child is on undocumented, undated family group sheets, copies now in my possession. If the dates on those records are correct, he would have been born and died between the 1820 and 1830 censuses. A few of the family records in my possession list a death date (no documentation) of 1827. Undoubtedly he died prior to 1833 when another son in the family was given the name Edward Follett.

William Alexander Follett, 1825–85

William Alexander Follett was King and Louisa's only child who followed the Mormons west under the direction of the Twelve Apostles. He and his wife, Nancy Mariah Fausett Follett, left Nauvoo in early 1846 and were somewhere in western Iowa close to Nancy's family by July of 1846. That month, William was one of the 520 Mormon men who enlisted in the Mormon Battalion, mustered at Council Bluffs, and set out on July 20, to march to Fort Leavenworth, Kansas. Most of the men were married and had wives and children.[35] In a record later referred to as the "Return List of Company B, July 16, 1846," William A. Follet, a private, is listed as supplying one cow and five sheep to the Battalion, and requesting that his wages of $10 per month be given to his family.[36] A month later on August 22 at Winter Quarters, Nancy gave birth to William King. The baby died about two weeks later on September 6.[37]

Appendix D: The Children of King and Louisa Follett

William Alexander Follett, date unknown. Photocopy courtesy of Wilola Follett, 1998.

William left no personal account or memoir of the group's lengthy and arduous march to San Diego, California, which they reached on January 29, 1847. During the next six months while the political situation stabilized, the battalion members built roads and other civic projects. When they were discharged on July 16, 1847, William went north with many of the men where he was one of the workmen employed by John Sutter in northern California. He would have undoubtedly been present in the area when gold was discovered in January of 1848.[38] He is listed as one of twenty-four Mormon Battalion veterans who left California in the Ebenezer Brown Company on August 12, 1848, traveled from "Pleasant Valley, California, over the newly constructed Carson Pass wagon road over the Sierra Mountains" arriving in the Salt Lake Valley on October 10, 1848.[39] Robert Bruce Dunbar in a Fausett/McKee family history identifies William Alexander as "one of those who fell sick and returned to their families, arriving back in Council Bluffs, Iowa, in September 1847."[40] This apparent family tradition date cannot otherwise be documented in battalion or Church records that I could find.

However and whenever William returned to Nancy in Council Bluffs, I next found him, Nancy, and two-year-old Warren listed on the federal census for Iowa, taken October 30, 1850, living in District 21 in the County of Pottawattamie.[41] In an Iowa state census taken in 1851,

Warren is still listed as age two, and another son, Isaac Alfred (my great-grandfather) is listed as one year old, having been born in June 1850.[42] Isaac, however, was not listed on the 1850 census taken four months after his birth. William Alexander is listed as head of family on an Iowa 1852 census, living in Kanesville Precinct, Pottawattamie County, with a total of three males (William, Warren, and Isaac) and one female (Nancy) female.[43] By 1852, population in the Council Bluffs area had dropped to about 3,000 from a high of 7,000 at the peak of the Mormon settlement.[44] On June 7, 1852, the Follett family left Kanesville/Council Bluffs with 293 other individuals, plus ten families and about sixty-five wagons in the Thomas C. D. Howell Company. That company reached the Salt Lake Valley between September 2 and 27.[45] By that same fall, the Folletts were living in the Provo's "Second Fort" as members of Provo Fifth Ward. The first settlers had colonized Provo, a three-day trip south from Salt Lake City, in 1849.[46]

William and Nancy stayed in the Provo area for approximately the next thirty years where ten more children were born to them.[47] William operated a lumber mill in Provo Canyon, farmed, and was elected a city alderman in February 1855.[48] He resigned in April 1855 after being one of about thirty men called by Brigham Young to "establish a halfway station for travelers between the Pacific Coast and Utah, maintain good rapport with the Indians and attempt to instruct them in the ways of farming and cleanliness."[49] The group settled the Las Vegas Fort, which later became the city of Las Vegas. During this mission, William and a few others took oxen and cattle to the Mormon colony of San Bernardino, California, where they sold them in return for wild mules and mares.[50] William was back in Provo by July 6, 1856, when he was elected as Third Major, Third Battalion, in the reorganized militia of Utah County, Provo Military District.[51] He was again elected to the Provo City Council for a term in 1861-62.[52] During the mid-1860s, he served simultaneously as bishop of Provo Fourth Ward and on the Utah Stake high council.[53]

William is listed in the 1860 federal census in Provo, Utah, taken on September 14, as "Wm. A Fowlett" and his wife "NYM Fowlett" with five children ages twelve to seven months, with real estate valued at $300 and personal property $600.[54] He appears in the 1870 census, taken on August 18, in the Provo City Third Ward as a farmer with real estate valued at $300 and personal property at $200, with seven children ages twenty to two years.[55] Sometime after 1870, he and Nancy's father, William McKee Fausett, obtained a government land patent in the area of northeast Provo known as Pleasant View.[56] Once again he served on the city council in 1874–75.[57] In 1874, Brigham Young encouraged Saints throughout Utah to live the United Order, something that had been tried in Missouri. This order required that Church members "consecrate" their assets to the Church by deed; William was elected as one of the Provo order's directors.[58] The consecration deed he signed read:

> Be it known by these presents, that I William Alexander Follett, of Provo City, Utah County, Utah Territory, for and in consideration of the good will which I have to the Church of Jesus Christ of Latter Day Saints, give and convey unto Brigham Young, Trustee in Trust for said Church, his successors in office and assignees, all my claim to an ownership to the following described property to wit: Lot one, Block 92, containing 72/160 of an acre, in Provo Survey of Building lots, with a log house $50. Also lot 2, Block 91, containing 72/160 of an acre in the above survey, $10. 2 yoke of 2 years old steers $50 per yoke.
>
> 3 cows at $20 each, one yearling steer at $12, 2 heifers at $18 each, 1 swine $5. 3 mules $150, 1 cooking stove $25, 40 bushels of wheat at $2 per bushel. Garden vegetables $15. One-half ton of hay $12, House hold furniture, beds, bedding, etc, $50, Ten head of sheep at $5 per head. Total value of Property $655. Together with all rights, privileges and appurtenances thereto belonging or appertaining. I also covenant and agree that I am the lawful claimant and owner of said property, and will warrant and forever defend the same unto the said Trustee in Trust, successors in office and assignees, against my heirs and assignees or any person whomsoever. Signed William Alexander Follett. Witnessed by three witnesses and acknowledged before Dominicus Carter, Probate Judge.[59]

In 1877–78 a number of families from Utah County were called by the Church to help colonize Arizona. According to family records, William and Nancy, then in their early fifties, traveled to Arizona with their son Isaac and his family. The 1880 federal census taken on June 10 lists William, Nancy, and five children, ages twenty-one to twelve years, living in Walker (now Taylor), Apache County, Arizona Territory.[60] Sometime after this census, William moved farther south to Smithville (now Pima), Arizona, where he died on October 19, 1885. Nancy Mariah died in Pima on April 1, 1886; both are buried in the town cemetery. The inscription on William Alexander's headstone reads: "The sweet re-

Headstone of William Alexander Follett in Pima Cemetery, Pima, Arizona. Photo courtesy of Irval L. Mortensen 2011.

membrances of the just shall flourish when they sleep in dust." Nancy's states: "A loving wife, a mother dear, a faithful friend lies buried here."

The *Utah Territorial Enquirer*, published in Provo, carried this notice:

> By letter received by Mrs. John W. Turner of this city from Smithville, Graham Co., Arizona, we learn of the death of W. A. Follet, which occurred on the 19th inst. The deceased was a former resident of this city and well known and highly respected. He was at one time bishop of the Fourth ward. He was taken sick last August with malarial fever and confined to his bed. About a month ago he was stricken with paralysis which affected the whole of his left side and partly deprived him of speech, which continued until death relieved him from his sufferings. The deceased was about 65 years of age and leaves a wife, 7 children, 15 grandchildren and a numerous circle of relatives and friends to mourn his loss.
>
> The mother [Louisa Tanner Follett] of Bishop Follett, over 90 years of age, is still living in the State of Iowa. The relatives and friends of the deceased residing in this city unite with us in sympathy to the family in their great bereavement.[61]

Emily Follett, ca. 1829

Mary Follett, ca. 1831

The only record I have been able to find of children born to King and Louisa between 1825 and 1833 are two girls by these first names on undocumented family records in my possession. The 1830 census for the

Appendix D: The Children of King and Louisa Follett

Edward Follett, n.d. Photo courtesy of Caron Whitesides.

Follett family lists one female under age five. This was probably Emily.[62] While living in Missouri, King and Levi Jackman bartered services, and one of the items provided to King by Jackman was: "December 26, 1832, one coffin."[63] This was probably for the death of either Emily or Mary. Some of the family records in my possession show a death date for Emily of 1833. By the 1840 census, no female of this age is listed in the Follett family and neither girl is on any records containing the rest of the family in Missouri or Nauvoo.

Edward Moroni/Marion Follett, 1833–92

Little is known about this son of King and Louisa Follett. His middle name is spelled variously as Moroni, Maroni, and Marion; but since he was born in 1833 after the Folletts had joined the Church, Moroni, a Book of Mormon name, seems most probable. Some family records use the spelling "Maroni" while still other family records, created years after his death, use "Marion," perhaps because they did not understand the Mormon source or may even have not wanted to acknowledge the Mormon connection.

When the Follett family left Nauvoo, Edward was about thirteen. By 1847, he was living with his sister Adeline and her husband, Nathan West, in Van Buren County, Iowa. By the 1850 census, the Wests and Edward were living across the state in Pottawatamie County, Iowa. In that census, his age is given as sixteen; no occupation is identified.[64] He apparently traveled to California with his sister Nancy and her second husband, Henry Sanford, or joined them there. The 1860 federal census lists him at Lafayette/Alamo Post Office in Contra Costa County, California, in the Sanford home. His surname is spelled "Folette" and his occupation is given as "laborer." His age is difficult to read but seems to be "23."[65] However, based on a birth year of 1833, he would actually have been twenty-seven. I have not been able to locate him on any other U.S. census records before his death, even though he remained in Contra Costa County until his death in 1892.

On July 9, 1866, he registered to vote in the Third Township of Contra Costa County and is listed as a voter on the 1867 voting register. That record, puzzlingly, gives his middle name as "Marion" and his age as twenty-eight, which is probably a transcription error. His occupation is given as "farmer."[66] He was one of several signers in a civil case on May 17, 1881; their affidavit swore that each man "lives near to and for four years last past [sic] has lived near the Colby Ranch in Contra Costa County." Edward signed as "E. M. Follett."[67]

The voter rolls for 1892, the year of his death, describes him as age fifty-nine (corroborating a birth year of 1833), and as a farmer in the Third Township. It describes him as six feet one inch tall, with light skin, gray eyes, and gray hair. He had a scar over his left eye.[68]

Edward, who never married, died on October 27, 1892, age fifty-nine years, four months, and eighteen days, of peritonitis (appendicitis). His name is listed in the Register of Deaths as "E. M. Follett." He died in Walnut Creek and no occupation is given.[69] He was buried in the Fales Cemetery near his sister Nancy Sanford, who had died in 1874, and his remains were also reburied in Mass Grave Plot 4, Lafayette Cemetery, as one of the "Pioneers of San Ramon Valley."[70] He left no known descendants.

Warren King Follett, 1838–97

Warren King Follett was about eight years old when the Follett family left Nauvoo. In 1847, he was probably living with his mother, and Adeline and Nathan West in Van Buren County, Iowa. He was still with the Wests at the time of the 1850 census, this time in Atchison County, Missouri, at age thirteen.[71] However, the 1856 Iowa state cen-

Warren King Follett with unknown child, n.d. Photo courtesy of Caron Whitesides, 2002.

sus describes him as an Iowa resident for ten years, though still with the Wests, along with his mother in Silver Creek Township, Mills County, Iowa. Here he spent the remainder of his life. That census lists him as an eighteen-year-old farmer with forty-three acres under cultivation that produced more than a thousand bushels of wheat, oats, and corn. The census also credits him as producing seventy-five pounds of butter, twenty-four pounds of wool, and thirty-five pounds of "domestic manufactures."[72] He and Louisa jointly bought land in 1858 and 1859 in Silver Creek.

Warren and Louisa were still living in the West household during the enumeration of the 1860 federal census. His surname was spelled "Fallet," and he was listed as a twenty-one-year-old laborer, with no value given for land or other property.[73] An 1881 history of Mills County states that Warren first resided in Silver Creek Township "on what is now the farm of David Emrick. He moved to the farm he now occupies in 1853.... His farm comprises some 220 acres all in splendid condition and well improved, with buildings and fruit. Mr. Follett is one of the oldest settlers in the county, and has always been closely identified with its improvements and advances."[74]

During the Civil War, the residents of Iowa, a border state, were split on their support for the North or the South. As early as 1860, Warren participated with other Silver Creek men in helping slaves escape to the North. A modern journalist has identified them as "zealous citizens who believed that if all couldn't be free their own freedom might well be endangered."[75] Warren, at age twenty-four, enlisted on August 13, 1862, in Company B of the Twenty-Ninth Iowa Infantry, with fellow Mills County men who served together until August 1865. Three weeks after he enlisted, he married Virginia Ann ("Jenny") Dunlap on September 6, 1862, with the ceremony being performed by John A. Martin, a Baptist minister.[76] Virginia's family was from Missouri and had moved to Silver Creek in 1856 when she was eleven. According to her great-niece, Frances Minthorn, Virginia's father, James Dunlap, "may not have approved of the match ... probably because Warren Follett had volunteered with the Iowa militia to serve on the Union side in the Civil War." However, Frances provides no documentation for this speculation and concedes that, at eighteen, Virginia was "not so young that she had to ask for her father's permission."[77]

Warren's infantry company's mustering-in roll, at Camp Dodge, Iowa, December 1, 1862, shows that he enlisted for three years as a "Fifer" in the company band. He was paid a bounty of $25 and a premium of $2 and is described as five feet ten with gray eyes and dark hair and complexion. When he mustered out at New Orleans, on August 10, 1865, his entry in the Company Descriptive Book reads: "This soldier has never been absent from the company, has participated in all the actions that the Co. has been in. Mustered out and honorably discharged from the U.S. Service."[78]

The Follett family had been active in the Silver Creek Baptist Church since that congregation's organization in December 1857. Services were sometimes held in homes in the Follett neighborhood.[79] An 1881 history of Mills County lists Warren as one of the original members of the First Baptist Church of Malvern when it was founded on December 6, 1870.[80]

On the 1870 census, Warren was listed as a farmer with real estate valued at $3,000 and personal property at $2,320.[81] By that time, Warren and Jenny had three children: William (born April 1866, died

Appendix D: The Children of King and Louisa Follett

Warren King Follett in old age; he died in 1897. Photo courtesy of Wilola Follett, 1998.

August 1867); Alberta (born 1868), and Hattie Belle (born 1870). Over the next twelve years, six more children were added to the family: Charles Montgomery (1872), Drusilla (1873), Ella Mae (1875), Frederick (1877, died 1882), James Garfield (1881), and Harvey Howard in 1882. Except for sons William and Frederick, the other seven children lived to adulthood, married, and raised families.[82]

A sampling of articles in the local newspaper reflects Warren's life. In October of 1884, he advertised: "After this date, I will be ready to furnish you with good Winter Apples at 50 cents per bushel and Fresh Cider at 20 cents per gallon at my farm two miles north of Malvern."[83] On October 22, 1885, an intruder awakened Warren in the middle of the night. Warren chased him out of the house, first with a chair, and then with an "unloaded" gun. "Mr. Follet had sold fourteen wagon loads of apples that day, which no doubt led to the raid but fortunately the returns from the sales had been deposited in town for safe keeping," the article noted.[84] In 1905, after his death, another newspaper article reported:

> When a boy he [Warren] was fond of playing the violin and hunting Coons.... After the war was over he returned to the old farm which he soon began to develop, and made it one of the best farms in the entire county, and where he constantly grew both in influence and power until he was recognized as not only one of the foremost men in his community but in southwestern Iowa. The name and fame of this unassuming strong man left a marked lesson to the young men of this day, as to what may be ac-

complished in this life if one will only devote his best energies in the right and proper direction.[85]

On May 13, 1897, the *Malvern Leader* reported that Warren fell about twelve feet into a ditch, suffering major head cuts and a broken leg. He lapsed into unconsciousness but was "doing nicely," according to the doctor who treated him at home.[86] However, on May 22 he died unexpectedly as the result of a blood clot. The funeral was held at the home on May 25, and the local chapter of the Grand Army of the Republic, of which he was a member, buried him with military honors in the Malvern Cemetery.[87]

He shares the plot with his two sons (Willie A. who died in 1867, age eleven months, and Freddie, who died in 1882, age five years), and his mother. His wife, name given as "Virginia A." on the headstone, died February 14, 1910.[88] Warren's death marks the earthly end of King and Louisa Follett's children. King's legacy was left to be continued by his grandchildren, who, I believe, numbered thirty, and their descendants. Only six of his nine children lived to adulthood and only four of them had children.

Notes

1. U.S. Census, 1850, Iowa, Pottawattamie County, District 21, Roll M432_188, p. 150, image 304.

2. *Iowa State Census Collection, 1836–1925*, Silver Creek Township, Mills County, Iowa, Roll IA_62, line 10, family 13. Living with the West family were Elisha Whiting, age seventeen, and Edmund Whiting, age twenty-five years. I believe these two men are relatives of Nathan.

3. U.S. Census, 1860, Iowa, Silver Creek, Mills County, Roll M653, p. 96, image 113. Nathan's name is given as "N. A." Warren and Louisa Follett and a thirteen-year-old male named Franklin Horne are living in the household. I have not been able to further identify Franklin.

4. U.S. Census, 1870, Iowa, Silver Creek, Mills County, Roll M593_411, p. 98, image 197. On this record Nathan's first name is recorded as "Nathanial" and in the household is twelve-year-old George Doughty, the son of Nathan's daughter, Tryphena West Doughty, and her husband, George Doughty Sr.

5. U.S. Census, 1880, Iowa, Silver Creek, Mills County, Roll T9_356, p. 354, image 10. Also in the household is Elsie Kearney, a twenty-five-year-old "farm hand" born in Iowa.

6. H. H. Woodrow, "History of Silver Creek Township," in *Standard Historical Atlas of Mills and Fremont Counties Iowa*, Section 2, p. 2.

7. *History of Mills County, Iowa: Containing a History of the County*, . . ., 631.

8. Journal History, April 20, 1851, 2. One of the other men was "W. Redfield" who may have been, William Redfield, the husband of Nathan's sister Tryphena.

9. "Died: West," *Malvern [Iowa] Leader*, August 3, 1884.

10. *Iowa Marriages, 1884*.

11. *Mills County, Iowa, Cemeteries*, 89. The cemetery records contain this information: "West, Adaline L wf of N A 21 Dec 1816—1 Aug 1884. . . Nathan A b Trumbull Co., Ohio 10 Apr 1808—8 May 1888."

12. I have various birth dates for her and her age is listed differently on family and Church records in my possession. I believe that the correct date is April 10, 1824, in Florence, Huron County, Ohio.

13. "Daley, Elizabeth M.," in *Early Mormon Latter-day Saints: A Mormon Trail Pioneer Database*, ID No. 14073.

14. "Emer Harris 1781–1869."

15. Mill Branch (Iowa), Record, 1847–1852.

16. Lyman Stephen Wood, *Biographical and Historical Sketches in the Life of Lyman Stephen Wood*, 5–6.

17. Notes available upon request.

18. U.S. Census, 1850, Iowa, District 21, Pottawattamie, Iowa, Roll M432_188, p. 133A, image 271.

19. Iowa General Assembly, *Census of Cedar, Clinton, Decatur, Gutherie, Iowa, Jackson, Jasper, Jefferson, Johnson, Madison, Mahaska, Page, Pottawattamie, Poweshiek, Scott, and Washington Counties, Iowa*, Microfilm #1022203, item 13, Roll 118, Line 8.

20. Iowa Census Board, *1852 Census of Various Counties in Iowa*, Kanesville Township, Pottawatamie County, p. 20, line 7. See also Ronald Vern Jackson, ed., *Iowa 1852*, p. 181.

21. *Iowa State Census Collection, 1836–1925*, Kane Township, Pottawattamie County, Roll IA_64, Family 1, lines 9–10.

22. Details available on request.

23. "Died: Forester," Obituary, *Contra Costa [California] Gazette*, January 2, 1875. This obituary dates her death as December 25, 1874, age twenty-six. Other family records in my possession are available on request.

24. U.S. Census 1850, Missouri, Atchison County, Roll M432_391, p. 153, image 308.

25. Biographical sketch of Nancy and Henry's son, Farmer Sanford, in J. P. Munro-Fraser, *History of Contra Costa County, California . . .*, 642–43. This sketch identifies Farmer as "one of Walnut Creek's most enterprising business men." He owned a livery stable, was a partner in an undertaking parlor, and was a "Constable of Township Number Two, having been elected in 1879."

26. Contra Costa County (California), County Clerk, Great Registers, 1867–1898, p. 13, No. 833.

27. U.S. Census, 1860, California, Township 2, Contra Costa County, Roll M653_57, p. 561, image 565.

28. U.S. Census, California, 1870, Township 2, Contra Costa County, Roll M593_71, p. 378, image 230.

29. "Died: Sanford," *Contra Costa [California] Gazette*, July 28, 1874. Some early family records gave her death date as 1847 rather than 1874, which forestalled further research on her for many years.

30. Documentation available upon request.

31. Darlene Appell, comp., *California Cemetery Records in Contra Costa County, Vol. 2: More Cemetery Records from the 1850s to the Present*, 424–25.

32. Darlene Appell, comp., *California Cemetery Records in Contra Costa County, Vol. 1: 1854–1964*, 20.

33. Walt (no surname), Letter to Mrs. John W. Clemson, Second Vice President, Walnut Creek Historical Society, July 5, 1978.

34. Information available on request.

35. Larry C. Porter, "Interrupted Exodus: Enlisting the Mormon Battalion as Iowa Volunteers," 141–42.

36. Ardath and Conrad Carlsen, transcribers, *Return List of the Mormon Battalion, July 1846*, 13–14.

37. Family records and LDS Ancestral File, details available on request. Some family records mistakenly omit this child's death in infancy and list him as having achieved adulthood and married Mary Ann Dunlap. This error probably resulted from confusion between the numerous "Williams" and "Kings" in the early generations of King's descendants. However, U.S. census records from 1850 forward show no living male child in William's family with this possible birth year.

38. Norma Baldwin Ricketts, *The Mormon Battalion: U.S. Army of the West, 1846–1848*, 169, 197, 285, 292, 299.

39. "Ebenezer Brown Company (1848)."

40. Robert Bruce Dunbar, *Fausett/McKee Family History from 1630 to July 2000: The Ancestors and Descendants of the Fausett and McKee Families of Orange County, North Carolina*, 133.

41. U.S. Census, 1850, Iowa, District 21, Pottawattamie County, Roll M432_188; p. 121, image 243. The Follett family is identified as "dwelling

house and family number 908. Next door in "dwelling house and family number 909" are Nancy's parents, William Fawcett and Matildia Fawcett, and three children.

42. *Iowa State Census Collection, 1836–1925*, 1851 census, Pottawattamie County, no township listed, Roll IA_118, lines 8–11.

43. Iowa Census Board, *1852 Census of Various Counties in Iowa*, Kanesville Precinct, Pottawatamie County, p. 22, Line 30. See also Ronald Vern Jackson, ed., *Iowa, 1852*, 181.

44. Marsha Pilger, ed., "History of Kane Township, Pottawattamie County, Iowa," 3.

45. "Thomas C. D. Howell Company (1852)" in *Mormon Pioneer Overland Travel, 1847–1868*. Follett relatives listed on this manifest are William A. Follet (age twenty-six), Nancy Mariah Fausett Follet (age twenty-five), Warren King Follet (age four) and Isaac Alfred Follet (age two).

46. Emma McDowell Jacobson, *History of Early Provo Cemeteries Moved: Fort Wall, Temple Hill, Grandview, 1849–1853, Moved to Block 4, Provo City Cemetery*, p. 10. See also *Registry of Names of Persons Residing in the Various Wards as to Bishop's Reports 1852–1853*, p. 19.

47. From family, Church, and census records (available on request), these ten children were: Louinda and Louise L. (twins) born 1853; William Lamoni born 1855; John born 1857; Joseph Edward born 1860; Lyman Leander born 1862; Nancy Ann born 1864; Sarah Maria born 1866; Annie Eliza born 1868; and Hyrum born 1870.

48. Marilyn McMeen Miller and John Clifton Moffitt, *Provo: A Story of People in Motion*, 101.

49. Kate B. Carter, comp., "The Las Vegas Fort," 18:97–99, 104–5.

50. Ibid., 104.

51. William M. Wilson, *Early, Pictorial Provo: An Illustrated Industrial Review of Provo, the Garden City of Utah*, 131–32.

52. Miller and Moffitt, *Provo*, 101.

53. Follett family records in my possession. The Follett family is listed as being in more than one ward after their arrival in Provo, so "ward" may have indicated an ecclesiastical and/or a civic division, in addition to the normal boundary changes as membership grew.

54. U. S. Census, 1860, Utah Territory, Provo, Roll M653_1314; p. 924, image 396.

55. U.S. Census, 1870, Utah Territory, Provo Ward 3, Roll M593_1612, p. 289, image 571.

56. Merle S. Foote, *Pleasant Views: A History of the Early Pleasant View Area of Northeast Provo, Utah*, 3. Those obtaining land grants during the 1870s may

have just moved to the area or they may have already been living on the land as squatters.

57. Miller and Moffitt, *Provo*, 101.

58. *Provo: Pioneer Mormon City*, 117, 118.

59. John Edge Booth, *A History of the Fourth Provo Ward*, 66–67.

60. U.S. Census, 1880, Arizona, Apache County, Walker, Roll T9_36, p. 40, image 100. This area, presently located on Silver Creek three miles south of present day Snowflake, was briefly named "Walker" but became "Taylor" (its present name) in 1881. William Alexander Follett's son Isaac Alfred, though not enumerated in the 1880 census for Arizona, was one of the founding settlers in March of 1878 of Forestdale, a small town southwest of Showlow and about sixteen miles from Taylor where William and Nancy and family were living. By 1879–80, Isaac Alfred and his family had moved from Forestdale to Smithville (now Pima) Arizona. James H. McClintock, *Mormon Settlement in Arizona: A Record of Peaceful Conquest of the Desert*, 166, 167, 170. Isaac Alfred Follett, my great-grandfather, and his descendants lived in Pima for two more generations (my grandfather Orren W. Follett and my father Afton Follett). I was born in Pima.

61. "Death of Bishop Follett," *Utah Territorial Enquirer*, October 27, 1885.

62. U.S. Census, 1830, Ohio, Portage County, Shalersville, Roll 138, p. 252, image 3.

63. Levi Jackman, Record Book (ca. 1832–1834). See Chapter 6 for a full discussion of this bartering.

64. U.S. Census, 1850, Iowa, Pottawattamie County, District 21, Roll M432_188, p. 150, image 304.

65. U.S. Census, 1860, California, Contra Costa County, Township 2, Roll M653_57, p. 561, image 565.

66. Contra Costa County, California County Clerk, Great Registers, 1867–98, p. 5, No. 422.

67. Affidavit, *G. W. Colby Plaintiff vs. Robert McCarger, Defendant*.

68. Contra Costa County California, County Clerk. Great Registers, 1867–98, p. 15, Line 1053.

69. Contra Costa County, California, County Recorder, Death Records, 1873–1921, 1:19, Line 20.

70. Appell, *California Cemetery Records in Contra Costa County*, 2:424–25.

71. U.S. Census, 1850, Iowa, Pottawattamie County, District 21, Roll M432–188, p. 150, image 304.

72. *Iowa State Census Collection, 1836–1925*, Mills County, Silver Creek Township, Roll IA_62, Line 10, family 13.

73. U.S. Census, Iowa, 1860, Mills County, Silver Creek, Roll M653_336, p. 96, image 113.

74. *History of Mills County, Iowa*, 628.

75. Allen Wortman, "Underground Railway Depended Entirely on Men Used to Cold Night Rides." Wortman was a Mills County historian who provided much information regarding the Follett family and their activities during an interview and visit with him in August 2001.

76. *Mills County [Iowa] Marriages 1851–1865*, Grooms F–H.

77. Frances Minthorn, Diary, undated, in Alice Minthorn Hall, email to Mortensen, December 4, 2002.

78. "Company Muster-in Roll" and "Company Descriptive Book," both undated, and "Co. Muster-out Roll," dated August 10, 1865, Company B, 29th Iowa Infantry.

79. Mills County History Book Committee, *First Baptist Church: Mills County, Iowa*, 99.

80. *History of Mills County, Iowa*, 583.

81. U.S. Census, 1870, Iowa, Mills County, Silver Creek, Roll M595_411, p. 98, image 197.

82. Follett and Dunlap family records in my possession; available on request.

83. "Notice to My Old Patrons and Friends," *Malvern [Iowa] Leader*, October 16, 1884.

84. "House Breaking," *Malvern [Iowa] Leader*, October 22, 1885.

85. "Stories of Mills County," *Glenwood [Iowa] Opinion*, July 20, 1905.

86. "A Very Sad Accident," *Malvern [Iowa] Leader*, May 13, 1897.

87. "Death of Mr. W. K. Follett," *Malvern [Iowa] Leader*, May 27, 1897.

88. *Mills County Iowa Cemeteries*. Microfilm #1421802, Item 4, p. 89. The headstone reads: "Follett, Warren K 22 Jan 1838–22 May 1897 (CIVIL WAR-GAR)."

Bibliography

Shortened Citations

Ancestral File. http://www.familysearch.org/eng/search/frameset_search.asp. On this webpage, navigate to Ancestral File, then search by the name of the individual of interest. This site is maintained by the Church of Jesus Christ of Latter-day Saints.
Bible. *The Holy Bible, authorized King James Version.* Salt Lake City: Church of Jesus Christ of Latter-day Saints, 1979. Cited parenthetically in the text by abbreviated book, chapter, and verse.
Community of Christ. Library-Archives, Community of Christ, Independence, Missouri.
D&C. Doctrine and Covenants. Salt Lake City: Church of Jesus Christ of Latter-day Saints, 1981. Cited parenthetically by section and verse.
Utah State Historical Society Archives. Salt Lake City, Utah.
History of the Church. Joseph Smith Jr. et al., *History of the Church of Jesus Christ of Latter-day Saints.* Edited by B. H. Roberts, 2d ed. rev. (6 vols. 1902–12, Vol. 7, 1932). Rpt., Salt Lake City: Deseret Book, 1976 printing.
Journal History. Journal History of the Church of Jesus Christ of Latter-day Saints. Chronological scrapbook of typed entries and newspaper clippings, 1830-present. LDS Church History Library.
Journal of Discourses. 26 vols. London and Liverpool: LDS Booksellers Depot, 1855–86.
Family History Department. LDS Church Family History Archives, Church of Jesus Christ of Latter-day Saints, Salt Lake City.
LDS Church History Library. History Library and Archives, Historical Department, Church of Jesus Christ of Latter-day Saints, Salt Lake City.
Lee Library. L. Tom Perry Special Collections, Harold B. Lee Library, Brigham Young University, Provo, Utah.
Marriott Library. Special Collections, J. Willard Marriott Library, University of Utah, Salt Lake City.

Bibliography

AncestralFile. See Shortened Citations.
Abbott, Myron. "History of Abigail Smith Abbott." *Nauvoo Journal* 3 (July 1991): 67–70.

Adkins, Edith. *Early Maps of Winchester New Hampshire, 1733–1892.* West Chesterfield, N.H.: Old Maps, 1983.

Affidavit, cited in G. W. Colby, Plaintiff vs. Robert McCargern, Defendant, Box B-42, Superior Court of Contra Costa County, California, Contra Costa History Center. Photocopy of holograph in my possession.

Audrey, Gertrude A., comp. "Abstract of Wills of Otsego County, New York, 1794–1850." Cooperstown, N.Y.: Surrogate's Office, 1941.

Allaman, John Lee. "Policing in Mormon Nauvoo." *Illinois Historical Journal* 89, no. 2 (Summer 1996): 85–98.

Allen, James B. "Nauvoo's Masonic Hall." *John Whitmer Historical Association Journal* 10 (1990): 39–50.

Allen, James B., and Glen M. Leonard. *The Story of the Latter-day Saints.* 2d. ed. Salt Lake City: Deseret Book, 1992.

"Amasa Lyman Autobiography." *Millennial Star* 27, no. 32 (August 12, 1865, 502–3.

"Ancestors of Tim Farr-aqwg121", http://cc.mscnscache.com (accessed June 21, 2007).

Anderson, Karl Ricks. *Joseph Smith's Kirtland Eyewitness Accounts.* Salt Lake City: Deseret Book, 1986.

_____. "Northern Ohio Settlements." In *Historical Atlas of Mormonism.* Edited by S. Kent Brown, Donald Q. Cannon, and Richard H. Jackson. New York: Simon & Schuster, 1994, 20.

Anderson, Lavina Fielding. "Dreams of Power: The Patriarchal Blessings of Joseph Smith Sr." Presentation at the 2010 Mormon History Association Conference, Independence, Missouri. May 2010. E-copy in my possession, courtesy of Anderson.

Anderson, Richard Lloyd. "Atchison's Letters and the Causes of Mormon Expulsion from Missouri." *BYU Studies* 26, no. 3 (Summer 1986): 3–47.

_____. "The Impact of the First Preaching in Ohio." *BYU Studies* 11, no. 4 (Summer 1971): 474–96.

_____. "Jackson County in Early Mormon Descriptions." *Missouri Historical Review* 65, no. 3 (April 1971): 270–93.

Appell, Darlene, comp. *California Cemetery Records in Contra Costa County, Vol. 1* and *More Cemetery Records from the 1850s to the Present, Vol. 2.* Concord, Calif.: Contra Costa County Genealogical Society, 1980–90.

Arnold, Isaac N. *A Centennial Offering, Being a Brief History of Cooperstown with a Biographical Sketch of James Fenimore Cooper.* Edited by Samuel M. Shaw. Cooperstown, N.Y.: Freeman's Journal Office, 1886. Microfilm #844652. LDS Family History Library.

Arnold, Ralph. "Van Buren County." In *The Iowa Mormon Trail: Legacy of Faith and Courage.* Edited by Susan Easton Black and William G. Hartley. Orem, Utah: Helix Publishing, 1997, 199–202.

Arrington, Leonard J., and Davis Bitton. *The Mormon Experience.* New York: Alfred A. Knopf, 1979.

Arrington, Leonard J., Feramorz Y. Fox, and Dean L. May. *Building the City of God: Community and Cooperation among the Mormons.* Salt Lake City: Deseret Book, 1976.

Asbury, Henry. *Reminiscences of Quincy, Illinois.* Quincy, Ill.: D. Wilcox, 1882.

Ashford, Connecticut. *Land Records, 1715–1902: General Index, 1715–1952.* LDS

Family History Library, Microfilm #3677.

———. *Proprietor Records, 1705–1770*. Microfilm 3676, item 31, LDS Family History Library.

Atkins, Edith. *Early Maps of Winchester, N.H., 1733–1892*. Westchester, N.H.: Old Maps, 1983.

Austin, Emily M. *Mormonism; or, Life among the Mormons, Being an Autobiogrqaphical Sketch; Including an Experience of Fourteen Years of Mormon Life*. Madison, Wisc.: M. J. Cantwell, 1882.

"Autobiography of Cordelia Morley Cox." n.d. http://www.oscox.org/fwcox/cordeliaccox.html. (accessed May 14, 2010).

"Awful Assassination of JOSEPH AND HYRUM SMITH! The pledged faith of the state of Illinois stained with innocent blood by a Mob!" *Times and Seasons* 5, no. 12 (July 1, 1844): 1.

Babbitt, Charles Henry. *Early Days at Council Bluffs*. LDS Family History Library Microfiche #6049057, 77–89.

Backman, Milton V., Jr. *The Heavens Resound: A History of the Latter-day Saints in Ohio, 1836–1838*. Salt Lake City: Deseret Book, 1983.

———. *People and Power of Nauvoo: Themes from the Nauvoo Experience*. Salt Lake City: Greg Kofford Books, 2002.

———, comp. *A Profile of Latter-day Saints of Kirtland, Ohio, and Members of Zion's Camp, 1830–1839: Vital Statistics and Sources*. Provo, Utah: Brigham Young University, 1982.

———. "The Quest for a Restoration: The Birth of Mormonism in Ohio." *BYU Studies* 12, no. 4 (Summer 1972): 346–64.

Backman, Milton V., Jr. and Richard O. Cowan. *Joseph Smith and the Doctrine and Covenants*. Salt Lake City: Deseret Book, 1992.

Baker, H. C. *Genealogical Record of John Brown (1755–1809) and His Descendants, also the Collateral Branches of Merrill, Scott and Follett Families*. St. Paul, Minn.: I I. C. Baker Publisher, 1912. Microfilm #6104844, LDS Family History Library.

Baker, Simon. Statement. Journal History. August 15, 1840, 1–2.

"Baptism for the Dead: An Epistle of the Twelve to the Saints of the Last Days." December 13, 1841. *Times and Seasons* 3 (December 15, 1841): 625–27.

"Baptisms for the Dead, 1840–45." Microfilm #183376 and #183379. LDS Church History Library,

Barber, Gertrude Audrey, comp. *A Collection of Abstracts from Otsego County, New York Newspaper Obituaries, 1808–1875*. Waipahu, Hawaii: M. & W. Reamy, 1993.

Barber, Gertrude A., comp. "Deaths Taken from the *Otsego Herald* and *Western Advertiser and Freeman's Journal*, Otsego County, N.Y. Newspapers, from 1795–1840." 1:81. Microfilm #0908217, item 2, LDS Family History Library.

Barlow, Israel, Quincy, Illinois. Letter to Miss Elizabeth H. Bullard, Holliston, Middlesex, Massachusetts, February 27, 1839. Holograph. Barlow Family Collection, 1816–1966. MS 941, LDS Church History Library.

Barlow, Ora Haven. *The Israel Barlow Story and Mormon Mores*. Salt Lake City: Ora H. Barlow and Israel Barlow Family Association, 1968.

Barney, Lewis. Autobiography and Diary, 1878–83. Holograph. MS 526. LDS Church

History Library.

Barrett, Ivan J. *Joseph Smith and the Restoration: A History of the Church to 1846*. Provo, Utah: Brigham Young University Press, 1973.

Bashore, Melvin Lee, and Linda L. Haslam. *Mormon Pioneer Companies Crossing the Plains (1847–1868): Guide to Sources in the Historical Department and Family History Library of the Church of Jesus Christ of Latter-day Saints*. Microfiche #6105191, LDS Family History Library.

Batchellor, Albert Stillman, ed. *Miscellaneous Revolutionary Documents of New Hampshire, Including the Association Test, the Pension Rolls, and Other Important Papers*. State Papers Series, Vol. 30. Manchester, N.H.: John B. Clarke Co., 1910.

Bates, Edward Craig. *The History of Westborough, Massachusetts, Part I and II*. Westborough, Mass.: The Town, 1891.

Baugh, Alexander L. *A Call to Arms: The 1838 Mormon Defense of Northern Missouri*. Ph.D. diss., Brigham Young University, 1971. Printed in Dissertations in Latter-day Saint History Series. Provo, Utah: Joseph Fielding Smith Institute for Latter-Saint History and *BYU Studies*, 2000.

———. "The Final Episode of Mormonism in Missouri in the 1830's: The Incarceration of the Mormon Prisoners at Richmond and Columbia Jails, 1838–1839." *John Whitmer Historical Association Journal* 28 (2008): 1–34.

———. "'For This Ordinance Belongeth to My House': The Practice of Baptism for the Dead Outside the Nauvoo Temple." *Mormon Historical Studies* 3, no. 1 (2002): 47–58.

———. "From High Hopes to Despair: The Missouri Period, 1831–1839." *Ensign*, July 2001, 44–52.

———. "Jacob Hawn and the Hawn's Mill Massacre: Missouri Willwright and Oregon Pioneer." *Mormon Historical Studies* 11, no. 1 (Spring 2010): 1–25.

Beecher, Maureen Ursenbach, ed. *Personal Writings of Eliza Roxcy Snow*. Logan: Utah State University Press, 2000.

Bennett, Richard E. "Lamanism, Lymanism, and Cornfields." *Journal of Mormon History* 13 (1986–87): 45–60.

Bennett, Richard E. "'Quincy the Home of Our Adoption': A Study of the Mormons in Quincy, Illinois, 1838–1804." In *A City of Refuge: Quincy, Illinois*. Edited by Susan Easton Black and Richard E. Bennett. Salt Lake City: Millennial Press, 2000, 83–105.

Bennett, Richard E., Susan Easton Black, and Donald Q. Cannon. *The Nauvoo Legion in Illinois: A History of the Mormon Militia, 1841–1846*. Norman, Okla.: The Arthur H. Clark Company, 2010.

Berg, Fred Anderson, ed.. *Encyclopedia of Continental Army Units: Battalions, Regiments and Independent Corps*. Harrisburg, Pa.: Stackpole Books, 1972.

Bernauer, Barbara, J., Assistant Archivist, Community of Christ. Email to Joann Mortensen, February 23, 2001.

———. "Gathering the Remnants: Establishing the RLDS Church in Southwestern Iowa," *John Whitmer Historical Association Journal* 20 (2000): 4–33.

Berrett, William E., and Alma P. Burton, eds. *Readings in L.D.S. Church History from* the Original Manuscripts: A Selection of and Extracts from Letters, Editorials, Private Journals, Records, Periodicals, Histories, Biographies, and Other Original Writings Contemporary with and Casting Light upon Early Events in the Church of Jesus Christ of Latter-day Saints. Salt Lake City: Deseret Book, ca. 1953–55.

Best, Christy, LDS Church History Library archivist, Letter April 16, 2003, and emails August 30, 2006; August 31, 2007, June 9, and June 13, 2008, to Joann Follett Mortensen.

Birdsall, Ralph. *The Story of Cooperstown: With Seventy Illustrations from Photographs.* Cooperstown, N.Y.: Arthur H. Crist Co., 1917.

Bishop, M. Guy. "'What Has Become of Our Fathers?' Baptism for the Dead at Nauvoo." *Dialogue: A Journal of Mormon Thought* 23, no. 2 (Summer 1990): 85–98.

Bitton, Davis. "Kirtland as a Center of Missionary Activity, 1830–1838." *BYU Studies* 11 (Summer 1971): 497–516.

———. *Millions Shall Know Brother Joseph Again: Perceptions and Perspectives.* Salt Lake City: Kofford Books, 2011.

Black, Susan Easton. "A City of Refuge." In *A City of Refuge: Quincy, Illinois.* Edited by Susan Easton Black and Richard E. Bennett. Salt Lake City: Millennial Press, 2000, 67–81.

———. "The Evils of Rumor: Richmond, Missouri, 1836–1838." In *Regional Studies in Latter-day Saint Church History: Missouri.* Edited by Arnold K. Garr and Clark V. Johnson. Provo, Utah: BYU Department of Church History and Doctrine, 1994, 119–35.

———. "How Large Was the Population of Nauvoo?" *BYU Studies* 35 (1995): 91–94.

Black, Susan Ward Easton, comp. *Membership of the Church of Jesus Christ of Latter-day Saints, 1830–1848.* Microfilm #889392, item 4. LDS Family History Library. Photocopy of relevant pages in my possession.

Black, Susan Easton, and Richard E. Bennett, eds. *A City of Refuge: Quincy, Illinois.* Salt Lake City: Millennial Press, 2000.

Black, Susan Easton, and Harvey Bischoff Black, comps. *Annotated Record of Baptisms for the Dead, 1840–1845, Nauvoo, Hancock County, Illinois.* 7 vols. Provo, Utah: BYU Center for Family History and Genealogy, 2002.

Black, Susan Easton, Harvey Bischoff Black, and Brandon Plewe, comps. *Property Transactions in Nauvoo, Hancock County, Illinois, and Surrounding Communities (1839–1859).* Wilmington, Del.: World Vital Records, 2006. Also http://www.WorldVitalRecords.com (accessed July 23, 2007).

Black, Susan Easton Black, and William G. Hartley, eds. *The Iowa Mormon Trail: Legacy of Faith and Courage.* Orem, Utah: Helix Publishing, 1997.

Blair, Alma R. "Conflict in Missouri." In *Historical Atlas of Mormonism.* Edited by S. Kent Brown, Donald Q. Cannon, and Richard H. Jackson. New York: Simon & Schuster, 1994, 46.

Bliss, Leonard, Jr., *The History of Rehoboth, Bristol County, Massachusetts.* Boston: Otis, Broaders, 1836.

Bloom, Harold. *American Religion: The Emergence of the Post-Christian Nation.* New York: Simon & Schuster, 1992.

Blum, Ida. "History of the Naming of the Streets in Nauvoo: Gateway to the West." In Church of Jesus Christ of Latter-day Saints and Nauvoo Family History and Property

Identification Department. *Reference Book for Nauvoo Family History and Property Identification Department.* Salt Lake City: Nauvoo Restoration, Inc., 1990, 193–96.

Blum, Ida. *Nauvoo: An American Heritage.* Carthage, Ill.: Blum, 1969.

———. *Nauvoo: Gateway to the West.* Carthage, Ill.: Ida Blum, 1974.

Boileau, Beverly (local historian, Mills County, Iowa). Email to Joann Mortensen, February 23, 2001.

"A Book of Records Belonging to the Church of Christ in Winchester, in the State of New Hampshire, in New England, 1736–1884." Photocopy of holograph. Courtesy of Historical Society of Cheshire County, Keene, New Hampshire.

Boone County, Missouri. Circuit Court Record/Docket Book, July 1839 to August 1840. Boone County Courthouse, Columbia, Missouri. Typed transcription of microfilm of holograph made by Stephen S. Davis, November 2003. Photocopy of typescript in my possession.

Booth, Bertha Ellis. *A Short History of Caldwell County.* 1936. Rpt., Independence, Mo.: Missouri Mormon Frontier Foundations, 2001.

Booth, John Edge. *A History of the Fourth Provo Ward,* 1901. Typescript copy. Brigham Young University, 1941. LDS Family History Library, Microfilm #1059491, item 3.

Bowen, Richard LeBaron. *Early Rehoboth: Documented Historical Studies of Families and Events in This Plymouth Colony Township.* 4 vols. Rehoboth, Mass.: Rumford Press, 1945–46. Vol. 2 in LDS Family History Library, Microfilm #6087441.

Bracken, James Bennett. Statement. November 6, 1881. Holograph. MS 2425. LDS Church History Library.

Brand, Twylia G., extractor. *Deeds, Jackson County, Missouri.* Vol. 1: Deed Books, A–K, 1827–1845; Vol. 2: Deed Books, L–R, 1845–1851. Independence, Mo.: Jackson County Genealogical Society, 2001–2003.

Bristol County, Massachusetts. Probate Court, Probate Records, 1687–1916: Index, 1687–1926.

Britton, Rollen J. *Early Days on Grand River and the Mormon War.* Columbia, Mo.: State Historical Society of Missouri, 1920. http://www.farweshistory.com/mcgee (accessed August 21, 2006).

Brown, James W., and Karen Powell. "From New England to Ohio." *Ohio Genealogical Society Quarterly* 43, no. 3 (September 2003): 153–58.

Brown, Lisle G, comp. *Nauvoo Sealings, Adoptions, and Anointings: A Comprehensive Register of Persons Receiving LDS Temple Ordinances, 1841–1846.* Salt Lake City: Smith-Pettit Foundation, 2006.

Brown, Robert Charles, and J. E. Norris, *History of Portage County, Ohio: Containing a History of the County, Its Townships, Towns, Villages, Schools, Churches, Industries, etc.* Chicago: Warner, Beers, 1885.

Brown, S. Kent, Donald Q. Cannon, and Richard H. Jackson, eds. *Historical Atlas of Mormonism.* New York: Simon & Schuster, 1994.

Buff, Newburn Isaac, comp. *Early History of Provo: From March 18, 1849, also Genealogical Information.* Holograph. Microfilm #26321, LDS Family History Library.

Bullock, W. P. *Atlas of Caldwell County, Missouri.* Hamilton, Mo.: Farmers Advocate, 1897. Rpt., Richmond, Mo.: Ray County Historical Society, 1991.

Burkett, Frank M., volunteer at Hancock (Illinois) Historical Society. Email to Joann

Follett Mortensen, June 3, 2004.
Burkett, George, Jr. Autobiography, n.d. Typescript. In my possession.
Burns, Helen, and Warren Burns. *Branches of My Family Tree: The Follett Branch.* Colorado Springs, Col.: H. C. Burns, 1993.
Bushman, Richard Lyman. *Joseph Smith: Rough Stone Rolling.* New York: Alfred A. Knopf, 2005.
———. "Mormon Persecutions in Missouri, 1833." *BYU Studies* 3 (Fall 1960): 11–20.
Butler, Margaret Manor. *A Pictorial History of the Western Reserve, 1796 to 1860.* Cleveland, Ohio: Early Settlers Association of the Western Reserve, 1963.
Cahoon, Reynolds, Diary, 1831–32. Holograph. Unpaginated. MS 1115. LDS Church History Library.
"Caldwell County Tax Lists." Liberty and Kingston, Mo.: *Caldwell Banner of Liberty* [newspaper], 1864. http://www.yourlaunchpad.com//terry/caldwell/taxlst.htm (accessed June 22, 2001). This website was not available after 2005.
Call, Ethan, and Christine Shafer Call, eds. *The Journal of Anson Call.* Afton, Wyo.: E. L. and C. S. Call, 1986.
Cannon, Donald Q. "The Founding of Nauvoo." In Church of Jesus Christ of Latter-day Saints and Nauvoo Family History and Property Identification Department. *Reference Book for Nauvoo Family History and Property Identification Department.* Salt Lake City: Nauvoo Restoration, Inc., 1990, 12.
———. "The King Follett Discourse: Joseph Smith's Greatest Sermon in Historical Perspective." *BYU Studies* 18, no. 2 (Winter 1978): 179–92.
———. "Licensing in the Early Church." *BYU Studies* 22, no. 1 (Winter 1982): 96–105.
Cannon, Donald Q., and Lyndon W. Cook, eds. *Far West Record: Minutes of the Church of Jesus Christ of Latter-day Saints, 1830–1844.* Salt Lake City: Deseret Book, 1983.
Cannon, George Q. *Life of Joseph Smith the Prophet.* 1888. Rpt., Salt Lake City: Deseret Book, 1986.
Cannon, Janath R. *Nauvoo Panorama: Views of Nauvoo before, during and after Its Rise, Fall and Restoration.* Nauvoo, Ill.: Nauvoo Restoration, 1991.
Carlsen, Ardath and Conrad, transcribers. *Return List of the Mormon Battalion, July 1846.* Salt Lake City: Privately published, 1986.
Carter, Kate B., ed. "The Las Vegas Fort." In *Our Pioneer Heritage.* 20 vols. Salt Lake City: Daughters of Utah Pioneers, 1958–77, 18:97–105. Microfilm #6101187, LDS Family History Library.
Cheney, Nathan. Letter to "Dear and Beloved Parents, Brothers and Sisters," Nauvoo City, October 17, 1841. Holograph. Historical Letters and Sketches, 1919, MS 480, fd. 2, item 3. LDS Church History Library.
Cheshire County, New Hampshire. *The Early Maps: With a Narrative History of the Town Grants.* West Chesterfield, N.H.: Old Maps, 1983.
Cheshire County, New Hampshire. Register of Deeds, 1770–1860. LDS Family History Library Microfilm #15615, 15617, 15620, 15622.
Chiat, Marilyn J. Online interview. *Monthly Aspectarian* on her book, *The Spiritual Traveler, Chicago and Illinois,* September 2004. http://www.lightworks.com/MonthlyAspectarian (accessed August 8, 2007).
Child, Hamilton. *Gazetteer of Cheshire County, N.H., 1736–1885.* Syracuse, N.Y.:

Hamilton Child, 1885.

Christensen, Clare B. *Before and after Mount Pisgah: Cox, Hulet, Losee, Morley, Tuttle, Winget, Whiting & Related Families.* Salt Lake City: Ross A. Nielsen, 1979, LDS Family History Library Microfilm #1697801.

Church Education System. *Church History in the Fulness of Times.* 2d ed. Institute of Religion manual. Salt Lake City: Church of Jesus Christ of Latter-day Saints, 2000.

Church of Jesus Christ of Latter-day Saints and Nauvoo Family History and Property Identification Department. *Reference Book for Nauvoo Family History and Property Identification Department.* Salt Lake City: Nauvoo Restoration, Inc., 1990.

"City of Streetsboro and Shalersville Township, 1809–1994. In *Portage County, Ohio, Cemeteries. Vol. 10.* Ravenna, Ohio: Portage County Genealogical Society, 1991, Microfilm #2055209, LDS Family History Library.

Clark, John W. Letter to "Dear Brothers and Sisters [David H. Clark, Dupage, Mill County, Illinois], July 13, 1839.

Clayton, William. "To the Friends of the Temple." *Times and Seasons* 5, no. 19 (October 15, 1844): 675.

Clegg, Michael Barren, comp. *Tax Records of Portage, Summit, and Portions of Medina Co[untie]s, Ohio, 1808–1820.* Microfiche #6100904. LDS Family History Library.

Clegg, Michael Barren, and Eleanor Schindler, comps. *Portage County, Ohio, Newspaper Obituary Abstracts, 1825–1870.* Microfiche #6087731, LDS Family History Library.

Clemens, William Montgomery, ed. *American Marriage Records before 1699.* 1926. Rpt., Baltimore, Md.: Genealogical Publishing, 1984.

Clements, John. *New Hampshire Facts: A Comprehensive Look at New Hampshire Today: County by County.* Dallas, Tex.: Clements Research, 1987.

Colby, Gertrude Follett (Beaumont, Texas). Letter to Mrs. Joyce Giaguinta (Iowa City, Iowa), September 21, 1977. Photocopy in my possession courtesy of Iowa State Historical Society.

Collier, Fred C., ed. *The Nauvoo High Council Minute Books of the Church of Jesus Christ of Latter Day [sic] Saints.* Hanna, Utah: Collier's Publishing, 2005.

Collins, William H., Cicero F. Perry, and John Tillson. *Past and Present of the City of Quincy and Adams County, Illinois: Including the Late Colonel John Tillison's History of Quincy, Together with Biographical Sketches of Many of Its Leading and Prominent Citizens and Illustrious Dead.* LDS Family History Library, Microfilm #934969, item 4.

"Commission Records, Illinois State Militia, 1835–1844." *Nauvoo Journal* 2 (January 1990): 1–12. Microfilm #908142, item 9, LDS Family History Library.

"Company Muster-in Roll," n.d,; "Company Descriptive Book," n.d.; "Co. Muster-out Roll," August 10, 1865. Company B, 29th Iowa Infantry. Photocopies courtesy of Beverly Boileau.

Conant, Frederick Odell. *A History and Genealogy of the Conant Family in England and America: Thirteen Generations.* Microfilm #896781, LDS Family History Library.

"Conference: 'First, Names of the Elders' June 3, 1836," *Messenger and Advocate* 2 (July 1836): 335–36.

"Conference Minutes." *Times and Seasons* 5, no. 15 (August 15, 1844): 612–17.

Conrad, Howard Louis. "Mormonism." *Encyclopedia of the History of Missouri: A Compendium of History and Biography for Ready Reference*. New York: Southern History, 1901, 481–87.

Contra Costa County, California. County Clerk. *Great Registers, 1867–98*. Microfilm #0976458, LDS Family History Library.

Contra Costa County, California. County Recorder. Death Records, 1873–1921. Register of Deaths, Vols. 1–3, 1873–1915. Microfilm #1294350, LDS Family History Library.

Cook, Lyndon W. *Nauvoo Marriages, Proxy Sealings, 1843–1846*. Provo, Utah: Grandin Book, 2004.

———. *A Tentative Inquiry into the Office of Seventy 1835–1845*. Provo, Utah: Grandin Book Company, 2010.

Cook, Lyndon W., and Milton V. Backman, Jr., eds. *Kirtland Elders' Quorum Record, 1836–1841*. Provo, Utah: Grandin Book, 1985.

Cowan, Richard O. "The Pivotal Nauvoo Temple." In *Regional Studies in Latter-day Saint Church History: Illinois*. Edited by H. Dean Garrett. Provo, Utah: Department of Church History and Doctrine Brigham Young University, 1995, 113–23.

———. *Temples to Dot the Earth*. Salt Lake City: Bookcraft, 1997.

Cowdery, Oliver, "Address." *Messenger and Advocate* (Kirtland, Ohio) 1, no. 1 (October 1834): 2.

Cox, Cordelia Morley. "Biography of Isaac Morley: A Sketch of the Life of My Father Isaac Morley, One of the Pioneers to Salt Lake Valley in 1848." http://www.boap.org/LDS/Early-Saints/IMorley,html (accessed May 18, 2010).

Craig, John. "Richmond, Mo.: Update on Location of 'Old Vacant Log House.'" *Missouri Mormon Frontier Newsletter* 41–42 (July 2007–May 2008): 1–7.

Crawley, Peter L. "Two Rare Missouri Documents (1834, 1838)." *BYU Studies* 14, no. 4 (1974): 501–27.

Crockett, David R. "The Nauvoo Temple: 'A Monument of the Saints.'" *Nauvoo Journal* 11, no. 2 (1991): 5–30.

Curtis, Annette W., ed. *1836 Clay County, Missouri State Tax List: All Taxpayers and Land Owners Are Identified Including Mormons and the 1835 Missouri Tax Law*. Independence, Mo.: Missouri Mormon Frontier Association, 2003.

———. "Historic Sites in Mormon Missouri: Richmond, Missouri." http://www.farwesthistory.com/mweb/mmff/richmo.asp. (accessed October 7, 2006).

———. "People and Places: Mormon Prisoners in Richmond, Missouri." *Missouri Mormon Frontier Newsletter* 36 (February 2005–July 2005): 1–10.

Curtis, Gates, ed. *Our County and Its People: A Memorial Record of St. Lawrence County, New York*. Syracuse, N.Y.: D. Mason, 1894.

Curtis, William J. *Jackson County, Missouri, Mormon Historic Sites*. Independence: Missouri Mormon Frontier Foundation, 2002.

Daggett, John, and Amelia Daggett Sheffield. *A Sketch of the History of Attleborough: From Its Settlement to the Division*. Boston: Press of Samuel Usher, 1894.

Daley, Elizabeth M. *In Early Mormon Latter-day Saints: A Mormon Trail Pioneer Database*, ID No. 14073, posted May 26, 2006. http://www.earlylds.com. (accessed June 21, 2007).

Daniell, Jere R. *Colonial New Hampshire: A History*. Millwood, N.Y.: KTO Press, 1981.

Davis, Harold E. "Sources of Immigration into Portage County." In Helen S. Dilley, ed., *Pioneer Life in Hiram Township*. Publications of the Hiram Historical Society, Vol. 2 (November 1930). LDS Family History Library Microfilm #1320903, item 10.

Davis, Inez Smith. "The Story of the Church." http://www.centerplace.org/history/misc/soc/index/htm (accessed June 9, 2008).

Davis, William C. *A Way through the Wilderness: The Natchez Trace and the Civilization of the Southern Frontier*. New York: HarperCollins, 1995.

"Death Listing." *New Hampshire Sentinel*. Photocopy of clipping in my possession courtesy, Historical Society of Cheshire County, Keene, New Hampshire, June 3, 2009.

"Death of Bishop Follett." *Utah Territorial Enquirer*, October 27, 1885. Photocopy of clipping courtesy of Wilola Follett.

"Death of Mr. W. K. Follett." *Malvern [Iowa] Leader*, May 27, 1897. Photocopy of clipping courtesy of Beverly Boileau.

"Death of Mrs. Follett." *Malvern (Iowa) Leader*, November 15, 1891. Photocopy of clipping in my possession courtesy of Beverly Boileau.

"Deaths." *Nauvoo Neighbor*, March 27, 1844, 3.

DeBarthe, Paul David Coit, and Haumana DeBarthe. "Archaeological Reconnaissance of a Caldwell County, Missouri, Log House." Independence: Missouri Mormon Frontier Foundation, 1997.

DeKalb Town Meeting, Book 1, 1806–45, 74–127. DeKalb Historical Association, DeKalb, New York. Photocopy of holograph, from Virginia Fischer, Town Historian, September 2006, in my possession.

DePlatt. See Platt, Lyman D.

Derby, C. Helen. *Centennial Home Coming in Celebration of the One Hundreth Anniversary of the Settlement of Shalersville Township, Portage County, Ohio, Held at Shalersville Center, August 30, 1906*. Ravenna, Ohio: Ravenna Republican Print, 1906.

Dibble, Philo. Quoted in Journal History, November 1831, 1; April 15, 1861.

"Died" [Obituary of King Follett]. *Nauvoo (Illinois) Neighbor*, March 20, 1844, 2.

"Died: Forester." Obituary. *Contra Costa [California] Gazette*, January 2, 1875. Photocopy of clipping in my possession courtesy of Contra Costa County Historical Society.

"Died: Sanford." *Contra Costa [California] Gazette*, July 28, 1874. Photocopy of clipping courtesy of Contra Costa County Historical Society.

"Died: West." *Malvern (Iowa) Leader*, August 1, 1884. Photocopy of article courtesy of Beverly Boileau.

Dilley, Helen S. "Pioneer Life in Hiram Township." *Publication of the Hiram Historical Society* 2 (November 1930). Microfilm #1320903, Item 10, LDS Family History Library.

Dinger, John S. "Joseph Smith and the Development of Habeas Corpus in Nauvoo, 1841–44." *Journal of Mormon History* 36, no. 3 (Summer 2010): 135–71.

"Divergent Paths of the Restoration." Description of walking tour led by Steven Shields. Preliminary program, Mormon History Association annual conference ("The

Home and the Homeland: Families in Diverse Mormon Traditions,") Kansas City, Mo., May 27-30, 2010, p. 12.

Document Containing the Correspondence, Orders, &c. in Relation to the Disturbances with the Mormons; and the Evidence Given before the Hon. Austin A. King, Judge of the Fifth Judicial Circuit of the State of Missouri, at the Court-House in Richmond in a Criminal Count of Inquiry, Begun November 12, 1838, on the Trial of Joseph Smith, Jr., and Others for High Treason and Other Crimes against the State. Jefferson City, Mo.: Missouri General Assembly, 1839. Microfilm #1670779, LDS Family History Library.

Dow, Joseph. *Joseph Dow's History of the Town of Hampton, from Its First Settlement in 1638, to the Autumn of 1892.* Portsmouth, N.H.: Peter E. Randall, 1988.

Dunbar, Robert Bruce. *Fausett/McKee Family History from 1630 to July 2000: The Ancestors and Descendants of the Fausett and McKee Families of Orange County, North Carolina.* Landsdale, Pa.: R.B. Dunbar, 2000.

Durant, Samuel W., and Henry B. Peirce. *History of St. Lawrence Co., New York: With Illustrations and Biographical Sketches of Some of Its Prominent Men and Pioneers, 1749–1878.* 1878. Rpt., Interlaken, N.Y.: Heart of the Lakes Publishing, 1982.

"Early Branches of the Church of Jesus Christ of Latter-day Saints." *Nauvoo Journal* 3, no. 1 (January 1991): 5–21.

Early Maps of Swanzey, New Hampshire: Anniversary Portfolio: A Collection of Historical Maps of Swanzey, 1734–1892. West Chesterfield, N.H.: Old Maps, 1983.

"Ebenezer Brown Company (1848)." In *Mormon Pioneer Overland Travel, 1847–1868.* http://www.lds.org/churchhistory/library/pioneercompany (accessed February 18, 2008).

Editorial. *Quincy [Illinois] Argus*, March 16, 1839. Quoted in Anna Scianna, "Missouri's Mormon Past," *Missourian*, October 15, 2006.

Edward Brothers. *An Illustrated Historical Atlas of Caldwell County, Missouri.* 1876. Rpt., Caldwell, Mo.: Caldwell County Historical Society, 1984.

Ehat, Andrew F. "'They Might Have Known That He Was Not a Fallen Prophet': The Nauvoo Journal of Joseph Fielding." *BYU Studies* 19, no. 2 (Winter 1979): 133–66.

1853–1905 Marriage Index. Grooms: Harrison County, Iowa. www.rootsweb.com/iaharris/marriage/e.htm. (accessed November 8, 2003).

"1842 Tax Records, Index of Hancock County, Illinois (A-Milton Kimball)." *Nauvoo Journal* 2, no. 2 (April 1990): 37–72.

"Eighty-Seven." *Malvern (Iowa) Leader*, April 22, 1886.

Eldridge, Vera Haworth. "Mormons in Clay County." In *Discover North.* Ferrelview, Mo.: Suburban Communications, April 1975, 4–10. M277.78 E37m 1975. LDS Church History Library.

Ely, Ruby. "July 4th in Caldwell County." In *A Peek in the Past*, 2 vols. Kingston, Mo.: Peek in the Past Committee, 1992, 49–50. 977.8185 H2c, LDS Family History Library. Originally presented as radio broadcasts June 30 and July 1, 1984.

Emanuels, George. *Ygnacio Valley, 1834–1970.* Fresno, Calif.: Panorama West Books, 1982.

"Emer Harris 1781–1869." In Ancestors of Tim Farr-aqwn108. http://webspace.webring.com/people/eu/um_5941/Aqwn108.htm (accessed February 26, 2010).

Encyclopedia of Missouri. St. Clair Shores, Mich.: Somerset Publishers, 1985.

"An Epistle of the Twelve, to the Church of Jesus Christ of Latter-day Saints in All the World." *Times and Seasons* 6, no. 1 (January 15, 1845): 779–80.

Esplin, Ronald K. "The Significance of Nauvoo for Latter-day Saints." In *Kingdom on the Mississippi Revisited: Nauvoo in Mormon History*. Edited by Roger D. Launius and John E. Hallwas. Urbana: University of Illinois Press, 1996, 19–38.

Essex County, Massachusetts. Register of Deeds. *Deeds, 1839–1866; Index to Deeds, 1640–1879*. Microfilm # 866022, LDS Family History Library.

Essex Institute. *Town Records of Salem, Massachusetts, 1680–1691*, Vol. 3. Salem, Mass.: Essex Institute, 1934. Microfilm #1425575, Item 3, LDS Family History Library.

Essex Institute. *Vital Records of Attleborough, Massachusetts, to the End of the Year 1849*. Salem, Mass.: Essex Institute, 1934. Microfilm #982348, Item 1, LDS Family History Library.

Essex Institute. *Vital Records of Salem, Massachusetts, to the End of the Year 1849. Vol. 1: Births, A–L*. Newburyport, Mass.: Parker River Researchers, 1988. Microfilm #974.45/S1 LDS Family History Library.

Essex Institute and H. Whipple. "Records of Baptisms of First Church of Salem, Massachusetts." In *Historical Collections of the Essex Institute*, Vol. 7. Salem, Mass.: H. Whipple, 1865. Microfilm #982475, Item 9, LDS Family History Library.

Evans, John Henry. *Charles Coulson Rich: Pioneer Builder of the West*. New York: Macmillan, 1936.

Everts, L. H., comp. and cartographer. *Combination Atlas Map of Portage County, Ohio*. Chicago: L. H. Everts, 1874. LDS Family History Library, Microfilm #0908223.

Explore Mills County [Iowa]: Find the Mormon Traces. Pamphlet. N.p.: n. pub., n.d. Copy in my possession courtesy of Beverly Boileau.

Farmer, John, Jacob B. Moore, and Abel Bowen. *A Gazetteer of the State of New Hampshire*. Concord, N.H.: Jacob B. Moore, 1823. LDS Family History Library, Microfilm #823666, item 2.

Far West Burial Ground. http://www.farwesthistory.com/mmffpp.asp (accessed July 4, 2005).

Faulring, Scott H. "Letter from David Whitmer to Nathan West Concerning Caldwell County, Missouri, Property Once Owned by King Follett." *Mormon Historical Studies* 1 (Spring 2000): 127–35.

First Baptist Church: Mills County, Iowa. Dallas, Tex.: Taylor Publishing, 1985.

"First, Names of the Elders," Kirtland Ohio, June 3, 1836, 2 *Messenger and Advocate* 10 (July 1836): 335–36.

Fischer, Virginia, town historian, Dekalb Historical Association, DeKalb Junction, New York. Letter to Joann Follett Mortensen, December 2, 2006.

Flakes, Marion. "Bonaparte on the Mormon Trail through Van Buren County." In *History of Bonaparte*, a scrapbook compiled by the Van Buren County Historical Society (1967): *Evidence of Presence of Latter Day [sic] Saint Families in Van Buren County Area in the 1840s*. Microfilm #967000, item 4, LDS Family History Library, filmed by the Genealogical Society of Utah, 1974.

Flanders, Robert Bruce. *Nauvoo: Kingdom on the Mississippi*. Urbana: University of

Illinois Press, 1975.

Follett, Adaline Louisa (West). File #13829. Nauvoo Restoration Land and Records Office. This record is a compilation of data from various sources, searchable by individual's name, with each assigned a unique filename. Information obtained by personal visit in 2008. CD and printout in my possession.

Follett, Alexander. Birth Record, Birth Records "F," Winchester Town Hall, Winchester, New Hampshire. Personal visit September 22, 1999.

Follett, John W. File #31139. Nauvoo Restoration Land and Records Office. This record is a compilation of data from various sources, searchable by individual's name, with each assigned a unique filename. Information obtained by personal visit in 2008. CD and printout in my possession.

Follett, King. Birth Record. Births "F." Winchester Town Records, Winchester Town Hall, Winchester, New Hampshire, Personal visit September 22, 1999.

Follett, King. Certificate of Membership and Elder's License, Missouri, September 12, 1835. Photocopy of original in my possession; location of original unknown.

———. Deed, July 28, 1838. Receipt and Registration Certificate, No. 10063. Land Office, Lexington, Missouri. Photocopy obtained from National Archives Land Entry Files, July 27, 1999, in my possession.

———. Father's Blessing for son William Alexander Follett, dated March 18, 1838. Photocopy of holograph in my possession; location of original unknown.

———. Nauvoo Restoration Land and Records Office. File #10091. This record is a compilation of data from various sources, searchable by individual's name, with each assigned a unique filename. Information obtained by personal visit in 2008. CD and printout in my possession.

Follett, King, and Adaline Louisa West Follett. Family Group Sheet. Prepared and submitted by Faun E. Fuller for proxy temple work. Arizona Temple's date-stamp December 12, 1944. Photocopy in my possession.

Follett, Louisa Tanner. "Affidavit." Holograph, LDS Church History Library; photocopy in my possession. Also in *Mormon Redress Petitions: Documents of the 1833–1838 Missouri Conflict*. Edited by Clark V. Johnson. BYU Religious Studies Center, Monograph Series No. 16. Provo, Utah: BYU Religious Studies Center, 1992, 201. See also Missouri Claims, 1839–45. MS 2703, fd. 11, item 3. LDS Church History Library.

Follett, Louisa Tanner. Diary, June 1844–September 1845. Microfilm of holograph and typescript copy, courtesy of Iowa State Historical Society, 1997. Typescript copy of holograph, n.d. MS 6383. LDS Church History Library. See Appendix C, this volume, for my transcription.

Follett, Warren King. Service Documents, 29th Iowa Infantry, Company B. Photocopy of holographs in my possession courtesy of Beverly Boileau, historian of Mills County, Iowa.

Follett, Mrs. William. "The Follett Family." *Connecticut Nutmegger* 48 (1975): 158–59. This periodical is published by the Connecticut Society of Genealogists, Hartford, Conn.

Follett, William Alexander. Father's Blessing, March 18, 1838. Photocopy of holograph in my possession.

Foote, Merle S. *Pleasant Views: A History of the Early Pleasant View Area of Northeast Provo, Utah*. Microfilm #908779, item 16, LDS Family History Library.

Forbes, Harriette Merrifield. *The Hundredth Town: Glimpses of Life in Westborough*. Boston: Press of Rockwell and Churchill, 1889. Microfilm #897450, item 4, LDS Family History Library.

Forester, Mary L. Obituary. *Contra Costa [California] Gazette*, January 2, 1875.

Freemasons. Nauvoo Lodge Account Book, 1840–45. MS 3433. LDS Church History Library.

Freemasons. Nauvoo Lodge Minute Book, October 1841–February 1846. LDS Church History Library. Holograph. MS 3436. Unpaginated. Contains "Record of Nauvoo Lodge under Dispensation," which lists first members.

Gannett, Michael R. *Cornwall Documents: Town Meeting Minutes, 1740–1875*. Cornwall, Conn.: Cornwall Historical Society, 1994.

_____. *The Distribution of the Common Land of Cornwall, Connecticut*. Cornwall, Conn.: Cornwall Historical Society, 1990.

Gardner, Hamilton. "The Nauvoo Legion, 1840–45: A Unique Military Organization." In *Kingdom on the Mississippi Revisited: Nauvoo in Mormon History*. Edited by Roger D. Launius and John E. Hallwas. Urbana: University of Illinois Press, 1996, 48–61.

Gardner, Nathan Hale. "Biographical Sketch of Lucina Streeter Snow, 1978." Typescript. MS 10530. LDS Church History Library.

Garr, Arnold K., and Clark V. Johnson, eds. *Regional Studies in Latter-day Saint Church History: Missouri*. Provo, Utah: BYU Department of Church History and Doctrine, 1994.

Garrett, H. Dean, ed. *Regional Studies in Latter-day Saint Church History: Illinois*. Provo, Utah: Department of Church History and Doctrine Brigham Young University, 1995.

Gates, Jacob. Journals, 1836–61. Holograph. MS 1501. LDS Church History Library.

"Genealogy of Jeremiah Levet." Item 111 in "A Record of Genealogies, Biographies etc., Appertaining to the 20th Quorum of Seventies." In Seventies Quorum, *Record of Members of the Quorum of Seventy, 1844–94*, Sixteenth Quorum, Microfilm #25554. LDS Family History Library.

Genosky, Landry, ed. *People's History of Quincy and Adams County, Illinois: A Sesquicentennial History*. Quincy, Ill.: Jost & Kiefer, n.d.

Gentry, Leland Homer. "Adam-ondi-Ahman: A Brief Historical Survey." *BYU Studies* 13 (Summer 1973): 553–76.

_____. "The Danite Band of 1838." *BYU Studies* 14 (Summer 1974): 421–50.

_____. *A History of the Latter-day Saints in Northern Missouri from 1836 to 1839*. Ph.D. diss., Brigham Young University, 1965. Rpt., under the same title in Dissertations in Latter-day Saint History Series. Provo, Utah: Joseph Fielding Smith Institute for Latter-day Saint History, 2000.

Gentry, Leland Homer, and Todd M. Compton. *Fire and Sword: A History of the Latter-day Saints in Northern Missouri, 1836–39*. Salt Lake City: Greg Kofford Books, 2011.

Gifford, Samuel Kendall. "Reminiscences, 1864." Typescript. MS 8167. LDS Church History Library.

Gilbert, A. S., and W. W. Phelps, Liberty, Clay County. Letter to Daniel Dunklin,

Governor of Missouri, May 7, 1834. *Times and Seasons* 6, no. 20 (January 1846): 1075.

Givens, George W. *In Old Nauvoo: Everyday Life in the City of Joseph.* Salt Lake City: Deseret Book, 1990.

Givens, George, and Sylvia Givens. *Nauvoo Fact Book: Questions and Answers for Nauvoo Enthusiasts.* Lynchburg, Va.: Parley Street Publishers, 2000.

Godfrey, Kenneth W. "Crime and Punishment in Mormon Nauvoo, 1839–1846." *BYU Studies* 32 (1992): 195–227.

―――. "The Nauvoo Neighborhood: A Little Philadelphia or a Unique City Set Upon a Hill?" *Journal of Mormon History* 11 (1984): 78–97.

―――. "New Light on Old Difficulties: The Historical Importance of the Missouri Affidavits." In *Regional Studies in Latter-day Saint Church History: Missouri.* Edited by Arnold K. Garr and Clark V. Johnson. Provo, Utah: BYU Department of Church History and Doctrine, 1994, 201–18.

―――. "Some Thoughts Regarding an Unwritten History of Nauvoo." *BYU Studies* 15, no. 4 (Summer 1975): 417–24.

Godfrey, Kenneth W., Audrey M. Godfrey, and Jill Mulvay Derr, eds. *Women's Voices: An Untold History of the Latter-day Saints, 1830–1900.* Salt Lake City: Deseret Book, 1982.

Goss, Mrs. Charles Carpenter. *Colonial Gravestone Inscriptions in the State of New Hampshire.* 1942. Rpt., Baltimore, Md.: Genealogical Publishing Co., 1974.

Goulty, G. Frank. "Nauvoo Photography Collection." ca. early 1900s. PH 1107, fd. 3, item 3. LDS Church History Library.

Great River Genealogical Society, comps. *Marriages of Adams County, Illinois. Vol. 1: 1825–1860.* Quincy, Ill.: Great River Genealogical Society, 1979.

Greene, John Portineus. Diary, November 1–16, 1838. Holograph. MS 5366. LDS Church History Library.

―――. *Facts Relative to the Expulsion of the Mormons or Latter Day Saints from the State of Missouri under the "Exterminating Order."* Cincinnati: R. P. Brooks, 1839. Microfilm #25592, item 2, LDS Family History.

Hale, Aroet Lucius. Letter to Ebenezer Beesley, ca. 1897. Hale Papers, 1855–1900. MS 17081, item 2. LDS Church History Library.

Hamer, John C. *Northeast of Eden: A Historical Atlas of Missouri's Mormon County.* Kingston, Mo.: Far West Cultural Center and Mormon Missouri Frontier Foundation, 2004.

Hammond, Isaac W., comp. and ed. *The State of New Hampshire: Rolls and Documents Relating to Soldiers in the Revolutionary War, Part 1.* Manchester, N.H.: John B. Clarke, 1889.

―――. *The State of New Hampshire: Rolls of the Soldiers in the Revolutionary War 1775 to May 1777, Vol. 1.* Concord, N.H.: Parsons B. Cogswell, State Printer, 1885.

―――. *The State of New Hampshire: Rolls of the Soldiers in the Revolutionary War, May 1775 to 1780, Vol. 2.* Concord, N.H.: Parsons B. Cogswell, State Printer, 1886.

―――. *Town Papers. Documents Relating to Towns in New Hampshire, A to F Inclusive.* 13 vols. Concord, N.H.: Parsons B. Cogswell, State Printer, 1882–84.

Hancock, Charles Brent. Autobiography, ca. 1882. Typescript. MS 5285. LDS Church History Library.

Hancock, Mosiah Lyman. Autobiography, n.d. MS 8175. LDS Church History Library.

Hanna, William F. *History of Avon, 1988.* January 1.1989. Town of Avon website. http://www.avonmass.org/about/centennial (accessed May 18, 2008).

Harder, Kelsie B., and Mary H. Smallwood. *Claims to Name: Toponyms of St. Lawrence County.* Utica, N.Y.: North Country Books, 1993.

Harned, Ellen D. *History of Windham County, Connecticut.* Worcester, Mass.: Ellen D. Harned, 1874.

Harrington, May Hamlin. "A Short Historical Sketch of Early Pioneers." In *Early Records of Places and People in the Following Counties of Ohio, Columbiana, Mahoning, Portage, Stark.* Daughters of American Revolution. Jane Bain Chapter (Alliance, Ohio). Columbus, Ohio: State Library of Ohio, D.A.R. Collection. Typescript 1941. LDS Family History Library, Microfilm #317349.

Harrison County Genealogical Society, comp. *Harrison County (Iowa) Cemetery Records.* Microfilm #1579041, LDS Family History Library.

Hart, John L. "Courage a Legend as She Faced Mob." *Church News*, June 19, 2004, 10–12.

Hartley, William G. "'Almost Too Intolerable a Burthern': The Winter Exodus from Missouri, 1838–39." *Journal of Mormon History* 18 (Fall 1992): 6–40.

———. "Letters and Mail between Kirtland and Independence: A Mormon Postal History, 1831–33." *Journal of Mormon History* 45, no. 3 (Summer 2009): 163–89.

———. "The McLellin Journals and Early Mormon History." In *The Journals of William E. McLellin 1831–1836.* Edited by Jan Shipps and John W. Welch. Urbana: University of Illinois Press/Provo, Utah: BYU Studies, 1994, 263–89.

———. "Missouri's 1838 Extermination Order and the Mormons' Forced Removal to Illinois." *Mormon Historical Studies* 2, no. 1 (2001): 5–28.

———. *My Best for the Kingdom: History and Autobiography of John Lowe Butler, a Mormon Frontiersman.* Salt Lake City: Aspen Books, 1993.

———. "Nauvoo Stake, Priesthood Quorums, and the Church's First Wards." *BYU Studies* 32, no. 1 (1992): 57–80.

———. "Pushing on to Zion: Kanesville, Iowa, 1846–1853." *Ensign*, August 2002, 15–23.

———. *"Stand by My Servant Joseph": The Story of the Joseph Knight Family and the Restoration.* Salt Lake City: Deseret Book, 2003.

Hatcher, Patricia Law. *Abstract of Graves of Revolutionary Patriots.* 4 vols. Dallas, Tex.: Pioneer Heritage Press, 1987.

Haynes, Tom, ed. *Sacred and Secular: Historic Meetinghouses and Churches of the Monadnock Region, 1750 to 1850.* Keene, N.H.: Historical Society of Cheshire County, November 2006.

Hayward, John. *A Gazetter of New Hampshire.* Boston: John P. Jewett, 1849.

Heitman, Francis B. *Historical Register of Officers of the Continental Army during the War of the Revolution, April 1775 to December 1783.* Frederick, Md.: University Publications of America, 1975. LDS Family History Library, Microfilm #6078147.

Hewwett, Janet B., comp. *The Roster of Union Soldiers 1861–1865, Iowa M541-1–M541-29.* Wilmington, N.C.: Broadfoot Publishing Company, 2000.

Hickman, W. Z. *History of Jackson County, Missouri.* Topeka, Kans.: Historical Publishing Company, 1920.

Hicks, Michael. "What Hymns Early Mormons Sang and How they Sang Them," *BYU Studies* 47, no. 1 (2008): 95–118.
Higbee, John Somers. Reminiscences and Diaries, 1845–66. Typescript. MS 1742. LDS Church History Library.
Hill, Gardner, M.D. "Old Methodist Meeting House in Winchester." Unidentified and undated newspaper clipping. St. Lawrence County Historical Society, Canton, New York.
Hill, Marvin S. *Quest for Refuge: The Mormon Flight from American Pluralism.* Salt Lake City: Signature Books, 1989.
History of Caldwell and Livingston Counties, Missouri. St. Louis: National Historical Co., 1886. Microfilm #844894, LDS Family History Library.
History of Carroll County, Missouri, Including a History of Its Townships, Cities, Towns, and Vvillages. . . Biographical Sketches of Prominent Men and Citizens. 1881. Rpt., Walsworth Publishing for Carroll County Historical Society, 1969.
The History of Daviess County, Missouri. Kansas City, Mo.: Birdsall & Dean, 1882.
History of Jackson County, Missouri: Containing a History of the County, Its Cities, Towns, etc., Biographical Sketches . . . History of Missouri, Maps of Jackson County. Kansas City, Mo.: Union Historical Co., 1881. Microfilm #962549, item 1. LDS Family History Library.
"History of Joseph Smith." *Times and Seasons* 6 (December 1, 1845): 1041–42 and 6 (December 15, 1845): 1057.
"History of Lyman Wight." *Millennial Star* 27, no. 29 (July 22, 1865): 455.
History of Mills County, Iowa: Containing a History of the County, Its Cities, Towns, etc., a Biographical Directory of Many of Its Leading Citizens, War Record of Its Volunteers in the Late Rebellion, General and Local Statistics. Des Moines, Iowa: State Historical Co., 1881.
History of Portage County. http://www.heritagepursuit.com/Portage/Portage518CXXIX.htm (accessed June 24, 2009).
History of Ray County, Mo. St Louis: Missouri Historical Company, 1881.
History of the Church. Joseph Smith Jr. et al., *History of the Church of Jesus Christ of Latter-day Saints.* Edited by B. H. Roberts, 2d ed. rev. (6 vols. 1902–12, Vol. 7, 1932). Rpt., Salt Lake City: Deseret Book, 1980 printing.
"A History of the Persecution of the Church of Jesus Christ of Latter Day Saints in Missouri." *Times and Seasons* 1, no. 5 (March 1840): 65–66.
History of Wyoming County, N.Y. 1880. Rpt., Interlaken, N.Y.: Heart of the Lakes Publisher, 1994.
Hogan, Mervin Booth. "The Vital Statistics of Nauvoo Lodge." Typescript, 1976. M230.91/H714v/1976. LDS Church History Library.
Holbrook, Joseph. *History of Joseph Holbrook, 1806–1865: Written by His Own Hand.* Salt Lake City: M. F. & W. C. Holbrook, 1977.
Holmes, Frank R. *Directory of the Ancestral Heads of New England Families, 1620–1700.* Baltimore, Md.: Genealogical Publishing Co., 1964.
Holmes, Gail George. "The LDS Legacy in Southwestern Iowa." *Ensign*, August 1988, 54–57.
Holmes/Holm, James B., and Lucille Dudley, eds. *Portage Heritage: A History of Portage County, Ohio; Its Towns and Townships and the Men and Women Who*

Have Developed Them; Its Life, Institutions and Biographies, Facts and Lore. Microfilm #1033821, Item 1. LDS Family History Library.

Holzapfel, Richard Neitzel. "Nauvoo Remembered: Helen Mar Whitney Reminiscences." *Nauvoo Journal.*
    Part 1: 6, no. 2 (Fall 1994): 3–9.
    Part 2: 7 (Spring 1995): 19–34
    Part 3: 6, no. 2 (Fall 1995): 3–16.
    Part 4: 8, no. 1 (Spring 1996): 7–29.

Holzapfel, Richard Neitzel, and T. Jeffery Cottle. *Old Mormon Kirtland and Missouri: Historic Photographs and Guides.* 2d ed. Santa Ana, Calif.: Fieldbrook Productions, 1991.

———. *Old Mormon Nauvoo and Southeastern Iowa: Historic Photographs and Guides.* Santa Ana, Calif.: Fieldbrook Productions, 1991.

Holzapfel, Richard Neitzel, T. Jeffery Cottle, and Ted D. Stoddard, eds. *Church History in Black and White: George Edward Anderson's Photographic Mission to Latter-day Saint Historical Sites, 1907 Diary, 1907–8 Photographs.* Provo, Utah: BYU Religious Studies Center 1995.

Holzapfel, Richard Neitzel, and Jeni Broberg Holzapfel. *Women of Nauvoo.* Salt Lake City: Bookcraft, 1992.

Horton, Loren N. "'The Worst That I Had Yet Witnessed': Mormon Diarists Cross Iowa in 1846." *Iowa Heritage Illustrated* 77 (Summer 1996): 70–73.

Hoskin Family. Family History Letters. http://www.rootsandroutes.net. (accessed May 3, 2001).

Hough, Franklin B. *A History of St. Lawrence and Franklin Counties, New York: From the Earliest Period to the Present Time.* Albany, N.Y.: Little and Co., 1853. LDS Family History Library, Microfilm #808345.

"House Breaking." *Malvern [Iowa] Leader,* October 22, 1885.

Hoyt, W. D., Jr., ed. "A Clay Countian's Letters of 1834: From John Chauncey of Liberty, Clay County, to Francis J. Dallam, City Collector of Baltimore, Maryland." *Missouri Historical Review* 45 (July 1951): 349–53. Microfiche M277.78 C498c 1951. LDS Church History Library.

Huff, Joe, and Madeline, comps. *Census of Clinton, Davis, Louisa, Marion, Scott, Van Buren, and Wapello Counties, Iowa, 1847.* Des Moines: Iowa General Assembly, compiled in 1974–75. Typescript. Microfilm #1022202, items 10–16, LDS Family History Library.

Hunt, Elmer Munson. *New Hampshire Town Names and Whence They Came.* Peterborough, N.H.: William L. Bauhan, 1970.

Huntington, Oliver Boardman. Autobiography, 1823–39. Typescript. L. Tom Perry Special Collections, Harold B. Lee Library, Brigham Young University, Provo, Utah. See also http://www.boap.org/LDS/Early-Saints/OBHuntington.html (accessed June 21, 2007).

Huntington, William. Autobiography-Journal, 1784–1846. Typescript. L. Tom Perry Special Collections, Harold B. Lee Library, Brigham Young University, Provo, Utah. Electronic version at http://www.boap.org/LDS/Early-Saints/WHuntington.html (accessed August 19, 2006).

Huntington, William. "Reminiscences and Journal, April 1841–August 1846." Typescript. MS 1801. LDS Church History Library.

Hurd, Hamilton D., ed. *History of Cheshire and Sullivan Counties, New Hampshire.* Philadelphia: J. W. Lewis, 1886.

Hyde, Myrtle Stevens, comp. "Kanesville Conditions." Microfiche #6067111. LDS Family History Library.

Illinois, Hancock Co., Nauvoo Precinct. Election Returns, August 1, 1842. MS 1532, item 9. LDS Church History Library.

"In this paper, we give the proceedings . . ." *Elders' Journal* 4 (August 1, 1838).

"Index to Historical Collections: Nauvoo Restoration, Inc.: Rowena Miller Files." Lands and Records Office, Nauvoo Restoration. Microfilm CR 387 1, items 1–4. LDS Church History Library.

"Index to Mormon Battalion and Nauvoo Legion Solders." *Nauvoo Journal* 2, no. 1 (January 1990): 28–36.

"Information Concerning Persons Driven from Jackson County, Missouri, in 1833." MS 6019, fd. 3, unpaginated. LDS Church History Library.

Inouye, Henry K., Jr. *Latter Day [sic] Saints in Early Independence, Missouri.* Independence, Mo.: H&H Enterprises, n.d.

Iowa Census Board. *1852 Census of Various Counties in Iowa.* Microfilm #1022205, LDS Family History Library.

Iowa General Assembly, *Census of Cedar, Clinton, Decatur, Gutherie, Iowa, Jackson, Jasper, Jefferson, Johnson, Madison, Mahaska, Page, Pottawattamie, Poweshiek, Scott, and Washington Counties, Iowa,* Microfilm #1022203, item 13, Roll 118, Line 8, LDS Church History Library.

Iowa Marriages, 1884. http://www.rootsweb.com/iamills/marriage (accessed July 20, 2005).

Iowa State Census Collection, 1836–1925. Mills County, Silver Creek Township, Silver Creek Township. Roll IA_62, Line 10, Family Number 13, http://www.ancestry.com. (accessed February 13 and 17, and March 13, 2008).

Iowa State Census Collection, 1836–1925. 1851 Census. Pottawattamie County, no township listed, Roll IA_118, lines 8–11. http://www.ancestry.com. (accessed March 13, 2008).

Jackman, Levi. Diary, May 1835–July 1844. Holograph. MS 8362. LDS Church History Library.

———. Drawing of the Battle on the Big Blue River, ca. 1871. Holograph. MS 4153, frame 43. LDS Church History Library.

———. Letter to Angeline Jackman, Liberty, Missouri, February 26, 1836. Levi Jackman Papers, 1835–46. Holograph. MS 4453. LDS Church History Library.

———. Record Book, ca. 1832–34. Holograph. MS 5940. LDS Church History Library.

———. "A Short Sketch of the Life of Levi Jackman." In "Reminiscences and Journal, 1851–1867." Carbon copy of typescript, prepared July 13, 1949, by Utah Historical Society. Also in LDS Church History, Ms 1583.

———. "A Short Sketch of the Life of Levi Jackman (1797–1876)." http://www.msnmscache.com/cache (accessed January 24, 2008).

Jackson, Brian D. "Preparing Kingdom-Bearers: Educating the Children of Nauvoo." *Mormon Historical Studies* 3 (2002): 59–72.

Jackson, Ronald Vern, ed. *Iowa, 1852*. North Salt Lake, Utah: Accelerated Indexing System, 1988.

Jacobson, Emma McDowell. *History of Early Provo Cemeteries Moved: Fort Wall, Temple Hill, Grandview, 1849–1851, Moved to Block 4, Provo City Cemetery*. Microfilm #10133821, item 1. LDS Family History Library.

Jaeckel, Nancy K. "Manti: The Life of a Shell-Bark Hickory Grove." *Nauvoo Journal* 6 (Fall 1994): 45–64.

"James M. Daley, Pioneer, Dies." *Contra Costa [California] Gazetteer*, July 28, 1923.

Jeffers, MeLinda Evans. "Mapping Historic Nauvoo." *BYU Studies* 32 (Winter/Spring 1992): 269–75.

Jennings, Warren A. "The Expulsion of the Mormons from Jackson County, Missouri." *Missouri Historical Review* 64 (October 1969–July 1970): 41–63.

———. "'Zion Is Fled': The Expulsion of the Mormons from Jackson County, Missouri." Ph.D. diss., University of Florida, 1962. Microfilm #M277.78 J54z. LDS Church History Library.

Jenson, Andrew, comp. *Church Chronology: A Record of Important Events Pertaining to the History of the Church of Jesus Christ of Latter-day Saints*, 2d ed. Salt Lake City: Deseret News, 1914.

Jessee, Dean C. ed. *The Papers of Joseph Smith. Vol. 2: Journal, 1832–1842*. Salt Lake City: Deseret Book, 1992.

———, comp. and ed. *The Personal Writings of Joseph Smith*. Salt Lake City: Deseret Book, 1984.

———. "'Walls, Grates and Screeking Iron Doors': The Prison Experience of Mormon Leaders in Missouri, 1838–1839." In *New Views of Mormon History: A Collection of Essays in Honor of Leonard J. Arrington*. Edited by Davis Bitton and Maureen Ursenbach Beecher. Salt Lake City: University of Utah Press, 1987, 19–42.

Jessee, Dean C., and David J. Whittaker, eds. "The Last Months of Mormonism in Missouri: The Albert Perry Rockwood Journal." *BYU Studies* 28 (Winter 1988): 5–41.

Jenson, Andrew. "Martin Wood." *LDS Biographical Encyclopedia: A Compilation of Biographical Sketches of Prominent Men and Women in the Church of Jesus Christ of Latter-day Saints*, 4 vols. Salt Lake City: Andrew Jenson History Company, 1901–36, 3:738.

Jenson, Andrew, ed. "Miscellaneous. FOLLETT (King)." *Historical Record: A Monthly Periodical*. Salt Lake City: Andrew Jenson, 1886, 5:31.

"John Follett, Attleboro, 1718." Bristol County, Massachusetts. Register of Probate. Probate Records, 1690–1881. Microfilm #5675140, LDS Family History Library.

"John Follett." File #31139, Lands and Records Office, Nauvoo, Illinois.

Johnson, Benjamin Franklin. *My Life's Review*. Independence, Mo.: Zion's Printing and Publishing Co., 1947. http://www.boap.org/LDS/Early-Saints/BFJohnson.html (accessed August 21, 2006).

Johnson, Clark V., "Missouri: LDS Communities in Jackson and Clay Counties." In *Encyclopedia of Mormonism*, 4 vols. New York: Macmillan Publishing Company, 1992, 2:922–25.

---. "The Missouri Redress Petitions: A Reappraisal of Mormon Persecutions in Missouri." *BYU Studies* 26 (Spring 1986): 31–44.

---, ed. *Mormon Redress Petitions: Documents of the 1833–1838 Missouri Conflict.* Provo, Utah: BYU Religious Studies Center, Brigham Young University, 1992.

Johnson, Clark V., and Ronald E. Romig. *An Index to Early Caldwell County, Missouri Land Records.* Independence, Mo.: Missouri Mormon Frontier Foundation, 2002.

Johnson, Eleanor Moliere. "The Gathering of the Mormons in Jackson County, Missouri." M.A. thesis, University of Nebraska, 1927. Microfilm M291 Ala, item 3. LDS Church History Library.

Johnson, Wm. Cumming, Jr. "List of Voters in Portage County, Ohio, 1816–1856." Typescript, July 1985. Western Reserve Historical Society, Cleveland, Ohio.

Johnston, Carrie Polk, and W.H.S. McGlumphy. *History of Clinton and Caldwell Counties, Missouri.* Tucson, Ariz.: W. C. Cox, 1974. Microfilm #908920, item 2 and #1000287, item 1. LDS Family History Library.

Jones, James. Letter to Henry Jones, May 19, 1846. In Henry Jones, Correspondence, 1844–95. MS 7188, LDS Church History Library.

Jordan, Gilbert J. *Yesterday in the Texas Hill Country.* College Station, Tex.: Texas A&M University Press, 1979.

Jorgensen, Danny L. "Conflict in the Camps of Israel: The 1853 Cutlerite Schism." *Journal of Mormon History* 21 (Spring 1995): 25–64.

---. "Cutler's Camp at the Big Grove on Silver Creek: A Mormon Settlement in Iowa, 1847–1853." *Nauvoo Journal* 9, no. 2 (Fall 1997): 39–51.

---. "The Fiery Darts of the Adversary: An Interpretation of Early Cutlerism." *John Whitmer Historical Association Journal* 10 (1990): 67–84.

---. "The Scattered Saints of Southwestern Iowa: Cutlerite-Josephite Conflict and Rivalry, 1855–1865." *John Whitmer Historical Association Journal* 12 (1992): 80–97.

Journal History. See Shortened Citations.

Kamas Ward, Summit County, Utah. Record of Members: Annual Genealogical Report, 1870–1948. Microfilm #26056, LDS Family History Library.

Kane, Colonel Thomas L. "The Mormons: A Discourse Delivered before the Historical Society of Pennsylvania," March 26, 1850. Philadelphia: King & Baird, Printers, 1850.

"Kidnapping." *Times and Seasons* 4 (November 1, 1843): 375–76.

Killpack, Garth Homer, ed. *Autobiography and Journal of Warren Foote, 1817–1903.* Springville, Utah: G. H. Killpack, 1974. http://www.boap.org/LDS/Early-Saints/WFoote.html (accessed August 13, 2006).

Kimball, James L., Jr. Interviewed by Joann Follett Mortensen, October 1999. Salt Lake City. Notes in my possession.

---. Quoted in "Historic Nauvoo Cemetery Being Restored." *LDS Church News,* June 17, 1989, 11.

Kimball, Stanley B. "Heber C. Kimball and Family: The Nauvoo Years." *BYU Studies* 15, no. 4 (Summer 1975): 447–79.

---. "Missouri Mormon Manuscripts: Sources in Selected Societies." *BYU Studies* 14, no. 4 (Summer 1974): 458–87.

———. "The Mormon Trail Network in Iowa 1838–1863: A New Look." *BYU Studies* 21 (Fall 1981): 417–30.

———. "The Mormons in Illinois, 1838–1846: A Special Introduction." *Journal of the Illinois State Historical Society* 64 (Spring 1971): 4–21.

"King Follett." File 10091. Lands and Records Office, Nauvoo, Illinois.

"King Follett . . ." [Palmyra] *Missouri Whig and General Advertiser*, 1, no. 11 (October 12, 1839).

Lacey, Robert. *Great Tales from English History*. New York: Little, Brown and Company, 2004.

"Lafayette (California) Cemetery Records to 1935." Typescript copy of original in my possession.

Larned, Ellen D. *History of Windham County, Connecticut*. Worcester, Mass.: Ellen D. Larned, 1874.

Larson, Carl V., comp. and ed. *A Database of the Mormon Battalion: An Identification of the Original Members of the Mormon Battalion*. Salt Lake City: U.S Mormon Battalion, 1997.

Larson, Stan, ed. "The King Follett Discourse: A Newly Amalgamated Text." *BYU Studies* 18, no. 2 (Winter 1978): 193–208.

Launius, Roger D., "The Latter Day Saints in Ohio: Writing the History of Mormonism's Middle Period." *John Whitmer Historical Association Journal* 16 (1996): 31–56.

Launius, Roger D., and John E. Hallwas, eds. *Kingdom on the Mississippi Revisited: Nauvoo in Mormon History*. Urbana: University of Illinois Press, 1996.

Launius, Roger D., and F. Mark McKierman. *Joseph Smith's Red Brick Store*. Macomb: Western Illinois University, 1985.

Lawrence, Ruth, ed. *Colonial Families of America*, Vol. 9. New York: National Americana Society, 1931.

Lawton, Dorris, comp. *Marriage Index, Hancock County, Illinois*. N.p.: Hancock County Historical Society, 1990.

Leavitt, Joseph Page. *Story of Jeremiah Leavitt (III) and Autobiography of Sarah Studevant*. Microfilm # 1036191, Item 16. LDS Family History Library.

Legal Dictionary. http://definitions.uslegal.com/p/prose (accessed October 6, 2010).

Leonard, Glen M., "Letters Home: The Immigrant View from Nauvoo." *BYU Studies* 31 (1991): 91–100.

———. *Nauvoo: A Place of Peace, a People of Promise*. Salt Lake City: Deseret Book/Provo, Utah: BYU Press, 2002.

———. "Picturing the Nauvoo Legion." *BYU Studies* 35, no. 2 (1995): 95–128.

Leonard, Glen M., and T. Edgar Lyon. "The Nauvoo Years." *Ensign*, September 1979, 10–15.

Leseman, Lucy (Mrs. Henry). "Follett Records: Descendants of Robert Follett, 1625–1708, Salem, Massachusetts." Unpublished. Photocopy of carbon copy in my possession, courtsey of Lucy Leseman.

LeSueur, Stephen C. "The Danites Reconsidered: Were They Vigilantes or Just the Mormon Version of the Elks Club?" *John Whitmer Historical Association Journal* 4 (1994): 35–52.

———. *The 1838 Mormon War in Missouri*. Columbia: University of Missouri Press, 1987.

———. "'High Treason and Murder': The Examination of Mormon Prisoners at Richmond, Missouri, in November 1838." *BYU Studies* 26 (Spring 1986): 3–30.

"Let Every Man Learn His Duty." *Evening and Morning Star* 1, no. 8 (January 1833): 61.

Lewis, Wayne J. "Mormon Land Ownership as a Factor in Evaluating the Extent of Mormon Settlements and Influence in Missouri, 1831–1841." M.A. thesis, Brigham Young University, 1981.

"Life and Journal of Eliza Marie Partridge (Smith) Lyman." http://www.partridge.parkinsonfamily.org/histories/eliza-diary-&-misc.htm (accessed July 26, 2006).

Lightner, Mary E[lizabeth Rollins]. "Mary E. Lightner's Life History." *Utah Genealogical and Historical Magazine* 17 (July 1926): 193–205.

Literski, Nicholas S. "An Introduction to Mormonism and Freemasonry." n.d. http://www.signaturebookslibrary.org/?p=418. (accessed July 17, 2011).

Littlefield, Lyman Omer. *The Mormon Martyrs: a Sketch of the Lives and a Full Account of the Martyrdom of the Joseph and Hyrum Smith*. Salt Lake City: Juvenile Instructor Office, 1882.

Livermore, Samuel Truesdale. *A Condensed History of Cooperstown: With a Biographical Sketch of J. Fenimore Cooper*. Albany, N.Y.: J. Munsell, 1862.

Livingston County History, Celebrating 150 Years, 1821–1981. Chillicothe, Mo.: Retired Senior Volunteer Program, 1981.

Ludy, Paul V., ed. *School Days in Old Nauvoo: Joseph Smith III*. Bates City, Mo.: n.pub., 2001. M277.73 S6532s 2001. LDS Church History Library.

Lupold, Harry Forrest. *The Latch String Is Out: A Pioneer History of Lake County, Ohio*. Fort Wayne, Ind.: Allen County Public Library, 1989.

Lupold, Harry Forrest, and Gladys Haddad, eds. *Ohio's Western Reserve: A Regional Reader*. Kent, Ohio: Kent State University Press, 1988.

Lyman, Albert R. *Amasa Mason Lyman, Trailblazer and Pioneer from the Atlantic to the Pacific*. Delta, Utah: Melvin A. Lyman, 1957.

Lyman, Amasa Mason. "Amasa Lyman's History." *Millennial Star* 27 (12 August 1865): 502–3.

Lyman, Edward Leo. *Amasa Mason Lyman, Mormon Apostle and Apostate: A Study in Dedication*. Salt Lake City: University of Utah Press, 2009.

"Life and Journal of Eliza Marie Partridge (Smith) Lyman." Typescript. L. Tom Perry Special Collections and Manuscripts Division, Harold B. Lee Library, Brigham Young University, Provo, Utah. Electronic version available at http://www.partridge.parkinsonfamily.org/histories/eliza-diary-&-misc.htm (accessed July 26, 2006). No editor, compiler, or author identified; D'Ann Stoddard is identified as "contributor."

Lynn, John W. *New Hampshire Lineages of Revolutionary War Regiments*. Grand Junction, Colo.: Lynn Research, 1986.

Lyon, T. Edgar. "The Account Books of the Amos Davis Store at Commerce, Illinois." *BYU Studies* 19 (Winter 1979): 241–43.

———. "Independence, Missouri, and the Mormons, 1827–1833." *BYU Studies* 13, no. 1 (1972): 10–19.

Mace, Wandle. Journal, 1809–46. Typescript. L. Tom Perry Special Collections, Harold B. Lee Library, Brigham Young University, Provo, Utah. See also

"Autobiography: Journal of Wandle Mace." http://www.boap.org/LDS/Early-Saints/WMace.html (accessed September 27, 2004, October 23, 2006, and August 7, 2007).

Madsen, Carol Cornwall. *In Their Own Words: Women and the Story of Nauvoo*. Salt Lake City: Deseret Book, 1994.

_____. *Journey to Zion: Voices from the Mormon Trail*. Salt Lake City: Deseret Book, 1997.

Madsen, Gordon A. "Joseph Smith and the Missouri Court of Inquiry: Austin A. King's Quest for Hostages." *BYU Studies* 43, no. 4 (2004): 93–136.

Mallory, Rudena Kramer, comp. *Clay County, Missouri, Marriages, 1821–81*. Kansas City, Mo.: R. K. Mallory, 1997.

Map. King Follett Land. DeKalb, New York, DeKalb Historical Society, DeKalb Junction, New York. Included without title or date in a letter from Virginia Fischer, Town Historian, DeKalb Historical Association, December 7, 2006. It seems to be the "1814 Goff and Spencer Survey Map, in DeKalb Town Historians' Collection.

Marquardt, H. Michael, comp. *Early Patriarchal Blessings of the Church of Jesus Christ of Latter-day Saints*. Salt Lake City: Smith-Pettit Foundation, 2007.

Martin, James D. *The Story of the John Daley Jr. Family: Westward Pioneers*. Ogden, Utah: J. D. Martin, 2000.

"Masonic Funeral Services," 1877. http://www.ilorlibrary.org/funeral (accessed June 13, 2008. Scanned courtesy of John Dorner, Librarian and Curator, Illinois Lodge of Research, Bloomington.

McBeth, Mildred, comp. *Alpheus Cutler: A Different Approach*. Salt Lake City: M. H. McBeth, 1994.

McBride, Matthew S. *A House for the Most High: The Story of the Original Nauvoo Temple*. Salt Lake City: Greg Kofford Books, 2007.

_____. Emails to Joann Follett Mortensen, February 17 and March 15, 2004.

McClintock, James H. *Mormon Settlement in Arizona: A Record of Peaceful Conquest of the Desert*. Phoenix, Ariz.: Manufacturing Stationers, 1921.

McConkie, Bruce R. *Mormon Doctrine*, 2d ed. Salt Lake City: Bookcraft, 1966.

McConkie, Joseph Fielding. "A Historical Examination of the Views of the Church of Jesus Christ of Latter-day Saints and the Reorganized Church of Jesus Christ of Latter Day Saints on Four Distinctive Aspects of the Doctrine of Deity Taught by the Prophet Joseph Smith." M.A. thesis, Brigham Young University, 1968.

McConkie, Joseph Fielding, and Craig J. Ostler. *Revelations of the Restoration: A Commentary on the Doctrine and Covenants and Other Modern Revelations*. Salt Lake City: Deseret Book, 2000.

McConkie, Mark L. *Remembering Joseph: Personal Recollections of Those Who Knew the Prophet Joseph Smith*. Salt Lake City: Deseret Book, 2003.

McReynolds, Edwin C. *Missouri: A History of the Crossroads State*. Norman: University of Oklahoma Press, 1962.

Memorial to Congress, November 28, 1843. MS 2145, fd. 6, LDS Church History Library.

Merrill, Eliphalet, and Phinehas Merrill. *Gazetteer of the State of New Hampshire*. Bowie, Md.: Heritage Books, 1987.

Mill Branch (Iowa), Record, 1847–1852. Microfilm #LR 5162-21. LDS Church

History Library.

Miller, David E., and Della S. Miller. *Nauvoo: The City of Joseph*, 2d ed. Bountiful, Utah: Utah History Atlas, 1996.

Miller, Marilyn McMeen, and John Clifton Moffitt. *Provo: A Story of People in Motion.* Provo, Utah: Brigham Young University Press, 1974.

Miller, Rowena. Memorandum. January 6, 1965. Nauvoo Restoration, Inc., Corporate Files, #CR 387 19. LDS Church History Archives.

Millet, Robert L. "Pearl of Great Price." In *Encyclopedia of Latterday Saint History.* Edited by Arnold K. Garr, Donald Q. Cannon, and Richard O. Cowan. Salt Lake City: Deseret Book, 2000, 900–902.

———. "Zion." In *Encyclopedia of Latter-day Saint History.* Edited by Arnold K. Garr, Donald Q. Cannon, and Richard O. Cowan. Salt Lake City: Deseret Book, 2000, 1397–98.

Mills County History Book Committee. *First Baptist Church: Mills County, Iowa.* Dallas, Tex.: Taylor Publishing, 1985.

Mills County Iowa Cemeteries. Microfilm #1421802, item 4, p. 89. LDS Family History Library.

Mills County Iowa County Recorder. Probate Records, 1854–1935. Microfilm #1491834. LDS Family History Library.

Mills County [Iowa]. "Explore Mills County: Find the Mormon Traces." Brochure in my possession, obtained 2001.

Mills County [Iowa] Marriages, 1851–1865. Grooms F–H. http://www.rootsweb.com/iamills/marriage (accessed May 3, 2001).

Minthorn, Frances Marian Huff. Journal. Quoted in Alice May Minthorn Hall. Email to Joann Mortensen, December 4, 2002.

Missouri General Assembly. *Document Containing the Correspondence, Orders, &c. in Relation to the Disturbances with the Mormons.* Microfilm #1670779, LDS Family History Library.

Mitchell, Gay Aleen. Letter to Joann Mortensen, September 29, 2004. Photocopy in my possession.

Moore, Beth Shumway. *Bones in the Well: The Haun's Mill Massacre, 1838, A Documentary History.* Norman: Arthur H. Clark, an imprint of the University of Oklahoma Press, 2006.

Mormon Biographical Registers. http://byustudies.byu.edu/Indexes/BioAlpha/MBRegisterA.aspx (accessed June 27, 2005).

"The Mormon Prisoners Escape." *Quincy [Illinois] Whig* 2 (July 20, 1839). Dale Broadhurst website, "Uncle Dale's Old Mormon Articles: Quincy Whig & Argus (1839). http://www.sidneyrigdon.com/dbroadhu/ILwhig1839.htm (accessed August 28, 2006). Rpt., *Daily [St. Louis] Missouri Republican,* 15 (Thursday, July 11, 1839).

"Mormonism." In *Early Days in Council Bluffs.* LDS Family History Library, Microfilm #2055216, item 7, 77–89.

Mortensen, Joann Follett. "Life Story of William Alexander and Nancy Mariah Follett" with supporting family documents and records. Typescript, 2003.

Mueller, Ellen Crago, Elnora L. Frye, and Leroy Robert Maki, eds. *Obituary Data, Albany County, Wyoming.* Laramie, Wyo.: Albany County Genealogical

Society, 1996.

Mulder, William. "Nauvoo Observed." *BYU Studies* 32, no. 1 (1992): 95–118.

Munro-Fraser, J. P. *History of Contra Costa County, California: Including Its Geography, Geology, Topography, Climatography and Description; Together with a Record of the Mexican Grants . . . Also, Incidents of Pioneer Life and Biographical Sketches of Early and Prominent Settlers and Representative Men*. San Francisco: W. A. Slocum, 1882.

Myers, Merrible E. "List of Names of As [sic] Belonging to the Enumeration of the White Males of 21 Yrs and Upward in Portage Co for the Year 1827." Typescript. Probate Court, Portage County, Ravenna, Ohio, Western Reserve Historical Society, Cleveland, Ohio. Another version under the title of "List of Names of as [sic] Belonging to the Enumeration of the White Males of 21 Yrs old and Upward in Portage Co for the year 1827–Located in Probate Court of Portage Co Ravenna Ohio," Western Reserve Historical Society, Cleveland, Ohio, typescript, n.d., unpaginated.

Nagel, Paul C. *Missouri: A Bicentennial History*. New York: W. W. Norton & Company, 1977.

"Nathan West." File #30219. Nauvoo Restoration Land and Records Office. This record is a compilation of data from various sources, searchable by individual's name, with each assigned a unique filename. Information obtained by personal visit in 2008. CD and printout in my possession.

"Nauvoo." *Times and Seasons* 3, no. 23 (October 1, 1842): 936.

"Nauvoo Additions." In Church of Jesus Christ of Latter-day Saints and Nauvoo Family History and Property Identification Department. *Reference Book for Nauvoo Family History and Property Identification Department*. Salt Lake City: Nauvoo Restoration, Inc., 1990, 88.

"Nauvoo Baptisms for the Dead in Mississippi River (September 1840–November 1841)." Microfilm #255501, LDS Family History Library.

Nauvoo Family History and Property Identification Department. "Hancock County: Township and Range." In Church of Jesus Christ of Latter-day Saints and Nauvoo Family History and Property Identification Department. *Reference Book for Nauvoo Family History and Property Identification Department* Salt Lake City: Nauvoo Restoration, Inc., 1990, 32.

Nauvoo Expositor 1 (June 17, 1844): whole issue.

Nauvoo First and Second Ward. List of Members, 1836–46. In Records of Members, 1841–1845. Microfilm #889392, item 4. LDS Family History Library.

Nauvoo House Association Records, 1841–1846. "Pinery Accounts, 1842 April–December." Holograph, MS 2375, Box 6, unpaginated, LDS Church History Library.

Nauvoo (Ill.) Assessor. Tax Lists for District No. 3, 1840, 1842, 1850. Microfilm #7706, Item 5, 163–236. LDS Family History Library.

Nauvoo Illinois. City Records, 1841–1845. Petitions, 1841 and 1842. MS 16800, Box 1, Fds. 23–25. LDS Church History Library. Photocopies of holographs in my possession.

Nauvoo Illinois. School Records, 1842–1845." LDS Family History Library, Microfilm #7705.

"Nauvoo Illinois Seventies License Record." Holograph. MS 3440. LDS Church History Library.

Nauvoo Legion (Ill.), Records, 1841–45. Holograph. MS 3430. LDS Church History Library.
Nauvoo Lodge. Minute Book, October 1841–February 1846. LDS Church History Library, CD #3436. Unpaginated.
Nauvoo Relief Society Minutes. See "Record of the Organization, and Proceedings of the Female Relief Society of Nauvoo, 1842–44."
Nauvoo Restoration, Inc., Church Service and Proselyting Missionaries (1987–89), comp. *Old Nauvoo Burial Ground: Church of Jesus Christ of Latter-day Saints; This List Contains Names of Persons Who Died in Nauvoo Area, 1839–1850 Period; Members and Others Possibly Buried in Old Nauvoo Burial Ground or in Other Cemeteries in Nauvoo.* Nauvoo, Ill.: Nauvoo Restoration, Inc., 1990.
Nauvoo Restoration, Inc. Old Nauvoo Burial Ground: Inventory of Markers and Graves, etc. Follett, King, Nauvoo RIN 10091. Transcript in my possession, obtained on personal visit to Nauvoo 2008.
Nauvoo (Ill.) Sexton. Cemetery Records, 1839–45, unpaginated. MS 16142. LDS Church History Library.
Nauvoo Temple Building Committee. Carpenter Time Book C. Microfilm #CR 342, Reel 5, item 9. LDS Church History Library.
Nauvoo Temple Building Committee. Records, 1841–1852. Microfilm #CR 342-9. LDS Church History Library.
Nauvoo Temple Endowment Register, December 10, 1845–February 8, 1846. Salt Lake City: Temple Records Index Bureau, 1974.
Nauvoo Trustee Land Book, 1836–1842. MS 3438. LDS Church History Library.
Neagles, James C., and Lila Lee Neagles. *Locating Your Revolutionary War Ancestor: A Guide to the Military Records.* Logan, Utah: Everton Publishers, 1983.
New Hampshire. Cheshire County. Probate Estate Files, 1769–1885, LDS Family History Library:
    Administrations, 1823–1869. "Estate of Captain John Follett," Microfilm #15727.
    Seth Alexander, Winchester 1781, 12–13, Microfilm #2230625.
    Dowers Claims, Settlement of Estate of Widows, 1814–1886, Vol. 46:52–54, Microfilm #15726.
    "Estate of Captain John Follett," 416, Microfilm #2257129.
New Hampshire. Registrar of Vital Statistics. *Index to Births, Early to 1900.* Microfilm #1000481 ("French–Folsom"), and 1000481 ("Andervil–Allen"). LDS Family History Library.
New York. St. Lawrence County. County Clerk, Mortgages, 1802–1850. Microfilms #885323 and #885325. LDS Family History Library.
Nibley, Preston. *Joseph Smith the Prophet.* Salt Lake City: Deseret News Press, 1944.
[No author]. "An Invitation to Do a Week Long Dig: Log House Archaeological Dig 22–27 June 1998." *Missouri Mormon Frontier Foundation Newsletter,* Nos. 16/17 (Winter/Spring 1998): 1–2.
"Notice." *Times and Seasons* 1 (May 1840): 112.
"Notice." *Times and Seasons* 6 (March 15, 1845): 847.
"Notice to My Old Patrons and Friends." *Malvern [Iowa] Leader,* October 16, 1884.

Oak, Henry Lebbeus. *Oak/Oaks/Oakes—Family Register. Nathaniel Oak of Marlborough, Mass.: And Three Generations of His Descendants in Both Male and Female Lines: With a Sketch of [the] Life of Henry Lebbeus Oak, Historical Writer and Genealogist.* Los Angeles: Out West Print, 1906. Microfilm #1012621, item 1. LDS Family History Library.

Oakes, Fred Arthur. *Oakes and Relatives.* Minneapolis, Minn.: Fred Arthur Oakes, 1974. Microfilm #962962, item 6-22A. LDS Family History Library.

Oakman, Walter F., comp. "Mount Caesar Cemetery." *Swanzey Cemetery Records, Swanzey, N.H.* Microfilm #15577, Item 10, p. 71, LDS Family History Library.

O'Driscoll, Jeffrey S. *Hyrum Smith: A Life of Integrity.* Salt Lake City: Deseret Book, 2003.

Ohio. Portage County. LDS Family History Library.

> Auditor. Duplicate Tax Records: 1816–38. Microfilm #528374, 52375, and 528378. LDS Family History Library.
>
> Probate Court (Portage County) Records, 1808–67. Probate record v. 3 1821–1832. LDS Family History Library. Alexander Follett, Probate Packet, #140, September 1826. Microfilm # 378318.
>
> Probate Court (Portage County) Probate Dockets, 1819–89. Probate docket v. 1 1819–1841. Microfilm #891354.

Olson, Earl E. "The Chronology of the Ohio Revelations." *BYU Studies* 11, no. 4 (Summer 1971): 329–49.

Olson, Ferron Allred. *Seymour Brunson: Defender of the Faith.* Salt Lake City: F.A. Olson, 1998.

"130 Years of Methodism in DeKalb." New York Historical Society website. http://www.DeKalbnyhistorian.org/LocalHistoryArticles/130YrsMethodism/Methodist.html (accessed April 20, 2010).

Openshaw, Rose. "History of Morris Phelps." http://www.morrisphelps.org/morris (accessed July 5, 2007).

Ostler, Craig J. "Nauvoo Saints in the Newspapers of the 1840s." *Nauvoo Journal* 8 (Spring 1996): 30–33.

Pace, William Byram. Autobiography, 1904. Typescript. MS 13067. LDS Church History Library.

Paden, Irene Dakin. "The Ira J. Willis Guide to the Gold Mine." MS 416, LDS Church History Library.

Palmer, James. *James Palmer's Travels and Ministry in the Gospel, 1820–1905: Pioneer of 1850.* Salt Lake City: Utah Printing, 1963.

(No headline). *Palmyra (Missouri) Whig and General Advertiser,* 1, no. 11 (October 12, 1839), not paginated. Dale Broadhurst's website: *Dale's Old Mormon Articles: Missouri, 1838–1840.* http://www.lavazone2.com/dbroadhu/MO/Miss1838.htm (accessed August 4, 2004).

Parkin, Max H. "Conflict at Kirtland: A Study of the Nature and Causes of External and Internal Conflict of the Mormons in Ohio between 1830 and 1836." M.A. thesis, Brigham Young University, 1966.

———. "A History of the Latter-day Saints in Clay County, Missouri, from 1833 to 1837." Ph.D. diss., Brigham Young University, 1976. Facsimile copy: Ann Arbor, Mich.: University Microfilms International, 1984, in my possession.

———. "Jackson County and Vicinity." In *Historical Atlas of Mormonism*. Edited by S. Kent Brown, Donald Q. Cannon, and Richard H. Jackson. New York: Simon & Schuster, 1994, 38.

———. "Latter-day Saint Conflict in Clay County." In *Regional Studies in Latter-day Saint Church History: Missouri*. Edited by Arnold K. Garr and Clark V. Johnson. Provo, Utah: BYU Department of Church History and Doctrine, 1994, 241–60.

———. *Missouri*. Vol. 4 in SACRED PLACES: A COMPREHENSIVE GUIDE TO EARLY LDS HISTORICAL SITES. LaMar C. Berrett, general editor. Salt Lake City: Deseret Book, 2004.

Partridge, Edward. "Family Record." 53. http://www.partridge.parkinson.org/history (accessed November 20, 2005).

Peck, Reed. *The Reed Peck Manuscript: An Important Document Written in 1839*. Typescript. Salt Lake City: Utah Lighthouse Ministry, n.d.

Perkins, Keith W., and Donald Q. Cannon, eds. *Ohio and Illinois*. Vol. 3 of SACRED PLACES: A COMPREHENSIVE GUIDE TO EARLY LDS HISTORICAL SITES. General editor LaMar C. Barrett. Salt Lake City: Deseret Book, 2002.

Perley, Sidney. *The History of Salem, Massachusetts*. Salem, Mass.: Sidney Perley, 1928:
Vol. 2. 1637–1670, 1926.
Vol. 3. 1671–1716: 1928.

"Petition to the President, 10 April 1834, Liberty, Clay County, Missouri." http://www.farwesthistory.com/petition.com (accessed June 8, 2005). Based on *Times and Seasons* 6 (December 1, 1845): 1041–42 and 6 (December 15, 1845): 1057. The internet version includes the signers; the *Times and Seasons* source does not.

Pettegrew, [also Pettigrew] David. "A History of David Pettegrew." David Pettegrew Papers, 1840–1857. Holograph, fd. 1. MS 2282, LDS Church History Library.

———. Statements, August 1862. Holograph. MS 4059. MS 2282, fd. 2, 1832, LDS Church History Library.

Phelps, Morris Charles. Reminiscences, n.d. Holograph. MS 271, item 1. LDS Church History Library.

Phelps, W. W. Letters, 1835–41. Holograph. MS 8711. LDS Church History Library.

Phillips, James Duncan. *Salem in the Seventeenth Century*. Boston: Houghton Mifflin Company, 1933.

"Philo Dibble's Narrative." In *Early Scenes from Church History by George C. Lambert: Eighth Book of the Faith-Promoting Series*. 1882; rpt. Grantsville, Utah: Archive Publishers, 2000, 74–96.

Pierce, Richard E., ed. *The Records of the First Church in Salem, Massachusetts, 1629–1736*. Salem, Mass.: Essex Institute, 1974.

Pilger, Marsha, ed. "The History of Kane Township Pottawattamie County, Iowa." *Frontier Chronicle* 7, no. 3 (July–September 2001): 2–6.

Platt, Lyman D. *Jeremiah Leavitt II and Sarah Sturtevant*. 1975. Microreproduction of typescript. Microfilm #940028, item 3. LDS Family History Library.

———., comp. "List of Church Members in Nauvoo, IL taken from 1842 Census." *Nauvoo Journal* 4 (Spring 1992): 5–7.

———., ed. *Nauvoo: Early Mormon Record Series, Vol. 1*. Highland, Utah: N.p., 1980.

Political History of Jackson County [Missouri]: Biographical Sketches of Men Who Have Helped to Make It. Kansas City: Marshall & Morrison, 1902. Microfilm #908755, item 3. LDS Family History Library.

"Poll Books and Certificates of Election for Units of the Nauvoo Legion at Nauvoo and Ramus, Illinois..." Vault MSS 76, Box 4, fd. 2. Nauvoo Legion, Military Records and Economic Records, 1833–1858. Perry Special Collections.

Pollard, Lorene Elizabeth Burdick. *Whitmer Memoirs.* Typescript, 2003. MS 18709, LDS Church History Library

Porter, Larry C. "Interrupted Exodus: Enlisting the Mormon Battalion as Iowa Volunteers." In Susan Easton Black and William G. Hartley, eds. *The Iowa Mormon Trail: Legacy of Faith and Courage.* Orem, Utah: Helix Publishing, 1997, 133–54.

Porter, Larry C., and Milton V. Backman, Jr. "Doctrine and the Temple in Nauvoo." *BYU Studies* 32 (1992): 41–56.

Porter, Larry C., and Ronald E. Romig. "The Prairie Branch, Jackson County, Missouri: Emergence, Flourishing, and Demise, 1831–1834." *Mormon Historical Studies,* 8, nos. 1–2 (Spring/Fall 2007): 1–38.

"Potter Goff Survey Classification of the Township of DeKalb." 1814. St Lawrence Historical Society, Canton, New York. Photocopy of holograph in my possession.

Pratt, Parley Parker. *Autobiography of Parley Parker Pratt, One of the Twelve Apostles of the Church of Jesus Christ of Latter-day Saints: Embracing His Life, Ministry, and Travels, with Extracts in Prose and Verse from His Miscellaneous Writings.* Edited by Parley P. Pratt Jr. Chicago: Law, King and Law, 1888; rpt. Salt Lake City: Deseret Book, 1935, 1985. Microfilm editions in LDS Church History Library, Microfilm 962830, Item 1, and Microfilm #9962830, item 1. LDS Family History Library.

"Preamble." *Nauvoo Expositor* 1 (June 7, 1844): 2.

"A Proclamation, to the Saints Scattered Abroad." *Times and Seasons* 2, no. 6 (January 15, 1841): 276.

Proctor, Scot Facer, and Maurine Jensen Proctor, eds. *Autobiography of Parley P. Pratt: Revised and Enhanced Edition.* Salt Lake City: Deseret Book, 2000.

Proctor, Scot Facer, and Maurine Jensen Proctor, eds. *The Revised and Enhanced History of Joseph Smith by His Mother.* Salt Lake City: Deseret Book, 1996.

Provo: Pioneer Mormon City. Writers' Program (Utah), American Guide Series. Portland, Ore.: Binfords & Mort, 1942.

Pry, Jean A., and Dale A. Whitman. "'But for the Kindness of Strangers': The Columbia, Missouri, Response to the Mormon Prisoners and the Jailbreak of July 4, 1839." In Thomas M. Spencer, ed. *The Missouri Mormon Experience.* Columbia: University of Missouri Press, 2010, 119–38.

Putnam, Mary L. S., and Lila Cahoon, comps. and eds. *Reynolds Cahoon: His Roots and Branches.* Bountiful, Utah: Family History Publishers, 1993.

Quincy (Illinois) Branch. Record of Members and Minutes of Meetings, l840–45. Microfilm #1919, Items 3–4. LDS Family History Library.

Quinn, D. Michael. *The Mormon Hierarchy: Origins of Power.* Salt Lake City: Signature Books in association with Smith Research Associates, 1994.

"A Record of Genealogies, Biographies etc., appertaining to the 20th Quorum of Seventies." In *Record of Members of the Quorum of Seventy, 1844–1894.*

Microfilm of holograph #25554. LDS Family History Library.

"Records of Members, 1841–1845." Church Records, 1836–1846: Nauvoo 1st and 2nd Wards, List of Members." Microfilm #889392, item 4. LDS Family History Library.

"Record of the Organization, and Proceedings of the Female Relief Society of Nauvoo, 1842–44." Smith Research Associates, *New Mormon Studies: A Comprehensive Research Library*, CD-ROM. Salt Lake City: Signature Books, 1998.

Reed, Benjamin. *The History of Swanzey, New Hampshire: From 1734 to 1890*. Salem, Mass: Salem Press Publishing and Printing, 1892.

Reed Collection, Miscellaneous holograph papers regarding Nathaniel Oake, 1741–42, Marlboro and Northboro, and John Rediat and John Rediat Jr. Located in Historical Room, Westborough Public Library, Westborough, Massachusetts. Photocopy in my possession.

Registry of Names of Persons Residing in the Various Wards as to Bishop's Reports, 1852–1853. Microfilm #823831, item 1. LDS Family History Library.

Revised Laws of the Nauvoo Legion. Nauvoo: John Taylor, Publisher, 1844.

Rich, Mary A. Phelps. "The Life of Mary A. Rich (1826–49)." Typescript. Perry Special Collections. Also http://www.boap.org/LDS/Early-Saints/MRich.html (accessed July 2, 2004, and October 23, 2006).

Rich, Sarah DeArmon Pea. "Sarah Dearmon Pea Rich, 1814–1893." N.d. Typescript. MS 1543. LDS Church History Library.

Ricketts, Norma Baldwin. *The Mormon Battalion: U.S. Army of the West, 1846–1848*. Logan: Utah State University Press, 1996.

Riggs, Mike. "Forgotten Sites in Caldwell and Daviess Counties." *Missouri Mormon Frontier Foundation Newsletter*, Nos. 7/8 (Summer/Fall 1995): 3.

Riggs, Michael S., and Ronald E. Romig. "The Land Holdings of Charles C. and Joseph Rich in Missouri." December 4, 2002. http://www.farwesthistory.com/'analysis.asp (accessed August 5, 2011).

Ripley, Alanson. "To the Elders Abroad." *Elders' Journal* 1 (July 1838): 38–39.

Roberts, Brigham H. *A Comprehensive History of the Church of Jesus Christ of Latter-day Saints, Century I*. 6 vols. 1930. Rpt., Provo, Utah: Brigham Young University Press, 1965 printing.

———. *The Missouri Persecutions*. 1900. Rpt., Provo, Utah: Maasai, Inc., 2001.

———. *The Rise and Fall of Nauvoo*. 1900. Rpt., Grantsville, Utah: Archive Publishers, 1999.

Robertson, R. J., Jr.,"The Mormon Experience in Missouri, 1830–1839, Parts 1–2." *Missouri Historical Review* 68, no. 3 (April 1974): 280–98; and 69, no. 4 (July 1974): 393–415.

Robinson, Ebenezer. "Items of Personal History of the Editor." *The Return* 2 (March 1890): 234 and 5 (May 1890): 1. http://www.boap.org/LDS/Early-Saints/ERobinson (accessed October 12, 2006).

Roles of Connecticut Men in the French and Indian War, 1755–1762. Vol. 2: *1758–1762*. 1903–6. Rpt., Bowie, Md.: Heritage Books, 1993–1994.

Romig, Ronald E. *Early Independence, Missouri: "Mormon" History Tour Guide*. Independence: Missouri Mormon Frontier Foundation, 2002.

———. *Early Jackson County, Missouri: "Mormon" History Guide. The "Mormon" Settlement on the Big Blue River.* Independence, Mo.: Missouri Mormon Frontier Foundation, 1996.

Rose, Samantha Dalena Rawson. "A History of Daniel Berry Rawson." n.d. In Rawson Family Histories, ca 1950. MS 8032. Typescript. LDS Church History Library.

Rounds, H. L. Peter, comp. *Abstracts of Bristol County, Massachusetts, Probate Records.* Baltimore, Md.: General Publishers., 1987–88.

Rowley, Dennis. "The Mormon Experience in the Wisconsin Pineries, 1841–1845." *BYU Studies* 32, no. 1 (1992): 119–48.

———. "Nauvoo: A River Town." *BYU Studies* 18, no 2 (Winter 1978): 255–71.

"The Saints Make Nauvoo." *Times and Seasons* 6, no. 6 (April 1, 1845): 856.

Salt Lake City Office of Vital Statistics. Death Records of Salt Lake City, Utah, 1848–September 1950. Microfilm #26558. LDS Family History Library.

Sam MB. [Samuel M. Brown]. "The King Follet [sic] Obituary." March 21, 2007. http://www.bycommonconsent.com (accessed July 8, 2007).

Sanford, Henry. On "Early Latter-day Saints Database." http://www.earlylds.com (accessed February 27, 2008).

Saunders, Richard. "A Contemporary View of the Nauvoo Legion: The General Return for the Second Cohort, 1843." *Nauvoo Journal* 5, no. 2 (Fall 1993): 110–11.

———. "Officers and Arms: The 1843 General Return of the Nauvoo Legion's Second Cohort." *BYU Studies* 35, no. 2 (1995): 139–51.

Savage, James. *A Genealogical Dictionary of the First Settlers of New England: Showing Three Generations of Those Who Came before May, 1692, on the Basis of [the?] Farmer's Register.* Salem, Mass.: Higginson, 1995.

Schindler, Harold. *Orrin Porter Rockwell: Man of God, Son of Thunder.* Salt Lake City: University of Utah Press, 1966.

Scholz, Charles W. "Remarks of Charles W. Scholz: Mayor of Quincy." In Susan Easton Black and Richard E. Bennett, eds. *A City of Refuge: Quincy, Illinois.* Salt Lake City: Millennial Press, 2000, xv–xvi.

Schultz, Eric B., and Michael J. Tougias. *King Philip's War: The History and Legacy of America's Forgotten Conflict.* Woodstock, Vt.: Countryman Press, 1999.

"Sealings in the Temple at Nauvoo, Hancock County, Illinois." Microfilm #183374. Special Collections, LDS Church Family History Library.

"The Season." *Evening and the Morning Star* 2, no. 13 (June 1833): 2.

Selections, First Council of 70: Selected Material from Seventies Book B, 1844–48. #CR 3/51. LDS Church History Library.

Senate Document 189: Document Showing the Testimony Evidence Given before the Judge of the Fifth Judicial District of the State of Missouri, on the Trial of Joseph Smith Jr., and Others, for High Treason and Other Crimes against That State. 26th Cong. 2d Session. Washington, D.C.: U.S. Government Printing Office, February 15, 1841.

The Seventies Hall at Nauvoo. Nauvoo, Ill.: Nauvoo Restoration, Inc., n.d.

Seventies Records, 1844–1975: 10th Quorum. LDS Church History Library. Microfilm no. CR 499, Reel 30, item 3.

Seventies Quorums. Record of Members of the Quorums of the Seventy, 1844–94. Twentieth Quorum Record, Provo, Utah, 1857. Family History Library,

Microfilm #25554.

"Shalersville." Portage County, Ohio. GenWeb Project website http://www.rootsweb.com/ohportage/hist016.htm (accessed August 12, 2004).

Sheridan, Judith. "The Connecticut Western Reserve." November 9, 2009. Bristol Public Library, Bristolville, Ohio, website. http://content.bristol.lib.oh.us/connecticut.htm (accessed April 22, 2010).

Shurtliff, Myrtle Ballard, comp. "Record of Family and Journal of Luman A. Shurtliff." Typescript. ca. 1968. Microfilm #1321330, item 6. LDS Family History Library.

Siegfried, Mary, comp. "List of Known Dead Buried in Old Mormon Cemetery, Nauvoo, Hancock Co., Illinois." Microfiche #6088852. LDS Family History Library.

Simmonds, A. J. "John Noah and the Hulets: A Study in Charisma in the Early Church." Paper presented at the Mormon History Association Conference, May 26, 1979. LDS Church History Library, Microfilm #M277:71S597j.

———. "'Thou and All Thy House;' Three Case Studies of Clan and Charisma in the Early Church." *Nauvoo Journal* 7, no. 1 (Spring 1995): 48–55.

Simon, Jerald F. "Thomas Bullock as an Early Mormon Historian." *BYU Studies* 30 (Winter 1990): 71–88.

Skidmore, Velma W. "Found at Last: The Final Resting Place of Frederick Granger Williams." *Mormon Historical Studies* 3, no. 1 (2002): 229–39.

Spencer, Thomas N. "Introduction." In Thomas N. Spencer, ed., *The Missouri Mormon Experience*. Columbia: University of Missouri Press, 2010, 1–18.

Smith, Calvin N., "King Follett: Quiet Fortitude, Prophet Speaks at Funeral." *Church News*, December 25, 1983, 10–11.

Smith, George D., ed. *An Intimate Chronicle: The Journals of William Clayton*. Salt Lake City: Signature Books, 1991.

Smith, Hyrum. Diary (ca. December 1831–February 1835). Typescript. MS 9476. LDS Church History Library.

Smith, James E. "Frontier Nauvoo: Building a Picture from Statistics." *Ensign*, September 1979, 17–19.

Smith, Joseph. "Answers to Questions Asked in No. 2." *Elders' Journal* 1 (July 1, 1838): 43–44.

Smith, Joseph. Letter to Jared Carter, April 17, 1833, *Times and Seasons* 5, no. 24 (January 1, 1844): 753. (The *Times and Seasons* was a Church newspaper, printed in Nauvoo from November 1839 until February 15, 1846.)

Smith, Joseph, et al. See *History of the Church*.

Stackpole, Everett S., and Lucien Thompson. *History of the Town of Durham, New Hampshire (Oyster River Plantation) with Genealogical Notes*. Durham, N.H: Town of Durham, 1913.

Staker, Mark Lyman. *Hearken, O Ye People: The Historical Setting of Joseph Smith's Ohio Revelations*. Salt Lake City: Greg Kofford Books, 2009.

Standard Historical Atlas of Mills and Fremont Counties Iowa. Chicago, Ill.: Anderson Publishing, 1910. Microfilm #989482, item 1. LDS Family History Library.

Starr, Edward C. *A History of Cornwall, Connecticut: A Typical New England Town*. New Haven, Conn.: Tuttle, Morehouse & Taylor Company, 1926. Microfilm #1320817, item 3. LDS Family History Library.

"State of Missouri against King Follett: Indictment for Robbery, Case No. 1380," 267–68. Boone County, Missouri, Circuit Court Record, 1821–1925; Index, 1859–1935, Circuit Court Record, Volume C: 1838–42: LDS Family History Library, Microfilm #981755.

Stillwell, Thomas Daniel. "Letter to Editor and Readers of the Lehi Post." In *Reminiscences*. Typescript, n.d. MS 7323. LDS Church History Library.

Stokes, Durward T., ed. "The Wilson Letters, 1835–1849: Six Letters from Andersen, Caleb, and Josiah Wilson, Written from Their New Home in Clay County, Missouri, to Their Relatives at Their Old Home in Orange County, North Carolina." *Missouri Historical Review* 60, no. 4 (July 1966): 495–517.

"Stories of Mills County." *Glenwood [Iowa] Opinion*, July 20, 1905.

Stout, Hosea. Diary, 1844–46. 2 vols. Typescript. Perry Special Collections.

———. "Diary of Hosea Stout: Supplemental Volume Containing Letters, Documents, etc." Typescript. Microfilm #962966, item 1. LDS Family History Library.

Struthers, Clifford, caretaker of Evergreen Cemetery, Winchester, New Hampshire. Interviewed by Joann Follett Mortensen, conducted in Winchester, New Hampshire, September 22, 1999.

Struthers, Clifford, comp. *Evergreen Cemetery Records, Evergreen Cemetery, Winchester, New Hampshire*. Typewritten transcript in my possession.

Swanzey, New Hampshire, Town Clerk. Records of Marriages, Births, and Deaths, ca. 1741–1915, Microfilm #2200234, item 1. LDS Family History Library.

Sweeney, John, Jr. "A History of the Nauvoo Legion in Illinois." M.A. thesis, Brigham Young University, April 1974.

Switzler William F. *Switzler's Illustrated History of Missouri, from 1541 to 1877*. St. Louis: C. R. Barns, 1879. Microfilm #1723772. LDS Family History Library.

Tanner, Elias F. *The Genealogy of the Descendants of Thomas Tanner, Sr., of Cornwall, Connecticut*. Lansing, Mich.: Darius D. Thorpe, 1893. Microfilm #1036365, item 3. LDS Family History Library.

Taylor, Alan. *William Cooper's Town: Power and Persuasion on the Frontier of the Early American Republic*. New York: Alfred A. Knopf, 1995.

Telford, John. *Nauvoo: The City Beautiful*. Salt Lake City: Deseret Book, 2002.

"The Temple of God in Nauvoo." *Times and Seasons* 4, no. 1 (November 15, 1842): 10.

Temple Index Bureau. Microfilm #1262904. LDS Family History Library.

"Thomas C. D. Howell Company (1852)." In *Mormon Pioneer Overland Travel, 1847–1868*. http://www.lds.org/churchhistory/library/pioneercompany (accessed February 20, 2008).

Thomas, Isaiah, and Ebenezer T. Andrews, eds. *The Perpetual Laws of the Commonwealth of Massachusetts*. 4 vols. Boston, Mass.: I. Thomas and E. T. Andrews, March 1801.

Todd, Jay M. "Nauvoo Temple Restoration." *Improvement Era* 71 (October 1968): 10–16.

"To the Editor of the Times and Seasons. Cold Comfort." *Times and Seasons* 24, no. 3 (October 15, 1842): 953.

Town Highway Records. Benton, Yates County, New York. n.d. http://www.yates-county.org/upload/12historian/townroad.htm (accessed April 20, 2010).

Town Meetings, Book 1:1806–1845." Holograph. DeKalb Historical Association, DeKalb Junction, New York.

Town Records of Dudley, Massachusetts, [and] Pawtucket, Rhode Island. Pawtucket, R.I.: Adam Sutcliffe, 1893–1984. Microfilm #599197, item 1. LDS Family History Library.

The Town Register: Marlboro, Troy, Jaffrey, Swanzey. Augusta, Maine: Mitchell-Cony Company, 1908; rpt., Salem, Mass.: Higginson, 1997.

Transactions in Nauvoo, Hancock County, Illinois, and Surrounding Communities, 1839–1859. http://www.WorldVitalRecords.com (accessed July 23, 2007).

Triggs, J. H. *History and Directory of Laramie City, Wyoming Territory*. Laramie, Wyo.: Powder River, 1955.

Turner, Elisha L., transcriber. "Baptisms, from Rehoboth Church Records." In *New England Historical and Genealogical Register*. 15 vols. Boston: Samuel G. Drake, 1861, 67–72.

United States.
    Adjutant General's Office. *General Index to Compiled Military Service Records of Revolutionary War Soldiers*. Washington, D.C.: National Archives, 1942. Microfilm #882858. LDS Family History Library.
    General Land Office. U.S. Land Sales in Missouri, 1827–1903. Microfilm #984767, item 291. LDS Family History Library.

U.S. Census.
    1790. New Hampshire, Cheshire County, Winchester. Roll, M637_5 image 0065.
    1800. New Hampshire, Cheshire County, Winchester. Roll 20, p. 1066, image 180.
    1800. New York, Otsego County, Otsego. Roll 25, p. 595, image 43.
    1810. New Hampshire, Cheshire County, Winchester. Roll 23, pp. 122–23, image 70. 1820.
    1820. New York, Genesee County, Attica. Roll M33_72, p. 11, image 15.
    1820. Ohio, Portage County, Shalersville. Roll M33_95, p. 60, image 68.
    1830. Illinois, Edgar, p. 36. NARA Roll M19-23; microfilm 07648, LDS Family History Library. No image number, but this record exists in both holograph and typescript format.
    1830. Ohio, Portage County, Shalersville. Roll 138, p. 252, image 3.
    1840. Illinois, Adams County. Roll 54, p. 60.
    1840. Missouri, Caldwell County, Blythe. Roll 176, p. 221, image 361.
    1840. Missouri, Caldwell County, Rockport. Roll 179, p. 221, image 367.
    1850. Iowa, Pottawattamie County. Roll M432_188, p. 121, image 243. http://www.Ancestry.com (accessed February 13, 2008).
    1850. Iowa, Pottawattamie County. Iowa: Roll M432_188, p. 150, image 304.
    1850. Missouri, Atchison County. Roll M432_391, p. 153, image 308.
    1860. California, Contra Costa County, Township 2. Roll M653_57, p. 561, image 565.
    1860. Iowa, Mills County, Silver Creek. Roll M653_336, p. 98, image 113. http://www.Ancestry.com (accessed February 13, 2008).
    1860. Utah Territory, Utah County, Provo, Roll M653_1314; p. 924; image 396.
    1870. California, Contra Costa County, Township 2. Roll M593_71, p. 378,

image 230.

1870. Iowa, Mills County, Silver Creek. Roll M593_411, p. 98, image 197. http://www.Ancestry.com (accessed February 13, 2008).

1870. Utah Territory, Utah County, Provo Ward 3, Roll M593_1612, p. 289, image 571.

1880. Arizona, Apache County, Walker. Roll T9_39, p. 40, image 100; Microfilm #1254036.

1880. Iowa, Mills County, Silver Creek. Roll T9_356, p. 354, image 10. #1254356. Enumeration district 131; image 0224.

United States Land Sales in Missouri, 1827–1903; Index to Land Sales, 1818–1893. Jefferson City: State of Missouri, 1969. Microfilm #984767. LDS Family History Library.

Van Orden, Bruce A. "Causes and Consequences: Conflict in Jackson County." In *Regional Studies in Latter-day Saint Church History: Missouri.* Edited by Arnold K. Garr and Clark V. Johnson. Provo, Utah: BYU Department of Church History and Doctrine, 1994, 337–47.

———. "From Kirtland to Missouri." In *Historical Atlas of Mormonism.* Edited by S. Kent Brown, Donald Q. Cannon, and Richard H. Jackson. New York: Simon & Schuster, 1994, 26.

———. "Writing to Zion: The William W. Phelps Kirtland Letters (1835–1836)." *BYU Studies* 33, no. 3 (1993): 542–93.

"A Very Sad Accident." *Malvern [Iowa] Leader,* May 13, 1897.

Vineyard, Mrs. John, abstracter and publisher. *Deed Books A, B, C, of Jackson County, Missouri.* Microfilm #982082, item 8. LDS Family History Library.

Vital Records of Dudley, Massachusetts, to the End of the Year 1849. Worcester, Mass.: Franklin P. Rice, 1908. Microfilm #873747. LDS Family History Library.

Vital Records of Salem, Massachusetts, to the End of the Year 1849. Vol. 1: *Births.* Salem, Mass.: Essex Institute, 1916–25.

Vital Records of Westborough, Massachusetts, to the End of the Year 1849. Worcester, Mass.: F. P. Rice/Boston: Stanhope Press, 1903.

Vosburgh, Royden Woodward, ed. "Records of the Presbyterian Church of Cooperstown, in Otesgo County, N.Y." Typescript. New York: New York Genealogical and Biographical Society, 1920. Transcribed by New York State Historical Association, Cooperstown, New York. Photocopy in my possession.

Wallace, R. Stuart, and Douglas E. Hall. *A New Hampshire Education Timeline.* n.d. New Hampshire Historical Society. http://www.nhhistory.org/edu/support/nhlearnmore/nhedtimeline.pdf (accessed April 17, 2010).

Walt [no surname]. Letter to Mrs. John W. Clemson, Second Vice President, Walnut Creek Historical Society, July 5, 1978. Photocopy in my possession courtesy of Walnut Creek Historical Society, Walnut Creek, California 94598.

Ward, Andrew H. *History of the Town of Shrewsbury, Massachusetts: From Its Settlement in 1717 to 1829, with Other Matter Relating Thereto Not Before Published, Including an Extensive Family Register.* Boston: Samuel G. Drake, 1847.

Ward, Maurine Carr. "John Needham's Nauvoo Letter: 1843." *Nauvoo Journal* 8 (Spring 1996): 38–42.

———. "'This Institution Is a Good One': The Female Relief Society of Nauvoo, 17 March

1842 to 16 March 1844." *Mormon Historical Studies* 3, no. 2 (2002): 87–203.
"Water from the Well: Buckets, Coopering and Wood." http://www.oldandinteresting.com (accessed May 27, 2008).
Webster, Noah. *American Dictionary of the English Language*, 2 vols. New York: S. Converse, 1828.: http://www.1828-dictionary.com
West, Nathan Ayres. File #30219. Nauvoo Restoration Land and Records Office. This record is a compilation of data from various sources, searchable by individual's name, with each assigned a unique filename. Information obtained by personal visit in 2008. CD and printout in my possession.
Westergren, Bruce N., ed. *From Historian to Dissident: The Book of John Whitmer*. Salt Lake City: Signature Books, 1995.
Whitesides, Caron. Letter to Janet Fuller, Mesa, Arizona, March 30, 1994. Photocopy in my possession.
Whitney, Orson F. "The 'Mormons' in Jackson County." In W. Z. Hickman, ed., *History of Jackson County*. Topeka, Kans.: Historical Publishing Company, 1920, 191–98.
Widger, Betty, extracter. *Portage County, Ohio, Marriages, Vol. 1, 1808–1850*. Warsaw, Ind.: Larry & Cynthia Scheuere, 1990.
Wight, Orange Lysander. Reminiscences, May–December 1903. Typescript by Winona Wittner and Viola W. Squires, 1966. MS 405. LDS Church History Library.
Wilcox, Pearl. *The Latter Day Saints on the Missouri Frontier*. Independence, Mo.: N.pub., 1972.
Willes/Willis, Ira Jones. Diaries, 1831–48. In "Willes Family Papers 1831–1871," Holograph. MS 2014, fd. 1. LDS Church History Library. Unpaginated.
Williams, Clyde J., comp. *The Teachings of Lorenzo Snow: Fifth President of the Church of Jesus Christ of Latter-day Saints*. Salt Lake City: Bookcraft, 1984.
Williams, Samuel. "Raymond Migrations: Alonzo Pearis Raymond, 28 Dec 1852." http://www.rootsweb.com/raymondfamily/AlonzoRaymondLineage.html (accessed July 12, 2005).
Wilson, William M. *Early Pictorial Provo: An Illustrated Industrial Review of Provo, the Garden City of Utah*. 1910. Rpt., Provo, Utah: S. K. Benson, 1974.
"Winchester." In *Gazetteer of New Hampshire Containing Descriptions of all the Counties, Towns and Districts in the State*. Boston: John Hayward and John P. Jewell, 1849.
Winchester, New Hampshire. Town Clerk. Records of Marriages, Births, and Deaths, 1733–1930. Microfilm #2208914, Item 3. LDS Family History Library.
Wixom, Hartt. *Edward Partridge: The First Bishop of the Church of Jesus Christ of Latter-day Saints*. Springville, Utah: Cedar Fort, 1998.
Wood, Lyman Stephen. *Biographical and Historical Sketches in the Life of Lyman Stephen Wood*. Microfilm #1421603, item 9. LDS Family History Library.
Wood, Ralph V., comp. *Jefferson and St. Lawrence Counties, New York State, 1810 and 1820 Federal Population Census Schedules: Transcripts and Index*. Cambridge, Mass: Ralph V. Wood, 1963.
Woodrow, H. H. "History of Silver Creek Township." In *Standard Historical Atlas of Mills and Fremont Counties Iowa*, section 2, p. 2. Microfilm 989482, Item 1, LDS Family History Library.
Woodson, W. H. *History of Clay County, Missouri*. Topeka, Kans.: Historical Publishing

Company, 1920.

Wortman, Allen, Mills County historian. Interviewed by Joann Follett Mortensen, August 2001, Malvern, Iowa.

Wortman, Allen. "Underground Railway Depended Entirely on Men Used to Cold Night Rides." Column in series: "Traveling Extensively in Southwest Iowa." *Malvern [Iowa] Leader*, September 30, 1999. Photocopy of clipping courtesy of Beverly Boileau.

Wright, Martin H. (groom), and Wilda Follett (bride). In *Marriage Records, 1869–1920, Albany County, Wyoming*. Cheyenne, Wyo.: State Archives and Historical Department, 1970.

Wright, Robert K., Jr. *Army Lineage Series: The Continental Army*. Washington, D.C.: U.S. Army Center of Military History, 1986.

Yankee Travel Guide. "Captain Wyman's Tavern Named Editor's Choice." *Historical Society of Cheshire County Newsletter* 20, no. 1 (July 2004): 2.

Young, Andrew W. *The Project Gutenberg E Book of the Government Class Book*. http://www.gutenberg.org/files/15319 (accessed April 20, 2010).

Young, Emily Dow Partridge. Diary and Reminiscences, February 1874–November 1899. Typescript from photocopy of holograph, n.d., no transcriber. MS 2845. LDS Church History Library.

———. "What I Remember." 1884. Typescript. n.d. MS 5718. LDS Church History Library.

Young, Joseph, Sr., comp. "Names of the Presidents and Members of the First and Second Quorums of Seventies, Ordained under the Hands of the Prophet Joseph Smith with His Two Counselors, Sidney Rigdon and Oliver Cowdery, on February 28th, 1835, in the Town of Kirtland, Geauga County, Ohio." In *History of the Organization of the Seventies: Names of the Presidents and the Members of the First and Second Quorums: Items in Relation to the First Presidency of the Seventies, also a Brief Glance at Enoch and His City*. M251.34 Y73h 1878 LDS Church History Library.

Index

A

Abbott, Myron, 454
Abbott Settlement, 116
Adam-ondi-Ahman, Mo.
   hostilities at, 196, 199–200
   refugees, 206
Adams, James, 352 note 56
ague. *See* malaria.
Alexander, Elias, 22–23, 27
Alexander, Seth, 5, 435, 510
Allen, James B., 348
Allred, Isaac, 239 note 32
Allred, James, 239 note 32
Allred, Martin C., 239 note 32
Allred, William, 239 note 32
Allred Settlement, 116, 129
Ames, Ira, 142
Anderson, George Edward, on Richmond Jail, 221
Anderson, Lavina Fielding, xiv, 143–44
Anderson, Richard Lloyd, 63, 201–2, 210 note 62
Andrus, Milo, 290
Angell, Truman O., 149
anti-Mormonism. *See* Missouri *and* Nauvoo.
Appleby, William I., 306
Ashley, Samuel, 4, 5, 10
Ashworth, Brent, 302 note 40
Atchison, David Rice, 210 note 62
Austin, Emily M. Coburn
   describes Missouri, 71
   in Missouri, 89 note 19, 110–11
   on Rigdon's July 1848 speech, 192–93
Avard, Sampson, 190, 211 note 70
Avery, Daniel, 370–71
Avery, Philander, 370–71
Ayers, Nathan, 116

B

Backman, Milton V., Jr.
   on cemeteries in Nauvoo, 398–99
   on healings in Nauvoo, 290
   on Kirtland, 139
   on Kirtland baptisms, 46
   on Kirtland Temple dedication, 141
   on School of the Prophets, 140–41
Baker, Joel, 38
Baker, Simon, 310
Baldwin, Caleb
   at Liberty Jail, 225, 245
   at Richmond, Mo., 239 note 32
   Battle of Big Blue, 106 note 7
   in high council case, 126
Baldwin, Wheeler, 76
Ball, Jonah Randolph, 311, 324 note 22
Ballinger, Morris T., 262
Bankdoll/Barkdoll, Isah, 434, 447 note 22, 509
baptism for the dead, 305, 310–13, 336
Barber, Andrew, 97, 106 note 7
Barlow, Elizabeth Haven, 290
Barlow, Israel, 270

Barlow, Watson, 274
Barney, Lewis, 454
Battle of Crooked River, 203–5, 222, 226
Battle of the Big Blue, 94, 106 note 7, 151, 167; map, 95
Baugh, Alexander L.
 assistance from, xiii
 baptism for the dead, 311
 Clay County, 115
 DeWitt, 198
 Far West, 217
 hostilities, 79, 93, 171, 193
 Richmond hearing, 240 note 40
Beck, Thomas, 239 note 32
Beebe, Calvin, 104, 125
Beebe, George, 106 note 7
Beebe (in Kirtland), 141
Belding, Christian King, 2
Belding, Samuel, 2
Beman/Beaman, Alva/Alvah, 146, 154 note 41
Bennett, David, 100
Bennett, James, 100
Bennett, John C., 362–63
Bennett, Richard E., 318
Bent, Samuel, 223–24, 239 note 32
Best, Christy, xiii
"Best Guide to the Gold Mines, 816 Miles by Trail," 130 note 14
Bidamon, Emma Hale Smith. See Smith, Emma.
Bidamon, Louis Crum, 406 note 49
Big Blue Settlement, 74, 76, 86, 242 note 68, 383
Billington, Ezekiel, 239 note 32
Bishop, Bridget Oliver, 473, 475 note 17
Bishop, Hannah, 475 note 17
Black, Adam, 196
Black, John, 471
Black River. See pineries.
Black, Susan Easton, 272, 318
Black, Susanna Shockley, 471
Blair, W. W., 462
blessing children, 188, 208 note 9
blessing meetings. See feasts for the poor.

Bloom, Harold, 420
Blue River, Mormon ferry on, 94
Blum, Ida, 394
Bogart, Samuel, 203, 205
Boggs, Lilburn W.
 assassination attempt, 362
 calls out state militia (1833), 97
 commissions Mormon militia officers, 171
 during Mormon War, 197–98, 202, 213, 219
 issues extermination order, 205, 213
 orders weapons returned, 246
 resident of Independence, 84
Boileau, Beverly, xii–xiii, 463, 466 note 48
Bond, Christopher, 237
Book of Abraham, 141
Book of Commandments, 68, 136–37
Book of Mormon
 rare in early Ohio, 46
 translation, 61–62
 witnesses, 62
"Book of the Law of the Lord, The," 338
Booth, Ezra, 52
Bozorth, Squires, 166
Brace (no first name), 106 note 7, 126
Bracken, James Bennett, 202
Brown (sheriff), 253
Brown, Benjamin, 149
Brown, Ebbery, 223–24
Brown, Ebenezer, 239 note 32, 525
Brown, John Zimmerman, 443–44
Brown, Samuel Morris, 125–26, 133 note 64, 390
Brunson, Seymour
 biography, 324 note 17
 funeral, 310, 395
 requested as witness in Washington, 292
 tries to help prisoners escape, 274
Brush Creek, 76
Brush, John, 104
Bryan, Thomas U., 262
Buchanan, John, 239 note 32
Buell Mills/Hudspeth Settlement (1831), 90 note 33

Buell, Presendia Huntington, 247
Bullock, Thomas
    and King Follett Discourse, 414–15
    Clay County refugees, 103
    Jackson County, map, 75
Bunyon, John, 257
Burkett, George, Jr., 122–23, 132 note 48
Burnam [sic], Enoch, 430
Burnham, Isaac, 431
Burnham, Louisa, 431
Burnham, Nancy Tanner, 431, 434–35, 511
Bush, John, 170
Bushman, Richard Lyman
    on Mormon militarism, 118
    on Nauvoo City Charter, 314
    on temple ordinances, 345–46
    on vigilantism, 62–63, 83
Butler, Armond, 166–67
Butler, John Lowe, 5
    at Far West, 217
    at Gallatin, 194–95
    at Quincy, 272
    stayed with Folletts, 195
    taxed in Nauvoo, 385

C

Cahoon, Reynolds, 51–52, 351 note 39, 386
Caldwell County, Mo. *See also* Far West, Mo.
    created, 161
    described, 162–63
    Mormon population, 163
    records destroyed, 234
Call, Anson, 206, 211 note 77, 230, 273
Cameron (judge), 217
Cannon, Donald Q.
    on dimensions of Nauvoo, 298
    on King Follett, 307, 379, 393, 407 note 74
    on King Follett Discourse, 419, 412
    on Nauvoo Legion, 318
Capron, Oliver, 5
Carlin, Thomas, 303 note 49
Carn, Daniel, 239 note 32
Carroll (in Kirtland), 141
Carroll County, Mo., 194, 202
Carter, Jared, 54
Carter, Simeon, 85, 124–25, 127
Cave Spring, school at, 77
cemeteries. *See* Nauvoo burial grounds.
chairs, possibly owned by King and Louisa Follett, 459–60, 465 note 34
Chamberlin, Solomon, 99–100
Chamberlin, Wyat, 27
Channing, Edward, 159
Chaplin/Chapin (no first name), 106 note 7
Chase, Darwin, 225, 239 note 32, 245
Chase Settlement, 116
Chauncey, John, 120
Cheney, Nathan, 305, 338
Cheshire County, NH, 1–10, 16–17
Chiat, Marilyn, 401–2
Christensen, Clare B., 106 note 7
Christmas celebration, 386
Church of Jesus Christ of Latter-day Saints. *See also* Mormon.
    name changed, 188
    organization of, 62
    priesthood ordinations in, 62
City of Joseph, 288, 374 note 38, 437. *See also* Nauvoo.
Clark, Jesse, 159
Clark, John B. (Missouri militia), 205–6
    on jurisdiction, 222
    orders Mormons out, 218–19
    on number arrested at Far West, 239 note 20
Clark, John Wesley, aids prisoners' escape 253–60, 266 note 51, 274
Clat Adams Bicentennial Park, 280–81
Clawson, Moses, 239 note 32
Clay County, Mo. *See also* Liberty, Mo.
    history of, 109
    hostilities in, 158–59
    kindness of citizens, 111–12
    Joseph Smith authorizes gathering in, 116
    Mormon refugees in, 99–105, 108 note 45, 109–29, 157–58

Clay County Stake, 123–25
Clayton, William, 336, 360, 414–15
Cleveland, Henry A., 96, 106 note 7
Clinton County, Mo., 191, 194, 202
Clothier, Ira, 166
clothing, home manufacture, 18
Colby, Gertrude Follett, 460, 446 note 19
Cole, Zera Smith, 142, 153 note 25
Colesville Branch/Settlement
    attacks on, 86–87
    defense of, 96–97
    in Missouri, 89 note 19, 75–76, 116
Colesville School, 77
Collins, William, 217
Coltrin, Zebedee, 124
Commerce, Ill., 300 note 7. *See also* Nauvoo, Ill.
Community of Christ archives, assistance at, xiii
Conant, Ezra, 4
Congregational Church, 6–7, 40
"Congress" land, 114, 163
Connecticut Western Reserve. *See* Western Reserve.
Connelly, Frances, 262
consecration, in Missouri, 69, 72
Coolidge, Joseph W., 317
Cooper, James Fenimore, 22
Cooper, William, 22
Coray, Howard
    biography, 404 note 11
    house, 379–81
    organizes whittlers, 439–40
Coray, Martha Jane Knowlton, 404 note 11
Cordon, Alfred, 419
Corrill, John
    as presiding elder in Missouri, 76
    dealing with hostilities, 97, 84, 115, 159–60
    ministry to Clay County Saints, 124
    on dissent in Missouri, 189
Cottle, T. Jeffrey, 293
Council Bluffs, population, 526
Covey (of Ohio), 45
Covey, Benjamin, 239 note 32

Cowdery, Oliver
    as Book of Mormon witness, 64 note 6
    as missionary, 63
    excommunicated, 188
    expelled from Far West, 189–90
    helps ordain Joseph Smith Sr., 153 note 22
    in Missouri, 68, 85, 160
    letter to Nathan West, 235–36
Cox, Cordelia Morley, 93, 96, 99
Craig, John, 221–22
Crandall/Crandle, Sarah ("Sally"), 127
Crandall, Daniel, 127
Crane, William B., 38, 42 note 20
Cunningham (drowned), 360
currency, in Nauvoo, 385
Cutler, Alpheus, 351 note 39, 461, 518

D

Daley, Elizabeth Ennis, 279
Daley, James
    at Battle of Crooked River, 280
    biography, 279
    contribution to Nauvoo Temple, 340
    death, 434, 438, 509
    in Samuel Brunson's Company, 182 note 46
    in Nauvoo, 290, 299
    misidentified as James Bailey, 155 note 47
    not in Nauvoo Legion, 317
    not in 1842 LDS census, 331
    ordained Seventy, 147, 366, 368
    signs removal covenant, 230
    taxed in Nauvoo, 297, 331
Daley, James Marion, 438, 521
Daley, John, 290
Daley, John, Jr., 279
Daley, Nancy Follett. *See* Sanford, Nancy Follett Daley.
Daley/Dayle, William King, 349, 521
Dallam, Francis J., 120
Daniels, Sheffield, 106 note 7, 239 note 32
Danites
    activities of, 189–90, 199, 201

Index 583

attack Gallatin and Millport, 200–201
at Gallatin election, 195
nicknames of, 211 note 72
Daviess County, Mo.
  creation, 161
  Mormons settle in, 186–87, 194
  population, 187
Davis, Amos, 300 note 7, 384
Democratic Association of Quincy, 271
Demster, John, 27
DePlatt, Lyman, on 1842 LDS census, 331
DeWitt, Mo.
  conflict at, 197–98, 291
  population, 197
Dibble, Philo
  and Battle of Big Blue, 96, 106 note 7
  as possible witness in Washington, 291
  biography, 47, 106 note 8
  in Clay County, 127, 166
  taxed in Nauvoo, 386
Dickamore, Jeffrey Hale, 415
dissenters, expelled from Far West, 189–90
Doctrine and Covenants, publication of, 137
Dodge, Erastus, 340
Doniphan, Alexander
  advises Mormon militia, 190
  at Richmond hearing, 223, 240 note 44
  refuses to execute prisoners, 217, 238 note 11
Dorner, John, 408 note 86
Doughty, George, Jr./Sr., 534 note 4
Doughty, Tryphena West, 151, 278, 428, 457–58, 534 note 4
Douglas, Ellen Briggs, 329–30, 384, 405 note 29
Douglas, George, 405 note 29
Dunbar, Robert Bruce, 525
Dunham, Jonathan
  at Richmond hearing, 223–24
  as Danite, 224
  nicknamed Captain Black Hawk, 224
  prisoner at Richmond, Mo., 239 note 32
Dunklin, Daniel
  and Jackson County hostilities, 121
  and petition, 85, 115, 160–61
  lack of support for Mormons, 119
Dunlap, James, 460, 533
Dunlap, Viola. See Huff, Viola Amelda Dunlap.
Dunlap, Virginia Ann ("Jenny"), 532–34
Dunn, John, 261

E

Eames/Ames, Ellis, 129, 133 note 80
Earl, John T., 239 note 32
East Branch Settlement, 116
education
  in Caldwell County, 170
  in New Hampshire, 19
  in Shalersville, Ohio, 35
  in Missouri, 77
Edwards, Elisha, 239 note 32
Egyptian mummies, 141
Elliott, John, 371
Ellis, Ann, 520
Ellis, W. A., 520
Elmer, Samuel, 20
Emrick, David, 531
endowment. See Kirtland and Nauvoo.
England, converts from, 306
English, Charles, 127
Episcopalian Church, in Ohio, 41
Esplin, Ronald K., 287
Evans, John Henry, 317

F

Fairbanks, Silas P., 6
Far West, Mo., 157
  cemetery, 167
  county seat, 171
  described, 168–70, 193
  establishment of, 163
  evacuation, 231–32, 247
  Mormon militia, 196
  refugees in, 198, 206, 214, 226–27
  surrender of, 213–19, 239 note 20
  temple site, 172, 188, 191, 232–33
Far West High Council
  and King Follett, 172
  and Mormon militia, 171

and Nathan West, 168, 172
Fausett/Fossett/Fawcett, William McKee, 448 note 35, 527, 537 note 41
Fausett, Matilda/Matildia Carolina Butcher, 448 note 35, 537 note 41
feasts for the poor, 141–43
ferries, across Missouri, 101
Field, William, 380
Fielding, Joseph, 419
Flanders, Robert B., 334, 357, 441
Fleming, Josiah Walcott, 405 note 22
Follett, Adeline Louisa. See West, Adeline Louisa Follett.
Follett, Afton, xiv, 538 note 60
Follett, Alberta, 533
Follett, Alexander
  death, 38
  in Ohio, 33–34, 37, 42 note 20
  marriage, 38
  name variants of, 41 note 1
  proxy baptism of, 312
Follett, Alitha, 312
Follett, Alwilda/Alwelda/Avilda/Awilda/Alvadilla, 520
Follett, Annie Eliza, 537 note 47
Follett, Benjamin, 474
Follett, Caroline Baker, 38
Follett, Charles (son of Warren), 460
Follett, Charles Montgomery, 533
Follett, Christian Belding, 2, 4
Follett, Drusilla, 533
Follett, Edward (1821–ca. 1827) 38, 524
  death of, 78, 104
  in Missouri, 77, 54
Follett, Edward Moroni/Maroni/Marion (1833–92), 104, 463
  biography, 529–30
  birth, 49, 54
  burial and reinterment, 523–24
  death, 50
  description of, 15
  in California, 522, 530
  in 1840 U.S. Census, 278
  in 1842 LDS census, 330
  in Iowa, 457–58, 529

  in Missouri, 168
  in Nauvoo, 308, 323, 382, 428
  physical description, 15, 530
  probable death date of, 313
Follett, Elizabeth Millicent Daley, 519
Follett, Ella Mae, 533
Follett, Emily (ca. 1829–before 1833), 38, 49, 54, 78, 104, 313, 528–29
Follett family,
  in 1840 U.S. Census, 278
  in 1842 LDS census, 330–31
  in Quincy, hypothesized activities of, 273
  origin and variant spellings of name, 469
Follett, Frederick, 533–34
Follett, Hannah Oak Alexander, 4–10, 16, 188
Follett, Harvey Howard, 533
Follett, Hattie Belle, 533
Follett, Hyrum, 537 note 47
Follett, Isaac Alfred, 526–27, 537 note 45, 538 note 60
Follett, James Garfield, 533
Follett, John (fl. 1640), 469
Follett, John (1669–ca. 1718) 471–73
Follett, John (1695–1747), 473
Follett, John (1727–ca. 1818), 473
Follett, John (1752–1829), 1–10, 16, 18, 39, 474
Follett, John (multiple ancestors by that name), 1–2
Follett, John III, 312
Follett, John IV, 312
Follett, John W./Wesley (1819–ca. 1849; son of King and Louisa),
  baptism, 49
  biography, 519–20 birth, 28, 37
  endowment, 441, 452
  in 1840 U.S. Census, 278
  in 1842 LDS census, 331
  in George A. Smith survey, 103
  in Missouri, 54, 77, 113, 168, 171–72, 193
  in Nauvoo, 307–8, 428, 438
  land purchases, 286, 297
  meets Laura Phelps, 260

not in Nauvoo Legion, 317
not taxed in Nauvoo, 296, 331
ordained Seventy, 366, 368
Follett, John (b. 1857, son of William Follett), 537 note 47
Follett, Joseph Edward, 537 note 47
Follett, Josephine Merrill, xi
Follett, King (1788–1844)
Chronological Biography
ancestry of, 1–10, 467–76
hospitality of, 123, 226–227
lack of personal records, x
map of residences, xvii
signatures of, 470
In New York, 19–28
birth, 14–15
marriage, 27
In Ohio, 28, 33–41, 45–54
anointed in Kirtland (1836), 146
baptism of, 48
distillery business, 37
elder's license, 47, 73, 128–29, 147
taxed in Ohio, 38
errors in Church records about, 48–49
ordained Seventy (Second Quorum), 73, 147, 309, 366
ordains Jeremiah Leavitt, 177
patriarchal blessing, 141–42
returns to Kirtland (1835–36), 129, 135–43, 147–48, 150
taxed in Ohio, 38, 42 notes 19–20, 54, 180 note 8
In Missouri
moves to Missouri, 71–73
and Clay County High Council, 125–27
age and health after imprisonment, 266 notes 54–55
arrested twice, 218, 230
as "Captain Bull," 203–4, 224
as Danite, 96, 198–99, 203, 224, 248
at Battle of Crooked River, 204, 248
at Far West, 162, 173–75; in militia, 97, 193, 195–96
at Quincy (Oct. 1839), 274, 291

at Richmond hearing, 223–24
baptisms by, 175–77
business with Levi Jackman, 77–78, 124, 150
business trip to New York, 149–50
father's blessing on William Alexander Follett, 177–79
returns from Kirtland (1836), 150–51
imprisonment (1838, 1839) and attempted escape, 166–67, 176, 239 note 32, 245–63
in Clay County, 157
in Hulet Settlement, 116, 123
in Whitmer Settlement, 75–77
not in Caldwell County militia, 171
owns land, 163–65, 167, 181 note 34, 235–36
signs petition, 119
steals powder keg, 248
taxes, 100, 162, 236–37
In Nauvoo
as Joseph Smith's bodyguard, 204, 363–64
as Mason, 348–49
compared to Orrin Porter Rockwell, 204, 364
helps rescue kidnap victims, 369–71
identified as constable, 371
in 1840 U.S. Census, 278
in 1842 LDS census, 330
in George A. Smith survey, 103
in Nauvoo First Ward, 308, 316
Nauvoo Legion, officer in, 316–21, 326 note 53, 334–35
owns land, 286, 293–96, 302 note 40, 307–8; map, 297
not listed as voter, 332
possible Nauvoo policeman, 365–66
probable farmer, 383
proxy baptisms for relatives, 312–13
purchases at Nauvoo Temple store, 339–40
requested as witness in Washington, 291

signs petitions, 316, 332–34, 372
taxed in Nauvoo, 296, 331, 350 note 11, 385
fatal injury and death, 388–89; death date, 406 note 45
Masonic funeral, 393–98, 408 note 86
obituary, 389–93
location of grave unknown, 400–402
endowed by proxy, 346
sealed vicariously to Louisa, 361
well near property uses bricks from temple well, 444–45, 449 note 62
Follett, LeRoy, 308, 465 note 21
Follett, Life/Life/Alitha, 325 note 26
Follett, Louinda, 537 note 47
Follett, Louisa Tanner. See also King Follett.
Chronological Biography
ancestry of, 20
as Methodist Episcopalian, 41
in New York, 20–28
In Ohio, 37
baptized, 48
In Missouri, 458
King in Kirtland, 129, 139
property losses in Missouri, 100, 162, 231
leaves Missouri, 230–31
In Nauvoo
in 1840 U.S. Census, 278
endowment of (and children), 346, 442
diary (1844–45), x, 27, 429–36
defends Mormonism, 495
expresses sorrow, 497, 502–3, 508
expresses faith, 498–500, 503, 508–9
provenance of, 446 note 19
reflects on King, 433–34
reflects on other deaths, 434
transcribed, 493–516
homemaking duties, 381–82
in 1842 LDS census, 330
in George A. Smith survey, 103
in Nauvoo First Ward, 308
in Relief Society, 343–44
on Smith assassinations, 427, 431–32, 500–501
proxy baptisms by, 312, 336
sealed to Nathan A. West, 442
signs petitions, affidavits, 276–77, 283 note 32, 291, 372
visits family after King's death, 428
returns to Nauvoo, 514–16
In Iowa, 451, 457–64
blindness, 460
joins RLDS Church, 461–62
death and burial, 462–63
Follett, Louise L. (b. 1853), 537 note 47
Follett, Luther, 8
Follett, Lyman Leander, 537 note 47
Follett, Martha Kellum/Cullum, 471–72
Follett, Mary (ca. 1831–33), 38, 49, 54, 78, 104, 313, 528–29
Follett, Mary Bishop, 473, 475 note 17
Follett, Mary Emily Hamblin, 183 note 70
Follett, Minnie Vista Peterson, 373 note 20
Follett, Nancy. See Sanford, Nancy Follett Daley.
Follett, Nancy Ann (b. 1864), 537 note 47
Follett, Nancy Maria/Mariah Fossett (wife of William Alexander Follett), 439, 448 note 34
biography, 524–28
endowed, 442, 452
in Nauvoo, 299
in Iowa, 524
in Utah, 526, 537 note 45
in Las Vegas, 526
in Arizona, 527
death of, 527–28
Follett, Orren W., xi, 352 note 46, 538 note 60
Follett, Persis Black, 470–71
Follett, Rachel Stevens, 312, 473
Follett, Robert (fl. 1655), 1, 469–71
Follett, Russell, 6
Follett, Samuel (b. 1706), 472
Follett, Sarah Fuller, 472–73

Follett, Sarah Maria, 537 note 47
Follett, Seth (King's half-brother), 22–23, 26–27
Follett, Sybil/Sibel Willard, 4, 10
Follett, Tonya, xiii
Follett, Virginia Ann ("Jenny"), 459, 462, 466 note 46
Follett, Walter, Jr., 474
Follett, Warren King (1838–97)
  biography, 530–34
In Missouri, 530
  birth of, 177
  possible blessing of, 188
In Nauvoo, 323
  description of, 15
  in Nauvoo First Ward, 308
  in 1840 U.S. Census, 278
  in 1842 LDS census, 330
  probable chores of, 382
In Iowa, 530–31, 457–63
  lives with Adeline and Nathan West, 530
  Louisa travels/lives with, 428, 430–32, 435, 497, 518
  buys property with Louisa, 531
  served in Union Army, 532
  married Virginia Ann ("Jenny") Dunlap, 532
  member of Baptist Church, 532
  physical description, 532
  repels intruder, 533
  death, 534
Follett, Warren King (b. 1848, son of William and Nancy), 515, 537 note 45
Follett, Willard, 8
Follett, William (1866–67, son of Warren and Virginia), 533–34
Follett, William Alexander (1825–85)
Chronological Biography
  biography, 38, 524–28
  in Missouri, 54, 77, 168, 170
  receives father's blessing, 177–79
In Nauvoo, 299, 307–8, 323, 330–31, 346, 428
  endowed, 442
  in 1840 U.S. Census, 278
  in George A. Smith survey, 103
  at the pineries, 359–60
  marriage of, 439
  ordained Seventy, 366
  probable chores of, 382
After Nauvoo
  in Iowa, 524
  in Mormon Battalion, 524–25
  at Sutter's mill, 525
  in Utah, 526, 537 note 45
  in Las Vegas, 526
  in Arizona, 527
  death of, 527–28
Follett, William Haynes, 373 note 20
Follett, William King (b. and d. 1846), 524
Follett, William Lamoni, 537 note 47
Follett, Wilola, 462, 525, 533
Folsom, Jeremiah, 4
food, raising and preparing, 17–18
Foote, Warren
  biography, 209–29
  describes Far West, 193
  on Joseph Smith's militarism, 199
  on flight of Missourians, 200
Forbes, Edmund M., 261
Ford, Thomas, 370, 427, 439
Fordham, Elijah, 142–43, 153 note 25
Forman/Foreman, John, 106 note 7
Fort Osage (1831), 90 note 33
Fourth of July celebration (1838), 191–92
Frampton, David, 100, 239 note 32
Freemasonry. *See* Masonry.
French and Indian War, 20
Fuller, Janet, 459

G

Galland, Isaac, 249, 264 note 14, 286
Gallatin, Mo., 194–95, 200–201
Galloway, Charles Wesley, 176
Galloway, John, 176
Garner, Mary Field, 380–81
Garner, William, 381
Gates, Gibson, 102, 113
Gates, Horatio, 4

Gates, Jacob, 169, 182 note 39, 239 note 32
gathering, principle of, 299
Gentry, Leland Homer, 117
Gibbs, Luman
   and Battle of Crooked River, 264 note 12
   at Richmond Jail, 225, 239 note 32, 245, 248–52
   released, 266 note 59
Gibbs, Phila, 249, 267 note 59
Gifford, Samuel Kendall, 230, 241 note 67, 289, 458
Gilbert, Algernon Sidney
   in Missouri, 68, 74, 97, 121
   signs petitions, 115, 119
   store damaged, 84, 87
Gilbert Settlement, 116
Givens, George, and Sylvia
   on artificial light, 381
   on Big Field, 383
   on burials, 394, 400
   on "the grove" in Nauvoo, 412–13
   on wells, 334, 387
Godfrey, Kenneth W., 385
Goff, James, 100
Goulty, G. Frank, 404 note 10.
Granger, Oliver, 302 note 48
Grant, George D., 239 note 32
Green, Addison, 203
Greene, John Portineus, 217
   biography, 238 note 12, 242 note 69
   on Caldwell County, 171
   on leaving Missouri, 230
Grimshaw, Jonathan, 415
grove, and Nauvoo preaching services, 412–13
Groves, Elisha H., 172
Gyman, Thomas, 73

H

habeas corpus, 315, 364
Hale, Aroet Lucius
   characterizes King as Joseph Smith's friend, 411
   in Nauvoo Martial Band, 396–97, 408 note 89
   on King Follett Discourse, 419
Hallett, Clark, 239 note 32
Hallwas, John E., 309
Hammond, Joseph, 3
Hancock, Charles Brent, 440
Hancock, Mosiah Lyman, 439–40
Hancock, Solomon, 72, 77, 125
Harris, Emer, 519
Harris, George W., 239 note 32
Harris, Martin, 64 note 6, 519
Hartley, William G.
   on Caldwell County, 169–70
   on Danites, 199–200
   on evacuation from Missouri, 230–31
   on extermination order, 237
   on Missouri-Ohio correspondence, 117–18
Hathaway, William S., 394
Haun's Mill
   Hawn/Haun, Jacob, correct spelling of name, 163
   massacre and looting, 206–7, 213
   word of reaches Far West, 214
Haven, Charlotte, 366
Haven, Martha Hall, 386, 422 note 33
Haws, Peter, 359
Head, Anthony, 239 note 32
Henderson, James M., 239 note 32
Hendricks, Drusilla, 203
Henry, Alonzo, 499
Heward, John, 442
Hewlet/Hewlett/Hulet, Charles, 296, 307, 393. *See also* Hulet.
Hibbard, Davidson, 287
Higbee, Elias
   biography, 301 note 23
   calls out Mormon militia, 199, 203
   lists possible witnesses, 198
   on Nauvoo Temple Committee, 351 note 39
   visits Washington, 291
Higbee, Francis M., 198, 291, 239 note 32, 426
Higbee, John Somers
   and Wight family, 99

at Quincy, Ill., 273
forced evacuation of, 99
in Missouri, 70–71, 110, 239 note 32
Hinckle, George M., 172, 174
Hinckley, Gordon B., 281, 444
Hitchcock, Jesse
   biography, 133 note 80
   patriarchal blessing, 142–43
   signs King Follett's elder's license, 129, 153 note 25
Hodges, Curtis, Sr., 166. See also Hudges.
hogs, slaughter yard in Clay County, 112
Holbrook, Chandler, 239 note 32
Holbrook, Joseph
   biography, 373 note 17, 464 note 4
   in the pineries, 360
   looting in Far West, 218
   Nauvoo Legion commission, 319–20
   on endowments, 443, 452
   on evacuating Nauvoo, 454
Holbrook Settlement, 116
Holzapfel, Richard Neitzel, 293
Holzapfel, Richard Neitzel and Jeni Brobert Holzapfel, 293, 377–78, 380
Hooper, H. P., 237
Horne, Franklin, 534 note 3
Horne, Lewis, 262
Hoskin (of Ohio), 34
Hotchkiss, Horace, 286
Howell, Thomas C. D., 526, 537 note 45
Hudges, Amos, 166–67
Huff, Viola Amelda Dunlap, 462, 466 note 46
Hulet Branch/Settlement, 116–17. See also Hewlett.
   dispute at, 151
   members of, 124, 126–27, 156 note 57
Hulet/Hulett, Charles, 116, 106 note 7, 302 note 44, 385
Hulet, Sylvester, 116
   Battle of Big Blue, 106 note 7
   biography, 131 note 29
   Clay County High Council, 125–27
   prisoner at Richmond, Mo., 239 note 32
   visits Louisa Follett, 127, 131 note 29, 431, 500
Hunter, Edward, 305–6, 367
Hunter, Jesse D., 239 note 32
Huntington, Dimick, 297
Huntington, Oliver B., 227
Huntington, William
   and removal committee, 227
   biography, 241 note 59
   hostilities at Adam-ondi-Ahman, 199
   Nauvoo sexton, 394, 399
Hyde, Orson, 303 note 49, 365
Hyde, William, 149

I

Independence, Mo., see also Jackson County, and Missouri.
   described (1831), 66–67
   headquarters of nine Joseph Smith movements, 65–66
Indians, Mormon beliefs about, 81, 158
Iowa, Mormon settlements in, 299, 456
Irving, Washington, 69–70

J

Jackman, Angeline, 147
Jackman, Levi
   as missionary, 73, 428–29
   Battle of Big Blue, 106 note 7; map, 95
   business with King Follett, 24, 77–78, 529
   business with Nathan West, 78
   encounters King Follett in New York, 150
   moves to Missouri, 73–74, 110
   on Clay County Stake high council, 125
   on hostilities in Missouri, 86–87, 96, 98–99
   on Kirtland Temple, 129, 139
   on Seventies, 147
   taxed in Nauvoo, 385
Jackson, Andrew, 63, 119
Jackson, Brian D., 323
Jackson County
   as Zion, 53, 56 note 27, 69, 111
   attempts to return to, 114–15

descriptions of, 69
Mormons in, 66–88; map, 75
property losses in, 113–14, 118
proposal to purchase land, 121
temple site dedicated, 137
Jacques, Vienna, 310
Jenson, Andrew
  biography, 407 note 73
  King Follett biographical statement, 392–93
Jessee, Dean C., 338
Johnson, Aaron, 371
Johnson, Benjamin F., 138, 152 note 4, 201
Johnson, Clark V., 83, 165
Johnson, John, and Elsa, 46
Johnson, Lyman E., 189–90
Jonas, Abraham, 347–48
Jones, Benjamin, 239 note 32
Jones, Henry, 454–55
Jones, Hollis, xii
Jones, James, 454
Jones, Peggy Follett, xii, 18
Joseph Smith Translation, 46
Journal of Mormon History, xiii

K

Kane, Thomas L., 388, 406 note 53, 455
Kearney, Elsie, 535 note 5
Kempton, Maria West, 151, 156 note 60, 278, 428, 457–58
Kendall, Samuel, 194
Killyon, John, 274
Kimball, George, 239 note 32
Kimball, Heber C.
  as Mason, 348
  endowed, 346, 352 note 56
  describes Nauvoo, 329
  performs sealings, 442
  taxed in Nauvoo, 385
  visits Joseph Smith in prison, 247
Kimball, Helen Mar. *See* Whitney, Helen Mar Kimball.
Kimball, Hiram, 307, 385, 393
Kimball, James L., 399
Kimball, Sarah Melissa Granger, 341

King, Austin, 196, 222, 225, 249–50
King Follett Discourse, 411–21, 477–92
  amalgamated by Jonathan Grimshaw, 415
  delivery of, ix, 411–12
  not funeral address, 411
  references to King Follett in, 416–17
  scribes for, 414–15
Kirby, Elizabeth, 442
Kirtland, Ohio
  apostasy in, 173
  cost of common items in, 144
  Mormons in, 135–51
  population of, 51, 136
Kirtland Camp, route of, 129
Kirtland High Council, 167
Kirtland Temple
  announcement of, 129
  construction of, 138–39, 144
  dedication, 145, 147, 149
  endowment in, 145
  revelation about, 137–38
  significance of, 135
Knight, Joseph, 76
Knight, Newel, 125, 141, 217, 302 note 48, 443
Kofford, Greg, xiv

L

Lacey, Robert, xiv
"Lady Byron[']s Farewell," 506–7
Lafayette County, Mo., Mormon refugees in, 101
Larson, Stan, 415–16
Launius, Roger D., 309
Law, William, 352 note 56, 425–26
Law, Wilson, 370, 426
LDS Church History Library, xiii
Leavitt, Jeremiah, II, 176
Leavitt, Sarah Sturtevant, 176–77
Lee, John D., 442
Leonard, Abigail, 104
Leonard, Glen M.
  on collective farms, 168
  on Kane's visit to Nauvoo, 455

on Nauvoo evacuation, 452
on Nauvoo Legion, 318
on reaction to Smith assassinations, 427
on temple endowments, 452
LeSueur, Stephen C.
on Mormon refugees, 206
on Mormon migration to Missouri, 186–87
on Richmond hearing, 240 note 40
letters, 19, 83
Lewis, Joshua, 75
Liberty, Mo., 109, 245
Liberty Jail, 245. *See also* individual prisoners.
Lightner, Mary Elizabeth Rollins, 101
Literski, Nicholas S., 396
Littlefield, Lyman O., 390
Livingston County, Mo., 194, 202
Loveland, Chester, 371
Lowrey Settlement, 116
Lucas, Samuel D., 207, 214, 217
Lyman, Amasa Mason
　and attempted escape, 274
　and Hulet Branch, 127
　and Zion's Camp, 122–23, 132 note 47
　at DeWitt, 198
　at Far West, 215
　biography, 132 note 50, 283 note 21
　prisoner at Richmond, Mo., 239 note 32
　requested as witness in Washington, 291
　witness for temple sealings, 442
Lyon, T. Edgar, 67

M

Mace, Wandle
　on King Follett Discourse, 419
　on King Follett's death, 392
　on refugees, 275
Madsen, Carol Cornwall, 307–8
Madsen, Gordon, 223
Maid of Iowa, 378
mail. *See* letters.
malaria, 289
Malvern Mills, Iowa, 177
Manship (justice of peace), 113
Mantua, Ohio, 49

maps
　Battle of Big Blue, 95
　Jackson County, 75
　King Follett's land in Nauvoo 297
　King Follett's residences, xvii
　LDS branches in Western Reserve, 50
　Mirabile Township, 165
　Mormon War (1838), 186
Marks, William, 320
Marquardt, H. Michael, 143
Marsh, Thomas B., 125, 141
Martin, John A., 533
Masonry. *See also* Nauvoo Masonic Lodge.
　activities, 368–69
　and temple endowment, 346–47
　established in Nauvoo, 347–48
　numbers of members, 348
Mather, Increase, 91 note 55
Maughan, Ruth Clark, 264 note 13
Maynard, Silas, 174, 239 note 32
McBeth, Mildred, 461
McBride, Matthew S.
　on Kirtland Temple, 145
　on Masonry, 346–47
　on Nauvoo Temple, 338, 357
McClary, David, 368
McConkie, Joseph Fielding, 420
McConkie, Mark L., 47–48
McGee, Joseph H., 194, 200–201
McHenry, Henry, and Lucy Ann, 261, 267 note 62
McLellin, William, 85, 97, 125
McRae, Alexander
　at Far West, 217
　at Liberty Jail, 225, 245
　at Richmond, Mo., 239 note 32
Menard, Christy, 9, 10
Menshall, Robert, 27
Merrill, Cyrena, 352 note 46
Merrill, Josephine, 352 note 46
Merrill, Philemon Christopher, 352 note 46
Methodist Episcopal Church, 27, 41, 463
Miles, Daniel S., 239 note 32
militia
　ambiguity with "mob," 83

in New England, 2–3, 317–18
Mormon, in Caldwell County, 191
Miller, George, 352 note 56
Miller, Henry, 407 note 75
Miller, Rowena, 293–96
Millport, Mo., 200–201
Mills County, Iowa, xii, 151
Mills, Rhoda Hulet, 116
Minthorn, Frances Marian Huff, 460, 462, 533
Mirabile Township, 163–66; map, 165
missionaries, appointed in Missouri, 128
missionary work, restricted in Clay County, 118
Missouri
    conditions in 1830s, 71
    descriptions of, 69–70
    hostilities in, 79–84, 86, 93–105, 159
    Mormon differences from Missourians, 79–82
    Mormons in Jackson County, 65–88, 101
    Mormons leave state, 228–30
    Mormons move to, 54–55, 73
    numbers of refugees, 229
    property losses in, 104, 107 note 28
Missouri Legislature, 227–28
Missouri Mormon Frontier Association, 220–21, 232
Monroe County, Mo., 129
Moore, Zelda, 16
Morley, Isaac, Sr.
    biographical information, 105 note 2
    in Kirtland, Ohio, 141
    in Missouri, 84, 93, 97, 99, 115, 124, 239 note 32
Morley Settlement, in Clay County, 116
Mormon Battalion, 456
Mormon beliefs, xiv–xv
Mormon converts, socioeconomic class, 47–48
Mormon History Association, xiii
Mormon War (1838), 185–207; map, 186
Morrison, Thomas, 426
Mortensen, Hal, 468
Mortensen, Halie, 468
Mortensen, Irval L.
    cartography by, 50
    photographs by, xii–xiii, 18, 39, 76, 117, 166, 233, 235, 367, 380, 399–403, 413, 415, 430, 444–45, 453, 524, 528
Mortensen, Jeanna, 468
Mortensen, Joann Follett
    personal benefits of research, 467–68
    research and writing, x–xii
    photograph, 18
Murdock, John, 45, 125
Murphy, John, 261

N

Nauvoo, Illinois
    arsenal, 369
    burial grounds, 398–99
    civil government, 313–16
    cost of typical items, 384–85
    descriptions, 285–87, 288–89, 292–93, 305–7, 329–31, 355, 377–78
    education in, 322–23
    entertainment in, 386
    evacuation, 441, 451–53
    frontier elements of, 377–78
    hostilities, 364–65, 423–25, 437, 440–41
    illness and death, 290, 386–87, 389
    meaning of name, 287–88
    population, 293, 307, 329–30, 350 note 5, 356, 437
    poverty, 381, 385
    preaching services in, 307–8, 356, 386
    stores and professions, 384
    wards, 315–16, 325 note 38
    wells in, 387
Nauvoo Brass Band, 386
Nauvoo Cultural Hall. *See* Nauvoo Masonic Hall.
Nauvoo Expositor, 420, 426
Nauvoo House, 311, 358, 367
Nauvoo Legion

activities of, 320–22, 334–35
authorized by legislature, 314
boys' units, 440
fears about, 318
organization of, 305–6, 316–17
number of members, 317
Nauvoo Martial Band, 396
Nauvoo Masonic Hall, 427–28, 430
Nauvoo Masonic Lodge, and Follett's funeral, 393–94
Nauvoo Restoration, Inc., 367
Nauvoo Stake, and ward structure, 308
Nauvoo Temple
  and Brigham Young's leadership, 437–38
  and tithing store, 337
  as public works project, 379
  baptisms for the dead, 313
  construction of, 336–41, 355, 379
  descriptions of, 335, 357
  endowments in, 441–43, 452
  reconstruction of, 444
  women's contributions to, 341
Needham, John, 364, 374 note 28
Nelson, Hilea Daley, 520
Nelson, Isaac, 520
Nelson, Ohio, 49
Newberry, James, 239 note 32
Newman, Elijah, 239 note 32
Neyman, Cyrus Livingston, 310
Neyman, Jane, 310

O

Oak, John, 4
Oak, Mehitable Rediat, 4
Oak, Nathaniel, 4
Oak, Susanna Allen, 4–5
Ohio
  cost of typical items, 39–40
  LDS Church established, 59–63
  settlement of, 33–34
Ohio Star, letters about Mormonism, 52
Old Nauvoo Burial Grounds, 398, 400–403
Old Pioneer Cemetery (Nauvoo), 398

Olmstead, Harvey, 310
Olney, Oliver, 142
Osler, Craig J., 420
Owen, Ephraim, 301 note 21
Owen, Mosby S., 96
Owens, Zedekiah, 239 note 32

P

Pace, William Byram, 440
Packman, John B., 261
Page, Ebenezer, 239 note 32
Page, Hiram
  and Battle of Big Blue, 106 note 7
  as Book of Mormon witness, 64 note 7
  biography 155 note 56
  Clay County High Council, 126
  married Adeline Follett and Nathan West, 151
Palmer, James, 387, 392
Paris, Mo., 129
Parker, Ellen Briggs Douglas. *See* Douglas, Ellen Briggs.
Parker, John, 405 note 29
Parkin, Max H, 74, 101, 120, 160
Parkman, Ohio, 49
Parks, Isaiah, 262
Parley Street Cemetery, 398
Parrish, Betsy, 122
Partridge, Edward
  and Clay County High Council, 126
  and consecration, 70, 72
  conversion of, 47
  in Kirtland, 141
  in Missouri, 53, 77, 84–85, 124, 226
  in Nauvoo, 302 note 38
  prisoner at Richmond, Mo., 224, 239 note 32
  signs appeals/petitions, 115, 119, 160
  tarred and feathered, 84
Partridge, Eliza, 114, 226
Partridge, Emily Dow, 71, 74
Partridge, Lydia Clisbee, 47, 74, 226
Partridge Settlement, 116
Peck, Reed
  biography, 210 note 69

Missouri experience, 169, 248
on King Follett's activities, 203, 211
  note 70, 224
witness at Richmond hearing, 223–24
penny subscription drive, 356–57
Petersen, Lauritz, 294
Peterson, Ziba, 46, 63
Pettegrew/Pettigrew, David
  and wife, 111
  hostilities, 99, 100–102, 112–13
  in Missouri, 76, 83, 111
  in Quincy, Ill., 273
  on Mormon militarism, 118
  prisoner at Richmond, Mo., 239 note 32
Phelps, Laura Clark, 253–60, 266 note 48
Phelps, Mary Ann. See Rich, Mary Ann Phelps.
Phelps, Morris
  at Battle of Crooked River, 204
  charged with murder, 211 note 71
  escapes from jail, 253–60
  in prison, 222, 225, 239 note 32, 242 note 70, 245, 247–52
Phelps Settlement, 116
Phelps, William Wine
  agrees to leave Jackson County, 84–85
  and anointings, 146–47
  biography, 152 note 9, 167
  clerk for patriarchal blessings, 143
  counselor in Clay County Stake presidency, 124
  describes Missouri, 69, 72
  excommunicated, 188
  hymns by, 142
  in Missouri, 68, 74, 77
  letters to wife, 139–41, 144, 146, 153 note 19
  Nathan West defends, 174
  on eternal marriage, 361
  on Far West High Council, 172
  on slavery, 83–84
  owns land, 166–67
  printing office destroyed, 84
  response to Clay County Committee, 159–60
  signs petitions, 115, 119
  taxed in Nauvoo, 386
  warned out of Far West, 189–90
Pilgrim's Progress, 257
pineries (Wisconsin), 358–60
Pinkham, Nathan, 203
Pioneer Cemetery (Nauvoo), 398–99
Pitcher (of Missouri militia), 97–98
Pitchforth, Ann H., 385, 414
Pixley, Benton, 86
polygamy
  and Brigham Young's leadership, 437–38
  confusion caused by, 425
  introduced in Nauvoo, 361–62
Poorman/Porman, John, 106 note 7
Pope, J. D, 237
Portage County, Ohio, 34–37, 40, 46. See also Shalersville, Ohio.
Potter, Amasa, 414, 421 note 14
Powell blacksmith shop, 222
Prairie Branch, 76, 116, 124, 131 note 29
Pratt, Mary Ann Stearns, 225, 247, 249, 264 note 15
Pratt, Nathan, 264 note 15
Pratt, Orson
  aids Parley Pratt's escape, 253–60, 266 note 51
  as Clay County Stake high councilor, 124–25
  biography, 154 note 34
  on Kirtland Temple dedication, 144
  on School of the Prophets, 140–41
Pratt, Parley P.
  and Allred Settlement, 129
  and Clay County Saints, 124–25
  arrested at Far West, 215
  as missionary, 47, 63, 107 note 21
  at Battle of Crooked River, 204
  charged with murder, 211 note 71
  conversion of, 46
  in prison/escapes, 221–22, 225, 239 note 32, 242 note 70, 245, 247–60, 263, 264 note 15, 274
  on Alexander Doniphan, 238 note 11
  on Alva Beaman, 154 note 41

on eternal marriage, 361
reports Missouri conditions, 115, 120
Pratt, Thankful Halsey, 264 note 15
Presbyterian Church, 20–22, 60
proxy baptisms. *See* baptisms for the dead.

Q

Quincy, Ill.
  aids slaves and Native Americans, 272
  Follett family in, 269–81
  kindness to refugees, 269–71, 280
  monument in, 280–81
  Mormon refugees, 229–31, 272–73, 275
Quinn, D. Michael, 204, 211 note 70

R

Randall, James, 325 note 25
Randall, Sally Carlisle, 311–12, 325 note 23, 384–85
Rathbun/Rathburn/Rathborn, Robert, 73
Ravenna, Ohio, 49
Rawson, Daniel Berry, 110
Ray County, Mo., 161, 202–3
recommends, for members going to Missouri, 53–54
Red Brick Store (Nauvoo), 341–42, 345
Redfield, Harlow, 301 note 21
Redfield, Tryphena West (Nathan's sister), 462, 535 note 8
Redfield, William, 535 note 8
redress petition (1833), 119
Rees, Amos, 223, 240 note 44
Reformed Mormon Church, 425–26
Refugee Committee, 270, 275
Relief Society
  activities of, 356, 382
  organization of, 341–44
removal committee, 176, 227–30, 234
Revolutionary War, 1–4, 20–21, 34
Reynolds, Edwin C., 81
Reynolds, Thomas, 253
Rich, Charles Coulson
  in Nauvoo Legion, 317, 321
  in Quincy, 273
  possible log cabin of, 232–35, 242

note 79
  requested as witness in Washington, 292
  taxed in Nauvoo, 385
  tries to aid escape, 274
Rich, Leonard, 126
Rich, Mary Ann Phelps, 253, 257, 266 note 48
Rich, Sarah DeArmon Pea, 234, 270–71, 289
Rich, Thomas, 239 note 32
Richards, Charles, 126
Richards, Franklin D., 443
Richards, Willard, 352 note 56, 412, 414–15, 427
Richardson (of Columbia, Mo.), 259
Richmond, Mo., 162
  description of, 248–49
  hearing at, 223–24, 240 note 40
  jails, 219–21, 224–25
  monument, 220
  Mormon prisoners at, 218–20
Rigdon, Athalia, 343
Rigdon, Nancy, 343
Rigdon, Phoebe, 246
Rigdon, Sidney
  as land agent, 293–95
  at Clay County Jail, 241 note 52
  at Far West, 215
  biography, 192
  conversion, 56 note 24
  counselor in Church presidency, 173
  helps ordain Joseph Smith Sr., 153 note 22
  imprisoned, 239 note 32, 245–46
  in Missouri, 53
  in Ohio, 46, 52, 91 note 73
  inflammatory oration, 192–93
  on Clay County hostilities, 160
  preaching of, 412
  visits Washington, 291
Ripley, Alanson
  biography, 181 note 22
  in Missouri, 163, 198, 239 note 32, 247
  requested as witness in Washington, 291
Rixford (of NY), 17
Roberts, Brigham Henry

on King Follett, 204, 211 note 71
on Mormons in Missouri, 70, 81, 97, 112
on Mormons in Nauvoo, 287
Robinette, William C., 261
Robinson, Ebenezer
  arrival in Quincy, 272
  biography, 282 note 10
  describes Nauvoo, 288
  imprisoned, 224–25, 239 note 32
Robinson, George W., 215, 239 note 32
Robinson, Joseph Lee, 419
Rockwell, Orrin Porter, 74, 99–100, 291, 385
Rockwood, Albert Perry
  estimates Clark's troops, 219
  on Battle of Crooked River, 204–5
  on Danites, 195
  on number arrested at Far West, 239 note 20
  protects Joseph Smith, 363–64
  Seventies quorum, 368
  taxed in Nauvoo, 386
Rollins, James S., 265 note 27
Rollins/Rawlins, James Henry, 239 note 32
Romig, Ronald E., 104, 163, 165
Rosati (Catholic bishop), 113
Roux (Catholic priest), 113
Rowley, Dennis, 358–59
Ruston (Nauvoo), 386

S

Salt Creek Branch, 129
Sanford, Farmer, 521, 536 note 25
Sanford, Fran, 448 note 34
Sanford, Henry
  biography, 448 note 34, 520–22
  endowed, 442, 452
  in California, 521–22
  in Iowa, 458, 521
  marries Nancy Follett, 366, 436, 438
  ordained Seventy, 366, 368
Sanford, Kate, 522–23
Sanford, Mary, 521–23
Sanford, Minnie, 522–23
Sanford, Nancy M. [Millicent/Mariah] Follett Daley, 509, 516
  Chronological Biography
    biography, 520–24
    birth, 38
    baptism, 49
    in Missouri, 54, 77, 168, 170
    in Nauvoo, 299, 331, 428, 436
    in 1840 U.S. Census, 278
    marries James Daley, 147, 278–79
    marries Henry Sanford, 438
    endowed, 442, 452
    in Iowa, 458
    in California, 103–4
    burial and reinterment, 523–24
    possible middle names of, 43 note 24
Sanford, Newill W., 521
Saunders, Richard, 318
Scholz, Charles W., 272
School of the Elders, 140–41
School of the Prophets, 140
Scott, Sarah Hall, 419–20, 422 note 33
Seely, William, 203
Seventies Building/Hall, 309, 367–69, 427, 437
Seventies, records of, 324 notes 13–14
Shaler, Nathaniel, 35
Shalersville, Ohio
  Follett family in, 28, 33–41, 45–54
  social conditions in, 35–37
Shearer, Daniel, 239 note 32
Shearer, Norman, 225, 239 note 32, 245
Sherwood (woman), 101
Sherwood, Henry F., 293, 296
Shurtliff, Luman A., 190, 217
Silver Creek, Iowa. *See* West, Nathan A.
Simmonds, A. J., 116
Slade, Clark, 167
Slade, Roxa, 126
slavery, in Missouri, 81
Smith, Agnes M. Coolbrith, 200
Smith, Alvin, 61
Smith, Amanda, 230
Smith, Bathsheba Wilson Bigler, 382–83, 404 note 21
Smith, Calvin N., 420

Smith, Don Carlos, 302 note 48, 324 note 18
Smith, Emma Hale
  adopts Murdock twins, 55 note 4
  as Relief Society president, 343–44
  attends blessing meetings, 142
  correspondence with Louis C. Bidamon, 406 note 49
  endowed and sealed, 346
  hires a well dug, 388
  in Ohio, 55 note 4
  visits Joseph Smith in prison, 247, 363
Smith, George A., survey of refugees, 103–4
Smith, Hiram (in California), 522
Smith, Hyrum
Chronological Biography
In Ohio
  as Book of Mormon witness, 64 note 7
  gives recommends to Missouri-bound members, 54
In Missouri
  contracts cholera, 122
  arrested at Far West, 215
  on Missouri hostilities, 160
  on Samuel Bogart, 203
  prisoner at Richmond, Mo., 239 note 32
  at Liberty Jail, 225, 245–46
In Nauvoo
  and penny drive, 356
  appreciates music, 386
  as land agent, 293–96
  as Mason, 347, 396
  blessings by, 143
  counselor in Church presidency, 173
  diary mentions King Follett, 50–51
  endowed, 352 note 56
  heads rescue party, 363
  on Nauvoo Temple Committee, 351 note 39
  preaching, 412
  taxed in Nauvoo, 385
  assassination and funeral, 396, 427
Smith, James E., 379
Smith, Joseph
Chronological Biography

biography to 1830, 59–63
First Vision, 60–61
In Kirtland, Ohio, 46, 52–54, 55 note 4
  and anointing meetings, 146
  and blessing meetings, 142
  blessings by, 143, 153 note 25
  revelations, 136
  tarred and feathered, 91 note 73
In Missouri, 65, 67, 73
  at Far West, 187, 215, 232; house, 232
  at preliminary hearing (August 1838), 196
  at Richmond, 220, 239 note 32
  contracts cholera, 122
  corresponds with Isaac Galland, 249
  endorses Rigdon's oration, 192–93
  describes Missouri, 67, 70
  forbids stealing, 202
  holds meetings at Rockwell home, 74
  in Clay County, 123–24, 160
  in Independence, 137
  in Liberty Jail, 225, 230, 245–47
  lawsuits against, 188–89
  militarism of, 199
  on suffering of Saints, 200
  priesthood titles, 173
  revelations, 120, 122
  temple site, 68–69
In Nauvoo, 285–90, 306. *See also* King Follett Discourse.
  and King Follett Discourse, 411–21
  and Red Brick Store, 384
  as candidate for U.S. president, 425–26
  as land agent, 293–96
  as Mason, 348–49
  attempts to arrest, 362–63
  city charter, 314
  describes Nauvoo, 287
  instructions to Relief Society, 341–42, 345
  journal of, 338
  on kindness in Quincy, 443–44
  Nauvoo Legion, 319, 334–35, 369–70
  new doctrines, 309–13, 361
  seeks federal redress, 291–92, 371–72

temple ordinances, 345–46, 356
taxed in Nauvoo, 385
assassination and funeral, 396, 427
Smith, Joseph, Sr.
as Book of Mormon witness, 64 note 7
marriage of, 60
patriarchal blessings, 141–43, 153 note 22, 177
Smith, Louisa, 55 note 4
Smith, Lucy Mack, 60, 226–27, 271, 343
Smith, Mary Fielding, 356
Smith, Samuel H., 64 note 7, 302 note 38
Smith, Thaddeus, 55 note 4
Smith, William, 129, 143
Snow, Eliza Roxcy
as Relief Society secretary, 343
biography, 152 note 6
memorial poem, 402–3
on Kirtland Temple, 138, 149
on leaving Missouri, 230
on Nauvoo, 289–90
on Quincy citizens, 271
Snow, Erastus, 419
Spencer, Thomas M., 102
St. Lawrence County, NY, 22–23
Staker, Mark Lyman, 142
Stearns, Mary Ann. *See* Pratt, Mary Ann Stearns.
Stearns, Nathan, 264 note 15
Steele, John, 454
Stevenson, Edward, 413, 419
Stillwell, Thomas Daniel, 185, 230, 242 note 68, 273
Stout, Allen J., 239 note 32
Stout, Hosea, 320
Streetsboro, Ohio, LDS branch in, 49
Strode, Clark, 166–67
Struthers, Cliff, 6
succession crisis, 461
Sunday services, 118, 307–8, 356, 386, 412
Swanzey, NH, 1–4
Sweeney, John, 320

T

Tanner, Anna Baldwin, 21–22, 312

Tanner, Anna Warren, 20–22, 149–50, 155 note 52, 312
Tanner, Florilla, 432
Tanner, Hay, 312
Tanner, John T., 239 note 32
Tanner, Joseph, 28, 432, 501
Tanner, Nancy, 312
Tanner, Nathan, 217
Tanner, Olive, 312
Tanner, Sidney, 239 note 32
Tanner, Thomas, II, 432–34, 501–2, 511
Tanner, Thomas, III, 20–22, 24
Tanner, Thomas, Jr., 20–21
Tanner, Thomas, Sr., 20–22
Tanner, Thomas William, 432, 501–2
Tanner, Warren, 312
Tanner, William, 432, 501
tarring and feathering, process of, 91 note 73
Taylor, John, 427
temple ordinances, 145, 345–46
Thanksgiving, in Nauvoo, 386
Thomas, Daniel S., 239 note 32
Thompson, Mercy Fielding, 356
Thompson, Robert B., 292
Timber Settlement/Branch. *See* Whitmer Branch.
Tippets, Alvin G., 239 note 32
Todd, Roger N., 262
tongues, gift of, 127
Tracy, Nancy Naomi Alexander, 149
Troost Lake/Park, 77
Turner (of Boone County), 262
Turner, John W. (wife of)
Turner Settlement, 116

U–V

U.S. Senate Judiciary Committee, 292
United Order, in Utah, 527
Universalist Society/Church, 7
University of the City of Nauvoo, 314, 322
Upper Shoal Creek Settlement, 116
Van Buren County, 111, 151
Van Buren, Martin, 291
Van Orden, Bruce, 70, 83–84
Veasey (traveler), 498

Voorhees, Washington, 239 note 32

W

Wait, Truman, 174
Wallace, James, 233
Walters, George, 261, 267 note 62
Ward, Maurine Carr, 344
Watson, W. J., 463
well–digging, process of, 387–88
Wells, R. W., 115
Wescott, Benjamin, 296–97
West, Adeline/Adaline Louisa Follett, 27, 517–19
   baptism, 50
   cemetery record, 535 note 11
   endowed and sealed, 442
   in 1840 U.S. Census, 278
   in 1842 LDS census, 331
   in Iowa, 457–59
   in Missouri, 54, 77
   in Ohio, 37, 38, 435
   land purchases, 297
   marriage of, 151
   obituary, 54
   performs proxy baptisms, 312
   signs 1843 memorial, 372
   travels after King's death, 428–29, 431–32, 495
West, Griffith, 312
West, James M., 262
West, Julia A. Johnson Fleming, 519
West, Maria (dau. of Nathan West), 151.
   See Kempton, Maria West.
West, Mary (Nathan's mother), 312
West, Mary Smith Hulet (Nathan's wife), 116, 131 note 29, 302 note 44
   death of, 151, 155 note 57
   sealed to Nathan West, 442
West, Nathan Ayers, 517–18, 435
Chronological Biography
In Missouri
   and Battle of Big Blue, 106 note 7
   and Clay County High Council, 125–27, 174–75
   business with Levi Jackman, 78
   clerk of Far West High Council, 168
   defends Whitmer Settlement, 96
   land ownership, 100, 168, 286, 297
   marries Adeline Follett, 131 note 29, 151
   not in Caldwell County militia, 171–72
In Nauvoo, 307
   as Mason, 349
   endowed, 442
   in 1840 U.S. Census, 278
   in George A. Smith survey, 103
   in Nauvoo Legion, 317, 369
   ordained Seventy, 366, 368
   performs proxy baptisms, 312
   signs petitions/appeals, 119, 332, 372
   taxed, 162, 331
   not in 1842 LDS census, 331
   sealed to three women, 442
   travels after King's death, 428–29, 431–32
In Iowa, 457–59
   Louisa lives with, 273, 511
   in Silver Creek, 103, 156 note 60
   letter to David Whitmer, 235–36
   excommunicated, 461, 518
   obituary, 518–19
   cemetery record of, 535 note 11
West, Tryphena (dau. of Nathan West).
   See Doughty, Tryphena West.
West, William, 312
Western Reserve, LDS branches in, 50
Westover, Mary C., 419, 421 note 14, 414
Whitcomb, Joseph, 4
White, Hugh, and William, 286
White, J. (sheriff), 371
White, James (Nauvoo), 300 note 4, 436
"White Pilgrim, The," 512–13
Whitesides, Caron Colby, 460, 529, 531
Whiting (in Ravenna), 499
Whiting, Edmund, 534 note 2
Whiting, Elisha, 534 note 2
Whiting, Nathan, 20
Whiting, Sally Hulet, 133 note 71
Whiting, William, 106 note 7
Whitlock, Andrew, 239 note 32
Whitlock, Harvey, 85–87, 92 note 85

Whitman, William, 223–24, 239 note 32
Whitmer Branch/Settlement, 75–77
Whitmer, Christian
   as Book of Mormon witness, 64 note 7
   in Clay County, 96, 105 note 6, 125
Whitmer, David
   and Battle of Big Blue, 106 note 7
   as Book of Mormon witness, 64 note 6
   as president of Church in Missouri, 76–77, 174
   defends Whitmer Settlement, 96–97
   excommunicated, 188
   expelled from Far West, 189–90
   fund-raising by, 51–52
   in Clay County, 116, 123, 126
   on Hulet Branch, 127
   sends items to Missouri, 150
Whitmer, Jacob, 64 note 7, 106 note 7, 172
Whitmer, John
   agrees to leave Jackson County, 84–85
   and Clay County high council, 125–26
   as Book of Mormon witness, 64 note 7
   counselor in Clay County Stake presidency, 124
   excommunicated, 188
   expelled from Far West, 189–90
   King Follett buys land from, 235–36
   Nathan West defends, 174
   on Far West High Council, 172
   sends items to Missouri, 150
   signs petition to governor, 115
Whitmer, Peter, 85
   as Book of Mormon witness, 64 note 7
   as missionary, 49–50, 56 note 18, 63
Whitmer Settlement, 86–87, 116
Whitney, Helen Mar Kimball, 194, 288, 321, 288
Whitney, Newel K., 140, 142, 320, 352 note 56
Whitney, William, 194
Whittaker, David J., xiii
"whittling deacons," 439–40
Wight, Harriet, 99, 107 note 21
Wight, Lyman
   at Adam-ondi-Ahman, 196
   at Far West, 215
   biography, 182 note 53
   Church callings, 76, 107 note 21, 125
   charged with teaching erroneous doctrine, 172
   hostilities, 98, 171
   in Jackson County, 85, 97
   imprisoned, 221, 225, 239 note 32, 245
   reports to Joseph Smith, 115, 120
Wight, Orange, 99
Wight Settlement, 116
Wilcox, Pearl, 170, 222
Wilke, William, 339
Willard, Catherine Field, 4
Willard, Eliza, 8
Willard, Josiah, 4
Willard, Seth, 8
Willard, Simon, 4
Willes, Ira Jones, 113, 130 note 14
Williams, Frederick G.
   and Egyptian scrolls, 141
   Church callings, 153 note 22, 173
   in Missouri, 160
   monument, 281
Williams, Newman B., 175, 183 note 66
Williams, Samuel, 175–76, 183 note 66
Wilson (Missouri militia), 215
Wilson, Moses, 105 note 6, 113, 215
Wilson's store, 93
Winchester, NH, 1–2, 4, 6–10, 15–16, 15–20
Winder, Ned, 294, 296
Wisconsin. See pineries.
Wixom, Hartt, 226
women, support temple construction, 356–57
Wood, Esther Cranmer, 176
Wood, Gideon Durfy, 519
Wood, Hannah Daley, 519
Wood, Henry, 176
Wood, Lyman Stephen, 519
Wood, Martin, 176, 183 note 67
Wood, Reese, Doniphan, and Atchison (attorneys), 85–86
Woodruff, Wilford, 349, 385, 414–15
Woods, Carlo M., 231, 283 notes 32–33
Woodson, W. H., 112

Woodward, George W., 217
Woolley, Edwin D., 396
Word of Wisdom, 174, 301 note 21
Workman, John, 380
Worthington, George W., 200–201
Worthman, Allen, xiii, 539 note 75
Wright, H. Martin, 520

Y–Z

Young, Brigham
    as Joseph Smith's successor, 436–39
    on evacuating Nauvoo, 454–55
    on temple, 346, 352 note 56, 452
    orders list of Clay County refugees, 103
    quotes Joseph Smith on move to Rocky Mountains, 424–25
    taxed in Nauvoo, 385
Young, Emily Dow Partridge Young, 112
Young, Joseph, 147, 206–7, 368
Younger, Joseph W., 239 note 32
Zabriski, Henry, 239 note 32
Zarahemla Stake, 299
Zion. *See* Jackson County.
Zion's Camp
    cholera, 122–23, 132 notes 47–48
    disbanding of, 123–24
    purposes, 120–21
    route, 129

About the Author

Joann Follett Mortensen, a third great-granddaughter of King and Louisa Follett, is an Arizona native. She graduated from the University of Arizona with a B.S. in secondary education, a major in business, and a minor in history. Her professional life has focused on working with school districts and school boards where she specialized in providing consulting services for personalized administrative searches, board and leadership training, and team-building activities. As a volunteer, she has participated on numerous councils and boards serving education and the arts in her community and in Arizona.

Not all Folletts followed Brigham Young, but her branch of the family did and was colonizing Arizona's Gila Valley by the 1880s. Joann, an avid family historian, began serious research for this book in the 1970s. She gave a paper at the 2003 Mormon History Association conference in Kirtland, Ohio: "King Follett: the Kirtland Years— One Who Bore the Burden," and followed up in 2005 with an article in the *Journal of Mormon History*: "King Follett: The Man behind the Discourse."

She and her husband Irval, an attorney, have three children, seven grandchildren, and one great-grandchild. They served an eighteen-month mission (2010–11) at the LDS Church History Library in Salt Lake City. Assigned to the Collections and Development Department, they are continuing that work as Church Service Missionaries from their home in Safford, Arizona.

Joann {jfmortensen@gmail.com} welcomes any input into the history of King Follett and his family.

Also available from
GREG KOFFORD BOOKS

Knowing Brother Joseph Again: Perceptions and Perspectives

Davis Bitton

Paperback, ISBN: 978-1-58958-123-4

In 1996, Davis Bitton, one of Mormon history's preeminent and much-loved scholars, published a collection of essays on Joseph Smith under the title, *Images of the Prophet Joseph Smith*. A decade later, when the book went out of print, Davis began work on an updated version that would also include some of his other work on the Mormon prophet. The project was only partially finished when his health failed. He died on April 13, 2007, at age seventy-seven. With the aid of additional historians, *Knowing Brother Joseph Again: Perceptions and Perspectives* brings to completion Davis's final work—a testament to his own admiration of the Prophet Joseph Smith.

From Davis Bitton's introducton:

This is not a conventional biography of Joseph Smith, but its intended purpose should not be hard to grasp. That purpose is to trace how Joseph Smith has appeared from different points of view. It is the image of Joseph Smith rather than the man himself that I seek to delineate.

Even when we have cut through the rumor and misinformation that surround all public figures and agree on many details, differences of interpretation remain. We live in an age of relativism. What is beautiful for one is not for another, what is good and moral for one is not for another, and what is true for one is not for another. I shudder at the thought that my presentation here will lead to such soft relativism.

Yet the fact remains that different people saw Joseph Smith in different ways. Even his followers emphasized different facets at different times. From their own perspectives, different people saw him differently or focused on a different facet of his personality at different times. Inescapably, what they observed or found out about him was refracted through the lens of their own experience. Some of the different, flickering, not always compatible views are the subject of this book.

Saints of Valor: Mormon Medal of Honor Recipients

Sherman L. Fleek

Hardcover, ISBN: 978-1-58958-171-5

Since 1861 when the US Congress approved the concept of a Medal of Honor for combat valor, 3,457 individuals have received this highest military decoration that the nation can bestow. Nine of those have been Latter-day Saints. The military and personal stories of these LDS recipients are compelling, inspiring, and tragic. The men who appear in this book are tied by two common threads: the Medal of Honor and their Mormon heritage.

The purpose of this book is to highlight the valor of a special class of LDS servicemen who served and sacrificed "above and beyond the call of duty." Four of these nine Mormons gave their "last full measure" for their country, never seeing the high award they richly deserved. All four branches of the service are represented: five were Army (one was a pilot with the Army Air Forces during WWII), two Navy, and one each of the Marine Corps and Air Force. Four were military professionals who made the service their careers; five were not career-minded; three died at an early age and never married. This book captures these harrowing historical narratives from personal accounts.

The Gift and Power: Translating the Book of Mormon

Brant A. Gardner

Hardcover, ISBN: 978-1-58958-131-9

From Brant A. Gardner, the author of the highly praised *Second Witness* commentaries on the Book of Mormon, comes *The Gift and Power: Translating the Book of Mormon*. In this first book-length treatment of the translation process, Gardner closely examines the accounts surrounding Joseph Smith's translation of the Book of Mormon to answer a wide spectrum of questions about the process, including: Did the Prophet use seerstones common to folk magicians of his time? How did he use them? And, what is the relationship to the golden plates and the printed text?

Approaching the topic in three sections, part 1 examines the stories told about Joseph, folk magic, and the translation. Part 2 examines the available evidence to determine how closely the English text replicates the original plate text. And part 3 seeks to explain how seer stones worked, why they no longer work, and how Joseph Smith could have produced a translation with them.

Fire and Sword: A History of the Latter-day Saints in Northern Missouri, 1836-39

Leland Homer Gentry and Todd M. Compton

Hardcover, ISBN: 978-1-58958-103-6

Many Mormon dreams flourished in Missouri. So did many Mormon nightmares.

The Missouri period—especially from the summer of 1838 when Joseph took over vigorous, personal direction of this new Zion until the spring of 1839 when he escaped after five months of imprisonment—represents a moment of intense crisis in Mormon history. Representing the greatest extremes of devotion and violence, commitment and intolerance, physical suffering and terror—mobbings, battles, massacres, and political "knockdowns"—it shadowed the Mormon psyche for a century.

Leland Gentry was the first to step beyond this disturbing period as a one-sided symbol of religious persecution and move toward understanding it with careful documentation and evenhanded analysis. In Fire and Sword, Todd Compton collaborates with Gentry to update this foundational work with four decades of new scholarship, more insightful critical theory, and the wealth of resources that have become electronically available in the last few years.

Compton gives full credit to Leland Gentry's extraordinary achievement, particularly in documenting the existence of Danites and in attempting to tell the Missourians' side of the story; but he also goes far beyond it, gracefully drawing into the dialogue signal interpretations written since Gentry and introducing the raw urgency of personal writings, eyewitness journalists, and bemused politicians seesawing between human compassion and partisan harshness. In the lush Missouri landscape of the Mormon imagination where Adam and Eve had walked out of the garden and where Adam would return to preside over his posterity, the towering religious creativity of Joseph Smith and clash of religious stereotypes created a swift and traumatic frontier drama that changed the Church.

Modern Polygamy and Mormon Fundamentalism: The Generations after the Manifesto

Brian C. Hales

Paperback, ISBN: 978-1-58958-109-8

Winner of the John Whitmer Historical Association's Smith-Pettit Best Book Award

This fascinating study seeks to trace the historical tapestry that is early Mormon polygamy, details the official discontinuation of the practice by the Church, and, for the first time, describes the many zeal-driven organizations that arose in the wake of that decision. Among the polygamous groups discussed are the LeBaronites, whose "blood atonement" killings sent fear throughout Mormon communities in the late seventies and the eighties; the FLDS Church, which made news recently over its construction of a compound and temple in Texas (Warren Jeffs, the leader of that church, is now standing trial on two felony counts after his being profiled on America's Most Wanted resulted in his capture); and the Allred and Kingston groups, two major factions with substantial membership statistics both in and out of the United States. All these fascinating histories, along with those of the smaller independent groups, are examined and explained in a way that all can appreciate.

Praise for *Modern Polygamy and Mormon Fundamentalism*:

"This book is the most thorough and comprehensive study written on the sugbject to date, providing readers with a clear, candid, and broad sweeping overview of the history, teachings, and practices of modern fundamentalist groups."
—Alexander L. Baugh, Associate Professor of Church History and Doctrine, Brigham Young University

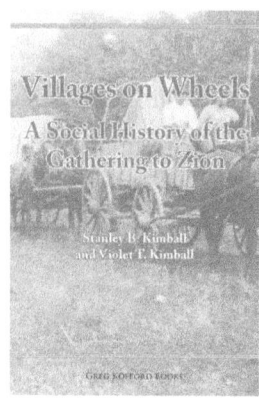

Villages on Wheels: A Social History of the Gathering to Zion

Stanley B. Kimball and Violet T. Kimball

ISBN: 978-1-58958-119-7

The enduring saga of Mormonism is its great trek across the plains, and understanding that trek was the life work of Stanley B. Kimball, master of Mormon trails. This final work, a collaboration he began and which was completed after his death in 2003 by his photographer-writer wife, Violet, explores that movement westward as a social history, with the Mormons moving as "villages on wheels."

Set in the broader context of transcontinental migration to Oregon and California, the Mormon trek spanned twenty-two years, moved approximately 54,700 individuals, many of them in family groups, and left about 7,000 graves at the trailside.

Like a true social history, this fascinating account in fourteen chapters explores both the routines of the trail—cooking, cleaning, laundry, dealing with bodily functions—and the dramatic moments: encountering Indians and stampeding buffalo, giving birth, losing loved ones to death, dealing with rage and injustice, but also offering succor, kindliness, and faith. Religious observances were simultaneously an important part of creating and maintaining group cohesiveness, but working them into the fabric of the grueling day-to-day routine resulted in adaptation, including a "sliding Sabbath." The role played by children and teens receives careful scrutiny; not only did children grow up quickly on the trail, but the gender boundaries guarding their "separate spheres" blurred under the erosion of concentrating on tasks that had to be done regardless of the age or sex of those available to do them. Unexpected attention is given to African Americans who were part of this westering experience, and Violet also gives due credit to the "four-legged heroes" who hauled the wagons westward.

A House for the Most High: The Story of the Original Nauvoo Temple

Matthew McBride

Hardcover, ISBN: 978-1-58958-016-9

This awe-inspiring book is a tribute to the perseverance of the human spirit. *A House for the Most High* is a groundbreaking work from beginning to end with its faithful and comprehensive documentation of the Nauvoo Temple's conception. The behind-the-scenes stories of those determined Saints involved in the great struggle to raise the sacred edifice bring a new appreciation to all readers. McBride's painstaking research now gives us access to valuable first-hand accounts that are drawn straight from the newspaper articles, private diaries, journals, and letters of the steadfast participants.

The opening of this volume gives the reader an extraordinary window into the early temple-building labors of the besieged Church of Jesus Christ of Latter-day Saints, the development of what would become temple-related doctrines in the decade prior to the Nauvoo era, and the 1839 advent of the Saints in Illinois. The main body of this fascinating history covers the significant years, starting from 1840, when this temple was first considered, to the temple's early destruction by a devastating natural disaster. A well-thought-out conclusion completes the epic by telling of the repurchase of the temple lot by the Church in 1937, the lot's excavation in 1962, and the grand announcement in 1999 that the temple would indeed be rebuilt. Also included are an astonishing appendix containing rare and fascinating eyewitness descriptions of the temple and a bibliography of all major source materials. Mormons and non-Mormons alike will discover, within the pages of this book, a true sense of wonder and gratitude for a determined people whose sole desire was to build a sacred and holy temple for the worship of their God.

Hearken, O Ye People: The Historical Setting of Joseph Smith's Ohio Revelations

Mark Lyman Staker

Hardcover, ISBN: 978-1-58958-113-5

2010 Best Book Award - John Whitmer Historical Association
2011 Best Book Award - Mormon History Association

More of Mormonism's canonized revelations originated in or near Kirtland than any other place. Yet many of the events connected with those revelations and their 1830s historical context have faded over time. Mark Staker reconstructs the cultural experiences by which Kirtland's Latter-day Saints made sense of the revelations Joseph Smith pronounced. This volume rebuilds that exciting decade using clues from numerous archives, privately held records, museum collections, and even the soil where early members planted corn and homes. From this vast array of sources he shapes a detailed narrative of weather, religious backgrounds, dialect differences, race relations, theological discussions, food preparation, frontier violence, astronomical phenomena, and myriad daily customs of nineteenth-century life. The result is a "from the ground up" experience that today's Latter-day Saints can all but walk into and touch.

Praise for *Hearken O Ye People*:

"I am not aware of a more deeply researched and richly contextualized study of any period of Mormon church history than Mark Staker's study of Mormons in Ohio. We learn about everything from the details of Alexander Campbell's views on priesthood authority to the road conditions and weather on the four Lamanite missionaries' journey from New York to Ohio. All the Ohio revelations and even the First Vision are made to pulse with new meaning. This book sets a new standard of in-depth research in Latter-day Saint history."
   -Richard Bushman, author of *Joseph Smith: Rough Stone Rolling*

"To be well-informed, any student of Latter-day Saint history and doctrine must now be acquainted with the remarkable research of Mark Staker on the important history of the church in the Kirtland, Ohio, area."
   -Neal A. Maxwell Institute, Brigham Young University

www.ingramcontent.com/pod-product-compliance
Lightning Source LLC
Chambersburg PA
CBHW071448250426
43671CB00042B/473